W. (William) Tweedie

The Arabian Horse, His Country and People

W. (William) Tweedie

The Arabian Horse, His Country and People

ISBN/EAN: 9783744760508

Printed in Europe, USA, Canada, Australia, Japan

Cover: Foto ©ninafisch / pixelio.de

More available books at **www.hansebooks.com**

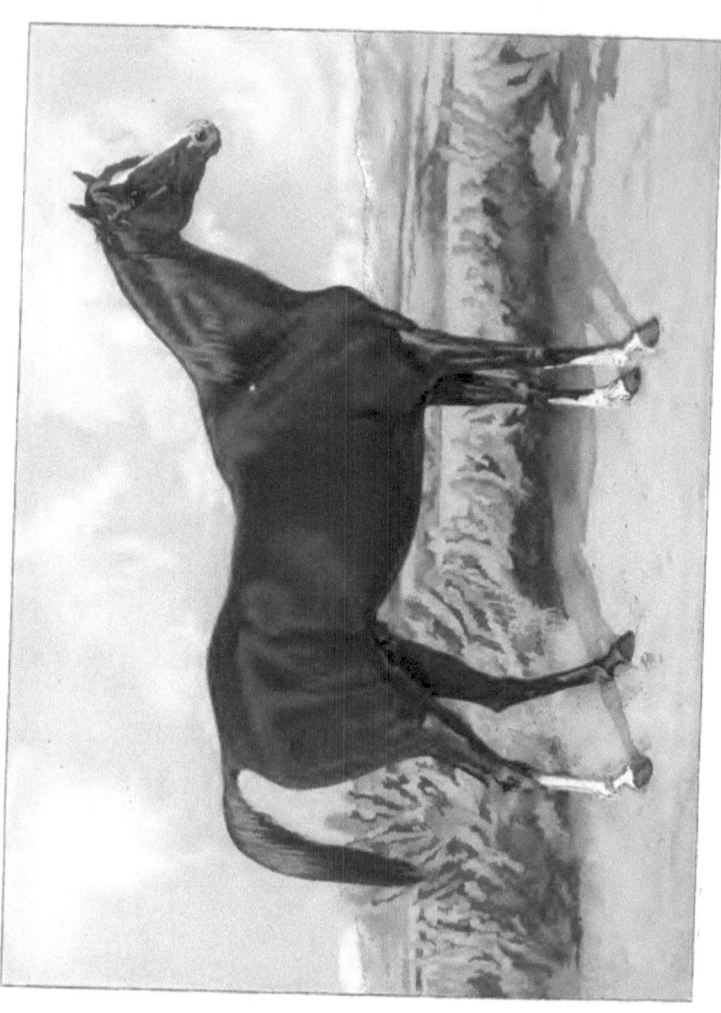

THE ARABIAN HORSE

HIS COUNTRY AND PEOPLE

WITH PORTRAITS OF TYPICAL OR FAMOUS ARABIANS

AND OTHER ILLUSTRATIONS

ALSO

A MAP OF THE COUNTRY OF THE ARABIAN HORSE, AND A DESCRIPTIVE
GLOSSARY OF ARABIC WORDS AND PROPER NAMES

BY

MAJOR-GENERAL W. TWEEDIE, C.S.I.
FOR MANY YEARS H.B.M.'s CONSUL-GENERAL, BAGHDAD, AND POLITICAL RESIDENT FOR THE
GOVERNMENT OF INDIA IN TURKISH ARABIA

WILLIAM BLACKWOOD AND SONS
EDINBURGH AND LONDON
MDCCCXCIV

All Rights reserved

PREFACE.

A LOVE of horses, even when it does not help to originate the military bent, seldom fails to be developed by active service. The Author of this volume, when still very young, found himself in the thick of a campaign which lasted for two years. In the harder half of that period, while the first shock of the Sepoy Mutiny and War was being confronted, he was not a mounted officer, but an ensign with a marching regiment. In India this makes little difference, as there, even in British regiments, the infantry subaltern, scarcely less than the cavalry and the staff officer, has his faithful horse as his partner in every duty, except on parade and when the battalion is formed for action. During the mid-day halt the shadow of the noble animal protects him from the sun's rays; and in cold wet nights, when riding round the pickets, he is often fain to thrust his feet into his horse's armpits for warmth. Impressions stamped upon the mind in this way have all the elements of permanence; and the Author, when the episode of the Mutiny was over, found himself an Arab as regards his love for horses.

Thus it came to pass, that when the changes and chances of official life removed him, many years afterwards, from India to the homes and haunts of the Arabs, one of his first thoughts was, that he would enjoy an opportunity of observing whether the Arabian Horse rises or falls in estimation, when seen, so to speak, through the eyes of the country which yields him.

The following pages have grown out of that idea. They were written at Baghdad, between 1885 and 1891, in such intervals of leisure as consular duties permitted. It is with the greatest diffidence that they are now offered to the public. This feeling does not arise from any doubt regarding the interest which surrounds the central figure. The Horse, according to a recent calculation, had, up to 1887, "at least 3800 separate works" devoted to him in the various languages of the civilised world.¹ Europe, it is needless to notice, vies with Asia in appreciating him. If, in the East, the "Lion of the Punjab" despatched two military expeditions, and spent about £6,000,000 sterling, to obtain possession of Laili,² did not the son of Darius, in the West, when Bucephalas³ died at the age of 30, found the city of Bucephalia in his honour? In Christendom, the idea of chivalry sets out with that of horsemanship; the knight's spurs form his essential badges; and cavalry takes precedence of the other arms. There are towns in England which have horses for their primary, and human beings for their secondary, inhabitants.

The Author's misgivings in bringing out his volume relate to what may be called its historical parts. It is not a book of the Arabian Horse only; but, as the title-page shows, of the Arabian Horse and his environment. The reasons which necessitate this panoramic treatment are stated in the opening chapters. The horse of the Bedouin Arabs holds so unique a place in natural history, and enters so completely into the lives of those who breed him, that it is impossible to describe him while adhering to the beaten track of works on horses. But one who is writing on the classic ground of ancient Babylonia labours under at least two disadvantages. In searching for historical standing-ground, he encounters questions which have already been considered in Europe by trained investigators, who live beside great libraries, and have made good use of them. And in choosing and shaping the materials which lie more or less before him, he finds it difficult to observe true proportions. In plainer language, there is a constant temptation to make the most of the opportunity, and to introduce details and accessories which may be regarded by many in the light of encumbrances.

Even in Baghdad, the feeling was always present that European readers might not relish too full accounts of Arabia and the Arabs. In busy Edinburgh, where this Preface is written, it may be imagined how much more forcibly the same apprehension presents itself.

But it is too late now for such reflections. Her Majesty the Queen-Empress rules over about as many Muslim subjects as the Sultan of Turkey and the Shah of Persia put together. Arabia is the "holy land," and Arabic the sacred language, of all those masses. If our countrymen have not so far formed any very strong desire to enlarge the area of their knowledge on Arabian topics, this book may

---

[1] THE HORSE (in "Modern Science" series), by W. H. Flower, C.B., LL.D., D.C.L., London, 1891; in preface. At least eighty-six of the 3800 works referred to are written in Arabic or Persian, and are specially devoted to the Arabian variety.

[2] The sex of Laili varies in different accounts; but see the story of this animal's acquisition in Sir L. Griffin's sketch of Ranjit Singh, in "Rulers of India" series.

[3] The name of Alexander's horse, we now know, was Bucephalas, not Bucephalus, which was the name of a famous breed of Thessaly.

stimulate the reader to take an interest in a nation which has made or moulded at least 1300 years of Eastern history.

It may be well here to explain that the religion which is called in Arabia the Dīnu 'l Islām, and in Europe, not too correctly, Mohammedanism, is looked at in the following pages, as far as possible, from the Arabian standpoint. Undoubtedly the Arab Prophet, as his system grew, sought to make it universal.[1] Under no other view of his mission could he have claimed to be the Messenger of God, not only to the Arabian tribes, but to the whole human family. Astounding progress, we know, has been made towards the realisation of this conception. An eighth or so of mankind now pray with the face turned towards Mecca. But this fact, however impressive, does not affect the essential truth that Muhammad was an Arab speaking to Arabs.

Copious sources of information about the Dīnu 'l Islām are open to English readers. When learning revived in the sixteenth century, the great leaders of the Reformation thought and wrote much on the subject of El Islām; and the theories which they propounded regarding it are not unrepresented in modern literature. Goethe and Sprenger, and, later, Nöldeke, Carlyle, and others, have severally applied newer methods to the study both of the faith and the man. Lastly, philosophic Indians have written books on Islamism which are to the Arab religion what *Robert Elsmere* is to Christianity. The Arabs themselves have not as yet conceived the idea of explaining away their ancient Semitic creed, so that it shall equally suit the believer and the unbeliever; and in the frequent references to their Faith which the general subject of this volume necessitates, the statement of outstanding facts forms the principal object. On the point of what Islamism is, and what it is not, Al Kur-ân, and the Prophet's authentic "Sayings," are the only witnesses which will be cited. It is said that there are people who condemn all books in which they find something different from that which they expect to find. But a very ordinary amount of reflection will be sufficient to show, that he who approaches Arabian subjects, on Arab soil, with an adequate command of Arabic, and in sympathy with the Arabs, is likely, even though a European, to gather fresh materials.

If all who have aided the Author were here enumerated, the list would be chiefly composed of persons who do not see European books, and do not know the English language. But it is impossible to refrain from mentioning that, but for the encouragement which has been given to this work, from its earliest stage onward, by Mr William Blackwood, himself a genuine lover of horses, it would never have been completed.

The most grateful acknowledgments are also due to Professor W. Robertson

---

[1] AL KUR-ÂN, Sū-ra xxxviii. 87.

Smith of Cambridge. One of the Author's first proceedings, after his return from Baghdad, was to submit the completed manuscript to this most eminent scholar, and solicit the favour of his reading it in proof. This request was willingly granted; and the result has been a great many valuable corrections and suggestions, not, of course, on matters of opinion, but on points of Semite lore and scholarship. Doubtless, in spite of all help, and in spite of many years of honest labour, deficiencies have to be admitted. How far these are to be held compensated for by the novel circumstance that this book, like the subject of which it treats, is a product of Arabia, others must be left to determine.

EDINBURGH, *15th March 1894.*

METHOD OF
TRANSCRIPTION FROM ARABIC TO ROMAN LETTERS.

I. It is impossible to convey to those who have no ear-knowledge of a language a correct idea of its pronunciation through the letters of another language; therefore we do not attempt too much in this direction. On the other hand, Arabic words will not be written without reference to their Semitic forms. A middle course is aimed at; and the reader whose patience serves to carry him through the following explanations may, in the case of most words, come near enough the right pronunciation.

II. In the 28 letters (all consonants) of the Arabic alphabet, there occur 2 forms of S; 2 of T, K, and H respectively; and 4 of D, only one of which is *our* D, while the other 3 forms are *variants* of D.[1] All these several symbols, each of which bears for the Arabs its own proper sound, are distinguished in European grammars by differently marked letters; but we stop short of this.

III. Next for notice are the 2 essentially Semitic letters ع (*a'in*) and غ (*ghain*). The former is a strengthened *a*, *i*, or *u*, according to the vowel-marks borne by it: *short*, when *only* the vowel-mark acts on it; *elongated*, when preceded or followed by one of the three consonants used by the Arabs to form their long vowels and diphthongs. This letter will be written, when *short*, *a'*, *i'*, *u'*, as the case may be; when *elongated*, *ä'*, *ï'*, *ü'*.[2] The other is that father of gutturals which has been described as a grinding together in the throat of Arabs of the Greek γ, the Northumbrian *r*, and the French *r grasséyé*. A recent traveller represents غ by *gh-r*; but *gh* contents us. As only the born Arab (and his camel) can utter it, the equivalent used is immaterial.

---

[1] Our *C*, *G*, *P*, *Q*, *V*, and *X* have no exactly correspondent signs in Arabic. For *C soft*, *S* answers; and for *C hard*, *K*. Our *G hard* chiefly appears in the sound given to ج by *par exemple* the Egyptians, who say *gamal* (*Camelus*), not *jemal*. The question of whether the hard or the soft sound of ج be the more primitive is perhaps an open one. [In this book *C* and *G* are but little used in transcription, because of the double sounds which belong to them: when, *e.g.*, *na-kib* is written *na-cib*, or *Nejd*, *Negd*, one reader will sound the *c* as in *cat*, and another as in *city*; one, the *g* as in *game*, and another, as in *gent*.] *X* with Arabs is *k* followed by *s*, e.g. *ik-sir* — with the def. art. our *el-ixir* (Gr. ξηρόν). The soft *ch* (as in *chop*) of Turkish and Persian is not Arabic; but multitudes of Arabs thus sound the weaker *K*, as *chord* for *kord*.

[2] These apostrophes are to be distinguished from the similar marks which are used with words *in construction*, and which indicate *elision*; as *beitu 'l Amír* — *house of the Amír*.

TRANSCRIPTION FROM ARABIC TO ROMAN LETTERS.

IV. The foregoing remarks may be thus tabulated and supplemented :—

a,[1] *i, u*, represent—(1) *when unmarked*, merely the (short) *vowel-signs* (in Arabic not *letters* at all), as in *moral, pin*, and *pull*.

(2) When capped thus ^, the elongated *a, i,* and *oo* of *father, intrigue,* and *good* respectively.

(3) When ticked off with an apostrophe (*e.g.,* A'rab, I'râk, U'th-mân), the first of the two guttural letters (*unelongated*) alluded to in par. III. *supra*.

(4) When thus distinguished by an apostrophe *and also capped* (*e.g.,* Fid-â'n, sha-i'r, Su-â'd), the same guttural *lengthened* or *made into a diphthong* through the action on it of a consonant. [*N.B.*—With gutturals, *i* approximates to *e*, and *u* to *o; e.g.,* I'râk may be written E'râk, and U'th-mân, O'th-mân.]

ai, as in *aisle*.
au, like *o* in *how*.
d, as in English (or rather Italian).
dh, is used in these pages indifferently for the 3 letters bracketed together in par. II. *supra* as lisping or aspirated variants of D. [The Turks, Persians, and Indians pronounce all 3 as *z*.]
e, as in *grey*.
g, [Merely a speech-variant of the deep *k*], as in *gang*.
j, As in *journey*.
o, as in *bone*.

th, kh, sh, gh, unseparated by a hyphen, represent in these pages—*th*, the Greek θ; *kh*, the Scottish *ch* of *loch*; *sh*, the terminal sound in *fish*; *gh* [the guttural above referred to as written by some *gh-r*] as in interjection *ugh*.

After all, we shall leave on one side the above transliteration when pronunciation may seem to be thereby aided—as by writing *Ae-ni-za* for *I'naza;* and further, retain such familiar forms as Yemen, Medina, Bedouin, Bussorah, Oman. The sole breach of the last-named principle is Mu-ham-mad.[2] Not even the classic authority of Washington Irving's *Life of Mahomet* can reconcile us to a form which is but little in advance of *Mawmet*.[3] "Muhammad" exactly reproduces the Arabic letters and vowel-marks.

---

[1] Grammarians recognise the tendency equally of *a* the vowel-mark (*e.g.,* Najd) and *a* in words like *al* the def. art. to *incline* to *e;* so that Najd may be written Nejd, and *al,* &c., *el*. Indeed one oftener sees *El Emîr* than *Al A-mîr*.

[2] This mode of separating foreign names into syllables is intended as an aid to pronunciation;

but it also follows the "shuttings-off," or truncations, in the Arabic block of letters. The Arabs attach much importance to the proper bringing out of syllables : *e.g., Kŭ-rân,* for *Kŭ-rân,* is as unclerkly as *di-seate,* for *dis-ease,* in English.

[3] " A whining mammet."
— *Romeo and Juliet*.

LIST OF THE PRINCIPAL WORKS CONSULTED.

N.B.—*In footnote references, the titles of the following works will seldom be given, but merely their numbers in this catalogue.*

Works marked with an asterisk are those to which the author hereby acknowledges his obligations.

1. AIDE-DE-CAMP, THE GRIFFIN'S. By Blunt Spurs. 3d edit. Madras, 1860.

2. *ARABIA DESERTA, TRAVELS IN. By Charles M. Doughty. 2 vols. Cambridge University Press, 1888.

3. ARABIA, DIARY OF A JOURNEY ACROSS, DURING THE YEAR 1819. By Captain G. F. Sadlier, H.M.'s 47th Regiment. (Compiled from Records Bombay Govt.: 1866.)

4. ARABIA, GLEANINGS FROM THE DESERT OF. By the late Major R. D. Upton, 9th Royal Lancers. London, 1881.

5. ARABIAN HORSES STUDIED IN THEIR NATIVE COUNTRY IN 1874-75. By the Same. *Fraser's Magazine*, Sept. 1876.

6. ARABIA, NEWMARKET AND: AN EXAMINATION OF THE DESCENT OF RACERS AND COURSERS. By the Same. 1873.

7. ARABIA, NARRATIVE OF A YEAR'S JOURNEY THROUGH CENTRAL AND EASTERN (1862-63). By William Gifford Palgrave, late of the 8th Regt. Bombay N.I. Original edit., 2 vols. 1865.

8. ARABUM, SPECIMEN HISTORIÆ. Auctore Edvardo Pocockio: accessit Historiâ Veterum Arabum, ex Aboo'l Fedâ. Curâ Antonii Sylvestre de Sacy; edidit Josephus White. Oxonii, MDCCCVI.

9. ARABIA, TRAVELS THROUGH, AND OTHER COUNTRIES IN THE EAST, PERFORMED BY M. NIEBUHR. (Condensed English translation in 2 vols. by R. Heron—Edinburgh, 1792—of the first 3 vols. of Niebuhr's Narratives.)

10. BENGAL SPORTING MAGAZINE (J. H. Stocqueler). Calcutta, 1833 to 1846.

11. BLUNT, LADY ANNE: *BEDOUIN TRIBES OF THE EUPHRATES. Edited, with a Preface, and some Account of the Arabs and their Horses, by W. S. Blunt. 2 vols. London: John Murray, 1879.

12. BLUNT, LADY ANNE. *A PILGRIMAGE TO NEJD, THE CRADLE OF THE ARAB RACE. 2 vols. London: John Murray, 1881.

13. BLUNT, MR W. S.: THE THOROUGHBRED HORSE—ENGLISH AND ARABIAN. *Nineteenth Century*, Sept. 1880.

14. BLUNT, MR W. S.: THE FORTHCOMING ARAB RACE AT NEWMARKET. *Nineteenth Century*, May 1884.

15. BURCKHARDT, J. L.: *NOTES ON THE BEDOUINS AND WAHABYS, collected during his Travels in the East. 2 vols. London, 1831.

16. BURCKHARDT, J. L.: *TRAVELS IN ARABIA. 2 vols. London: H. Colburn, 1829.

17. CAVALRY: ITS HISTORY AND TACTICS. By Capt. L. E. Nolan, 15th Hussars. 3d edit. 1860.

18. EL KAMSA (AL KHAMSA): Il cavallo Arabo Puro Sangue: studio di sedici anni, in Siria, Palestina, Egitto e nei Deserti dell' Arabia; di Carlo Guarmani di Livorno. Traduzione dal manoscritto originale Francese del dottor Ansaldo Felleti di Bologna. Bologna, 1864.

19. *ENCYCLOPÆDIA BRITANNICA. 9th edit. 1875-1888.

20. HORSE-DEALING IN SYRIA, 1854. Two Articles in *Blackwood's Edinburgh Magazine*, vol. lxxxvi.

21. HORSES, ENGLISH AND EASTERN. By Sir F. H. Doyle. *Fortnightly Review*, vol. xxix., N.S.

22. HORSE, NATURAL HISTORY OF THE. By Lieut.-Col. C. Ham. Smith, forming vol. xii. of the Naturalists' Library, edited by Sir W. Jardine, Bart. Edinburgh, 1843.

23. HORSES OF THE SAHARA, AND THE MANNERS OF THE DESERT, THE. By E. Daumas. With Commentaries by the Emir Abdel Kader. Translated from the French by James Hutton. London: W. H. Allen, 1863.

24. HORSE, THE HISTORY OF THE. By W. C. L. Martin. London, 1845.

25. HORSE, THE BOOK OF THE. By S. Sidney. London and New York: Cassell, Petter, & Galpin.

26. INDIA SPORTING REVIEW, edited by "Abel East." N.S. Calcutta, 1856 to 1857.

27. ITINERAIRE DE JÉRUSALEM AU NEGED SEPTENTRIONAL. Par M. Guarmani. Extrait du bulletin de la Société de Géographie. (Nov. 1865.)

28. JOURNEY TO THE WAHABEE CAPITAL OF RIYÁDH IN CENTRAL ARABIA, REPORT ON A. By Lieut.-Col. L. Pelly, Political Resident Persian Gulf. Bombay (printed for Govt.), 1866.

29. *KUR-ÁN, AL. Medina, c. A.D. 635 et 650. [Every Kur-án extant, no matter when copied or printed, might properly bear the later of the above two dates. There is nothing to show that the Prophet made any provision for the handing down of his "revelations" in a firm and solid form. He caused, indeed, to be recorded, in *Sú-ras*,[1] the heart-moving words which came to him; but the freed slave Zaid who performed this service observed no method. The tablets which received the writings consisted of flat stones, skins, the woody parts of palm-branches, and the like.[2] After the Prophet's death, Zaid collected these literally "fugitive pieces," and made a fair copy. This first transcript, traditionally known as *As Suhf*, or *The Leaves*, was afterwards destroyed, so as to give finality to a later edition which was made, in U'th-mán's Caliphate, by Zaid and three associates. It is known from a sure tradition that the four men wrote exactly four copies; and all later manuscripts are reproductions of this second redaction. The text thus formed by the care of the Caliph U'th-mán was accepted at the time with wonderful unanimity by those who had heard the Kur-án from the mouth of the Prophet. In our day, an eminent European critic pronounces the opinion that it "contains none but genuine elements—though sometimes in very strange order."]

30. LAYARD, SIR HENRY: *NINEVEH AND ITS REMAINS, by. 3d edit. 2 vols. 1849.

31. LAYARD, SIR HENRY: *DISCOVERIES IN THE RUINS OF NINEVEH AND BABYLON, WITH TRAVELS IN ARMENIA, KURD-ISTÁN, AND THE DESERT. 1853.

---

[1] In late Hebrew, *shū-rah* means a *series*; or, a *row of stones in a building*, whence a *line of writing*. Accordingly, it is supposed by European investigators that Muhammad borrowed the term "Súra" from the Jewish parlance of the period. If this be so, it is not surprising that the word puzzled the old Medina scholars. Even now many of their successors exercise their ingenuity in finding Arabic roots for it. But if the Arabs have the orthodoxy, the Germans have the etymology.

The constituents of the written Kur-án appear in 114 *Sú-ras*, each of which bears its own title, generally one of the leading words which occur in it. In translations, *Sú-ra* is commonly rendered by "chapter." But it is only *in part* that the division into *Sú-ras* corresponds with the separate "revelations"; and in these pages we write, not Ch., but S., for Sú-ra.

[2] Many add the shoulder-blades (*al-túf*) of sheep to this narration: and such have the support of the commentator Bu-khâ-rî (v. *Ki-tâbu 't tafsîr*, vol. v. p. 196, Egypt. edit.)

LIST OF THE PRINCIPAL WORKS CONSULTED.

32. LAYARD, SIR HENRY: EARLY ADVENTURES OF, IN PERSIA, SU-SI-A-NA, AND BABYLONIA. 2 vols. 1887.

33. *MAD-DU 'L KĀ-MŪS (lit. *Tide of the Ocean*). An English-Arabic Lexicon. By E. W. Lane. London: Williams & Norgate, 1863-93.

34. MESOPOTAMIA, TRAVELS IN. By J. S. Buckingham. 2 vols. London: H. Colburn, 1827.

35. *MU-A'L-LA-KĀT SEPTEM: Carmina antiquissima Arabum. D. F. Aug. Arnold. Lipsiæ, 1850. (*V*. Index I., art. MU-A'L-LA-KĀT.)

36. ORIENTAL SPORTING MAGAZINE (Bombay Presidency). June 1828 to June 1833. Reprint of 1873. 2 vols. London: Henry S. King.

37. ORIENTAL SPORTING MAGAZINE (Calcutta). Edited by "Raymond." December 1865 to December 1866.

38. ORIENTAL SPORTING MAGAZINE (N.S.) Calcutta. From Jan. 1868 to Dec. 1878 (soon after which it ceased to exist).

39. PURE SADDLE-HORSES AND HOW TO BREED THEM IN AUSTRALIA; TOGETHER WITH A CONSIDERATION OF THE HISTORY AND MERITS OF THE ENGLISH, ARAB, ANDALUSIAN, AND AUSTRALIAN BREEDS OF HORSES. By Edward M. Curr. Melbourne, 1863.

CONTENTS.

BOOK FIRST.
COUNTRY OF THE ARABIAN.

CHAP.		PAGE
I.	PRELIMINARY,	3
II.	DEFINITIONS,	15
III.	PENINSULAR ARABIA,	25
IV.	EXODUSES OF BEDOUIN OUT OF NAJD,	62
V.	SHÁ-MÍ-YA: OR DESERTS WEST THE EUPHRATES,	65
VI.	AL JA-ZÍ-RA: OR DESERTS EAST THE EUPHRATES,	70
VII.	EL I'RÁK; OR TIGRIS-LAND,	78

BOOK SECOND.
THE BREEDERS OF THE ARABIAN.

I.	THE HORSEMAN MAKES THE HORSE,	89
II.	WHERE DID THE ARABS COME FROM?	92
III.	OF THE BEDOUIN AS HORSE-BREEDERS,	121
IV.	HORSE-BREEDING AMONG THE SETTLED ARABS,	146

BOOK THIRD.
A GENERAL VIEW OF THE ARABIAN.

I.	THE ARAB'S LOVE OF HIS HORSE,	157
II.	FOREIGN ESTIMATES OF THE ARABIAN,	167

III. THE ARABIAN COMPARED WITH OTHER VARIETIES, IN RESPECT OF CONSTITU-
TION AND CHARACTER, . 173
IV. DEFECTS OF THE ARABIAN, 197
V. A SUMMARY, 205

BOOK FOURTH.

THE ARABIAN AT HOME.

I. ON THE ORIGIN OF THE ARABIAN BREED, . 225
II. THE TYPICAL ARABIAN, . . . 245
III. THE ARABIAN IN SHÁ-MÍ-YA AND AL JA-ZÍ-RA, . 269
IV. THE ARABIAN IN EL I'RÁK AND EAST THE TIGRIS, 277

CONCLUSION.

SECT.
I. OF BUYING STRAIGHT FROM THE BEDOUIN, 290
II. OF BUYING IN ARABIAN AND I'RÁKÍ TOWNS, 296
III. OF PROCURING THROUGH CONSULATES OR CONSULS, 297
IV. OF BUYING ARABIANS WHICH HAVE BEEN EXPORTED, . 299
V. ON THE PROPER TREATMENT OF THE EXPORTED ARABIAN, 314

INDEXES.

INDEX
I. BEING A GLOSSARIAL INDEX AND SUPPLEMENT TO ALL REFERENCES TO ARABIC
AND OTHER FOREIGN WORDS, 325
II. INDEX OF SUBJECTS, . 401

LIST OF ILLUSTRATIONS.

HEAD OF THE AUTHOR'S G.A.H. "RA-SHÎD,"   .   .   .   *On the Cover*
From a sketch made from life by Mr R. Alexander, R.S.A., Edinburgh.

FULL-PAGE PICTURES.

H.H. AGHA KHAN'S C.A.H. "SHÂH-RUKH,"   .   .   .   .   .   *Frontispiece*
From a portrait in oil presented to the author by H.H. Agha Sultân Muhammad Shâh of Bombay, the present head of the Agha Khan family.

GROUP OF FOUR HORSEMEN, ...   91
To illustrate the connection between different forms of horsemanship and different types of horses. Nos. 1 and 4 are taken, by Messrs Longmans, Green, & Co.'s kind permission, from Richardson's *Art of Horsemanship*; and No. 2 from an old work, by Peters, on Equitation.

FACSIMILE OF A PEDIGREE RECEIVED WITH AN ARABIAN COLT,   136

BAY ARABIAN HORSE, "CLAVERHOUSE,"   182
From a portrait in oil by the late Mr Roods.

GROUP, CONTAINING SEVEN STUDIES OF SELECTED ARABIANS,   .   .   252
No. 2 is reproduced, by the obliging permission of Mr John Murray, from *Bedouin Tribes of the Euphrates*, by Lady Anne Blunt; No. 3, by arrangement with Messrs Cassell & Co., Limited, from Sidney's *Book of the Horse*; No. 6, by the obliging permission of Messrs Longmans, Green, & Co., from Youatt on *The Horse*; and No. 7, by arrangement with Messrs Routledge & Sons, Limited, from *The Horse in the Stable and the Field*, by Stonehenge.

DR JOHN COLIN CAMPBELL'S G.A.H. "GREYLEG,"   .   .   .   254
From a portrait in water-colour made at Bangalore.

GENERAL M. J. TURNBULL'S G.A.H. "HERMIT,"   .   .   .   256
From a portrait in oil painted for this work by Mrs Turnbull, The Hermitage, Southwick, Sussex.

H.H. THE MAHARÂJAH OF JODHPORE'S B.A.H. "REX,"   .   .   258
From a portrait in oil presented to the author by H.H. Jeswunt Singh, G.C.S.I., Maharajah of Jodhpore.

AN ARAB HORSE-MART, BYCULLA, BOMBAY,   .   .   .   300
From a photograph taken for this work.

LIST OF ILLUSTRATIONS

THE BAY ARABIAN HORSE "EUCLID," . . . From a portrait in oil by Mr JAMES CLARK, animal painter, London.	309
THE BAY ARABIAN HORSE "LANERCOST," From a portrait in oil by the same artist.	310

ILLUSTRATIONS IN THE TEXT.

SPECIMENS OF THE MARKS WITH WHICH THE DESERT ARABS BRAND THEIR CAMELS,	67
THE AUTHOR'S FLYING CAMP BETWEEN SIN-JĀR AND THE EUPHRATES, From a sketch made locally.	77
IN THE AUTHOR'S GARDEN, BAGHDAD, . From a water-colour sketch by Mrs R. BOWMAN.	86
WILLIAM I. AND TONSTAIN, From an old book.	90
PORTRAIT OF A HACKNEY, ... From *The Horse and the Hound*, by Nimrod. (By the kind permission of Messrs A. & C. Black.)	90
THE "NA'L," OR SHOE, OF THE SEMITES, . From a sketch made locally.	97
À LA BEDOUIN, . . From a sketch made locally.	139
THE BEDOUIN RIDING-HALTER, From a sketch made locally.	140
THE BEDOUIN SADDLE, ... From a drawing made for this work by Captain F. G. MAUNSELL, R.A.	141
THE BEDOUIN SPUR, . From sketches made locally.	142
SADDLE OF THE TOWN ARABS AND THE KURDS, From a drawing by Captain MAUNSELL.	147
STIRRUP OF THE TOWN ARABS, THE PERSIANS, AND THE KURDS, From a sketch made locally.	148
ARAB HORSEMAN'S BIT AND BRIDLE, From sketches made locally.	151
A MOSQUE NEAR BAGHDAD, . . From a water-colour sketch by Mrs R. BOWMAN.	154
THE ASIATIC HORSE-SHOE, . From a sketch made locally.	180

LIST OF ILLUSTRATIONS.

A HORSEMAN OF THE INDIAN IRREGULAR CAVALRY OF THE OLDEN TIME, *From an old book.*	188
A PAIR OF CROOKED FORE-LEGS, *From a sketch made locally.*	200
HORSE-SHOE "TURNED UP" AT THE TOE,	201
"CENTRAL" HORSE-SHOE,	202
A MODIFICATION OF THE "CENTRAL" HORSE-SHOE,	203
A BIT ON THE TIGRIS, *From a water-colour sketch by Mrs Bowman.*	222
CENTAUR, *From an old book.*	238
B.A. HORSE, "AKBAR,"	257
AN INTERIOR IN BAGHDAD,	285
CAMEL HOWDAH USED BY THE BEDOUIN LADIES, *From a sketch in Sir H. A. Layard's Nineveh and its Remains. (By the kind permission of Mr John Murray.)*	321

MAP AND TABLES.

MAP OF THE COUNTRY OF THE ARABIAN HORSE,	*In pocket at end*
A TABLE OF THE MAIN DIVISIONS AND SUBDIVISIONS OF THE AL-NI-ZA NATION,	121
A TABLE OF THE FIVE ["AL KHAM-SA"] PRIMARY DIVISIONS OF THE PURE-BRED HORSE STOCK OF THE DESERT,	235
A TABLE OF THE COLOURS PROPER TO ARABIAN HORSES—	
A., COLOURS AKIN TO BAY,	262
B., THE WHITE, GREY, AND ROAN COLOURS,	263

CORRIGENDA.

PAGE
19, line 27, *pro* "accepted there," *lege* here accepted.
32, f.n. 1, line 4, *pro* "Ar-Ri-àdh," *lege* Ar Riàdh.
84, f.n. 1, heading Du-laim, *pro* "v. p. 135," *lege* v. p. 85 ; *cf.* under heading Mun-ta-fik, *pro* "v. p. 135," *lege* v. p. 85.
148, line 11, *pro* "khur-jen," *lege* khurj-ìn.
198, in f.n. 2, *pro* "Stonehenge's *Book of the Horse*," *lege* The *Horse in the Stable and the Field*, by Stonehenge.
254, inscription under full-page illustration, *pro* "Collin," *lege* Colin.
256, " " " *pro* "Major-General M.," *lege* General M. J.

BOOK FIRST
COUNTRY OF THE ARABIAN

THE ARABIAN HORSE.

CHAPTER I.

PRELIMINARY.

UR subject is the Horse of the land, not the land of the Horse; yet in treating of the Arabian, the first step must be an attentive survey of the soil which yields him.

"He who will the poet see
Must in the poet's country be."

says Goethe. For others than Arabs the Arabian horse is apt to be more a creature of the imagination than of observation or experience. Even when one thinks of specimens which have actually come before him, such may either not have been strictly speaking Arabians, or, otherwise, Arabians of that high and typical degree of excellence which is not met with oftener than once or twice in a lifetime.

The farther afield we travel, the broader and firmer our view becomes of the power or force of "the environment," especially *climate*, in moulding plants and animals; and considering how constantly this belief will keep showing itself in these pages, it seems best to begin by stating it. The Eastern mind, as is well known, has stood since time began till now at the stage when the abstract is lost in the concrete. The Arabs, when they would speak of what we call "climatic conditions," sum them up under the general name of *Al Má-e*, or the water. Similarly the Persians, and after them Indian Muslim, when they would talk of the same occult agencies, set them all down to *Áb wa Ha-wá—i.e.*, water and air; *soil* probably forming in their minds part of one and the same idea with the water which dissolves it. Speaking of the skyey element in climate, when Count de Lagrangé named Foig a Ballagh's famous daughter "*Fille de l'air*," he followed an idea which runs through ancient poetry and mythology. According to the Grecian poets, it was the wind that impregnated the mares of Thessaly—the cracks or "fliers" of their epoch. Early Arabian tradition delights in the same fancy. The epithet "daughters of the air" is said to have been applied by the Prophet Muhammad [1] to certain highly vaunted mares. It is even fabled that the Most High, when, before creating man out of wet earth, He willed that the horse should be, commanded the south wind to condense itself; and on a handful of the plastic matter thus obtained being presented to Him by the Spirit Jab-rá-il,[2] or Jab-ril —angel of revelation of Kuranic story—made from it a dark bay or dark chestnut—in Arabic *ku-mait*. Our only object in here introducing this very ancient material is to illustrate the sure truth which appears in it, like one of those glimpses of sound natural history in Aristotle and Pliny, that Heaven's free air forms a very great factor in the development of vigorous animals. Horses which are bred upon open plains will always be better travellers than stable-bred ones. With regard to the element of water, the ground is not less sure. Among things that strike us in the East, one is the stress which is laid by people everywhere on the natural qualities of the water; and another, their apathy about its being kept from contamination. Good water, they seem to think, can never be turned into bad, or bad into good, by anything that man or beast can do to it. Healing springs are still resorted to as believingly as in the time of Naaman [3] the Syrian leper; and on water more perhaps than on any other element or agency are thought by them to wait health and disease, longevity and premature decay.

---

[1] The above reference to this greatest figure in Arabian history may be taken advantage of to explain the sense in which he is a "Prophet." Not confined to our day, but on the contrary very ancient, is the conception associating the *foretelling of events* with the prophetic voice; but in speaking of Muhammad, this idea has to be discarded; Al Is-lám is never tired of inculcating that *the future is known to God only*; and no Arab will so much as say in the morning that it will rain before night. The two Kuranic terms translated Prophet are *Na-bí* and *Ra-súl*. Both words were fixed in Arabic long before the Kur-án, with practically the same signification: *ra-súl, one who carries on by consecutive progressions the relation of the tidings of him who has sent him*—*i. e.*, our *apostle*; *na-bí* (in Arabia, whatever it may have meant in Canaan, and afterwards in the religion of Israel), *one who informs others, or perhaps one who is himself informed, respecting the Divine.* And as showing how in these days knowledge is advancing, we observe an eminent Scottish theologian teaching that in this sense Muhammad was a Prophet. "Certainly," writes Professor Marcus Dods, D.D., in *Muhammad, Buddha, and Christ*, p. 17, "he had two of the most important characteristics of the prophetic order. He saw truth about God which his fellow-men did not see; and he had an irresistible inward impulse to publish this truth."

[2] The Biblical "Gabriel"—in Hebrew, *God's man*. Muslim believe that in the "Night of Power"—the night of the month Ra-ma-dhán in which Muhammad received his first "revelations"—the whole body of the "eternal and uncreated" Kur-án was miraculously injected, straight from the "sacred tablet" in the seventh or highest heaven hard by God's throne, into the heart of this chief of the angelic hierarchy, for enunciation to the Prophet as occasion required, from out the lowest heavenly vault. Yet further eminence belongs to Jab-rá-il as the "Holy Spirit," or "Spirit of Truth," of Al Kur-án.

[3] The name Na'-mán is common among Arabs still.

fecundity and barrenness, comeliness of form and feature and sallow skinniness.[1] Supposing the Arabs ever to grow civilised enough to take up horse-breeding on stud-farm principles, the first thing which they would look for, in selecting runs or sites, would be what they call "strong water"—that is, water proved by experience to favour animal growth. Our readers may consider this view too fully established to require illustration; but the mention of it recalls how remarkably, in the course of a journey of over two thousand miles, made in 1886-87 across the great river-valleys of the Tigris and the Euphrates, the horses and mules improved during halts in some localities more than in others. One such spot was Sin-jâr, now an Ottoman station, as of old a Roman outpost, holding in check the Sin-jâr mountains, by which the steppe between the middle reaches of the two rivers is divided into a northern and southern portion. On encamping beside the town or *ba-lad*, the capital a thousand years ago of a prosperous Arab principality, but now dwindled to at most two hundred houses, the animals seemed almost exhausted. Sin-jâr afforded them no luxuries; no shelter from the January blasts; nothing but the stony ground to lie on; no green food or carrots; only the invariable chopped straw and barley, with water in abundance. Yet it was amazing how they recovered. We had taken with us several valuable, or at all events highly valued, desert colts, merely to keep them moving, and favour their growing into horses of note. These in particular, after a fortnight of Sin-jâr, looked new creatures: never before or afterwards did they appear so promising as on the winter morning when their Arab grooms rode them with us out of Sin-jâr. The virtues of the ground were attributed by the dwellers on it to its water, drawn chiefly from champagne-like brooks, which, after issuing out of springs and watering a few miles of cultivation, lost themselves in the thirsty soil. The men and women of Sin-jâr, though living on poverty's brink, and not unacquainted with starvation, bore witness equally with their cattle to the excellence of its climate. Most of the inhabitants are Kurds; and the traveller has uncommon opportunities of admiring their *physique*, owing to the unconcerned manner in which their wives and daughters strip to bathe by the margin of their little river. Nothing could be more Arcadian, or at the same time chaster, than the method of their ablutions; their radiant black tresses forming, in the postures which the nymphs assume while they pour the water over one another with cups, far more modest

---

[1] Easterns send as far for water as Englishmen for wine or brandy. Herodotus relates how Persian monarchs, wherever they went, would keep themselves supplied through couriers with draughts from the Choaspes, perhaps the modern Karkha, western boundary of Persia; Burckhardt, how Mehemet Ali, in his campaigns in Arabia, had water from the Nile delivered daily at his tent. The princes and nobles of India maintain the same wholesome practice. To all this the West, as usual, abounds in contrasts. Once we heard a young gentleman fresh from Rugby say that water was meant only to wash in!

drapings than the bathing-dresses and transparencies of later stages of civilisation.[1] A large house overhangs the part of the stream resorted to; while, skirting the spot, and leading across the river, is one of the approaches to the town. But the bathers show the finest unconsciousness; nor do others notice them any more than if they were water-hens.[2] Turks and Persians new to Kurdi and Ya-zi-di manners, when they come on such a tableau, exclaim, "Out upon the ká-firs!" An old-school Pâsha sent to govern Sin-jâr would, we make no doubt, if he did not empty the town the sooner, "civilise" its ladies with whip and slipper. But even in Turkey the times grow easier. The present Sin-jâr governor has found out a better system—when he passes he looks another way.[3] Sin-jâr, though familiar ground to Arab nomads, is reckonable not to Arabia but to "Mesopotamia," a term which will be spoken of further on. The reader will not, therefore, place to the credit of Arabia the happy effect on animal life of the Sin-jâr climate; that having merely been noticed by way of showing how, in the East as well as in the West, soils and waters favourable to horses often run conterminous with others the reverse. The climate of Arabia proper, while improving, naturally, as one rises higher above the sea, is on the whole remarkable for its intensity. Hence the force and clearness with which its physical features reflect themselves in its characteristics.

> "'Tis the hard grey weather
> Breeds hard Englishmen,"

says Kingsley. Similarly in Arabia do even its institutions, not excepting its religion, certainly, too, its history, and most of all its living creatures, speak to us

---

[1] Nature's crowning the human head, especially in females, with a covering capable of being let down to form a canopy, is very wonderful. Without going back to Eve, who, if she had been thus equipped, would not have needed a leafy cincture, wherever we look, outside of civilisation, we see the same amplitude of natural drapery in woman. Among Sir H. Rawlinson's Cabul *notunds* (1838-40) was a ká-fir slave from the pagan land north of Afghân-istân, who, "by loosening her golden hair, could cover herself completely from head to foot as with a veil."—(*Ency. Brit.*, 9th edit., vol. xiii. p. 822.) An Arabian writer, describing a sleeping beauty wrapped in her tresses, uses the same word as he would have done for *wrapped in a blanket*. In the lower animals, we know, long-haired equally with short-haired breeds are producible. Yet even in their case the tendency of "high breeding" is to thin the hairy covering. Just as certainly in the human species decadence of the hair waits on civilisation. If Ká-fir, Kurdi, or *paysanne* from Southern France were to be transplanted to a European capital, all its hairdressers, brushes and combs and unguents, would hardly save her children from having to eke out Nature's failing bounties with "combings" and "raw material" brought from various quarters.

[2] The reader who is interested in the manners of different countries at different periods may compare, or contrast, with the above description the observations of an English traveller in Mid-Lothian in 1704; an extract from whose *Tour* was published in one of the earliest numbers of 'Blackwood's Magazine' (February 1818).

[3] Between our visit and those of Layard (1843 and 1850), Sin-jâr, we believe, had seen no European. In 1838, Mr Forbes, Bomb. Med. Staff, explored it, and in 1816 Mr J. S. Buckingham. *V.* in *Journ. Roy. Geograph. Soc.*, vol. ix. Part iii., former's "Visit to the Sin-jâr Hills, with some Account of the Sect of Ya-zi-dis;" and in *op. cit.*, in Catalog. No. 30, vol. i., latter's narrative. Dr E. A. W. Budge of the British Museum has been there more recently.

of its alternating droughts and tornadoes; simooms and upland breezes; burning sands and juicy pastures. And here occur two views of Arabia and the Arabian horse which, before setting out on the geographical survey next awaiting us, it may be useful to consider. One is the claim often put forward on behalf of Arabia to be regarded as the primeval habitat of the Horse; the other, the common idea of the same country being rich in horses. First, let us speak of the probability, or possibility, of Arabia's ever having contained wild horses. To do the Arabs justice, this is not their idea. The paternity of it belongs to Europeans, beginning probably with the imaginative Buffon, and brought down to date by Mr Blunt. On the one hand, the great French naturalist pictured to himself the boundless spaces of Araby, and the perfection to which the horse had been brought there : on the other, he saw a gregarious creature, full of *élan* and velocity, and chiefly dependent for safety on speed, as evinced by his sonorous and expressive voice, and his hatred of being left alone, by his power of covering great distances, and by the incredibly short period in which the newly dropped foal is able to scour along after its dam. And so, without dwelling on details like food and water, the conclusion was come to that the one had been made by Nature for the other. Alas for the theories of stay-at-home philosophers! An unkempt Arab who once piloted us from Bussorah to Al Ha-sà knew better. For when a baggage-pony had been lost, and the question of wild horses thus came up, his idea was that horses divorced from man could not live in the country of the Arabs, unless able to draw water for themselves from deep wells, and lay in fodder as the Bedouin does dates. How this may have been in remoter periods, when the geological formation of Arabia may have been different from now, it does not concern us to conjecture. Here we content ourselves with noting that not only has no living explorer, or any one who has left a book of travels, ever seen or heard of a wild horse in Arabia,[1] but even the Tigris and Euphrates valleys are devoid of those "mobs" of feral horses so numerous in Australia and S. America, which, though at the most only reversions, are sometimes mistaken for *feræ naturæ*. In regard to Mr Blunt, mentioned above as favouring Buffon's theory, it is but fair to add that the facts last glanced at arrested his attention, and that of the Lady Anne, during their travels. Mr Blunt, in the chapter on horses which is contributed by him to *Bedouin Tribes of the Euphrates*,[2] is "content with accepting the usual belief that Arabia was one of the countries where the horse was originally found in his wild state, and where he was first caught and tamed." But he qualifies this statement by explaining that by Arabia he would

---

[1] "That horses are to be found in a wild state in the deserts of Arabia is a fallacy. I never heard of such a thing hinted at in the desert."—Major Upton, *op. cit.* in Catalog. No. 4. p. 273.

[2] Vol. ii. p. 245.

not imply *peninsular* Arabia; which he truly describes as unsuited to the horse in his natural condition, owing to scarcity of water and pasture. Unable to lose hold of a conclusion supporting the idea of the Arabian forming the progenitor of all the horses in the world, Mr Blunt then informs us that "in Mesopotamia and the great pastoral districts bordering on the Euphrates, where water is abundant and pasture perennial," the "original stock" must once have roamed, and "the wild horse been captured, just as in the present day the wild ass is captured and taken thence by man to people [*sic*] the peninsula." This view, especially as held to be confirmed by the habit of the wild ass, will meet us again. It may not be so impossible as the theory which supposes wild horses to have existed in the inaccessible heart of Arabia. But that Mr Blunt himself was but half satisfied with it appears from his subsequently returning to his first and favourite standpoint. In a second journey, the outcome of which was *A Pilgrimage to Najd*, by Lady A. Blunt, on finding in the red sand, "quite one hundred miles from any spring," tracks of the antelope, which the Arabs, by the way, affirm needs no water, also signs of the wolf, fox, and hyæna, Mr Blunt makes the observation, in an addendum contributed by him to the record, that the "ancient tradition of a wild horse having been found" in Central Arabia "may not be so improbable as at first sight it seems." He at the same time disposes of the food question by remarking that "there is certainly pasture, and good pasture, in every part of" certain valleys which he indicates. While, when it comes to water, the height of the argument is reached; the fact, if fact it be, of the sheep of Najd needing water but once a-month is cited, and the conjecture hazarded that the horse of the same country "may have required no more."[1] One who can imagine this can imagine anything. Among the points lessening the horse's usefulness is his losing so much moisture through the skin, and requiring in consequence such frequent draughts of water. Of all the cattle used by the Arabs he is the most impatient of thirst—a character evidently depending on natural habit, not subjugation, and indeed going far to prove him the native of a different clime. Even crossing between his species and the asinine, while rendering the progeny hardier, does not make it more independent of water.

Passing next to the view of Arabia forming naturally a nursery of horses, all the facts available will be stated with reference to each division as we proceed. But looking at the country as a whole, let us understand at starting that only an Eastern poet could style it fertile. Nothing like a third of its surface is cultivable without irrigation; the task of extending which, outside of valleys and natural oases, probably is beyond the power of Turk or Arab. Vast spaces of unchanging and unchangeable plutonic barrenness spread themselves over it. Joining themselves

---

[1] *Op. cit.* in Catalog. No. 12, vol. ii, p. 249.

to these are larger and scarce less dreary regions, occupied by precipitous frowning mountains, accessible only to the goat; by unwatered tracts of stony nakedness; by labyrinthine, sandy ravines or gorges, bearing only the hardiest shrubs; and by tepid, cultivated palm-oases, thick with semi-tropical vegetation. Even in its best parts, if we except the coffee-yielding Yemen, pasturage distributes itself grudgingly; aridity everywhere dogs the heels of fertility. Worst of all, perhaps, for horse-breeders, the mountains of Arabia proper do not collect sufficient water to send out of its vast central plateaus one perennial river, whether to the Red Sea, the Gulf of Persia, or the Indian Ocean. A travelled wiseacre once remarked on the habit of rivers to turn towards cities! But if one were to say of nomadic horse-breeders that wherever the circuit of their migrations has not been traversed by a river, they have, opportunity serving, exchanged it for a watered territory, Arabian history would bear out the statement. It is the same all over the world. In the country of the Oxus—as many believe the primeval home of the Horse; in England, India, and America; in the Orange River State in South Africa; and in Australasia,—it is to be desired above all things by horse-breeders that a never-failing river should run through their pastures.[1] Such being the physical features of the Arab peninsula, there is little wonder that at the first sight of it our countrymen ask themselves where and by whom its far-famed coursers can be bred. The clearing up of this "mystery of horse-breeding in Central Arabia," as Mr Blunt calls it,[2] ranks among the objects proposed in this chapter and the next. One difficulty is on the surface, and that is the getting at, even approximately, the actual yield of horses in past and present times in the country indicated. Here we quote from Burckhardt (1784-1817), the traveller sharing with Carsten Niebuhr (1733-1815) the merit of opening up Arabia to Europeans:—

"It is a general but erroneous opinion that Arabia is very rich in horses; but the breed is limited to the extent of fertile pasture-grounds in that country, and it is in such parts only that horses thrive, while those Bedouins who occupy districts of poor soil rarely possess horses. It is found, accordingly, that the tribes most rich in horses are those who dwell in the comparatively fertile plains of Mesopotamia, on the banks of the river Euphrates, and in the Syrian plains. Horses can there feed for several of the spring months upon the green grass and herbs produced by the rains in the valleys and fertile grounds, and such food seems absolutely necessary for promoting the full growth and vigour of the horse. We find that in Najd horses are not nearly so numerous as in the countries before mentioned, and they become scarce in proportion as we proceed towards the south."[3]

[1] And not only that, but confirming the remarks already made as to water, experience teaches that all rivers are not alike. "The best of our horses in proportion to his figure," says an Australian writer, "the most abstemious, stout, and sound, and the most neglected in his breeding, drinks of the waters that flow into Lake Alexandrina—that is, the horses bred on the rivers Darling, Lachlan, Hogan, Murrumbidgee, and other tributaries of the Murray, after they leave the mountains, and before the Murray approaches the sea."—Op. cit. in Catalog. No. 39, p. 174.

[2] Op. cit. in Catalog. No. 12, vol. i. p. 158.

[3] Op. cit. in Catalog. No. 15, vol. ii. pp. 50, 51.

The soundness of the above is not to be disputed. It stands to reason that the same physical causes which have kept back the Arab people have prevented the multiplication and distribution of the Horse among them beyond a certain point. But it has to be remembered of Burckhardt that, though able, from his command of Arabic, and his painstaking philosophical habit, to inquire successfully on any topic, his actual travels, so far as his published journals show, carried him no farther in the direction of Central Arabia than about three hundred miles inland from the Red Sea. If he had seen one of the warlike clans of the interior, like the Im-tair or U'tai-ba, mustering its chivalry, the number of their mares would probably have exceeded by ten or twenty times what the accounts of Yam-bú' and Medina townsmen had prepared him for. Starvation is the same thing everywhere; all the world over, drought and aridity, equally with their opposites, produce their inherent effects on plants and animals. And yet Nature's laws are not so fixed as to be beyond the modifying or controlling power of circumstances. Accordingly, horse-breeding is not the same thing everywhere. In cities, given the necessary skill and capital, and it may proceed pretty much alike in one quarter of the world as in another—just as pheasants may be reared in cellars, or salmon in fish-ponds. Among soil-bound rural populations again, the same art, as seen above, has its localities assigned to it, and its results determined, in part by climate. But no sooner is it taken up by nomads than its conditions alter. Followers of the robust pastoral life are not to be stopped by a bad season. One set of wells or pastures failing them, they have but to move off with their flocks and herds in search of others. The bearing of this view on the horse-producing capabilities of Arabia is evident. Akin to it is the power which the horse, like so many other animals, possesses of adapting himself to new foods. Even his love of corn, let us bear in mind, comes to him as an acquired taste. His every feature speaks of a grazing, not granivorous, habit. Look at his mouth—what machine could shave earth's surface closer than his trenchant nippers! Not the most delicate leaf or seed escapes his prehensile upper lip; which may sometimes be seen long enough to suggest a rudimentary trunk—one fact more for Darwinism. In two desert paragons sent a few years ago through Baghdad to Bombay, this peculiarity was so marked as greatly to interest the Surgeon of the British Consulate. One of them especially, when he spied a green tuft behind a stone, would curl his snout round it, precisely as his brother pachyderm would his more perfected proboscis. We never learned whether he proved a race-horse. If he did so, he had but to shoot out his long elastic upper lip on the winning-post, to enrich turf language with the new expression of "won by a lip"; from all which excruciatingly near things may even the harshest critic be delivered!

Equally indicative of his habit is the horse's foot. The Arabic language,

with its way of making names descriptive, calls this his *hi-fir* or *digger*—our hoof;
and truly it forms for him spade, shovel, and bludgeon in one. On the Mongolian
steppes he scrapes away the snow with it, so as to get at the vegetation; or in
summer, when the earth is sun-baked, ploughs into it in quest of roots. The
association of ideas cleaves to him even in his stall in England; as shown by the
way in which he paws at feeding-time, unmindful of the stable floor. This last-mentioned trait suggests it to us to notice how in more important ways the horse,
when reduced to servitude, reminds us that he is herbivorous. Thus, in Australia
horses will carry the heaviest riders thousands of miles without once tasting corn,
and be bigger after than before it, if only the bivouacs where the nightly tea-kettle
is set a-boiling yield, as they generally do, plenty of grass. This first want of the
horse appears in every campaign. The commissariat may lay in as much barley
as ever it likes; but without plenty of hay or grass, the horses and transport-
animals will fall off. In an Indian light cavalry regiment[1] famed in Afghán-
istán for its working power, each trooper carried at his cantle a net which he
filled with grass, were it but from the roadsides, as often as he had the chance,
so that a ration of it was ready for the horses at every halt. Even in ordinary
circumstances, perhaps if more care were bestowed on the grass or hay, and the
corn reduced, good would follow.

Let us next observe the readiness with which the horse adapts himself
to different diets under different masters. See him first among the civilised
and luxurious, drifted almost as far away as the furthest from the primitive
maxim that the more simply life is sustained the better. Not content with
his oats and beans, his water thickened with meal, and his grass made into
sound old hay, there is hardly anything for which he may not conceive a fancy,
from roast-meat to sweet biscuits. See him among the robber Turk-u-máns,
or after being drafted into the service of their Russian conquerors, how with
raid or expedition, pursuit or flight, in front of him, he asks for nothing more
than a piece of raw and juicy beef wrapped round the mouthpiece of his bit.
Or see him in Arabia. In no other part of the world—none at least where he
has been so perfected—does necessity introduce him to such novelties of diet.
Truth to tell, both the Arab and his horse eat just what is to be got; and judging
from the effect produced on them, it would be well if more of us did the same.
The first Highland hut entered by Dr Johnson in his famous "Journey" was that
of an old woman, who informed him that in spring, when the goats gave milk,
her five children could live without oatmeal, which she considered expensive
food! The parallel of this in Arab tent-life will offer itself in another chapter in

---

[1] Central India Horse.

respect of camel's milk. Meanwhile, speaking of solids, the corn *par excellence* of Bad-u land is the date fruit. Farther north than about A'na on the Euphrates, the date-palm[1] does not bear; but in Arabia proper, horses know the taste of its luscious fruit as well as that of barley. On the shores of the Red Sea and the Gulf of Persia, fish, both fresh and dried, are given to horses. They who hold with the philosopher-poet of Persia, Sa'-di, that "the travelled deal hugely in fables," may be inclined to doubt this. Nay, say we with Sa'-di's great-great-grandfather—

"Travellers ne'er did lie;
Though fools at home condemn them."

And, in truth, numerous books mention the same fact—for example, the journal of a French naval officer, who visited Shetland in the seventeenth century. "The horses," says the lieutenant, "are no bigger than donkeys, with large heads and badly shaped bodies. They [the Shetlanders] catch a great quantity of cod, which they dry, without salt, by the cold; the heads and bones of these they dry thoroughly, and pound, and give to their cattle instead of corn."[2] This may prepare the reader for what has next to be added, of how in Central Arabia the locust is made into provender. This gigantic grasshopper—in Arabic *ja-rád*, or *stripper*—enters much into the life of the Arabs. Their poets mention him side by side with the wild ass and the ostrich. He is not forbidden to Muslim, though all Arabs do not think him eatable,—a fact perhaps due to different species visiting different districts, or to the flavour varying with their food. Once, towards Central Arabia, we were served with locusts. Thinking of John the Baptist, whose peculiarities of costume and diet, equally with his eloquence and courage, all speak of nurture in the Arabian desert, we did our best, but failed. Roasted, they eat like sawdust; boiled, like stewed snails. Yet once upon a time, according to desert story, a single locust fed an army; when the hoopoe[3] invited Solomon to a banquet on a barren island, and on the guests arriving soared aloft, caught a locust, broke it up, and dropped it in the sea, exclaiming, "Eat, O Prophet of God! they

---

[1] *Phœnix dactylifera—alma mater* of all Arabia. At least a hundred varieties of this tree, each distinguishable by its fruit, grow around Medina. They who know the date merely as one of the superfluities of European tables, little imagine what a compendium of all food it forms for Arabs. Trade-returns show the importation of it into England greatly to exceed the apparent consumption; and one explanation of this may be its use in the manufacture of cattle foods and *Revalenta arabica*. It is also said that our mining population know what a repairer of human tissue and stamina the date is.

[2] *Journal du Corsaire Jean Doublet de Honfleur, lieutenant de frégate sous Louis XIV*. Paris: 1884.

[3] Asiatic fable occupies itself with the hoopoe, as our own does with Robin Redbreast. In the Kur-án, she acts as courier between Solomon and the South Arabian queen who visited him. Traditionalists say that Solomon had her from Ophir; that her crest was of gold; that for the sake of it she was in danger of extermination; that she then petitioned Solomon, among whose miraculous endowments, according both to Jewish and Arabian legend, was the power of understanding the speech of all beasts and birds; and that the result was the changing of her golden crown into a plume of feathers of equal beauty.

who get none of the meat are sure at least of the broth!"—to this day proverbial with Arabs. The reception which awaits a "dropping from the clouds" of locusts differs widely in different places. Towards the Tigris and the Euphrates, the object is to prevent their eggs from being deposited, or, if too late for that, to destroy them; so that they may not be hatched in spring, when the crops are ripening. Here and there, an old-fashioned Mulla may utter a protest against coming between insects sent by God and their appointed work; but in these modern times, the Governments even of Baghdad and Mosul have grown distinctly secular; and in garrison towns the soldiers are employed in winter camping-out to dig for spawn. A poll-tax, payable in bushels of larvæ, is imposed on the inhabitants; and business halts while all who cannot afford to collect their quotas by proxy rush over the country like crusaders, often with music and banners,

"To extirpate the vipers."[1]

As so often happens in Turkey, the result is mostly of the "much-cry-and-little-wool" order. In due time the locusts issue, at first very like tadpoles. Myriads of them then overspread the desert. The mazy dances which they indulge in when first they feel their wings, half-jumping, half-flying, one inch from the ground to-day, and two inches to-morrow, with the buzzing made by them, give one almost a feeling of dizziness as he passes over them. The peasant's only chance is to cut his crops, ripe or unripe, before these harpies are strong enough to seize them. The prevailing belief is, that the locusts die, and are eaten by birds, after they have laid their eggs. The May winds often blow millions of them half-torpid into towns, carrying them even into the inner rooms of houses. But whether all thus perish, or flights of them depart with the storks and swallows, they generally leave their eggs behind. The only thing for it is patience, till some year, as is sure to happen, the two great rivers overflow, and, turning miles of dry land into sea, bring a Noah's flood on the seed of the locusts. How different the welcome given to the same visitants in the arid parts of middle Arabia! Everywhere the fat have much to fear which the lean have not; and the voracious pest of cultivators forms a precious resource of nomads. When the rustling of their wings is heard in the sky, every tent wakes up. "With all the body turned into an eye," as Persians say, men and women keep gazing, and, if the cloud settles, fall on it eagerly. In a short time, piles of locusts, stripped of their wings and legs, and roasted in holes in the sand, cover the ground. These are dried, made into powder, and stored in sacks. If saved from damp, powdered locust will keep good for years. Not only does this yield as animal food much nutritive

---

[1] *Bon Gaultier.*

matter; it has the great advantage of being easily carried. Arabs consider one measure of it equal to two of barley; and thus, among the many compensatory arrangements of Nature's plan it has to be reckoned that within the Arab peninsula an acre of sullen wilderness may yield in a moment, without forethought or labour, a richer supply for men and cattle than the plough could wring from it if it were corn-land.

The several views which we have been illustrating should now be fully before the reader; at least, if they are not, we do not know how to elucidate them further. The first is, that the Arabian horse greatly follows the Arabian climate; the second, that the epithet of "horse-pasturing" bestowed on ancient Argos by Homer is but little applicable to Arabia; the third, that if, nevertheless, it forms a mother of horses, the explanation lies partly in the migratory impulse of the Arab race, and partly in the horse's aptitude to thrive and multiply on so many different kinds of food.

CHAPTER II.

DEFINITIONS.

FOREIGN words are being explained, it will be noticed, partly in the text and partly in footnotes. Further information of the same kind is contained in Index I. But there are terms requiring immediate treatment; and the present chapter will be given to these, so that different readers may not understand them differently.

At least two such names have been already used: BEDOUIN, and DESERT.

The former is one of the key-words of these pages. In Index I. it is shown, under *Bad-w*, how *Bedouin* comes into European languages. Its common meaning follows so far its derivation. Etymologically, the Bedouin[1] are, *they who keep to undemarcated spaces*, or open country; also *of, or belonging to, such places*, or to their inhabitants. The opposite designation is *Ha-dha-rí—one or more whose location is in definite areas*, especially in towns or villages. Of all possible divisions of the inhabitants of Arabia, this is at once the most comprehensive, the most apparent, and the most important. We at least, as just now hinted, have to carry it with us from title-page to *finis*. Hardly a statement can be made about the Arabs, certainly not about their horses, which shall be applicable equally to the wandering and the settled. Strictly, the division should be threefold. First, they who hold absolutely to the moving life. Then, the clingers to the soil, *Ahlu 't tín*, or clodhoppers—perhaps rather, *people of clay*, in the sense of building homesteads of it, followers of the noble industry — " the invention of gods and the occupation of heroes."[2] Finally, townsmen, whose wealth has taken on other forms than sheep and cattle; whose trust is in walls and governments, not mares and *razzias*.[3] But for our present purpose, peasants (*fal-láh*, pl. *fal-lá-hín*) and townsmen,

---

[1] Classically, *Ba-da-wí;* often pronounced, esp. in Irák, *Ba-dá-wí*. In these pages, following the best spoken form, we shall use *Bad-u*.
[2] Lord Beaconsfield.
[3] *V.* in Index I., GHAZ-U.

shading into one another as they do by imperceptible gradations, may be taken together.

It was just now stated that of all the divisions of the Arab race, that being here noticed was the most inclusive. And this, in truth, forms its weak point. It is too extensive to be scientific. A good many explanations and qualifications are necessary before it can be safely applied. Thus, one modern writer—Palgrave —in his first chapter leaps boldly to the conclusion that "a fair specimen of the genuine and unalloyed Bedouin species" are the half-savage hordes of the Sha-rà-ràt, whose *dî-ras*, or *circles* of migration, lie in and around the great approach to Central Arabia from the north-west.[1] No one will dispute that these Sha-rà-ràt are nomads—nomads of the lowest type. But ask over all Arabia whether they be Bedouin, and the answer will be No. Even their claim to rank as Arabs is uncertain. Compared with the indescribable motley of Kurds, Persians, Indians, Africans, Chaldeans, Jews, Turk-u-màns, Syrians, Armenians, Greeks, Copts, Albanians, and others mixing itself with Arabs in the Tigris and Euphrates valleys, the population of Central Arabia, especially Najd, exhibits many features of homogeneousness. Yet it, too, is composite. Apart even from modern inundations, chiefly pilgrims, and apart from the Osmanli, ethnic chips of high antiquity traceable to no known branch of the Arab stem — home-born aliens, between whom and Arabs of the blood there is no intermarrying—are scattered over it; and of such are the Sha-rà-ràt. This allusion to the Arab view of a *race* distinction being in the name of Bedouin, just as in Scotland a race distinction is in the name of Highlander, is here only preliminary. What, if any, traces offer of an ultimate diversity of *blood* underlying, or running parallel with, the divergence of habit distinguishing Ba-da-wî from Ha-dha-rî, will demand inquiry further on; in connection mainly with the theory which derives the wandering Arabs from Ishmael. Meanwhile, the outstanding fact is noted, that swarms such as the Sha-rà-ràt by no means are authentic specimens of the Bedouin stock.

But further, and equally important. If not every roaming camel-breeder be a Bedouin, except in the bare etymological sense to which in the case of special terms it is useless to cling, neither does every Bedouin exhibit fully the nomad habit. Especially in the towns of Najd, families of well-kept desert lineage are settled; some wedded to commerce; others forming part of the *entourage* of one of their own kith and kindred who is pushing his fortunes. With all their contempt for ploughing, the bluest-blooded of desert clansmen dearly love a trading enterprise. From very early times the favourite outlets for the masterful qualities and irrepressible spirit of pastoral shekhlings have lain in this direc-

---

[1] *Op. cit.* in Catalog. No. 7, vol. i. p. 10.

tion. Next to leading a *ghaz-u*, nothing suits a Bad-u better than "personally conducting" a troop of merchants or a train of pilgrims. When owing to his protection, out of some mere *ma'gil*, or resting-place for camels, a centre of trade or industry is formed, the lordship over it falls naturally to him and his connections. In our country, also, in olden times, even royal burghs found shelter under the shadow of some territorial magnate chosen as chief magistrate or provost; but it is fine to mark the mere personality of a desert chieftain thus serving in Arabia as a nucleus, like the natural eminence with its castle atop in Europe. Inside his walls the Shekh is AL MU-II.Á-FIDH, the Protector; at most AL A-MIR, the Orderer,—nearest approaches to kingly title which primitive Arab usage favours. For the time being his striped cloak is exchanged for the furred purple; while camel-driving and the organisation of caravans yield to the wider aims of barbaric statecraft. But no sooner does he, or rather his mare, set foot in the open, than his name is Muhammad, and all his town manners and tinsel drop off him. The name just mentioned may suggest to many a case in point. The greatest and best who ever bore it [1]— deliverer of untold millions from polytheistic faith and worship—was born, as every one knows, a Meccan townsman: yet was he none the less what his Ku-raish lineage made him—a son and freeman of the desert. A posthumous child, and early bereft of his mother, he received, like Scott at Sandyknowe, part of his nurture among herdsmen and shepherds; and it was as manager of the business, and conductor of the trading caravans, of his future wife, the well-endowed Meccan widow Kha-di-ja, that his first start in life was made.

Not even with all this does the explanation of *Bedouin* as a term of classification exhaust itself. The Highlander of long ago at the tail of a herd of black cattle took care not to be mistaken for a common plebeian drover.

---

[1] It may not be superfluous to inform the reader that the above is not a mere Arab estimate of Muhammad, but is confirmed by high European authorities. As noble of heart as of lineage, as abounding in brotherly love as in moral force, all that was most elevated in the ancient Arab character came to perfection in him. Of the censures commonly passed on him, some are shaken when the Kur-ân is studied; and others count for little alongside of the facts of his being first a mere mortal, then a sixth-century Arab. Take, for example, his legislation regarding marriage. Here should be remembered the old-world view, nowhere stronger than in Semites, of the obligation to perpetuate the name and family. From Noah to Muhammad, no patriarch ever dreamt of moral evil in promoting as many expectant maidens as circumstances justified to be mothers of men; provided that no one's domestic peace was broken; no wife or daughter forced (except in war) from her own people; no woman deserted whose hand had once been taken. If the Meccan had realised the "bone of my bone and flesh of my flesh" ideal, if he had dealt with the idols of the harem as he did with those of the temple, he would have been other than an Arab. A graver accusation is that of issuing as God's revelations dogmas and precepts of his own shaping and re-shaping. But as to this, only they who have weighed the facts are fair judges. With, e.g., the outbursts of supposed miraculous voices in the church of the excellent Edward Irving in the heart of busy prosaic London before us, extreme allowance is necessary for exaltations of feeling and attendant visions or hallucinations—only too apt to become stereotyped or habitual—in one who at the mature age of forty emerged a Prophet from the mountain solitudes over against Mecca, like Amos from the deserts of Judah.

At the time of writing, a gipsy "king" or "duke" or "earl," if such survives, is in little danger of being confounded with the pariahs of the strolling order. But it is otherwise with the subject of our picture. Of all uncertain and irregular lines, none is more so than that which demarcates, if it can be said to do so, the partly localised and tributary from the perfectly nomadic and unbridled Arabs. Postponing race questions, and speaking only of characteristics, the facts are in this wise: In Arabia, as in other backward countries, the merest peasants are often half nomadic. Only the unapproachable clans of the interior remain untouched by the hand of civilisation. Over all the country the current in the main is running away from the predatory and towards the peaceful life. Further on we shall observe great communities actually in the transition stage from one condition to the other. With ethnic differences even—how much more habit—thus ever dissolving and disappearing, in Arabia as all the world over, in the crucible of circumstances, philosophic certainty need not be looked for in any delineation of Bedouin nations. But so much stated, the reader will not be drawn into error if for the purposes of this book, as Act-makers have it, the term Bedouin be declared to designate those archaic hordes of camel-pasturing horsemen, many of them nations in all but the fluidity and variability of their component parts; haughty, independent, yet the reverse of barbarous; impatient of all authority or organisation outside the tribal group or confederation; whose roof-tree is the tent-pole, and their reaping-hook the spear; whose tent cities are

"Like the borealis race,
That flit ere you can point their place;"[1]

and whose multitudinous chivalry, though now as little heeded as if in another planet, may for all that have some highly interesting part in Eastern history in store for it.

Then as to *desert*.

The picture which this word suggests to many is that of troughs of ribbed sand, devoid alike of green blade and of animal life higher in the scale than scorpions. In Arabia, as already stated, there are many such. But generally we may be safely guided here by the etymological sense of *terra deserta*, or tract without settled population, over which Nature's "ancient solitary reign" is unmolested. In Arabic the commoner terms are *bá-di-a*, from the same root as *Bedouin*; *bai-dá*, from a different root; *Al kha-lá, the void; sah-rá*, in maps written Sahara;

---

[1] Burns, in *Tam o' Shanter*.

fa-lát; ha-mád; and to name no more, where Turkish and Persian words prevail, *chol.*

The "Arabian desert" of these pages, the reader will please to understand, is not worse off, or sterner, than the average American prairie-land, Australian "bush," or Indian jungle. Acacias, euphorbias, cactuses, myrrhs,[1] tamarisks, with other shrubs as frugal of water as the camels whose favourite food they form, soften even its hardest parts. In good years and at the proper seasons, vast surfaces of it, owing nothing to man and all to nature, yield luxuriant pasture.

Only two other questions of nomenclature remain. How far extends the "country of the Arabian horse"? and what breed, or breeds, of horses are here included in the name Arabian?

Beginning with the topographical, it is evident that the two terms "Arabia" and "country of the Arabian horse" are no more synonymous, in the sense of coextensive, than "North Britain" and the country of the Scots! This will be illustrated presently. But much as we shall try to keep out of questions of mere delimitation, not only as hard to settle, but as belonging to works of a different order, here it may be expected of us to consider what exactly is the country which the name Arabia covers. The history of so ancient a word is little likely ever to be got at through etymology; we, at least, have no rope long enough for so deep a well.[2] After all, common use is probably a better guide than lexicography. Thus far, in speaking of *Arabia*, we have chiefly had in view what is often called "Arabia proper," or "peninsular Arabia"—south-eastern prolongation to the Indian Ocean, between the Red Sea and the Gulf of Persia, of the Syrian plateau. But this has merely depended on the space thus indicated much identifying itself with Najd, the soil and climate of which are so interesting to us. The time has come to intimate that the narrower definition of Arabia is by no means accepted there. Surface configuration does not conform to it; the Arabs do not know it; the principal modern upholder of it is Palgrave, whose book already quoted contains the following: "Arabia and Arabs begin south of Syria and Palestine; west of Bussorah and Zubair; east of Kerak and the Red Sea. Draw a line across from the top of the Red Sea to the top of the Persian Gulf; what is below that line is alone Arab; and even then do not reckon the pilgrim route, it is half Turkish; nor Medina, it is cosmopolitan; nor the sea-coast of Yemen, it is Indo-Abyssinian; least of all Mecca, . . . where every trace of Arab identity has long since been effaced by promiscuous immorality and the corruption of

---

[1] In Arabic, *murr; q. v.* in Index I.
[2] If Lane's suggestion in his Arabic dictionary connecting *A'rab* (name of people collectively) with ערב a *mixed collection,* which certainly the Arabs have been from time immemorial, be accepted then the names Arabia and Abyssinia have the same etymological meaning.

ages. Muskat and Kateef must also stand with Mokha and Aden on the list of exceptions"—(vol. ii. p. 163). But all this carries with it its own contradiction. It may be *magnifique*, in the sense of sweeping; but it is not geography: on similar grounds London might be put outside of England! We spoke just now of Arabs. One of them, Abû 'l Fi-dâ, the very great fourteenth-century historian and geographer, carried Arabia as far north as Aleppo. If we do not follow him here, it is partly because Niebuhr's conclusions on this point are taken as superseding those of earlier writers. It did not escape this prince of scientific travellers that the ancients had imagined a line like that drawn by Palgrave; but he mentions it only to impute it to their ignorance. After doing so, he thus continues: "Whatever may be thought of the limits assigned to this country by the ancients, a much wider extent must at any rate be allowed to present Arabia. In consequence of the conquests and settlements of the Arabs in Syria and Palestine, the deserts of these countries are now to be regarded as part of Arabia; which may thus be considered as being bounded on one side by the river Euphrates, and on the other by the Isthmus of Suez."[1] The above description is read as comprehending (1) all the steppe-land interposed between Palestine and I'râk, in Arab speech, *Shâ-mî-ya*, in European, not too correctly, "Syrian desert"; (2) the same diffusing itself southward adown the western side of the lower Euphrates, both above and below its junction with the Tigris at Gurna, to form the Shattu 'l A'rab, or river of the Arabs. How essentially all these lands enter into Arabia, not only because inhabited by Arabs, but in respect of physical aspects, will appear hereafter. Meanwhile the question is, What is the country of the Arabian horse? The spreading character of the Arab race has already been noticed. Not to let this draw on digression; not to refer to conquests, notably that unparalleled efflorescence of martial vigour which under Muhammad and his successors carried the Meccan standards over half the world,[2] we confine our view here to emigration. And this from the earliest ages has come to Arabs like an instinct. Nobody can presume to say when or how Arabia became their country; but in the first dim light of history we see them issuing out of it. A 'Saying'[3] of the Prophet directed against sea-going is sometimes quoted; but it is absolutely unauthentic. In the Kur-ân, passages having

---

[1] *Op. cit.* in Catalog. No. 9, vol. ii. p. 6.
[2] On the west, we know, the Arab empire, when most extended (middle of 8th Chr. cent.), touched the Loire; and for 500 years and more included Spain. On the east, it crossed the Oxus, beyond which its province of Mâ-wa-râ 'n na-har reached to the Jaxartes.
[3] The Muslim view of the Kur-ân's "down-send-ing" (*v.* p. 4, *ante*, in f.n. 2) is incompatible with the idea of translating its smallest word into another language; while owing to the precautions adopted after Muhammad's death in finally making a book of it (*v.* Kur-ân in List of publications consulted), even European criticism finds few openings for impugning its textual authenticity, and Muslim easily persuade themselves that in it are the *ipsissima*

DEFINITIONS.

the opposite tendency meet us—one in particular,[1] which in thirteen centuries has encouraged and delighted millions upon millions of mariners. Circumstances more than books and sayings doubtless have determined it; but at all events the superiority of the Arabs as navigators over most other Eastern nations is established. Star-craft seems born in them. Out of sight of paths and landmarks, he who is not the veriest townsman will shape a course as truly as if his nose contained a compass. Add to this a spirit of enterprise second only to the Anglo-Saxon —a power of making the most of immutable deserts, not less than of fastening upon trade-points where cities can be founded and wealth acquired by commerce —and we cease to wonder at colonies of Arabs having spread east and west from the Senegal to the Indus, north and south from the Euphrates to Madagascar. We aspire not to carry the reader over all the lands into which the Arab and his horse have passed. Our personal acquaintance with the Arabian in Africa is as slight as is that of most of our countrymen with the Arabian in Arabia; and, that apart, the subject would prove too wide. On the other hand, too much narrowing of the surface would afford an imperfect picture. The following are among the facts soon to appear. If all the Bedouin nations of the peninsula come under two divisions—namely, such as have never left inner Arabia in considerable bodies, and such as have overflowed into adjacent spaces—so does the emigrated portion separate itself into those who still have one foot firm in Najd, going to it, and to their kindred in it, for wives to their sons, and husbands to their daughters; and those who have not been equally careful "in the land of Canaanites" to keep their blood and manners free from Syrian or Kurdi admixture. Of all the cities washed by the Tigris and Euphrates, there is none, however non-Arab its population, from whose minarets may not occasionally be made out on the far horizon the blackness of a Bedouin encampment, having its winter *dí-ras* towards the interior of the peninsula. Lastly, there is none of all these Bedouin with whom there goes not the Bedouin mare. Wherefore necessarily in our pages are counted to the country of the Arabian horse all localities situated in western Asia, and

---

verba of "revelation." When in these pages a 'Saying' is quoted, perhaps as genuine perhaps as apocryphal, the reader will please therefore take the reference as applying not to a Kuranic text, but to one of the handed-down *A-ká-díth* (pl. of *ha-díth*, q. v., Index I.) of the Prophet. Barefaced fabricators of such have flourished. After much sifting, between seven and eight thousand 'Sayings' are now alone admitted into what, for want of better, form the standard collections of "orthodox traditions." But very many of these have variants; partly through the inaccuracy natural to the illiterate of two hemispheres, and partly through sectarian and polemic garbling.

[1] *He it is Who travelleth you by land and sea; so that when ye are in ships which sail away with them* [here pronoun changes from 2d to 3d person] *before a favouring breeze, and they rejoice in it, there comes upon them a gale; and the waves beat them from every side; and they think that truly they are whelmed by them:—they call on God as true believers in Him only;* [saying]—*Wouldst Thou but deliver us from this, then surely be we of the thanksgivers; and when He hath delivered them, then transgress they on the earth with what is outside of Right.*— Kur-àn, S. x.

tenanted in whole or part by Semites, over which it may be said of him, when occurring, that he is at least among his own people, if not always strictly on his native soil. Our map follows this view. Many good maps of the Arabian peninsula exist.[1] The portions of Arabia falling outside the peninsula are included in even better ones.[2] But we know of no map—short of maps of Asia—uniting all the country of the above definition. That now offered is compiled from those enumerated below; not without the addition of routes, seats of tribes, and other particulars derived from personal observation or inquiries.

Lastly, what is an Arabian? Some would answer, The pure-bred horse of Najd only; but this leaves us in a difficulty. Hard-and-fast lines are not to be laid down in Asia as in Europe; and in any case, to hold that in Arabia only horses of the highest class are Arabs would be like narrowing the term "English horse" to strains in the stud-book. True, there is less diversity of size and form among Arabian than among English horses; but this depends chiefly on the phase of civilisation in which the Arabs still are. They have no coaches requiring grand horses; or cabs in which to show off steppers of the "own brother to Cauliflower" stamp. In mere travelling they ride their own beasts, without minding what they are like. As draught is still rare among them, their strains are free from the cart-horse blend which is so ineradicable when once it is established. Not as yet having thought of turning their rivers into beer, they have none of those enormous dray-horses which excite in our cities the admiration of the inhabitants and the jealousy of foreigners. All their goods-traffic, as varied in character as it is considerable in extent, passes noiselessly on the backs of camels and horses, mules and asses: the last in all the greater request owing to the Bedouin despising them too much to "lift" them. For the simple water-wheels and antediluvian wooden ploughs of the cultivating classes, when horse-power is used, and not mules or horned cattle, it is in the form of nondescript ponies, coming, like the loads carried by them, from the four points of the compass, and called in Arabia *ku-dush* (pl. of *ka-dish*). Wanting thus the spur of necessity, not less than the needful knowledge, the Arabs, as a whole, cannot claim the title of scientific breeders—that is, manufacturers and cultivators *ad infinitum* of artificial varieties. But an im-

---

[1] *E.g.*, Walker's, compiled 1849, for E.I. Company; Palgrave's, to illustrate his journey (1862-63); and Mr C. M. Doughty's, in *op. cit.* in Catalog. No. 2.

[2] I. Die Euphrat-Tigris-Länder oder Armenien, Kurdistan und Mesopotamien zu C. Ritter's Erd-Kunde, Buch iii. West-Asien, Theil x. und xi. Bearbeitet von H. Kiepert, Herausgegeben von C. Ritter. Berlin, 1854, Verlag von Dietrich Reimer.

II. Carte Générale de l'Empire Ottoman en Europe et en Asie, dressée par Henri Kiepert. James Wyld, Geographer to the Queen, 457 Strand, W.C. 1867.

III. Nouvelle Carte Générale des Provinces Asiatiques de l'Empire Ottoman (sans l'Arabie), dressée par Henri Kiepert Berlin, 1883. Berlin, Dietrich Reimer, Editeur, 1884.

portant factor here is the size and diversity of their country. Not merely the Arab peninsula—1300 miles long, from the head of the Gulf of A'kaba to the Straits of Bâbu 'l Man-dab, by from 900 to 1500—comes into the prospect. To that has to be added not only all the undemarcated northern deserts which Niebuhr gives to Arabia; but further, the several conterminous lands included in our map, over which, in town and country, nomads mix with settlers. Over so great an area, necessarily, though there are no Shetland or Orkney Islands producing shaggy and stunted ponies almost as naturally as the mountain-grasses, there occur differences of soil and climate distinct enough to stamp themselves on all animals. Over the same surface, it is absolutely certain, crossing has had, or has still, a more or less free hand given to it. All who are what is called in India "Arab-mad"—that is, such fanatical believers in Arabs as to consider pure breeding, with every other attribute of perfection, implanted in them from the time of Noah—may start at this. But in all the world there is no more proper subject for wholesome scepticism than Arab genealogy, both of men and horses. This will appear as we proceed. Meanwhile, only this point is being made for, that, considering how many Arab tribes will breed from any horse or mare available; also, the diversity of character and conformation which is produced in horses by the varying degrees of "breeding" present in them, by the physical aspects of their native districts, and by what has been done with them in colthood, our labours would be futile were we to occupy ourselves exclusively with ideal animals. In the sequel it will be brought out most fully that the Central Arabian highlands possess the highest title to rank as nursing-mother of the far-famed steed of Araby. That fact will never be lost sight of. The typical horse of Najd, it will be seen, has a separate chapter given to him. They who accept him, and him only, as an Arabian, are at liberty to do so. But for the subject of this book are taken the horses bred by Arabs all over the territory which our map exhibits.

Pursuing the plan laid out at starting, several chapters must now be devoted to the country of the Arabian horse. First, the peninsula of the Arabs will be looked at. A brief account will next be given of how and when so many of its nomadic inhabitants have left it. Following in the track of the two greatest hordes which in modern times have done so, we shall then carry the patient reader into the so-called "Syrian desert," or *Shâ-mí-ya*, which is now appropriated by the Ae-ni-za: and thence, across the Euphrates, into the pastures of the Sham-mar. Lastly, with the face still Persia-wards, we shall find ourselves, now on this side the Tigris, now on that, in I'râk—capitals Baghdad and Bussorah—least Arabian of all these countries, but still running over with Arab men and Arab horses. To many who have booked themselves with us, the above may suggest heavy going for the next few stages. It may be so; but by "springing the team" over the driest bits, perhaps even sometimes pulling up before a picturesque prospect, we shall do our best for all who go on with us. The original route, it may be mentioned, was a shorter one. No separate stages were thought of for excursions through Arabian countries. To drop the figure, we tried during more than a year so to arrange our materials as that the Arabian horse should form not our central subject only, but our single one. The consequence was, that on the first appearance of terms such as Najdi horse, or as some would write it Nedgdi horse, Ae-ni-za horse, and I'-râ-ki horse, long digressions into geography and tribal history proved necessary. To obviate this, and for other reasons, the lines which are being followed seemed the proper ones. And thus it happens that not the Arabian horse alone, but with him large portions of country, as well as numerous peoples, are appearing in these pages.

CHAPTER III.

PENINSULAR ARABIA.

GREATLY as geographical knowledge has been advanced by Arabs, both in the fields of travel and book-making, the boundaries and delineations current among the inhabitants of the peninsula are as indeterminate as they are fluctuating. For "imaginary lines," as for "ethnic frontiers," we are indebted to Europeans, from the Greeks and Romans downward. By way of surface divisions, land and water, plain and mountain, main portion and "flanks," content the natives; "our limits and other peoples' limits" make up their political geography. Our purpose of shunning details of boundary has been stated. We are, however, occupied with a race of horses partaking in some slight degree of the character of a fauna. It has been seen how largely the moulding of that breed, equally with its diffusion, follows physical conditions. The further influence which foreign wars, internal disorders, and political changes have had on it will also continually display itself. Therefore, if, in place of topics of delimitation, slight glances at past and present passages of Arab history are here indulged in, we trust to the forbearance of the reader. First of all, vast spaces of the peninsula may be separated as entering but slightly into the country of the Arabian horse. To begin with, there is the triangle between the Gulfs of Suez and A'kaba—the "Sinaitic peninsula" of geographers. However interesting in connection with the question of whether Sinai, the Olympus, as it has been called, of the Hebrew peoples, be identifiable with this summit, or the other, of its mountain-masses—collectively Ja-bal Tûr of Arabs—a region pasturing only sheep and goats, does not allure us. Similarly may be eliminated the great block of desert—covering, as is computed, about 50,000 square miles—between, on the north, the medial plateau of the peninsula; and, on the south, Yemen, Hadhra-maut, and Oman. In books this is called *Ar Rub-u' 'l khá-lî*, or *The Empty Quarter*. The *Dah-ná*, or Red, from the orange colour of its drifting and treacherous sands, is a more common name for it. As will appear presently, the

Chinese designation of Dry Sea would well describe it. This is said never to have been traversed in its full width, even by Bedouin. Hunger and thirst, with the extreme of tropical heat, keep guard over it. The wild ass knows it; and its skirts are full of sun-scorched ostrich-hunters; but human settlements are impossible where a track is no sooner made than obliterated, and where an accident to the water-skins may mean a lingering death. Not towards the Indian Ocean and the Gulf of Oman only, but on the Red Sea and the Gulf of Persia littorals also, a varying breadth or belt of coast and mountain may also be excluded. Australians tell us, that the worst horse in all their country is that bred in tropical Queensland *near the sea*; and that throughout both Victoria and New South Wales, maritime districts will not produce horses equal in working power or stamina to those of the interior. To realise how in Arabia also this is so, it needs but to enter the peninsula where so many of us obtain our first and only glimpse of it, at Aden; then pass northward, cross the desert from west to east in the latitude of Suez; and, holding south again, observe what meets us. Aden, the reader may need reminding, is the port of Yemen; as Yemen is the "Sheba" or Sabæan kingdom of the ancients. Palgrave quotes an old tradition that the Arabian breed of horses originated in Yemen.[1] But probably he did not know that Yemen, and its mistranslation "Arabia Felix,"[2] included down to at least Ptolemy's time (prob. 100 to 150 A.D.) all Arabia, except the peninsula of Sinai (*Arabia Petræa*),[3] and Shâ-mi-ya or *Arabia Deserta*. Rejecting as obsolete this application of the name Yemen, we shall, here and henceforth, use it as did the very early Arabian poets, and afterwards the Muslim geographers. That is, we shall restrict it to the south-western province of the peninsula, as demarcated not alone from Al Hi-jáz and Najd, but also from its own proper extension along the sea-coast, from Aden to Cape Râsu 'l Hadd.[4] And that Yemen thus defined never was, and never can be, a natural horse-land is written on the face of it, as well as in numerous records. The sweltering heat of its littoral strip—Ti-hâ-ma —is like that of Bengal when the monsoon is gathering. Inland, cooler breezes blow; mountain-ranges, some of them of a fine elevation, mix with fertile valleys. But such afford no space to nomads; and their teeming industrious inhabitants have other pursuits than horse-breeding. Burckhardt says of Yemen, that both its climate and pasture are injurious to horses; that they never thrive in it, and even die in numbers from disease; as do, he might have added, English, and even

---

[1] *Op. cit.* in Catalog. No. 19, vol. ii. p. 241.
[2] *V.* in Index I., art. YEMEN.
[3] "Arabia Petræa" did not mean originally, as supposed by Palgrave, "Stony Arabia" (*Ency. Brit.*, vol. ii. pp. 236 *et* 239), but the Arabia of which the capital was Petra—*i.e.*, the Nabatæan country.
[4] *I.e.*, coast strip of Hadh-ra-maut.

Arabian, horses in Lower Bengal. When he visited it, he found it drawing on Najd for horses; also by way of Sa-wâ-kin, on the countries watered by the Nile.[1] This observation may safely be thrown much further back. Not mere probability, but good evidence, shows the importation of horses into Yemen to have begun tolerably early. "Antiquity" is one of the vaguest of terms: the ages denoted by it may either be immeasurably distant or comparatively near us. To a considerable extent, the facts of Arabian geography cited above on the Wild horse question prevent *Equus caballus* from being reckoned among the earliest possessions of the Arabs. In the records of the Assyrian kings who took tribute from Arabia, camels and asses are mentioned, but not horses. Strabo, referring to the time of Augustus, observes that there were neither horses nor mules in Yemen.[2] The great Greek geographer, so far as appears, never was nearer Yemen than Egypt. No doubt he had excellent information; but his statement on this point is surprising. At the period in question, Yemen formed the seat of a far-spread Arab empire; the "Sa-bà," or "Kingdom of the Himyarites and Sabæans," of whose wealth and trading importance, from the days of Solomon to those of Cyrus, we obtain glimpses in the Biblical books;[3] and in numerous inscriptions both Assyrian and South Arabian. In works like Pocock's[4]—at the time marvels of research, but now out of date—more than forty-nine successions of native Yemenite sovereigns are given; a queen whose name was Bil-kis coming twenty-second on the roll. Arabian lore identifies Bil-kis with the Queen of Sa-bá who, according to traditions noticed slightly in 1 Kings x. 1, 13, and more copiously in the Kur-ân,[5] visited Solomon; but the identification has so far not been verified. Solomon's ships plied on the Red Sea; and his trading caravans opened up new land-routes. He built "cities for his chariots," and "cities for his horsemen" (2 Chron. viii. 6). At that rate, ancient Jerusalem must have been full of horse-dealers. If even the officers of the royal household, when they entertained the Queen of Sheba, failed to seize so magnificent an opportunity of exchanging their used-up horses for gold of Ophir, it was contrary to all modern practice. Strabo's statement may only mean that horses and mules were not to be seen every day, and everywhere, in Yemen at the time alluded to. But the point is of small importance. If down to B.C. 50 no Tobba',[6] or sovereign, of Yemen received horses as presents, or imported them, the several Roman invasions of Arabia in the reigns of Augustus, Trajan, and Severus must have left foreign

---

[1] *Op. cit.* in Catalog. No. 15, vol. ii. p. 54.
[2] Bk. xvi. p. 768.
[3] Jer. vi. 20; Ezek. xxvii, *passim*; Isa. lx. 6; Job vi. 19.
[4] *Op. cit.* in Catalog. No. 8.
[5] Sû-ra xxvii.
[6] Tobba'—the most approved rendering of which is *powerful*—formed the distinctive hereditary title of the Sabæan emperors, as Pharaoh formed that of their Egyptian neighbours.

horses behind them, as our expedition against Theodorus did in Abyssinia.[1] Later (c. 356 A.D.), two hundred well-bred Cappadocian horses were among the presents carried by the embassy which the Emperor Constantius sent to Yemen, to incline the Homeritae towards Christianity.[2] Even the elephant, so much more like transporting others than being himself transported, was carried from Africa into Yemen. No one knows when the Sabæan kingdom began. But it lasted down to our sixth century; when the Himyarite king Dhû Nu'-âs (Dhû Nu-wâs of the Arab chroniclers) was defeated, and Yemen subjugated by the Ethiopians. All the Arabic stories about the Abyssinians speak of their elephants; which evidently were a novelty, and greatly impressed the Arabs.[3] When Ab-ra-ha, the second Abyssinian king of Yemen, marched from his capital, San-á', to pillage Mecca, he rode an elephant; but fortune did not attend him. The day he halted before the far-famed temple town, his army suffered a disaster, which prepared the way for the Persian conquest of Yemen (c. 570 A.D.) The year which witnessed Ab-ra-ha's destruction was that of Muhammad's birth. The Kur-ân alludes, in its oracular style, to the occurrence. Allah is represented as siding with the heathen Meccans against the Abyssinian Christians; and sending birds to hail down stones on the "People of the Elephant," *so that they became as corn eaten up all but the stalks*.[4]

Marching with Yemen on the north, the "barrier land" of Al Hi-jâz completes the Red Sea coast of Arabia. Here, and in western Najd, Is-lâm and the Arab empire began. Here are its two sacred cities—Mecca, where persecution first gave point to Muhammad's mission; Medina, where he died and was buried. But not to let this detain us, it has been seen how far from fertile Arabia is; and sterile, even in the midst of sterility, is Al Hi-jâz. To rear horses in it costs

---

[1] Mostly as gifts. But sometimes a charger which had broken loose would elect for an Abyssinian career. Thus a distinguished staff-officer landing in Annesley Bay with a couple of English chargers and a groom who didn't know how to picket them, found himself, the first or second morning, with nothing but the groom: Ultimately one was brought back; but the other remained.

[2] This fact has come down in an epitome by Photius (853 A.D.) of Constantinople, of a fifth-century work, no longer extant, by Philostorgius, v. *The Syrian Church in India*, by G. M. Rae, 1892, p. 97 *et seq.* The religion of the Sabæans is obscure. As tracing their descent from Abraham and Keturah, they practised circumcision; and many of their cult terms are common Semitic words. The worship of the heavenly bodies had a great place among them. The old confusion of the people of Sa-bâ, or Sheba, with the sect, or sects, of the *Sâ-bî-â-no*, is now dispelled. The two names are not written with the same S.

[3] Nations which do not see to it may go back, instead of forward, in civilisation, religion, arts, and manners. The modern Abyssinians shoot down their wild elephants; but they have lost the power of taming them. The spectacle of Sir R. Napier's Indian elephants working harder than paid labourers filled them with mute astonishment. An elephant picketed near a village would attract all the inhabitants. When the beast trumpeted, the crowd would flee as if the last trump had sounded.

[4] Kur-ân, S. cv. One of the traditional Arabic accounts of Ab-ra-ha's expedition, the preservation of which we owe to the historian Ta-ba-ri, of Baghdad, speaks of an outbreak of smallpox in his army; but this explanation of the bird miracle is caviare to all true believers and sticklers for literal interpretations.

too much money; and they can be but little used on expeditions, owing to the scarcity of water above ground, and the wells being so often dry.

"The settled inhabitants of Hi-jáz and Yemen," says Burckhardt, "are not much in the habit of keeping horses; and I believe it may be stated as a moderate and fair calculation that between five and six thousand constitute the greatest number of horses in the country, from A'kabah, or the north point of the Red Sea, southwards to the shores of the ocean near Hadh-ra-maut."

And again—

"The Bedouins of Hi-jáz have but few horses, their main strength consisting in camel-riders and foot-soldiers. In all the country from Mecca to Medina, between the mountains and the sea, a distance of at least 260 miles, I do not believe that 200 horses could be found; and the same proportion of numbers may be remarked all along the Red Sea from Yam-bú' up to A'kabah."

Observations as to numbers made in Burckhardt's day, if revised in ours, would probably give lower, not higher, figures. The studs of the great are outside the question. These merely indicate their owners' wealth and power, and the energy used in getting them together. At mid-winter in Cabul, when outside it was like Siberia, we raised vegetables in a warm corner of our hut; and so may horses be bred in Al Hi-jáz. Thus, we are told by Burckhardt of the Sha-rif of Mecca, that he "possessed an excellent stud"; that "the best stallions of Najd were taken to Mecca for sale"; and that "it became a fashion among the Bedouin women going on a pilgrimage to Mecca that they should bring their husbands' stallions as presents to the Sha-rif; for which, however, they received silk stuffs, ear-rings, and similar articles."[1]

Crossing now the stony desert which trends from the top of the Red Sea to the Persian Gulf, we come to the oasis of Al Ha-sá. Some 50 miles long, by about 15 at its broadest, this occupies almost the whole region skirting the upper half of the Gulf. Its settled inhabitants have been guessed at 150,000; all busily engaged in trade and cultivation. But hordes of nomads revolve round it; and the *ga-sá-ib*, or long plaited locks,[2] of the U'j-mán, Mur-ra, Ba-ni Khá-lid, and other divisions of the Bedouin, everywhere appear in it. The climate is more Indian than Arabian. To one entering it from the desert, the shade of its date-gardens, the coolness of its rice and corn fields, and the sound of its waters bubbling up from springs, and careering through green places, seem too delightful to be real. Cæsar, and others after him, have it that the natives of coast districts exhibit in their manners the liberalising effects of commercial

---

[1] *Op. cit.* in Catalog. No. 13, vol. ii. p. 36.
[2] Called also *ku-rún*, or *gu-rún*, lit. *horns;* and by the Ae-ni-za and Sham-mar, *ja-dá-il—i.e., twists* or *braids.*

intercourse. In certain of their aspects the inhabitants of Al Ha-sâ exemplify this; or perhaps they are not Arabs, in the sense that the tribes of the interior are Arabs. At all events, Aryan leaven from across the Gulf of Persia has often stirred them. In the third century A.H., when Carmathian rationalism was waging war on Allah-worship, the forces which shook the Arab empire gathered in Al Ha-sâ.[1] Nearer our time, when the Wahabite theocracy radiated outward from the centres of Bedouin life in Najd, the merchant princes and oases-planters of the eastern coast-land, though compelled to accept it, never loved it. This Wahabyism will often again be mentioned.[2] In our day, as most readers know, not only the Wahabite kingdom, but the fervid theological development which inflated it, are in a state of subsidence. Al Ha-sâ now forms as completely an Ottoman province as Al Hi-jâz and Yemen— more so indeed than the latter, in which is the British settlement of Aden. A Turkish garrison is posted in its chief town, Huf-huf; the Turkish flag flies, or droops, over the old Carmathian fortresses. Constantinople-coloured Islamism suits the temper of its people better than sectarian rigorism. Articles of taxation, not articles of religion, occupy the thoughts of the Osmanli. Embargoes on silk and other luxuries as unbefitting a "true believer" have gone out with Wahabyism: the products and manufactures of China, India, and Persia now freely enter the province through many a harbour. No longer dragged off to holy wars or crusades against "infidels," its inhabitants are prospering. The

---

[1] The reactionary movement of the Carmathians or Ka-râ-mi-ta [v. Index I.] is distinguished sharply from protests like those of the Kha-wâ-rij [v. Index I.] and Wa-hâ-bis. The two last named were directed at the *straightening*, or reform, of Islamism. The Carmathians rather followed in the footsteps of the Najdian Shekh nicknamed Mu-sai-li-ma [v. Index I.], who in the Prophet's lifetime headed a revolt on the lines of paganism. Their first appearance was in Babylonia. Welded together by a Knight Templar-like discipline and organisation, during two centuries they maintained their tenets of perfect freedom from every code of morals or theology. It is a matter of history how, under their warlike leaders, they wrested large portions of l'râk, Syria, and Arabia from the Caliphs: how at the pilgrimage season of 930 A.D. a Carmathian horde under Abû Tâ-hir sacked Mecca; carried off the "black stone" (ransomed 22 years later); and perpetrated deeds worthy of Hulagu and his Tatars (v. Gibbon's fifty-second chapter). The fruitful parent, Ismailism, of the Carmathian movement is known to moderns through another of its progeny, the Druses. Offshoots of the same stem are the Assassins; said still to exist in Lebanon, and certainly flourishing in Persia.

[2] Most have read how in the beginning of our century Turkey, or rather Egypt, was forced to send expeditions into middle Arabia to curb the Wahâbis; how from 1819-49, Egyptian Pashas maintained a grip of the Najdian table-land; how in the latter year Najd rose on the foreign garrisons, and restored the Wahabite empire. The second break-up of the revived sectarian sovereignty is also a matter of history. In due time (c. 1871) its fall was followed by the occupation of its seaboard province of Al Ha-sâ by a small force from Baghdad. The Turkish commander then proclaimed himself "conqueror of Najd"; and his master the Sultân sent him a sword of honour, with "Najd" studded in diamonds on the scabbard. This is all very well; so long as it does not produce the impression that Al Ha-sâ is part of Najd; or that governors are now sent from Constantinople into Central Arabia proper. Notwithstanding very great changes, Najd still forms what it did when the first glimmer of tradition falls on it, the heart of Arabian nationality and autonomy —the most Arab portion of Arabia.

sister arts of agriculture and horse-breeding flourish round their hamlets. Speaking of this suggests that here may be a convenient place to notice two of the many descriptives under which Arab horses pass in India—"Gulf Arabs," and "Najdi Arabs." The former name is often given loosely to such as are not good-looking, when the "coarseness" is unredeemed by racing form; the latter, to "little pictures," of a stamp which every self-constituted judge carries with him in his eye, though he scarcely could describe it. As for the coarse ones, directly we get outside of the peninsula we shall see many localities which produce them: here it merely is the counting of them to "the Gulf" that calls for a remark. If by "Gulf" the Persian side of it be intended, then, whatever share of Arab blood belongs to them should not save them from the name of Persians, if it be Persian breeding, or want of breeding, that has shaped them. Speaking, however, of the Arabian border, that is Al Ha-sá, not only are big and vulgar ones unfrequent there, but if a type exist at all for the miscalled "Najdi" of the Indian market, the Ha-sá bred one, we rather think, supplies it. Not that in Al Ha-sá there is only one type. Bad-u land, as just seen, has this oasis for its horse-market. Well-grown colts, or, oftener, aged stallions, of the best desert strains, are brought into it, and sold, by Bad-us; while others are bought by townsmen from passing foray parties. Yet withal, innumerable "wretches" grow up under its palm-trees. Blood and "manners" may seldom be wanting. It is easier to find a blood one in Al Ha-sá than the opposite. The "sweetly pretty," if sometimes characterless, head is present; also a glossy coat: the former Najdian; the latter due to the warmth all the year round of the Ha-sá climate. But these things no more make a horse than French gloves and shiny boots do a man. Herding from foalhood with cows and buffaloes develops neither bone nor barrel. Crops of *jat* or lucerne are excellent things in their way; but they belong to the stall-feeding system. For want of having had the temper chastened with work in colthood, the village-bred horse of Al Ha-sá generally is of the tear-away division,— the kind that at the starting-post take two grooms to hold them; the moment the flags are down, if not before it, shoot out like northern streamers; coming up the distance, look like half-drowned cats. Remount officers should not go to Al Ha-sá, unless it were for an Indian regiment of the very lightest of light, and shortest of short, riders. On the other hand, thousands of camels could be collected by a European or Indian agency making Huf-huf its headquarters. A speciality of the province is its breed of white asses, and these are reared within the oasis. India takes a considerable number of them for mule-production. All over Asiatic Turkey, the more of Al Ha-sá blood a donkey has in him, the higher is his value.

And now enough by way of survey of the girdle of coast, desert, and mountain, making up, let it be said, the outer third of the peninsula. True, nothing has been told of the extensive south-eastern province Hadh-ra-maut, with its continuation northward, Mah-ra; but these are still unexplored, and facts relating to their animals are wanting. The maritime kingdom of Oman is also being passed over. Inland, this abounds in features as soft and pleasing as its sea-coast is threatening and volcanic. Wells and fountains enrich it agriculturally. Of all the "concessions" awaiting European enterprise, that of mining into the mineral treasures of Oman may perhaps be put high up the list. Its dromedaries are among the best in Arabia; but we hear nothing of its horses. In two successive reigns, we have looked over the stud of its Sultân, without seeing in it a very superior mare or stallion. The attendants said that there were better collections at others of the royal palaces and pasture-grounds; and that Najd was where such were recruited from. With every indication thus converging Najd-ward, it is time to view the kernel the shell of which has now been opened. Etymologically, Najd means Highlands. Never had that word a deeper place in the heart of Celts in Scotland than Najd has now in that of Arabs. The tribal offshoot settled on the Tigris or Euphrates valleys itself, and is valued by others, according to its claims to Najdian origin. The family domiciled for generations in a Syrian or Levantine city, if it would find, or make, for itself an Arab pedigree, goes to Najd for it. Most of all the Bad-u, however wide the circle, to use a Persian figure, which the compasses of his heart describes, has Najd for central spot. From distant Africa even, not an Arab who has kept his pedigree turns his footsteps Najd-ward without good hope of finding kinsmen. For alignment's sake we have adopted in our map the boundary, founded on geographical feature, which Palgrave gives to Najd;[1] but, for our present purpose, a less unbending definition is necessary. Once we chanced to spend some time in Zu-bair, a town near Bussorah, at the sea extremity of the Euphrates deserts. Even there, within sight of Persia, on the debatable land between Semite and Aryan, the inhabitants, whose long, pensive, feminine features, equally with their grave yet

---

[1] Namely, these 9 provinces, laying themselves out diagonally from N.E. by E. to S.W. by W., at an elevation of from 1000 to 4000 feet :—

A'ridh, capital *Ar-Ri-ádh*; centre of all the most Pharisaical leaven of Najd.
Sa-dîr: bearing the flower of the population in respect of martial qualities. Ch. town, Al Maj-ma'.
Ya-má-ma: Wa-hâ-bî to the core. Ch. town, Khark or Kharj.
Ha-rîk (oftener Hâ-rich). Ch. town, Hû-ta.
Fa-laj (pl. *Af-láj*).
Da-wá-sir: nearly all valley.
Sa-fl-la: a poor and little known region.
Washm: important district; key to A'ridh. Has historical towns of Dhû 'r run-ma; Shak-râ or Shag-râ (commercial centre on route between Mecca and Bussorah); Kuw-wa. An army in Najd, cut off from Washm, would be in danger of starvation.

Ka-sîm: nearest approach to settled country in Central Arabia; tempting to raiders; its valleys studded with villages, granges, and gardens, wrapped in winding-sheets of sand. Wahabite fanaticism here tempered by foreign travel. About a third of its population, says Doughty, have been to Mecca and Medina, Ku-wait and Bussorah, as caravaners. Important towns, U'nai-sa, Bu-rai-da, Râs. Swarms with horse-buyers.

cheerful manners, revealed their Najdian origin, fondly imagined themselves unseparated from Najd. But when questioned they admitted that, although the air around was Najdian, the ground itself belonged not to Najd, but to its *ju-núb*, or flanks. Following the lead thus afforded—the prevailing one with Arabs—by Najd will hereafter be indicated, not the Najd only of the strictest geographers, but Najd with its "flanks" added: that is, every central district, however prolongated, the aspects of which, as distinct from oases like Al Ha-sá, are Najdian. Considering that we have here the spaces making up the very own country of the pure-bred Arabian, it is a pity that they have been but slightly, if at all, explored by European horsemen. The Arab says, *He who enters Najd does not come out again*. Wahabite fanaticism may have had, and still may have, its share in this. But there are sound secular reasons also for Najdian exclusiveness. The Arabic word for conquest literally means *opening*. And the Central Arabian people, with their seaboard encroached on by the Osmanli, and with other foreigners even more distinctly of the *veni, vidi, vici* order supposed to be perpetually on the hover, live in such fear of spies or forerunners that their doors, they think, cannot be kept too strictly bolted. A Sultân of Najd once boasted to a British officer that, although his agents were everywhere, and kept him well informed, he had few relations with foreign States. His Minister spoke of us as "successful pirates"; laughed outright at the notion of our philanthropy; and eyeing hard a naval cap, asked whether the wearer was "one of those commodores who used to seize vessels in the Persian Gulf"![1] The accredited official of a foreign Power who enters Najd will, so long as he keeps to governed parts, be taken such jealous care of, that, unless some one kill him to bring trouble on his protector, his life will be safe enough; but he will hear or see comparatively little except by order or permission. The private traveller who avows himself a European and a Christian will, if he escape with life, be passed from place to place with blows and buffetings, as mad dogs are in Europe."[2] As for

---

[1] *Op. cit.* in Catalog. No. 28, p. 49.

[2] Let them who question it consult the pages of one who tried it—"the seeing of an hungry man, and the telling of a most weary one"—the traveller Doughty. The mention of "mad dogs" suggests certain facts bearing on *rabies* which Baghdad affords. Except only, thanks to the Tigris, want of water, every condition favourable to this *peste* flourishes. The "dog-days," lasting half the year, are intense. A wet and cold winter follows. Every man's house is his dungheap. Corruption rots in the ways. Not the smallest precaution is taken. If any native of Baghdad were to spy a dog in a muzzle, he might, or might not, have the humanity to free him of it; but he would think that the man who had put it on was beside himself. Well, with all this, not only does rabies not produce itself in the large free community of dogs distributing themselves in guilds over the several *quartiers*; but not all the jackals, foxes, and wolves of the surrounding country introduce it. Perhaps even stranger; in ten years' residence we have known two packs of English fox-hounds, with German boar-hounds, and sporting and house dogs of every breed and no breed, imported by Europeans. Curs are also always being brought in by caravaners, and by the military, from all parts of Turkey, Central Asia, and

disguises, they are as precarious as in certain circumstances they are humiliating: for the ass to put on the lion's skin shows a laudable ambition, if a foolish one; when the lion dons the ass's, not only is there fear of the cudgel, but the best qualities of the king of beasts may go out of him.

But to proceed. In viewing a little while ago the barriers of the peninsula, we saw, on the north and north-east, a gravelly desert sloping from Al Hi-jâz to Al Ha-sâ: on the south, the "boundless continuity" of desolation of the Dah-nâ, or great red desert, rolling its sandy billows upward to the Najdian confines. Next it has to be mentioned, how out of the Dah-nâ there proceed northward, eastward, and westward, courses within courses of arms or offshoots; the tendency of which is to soften as they go, much as ocean flowing inland loses by degrees its brine. These are the Nu-fûdh, literally *piercers*, or passes. As natural phenomena they perplex geographers; but we cannot touch on that. One result due to them is that, not on the north and south only, but on every side, a girdle of desert encloses inner Arabia. It was the outer rim of this which, when encountered here and there by the Greeks and Romans, led them to imagine that all the inner peninsula was unpeopled save by dragons. The name "Daughters of the desert" given to the Nu-fûdh by Arabs[1] describes them perfectly: earth's surface undergoes transition in them from the uninhabitable to the habitable. Slightly in the same manner as the populated portion of Egypt, while guarded on the whole by deserts, is intersected by branches of the Nile, the central table-land of Arabia submits itself to the embraces of this progeny of the southern sand-waste. The Nu-fûdh form deep indentations in it, like gulfs in a mainland, and much determine its contour. In many parts, they go through and through it. Thus, in Central Arabia, plateau land makes one country, and Nu-fûdh land another country. The vast sierra-broken plains of the former, not unstudded with historical cities, and rich in oasis hamlets, here but slightly claim us. The interest for us is in Nu-fûdh land — but another

---

Egypt; yet we have never seen or heard of either a case of rabies in the canine, or hydrophobia in the human, species. How widely different the case is in India! The greatest legislators in the modern world — those of Simla — make and amend Acts about it: piles of dogs are done to death annually, to the horror of the natives, by the magistracy; and still do mad dogs rank with snakes and swollen rivers as among the checks to horse-breeding. Once in the Deccan it was ours to breed, and feed on corn till he was a four-year-old, a colt destined only to be bitten in his hovel by a running cur. After about a month rabies followed; before the scene ended, the poor animal had half destroyed himself with his teeth, and by knocking himself about.

[1] At the very heart of the Arab's speech is personification. Everything is with him *father, mother, son, sister,* or *daughter,* of something else. Thus Abû 'l khashm, *father of the nose,* common name for the carrier-pigeon, from the size of his beak, and the fleshy protuberance at the base of it; Ummu 'l kha-bâ-ith, *mother of crimes,* a name often given to wine; Ibnu âwi (vulg. *wel-wel*), the jackal; yet more poetically Bintu 'l ja-bal, *daughter of the mountain* — *i.e.*, the echo; and so forth.

word for Bad-u land. We know of but two of our countrymen who have crossed the peninsula from sea to sea, necessarily taking in their way two or more courses of the Nu-fûdh. In 1819 Captain Sadlier of the 47th Foot, sent by Government to congratulate the Egyptian Commander Ib-râ-him Pâsha on his successes against the Wahabis, marched 1200 miles, in European dress, across every natural obstacle from Ka-tîf to Yam-bû'. On reaching the Pâsha's camp near Medina, he found him to have acquired in the campaign three hundred mares and horses. "These," says the Captain's Journal, "his Excellency has collected from the different tribes of the districts which he visited, who scarcely retain either horse or mare to propagate the species; these parts of Arabia will therefore remain destitute of good horses, which will now be transferred in a great measure to Egypt, whither his Excellency has heretofore despatched a great number, independently of the number carried out of Arabia by the soldiery."[1] The same traveller also states, that if any of the Bedouin near his route had still a good horse, he would not venture to bring it for sale, lest it should be seized, and he himself dismissed empty-handed and on foot, to be laughed at: a sounder view than that of some others who, because of their having passed through portions of the same country without seeing horses, have concluded that there were none in it; the finding of horses to buy being in truth as much a special gift as the buying of them when they are before one.[2] Half a century after Captain Sadlier, Mr W. G. Palgrave (1862-63) posing as "a native travelling-doctor," he and his Syrian comrade "dressed like ordinary middle-class travellers of inner Syria,"[3] passed right over the peninsula, traversing three main segments of Nu-fûdh land. The season was midsummer: Nature's aspects in the Nu-fûdh were so Tartarean as to make "clothes, baggage, and housings all take the smell of burning;" the "suffocating

---

[1] *Op. cit.* in Catalog. No. 3.
[2] Arabia is not singular in this respect. The following passage in a paper on "Cape Horses" in an old Review deserves reprinting :—

"A purchasing officer at the Cape should not only be gifted with the *leather* of a post-boy and the patience of a Job, but he ought to have time for the exercise of a painstaking search; steering a zigzag course, passing by no *horsy*-looking farm-house without a 'peep into the stable,' to see what manner of 'paards' (nags) are there. . . . As was our wont, we were in the saddle one fine morning at early dawn. . . . Our first halt was at the farm of a person who rejoices in the sobriquet of 'Zwart Cop' (Black Pate). . . . 'Come in and eat whilst your horses have a feed.' . . .

"During our repast the conversation was drawn to horses. Our host protested he had none. Le Merchant's chin dropped into his waistcoat in despair. I gave him a nod of encouragement, and proposed a stroll. Mynheer said 'Ja,' and in a very few minutes we were in the stable, where we found ten uncommonly neat bay geldings. I inquired as to their ownership, seeing that our host had none of his own. The answer was, 'Oh; these are my 'span' (waggon teams), and not for sale.' Knowing what that meant, I begged to see the horses trotted out—a bit of flattery a Boer is open to, his span being his pride—and we noted 5 as fit for troopers. A second span was brought up from the field, from which we picked 4 more. Money was offered, and accepted after the usual amount of coquetting, and by the time our hacks had finished their bait we had added 9 good horses to the roll of the 7th Dragoon Guards."—*Op. cit.* in Catalog. No. 26, vol. iv. pp. 112, 113.

[3] *Op. cit.* in Catalog. No. 7, vol. i. p. 5.

sand-pits," "burning walls," with ever and anon a prospect seeming "a vast sea of fire ruffled into little red-hot waves,"[1] threw the writer for further metaphor on the poet of the 'Inferno.' The traveller who, to display his powers or beguile his readers, indulges in such extreme descriptions, must expect to be called to account for it; but we prefer discounting the excess, and accepting the remainder. Certainly we have never seen any such terrible abysses; but then we have never sought for them. The only "daughters of the desert" encountered by us have been such as, after meandering far from home, had turned comparatively gracious and amiable: not hundreds of feet deep, but more like empty river-beds; striped with cattle-paths; entwined with marks of coming and going; well spread with bunch-grass, and with shrubs a man's height or more, especially the tufted camel euphorbia called *gha-dhâ* —the distinctive feature always being the dunes, or ridges of red sand, which rise abruptly on either hand. And yet one summer a mare was brought to us at Baghdad from the Bedouin of Western Arabia whose state suggested the "burning lakes" of Palgrave. Her hind-legs had got as scorched and seared in crossing the Nu-fûdh as if fire had done it. One of the limbs it chanced was white, and as long as she lived remained red and hairless—a proof, perhaps, that skin producing white hair is naturally weaker than the dark-coloured.

In 1865 an explorer of a different school, the well-known military pioneer Lewis Pelly,[2] then Political Resident in the Persian Gulf, striking right down from Ku-wait, at the head of the Gulf, to beard the aged Fai-sal, Head of the Wahabite empire, in his capital, Ar Ri-âdh, crossed, and described in plain official language, the broad belt of unmitigated desert which shuts in Central Arabia on the east. The dashing march of sixteen days, including halts, which it took the party to make Ri-âdh, introduced them to one of the worst of the Nu-fûdh, called the "lesser Dah-ná," from its resemblance to its "mother," the great southern desert—a long strip of bareness, at one place fifty miles broad, running up towards the stony wastes at the head of the Gulf of Persia. The Journal kept has been printed, but not, we believe, published; and perhaps the reader might relish an extract from it. But first a word in regard to horses. For the purpose of helping them to fall in with likely colts, a professional buyer went with the camp; but not one was forthcoming. The few groups of Bedouin met were mostly camel-riders. A day's journey from the sea, a plump of desert spearmen—the wildest-looking of creatures —came up to them at a scamper, mounted on camels and mares.[3] Only once

---

[1] *Op. cit.* in Catalog. No. 7, vol. i. p. 92.
[2] Whose death as Lieut.-General Sir L. Pelly, K.C.B., K.C.S.I., and M.P. for Hackney (N.), has happened while this is being printed.
[3] Some years ago, a Swiss merchant of Baghdad, when crossing the same desert on a dromedary, had the misfortune to meet a similar party riding two and two on camels; the front rank man, so to call him, armed with a short spear or sword, and the fellow behind him (in Arabic his *ra-dîf*) with a lighted match-

a colt was brought for sale. As above observed, it no more follows necessarily that the country along their route had none to yield, than it would follow from one's crossing India without seeing any robbers that they had all been laid by the heels. But evidence is accumulating that in large portions of Arabia proper, were it not for its Will-o'-the-wisp-like nomads, horses would be rare. Among the glimpses of the "lesser Dah-ná" given in the Journal are the following :—

"There are altogether seven distinct lines of sand-hills with their intervening plains forming the breadth of the (lesser) Dah-ná at the line where I crossed it. But this particular line is selected on account of its comparative easiness; and we could observe that on either hand the region became more confused and broken up.... On the whole, the (lesser) Dah-ná, as we saw it, resembles seven huge rollers, with intervening plains of sea. Standing on the top of the last or westernmost ridge, which may be about a couple of miles wide, you overlook an horizon-bounded plain, scrubby with brushwood, and flushed here and there with scud and sand. You might fancy yourself standing on a sandy cliff and overlooking the ocean, so clearly defined is the base of the sand-ridge and the commencement of the plain. . . .

"Compared with the vast waste we have now crossed, even the most desert parts of Persia seem wooded and peopled; for we have seen neither tree, hut, nor fowl, and scarce a goat, since we left Ku-wait."[1]

What Sadlier and Palgrave did for the girth of the peninsula, and Pelly for its north-eastern quarter, a brave Englishwoman and her husband did for its north-western shoulder. All her countrymen, and still more her country-women, may be proud of Lady Anne Blunt's journey. Entering from towards Damascus, and holding south-east along the deep serpentine depression called Wá-di Sir-hán, a principal line of communication both for merchants and Bedouin between Shá-mi-ya and middle Arabia, they made their way past the oval oasis of Al Jauf—place of wells, corn-fields, and date-plantations—through a course of true Nu-fúdh to the province of Ja-bal Sham-mar, the capital of which, Há-yil, stands near the Hajj road between Bussorah and Medina. And here it more and more comes out how even these Central Arabian sand-streams participate in Nature's blessed diversity of feature. True, it was winter. Still, had the Nu-fúdh been all of one pattern, Lady A. Blunt could not have written of the one threaded by them that it was

lock. If he had chanced to come on them in their tents, the desert law of *dakhíl*, or *hospitium*, would have protected him, and a sheep would have been killed for him. But meeting him in the open, where with Arabs it is "no sin for a man to labour in his vocation," after some discussion on the vital question of his throat, they stripped him and his two men not only of their arms and dromedaries, but of every rag of clothing, and turned them adrift in the desert. Happily the Euphrates was near, so that the subject of the incident is still alive to tell of it. Lovers of a certain weed will hear with interest that his one appeal was for a few of his own havannahs; by refusing which the ruffians put themselves very low down among the world's caterans. They showed also, it is worth noting, the same scruples about taking a prize unawares as their Zulu congeners did with the Prince Imperial. Having marked down their bird while on the ground, they waited till he was up again, before actually falling on him.

[1] *Op. cit.* in Catalog. No. 28.

"better wooded and richer in pasturage than any part of the desert passed since leaving Damascus," containing "several kinds of camel-pasture, especially one new to us called *adr*, on which they say sheep can feed for a month without wanting water; and more than one kind of grass," so that "both camels and mares are pleased with the place, and we are delighted with the abundance of firewood for our camps." Out of this there proceeded the discovery that "the Nu-fûdh account for everything"—that is, for Central Arabia yielding horses. "In the hard desert," it is stated, "there is nothing a horse can eat; but here [in the Nu-fûdh] there is plenty. . . . It is in reality the home of the Bedouins during a great part of the year. Its only want is water, for it contains but few wells; all along the edge it is thickly inhabited; and Râ-dhî [their guide] tells us that in the spring, when the grass is green after the rain, the Bedouins care nothing for water, as their camels are in milk, and they go for weeks without it, wandering far into the interior of the sand desert."[1]

With such high authority confirmatory of the conclusion that Nu-fûdh land means Bad-u land, we do not think that the reader's time has been wasted in this survey of it. Austere as are its features, every breed, let us remember, in order to be thriving and permanent, must be in harmony with its environments. For the production of those overgrown horses, having watery bodies supported on thin legs, which are too often seen in greener, and for horse-show purposes more fostering, pastures, nothing could be more unpromising. But the conditions here presented, and the way in which the mares and foals, in order to pick up a living, are kept constantly on the rummage, form great aids of pure breeding in refining the Najdi horse from dross or lumber, and making him what he is, a desert diamond. If, as seen above, Najd is to every Bad-u what Al Hi-jâz is to every Muslim, the Caaba of the former is its Nu-fûdh. *To love one's birthplace is of religion*, taught Muhammad;[2] and to life's last moment the heart of nomad goes out to the pure soft sand of his Nu-fûdh as affectionately as if, like the young of the wild ass and antelope, he were born in it, as indeed may happen. When a tribe on the move is holding Najd-ward, and the swelling white brow of one of these great natural defiles upraises itself, "*Al hamdu l' Illah!*"[3] the Nu-fûdh

---

[1] *Op. cit.* in Catalog. No. 12, vol. i. pp. 157, 158.

[2] A 'Saying' [v. p. 20, in f.n. 3. Also Index I., art. HADITH].

[3] *Praise be to Allah*, one of three phrases ever rolling off the tongue of Arabs. The other two are *In shâ Allah, if it please Allah;* and *Mâ shâ Allah, What has pleased Allah,* used to indicate surprise, admiration, approval, also by way of (half-and-half) welcome. In an old magazine article (*op. cit.* in Catalog. No. 10, vol. vii., "Selections," p. 4), containing an account of "the Bedouin Arabs of the desert and their horses," it is amusing to read that, from fear of the evil eye, when showing a horse to a stranger they never omitted to pray to the great "Machâ Allaa:" This is like Marco Polo's saying of one of the populations of Central Asia, that they were "worshippers of Mahommet"!

again," goes trilling out from thousands of women's voices. Bare, and no more than habitable, as his country may appear to us, the Arab perfectly realises that it was made for him, and he for it.

Before leaving these "flanks of Najd" we must well view their northern segment, the important province of Ja-bal Sham-mar, but just now mentioned. Natural features, boundaries, and population,[1] may all be dismissed with a word. Of the first, the most prominent are the two parallel mountain-ranges of Ja-bal A-jâ and Ja-bal Sal-mâ. The inhabitants, as everywhere, are mixed nomadic, agricultural, and industrial; spread over a stony yet not unfertile surface of variegated oases, towns, villages, and homesteads. The authorities on these points are, up to 1862, Palgrave; thereafter, to 1877, Doughty; to 1879, Lady A. Blunt. The first resided for a considerable time, in his disguise, in Hâ-yil, a town easily accessible from Baghdad in twenty long marches. The second did the same in Arab clothes, or rags rather, but not concealing his nationality. While the third, and her husband, made their entry in the character of "persons of distinction, in search of other persons of distinction." How all these fared, and what they saw, will be found written in their several narratives. Yet it is essential to our subject that, instead of merely referring to works which all may not possess, we should pause to open up to the reader how, within the memory of those still living, a Shekhly filibuster, of the type alluded to in a previous chapter, erected in Ja-bal Sham-mar a petty royalty over townsmen first, and Bedouin afterwards; how, at the time of writing, whatever of government, in the European sense, middle Arabia enjoys has Hâ-yil for its centre. It has been seen how the Wahabite empire,[2] twice in its history, has suffered suppression, — early in the century from Egyptian armies; in our day from internal causes. Among the numerous gallants of desert lineage stirred by the

---

[1] In illustration of the variability of statistics, especially of population, compare Palgrave's estimate with Doughty's. The former, in *Ency. Brit.*, vol. ii. p. 254 (1875), gives 162,000 as the "total population" of Ja-bal Sham-mar, exclusive of an oblong strip, called by him "Upper Ka-sîm," between Sham-mar mountains and valley of Lower Ka-sîm; to which strip he assigns, on hearsay, a further population of 35,000. According to Doughty, the settled population may be "hardly 20,000 souls: add to these the tributary nomads, Ra-ni Wah-hib, 2500; the Bishr in the south, say 3000, or they are less; northern Harb in the obedience of Ibn Ra-shîd, say 2000; southern Sham-mar, hardly 2000; midland Heteym, say 1500; Sha-rá-rát, say 2500; and besides them no more. In all, say 14,000 persons or less; and the sum of stable and nomad dwellers may be not much better than 30,000 souls" (*op. cit.* in Catalog. No. 2, vol. ii. p. 20). Possibly this huge discrepancy depends on different limits being given to Ja-bal Sham-mar by the two authorities respectively. But how shall we explain Palgrave's (*loco cit. supra*) allowing "about 15,000 or 16,000 souls" to Hâ-yil; while Doughty states the number at 3000 souls only—(vol. i. p. 617)? For a reason which it is unnecessary here to mention, we hold Palgrave's figures of no account.

[2] Called also, after the prince whose prowess shaped it, the empire of the Ibn Sa-â'ds. As disposing the sword-power of all subject to it, the Head of it has, or had, A-mîr for title, also Sultán; and as religious exemplar, I-mâm.

troubles of the former epoch to couch the spear at fortune's prizes was A'bdu 'lla of Ja-bal Sham-mar; whose family name was Ra-shid. Finding his native province in the grip of others, this young blood rode out of Há-yil, with little but his good Sham-mar pedigree to help him. What was written for him proved to be the foremost rank, first in A-mir Tur-ki's, then A-mir Fai-sal's, armies; till when, after many "feats of broil and battle," chiefly through his eminent qualities, Najd recovered its independence, A-mir Fai-sal rewarded him with the viceroyalty of its northern appanage, Ja-bal Sham-mar. As always happens in the East, vicarious gradually merged in independent power. A'bdu 'lla himself before he died (c. 1844), by knitting to himself his powerful desert kinsfolk, half accomplished this object. His son and successor, Ti-lál, completed it. Numerous influences deadly to Wahabyism issued in his time out of Há-yil; great pieces of the Najdian empire, loosened through intrigue or by natural processes, included themselves, seemingly of their own accord, within his southern and eastern frontiers. In other directions also he put out his hand further and further. His death might easily have undone this; but it was otherwise ordered. If revolutions are not made with rose-water in Europe, no more are successions always from sire to son in Arabia. Ti-lál left several sons; the eldest, Ban-dar, barely arrived at manhood. But two formidable brothers also survived him—sons of A'bdu 'lla—and one of these took up the Shekhate, only to be cut off after two or three years.[1] Then Ban-dar had a turn of it: but all the time the true hero was being kept waiting; exercising his talents in the office of A-mir, or marshal, of pilgrim armies on the road to Mecca. This brother of Ti-lál was Muhammad—to give him his full name, Muhammad ibn A'bdi 'lla, al Ra-shid—at this moment prince of Ja-bal Sham-mar, and foremost man in all Arabia: that is, if before these pages are printed, the fate which he has meted out to so many do not overtake him.

> "The tug of your heart is the voice of your fate,"

says Schiller;[2] and with the proclamation of Ban-dar the "tug" came to Muhammad, then, as it chanced, at a distance from Há-yil. After a time he returned, apparently submissive; but in reality most dangerous. If all that we have to do is to accept Carlyle's word for it that the true *Könning*, King, or Ableman, supposing him to be discoverable, has a "divine right" over us; if the world's handed-

---

[1] It is said that Ban-dar, aided by his next brother, Badr, obtained the chiefship by shooting down his uncle, Mot-a'b. Doughty gives one version of it in vol. ii. pp. 14 and 15 of his "Travels"; the only feature of improbability in which is, that a brother of Ti-lál, himself a travelled man, should have suffered two such young scapegraces to make a target of him from a loophole inside his own castle.

[2] In *Wallenstein*.

down traditions both east and west the Caucasus have aught of prescription in them,—then may the method in which, on a spark falling on the powder, this man made himself master of Ja-bal Sham-mar, admit of justification; but Arabia, to her credit, does not think so. The massacre by him of his nephews and cousins is described both by Lady A. Blunt and Mr Doughty—with some variety of detail naturally, seeing that Hâ-yil has no newspapers. In its essential features, the story appeared long ago in Judges (ch. ix. 5); where we are told how "Abimelech went unto his father's house at Ophrah, and slew his brethren, the sons of Jerubbaal, being threescore and ten persons, upon one stone." Muhammad's victims were not so many; but his work was equally well finished. In one day he despatched with his own hand A-mir Ban-dar; and seizing the castle, or palace, had every male who could be found of the stock of A'bdu 'lla butchered before him. In Arabia a man is not considered murdered till every one on whom devolves, or may at a future time devolve, the sacred duty of avenging him is sent to the same bourn; and this, if restraining the wolfish appetite, makes the work go merrily on when started. It further seems—and here the Arab resembles the tiger—that no one who has once discovered the fine effects of man-killing will afterwards condescend to smaller practice. A-mir Muhammad's dagger-exploits now amount to a large number. The first to bring such topics under artistic treatment speaks of a "most brilliant constellation of murders, comprehending three Majesties, three Serene Highnesses, and one Excellency," as all lying "within so narrow a field of time as between A.D. 1588 and 1635."[1] No Arab since the Crusades ever had the chance of making a score like that. But from the latest accounts it is evident that the "diamond cut diamond" policy of the Ja-bal Sham-mar professional—the "murder him before he murder you" method—is progressing. We do not feel discourse of this nature to be a straying from our subject. If any reader incline to think so, we ask him to reserve his judgment. The connection between Arabian politics and Arabian horses came out just now, when it was seen in Captain Sadlier's journal how the wars of Wahabyism stripped the country of its mares. The effect of the Ja-bal Sham-mar programme on the stock of the desert will appear presently. Meanwhile we are not done with A-mir Muhammad. Several allusions have been made to the diminished state in our day of the Ibn Su-ủ'ds of Najd. The last great prince, so far, of their line, A-mir Fai-sal—he who received Sir L. Pelly—died in 1865. Then broke out those dissensions, at first between his two sons, and afterwards throughout the family, which favoured the growth of the Ibn Ra-shîds. So mutually interconnected are the stunting

---

[1] *Murder considered as one of the Fine Arts:* Thomas De Quincey.

of the central stem and the out-branching of its Ja-bal Sham-mar offshoot, that the Najdian empire is sometimes even said to have died down in southern, to revive again in northern, Arabia. But this view is superficial. True, in 1888 A-mir Muhammad crowned his House's triumph over its *ci-devant* suzerains by swooping down on Ar Ri-âdh with machine-guns and breech-loaders, and forcing on it a puppet Government. Not content with that, he accomplished a few months afterwards another piece of family extermination, this time rather in the Tarquin style—that is, by the hand of horsemen sent from Hâ-yil struck down mercilessly the tallest poppies in the Najdian garden, Fai-sal's three princely grandsons, Sa-â'd, Muhammad, and A'bdu 'lla; who, unable to brook the family downfall, had fled to Kharj in the adjacent district of Ya-mâ-ma, called for its fertility the Paradise of Najd, and famed in Arabian story for the bravery of its men and the *esprit* of its women. Out of the last-cited performance blood-revenge has followed: numerous panoramic scenes are, as we write, evolving themselves in the desert. Muhammad, if report say true, has sometimes had the worst of it. In a "God-governed" country like Central Arabia it may even be that the "writing on the wall" has appeared to him. We make not this remark to speculate or prophesy of the future. In the prime of life, and full of activity and projects, the Ja-bal Sham-mar chief may not even yet have reached his limits. In 1887, when the writer passed through Shâ-mi-ya, he found the two great palm oases of Shi-thâ-tha and Rah-hâ-li-ya all in a flutter after one of his *ghaz-us*. Scorning to strike settled folk, he had swept northward like a hurricane—as a few years previously he had done to within sight of Damascus—driving before him his natural enemies the Ae-ni-za. With him were the big caldrons, each able to take in three camels, which the Blunts saw at Hâ-yil. Everything about him was magnified by rumour: the size of his squadrons; the sacks of dollars carried on his camels; the arms and dresses of his *ri-jâ-jil* or followers. The Arab ideal is thus depicted by the poet A'mr :—

> [The tribes know] that we are spurners when angry,
> And acceptors when pleased;
> Defenders when submitted to,
> And the devil when defied.[1]

Similarly another poet : [2]—

---

[1] The idea in the first two lines probably is that of *rejecting and accepting presents*—one of the high points of diplomacy with Orientals. Military commanders who do not understand it may one day so misbestow their gifts as to be mistaken for suppliants; and the next, accept an offering from those whom they intend to punish, without realising that their doing so means alliance. An excellent proverb of the Arabs is: *Be none so sweet as to be swallowed; and none so bitter as to be spat out.*

[2] In the classical anthology *Al Ha-mâ-sa*: Freytag's edit., p. 47.

White [i.e., bare] are the parting-places of our hair:[1] ever on the boil our flesh-pots:
We compromise from our flocks and herds the blood-revenges due by us:[2]
Mine the race to whose founders ever was fatal
The cry of the combatants, "Ho! where are the front-fighters!"

All this well describes Muhammad. *Starve your dog and he will follow you, fatten him and he will bite you,* is an Arab proverb; but such churlishness has no place at Há-yil. Fear first, brotherhood afterwards; pitiless smiting to-day, kissing and feasting and being friends to-morrow, is the A-mîr's method. Out of an annual revenue of, as estimated, £40,000 (in kind and silver), Doughty sets down £1500 as going up the chimney of the public guest-house. Another secret of his popularity is the firmness of his rule, and the even-handed justice, free from bribery and the craft of clerks and lawyers, which, seated literally "in the gate" like David, he daily dispenses at Há-yil.[3] None can level at him the reproach cast on Mah-múd of Ghaz-nî by an old woman whose son had been taken by banditti in his Persian provinces—"Keep no more territory than you can rightly govern." Travellers know that they are in his country from there being no longer any robbers. Yet with all this let none suppose that Ja-bal Sham-mar fills, or ever will fill, the place of the old Najdian empire. Patriotism may be put aside. The use and purpose of all the web of confederacy which the A-mîr's wits have woven is simply what the immortal Squeers so racily described, the "swelling of one" at the cost of many,—the putting into Master Wackford the fatness of twenty, or twenty thousand. So far as that goes, the Ibn Su-û'd dynasty also might perhaps be included in the same category. But in one highly important respect, as must be familiar to many of our readers, that was *sui generis.* Not only because of its extension; at its best it reached from shore to shore, and a Su-û'd was able to dictate to the Porte the terms on which the pilgrimage to Mecca would be permitted. Not even because of its intensely national character; the central provinces of A'ridh, Ya-má-ma, and Sa-dîr produce the flower of the Arab race. To understand what the Najdian empire was, its other epithet of Wahabite needs recalling. How the Islamic new-birth termed Wahabyism was developed: how the author of it

---

[1] That is, from helmet. Compare Ezek. xxix. 18. In the Abyssinian expedition the writer, from wearing every day and all day an unventilated helmet, turned partially bald—a hint for young soldiers.

[2] This refers to the Arabs' insistence on blood for blood. So powerful was the speaker's tribe, that those who had vengeance to wreak against them were fain to accept the blood wit, instead of carrying on the feud.

[3] Thus Mr Doughty: "I have never heard any one speak against the Emîr's true administration of justice. When I asked if there were no hand-ling of bribes at Há-yil by those who are near the Prince's ear, . . . a tale was told me of one who brought a bribe to advance his cause at Há-yil; and when his matter was about to be examined he privately put ten *rials* into the Kádhi's (judge's) hand. But the Kádhi rising with his stick laid load upon the guilty Bedouin's shoulders until he was weary; and then he led him over to the Prince, sitting in his stall, who gave him many more blows himself, and commanded his slaves to beat him."—(*Op. cit.* in Catalog. No. 2, vol. i. p. 607.)

—himself but a scholar and preacher—made kings and warriors repeat its stern negations and advance its banners, will be glanced at when we come to speak in another chapter of the Bedouin. Here this passing reference is merely to the essential difference between a religious kingdom of that description and the purely secular edifice of the Ibn Ra-shíds, founded on the Kur-án but slightly; on fanaticism and orthodoxy not at all; on dollars, Martini Henrys, and personal force of character chiefly. At Hâ-yil all is compromise. Toleration and the promotion of free coming and going is the key-stone: yet even Wahabyism is not utterly broken with. The Ottoman Government also has to be humoured. No such burning deserts intervene between Baghdad and Ja-bal Sham-mar as those defending the southern capital; in one of which a whole Egyptian army died of thirst. A Turkish division marching from Na-jaf would pitch its tents before Hâ-yil in less than a month; and although the town is fortified, shelling would astonish it. To avert such unpleasantnesses the A-mir has no objections to call the Sultán Master, and even pray for him, provided it pass no further. A see-saw goes on between them in respect of making use of one another. The "successor of the Caliphs" hates the Wa-hâ-bis; by whom "Turks and infidels" are classed together: but he sees the advantages of having his rough work in Central Arabia done for him by a policeman of Muhammad's calibre. So also does it please the other to maul his rivals in the Sultán's name. After every feat of free-fighting he writes a letter to the nearest Turkish governor, describing himself effusively as the Sultán's servant. This adroit foreign policy is played by him as much as possible over the head of his tribal following. If he were to show it too much, for instance, by letting himself be dubbed a Pásha, half of his strength would fall from him. The shadowy claim indulged in by the Sultán of Rûm, in virtue of an alleged inheritance from the Arabian Caliphs to sovereignty over all Arabia, counts for nothing with the "nation that is at ease, that dwelleth without care; which have neither gates nor bars, which dwell alone."[1] So opposite is the effect of titles of honour in natural and artificial bodies respectively, that the Ja-bal Sham-mar chief would take less harm from a series of checks in *ghaz-u* than from putting on a Constantinople robe and ribbon. Without dwelling further on the contrast between this composite northern structure and the severely simple Najdian monolith to the south of it, let us note in passing the A-mir's own full perception that Ja-bal Sham-mar is not Najd. The Blunts had proof of this. When they talked of going from Hâ-yil to Ar Ri-ádh, the A-mir "made rather a face at the suggestion, and gave such an alarming account of what would there happen" to them, that they thought it wiser not to attempt it.[2]

---

[1] Jer. xlix. 31 : Revis. Vers.   [2] *Op. cit.* in Catalog. No. 12, vol. i. p. 254.

Even the Diogenes-tempered Doughty, though he visited many parts of Najd, did not venture to approach the dangerous centre of Reformed Islamism.[1] In one respect if in no other, Hâ-yil may be considered now to fill the place of Ar Ri-âdh. Partly because he is an Arab, partly to mount himself and his paladins in foray, its A-mir has a stud of horses rivalling Solomon's. Doughty says of him that he

"is a rich cattle-master; so that, if you will believe them, he possesses forty thousand camels. His stud is of good Najd blood; and as A'li 'el Ayid told me (an honest man and my neighbour, who was beforetime in the stud service—he had conducted horses for the former Amirs to the Pashas of Egypt), some 300 mares and 100 horses with many foals and fillies. After others' telling, Ibnu Rashîd has 400 free and bond soldiery; 200 mares of the blood; 100 horses; they are herded apart in the deserts, and he has 100 bond-servants (living with their families in booths of hair-cloth as the nomads) to keep them. Another told me the Amir's stud is divided in troops of 50 or 60—all mares, or all horses, together: the foals and fillies, after the weaning, are herded likewise by themselves. The troops are dispersed in the wilderness, now here now there, near or far off, according to the yearly springing of the wild herbage. The Amir's horses are grazed in nomad wise; the fore-feet hopshackled, they are dismissed to range from the morning. Barley or other grain they taste not; they are led home to the booths and tethered at evening; and drink the night's milk of the she-camel their foster-mother. So that it may seem the West Najd prince possesses horses and camels to the value of about a quarter of a million of pounds sterling, and that it has been gotten in two generations of the spoil of the poor Bedouin."

Not a doubt of it; and many a curse is on his head for it. Sa'di says that ten dervises can sleep on one blanket, and two emperors cannot be contained in one continent. And the nomad needs an ample elbow-room. Fertile of rulers as is the Arab blood, the spread of big Governments affects the martial clans of Najd much as that of drainage and cultivation does certain classes of animals. Turkish rule reaches them only here and there. In the Porte's Asiatic provinces, the problem of the submission of superior races to an inferior one has its solution partly in the looseness with which the Osmanli sit. Inside of flag-towns, were it not for the power of a gift over them, the Government establishments would be intolerable: for the surrounding country they form little more than a Sultân's sign-board. If Turkey had it in her to hold her Asiatic provinces as rigidly as England holds her Indian empire, the end would soon come. But a *régime* like A-mir Muhammad's is another matter. Rooted firmly in Arab soil, and everywhere interlacing with the *noblesse*

---

[1] "Persecution," says Hallam, "is the deadly original sin of the Reformed Churches." But why of the "*Reformed*" only? If "Reformed" Christianity approved of Geneva's burning Servetus for "heresy," had not Roman Christianity also its Inquisition? Tolerance is easy to a Gallio; persecution, it should rather have been said, is the "original" (if by that be meant besetting) "sin" of Pharisee, Wahâbbi, Papist, Puritan—all who have not discovered that no mortal man can possibly make certain that he and they who think with him are right in their beliefs and conclusions.

of the desert, this puts the hook in the nose of all Bedouin who can neither defy nor escape it. As for defiance, the A-mir's imported cannon and ordered troops of horse and camel-riders raise him in Arab eyes to the rank of a "Government." Yet may a pebble bring down a giant: eloquence especially is still a power in the practical politics of the desert; combinations kept together by the spear admit of being broken up by the tongue. Islamism, as long as it lasts, will infold within it the seeds of Wahabyism; and out of the latter there may come again, what has come before, empire; though the likelihood of it decreases with every year of the world's growth. Apart from life's natural period, a stroke of the Najdian *kid-dā-mi-ya*,[1] or crooked girdle-knife, may any day remove the A-mir. It has been seen how his stock was extirpated by him. As if in punishment and reprobation, the first craving of every man's heart—a son—has been denied to him: his house's interminable list of deaths and marriages has never had a birth inscribed in it. Whether, when death claims him, another like him will step out, or all this Ja-bal Sham-mar pageant will dissolve and leave not a wrack behind, is a question often mooted by lovers of the wild ways of the desert, the " simple blessings " of Bedouin. Meanwhile, happily for the true nomad, there are

"Hills beyond Pentland, and lands beyond Forth,"[2]—

spaces in which every freeman is still the other's equal, and the brisk desert air contains no germs of kingship. Not the Osmanli, not the Wa-hā-bī, least of all the Hā-yil princeling, will ever make a Pax Arabica resembling the Pax Britannica. We know of no large portion of the East, except, perhaps, British India, in which the "cankers of a calm world" are among the dangers to be apprehended. In connection with the A-mir's stud of Arabian horses, the first thing for the reader to remember is Mr Doughty's above-quoted remark, that it has been collected in two generations from the Bedouin proper. Not content with taking the mares of the Ae-ni-za and others from them in foray, he is always on the watch to buy. One day, perhaps, in Damascus or Aleppo coffee-houses the talk is all of some superior colt growing up in this tribe or that. And then, before anything can be done about him, the news comes in that he has been bought for Ibn Ra-shīd. All the Sham-mar, wherever distributed, are eager to serve him; every now and then a stalwart African or other messenger passes through Baghdad, taking to him two or three colts or fillies from far-away pastures. Not in the imperial stables at Constantinople, or in any other one place in the world probably, may

---

[1] So called because worn towards *front* of girdle. In other districts, where worn more on one *side*, it is called *jan-bī-ya*, or "side-arms." A third name is *shib-ri-ya*, lit. *span-length;* like "yard of clay" for a tobacco-pipe. In Arab hands two bites of a cherry are seldom made by it.

[2] Scott, in *Doom of Devorgoil*, Act ii. sc. 2.

modern traveller feast his eyes on so many picked Arabians as in his enclosures and pastures. His own favourite mares,

"In shape and gesture proudly eminent,"[1]

are the flower of the desert. Outside of these are high-class colts and fillies, designed for presentation to majesties. Then we reach the commoner brands, whether home-bred or *ghaz-u*-taken; yielding the lots sent annually to the Indian market, likewise animals to serve as presents — only another form of selling — to Páshas, visitors, and inferiors. Proverbially, when the Arab gives a cat, he expects a she-camel. Not to speak of the romantic figures of antiquity, even princes seldom bestow gifts for nothing: in ten years we have seen numbers of these Há-yil gift-horses in the stables of Baghdad officials; their quality graduated according to the A-mír's idea of what each several recipient's friendship was worth to him. Pilgrims of condition returning through his country from Mecca do not approach him empty-handed. An ancient Indian dame resident since the annexation of Oudh at Kar-ba-lá once showed us a very common mare and filly which had been given to her by the A-mír, as a return present for a Georgian beauty bought by her for him in the "Holy City."[2] The bestowal of a first-class horse or mare on an old Indian woman would seem to every Arab contrary to nature; so that the inferiority of the above, as of certain other specimens which we have seen of the A-mír's presentation-horses, is noticeable merely as showing that ka-dish-es may come out of Há-yil. Peninsular Arabia, it is true, does not form, as the country round Baghdad does, a breeding-ground of the animal last mentioned. The poor ka-dish[3] finds one of his chief

---

[1] *Paradise Lost*, Bk. I.

[2] If anywhere inland a blow is to be struck at the transport hither and thither, for sale, of human beings, it is at Mecca; but so far, not even a Consular Agent represents any foreign Power in the chief town of Al Hi-jáz. The Transcaucasian kingdom described by Marco Polo in his 4th chapter as Georgiana (in Persian *Gurj, et* Gurg-istán), Christianised since our fourth century, and now merged in the "holy Russian empire" (seat of government, Tiflis), shares with Circassia the distinction of supplying wives to Turkish harems. These are of the Caucasian type, and in youth more like boys than girls. A bevy of them forming the collection of a late aged Indian resident of Baghdad no sooner perceived their master moribund, than they asserted their independence Amazon fashion; each procuring for herself a husband with the ornaments which the old man had given to her! If, in that instance, the "whirligig of time" righted a great injury, so very often Georgians bought from Constantinople brokers receive an honourable and wifely status. In many other cases, especially in families of Páshas, they are handmaidens only; till one day Sarah "arranges" a marriage for Hagar; and some subaltern officer, or other candidate, hopeful of the Pásha's further favours, plays bridegroom to the serving-maid.

[3] All the rude hydraulic gear included in India under the name of *mdth* (i.e., bucket) is in Irák a *kard* (pronounced *chard*), and in Central Arabia *sa-ni-ní* (q. v. in Index I.) A cross-beam raised above the well-mouth (or projected over the river) with uprights, and supporting a wooden wheel or roller, forms the framework. Ropes having a huge leathern bag tied to one end, and a camel, ass, or pony harnessed to the other, pass over the wheel or wheels. The plash of the bag in the depths below notifies to the quadruped that he must put his shoulder to it, repacing the descent which leads from the brink, so that the bucket shall tilt into a reservoir or channel what portion of its contents may not have fallen back again through its leaky places in the process

walks in life—water-drawing—closed to him in Arabia proper. In Al Ha-sá, as seen above, springs and runnels serve the cultivator; in arider parts *sa-wâ-nî*, or camel-tackle, not ka-dish *chards*, are fitted to the wells. Yet, for one thing, there is the pilgrim route—Turkish, Persian, Bohemian, quite as much as Arabian. A convenient place as Há-yil may be to go to, as long as Muhammad's state continues, for those who without much labour would buy, at the A-mír's prices, genuine horses, such have need to be careful that they take not nondescripts, left behind by Constantinople Páshas, Tatar couriers, or Persian Aghas.

The "flanks of Najd" having thus been looked at, in a more systematic work the nine central provinces enumerated above in a footnote would next be visited. But this would prove interminable; and our design does not require it. Had it been otherwise, Najd proper would have shown to us, here, continuations of Nu-fûdh land—the towering sides of the valleys as sharp and sheer, but for torrent tracks, as if they had been cloven out of the limestone or sandstone plateau; there, elevated, and but slightly fertile, champaign-land, checkered by peaked and rocky mountain-barriers. In the depths of the Nu-fûdh, oasis-hamlets of the *ahl ma-dar*[1] would have attracted us; many of them cultivated by families of a horde or nation the main body of which is nomadic. In the busy upland townships, more of buying and selling, irrigating and ploughing, than of horse-breeding would have been noticed. But enough for the present of attempts at description. In our opening pages, as will be remembered, we saw how Najdian Bedouin make shift when pasture fails. The remainder of this chapter will be given to considering how, in the riverless peninsula, they whose heritage is the thirsty desert contend with the want of water. The inhabitants of countries in which no sound is more familiar than that of the falling rain, and clear streams are always running, can scarcely realise the opposite conditions, or how natural they appear to those who are accustomed to them.

Najdian ballads afford frequent glimpses of how, in good years, the land receives its allotted share of water. The masters of Arabian poetry, in the scarcity equally of animate and inanimate objects which the desert life offers, never tire of describing how, in winter, sterile mountains bring down the rain-clouds; how, for several days afterwards, the Nu-fûdh below run like rivers, so that plashes remain till early summer; while the main body of the current, sinking underground, reissues in the form of springs in distant lowlands. Such a sketch from Nature is

---

of ascent. Such is the force of association, that the undescribable creak of this rickety construction, in all which there is not a piece of sound carpentry, and which needs mending daily, though it may irritate the fretful, makes sweet music to those who have known what it was to hear it after spells of desert travel.

[1] Lit. *mud-folk*: opp. of *Ahl-wabar*, *tent-* (lit. *hair-*) *folk*.

the following, having for its scene the palm oasis of Tai-má, where, on the west, Nu-fúdh land slopes into Al Hi-jáz:—

Comrade, seest thou the lightning? look how it gleams! like the flash of a pair of hands amid the turreted clouds:[1]
Was yon its light? or the lamps of an anchoret[2] who has turned the oil on the twisted wicks?
I sat watching it [the cloud] with my companions, between Dhá-rij and Al U'-dhaib; far away was the object of our gaze:
On Ka-tan, I guess, the downpour of its right; and of its left, on Si-tár and Yadh-bul:
Then it poured out its deluge on Ku-tai-fa; throwing down on their chins the great trees of Ka-han-bul:
And there passed over Ka-nán of its flying scud; making the mountain-goats come down from it by every path:
And in Tai-má it spared not the stem of a single date-palm; and not a keep save those built of stone:
(Mount) Tha-bir, in the first burst of its rain, was like an Elder of the people in his striped cloak:
The top of Al Mu-jai-mir's head, in the midst of the torrent and its wrack, looked in the morning like the whorl of a spindle.[3]
And it [the rain-cloud] cast down on the plain of Al Gha-bít its burden; the alighting of a merchant of Yemen—him of the bales,—the caravaner.
In the morning, 'twas as if the singing-birds of the valley had sipped for their early draught the first flow of the grape's pure juice, mixed with spices;[4]
Thick at eve as the roots of the wild-onion, on its [the torrent's] distant margins, the beasts of prey drowned in it.

Nearly fourteen hundred years have passed since these verses of Im-ru 'l Kais[5] first won the hearts of Arabs. Here they are used to illustrate the Najdian climate rather than for ornament: wherefore fidelity to the original is better than metrical paraphrase. But he who would have them in long metre imitating, with variations, the original, will find them so reproduced, as elegantly as truly, in Mr C. J. Lyall's *Translations of Ancient Arabian Poetry*.[6] Apart from views of inanimate nature, the poem which contains them, consisting of some eighty couplets, descriptive, lyrical, and rhetorical, sets us down in the midst of the old life of Arabia, much as Burns's poems do in the kirks and farm-houses of western

---

[1] A simile perhaps referable to the great natural, or unnatural, order of "conceits"; yet the reverse of whimsical for Arabs, in whose discourse the hands move as rapidly as the tongue. La-bid says, in a poem contained in the Vienna edition of his Di-wán—
As if in the tops of the clouds, there were women clapping their hands.

[2] *V.* Index I., art. DER.

[3] The above place-names, except Gha-bít and Mu-jai-mir, belong to mountains bounding the view from the only slightly elevated site of Tai-má. Camels are still unloaded in the hollow of Gha-bít; the landmark of which is the low hill (perhaps only cairn) of Mu-jai-mir. The likening of the top of this, standing out amid the drift, to the notched "whorl" of the Arab spindle showing through a coil of twisted wool—"metaphor with a surprise" of Aristotle—like the comparison in Canticles of a black beauty with the "tents of Kedar,"—fulfils at least one poetic canon, adaptation to the audience. In Persia it is proverbial that the wise man who is seated with Maj-nún speaks to him of no other subject than Laila's beauty.

[4] "I would cause thee to drink of spiced wine."—Cant. viii. 2. A well-annotated collection of the parallelisms, not in allusion only but in colouring and texture, occurring in "the choicest of the songs of Solomon" and the earliest known Arabian poems respectively, might prove useful to students of the former.

[5] *V.* Index I., art. IM-RU 'l. KAIS (more classically, Im-ra-u 'l Kais).

[6] Williams & Norgate: 1885.

Scotland a century ago. Im-ru 'l Kais's period was before Muhammad's; and he lived and died a pagan. Having it in view, in another chapter, to cull from his ballad a further passage illustrative of a different subject, we may here observe that in his case the "blind minstrel" myth or theory is happily excluded. Not his laurel wreath only, but much of his personal history has been preserved. Authentic records describe him as a prince of Kin-da; a fifth-century offshoot from the Yemen empire. He seems to have made as much noise in his time with his exploits of war and adventure as with his compositions; and to have been the hero, and not merely maker and reciter, of his pieces. The name *Ma-liku 'dh dha-lil* which has come down with him, when rendered *Wandering King*, has been taken as showing that even in the days of Arabia's fullest licence he was famed for "roving." His own accounts of himself in his poem fit this view perfectly; but other stories have it that his loves were not returned. At any rate, his above-quoted title takes other meanings more naturally. But to revert to physical feature. No account of passing deluges, especially in districts which receive some of the rain brought up by the S.W. monsoon from the Indian Ocean, should obscure the view of Najdian aridity already given. Towns, of course, may be omitted; every permanent settlement of human beings has for its first essential a well or river. Neither need we recur to areas "as empty," to use an Arab figure, "as the belly of an ass." Apart from these, and speaking of its Bedouin-tenanted spaces, some of them representing three or four hundred miles of surface, the Arab peninsula, it may be here repeated, has want of water for the most potent cause of its peculiarities. In the Kur-ân it is said, *We* [God] *gave life to everything by means of water;*[1] and the changes which would follow in middle Arabia from artificial watering may perhaps be destined in the remote future to yield another illustration of it. It is not surprising that the Bedouin do not think of this; for, as seen already, the irrigation of their deserts would mean for them a notice to quit. But considering the deficiency, as well as the irregular seasonal[2] distribution, of their rainfall, their making not the smallest attempt to store it says little for their understandings. Or rather perhaps it is that, expecting in their dim natural religion to have everything done for them by Allah, their active energies run only in the narrowest traditional grooves. In other ways, also, this extreme dryness tends to stereotype the conditions favouring it. A country thus sealed against all mankind save Bad-us, and all transport save camels, is harder even than Afghân-istân for "openers" to enter; harder still to retire from; hardest of all to retain. Pelly

---

[1] S. xxi.
[2] With Bedouin the seasons are: *Ra-ti*, or spring; *Kahth*, time of greatest heat, from (auroral) rising of Pleiades to appearance of *Su-hail*, or Canopus; *Sa-fa-ri*, "fall of the year," between moderating of the heat and setting in of cold, or cool; lastly *Shi-ti*, our winter: each three months.

and other explorers mention having seen the remains of ancient aqueducts in the hills of Najd; but it is not known whose works they were. The Wahabite empire at all events cannot be credited with them. Instead of repairing the old reservoirs and conduits, the Ibn Su-ú'ds demolished them further. The reason given for this, it is curious to notice, corresponds with that alleged by certain religious oddities long ago in our country, against all contrivances designed to produce artificially benefits which God does not bestow spontaneously! For common use this argument may have answered; but any one can understand an A-mír of Najd having the same objection to large-scale irrigation which we islanders have to a Thames tunnel. Here it is needless to dwell too much on the years, or successions of years, of water-famine which periodically smite Arabia; when, except perhaps within the border of the monsoon, not a shower falls. Then, truly, the nomad's lot is cruel. All the associations of wooing, feasting, and fighting which endear to him the name of Spring vanish out of his life. No filling of the watering-places; no clothing of his Nu-fûdh with white-headed *un-sí*, most nutritious of herbage; no milk-flow; no wandering forth with his flocks and herds over fragrant pastures. The while the stricken tribesmen scatter in search of grass, or gather round any grimy pits or sand-pools in which a little water thick with drift and camel-ordure may have stagnated, a great mortality sets in—greater than one may often see among sheep in Scotland in severe winters. The mares perish first; then the small cattle; at last the camels. The children are given away to any one who will take them—thrown, as it were, on Providence: a better way, very likely, than collecting them in parochial "farms" and workhouses.[1] Not only in Arabia, but in every other country where horse-breeding is still on primitive lines, hard times similarly come to stock-masters. In Australia and southern Africa, droughts and murrains every ten or twenty years thin the horse-runs. In Najd, the speciality is the scarcity *every* year, and, more or less, all the year, of the pure element. Mr Doughty thus sets down his experiences in western Arabia, in the tents of the Ae-ni-za; not in late summer, when the water-supply falls to zero, but in the early spring, when it is at its best:—

"Sweet and light in these high deserts is the incorrupt air, but the water is scant and infected with camel-urine. Hirfa [wife of his nomad host] doled out to me at Zeyd's commandment hardly an ounce or two of the precious water every morning, that I might wash 'as the towns-people.' She thought it unthrift to pour out water thus when all day the thirsty tribesmen have not enough to drink. Many times between their waterings there is not a pint of water left in the greatest Shekh's tents; and when the goodman

---

[1] In towns of Arabs, the newly born infant whose mother may not own or rear it is left on the threshold of a mosque towards morning prayer-call; so that the first comer may take pity on it, and adopt it.

bids his housewife fill the bowl to make his guests' coffee, it is answered from their side, 'We have no water.'"[1]

Another traveller, the Italian, or Levantine, Guarmani,[2] who in 1863 went over the peninsula buying horses, has it in his journal that among the pariah hordes of the Sha-râ-rât, referred to by us already[3] as having Wâ-di Sir-hân and the country between Al Jauf and Ja-bal Sham-mar for their *dî-ras*, he heard old men declare that they had never tasted water in their lives! If it had been in Europe, this would not have sounded so incredible. He might have met the very man of whom the story goes, that once he undertook, for a wager, to tell, blindfolded, the name of every liquor offered to him; which he did successfully, till there was put in his hand a glass of "Adam's ale"—a tap so strange to him that he had to own himself defeated, and pay up! But we have never seen or heard of a wine-skin in tent of true nomadic Arab. Arabia is no exception to the statement that all countries have contrived the means of intoxication. It is told in Genesis how the "mocker" obtained possession of Noah.[4] That—and the connection is significant—occurs in one and the same passage with the intimation that the patriarch "began to be a husbandman" (*i.e.*, a *ha-dha-rî*), "and he planted a vineyard." It is also remarkable that when Abram, or Abraham—for Arabs the type of Bedouin manners—entertained the three heavenly visitors,[5] he set bread and flesh, butter and milk, *but not wine*, before them. Still more strikingly, we read in Jer. xxxv. of "the whole house," or clan, of the sons of Rechab refusing to drink wine; not, like the Nazarites (Num. vi. 2-8), under a self-dedicatory vow voluntarily assumed by individuals, but to preserve the rule of life coming down to them through the ages from their eponymous Shekh or "father," Rechab.[6] Even if the inference were to be drawn from these and other indications that the disseverance to this day of Bad-u land from the all but universal realm of Bacchus is of twin growth with the nomadic system, to our thinking many a lamer conclusion has been supported. The surface explanation, lack of means, may at all events be rejected: the Bad-u no more cultivates the tobacco-plant than the vine; yet it will be seen in another chapter that his pipe is seldom out. Nor does Islamism offer a solution. Certainly Muhammad must be regarded as the founder of the greatest total abstinence league in history; but it will appear elsewhere how indifferent the wandering Arabs are to Kuranic ordinance, except where it is drilled into them by Turks or Wahabis. In the "Days of Ignorance,"[7] fermented juice from Syrian vineyards, with

---

[1] *Op. cit.* in Catalog. No. 2, vol. i, p. 218.
[2] *Op. cit.* in Catalog. No. 27, p. 218.
[3] *V.* p. 15, *ante*.
[4] iv. 20, 23. *Et v.* Gen. xliii. 34.
[5] Gen. xviii. 1-8. [6] *V.* in Index I., art. Ri-kâb.
[7] Name given by Muslim to all the ante-Islamitic

stronger date-spirits, washed down the boiled mutton and camels' flesh at feasts of *ha-dha-rí* warriors and hunters. At the religious fairs of pagan Arabia, the Bedouin must have witnessed, probably even experienced, all the phantasmagoric symptoms of inebriation, from the first disturbance of the faculties, to the *dead-drunk* condition. But speaking of the central bodies of the nomad Arabs, we are mistaken if all this did not deepen in them their love of their own mode of life.[1] Some would have it that these things follow race; that the Arab inclines to sobriety as naturally as the Teuton, from Tacitus' time downward, does to free drinking; and that the notion of Muhammad's sermonisings having in this respect changed his countrymen is due to references to wine and wassail in the pre-Islamic poetry being too much taken *au sérieux*. But we demur to this. If the praises of wine may be sung by bards whose beverage is water, such effusions presuppose at least a sympathetic audience. Let the finest thing of this kind in European literature be put out, in Arab dress, in Najd, and no one would listen to it, any more than Englishmen would to verses going over the points of a riding-camel. Moreover, it was not all at once that Muhammad saw the necessity of making the rule against strong drink absolute. In one passage of the Kur-án, the fruits of the palm and vine, and the saccharine fermentations obtained from them, are cited as proofs of God's goodness;[2] in another, *rivers of wine* are included in heaven's charms.[3] Further, and more conclusive even than the early poetry on the point of old Arabian manners, might be quoted the

---

ages. Next to our own, no era ever set out with a more epoch-making incident than that dating from Muhammad's Flight to Medina (June 20th, A.D. 622). In a few years almost every feature of Arabian civilisation and town-life was altered by it. Arabian annalists have taken full advantage of the marked division in the national history which is thus presented, to crowd into the later period all the lights, into the earlier all the shadows. This may pass from the religious standpoint, but not from the secular: witness the greatness, both politically and commercially, of the old Sabæan and Minæan Arab sovereignties.

[1] Here an objection may be anticipated. Further on it will be illustrated how full the legendary and poetic lore of Arabs is of drinking-bouts. Such passages may seem to support the inference that the Bedouin before Muhammad were always ready for a revel when a travelling merchant came round with wine, and they had the means to purchase. But, first, it is impossible to determine how far these descriptions referred to Had-ar proper. The Arabian "makers" whose verses have come down, whatever they may have been by blood, were not Bedouin by

habit. It is idle looking for primitive manners in or near the seats of centralised governments. But the question is, If in prehistoric times the genuine Bedouin drank wine when they could get it, when and wherefore did they cast off this propensity? Apart from the operation of adequate causes, nations do not reverse their social customs. In countries partly tenanted by Arabs, wherever we have travelled with baggage-mules, we have been much applied to for brandy, by Osmanli military officers and others, but never by Bedouin. The passages of the old poetry which go round in desert circles are not those about the wine-jar, but those introducing the *bint* (maiden) and *ghazw*; mare and camel. We have never seen signs even in the Bedouin who approach Baghdad and Mosul, that the tradition of Jonadah the son of Reehab is observed by them only in the presence of strangers. But even supposing some of them to love the bottle secretly, why *secretly*, seeing that they do not profess Islamism?

[2] Sû-ra xvi.: word used for wine, SA-KAR, *q. v.* in Index I.

[3] S. xlvii.: word used for wine, KHAMR, *q. v.* in Index I.

injunction, put out doubtless on some special occasion, against the *coming to prayer in a state of intoxication*.[1] Not till later did it reveal itself to the Reformer that rules of moderation, however sufficient for well-off people, are but ropes of sand for the classes who take to drink not from the love of it, but because a dram is easier come by than clothes for the back or food for the belly. And after that there was no more parleying. In utterance upon utterance wine was condemned unreservedly. One text *declares heinous sin to be in it*: another ranks it with *abominations proceeding from Satan; . . . one of the Tempter's means of sowing enmity and hatred, and turning men aside from the remembrance and worship of God*.[2] Here we cannot occupy ourselves with the question of whether this rule of total abstinence, in so far as adhered to, has in a thousand years and more acted beneficially, or the opposite, on the Arab race, and on all the peoples which have received Islamism. Authorities are not wanting for the view that "a national love for strong drink is a characteristic of the nobler and more energetic populations of the world;" that "it accompanies public and private enterprise, constancy of purpose, liberality of thought, and aptitude for war."[3] If, instead of a Muhammad, a Bass or an Exshaw[4] had come to Arabia, perhaps the qualities which

---

[1] S. iv.; word used for *intoxicated*, *su-kâ-râ*, pl. of *sak-rân*, *v.* Index I., art. SA-KAR.

[2] Kur-ân: S. ii. *et v.* Three other usages of old Arabian life are pilloried with wine in the above quoted "revelations." The first is (Al) MAI-SIR, a round-game much associated with pagan feasts and hospitalities, in which differently marked arrows formed the "tickets" or "numbers," and hunks of slaughtered camels the stakes. In those early days it is doubtful if even chess (*shit-ranj*) was known to Arabia: more probably it came later, with cards (*gua-jî-fa*), backgammon (*nard*), draughts (*kâ-una*), and the rest, as the world opened to her. Nevertheless all such diversions, except perhaps chess, are held by strait-laced Arab Muslim to stand tabooed *by implication*. Sin is in the mere condition that *the winner shall receive from the loser*: not, apparently, with much reference to the effects of it on the latter, or to the casuistry of whether money thus pocketed belongs really to its new, or to its quondam, master; but because of Muhammad's condemnation of *Al Mai-sir*. The second prohibited thing was the setting up of "sacred stones" (*an-sâb*); as to which see in Index I., art. BAITU 'LLAH: and the third, the having recourse to *lots*, like the old Homeric heroes, to ascertain what God or fate had willed. In this also arrows (*az-lâm*), otherwise white pebbles, or ossicles ("bones") formed the implements; each having its own "message" or intimation marked on

it. It is impossible to consider in a footnote what effects Muhammad produced at the time and afterwards on these several phases of primitive manners. One of them, the symbolising of the divine by the erection of stones, received from him unquestionably a final blow. In regard to the others, all depends on the type of Islamism. Where that is lax and devious, poets like Hâ-fiz extol the grape-juice as *more to be desired and sweeter than the kiss of maidens*: before a journey millions draw a *fâl* (omen) from poet's verses, as in Europe "pricking for texts" is practised on the Bible: from Indus and Oxus to Mediterranean gambling flourishes among Muslim. Yet there are in all those spaces, as well as in India, middle Arabia, and Africa, millions who refuse the wine-cup, not like the Bedouin merely on traditional grounds, but because their Prophet has forbidden it: to whom, for the same reason, divination is accursed. Leaving the question of the good or evil of this, it surely is very remarkable that a growth of darkness like divination, uneradicated to this day in Europe, should in Arabia have so far yielded to one man's fiat; and that the same influence should so many hundred years ago in the same country have developed an attack on strong drink such as only the present century has witnessed in the United Kingdom and America.

[3] Quoted in *Ency. Brit.*, vol. vii. p. 482.

[4] Not long ago there lived in Bengal an old Hindû

advanced her to the height of greatness would have been so sublimated as to fix her there for ever; though it deserves remembering that even now, by her religion and institutions, she gives law to many of the realms which have been lost to her. Contenting ourselves with the conclusions that not only the Kenites, of whom was Rechab, and who as a branch of the Midianite nation are traceable to Abraham and Keturah, but the nomadic Arabs generally, have from the first "drunk no wine"; and that the Mecca lawgiver, sent as he believed to restore the faith and traditions of Abraham, exerted his authority to transmute this natural piece of desert abstinence into a taboo resting on a "revelation,"—it is time to notice how the Bad-u, importing no artificial beverage, and often for long periods without water, is saved from drying up. The Moses of his wilderness, as but few readers can need reminding, is his she-camel. Speaking for a moment generically of this oldest of living mammals,[1] the slightest glance at Arabia shows the magnitude of the services that have been rendered by him, in enabling mankind to explore and populate portions of the earth's surface which but for him would have remained uninhabited. Townsmen may call him "stupid"—the stupider, in many instances, the servant, the better for the master—or laugh at his long legs and hump back; but Najdian nomad prizes him as "God's own bounty."[2] Truly he is so: and whether the earth "brought him forth" suddenly, or he was developed joint by joint in the course of ages, is not very material. The Arab life could not go on without him. Almost every word in the Arabic dictionary, whatever may be its first mean-

---

who was very fond of brandy. When his eldest son returned from a visit to London, and began recounting the Presences into which he had been admitted, the father eagerly asked him whether he had seen John Exshaw! Yet this state of things in India should not be too much identified with English rule. Buddhism and Hinduism go back to such remote ages, that it is useless now quoting them for practical purposes. In the eleven centuries of partial Muslim conquest and rule in India, the masses were in a very primitive condition; but even then, a taste for noxious liquors pervaded considerable sections of them. The late Nizam of Hyderabad, in his zeal for the Kur-ân, prohibited the sale of strong drink. The revenue realisable from it he considered would be swallowed up in paying police magistrates and building prisons for its votaries. But never did a well-laid theory prove more futile. A Parsee merchant having a shop outside the city, in British limits, drove a great ready-money trade in champagnes and brandies; his customers' only scruples being against the *writing of their names in his books!* Casks and bottles of the nectar passed into the very palace, in curtained vehicles supposed to contain noble dames and veiled beauties! No such furtiveness, we hear, is now necessary anywhere in India. Every choice brand in Europe, equally with the most deleterious arracks, is imported. If "the invisible spirit of wine," as Cassio called it, the "enemy which men put into their mouths to steal away their brains," really be what casts a nation, then India's prospects were never fairer.

[2] 6000 camels formed part of the wealth of Job; one link more between the Uz Shekh and the Arabian Bedouin. From a name for the camel (*je-mal*) now being common to all the divisions of Semitic speech, while there is no such common name for the ostrich, or for the date-palm and its fruit, a high authority supposes—(1) that the Semites knew the camel while as yet one people dwelling together; (2) that the central table-land of Asia, near the sources of the Oxus and Jaxartes, the Jaihûn and Saihûn, where there is the camel, but not the palm or ostrich, was their location before the breaking up of their language.

[3] *Ba-ra-ka* (pl. *ba-ra-kât*), now the current word with Arabs, Persians, and Muslim Indians for *God's blessing*, means literally *Increase of camels*.

ing, denotes before we are done with it some part, or product, or habit of the camel. All Arabia is as redolent of the living beast as a country church in pastoral parts of Scotland is of sheep and shepherds on a wet Sunday. And little wonder, seeing that even his droppings, like those of the cow to Brahman, are pure to nomads. Bedouin mothers wash their babies, and Bedouin girls comb their tresses, in his urine : the desert caravaner who has been baking will run up to his staling camel, collect in his hands the acrid fluid, and clear his fingers with it.[1] The *dha-lûl*, or pacing-camel, may be either male or female; but Arabs naturally prefer for journeys the *nâ-ga*, or cow-camel, who as she goes can turn the weeds of the desert into milk that is meat and drink in one. In good seasons the camel kine are in milk most of the year; and that without requiring, as long as the spring herbage is fresh—two and a half to three months—to be taken to water. At night, when they are driven home, the lads milk them, while their sisters take in hand the smaller cattle. A bowl soon foams under every nâ-ga, and the sound of the milk-flow sets the mares a-whinnying, so that they are served first; and then they draw again for the tent-people. A foster-camel is told off for every mare; and so insufficient is the thin grass of the summer desert to keep the mares fit for *ghaz-u*, that when, as the year advances, the camels have to be sent botanising for days together, the mares go with them to drink the nightly draughts. We have seen offence unintentionally given at tables where *recherché* wines were flowing, through a guest's asking for a glass of water. But the greatest sounder of vinous depths never was more disturbed from this cause than a Shâ-mî-ya Shekh once was, on our mentioning water, with a skinful of camel's milk hanging on trestles at the tent door. "When the butt is out"—meaning the butt of this chief sustenance of nomads—" we will drink water,—not a drop before," say Bedouin. Four things in the desert life have chords of their own in every heart—the newly-born male child; the guest; the mare; and the she-camel; but the last holds a unique place, at once as nursing-mother, and type of wealth or increase. In Im-ru 'l Kais' ballad the horse is not introduced till near the end. But the same effusion cannot go further than its fifth couplet without bringing in the camel; while further on are two vivid sketches, depending for their interest not so much on the poet's charmers as on how, in the first, he slaughtered his dha-lûl to feast a band of maidens, and amused himself by making them carry on its trappings; in the second, got up into the fair U'nai-za's camel litter. His contemporary, A'n-ta-ra, or A'n-tar, happening in his third couplet to mention his nâ-ga, instantly breaks off into a laudation of her. So much does perception wait on association, that the nâ-ga actually forms a type of beauty for

---

[1] These several statements rest on the authority of Doughty (v. his vol. i, pp. 212, 237, et 340). But the writer, from what he has either seen or heard, can bear witness to them. Compare the Scottish custom noticed in *Adam Black's Memoirs*, p. 27, of *washing the head with whisky!*

Arabs.[1] Even her voice, so harsh to us, furnishes them with an ideal. Another member of the "tuneful quire" just quoted from [2] admiringly compares the warbling [3] of a beautiful glee-maiden with *the utterances of a nursing-camel over a dead young one!* Tried by more practical tests than the poetical, the relative value of the mare and the nâ-ga is regulated by circumstances, and above all by locality. When either animal is pitted against a bag of sovereigns, the choice depends on how much the bag contains; and the nomad's spiral fingers may be seen counting every coin through the material of the bag, all the time that he is saying how useless money is, compared with his four-footed treasure, the bringer forth of others like her. But when the same man has to choose between the mare and the nâ-ga, sometimes his wits are puzzled. Guarmani mentions his once giving a hundred camels in Najd for three desert stallions in the full vigour of their age; two, deep bay, nearly black—we take it "Voltigeur's colour"—the other, bay with black points. He at the same time informs us, after the manner of horse-buyers, that this deal was effected only because of certain favouring circumstances; and that often a hundred camels are given for one stallion of the very highest class, such as, according to his statement, Bedouin prize above the mare, keep in separate pastures, and ride only in the hour of peril.[4] This representation, in so far as it shows to us the Bedouin riding stallions, is too novel to be accepted on one man's authority; but without doubt Najd is incomparably more prolific in camels than in horses;[5] so that a whole string of the former may be bartered in it for one of the latter. It will be seen further on that the conditions in this respect are very different in Euphrates land.

The central thread of these remarks, it will be remembered, is, how does Najdian nomad overcome the want of water? Such further details as belong to this subject will fall in conveniently if we now recur, adverting more particularly to Central Arabian Bad-u land, to the question approached, with reference to all the peninsula, in our preliminary chapter,—is the horse-yield full or inconsiderable? Palgrave has the following observations:—

In Najd—"a horse is by no means an article of everyday possession, or of ordinary and working use. War and parade are, in fact, almost the only occasions on which it is employed; and no genuine Arab would ever dream of mounting his horse for a mere peaceful journey, whether for a short or a long distance. Hence horses are the almost exclusive property of the chiefs; who keep them for themselves, and often for the equipment of their armed retainers; and of a few wealthy or distinguished individuals, who regard them as an investment of capital or an ornament of social rank. . . . Military enterprise and the cen-

---

[1] *Ja-mal*, generically in Arabic The Camel (also, *par excellence*, the male), has among its essential meanings that of *comeliness*, or *beauty*.
[2] Ta-ra-fa, c. 600 A.D.: v. Index I., art. (*Al*) MU-'AL-LA-KAT.
[3] Lit., *making a note come back*.
[4] *Op. cit.* in Catalog. No. 27, p. 41.
[5] Arabs call it *Ummu 'l Ib-il*, or *Mother of camels*; not *Ummu 'l khail, Mother of horses*.

tralisation of wealth and power enabled the Wa-há-bi chiefs of recent date to collect and rear a greater number of horses than had perhaps ever before been possessed by a single Arab potentate; and the stables and pastures of the Sultán of Du-rai-î-ya may well have, as has been stated, contained 10,000 horses, since those of his much enfeebled successor at Riádh are told off at nearly half that amount. But if we allow 20,000 for the total census of pure breeds in Najd, a full allowance, and assign an equal number to the rest of the peninsula, thus making 40,000 in all, we shall still be rather in danger of an over than of an under statement."[1]

Now all this is the merest talk of a townsman; one who, as touching horses, has not thought out the subject, but would not leave his book unadorned with references to it. From first to last there is not a word of nomads. "Chiefs," whether urban or rural; "a few wealthy or distinguished individuals;" and "potentates," so engross him that he never gets within sight of the clans of the open. Lady A. Blunt, as has been seen, on realising at Há-yil that it would be impossible in Najd to go among the Bedouin, felt her curiosity sated; and joining a train of pilgrims, soon reached Baghdad[2]—no more Arabia than Cairo is Arabia. The following remarks by her, therefore, too much follow Palgrave:

"Whatever may have been the case formerly, horses of any kind are now exceedingly rare in Najd. One may travel vast distances in the peninsula without meeting a single horse, or even crossing a horse-track. Both in the *Nu-fúdh* and on our return journey to the Euphrates, we carefully examined every track of man and beast we met; but ... not twenty of these proved to be tracks of horses. The wind no doubt obliterates footsteps quickly; but it could not wholly do so, if there were a great number of the animals near. The Ketherin, a true Najd tribe and a branch of the Ba-ni Khá-lid, told us with some pride that they could mount a hundred horsemen; and even the Muteyr, reputed to be the greatest breeders of thoroughbred stock in Najd, are said to possess only 400 mares. The horse is a luxury with the Bedouin of the peninsula; and not, as it is with those of the North [Shá-mi-ya], a necessity of their daily life. Their journeys and raids and wars are all made on camel, not on horseback; and at most the Shekh mounts his mare at the moment of battle. The want of water in Najd is a sufficient reason for this. Horses there are kept for show rather than actual use, and are looked upon as far too precious to run unnecessary risks."[3]

A great deal in the above requires, with all conceivable deference, to be qualified. Why, even taking the slight data which are stated in it, if it had been the case that "horses of any kind are now exceedingly rare in Najd," a sub-branch like the Ketherin would not have boasted 100 mares, and the Muteyr or Im-tair 400. Darwin made the calculation of the elephant that, supposing a pair to begin breeding at 30, and to go on to 90, bringing forth in that space three pair of young, then at the end of 500 years there would be alive 15 millions of their descendants. Where, then, is the progeny even of the above 500

---

[1] *Op. cit.* in Catalog. No. 19, vol. ii. p. 241. [3] *Op. cit.* in Catalog. No. 12, vol. ii. p. 13.
[2] *V. supra*, p. 44.

mares? The numbers of the clan U'tai-ba are given in a footnote below, on the sound authority of Doughty, at 6000; out of which must surely come, say, 2000 horsemen, or more. We regret that no positive evidence on this subject, resting on our own eyesight, is with us. Nomads and their mares are as difficult to count, even when one is in the thick of them, as the leaves of a forest-tree when a gale is blowing. The fact of large bodies of those Bedouin who have extended outward from Najd, notably the Ru-wa-la, re-entering it most years in winter, adds to the uncertainty. We cannot assign any substantial foundation to Palgrave's figures. Mr Doughty might have collected statistics worthy of acceptance; but horse subjects occupied him only casually. The professional horse-buyer Guarmani, on finding himself within the enchanted Najdian cavern, may have overdrawn his description of its treasures. As for the Arabs, exaggeration on points of number, habitual to all of us, is carried by them to its highest pitch. But looking at all the evidence, from that of the ancient poetry downward, and avoiding equally the one extreme and the other, we can but repeat the statement made in a previous chapter,[1] in connection with a view of Burckhardt's, that if from all the *ái-ras* of the untamed nations of the peninsula[2] all the squadrons could be mustered, a horde, or *Urdú*, of light-horsemen not wanting at least in numbers, whatever it might lack in discipline and coherence, would display itself. It almost counts for a rule of nature that wherever in Asia or Africa the *ghaz-u* life is led by Bad-us, there shall be found the Bad-u mare; and Najd is no exception. What

---

[1] *V.* p. 10, *supra*.

[2] The following list of the nomadic nations of the peninsula, made from records or inquiries, not travel, may serve for want of better. The several headings are comprehensive; each including an immense number of ramifications. All the nations shown in it are not of the same class. Many consist of warlike mare and camel Bad-us; while others rather resemble helots. Not impossibly, several of the headings may be those of peoples now absorbed or replaced by others:—

AL MUR-RA, south of Al Ha-sá.
BA-NÉ HIJR, adjacent *di-ras*.
BA-NÉ KHÁ-LID, north of Al Ha-sá.
DA-WÁ-SIR, ostrich-hunters on skirts of great Red Desert.
DHA-FÍR, towards Euphrates.
HARB, great and warlike nation, much ramified, of Al Hi-jáz.
HI-TAIM, nomads; spread all over north of peninsula, but not accounted Bedouin; famed for their *she-láls*.

HU-DHAIL, shepherd nation of Meccan Arabia.
HU-WAI-TAT, nation (widely diffused and much mixed in character) of Red Sea littoral.
JM-TAIR, the hornets of the south; great horse-breeders.
KAH-TAN, nation of the south; noble in blood, rich in horses, but in last degree fanatical, truculent, unapproachable. Desert fable imputes to them many savageries, including even the drinking of an enemy's blood as a mark of irrestrainable fierceness.
MA'Z, N.E. Red Sea littoral, whence, like so many others, they have pushed into Africa.
SHA-RA-RAT, all round Al Jawf; nomadic, but squalid.
TAI, a noble race; long ago migrated out of Arabia proper, though its roots are still in Najd.
U'J-MÁN, Persian Gulf littoral, from Ku-wait southward.
U'TAI-BA, hardy warriors. Desert between Tá-if and Ka-sím. Their horses excel. "May be nearly 6000 souls," says Doughty. Stubborn resisters of Ja-bal Sham-mar yoke.

the desert Shekh rides or does not ride when merely on the move or hover is immaterial: in order to his mounting his mare when spear-blades shimmer on the horizon, he must always have her with him. As for "luxury" and "show," everything of the kind belongs to townsmen. It has just been noticed how in Nu-fûdh land the mare, instead of, as on the grassy steppes of Turk-istân, supplying her master with pailfuls of his favourite *kumis*,[1] herself drinks up the milk-flow. During an expedition she is a very great charge and trouble. How far the Arabian excels other varieties in power of doing without water will be spoken of elsewhere. Here we need only tell the reader that, although the mare of Najd may not need such bumpers as others that have never thirsted, yet she is not a little burdensome in this way to her master. Water once a-day is the least that will serve her: to keep her like what the Arabs call her, and what she has to be for foray, a "bird without wings." she must dip her muzzle in it oftener. Long ago, when Clive was conquering Bengal, an observant Rajah said that if he had a regiment of Englishmen he would send them to the field in palanquins, to be slipped like bull-dogs under the enemy's nose. The Bedouin's treatment of his mare somewhat carries out this idea. Like the knight's war-horse behind his palfrey, she is led in the wake of her master's riding-camel. A second camel takes the water-supply—a great pile of gurgling goat-skins, which she empties in perhaps a couple of days. These facts speak for themselves. Ere now the reader will have discovered that the Arabian Bedouin, whatever else he may be, is not fool enough to take all this trouble with a servant not worth it. If the camels provide the mares with sustenance, the mares defend the camels:—

"Useless each without the other,"

as the youthful Hiawatha, deep in dreams of Minnehaha, said within himself of man and woman. "No one in the Sah-râ," says the A-mir A'bdu 'l Kâ-dir,

---

[1] Also spelt *koumiss*, the staple drink and nourishment of the Mongols; described in Schuyler's *Turk-istân* (1876) as "sourish to the taste, but not unpleasant, and possessing agreeable exhilarating, though not intoxicating, qualities." Marco Polo likens it to *white wine*. The mares are milked into bottle-necked horse-skins; some stuff is added to set up acetous fermentation; after which they have to keep at it every now and again during several days with a churn-stick. The Turk-umâns take their horses in spring to opener places than their winter quarters. Foaling follows; ten days after which the foals are weaned, and their dams driven off in herds, each herd headed by a stallion. Thereafter nearly all their milk goes to the sustenance of their masters. Three times in the twenty-four hours they are brought in droves to the tents to be milked, when every weanling is allowed about a couple of minutes at the udder. Among all the hordes of Turk-istân and Turk-menia the Khirghiz come nearest the Arabs in cleverness at "lifting," not sheep and camels, but whole herds, perhaps 500 head, of horses. There is this great difference between them, that the Khirghiz seldom ride mares, but either geldings or entire horses. These they back as yearlings, alleging that otherwise they would grow up unapproachable. Hence their horses are more or less stunted, while their mares excel in size. Often the Khirghiz get up what they call a *baiga* or horse-race on a grand scale, over from 30 to 50 miles. Their system of training turns on gradually reducing the grass to about two straws a-day—for the last four or five days not even so much—while mare's milk, fresh or fermented, is substituted for water.

"cares to possess ten camels till he has a horse to defend them against those who might assail them." And again: "When you see the horses of the *gom* [enemy] marching proudly, their heads up, and making the air re-echo with their neighings, rest assured that victory accompanies them. But, on the other hand, when you see their horses marching sadly, with their heads down, without neighing, but lashing themselves with their tails, be sure that fortune has abandoned them."[1] In desert warfare there is no foot-soldiering. Slow-shooting matchlock-men, perched on camels, represent at once the infantry and artillery. When, if it be a mere foray, the prey is sighted, or if it be a heavier affair, the hostile squadrons, with the help of his long spear every Shekh springs to the ground. Another jump, and the mares are mounted; and all the riders scour over the empty wilderness, devil take the hindmost, cloaks and shirts and long tresses streaming out as in a flight of witches. Meanwhile the front place in the camel-saddle is taken by the *ra-dif*, or second man, commonly a kind of henchman, but often a Shekhling who has lost his mare. This fellow opens fire with his clouted musket; but as for charging on a camel, Balaam might as well have tried it on his ass! All the fire of her rider's Semitic nature enters into the generous mare. The star on her forehead, or blaze[2] on her face, is the oriflamme of victory. The big ruminant, on the contrary, for once misplaced, is little better than a magnified sheep. Press her, and she will very likely stop and bray; perhaps sink on her knees and wallow. If, when her rider's piece is empty, a horseman swoop down on him, all that he can do is to jump off and run for it, leaving her as prize of war. When the Bad-u's mare is bounding under him, and the fresh morning air raises his spirits to the highest, one of his cantatas is this:—

> Not for me the dullard camel,[3]
> Deck her saddle as they may!
> Bounding with her crest uplifted,[4]
> Dearer far my blood-red bay!
> My blood-red bay—a touch will turn her
> In the hottest of the fray!

---

[1] *Op. cit.* in Catalog. No. 23, pp. 14 *et* 241.

[2] Arabs call a dash of white passing out of the forehead a *ghur-ra*, meaning a *whiteness*: the colour in their simple minds of good-omened things generally. The Romans, we know, marked their good days with white pebbles, and their bad with black. In Najd, one who meets a white camel goes on his way rejoicing. *May thy black days become white ones*, is one of their forms of good wishing.

[3] The word thus translated is *dha-lûl*- lit. meaning, *broken*; from *dhull, subjection,* or *abasement*. Qu.

have we in *dhull* and *dull* a root common both to Semitic and Indo-European languages? Or is it a mere accidental correspondence of vocabularies?

[4] *Arduus cervix* of Horace. Some desert horses, when they are cantering, lift up the neck and crest like a serpent, while carrying the head perfectly. La-bîd depicts his mare as elevating her neck till it resembled the stem of a palm-tree too passingly smooth for the date-gatherers to ascend it. Another poet likens the long and lifted-up neck of his riding-camel to the rudder of a skiff sailing up the Tigris.

CHAPTER IV.

EXODUSES OF BEDOUIN OUT OF NAJD.

THE aspects of Arabia proper, including the food and water question, in so far as affecting horse-breeding, have now been examined. It might have been stated further that, even inside of the peninsula, a difference between tribe and tribe, in respect of the size and number of their horses, is perceptible, according as its *dî-ra* lies in the more rainless middle tracts, or, like the country of Kah-tân and U'tai-ba, nearer the south, within reach of the yearly monsoon.[1] It will be seen in the sequel how this view is confirmed by observations made outside of Najd, in the desert pastures of the Euphrates. The mere fact of those trans-peninsular regions which we are to enter in the next succeeding chapters being tenanted partly by Najdian nomads yields an illustration of it. We have already reckoned among the causes of Bedouin migration northward all the political passages which were glanced at in connection with the Wahabite empire and the Ja-bal Sham-mar Shekhate. But, that admitted, it is well in evidence that the movements out of Najd chiefly have depended on what has sent, with us, the Celt into the Lowlands—nay, the Scot himself into England, and into "New Caledonias" all over the world—want of food at home!

Not to go back to the migrations of antiquity, like that of the Tai[2] into the

---

[1] "The men of the north; the horses of the south," is a saying in Najd; where it is not the case that the pure-bred Arabian everywhere is of small stature or stunted. Once, on the Euphrates, we met officers of the Sultán's stables leading to Constantinople a bay horse very like one of our own Beacon course performers, which we were informed had lately been taken in foray from the southern nation of Kah-tân. At the time we doubted it, owing to what is stated in books about Najdian horses all being small. Subsequently we have come to know better; and the pity is that these Kah-tân are too dangerous and fanatical for anybody who is not one of them to venture near them.

[2] In Aramæan or Syriac, Ta-yô-yê supplies a comprehensive name for all Arabs; from which we learn that the Aramæans anciently had the Tai for neighbours. The tallest and noblest-looking Arab ever seen by us was a snowy-bearded patriarch of the Tai—a wealthy camel-owner of Arbil (τὰ Ἄρβηλα), not far from Mosul. Hâ-tim, whose generosity is still proverbial, was of the Tai. A legend of him is related by Layard: how when the fame of a mare

Tigris pastures, the exits chiefly bearing on our subject are the pushing northward, not so very long ago, of the two great rival nations of the Ae-ni-za and Sham-mar: the former into Shá-mi-ya, better known to Europeans as the "Syrian," also "Palmyrene," desert; the latter, into the important territory between or on the upper and middle Tigris and Euphrates, having for its best-known landmarks Urfa and Rak-ka, Mosul, Na-si-bin, and Di-ár-bakr, and called by Arabs Al Ja-zi-ra. Nothing could be closer than the connection between both those great departures of the *Arabes Scenitæ*, or Tent Arabs, and the later history of the Arabian horse. For one thing, he has enormously increased in numbers in the "pastures new" thus opened out to him. For another, Najdian race purity has undergone considerable alteration in the new localities. Reserving such topics, here let us speak merely of the exoduses. It is not in question that both proceeded from Najd. It is also well ascertained that the Ae-ni-za, said by Lady A. Blunt to be to the Sham-mar as seven to three,[1] were the first to migrate. No records exist of the several detachments in which, tribe after tribe, or family after family, these first entered Shá-mi-ya.[2] But the famous Darley Arabian came from the Ae-ni-za. It is further known that he was procured from his breeders, and sent to England, in the beginning of the eighteenth century. And hence it is to be inferred that two hundred years ago the pointing northward of the Ae-ni-za had begun. Soon Shá-mi-ya was overrun by them; and that it formed, say a hundred years ago, what it still is, one of the greatest breeding-grounds of the Bedouin horse in all Arabia, may be gathered from Burckhardt's writing that if any of the European Powers required

in his possession had travelled to the Golden Horn, and the Greek emperor 'it happened before the Turkish conquest' sent men to buy her, it was found on their disclosing their errand that the priceless treasure had been slaughtered for their entertainment, a time of famine having spared neither sheep nor camel. Comparatively recently a minor difficulty—want of firewood—was thus got over by a Shekh of the Sham-mar when strangers came to him. A travelling merchant happened to be passing, with bales of coarse cotton cloth upon his camels. A number of his bales were taken to the guest-tent, and their contents torn up and soaked in melted butter. A fire was made with this, and the coffee-pot set a-boiling, and a dinner cooked that satisfied every one. Such is desert hospitality.

[1] By this authority the Ae-ni-za tents are estimated approximately at 30,000, and the Sham-mar at 12,000 or 12,500; representing, at four to a tent, the former 120,000, the latter 50,000 souls. Palgrave, while giving as the principal subdivisions of the Ae-ni-za, the Sba' on the north, and the Wald Ali on the west, and the Ru-wa-la on the south, and assigning to them all the space between Syria and Ja-bal Sham-mar, guesses about 30,000 lances as what, if united, they could muster. Burckhardt's estimate, made fully half a century earlier, allowed to the Ae-ni-za a total of no fewer than from 300,000 to 350,000 souls.

Of the Sham-mar Palgrave says that their numbers about equal those of the Ae-ni-za; but this view is at variance with common Arab belief. All Arabia has it that the palm of valour is as clearly with the Sham-mar as superiority of numbers is with the Ae-ni-za; in fact, that if the Sham-mar were anything like as many as their rivals, there would be no Ae-ni-za left.

[2] Once when marching down the Euphrates valley, west the river, we halted for the night on a rocky slope called *Tal-at Mil-hem*: according to local tradition, the spot where a detachment of Ae-ni-za made its first lodgment in Shá-mi-ya, led by a certain Shekh Mil-hem.

Arabians to ennoble their studs, Damascus—western gateway of Shá-mi-ya—was the best place for their purchasing agents to visit.[1]

The Sham-mar exodus from Najd occurred about a hundred years ago. At Mosul old people still refer to it almost as if it had happened in their time, in words reminding one of the mission sent by Moses to spy out Canaan.[2] About 1804, they tell us, a Sham-mar free lance, called Abu Ru-wais, or *the man with the little head*, evidently, however, having a good deal in it, chancing to ride a foray in Shá-mi-ya, followed it up to the Euphrates; and obtaining from the river's western bank a view of the pastures on the further side, pushed across to explore. Finding the land as fat as Najd was lean, he and his comrades carried back such a description as made every mouth water: nay, even took with them bundles of produce; like the Israelitish tribes, and the "grapes, pomegranates, and figs." Drought, it happened, had brought Najd that year to starvation-point: so that the Shammar were only too glad to issue out of it, like eager hornets; till by degrees, after beating off every opponent, they occupied, Arab fashion, Al Ja-zi-ra.

Leaving the above two important departures to serve as specimens of very many others, some account of the three geographical spaces which have thus been added to the country of the Arabian horse has to be attempted in the next three chapters.

---

[1] *Op. cit*, in Catalog. No. 15, vol. ii. p. 57. [2] Numbers xiii.

CHAPTER V.

SHÁ-MI-YA; OR DESERTS WEST THE EUPHRATES.

ALL the regions watered by the Tigris and Euphrates, from about Ba-lis on the latter, in lat. 36°, to the Persian Gulf and Arabia proper in the south, are divided by the Arabs into *Bá-di-atu 'sh Shám*, or "desert of the North," oftener Shá-mi-ya; *Bá-di-atu 'l Ja-zí-ra*, or "desert of Al Ja-zi-ra"; and *Bá-di-atu 'l I'rák*, or "desert of I'rák." Practically, *Shám* means *the North;* and Shá-mi-ya, *towards the North*. But Shám also is the Arabs' name at once for the country which we call Syria, extending for some 400 miles between the Mediterranean and the Euphrates, and for its capital Damascus, a very ancient settlement of Semites.[1] The translation "Syrian desert" commonly serving for *Shá-mí-ya* is right, if by "Syrian" be understood *northern;* misleading, if it suggest that Shá-mi-ya forms part of Syria. Filling up the space between Palestine and the middle Euphrates; insensibly merging in Syria towards the north; entering on the south the peninsula, Shá-mí-ya belongs to Arabia. No one who has crossed its harsh and arid uplands, formed mostly of gypsum and marls; thirsted in its waterless wá-dis; and shared the life of its *ghaz-u* riders, will hesitate to reckon it to the great lone land of the Ba-da-wí. The "Arabia" into which Paul "went away" from Damascus apparently was Shá-mi-ya.[2] Compared with the circle of foliage and verdure which surrounds Damascus, one might rashly say of Shá-mi-ya, "there is no good in it"; but after most parts of Arabia proper, it must well content the nomad. The Euphrates washes all its eastern margin. Out of its stony central region, called, *par excellence*, the *Ha-mád*, or desert, the Ae-ni-za issue in summer to dress their water-skins in the river, and freshen up their mares with green grass and barley. A striking feature of the valley of the Euphrates is the numerous perished cities—awaiting the labours and discoveries of another

---

[1] Gen. xv. 2.   [2] Gal. i. 17.

Layard—of which it contains the traces. But it is also studded with villages, one or two of them almost towns; indeed everywhere are scattered over it, in tents and hamlets, communities engaged in husbandry. The Ha-mád itself contains oases to which, in a general way, the description given above of Al Ha-sà is applicable. Chief among these is Tadmor, or Palmyra,[1] about 160 miles north-east from Damascus, and five days' camel journey from the Euphrates. Whether this belongs more to Syria or Shâ-mi-ya need not here be debated. Neither does it concern us to recall the picturesque events of which in the third Christian century it formed the theatre: how, from a mere ploughland of settled Semites taken by some desert lord under his protection, Tadmor, aided by the convenience of its site on the caravan route between Asia Minor, Europe, and the Indian and Chinese east, expanded into a commercial emporium: how, after its incorporation by Rome with her own imperial system, it figured for 150 years and more as mistress of the Roman east: how its widowed queen, Zenobia—the Boadicea of her race and country—aiming at political independence, with the desert at her back, and all its chivalry united under her, defied Rome's veteran generals: how, at last, the Emperor Aurelian marched against the "Queen of the East," after an arduous siege took her city, and carried off the swarthy heroine to attend his chariot to the Capitol. More to the present purpose are these two views of Tadmor. In the poor hamlet now disposing itself among its fallen fortifications and long lines of Corinthian columns, supplies are procurable; so that if one can but master the objections, or elude the vigilance, of the Osmanli revenue officer posted in it, there is no better place to start from in search of the wasp-like legions of the Ac-ni-za.

What a mighty difference it must make to Shâ-mi-ya horse-breeders to have the Euphrates to fall back on, may be imagined. Here, in its middle course, the historical river formed the boundary long ago between the Assyrian empire on the east and the great nation of the Hittites on the west; rather later, the standards of the Greeks and Romans often were reflected in its waters.

"But something ails it now: the spot is cursed."[2]

---

[1] The derivation of the name *Palmyra* bestowed by the Greeks and Romans is obvious enough. Its Semitic name of Tadmor, substantially the same both in Arabic and Hebrew, from *tamar*, a palm, equally indicates what still forms the principal natural feature of the same spot. But when it comes to pronouncing this the identical "Tadmor in the wilderness" of 2 Chron. viii. 4, as built by Solomon, recent Biblical criticism follows, as usual, two courses. Be this as it may, the ruins still throwing their shadows over Tadmor belong to the same imposing order as those of the Temple of the Sun at Baalbek, the Temple of Jupiter at Athens, and the Parthenon. In 1694 this mine of archæology was rediscovered by a party of English merchants settled in Aleppo, distant about seven days for dromedaries. Half a century later another Englishman (R. Wood) published large-scale drawings of the ruins, with historical preface, under the title of *The Ruins of Palmyra, otherwise Tadmor in the Desert* (1753).

[2] Wordsworth.

Nothing more heroic than a *ghaz-u* of the Ae-ni-za on the Sham-mar, or the Sham-mar on the Ae-ni-za, now crosses it. In winter, when the nights are long, the water cold and swollen, and the formidable *ghai-lân*[1] blowing, raids are out of season. In spring also, when the mares are foaling, they are as far as possible avoided. At such times we have ridden up and down the Euphrates valley without ever catching a glimpse of Bedouin. But later on, when the fords are easy, and the interior of the Ha-mâd is glowing like a brick-kiln, and water and pasture have to be made a push for, among the features of the landscape sometimes are clouds of spearmen, passing like sandstorms over the rocky ground, or emerging, mares in hand, naked and dripping from the river. Of the extent to which, from ancient times, as now under the very eye of the Osmanli, the Euphrates is thus held in fee by nomads, proofs may be seen near A'na, on its Shâ-mi-ya border. On either side of a gully stand two piles of masonry, evidently once the props of a bridge across it.[2] These are covered with rude scratchings, not unlike those which, when copied and sent to Europe, open up new alphabets and histories. But the Arabs came to I'râk too late to use the old proto-Arabic letters. The Khaz-ga hieroglyphics merely are reproductions, made by all the nations of Arabia, of the distinctive marks with which they brand their camels,[3] as Australian horse-breeders do their horses.

Next to its river, the great advantage of Shâ-mi-ya is the opportunity of buying barley which its cultivated borders and oases afford to nomads. Otherwise, the physical conditions are essentially those of Central Arabia. Springs known only to Bedouin must exist; but we never saw one — only wells at long intervals on the caravan tracks; with, at most seasons, collections of rainwater in natural depressions. The rainfall is greater and less precarious than

---

[1] According to some, the *ghai-lân* is a piercing wind; according to others, merely an extraordinary coldness. They who go out in it muffle their heads; and Bedouin put stitches through certain of their mares' parts, to exclude it from their vital organs. The name may come out of the Arabic verb *ghâla*, used of mischief or destruction, *falling on one unawares; ex quo*, the Arab *ghûl* (our ghoul or bogle), i.e., a demon, which, appearing to travellers, causes them to wander, and destroys them. Even in mild forms of *ghai-lân* experienced by us, with the sun at noon as powerful as at the same season (January) in Lahore, and the temperature well above freezing, we have felt in Shâ-mi-ya the cold as piercing, where the wind was blowing, as ever we did at Cabul with snow on the ground, and the thermometer near zero. In the Ha-mâd a legend runs of a whole *ghaz-u* having perished, man and beast, in the *ghai-lân;*

except one rider, who, by disembowelling his camel and taking shelter inside, contrived to keep himself alive till its worst was over.

[2] A'na townsmen call this spot *Gan-ta-ra Khaz-ga*, or *Bridge of Khaz-ga*. Bedouin, confining themselves to what they see, call it *Ha-ja-rat Khaz-ga*, or, as we might say, the *Standing Stones of Khaz-ga*.

[3] These marks, made with a hot iron, are called *ssimu* (pl. *aw-sâm*). Such of them as we have seen have not been pictorial, but vague scrawlings, like the following:

Nevertheless, travellers should not despise these old *wsrm*, because of their being "only camel brands."

in Najd; but it all comes in winter and spring. They who traverse Shá-mi-ya, as the writer did, at the end of summer, must wonder what the Ae-ni-za mares live on. But for a low thin grass and a few sapless shrubs, all is barrenness. When, after going all night, one dismounts towards morning, to snatch a little sleep, his fear of losing hold of his horse's bridle is almost like one's clinging to the boat after a capsize in a river. Only a fool of a town-horse, it is true, one all bubble and squeak, fresh from a manger, would run off in such a place; and even he would, if left alone, probably soon come back. Still, just as a Bramah lock is better than the trustiest servant, so is precaution always best; and however superior the desert mare's intelligence may be, her master, we notice, as often as he calls a halt in Shá-mi-ya, slips a pair of irons round her fore-pasterns. One thing with another, for a fine sense of "pastoral melancholy" we recommend the reader to Shá-mi-ya in the dog-days. In the morning, when the sun comes up like a fire-ball, the flinty plain looks in its emptiness as if created merely to form a temple for him. How changed all this becomes when the spring rains have fallen, the descriptions in *Bedouin Tribes of the Euphrates* show. The authoress and her husband, leaving the Euphrates at Der, penetrated in March and April, by way of Tadmor, far into Shá-mi-yá; meeting the Ug-mu-sa, Ru-wa-la, Wald A'li, and other horse-breeding septs of the Ae-ni-za. They often came on shallow pools, or successions of pools, covering several acres; also on wá-dis, "some forty feet below the level of the plain; and on at least one vast bed of grass and flowers." In one place was "a splendid plain of rich grass, enough to feed all the Ae-ni-za for a week;" in another, "a dry water-course thick with grass," in which quails and the cuckoo were calling.

Elsewhere we shall speak of the nomadic herdsmen of Shá-mi-ya and their horses. Here we are but noting the principal features of their location.

A good starting-point for the interior of Shá-mi-ya is Der, about 140 miles higher up the Euphrates than A'na—nine caravan stages from Aleppo, ten from Damascus, and eight from Mosul. Lady A. Blunt says of Der that "it is, for a stranger, by far the best market for thoroughbreds [*i.e.*, thoroughbred Arabians] in Asia."[1] This, and the companion statement of there being "no horses at Der but thoroughbreds," she explains by saying that its townsmen, being but a single step removed from their undoubted ancestors the Bedouin, buy their colts as yearlings, either from the Ug-mu-sa or from some other of the Ae-ni-za tribes, and sell them as three years old to Aleppo merchants. The authority for this is not given, and our experience is different. Once we visited Der in search of horses,

---

[1] *Op. cit.* in Catalog. No. 11, vol. i. p. 117.

and saw none worth buying. Dealers were there from Aleppo, Baghdad, and other places. But these were either bound for the Ae-ni-za, hordes of whom were near; or were on the watch to buy any nondescript animals, resaleable at a profit, on which travellers, or their escorts, might ride into the town. In truth, the population of Der and of the hamlets round it is very mixed. The town is full of Ottoman officials, who are apt to pounce on good horses whenever they see them, and pay little or nothing for them. Not only does this stop the Bedouin from bringing in colts, but it makes even dealers, after a successful visit to the Ae-ni-za, take their purchases towards the intended market by another route than Der. And thus in all such towns the outsider's chance of finding a treasure dwindles. Among the horses in the possession of influential residents, one may now and then occur which has stood for a year or two only because of the largeness of the price put on him. Oftener the reason is that dealer after dealer has rejected him. At the best, such will generally prove to have been reared from foalhood tied to a manger; and after that, let a horse's blood and figure be what they may, he is not the same as if he had been left for his first year or two in the desert. Certainly there is always fresh news of the Ae-ni-za in Der. The talk of its coffee-houses is of the Bedouin. Riding-camels can be bought in it: with water-skins, Arab saddles and saddle-bags, and all the paraphernalia of travel; many of which articles, as might be expected, considering that horsemen and "sons of the road" have invented them, excel at once in lightness, strength, and utility. But he who would buy Bedouin horses in Shâ-mi-ya, as in Najd, should go to the Bedouin for them; and if using at all the *dal-lâl*,[1] or go-between, believe nothing of what is said, and only half of what is shown, to him.

---

[1] Lit., *one whose avocation it is to show*. In towns, open-air auctions of mules, donkeys, and inferior horses are daily held. A different form of auction is in vogue for superior horses. The animal is sent from house to house with a paper, in which every one who would buy him enters the price which he will pay; and thus a deal is effected. Over and above all this, or rather as part of it, the *dal-lâl* is always on the alert.

CHAPTER VI.

AL JA-ZI-RA: OR DESERTS EAST THE EUPHRATES.

APOLOGY may be necessary in again introducing an unfamiliar geographical term; but if "Mesopotamia" had been written, would the locality of reference have been any the clearer? The bestowal by the Greeks and Romans of names of their own mintage on the Asiatic countries invaded by them was only natural; but it is not surprising that, except in books, such pieces of nomenclature have faded. Mesopotamia, a rendering of the far older Aramæan name *bêth nahrîn* = country between the two rivers,[1] dates only from the time of Alexander. Yet it is in all our translations of the Bible, from Genesis to Chronicles; one of those sonorous words which are the more edifying from neither reader nor hearer knowing too much about them. In modern European literature Mesopotamia bears now an exceedingly extended, again a narrower, application. We cannot lend ourselves to the view which would understand by it the Tigris and Euphrates valleys, from the Alpine heights of Armenia to the Gulf of Persia; but neither can we consider here all the questions which require to be discussed before this foreign term can be used intelligently; wherefore in these pages it will be introduced but sparingly. Inasmuch as Al Ja-zî-ra is an Arabic name bestowed by the Arabs on a land outside of Arabia overrun by them about their Prophet's era, perhaps it too should be accounted foreign. But here the difference is that, notwithstanding the Turkish conquest nearly 400 years ago, Arabs with varying pretensions to the name, and greatly mixed with Kurds, Turk-u-mâns, and others, still occupy it. The name means *The Cut off.* But etymology is not to be pressed against usage; and a *Ja-zî-ra*, whether an *island* or a *peninsula*, necessarily is a

---

[1] Till recently it has passed for certain that the two rivers meant are the Tigris and Euphrates; and no different view is adopted in these pages. But the possibility should be mentioned of the boundary rivers having been the Euphrates and its principal affluent the Chaboras or Khâbûr. This would limit the designation of Mesopotamia to the western half, or less, of the territory here included in it. *V*. p. 74, *infra.*

space marked off by waters. Al Ja-zi-ra of the present description does not carry its irregular northern confines higher than, say, Mosul on the Tigris, and Su-mai-sât on the Euphrates. Its southern extension similarly is, not to the sea of Persia, but only to a little above the parallel of Baghdad. Within those limits, neither does it embrace all the area between the rivers, nor refuse numerous trans-riverine pieces. Much of the space between the rivers, as will appear in the following chapter, includes itself in I'râk; while many strips west of the Euphrates, with many others east of the Tigris, are properly Al Ja-zi-ra. In fine, and subject to these qualifications, if the Greeks meant by their Μεσοποταμία the territory on, or between, the *middle portions* of the two historic rivers, then is Mesopotamia very nearly Al Ja-zi-ra. Leaving these topics, we here restrict ourselves to the aspects of Al Ja-zi-ra as a Bad-u land expatiated in by the race of Najd. So far as this goes, if the mission of its Ottoman masters had been to hold it in trust for nomads, they might boast to-day of having succeeded. From Mosul, Aleppo, and Baghdad, and from numerous posts on both the rivers, they are supposed to grasp it. But in all the great triangle, 250 miles long, with an area of at least 55,000 square miles, which composes it, the Turkish fez is seldom seen outside of towns. The Osmanli official when he is travelling in it condescends to cover his head with the Arab handkerchief. Over most of it Shekh is a better name to conjure with than Sultán or Pásha. The Sham-mar free-lance, when saying "stand" to a raft of merchandise on the Tigris,[1] or driving before him the flocks of townsmen, realises what a far cry it is to the nearest garrison. And yet occasionally proof is given that if the Osmanli cannot govern, he has ways of his own of striking. A few cajoling letters, ending in a cup of poisoned coffee, or in the deputation of an executioner pretending to be an ally, sometimes serve with Turks all the uses of police and courts of justice. Within the memory of living people, the Shekh of all the Sham-mar slew in his sacred guest-tent a desert rival, contrary to every obligation of Arab honour; and when the Governor of Baghdad was apprised of it he feigned approval; sent one of his partisan leaders ostensibly to support the homicide, in reality to deal with him as he had dealt with the other; and soon the culprit's head was brought into the town. More recently a cockerel of the same nest rose to eminence as a public enemy. Goaded into a kind of fury, as some say by a luckless wooing, this hero of not a little desert fable long played the Rob Roy against all villagers and peaceful folk; till at last the Mosul Government, on his being delivered up by one with whom he had taken refuge, hanged him publicly. But such things do not often happen. In the main, "live and let live"

---

[1] As we write (1890), an Assyriologist from the British Museum informs us that in coming down the Tigris on a raft from Mosul, he showed a Constantinople *Bál-yúrí-di*, or order, to a band of roaming Arabs, and that the innocent, if futile, document, so far from being respected, was subjected before his eyes to indignity.

is the policy. On the one hand, Al Ja-zí-ra Bedouin restrain their lawlessness; on the other, Turkish authorities seldom bring things to an issue with them. Not remoteness of situation, not aridity, not the strength of its Bedouin, not religion, but only the Turk's way of taking countries and letting others use them, lies at the root of this. There is no Wahabyism in Al Ja-zi-ra, and not much even of Islamism; the unwritten laws of the desert, not the Mecca Prophet's Institutes, govern its nomads. A political mosaic like that of Hâ-yil, having a castle in the middle of it, is impossible so near the Osmanli. Either the ancient and natural strength of the desert must be held fast to, or, as Persians say, the saddle-cloth of obedience to foreign governors more and more carried on the back of the national life. The last great "desert king" of Al Ja-zi-ra was he whose head was fetched off by a Baghdad Pâsha in the circumstances above alluded to. What a falling off there was in him from the old Najdian ideal appeared in his disposition to lean on the Osmanli; his treacherous murder of a guest; and his taking to wife a towns-woman. After his tragic ending he was followed in the Shekhate by his son Far-hân, who died at a good old age only the other day, in the Arab quarter of Baghdad. The last order which Far-hân ever gave was, that the Surgeon of the British Consulate should be summoned to save him; but his hour was come. Happen-ing to pass the spot where they were burying him, we heard it bitterly remarked by many how, while accepting several thousand pounds a-year of Turkish money, under the pretence of settling his people at Kal-a' Sher-gât on the Tigris, he had permitted, if not encouraged, the plunder of flocks and merchandise. And now his son Mij-wal has succeeded him, always under Osmanli favour and patron-age. For the last twenty years, however, all the more stubborn heads of tents in these northern Sham-mar, deserting Shekh Far-hân, have kept gathering round his half-brother and rival, Fâ-ris.[1] Perhaps it belongs to the Osmanli policy to cajole, and be cajoled by, only a section of a clan or nation. Too many Far-hâns and Mij-wals—that is, if the latter walk in his late father's steps—may be considered not worth the price. Or perhaps it is that Fâ-ris, warned by the fate of his brother, born of the same father and noble Arab mother—him above referred to as hanged at Mosul—has deliberately chosen to play the game of desert politics

---

[1] How Lady A. Blunt spent some days with Fâ-ris near the town of Der, in March 1878; how she found him "very good-looking, with a clear olive complexion not darker than that of a Spaniard, an aquiline nose, black eyebrows meeting almost across his forehead, and eyes fringed all round with long black lashes, smile, one of the most attractive one can see;" how "Wilfrid" and Fâ-ris solemnly swore an oath of brotherhood for all their lives; how Fâ-ris immediately thereafter borrowed from his big brother a £10 note, there being in the Sham-mar camp "no clothes to the women's backs," the coffee and sugar all used up, and an Israelitish creditor dunning; and, lastly, how Fâ-ris, not ungrateful, made a raft for his generous visitors to ferry them across the swollen Khâ-bûr,"—all these things, and more, any one may read in *Bedouin Tribes of the Euphrates*, vol. i. ch. xv.

apart from foreign leading. Be all this as it may, with the Ae-ni-za kept out of Al Ja-zi-ra by the Sham-mar, and the latter so open to town influence, another than the Turkish Government would probably ere now have realised that a region anciently so civilised and flourishing need not necessarily be left to nature, pending the success of dubious projects for the changing of Bedouin into peasants. In the main, and excepting the limestone ranges of Sin-jár[1] (fifty miles long by seven broad) and A'bdu 'l A'ziz, with between them the isolated basaltic hill of Kau-kab, which traverse more or less its northern portion, the whole region is as flat and tractable as it is accessible. In October 1886 we marched across the southern or steppe division of it; and three months later, across the northern. A country having less of feature than the former it would be hard to find. Our Arab guide kept steering by the Thar-thár wá-di; but for the life of us we could not see a line of it. He must have picked it out from the surrounding monotony, in the same way as a shepherd is said to know his sheep's faces. Between Hit and Tak-rit, three and a half days for laden mules, or say about eighty miles, no human vestige, other than, few and far between, the black tents of the Sham-mar, came before us. Everywhere was fallow; the natural flora ousted by cultivation thousands of years ago; and little save bent-grass—the golden *him-rí*—now replacing it. Though the year's round of vegetation was then only beginning, this *him-rí* rose as high, but not as thick, as barley. It is fine pasture; but owing to our horses being entire we could not turn them out in it, as the Bedouin do their mares. Skins of Tigris water had to be carried with us on mules. At long distances were wells, with nomad camps spread round them; deep and gruesome pits, containing, when not run dry, scanty supplies of saline fluid. Frogs and toads sat blinking in the sides of them; and in several floated dead gazelles which, perhaps to drink, perhaps merely by accident, had gone headlong into them. In Arabic the word for *watering* a horse or mule literally means the *causing*, or *helping*, him *to go down*—i.e., to the water: a derivation guiding us to at least one explanation of the poverty of the Arabian fauna outside of certain swampy regions. The rivers of Al Ja-zi-ra are too deep-set for animals to get at them, except where an approach, called a *sha-rí-a'*, has been made. At Hit a town dog having business of his own at Tak-rit joined our party uninvited, knowing how dependent he would be for water on some friendly biped and his rope and bucket. As a feature still further handicapping Arabian agriculture, this very general depression of running waters between steep banks is noticeable. On the Tigris and the Euphrates, were land to be had for the taking, capital for the erection of water-wheels and purchase of well-cattle is thus necessitated; and in so poverty-stricken a country very little serves to turn the cultivators into

---

[1] *V. supra*, p. 5; also in Index I., art. Ya-zi-ri.

the bondsmen of Jews and others. No other Arabian crop or culture is so profitable as a date-grove. When planted in spots like Bussorah, close to ocean carriage, and where sweet water can be distributed everywhere from the Shattu 'l A'rab, it must be like a little gold-mine.

In recrossing Al Ja-zi-ra higher up, from Mosul, by Sin-jâr and Lake Khâ-tû-nî-ya, past Mâr-din and Na-si-bin to Bîr on the Euphrates, the best part was struck —the well-watered land N.W. of the Khâ-bûr river, which is recognised by many as the true ancient *Aram Naharayim*, or *Padan-aram* of Genesis.[1] By that time it was January, and plenty of rain had fallen. All the arid undulating plain west of the Tigris was spread with sheets of rain-water. First the Ja-gha-jagh was forded; then, with difficulty, the Khâ-bûr. The best known modern describer of these parts is Layard;[2] but the trees and thickets which he gives to the Khâ-bûr are now things of the past; and its last lion has either been hunted down or has joined his kindred in the impenetrable cane-brakes which fringe the Shattu 'l A'rab. The beaver settlements have been exterminated so completely, that only the old remember how once upon a time Pâshas sent far and near for a certain bitter product (*castoreum*) of the amphibious sapper, prized by them as a restorative. Among Nature's subjects still remaining, the most interesting is *Asinus onager*, or wild ass; *Gur khar* of Persia, and *Kulan* of Tatars. He is who, crossing the plain in small brown herds, excites the ardour of the Sham-mar horsemen, and tests severely their mares' speed and bottom. The only one whose flesh we ever tasted had been snared by a Sle-bi pot-hunter; not ridden into by a straight rider. Numbers of these Sle-bi cross the Euphrates in winter in pursuit of game; and we have heard the beauty of their breed of asses ascribed to their using as stallions wild specimens. It was seen above how some have argued that if Al Ja-zi-ra still have the wild ass, why may it not once have had the wild horse? Possibly it may; for who can prove a negative? But the watered part of it, with all its extensiveness, is relatively to the vast arid spaces lying contiguous little more than an oasis. The same tract, as its numerous mounds and ruined cities show, during all the time that the Assyrian empire was spreading over western Asia, supported a settled and industrious population. Even the Biblical literature gives us little help in realising how immeasurable are the past periods of time; and the eighteen Christian centuries may be carried back through eighteen, or twice eighteen, more, without the problems of natural history being thereby affected. But one fact at least appears to guide us, and that is, the essential difference between the wild ass's and the wild horse's natural habits. The former is ranked by the Arabs with the Antelopidæ rather than the Equidæ. In their poetry he is held up to admiration, or used in similes, side

---

[1] Chap. xxviii. 2, *et passim*.   [2] *Op. cit.* in Catalog. No. 31, chaps. 12 to 15.

by side with the ostrich and the camel. As long as a succulent bite can be found, he is as independent of water as the hare or rabbit. Notwithstanding what has just been said of the populousness in ancient times of this north-western shoulder of Al Ja-zi-ra, we know from the figures of camel-riding Arabs found in its buried cities that then, as now, nomads flitted over it; that Sennacherib and his predecessors had to cope with the irrepressible, ubiquitous Bad-u in the intervals of their grander undertakings. And so at this day, there falls on all the land the shadow of the Arab *rumh* or *shal-fa*—its shaft perhaps an Indian bamboo, perhaps a quivering reed from the Euphrates marshes; its tuft of sable ostrich-feathers serving the same impressive purpose as the death's-head and cross-bones device of a famous lancer regiment. For fear of it, all the less warlike populations of Al Ja-zi-ra, if stationary, hug the mountains; if nomadic, purchase with tribute the protection of the Sham-mar. In the dry months thousands of the Bedouin assemble between Sin-jâr and Ba-tin.[1] There in truce times the Sham-mar meet the Ae-ni-za; in the natural nomad life the female character is unblighted by face-veiling; hearts go out to hearts; passages of love and friendship soften blood-feud and foray. Other tribes, notably the A'd-wân and the Jais, immigrants like the Tai from Najd, tend their flocks and breed horses in the same pastures. Both banks of the Bi-likh, another feeder of the Euphrates, are occupied by the Ba-râ-zi-ya. The common view taken of these is that they are Kurds; but some say that they are Najdian. One thing worth mentioning before leaving Al Ja-zi-ra is this: Between Hit and Tak-rit we saw, as has been stated, round every well hordes of the Sham-mar with their mares. But in nearly a month of travel over the tract watered by the numerous head-streams (*Râsu 'l a'fu*) of the Khâ-bûr we fell in with even fewer Bedouin than Sir L. Pelly did between the Persian Gulf and Najd, or Lady A. Blunt in Wâ-di Sir-hân, for we in fact saw none at all. The margins of the river were white with flocks. At spring's first touch a luxuriant growth of natural grasses, variegated with flowering herbs, was turning the desert into a meadow; in the soft depths of which the newly dropped lambs were hidden. But with grass and water everywhere, the Sham-mar were so scattered that for all that we saw of them we might as well have been in Yorkshire. Perhaps, if our route had lain in peninsular Arabia, we should have concluded from seeing no Bedouin or Bedouin horses that there were none to see. But in Al Ja-zi-ra no one can fall into this error. In 1836 and 1837, Dr Ross, Surgeon to the British Consulate, Baghdad, in the course of two journeys to the Ruins of Al Hadhr,[2] saw a

---

[1] In nothing is nomad speech more delightfully general than in its names for natural features. Thus *ta-wil*, long or tall, is as generic a name for mountainpeaks as "Taffy" is for Welshmen. Similarly every headland is a *khashm* (lit. *snout*); every blunt height, a *ba-tin* (lit. *bellying*); and so forth.

[2] V. his narrative in *Journal Roy. Geog. Soc.*, London, vol. ix. part 3, 1839.

good deal of Southern Sham-mar-land. In one day's march he passed about a dozen large encampments, in which were upwards of 10,000 or 12,000 camels; yet he considered that he had seen "only a very inconsiderable part of this enormous tribe." With the discovery awaiting us that Bad-u horsemanship, though not without its strong points, falls far short of the English hunting-field model, it is the more worth noting, on the authority of so matter-of-fact a witness, how in the use of the queen of weapons for all who have taken pains to master it, the seat and hand and eye of the Sham-mar lancer serve him truly. A snake having started, a shekhling drove his spear through its head. The Arabs applauded, but the doctor declared that it was an accident. Thereupon the other threw the reptile on the ground again, saying, "Where will you have me hit it this time?" and on the tail being named to him, made a charge at it, so that in an instant it was whirling in the air, transfixed in the part in question. Probably this is one of the Bedouin virtues the decline of which is held to result from intercourse with townsmen; but some pretty spear-play may still be seen among the loose-robed chivalry of Al Ja-zi-ra. They have fallen off in numbers since Dr Ross's day. Also, their war-howl less often wakes the echoes now than then. Except when some unusual occurrence has set the contumacious swarms a-buzzing, European travellers have but little to fear in Al Ja-zi-ra. Nevertheless the view is still well supported, that while its towns and cultivated spaces are held by the Osmanli, the genii of the interior are the Sham-mar.

The better to command the deserts which we have been describing, our camp had been reduced to the scale shown in the sketch opposite.[1]

Unfortunately, the mistake had been committed of employing mules, instead of camels, to carry the baggage. Camels will browse as they go, and still make progress. If unloaded early enough, in Al Ja-zi-ra at least, they will do very well; and when collected at sunset round the tent, they sit ruminating contentedly, like the elders of a tribe, far into the night. But mules must have their chopped straw and barley. At any rate their owners say so: and as ours were not our own property, the slightest mention of taking them into places where rations might fail made the muleteers rebellious. Even mares and horses, especially town ones, are not well adapted for forced marches over arid and uninhabited spaces. The dromedary alone commands the desert. Mounted on her, the traveller can go anywhere. If there be Bedouin about, he will find them; while supposing him, after days of travelling, to reach a spot where he had thought to catch them, only to

---

[1] In towns like Baghdad, the traveller need anticipate no difficulty in procuring tents. If he should desire large ones, of Turkish, Persian, or Arab shapes and materials, he will generally be able to buy them; but, outside of India, there are no servants who understand how to pitch a tent of European design. If *tentes d'abris* will serve him, the local tent-makers will soon equip him.

discover that they had left it, he has at least his wallets, water-skin, and blanket; and instead of a mare almost certainly saddle-galled, and half dead for want of barley, a ruminant fit to start again when wanted. A course of camel-riding in these Euphrates deserts greatly develops the foraging faculty. The traveller who has reached Baghdad from that quarter may be known by the zeal with which he hunts up provisions. It is scarcely possible for him to hear a hen intimate that she has laid an egg in his vicinity, without setting out to look for it. When invited to dinner, he carries his empty canisters with him, and by a combined process of begging and taking, refills them from his hosts' dishes or pantries.

THE AUTHOR'S FLYING CAMP BETWEEN SIN-JÁR AND THE EUPHRATES.

CHAPTER VII.

I'RÁK: OR TIGRIS-LAND.

IF the interest of Najd for horsemen turns on the Arabian horse having been perfected there, I'rák has this claim to notice, that it yields large numbers of him. True, the I'ráki, or as he is sometimes, though less appropriately, called, the Baghdad horse, is not an Arabian of a high stamp. Still these two facts about him are evident: they who breed him, equally with their horse and mare stock, practically are, allowing for admixture and exceptions, Arabs; and of every hundred Arabians exported, a large percentage are from I'rák. Leaving the animal himself for description in the proper place, we therefore now invite our readers to cast an eye over his native districts. With the ancient history of I'rák, according to a venerable tradition one of the first countries occupied by man after the deluge, nay, even supposed by some to contain the site of Eden, we do not here occupy ourselves. The Shinar of Genesis;[1] later, the "ancient land of Chaldea"; still later (after its capital), the "country of Báb-il";—the "I'rák A'ra-bi"[2] of geographers may be said to fit itself to the surfaces making up the present Ottoman pashaliks of Baghdad and Bussorah; to which, however, large portions of the pashalik of Mosul also require to be added. In some curious way I'rák has come to be called "Turkish Arabia": but no such name, so far as we know, is given to it by the Báb-i-A'li or Sublime Porte.

A very large slice of I'rák perhaps admits of being regarded as what geographers call "the further present" of Al Ja-zi-ra.[3] That is, we may so consider the

---

[1] Chap. xi. 2.
[2] So qualified to distinguish it from "I'rák A'-ja-mi," one of the eleven provinces of Persia.
[3] The traveller who is holding southward perceives after Hit on the Euphrates and Sá-mar-rá on the Tigris, a marked difference both in the character of the ground and in the landscape. From a slightly elevated plain of secondary formation he descends to a mud-flat, the creation of the two rivers in the course of ages. "At a comparatively recent period," says Loftus, in *Quart. Jour. Geol. Soc.*, 1853, p. 251, "the littoral margin of the Persian Gulf extended certainly

tract beginning, in the parallel of Hit, where the Tigris and the Euphrates approach within twenty or thirty miles of one another, to diverge again lower down; and stretching south, between the rivers, towards the Gulf of Persia. This does not mean that I'rák is bounded by those rivers. Three important rivers, the Euphrates, the Tigris, and the Dhi-á-la, water it; but its limits are not determined by them. According to the Arabian geographer, Abú 'l Fi-dá, it lies on one of them—the Tigris—like Egypt on the Nile; that is, the Tigris runs through the middle of it. The same authority assigns to I'rák for boundaries, in the west, Al Ja-zi-ra and Shá-mi-ya; in the south, the flanks of Najd, Gulf of Persia, and Khúz-istán; and in the east, the mountainous country of the Zagros range.[1] It is impossible to apply to so large a tract a general description, whether in its horse-breeding or other aspects. One thing soon strikes the horseman—the difference in its horse-supply east and west of the Tigris. In the former direction, the further we go, the more do Persian influences prevail among the population; and Persian strains, or, to be more accurate, the absence of any particular strain at all, among the horses. In the latter, the nearer we approach the Euphrates, the more we feel that our faces are turned towards Arabia. Over its steppe portions, I'rák is fiercely hot from May to September, cold and wet in winter, charming in spring, and at all seasons more or less conducive to vigour of mind and body. Even the sedgy swamps of its southern part, however distressing to Europeans, maintain rice-growing, fish-eating, hardy races, scarcely anywhere to be surpassed for breadth of chest and length of limb. As horse-breeders these are not worth mentioning. Their mare is the canoe; their sheep and camels white-polled buffaloes. At present the Government has them well in hand. Their ancient avocation of fresh-water pirates is more or less suspended. Perhaps in their homes, and towards one another, they exhibit some traces of politeness; but the aspect which they present to strangers is that of savages. Closely connected with the extraordinary productiveness which I'rák displayed, and with the high degree of civilisation which belonged to it, not only in remote antiquity but partly even under the Baghdad Caliphs, was the cyclopean network of canals by means of which the men of old converted vast surfaces of it, especially between the rivers, into a garden. Not a hundredth part of the ancient irrigational system now exists; but enough remains to give birth in many places to rich crops and pastures. Canals apart, an enormous deal of cultivation, with many hundred miles of date-palm, spreads itself over the banks of the three rivers.

---

250 miles farther to the north-west than the present embouchure of the Shatt-l-A'rab. Another authority estimates that in Alexander's time at least a day's journey separated the mouths of the Tigris and Euphrates.

[1] I'rák consequently lies between 30° and 34° N. latitude, and between 44° and 48° 30′ E. longitude.

Early in October wheat and barley are put down, not only under wells and rivers, but—near towns—in the desert also, in dependence on the rain.[1] By midwinter the husbandman begins to be rewarded. With frost in the air, and a wintry sun looking through naked trees, irrigated lands are then knee-deep with crops of wheat and barley. These are not at first allowed to come to ear. They are either cut, and sent in ass-loads to market, or mares and cattle are turned out in them to eat their fill. By the time that this has been twice or thrice repeated, spring is well advanced. Then at last the corn is left to form and ripen. After all, the yield is greater than if it had never been eaten down. Our farmers should make a note of this, and not be in too great a hurry with their "ware wheats," when for all that they know a flight of fox-hunters may be the very thing for them. Beautiful in I'rák are March and April, with autumn's treasures thus pouring themselves into the lap of spring. Vernal showers, expressive of Nature's copiousness, with not an ache or rheum in them, have succeeded to the sterner rains of winter. The days grow longer and longer; and the genial sun, receiving the crisp north wind in its embraces, produces the perfection of climate.[2] Here and there among the standing crops sheets of rain-water glisten brighter than mirrors. All along the water-courses wild-flowers hide themselves in a wealth of sweetly scented grasses. Mothers of every kind are in milk; and near towns, where the plain is not under crops, it is studded with black tent-circles. In good years, when the devil leaves Eden alone, and there are neither locusts nor inundations, May sees the last field harvested. Then, in June and July, the I'ráki husbandman is seldom disappointed of a strong *shi-mál* or north-west wind. This does his winnowing for him; after the corn has been trodden out, either literally under the feet of cattle, or by passing over it a spiked wooden roller which is called a *jar-jar*.[3] The simple

---

[1] Rain-cultivation is locally called *dalm* or *dem*.

[2] If but the wind would never veer! The "Father of the tempest" in I'rák is a wind called *shar-ki*, from the south-east. Nothing could be more disagreeable than this jarring blustering blast when it sets in cold and moist (happily only for a day or two at a time) in March, except the same wind in August, when it comes hot and humid as the sirocco, laden with dust and yellow vapours; as unwholesome to breathe as to look at; unstringing the bow of animal life; bringing old wounds and old pains back again—nay, making the joints of the very chairs and tables creak. Men, we are told, should never let their tempers rise; but this is the wind to ruffle them, much as it whitens into waves the Tigris and Euphrates. In towns the force of it is broken; but out in the desert it rages round and round, through and through, one's head. The Arab takes it patiently as a "thing sent," wraps up his head, and says nothing. The European keeps out of it as much as he can.

[3] Thus inevitably the stalks (*jill*), except of rice crops, get chopped or triturated into what Persians call *káh*, and Arabs *tibn*. Hay, as we know it, is seldom seen in I'rák. Wherever we have been among Arabs, *tibn* and *sha-I'r* (barley) make up the horse provender; and these two words occur in the only slightly varied forms of *tében* and *sio'rim* in the passage of the Hebrew Bible (1 Kings iv. 28) in which a glimpse is given of King Solomon's stable management. So much is food a matter of habit, that once when we imported to Baghdad for a growing colt a supply of English meadow-hay and oats, he refused to leave his *tibn* and *sha-I'r* for it! For lack of straw, the method is in vogue of spreading the stalks with sundried droppings. This so gets into the coat and

harvest is barely over when the months of extreme heat begin. Then the ground is iron-bound. From an hour or so after sunrise, the sportsman's horses stand idle before their mangers; while his hawks and thin greyhounds are being summered in cool dark places. In towns business is chiefly transacted in the morning and evening, and at night. For an hour or two after noon the siesta[1] waits on all; on the merchant in his *sard-áb* or watered *chár-dák*; on the porter stretched atop his load; on the sentry at his post. In the open country garden cultivation is continued. For that the water-wheels of the Euphrates still revolve;[2] and all along the Tigris and the Dhi-á-la ponies draw up water.[3] But agriculture proper is interrupted; and the hardy Arab sheep, though still able to make a shift on ground where ours would die, have to be helped with chopped straw. All who have houses exchange the open fields for them. Many of the tent-dwellers set up sheds, called *sá-bát*, under some river-bank, and as near the current as possible. Vast portions of the country between the rivers resemble the merest sand-plain. Elf-lock shoots of wild colocynth and wild caper[4] stray over the desert, which is rough with stones and bits of coloured pottery. But for the traces of cities whose very names are lost, nothing could be more featureless. Where the Tigris or the Euphrates bounds the horizon, masses of date foliage darken it. Otherwise the fantastic images of the mirage[5] are all that the traveller sees before him. And yet it is not like this invariably. The changes which are caused perhaps in a night by overflowings of the great rivers sometimes maintain themselves through the summer. And apart from this, the Tigris and the Euphrates, wherever a natural depression affords an opening, send into it a body of running water, which is called a *khirr*. Streams of this kind do not go far; but many of them last all

---

mane that, with but one groom to three or four horses, is in Arabia one's favourites may be healthy, but they can hardly be clean. Horses doing daily marches have to lie on the bare ground. If *tibn* were put down as bedding the wind would blow it away.

[1] In Arabic *kai-lú-la*. The Prophet said, *Sleep at mid-day; verily the devils sleep not.*

[2] A great feature of the Euphrates is the waterwheel, called from its creaking *ná-ú·r*. The bed of the river being first of all raised by the running into it of dams of masonry, the water-power of several feet in height thus obtained is made to turn a rough wooden wheel of 30 or 40 feet diameter, having 100 or 150 rude clay-cups slung on the outer edge. The aqueducts with which these wheels are fitted form not the least picturesque part of them, being for the

most part supported by a series of well-built Gothic arches.

[3] The *ná-ú·r* cannot be put on the Tigris and the Dhi-á-la, owing to the softness of their beds.

[4] In old Arabic *la-táf* (Heb. *niphık*, Syr. *neqbi*). But now the Arabs call it *ka-bar*. That is, the Greek name κάππαρις has displaced the Semitic one.

[5] In Arabic *sa-ráb*. *More deceitful than the sa-ráb* is an Arab saying. Irák is seldom rained on between June and October. The drier the atmosphere the more remarkable the mirage. The air-strata, unequally heated, and therefore differing in rarity, in refracting the rays of light, here distort the objects seen through them; there make them appear raised off the ground; and again by a reproduction of their image which is reflected in a lower stratum, present them as if rising up out of a lake.

through the hot months; and fishermen sail up and down them in little skiffs. Delicate and nutritious grasses[1] spring up wherever the moisture reaches. When the *khirr* dries up towards September, cultivators raise in it heavy crops of beans or *lû-bia*, the very best of horse-keep. More considerable than the *khirr* are the marsh (*haur*) and salt-lake (*sab-kha*), many of which yield saline herbage almost as good as barley for horses.[2] All that has so far been said applies in the main to I'râk west of the Tigris. East of the same river, between it and the Turco-Persian frontier, lies a pastoral steppe called *Al Ha-wi-ja*, or, from its occupants, *Ha-wi-jatu 'l U'-baid*. Arabia contains as many *hâ-wís* and *ha-wí-jas* as India does *do-âbs*, or England holms. Both are geographical terms, descriptive of certain conformations or dispositions of land. Their etymology being obscure, the two names are difficult of definition; but generally they seem to indicate mud-flats. With regard to the Ha-wi-ja now before us, a glance at the map will show that, while divided by a range of low mountains into a northern and southern portion, it is much enclosed by rivers. Unlike the Euphrates, which, after receiving in its upper third the Bi-likh and the Khâ-bûr, holds on for some 800 miles without an important affluent joining it; the sister Tigris is enriched at every stage by snow-fed and considerable tributaries, notably the greater and lesser Zâb, the U'-dhaim, and the Dhi-â-la. Between two of these, the lesser Zâb and the U'-dhaim, lies the territory of the U'-baid, the—in the main—desert of *Al Ha-wi-ja*. In November 1886 the part of this called *Al A'ith* was wandered over by us without a fixed abode appearing. All the features of the ground were Najdian. He who has crossed its billowy sands, scourged by the prevailing winds into elevated masses and intermitting spiral ridges, with here and there in the rainy months surfaces of *nu-sî* pasture, may almost consider that he has seen Najd itself. In 1856 clouds of apparently ensanguined sand were, for the first time that any one remembered such a thing, blown into Baghdad day after day by the strong winds of the desert. As English gunboats were just then pounding Mu-ham-ma-ra, the red material alarmed the superstitious. Some

---

[1] In Arabic *green-food* is *ha-shîsh*. Grasses such as those of which we make hay are *í shb*; among which is *thui-yil*, the *dâb* of Northern, and *harýáli* of Southern, India, *Agrostis linearis* of botanists. Spreading from point to point both below and above the ground, loving the shade, yet not fearing the sun, this grass, wherever it may have come from originally, has so spread over east and west, that we have heard Turkish Pâshas bitterly call it an emblem of the British power! Long may it continue to be so.

Another I'râki grass is the *dow-asr*, a kind of wild oat, fresh and beautiful to look at, and much liked by horses; not, however, yielding a grain.

Outside the natural flora are innumerable cultivated herbs. The tall bean (*bâ-kil-lâ*) diversifies with its dark green the wheat and barley fields. The graceful *hur-tu-mân*, an excellent horse-keep, comes up half-wild along with it; and later on the *mâsh*, type of the vetch family.

[2] This applies particularly to the *I'l-rish*, mispronounced *itsh-rish*—a saltish herb lying close to the ground, having on it rough capsules like very small grapes. An inexhaustible supply of this is brought into I'râki towns in the hot months.

say that it came down the Tigris valley from Al A'ith. But if there be red sand-dunes in Al Ha-wi-ja, we did not see them. For many years, the wells and pastures of Al .\'ith have been, by the favour of the U'-baid, in the possession of the purely Bedouin tribe of Sá-yih, a sept driven by family quarrels across the Tigris,[1] and these were found by us leading the Najdian life; rich in mares and camels, and prone to foray. The horse-stock both of the U'-baid and Sá-yih will be looked at in another chapter. Al Ha-wi-ja, taken as a whole, is a fine natural horse-run; indeed the reader may be inclined, from much of what has just been stated, to form the same opinion of I'râk generally. But there are many things to handicap the Baghdad province under the existing *régime* in this respect; and although it would hardly do to consider every horse reared, or even got and foaled, in I'râk an I'râki, yet the local horse-stock is so inferior that one cannot but regret the fact of so much of it passing in distant countries as typical of Arabia's better strains.

As a rule, the Bedouin proper, when they enter I'-râk, avoid long sojourns in it. But considerable bodies of the Ae-ni-za, notably the Ibn Hadh-dhâl, are more and more tending to make it their *di-ra*. It is a fine thing for a fighting horde of the Ha-mâd thus to possess a special desert, into which, through fear of the Baghdad Government, their enemies can scarcely follow them. The present Head of these Hadh-dhâl Arabs, Shekh Fahd, even has a title and stipend from the Osmanli; and owns, though he seldom occupies, a house in Kar-ba-lá. In September and October he and his kindred swarm like locusts out of Shá-mi-yn towards culti- vated parts; and set up their blanket cities in the pastures west of the Euphrates, between Kar-ba-lá and Raz-zá-za. Nominally, they come to buy dates; but their camps form great camel-markets, which attract crowds of buyers. In fact, the Ibn Hadh-dhâl, though there is no better blood in the Ae-ni-za, are every year taking on more of the character of horse and camel sellers. It is not so to the same extent, perhaps, with their natural enemies, the Sham-mar. They, too, sell their colts as they go; but their first thought is to "see what God will give them"—*i.e.*, make free on every opportunity with other people's pro- perty. Lower down the Euphrates on the same side, round Sûku 'sh Shu-yûkh and Zu-bair, another Bedouin nation, the Najdian Dha-fir, has its pastures. But speaking broadly, excluding birds of passage, and allowing for exceptions, the horse- breeding peoples of the Tigris are of the most mixed description. A list of them

---

[1] A refugee tribe, or part of a tribe, thus attaching itself to another and possibly hostile tribe is called *ga-sir*. Fragments of the Sham-mar always are *ga-sir* with the Ae-ni-za, and *vice versâ*; and this is one of many other ways in which the several strains of horses are carried hither and thither.

would fill a gazetteer: the best known group-names are those given below.[1] Many are Bedouin by descent, and all but equally so by occupation — warlike, predatory, restless. Others, though settled, are able, owing to the inaccessibility of their haunts, to hold themselves safe from interference. Vast numbers are little else than peasants; milch cows of the Government;[2] a prey to all stronger than themselves; but not without some power of biting when too roughly handled by officialdom. Both extremes alike, including all the intermediate stages and gradations, are looked down on by Bedouin whose tails have escaped. Even when a common origin is admitted, the view taken is that of Rob Roy's wife when she asked the "Bailie" if a "stream of rushing water acknowledged any relations with the portion withdrawn from it for the mean domestic uses of those who dwelt on its banks?" This is all very well among the Bedouin; but it is a mistake when civilised people push the same fancy too far. For all whose proper concern it is to keep the life of the desert on its pristine lines, the utmost possible stiffening of the bristles may be advisable. But, this admitted, the European surely has no call to conclude that sixteen quarterings of Najdian blood count for nothing, as soon as a tribe takes to raising crops and contributing to the Government treasury. Notwithstanding the caution given above against regarding I'rák as demarcated by any river, the fact already stated may be remembered, that, in respect of the character of the people spread along it, the Tigris is far less Arabian than the Euphrates. The latter, in entering I'rák near Hít, strikes too decidedly eastward to retain much further connection with the pastures of the Ae-ni-za; but

---

[1] Bai-át, E. of Tigris, between Dúr Khur-má-tú and Kif-ri. Of Turanian, not Arab, stock.
Ba-nú Lám, E. of Tigris, from Kút to Persian frontier. W. of Tigris, S.E. of the Hai. Najdian origin.
Dá-war, same ground generally as Sham-mar Toga: guides and messengers.
Da-laim, v. p. 135.
I'-má-ra, pl. I'-má-rát, N. and S. of Hai river, formerly one of the most considerable nations in I'rák.
Ju-bór, W. of Tigris, tract called Tá-ji, between Baghdad and Tall Gúsh. Cattle-breeders and horse-dealers.
Kha-zá-il, Lower Shá-mi-ya, S.W. of Sa-má-wa, marching with Mun-ta-fik. Those having neither camels nor mares, cultivate; those better off, raid on their neighbours. Carriers and camel-dealers. Numbers of their colts are taken every year to India.
Mi'-dán, chiefly round I'-má-ra. Live in huts of reeds. Have enormous herds of buffaloes.
Mun-ta-fik, v. p. 135.
Sar-rá-e, between Tigris and Euphrates, S.E. of Hai river as far as the Hid.
Sham-mar Toga, plains E. of Tigris and S. of Dhi-á-la

to Kút. With them the Di-fá-fa'. Branch of them the Bú Mu-ham-mad; filling marshes N. of Gurna as far as Híd river. Propellers of canoes (m-a-shá-híf). Resembling them as living in huts and breeding buffaloes, but of better stock, and more peaceable, are the Ja-zá-ir inhabiting the marshy districts of the Euphrates.
U'-baid, from E. bank of Tigris to Him-rín hills, and round Kar-kúk. Ancient lineage; rich in mares and camels.
Zu-baid, a great, if mixed, people, between Tigris and Euphrates, N. of the Hai to Sak-lá-wi-ya canal, W.N.W. of Baghdad.
Add to the above a very large Kurdí element, in every stage between settled and nomadic.

[2] In I'rák, Government takes a sheep-tax (called ku-da) in money, at so much per head, and a similar one (called sar-af) on camels. On crops a tenth, or whatever it may be, is taken in kind. Wherever a patch of cultivation shows itself, down upon it, sooner or later, swoops a revenue officer, when the locusts are not beforehand with him.

this is more and more made up for, the nearer that it approaches the flanks of Najd. Even so high up as Hit, a great and aristocratic Bedouin people, preserving much of the old manners, occupies both its banks. These are the Du-laim or Di-lem, not long ago nomadic and strictly pastoral, but now half-way between that phase and the agricultural. The tribal form, with its essential "touch one touch all" organisation, is still indeed illustrated by them. A few years ago the irresistible tendency to stand by a friend drew them into a raid on the Sham-mar. Contrary to Arab usage, much blood was spilt; and the Du-laim, besides being defeated, were called most severely to account by the Baghdad Government. When they ride abroad it is still on blood-mares, with tufted spear on shoulder; and their home is still in open spaces. But mule-breeding is on the increase among them, and horse-breeding on the decline; the plough more and more attracts them; and sheds rise up beside their tents. Descending the Euphrates, we soon enter the country of the Mun-ta-fik. These expand over both sides of the river, from Sa-mâ-wa to the Gulf. On the Tigris, they possess the tracts which are crossed by the rivers Hid and Hai. Fifty years ago, the Arab settlement of Sûku 'sh Shu-yûkh, or Market of the Shekhs, near Gurna, which had grown up in connection with them, was a great centre of trade; but now it is close upon collapse. The Ac-ni-za say that the clans of the lower Euphrates are not sufficiently careful to ascertain the pedigree of a horse or mare before they breed from it; and that many of their mares are no better than those of the half-Persian Ka'b whose seats are on the opposite side of the Shattu 'l A'rab. To some extent this may be so; but the Mun-ta-fik are too near Najd, and their connection with it is too intimate, for them to be left without a certain number of pure-bred mares and stallions. Buyers from Zu-bair and Bussorah take away their colts; and India receives many good Arab horses from this source. Osmanli influences have been unsparingly exercised to weaken the bond which unites these people; and in some respects they now are in a somewhat shattered condition. But the warlike Arab spirit which they inherit is as strong as ever; and their interminable rice-fields and date-groves, added to their wealth in sheep and camels, serve to keep them in the foreground. The approaches to the Arabian littoral in this quarter, though not unguarded by the establishments of the distant central authority at Constantinople, are largely in the keeping of survivals like the Du-laim and the Mun-ta-fik, whose vitality it seems impossible to crush. To reach eastern Arabia by the open water-ways, and seize the towns of the seaboard, is an enterprise within the capacity of any foreign power possessing naval superiority. But it is one thing to defeat mercenaries, and a very different thing to be confronted by chieftains who, although destitute of what we should regard as military forces, hold in their hands the resources of important districts, and are possessed of singular ability. When recently enjoying the hospitality of one of the proudest of the Mun-ta-fik patriarchs, we more than ever realised the difficulties which would beset the European commander who should be called upon temporarily to establish his authority, and pass on troops from base to base, in these immense regions. We do not know how many, or how few, staff-officers who are able to speak to the Arabs in their own language, and interpret to others their characteristic traits and sentiments, would be available in such circumstances. But if ever it come to pass that, for want of such assistance, military chiefs are compelled to rely, in their Intelligence and Supply departments, on the legion of Levantines and I'-râ-kis who, on the grounds of their speaking English, or French, and Arabic, will proffer their services, very great difficulties will be experienced.

IN THE AUTHOR'S GARDEN, BAGHDAD.

BOOK SECOND

THE BREEDERS OF THE ARABIAN

CHAPTER I.

THE HORSEMAN MAKES THE HORSE.

THE moment that we leave the domain of Nature, and notice domestic breeds of animals, man's share in the making and moulding of them demands attention. He who would see a horse, for example, which should be wholly a product of climate, must necessarily catch a wild one.[1] Even the ponies which run in mobs in certain islands, though their owners may have but little to do with breeding them, at least receive protection.

No picture has come down of the horses of the cavalry and scythe-bearing chariots which the Romans encountered when they invaded Britain. But from the descriptions of their prowess in Cæsar and Tacitus, it is safe to infer that they showed *breeding*: that if climate made the web of them, the woof was shaped by the methods used to bring them to the proper standard, chiefly through the selection of parents, but also in the individual by means of work and training.

---

[1] With reference to the theory that the Horse's primeval home lies about the 40th degree of latitude on the highlands of Asia, we took advantage in 1886 of an adjoining region being under inspection by representatives of the Englishman and Slav—the two rival branches of the Aryan race—to inquire of a scientific friend, Surgeon Owen, C.I.E., medical officer with the "Boundary Commission," whether any facts bearing on this point had been seen or heard of. His answer was that, although in the localities visited by the Commission wild horses had not been seen, yet there were indications of the present existence of distinctly wild or aboriginal horses in Mongolia—that is, be it observed, the very region whence, eight centuries ago, Jenghis Kaan—the Bonaparte of the Eastern world—carried the Mongol arms, chiefly by means of clouds of horsemen, from the China sea to the banks of the Dnieper. As his authority in part, Dr Owen quoted his companion, Mr Ney Elias, who traversed in 1872 a line of upwards of 2000 miles, through the almost unknown tracts of western Mongolia, from the gate in the great wall of Kalgkan to the Russian frontier in the Altai. In Sir Douglas Forsyth's report on his mission to Yarkand it is stated that herds of wild horses (also wild camels) had been seen, not, indeed, by Sir Douglas, but by a native informant, in Northern Thibet. The country in question highly favours the natural habit of the horse; and from prehistoric down to recent times it has been famous for the excellence and numbers of its studs. *Vide* Marco Polo, Col. Yule's [1875] edit., ch. lxi. (vol. i. p. 261). In ch. liv., Ser Marco says, that the Tatar horses "will subsist entirely on the grass of the plains, so that there is no need to carry store of barley, straw, or oats."

The subjoined tableau from the famous roll of 12th-century embroidery which, from having been piously presented to the cathedral of Bayeux, is known as the "Bayeux tapestry," represents the horse and man-at-arms with which Norman William hammered Britons, Teutons, Danes, and other elements into a great nation; when the armour was as yet comparatively light; and war-steeds were not required to carry figures resembling our modern ironclads.

WILLIAM I. AND TOUSTAIN.

Where are now the stamps of horses which England possessed at the period of the Conquest? Where the square-set and untiring hackney, shaped like this,

(1)

(2)

on which our grandfathers covered the Great Northern Road? Or the "bonnie black mares" of the gentlemen who so often stopped them? Or, to name no more, the pack-horses of which the goods trains of long ago were formed?—

"How are they blotted from the things that be!"[1]

is the epitaph of them all. In this, as in other respects, old fashions have but given place to new: in the picture-gallery opposite, the characteristics and pursuits of Englishmen are reflected in their horses as completely as they were in those of long ago. The same thing has come to pass in other countries also. A century ago, Hindustan yielded breeds of horses second to none in stamina. Those were the days of free fighting: when hordes of mounted marauders swept the peninsula; when a blood mare might easily carry a shepherd or a slipper-bearer to the highest station; and when the true uses of light cavalry were understood as they have seldom been in Europe. Gradually all this was arrested by the growth of the British power. Their occupation gone, the old breeds then found their bourne on the other side of what some one has well called the "unjumpable Styx." In other lands, they would merely have taken on different forms. But unhappily among Indians generally there is no chord responsive to the epithet of "horseman," which is as dear to Englishmen as "horse-compelling" was to the Greeks and Romans. In India all the ploughing, and a great deal of the roadwork, are carried on by means of bullocks. And thus, in spite of much encouragement from Government, that country is now at a disadvantage in respect of the production of superior horses; compared with countries where colts are bred and reared at slight expense from the mares that work the farm, take the farmer to church and market, or occasionally even give him a look at the hounds.

All this is intended to illustrate how, next to climate—in highly civilised countries possibly even beyond and above it—'tis the man and the work that make the horse: and this view is so essential, that before in due time proceeding to consider the Arab horse, we wish to devote the following three chapters to the breeders of him; both the *Ahl bait*, or tent-folk, and the *Ahl há-yit*, or people of boundaries.

[1] Scott, in *The Lady of the Lake*.

CHAPTER II.

WHERE DID THE ARABS COME FROM?

ALL have heard of Queen Elizabeth's gunner, who, when he was called to account for not having fired a salute, gave twenty reasons, the last of which was that he had no powder! Not to follow suit, our best reason for failing in the sequel to answer the above-stated question may be given at the outset, and that is inability to do so. The discussion of it seems to suggest more difficulties than it solves. For example, the following. In all the "fragments of an earlier world" which lie imbedded in the Hebrew Scriptures, by what test are the substantial and permanent to be distinguished?[1] In what degree are we to consider the Hebrews and Arabs—so constantly in touch historically—inter-related ethnically? How far back falls the epoch when the Semite[2] consolidation, disintegrating, spread its portions, now spoken of as Arabs, Aramæans, Canaanites, Hebrews, Assyrians, Babylonians, and, lastly, the Ge'ez, or Abyssinians, over the several spaces which now contain them? Does Arabia proper, or Babylonia, or any other region where they are historically known to us, form the primitive seat of the Semitic peoples? Or came they as masterful immigrants from some nursery of nations outside of their present limits? Lastly, of all the Semitic tongues, which holds the same position towards the others that Sanscrit does in the Aryan family of speech? We do not mean that all, or any, of these formidable questions now await us. Most of them, we believe, are still undetermined. If we at least were to go into them, the very ancient Eastern figure of *diving into an ocean and bringing up a potsherd* would

---

[1] V. p. 113, *infra*, fn. 1.
[2] With reference to the term *Semite* or *Shemite*, the general reader may be glad of the information that it was first introduced (1787) under the impression that the division of mankind, so far as known to the Jews, in Gen. x., made most of the nations to whom it was applied descendants of Shem, the son of Noah. It is now known that the classification in question, whatever facts of political history or civilisation may be adumbrated in it, is neither ethnographic nor geographic. Nevertheless, for want of a scientific term, the universally received names "Semites" and "Semitic" continue to be borne by those nations collectively; and by the languages, some living and some dead, which are proper to them.

find one more illustration. Why, then, it may be asked, the present chapter? First, because the differences between the settled and nomadic Arabs cannot be elucidated apart from references to ethnology; in connection with which the preceding general statement may prove useful. Secondly, because in speaking of the origin of the Arabs we shall have an opportunity of stating certain facts about the Bedouin which most readers will find interesting.

Among the views of the Arab horse dealt with in previous chapters, one was that of his being indigenous to Arabia, in a sense in which the English horse is not indigenous to England; and another, that the pedigree of every genuine specimen of him issues pure and undefiled from some mysterious source. The unreasonableness of the former theory was then, let us hope, demonstrated; while the latter was reserved for consideration in its proper place. We have not yet come to that: meanwhile we wish to mention two more or less similar views with respect to the Arab man. The first is, the claim to purity of race in a very special sense which every Arab, at any rate every Bedouin, asserts for himself. The second, the vague belief prevailing that the ancient Arabs, while yielding numerous colonies, owed to the isolation of their peninsula a singular degree of freedom from foreign intrusion, and consequent race admixture. The latter opinion, it will soon appear, is not remote from the subject which is chiefly to occupy us in this chapter— the history of the Bedouin, considered separately from the whole body of the Arabs both nomadic and settled. Before passing on to that, if we slightly illustrate the individual Arab's claim to *sangre azul*, our remarks will not seem too irrelevant, when the Bedouin practice of horse-breeding afterwards comes under notice.

One of the pearls of wisdom which the Muslim ascribe to their Prophet is, *Preserve* [commit to memory] *of genealogies only as much as will keep pure your line.*[1] How far such an admonition was needed, and how far it has been followed, are nice questions. The world contains no greater recounters of pedigrees than the Arabs; but the "fatal facility" with which their handed-down material lends itself to the myth-making process is anything but a satisfactory feature.

---

[1] V. f.n. 3, p. 20, *ante*. Mr Stanley Lane Poole, in a little book (1882) about Muhammad, calls his 'Sayings' '*Table Talk*.' To which a captious critic might offer the two objections; that the Arab *sufra*— merely a skin spread on the ground—is not a *table*; and that eating, not talking, is the business to which Arabs and all primitive Asiatics address themselves at meal-times. Certain non-Muslim relics of the ancient Semite population of Babylonia, whose sect-name is Mandæans, even have the superstition that evil spirits live on food which they snatch from before talkative people.

After the Prophet's death Islamic piety constructed for him a family-tree connecting him through upwards of forty descents with Abraham; and this view, in whole or part, is now a point of faith with more than a hundred millions.

Let us try to state simply a series of facts, without attempting to build on them :—

I. Nobility depending on letters-patent is a thing undreamt of by the Arabs. Titled travellers in Arabia have sometimes thought that their connection with the peerage raised them in the eyes of the Bedouin. But any impression thus produced can only have depended on all the words by which the conventional English idea of "nobility" admits of presentation to an Arab being pre-associated in his mind with different ideas. When the old-fashioned Highlander said that King George could make any one he liked a Duke, but that "nobody could make a Mackay," he exactly expressed the Bedouin view. This comes out in the word *a-síl*—having for primary idea *established on a sure foundation*—which in Arabia forms the equivalent of our "old," as applied to birth. What the arch is in masonry, *a-sá-lat*, or a *deeply laid foundation*, is in the Arab's view of breeding. In modern Europe, at all events our portion of it, we ask, What has been a man's or a woman's history, subsequently to being born? and what improvements has he undergone through education? In the East, especially Arabia, the point is, How has he, or she, been *bred*? That a man's grandfather should have been rich or poor, front rank or rear rank, is secondary. All that is essential is, that his genealogy should be traceable to established stock. *Omne ignotum*, &c., goes but a short way in Arabia proper: and for one whose progenitors may have been Turks or Levantines to put himself on a level with him whose pedigree every one knows to be Arab, all Arab, and nothing but Arab, would there be looked on as utter presumption. The Bedouin, it should further be observed, do not think it possible for blood that has suffered mixture to recover itself. A son of Kah-tán by an African woman, even if a daughter of the tent *noblesse* be given to him to wife, cannot, in the opinion of his kindred, make so much as a beginning to restore to his offspring the true Arab purity and impress. The same romantic ideal finds expression in the desert law reserving for every youth the right of claiming the hand of his father's brother's daughter, at a lower dowry than that for which the maiden's parents would accept a stranger. In the speech of Bedouin, *bintu a'mm*, or cousin, passes as the accepted euphemism for a man's wedded wife. It would be useful to ascertain whether or not these consanguineous marriages[1] prove injurious, in respect of longevity, fecundity, and soundness. But with this problem still unsolved in Europe, where the necessary questions could

---

[1] Abraham's wife, Sarah, we know, was his half-sister—Gen. xx. 12.

be put in the census paper, the effects of such unions on the Bedouin Arabs are not likely soon to be discovered.

II. As a result, more or less, of this custom of close marriages, a considerable degree of "type fixity," displaying itself in inter-resemblance, runs in the several Bedouin stock-groups, and even circles of stock-groups. In the most "aristocratic" assembly of Englishmen, how diverse the shapes and features; how uncertain the presence even where most to be expected of outward or physical marks of race superiority! And one reason of this may be the freedom with which our ancient families, unscared by the Frenchman's fear of *mésalliance*—for which, by the way, our language contains no word—mate with others less artificial. On looking round a tentful of Bedouin, on the contrary, though different ethnic types may not be wanting, one generally sees sufficient evidence that the tribal bond, however it may have originated, has long been one of well-kept mutual kinship.

Traces of *breeding* are in the pose and figure; the head is well made and well set on; the small hand, and foot, and ear are prevalent; the most common cast of nose is the Wellingtonian—neither a beak nor a battering-ram, but a prominent and straightforward feature.

III. Whether as resulting from its fixity of type, or from other causes, Arab blood seems to possess a special virtue. If in our own island the pedigrees of those famed in field and senate be examined, from the Stuarts and Plantagenets to the Roses, Napiers, and Wolseleys, a high percentage will be found to be Norman. In the historical and old territorial aristocracy of the three kingdoms, names but slightly if at all altered from those in Froissart are conspicuous. Nay, even north of the Highland line in Scotland, half the Dunniewassals who, in compliment, as they think, to the nakedness of Celtic ancestors, refuse trousers, are descended from Norman immigrants, like Baliol and the "Bruce of Bannockburn." The Norman blood of the Eastern world—the unbridled, masterful, enterprising, conquering, and it may be added eloquent, stock—clearly is the Arab. Not only is this, when pure, a well-spring of powerful qualities; but even a little of it, when infused into families of wholly different derivation, has often led to greatness. For example, among the historical figures of native India the soldier-adventurer Hyder Ali, father of Tippoo, Sultân of Mysore, was the offspring of an Arab mother. The celebrated Sir Sâlâr Jung, from 1853 to his death in 1883 Minister of Hyderabad—type of high breeding and nobility alike of mind and aspect—was the thirty-third in descent from a family of Medina. Truly, there may be more in "blood," as it is called, than we know of; though this, to be sure, applies to most things.

IV. Not only the Arab man, and the Arab horse, but also very many of the creatures of the Arabian plain, from the largest antelopes down to the tiny *yar-bú*, or jumping-mouse, are remarkable for the grace and beauty, the absence of all useless substance, and the signs of "blood" or "quality," which belong to them. In this respect the Arab greyhound resembles the Arab horse. A more sprite-like creature, or one more completely made for speed, was never moulded by man or nature. So far as these observations refer to tent-bred animals, they more or less point to the force of *pure breeding;* but the hawks and bustards, antelopes and wild asses, of the desert, must owe their refined proportions to the soil and climate. A country the fauna of which is of this description may undoubtedly be regarded as offering special facility for the production of high-bred domestic animals. We never have felt tempted to breed Arabians in England. But if, in spite of the enormous initial outlay, and the difficulty of afterwards maintaining the necessary establishment, the English thoroughbred horse could be bred, and galloped, and fed, say on the Ja-bal Sham-mar plateau, and the two-year-old produce sent to Newmarket, the experiment would be interesting.

In Arabia, as in other countries, an epoch of obscurity, thick with gods and demons, giants and giant-killers, fabulous tribes and peoples, lies behind the beginnings of history. Many diffused legends of those remote centuries were afterwards quoted by Muhammad, for the purpose of producing the strongest possible moral impression on his countrymen. Hence the Kur-án abounds in references to very ancient Arabian kingdoms, and to the miraculous interferences by which they were destroyed. The action of "sacred books" in preserving material of this description has been noticed by writers as divergent as Gibbon and Dean Stanley ;[1] to a great extent, it forms a necessary feature of their antiquity. We allude to it only to say that a middle course will here be aimed at, relatively to all that has thus come down. On the one hand, mere fossil remains will not be treated as necessarily important; on the other hand, it will be remembered that many an undiscovered fact of history probably is imbedded in the strange conglomerate of ancient fable.

---

[1] We cite of Gibbon's references, that in his 33d ch. to "the memorable fable of the Seven Sleepers" of Ephesus: the currency of which in the East is testified, while its diffusion has been enormously increased, through its having been brought into the Kur-án (S. xviii.); and further, his suggestion, in his 50th ch., that the tenet of the immaculate conception of the Virgin Mary was "borrowed from the Kur-án." The late Dean of Westminster (*Lect. on Hist. East. Church*, p. 253) mentions, *inter alia*, the latter legend as one of those which Muhammad "derived from Christian sources;" and which were "received back from him into Christendom." The first page reference under this statement is "Kur. iii. 31, 37." As two such eminent writers have noticed this point, we may just say that, according to the best Baghdad scholars, the Arab Prophet taught,—(1) that Mary was, while yet unborn, dedicated by her mother to God's service: (2) that her Lord accepted her; (3) that at her birth she was miraculously shielded from the touch of Satan; (4) that all her life she was endowed with immaculacy. The Roman view, which, though only in our day (1854) made binding, has long been favoured by the Jesuits, goes further than the Arabian, in representing the act of sanctification as *simultaneous with conception.*

Accordingly, all that need here be said of the very early period of Arabia is that, although several of the peoples — *e.g.*, the Amalekites and the nation of Tha-múd—who then existed lasted well into historic times, they are now no more. This fact is embodied in the name,[1] meaning the *lost*, or *cut off*, Arabs, which adheres to them.

Advancing from spaces of Cimmerian darkness to those of dawning light, we soon perceive an essential fact. Not all the mountains of futile explanation which have been raised over it, can obscure this circumstance in the conditions of Arabia, that from the earliest times of which we have cognisance two populations as dissimilar as the typical Ba-da-wí and the typical Ha-dha-rí have divided its area between them. A passing glimpse of the Sabæan period of Arab history was afforded in a previous chapter. Strabo[2] has preserved the information that before our era S. Arabia contained not only the people of Sa-bá, but several other settled nations.[3] Succeeding capitals of ancient Yemen—Má-rib and San-á', and others before them—teemed with aristocratic figures; builders of palaces; hard-fighting Cæsars; satraps or governors of subsidiary provinces. Under the same regime towns and villages grew up. Commerce, agriculture, and the industrial arts[4] prospered. Im-ru 'l Kais uses *Ya-má-ní*, or Yemenite, as a synonym for *travelling merchant*. Traders, and leaders of successful or unsuccessful military expeditions, told in many lands their stories of

" Sabæan odours from the spicy shore
Of Arabie the blest." *

But these influences, as has also been seen, hardly if at all affected the middle zone of the peninsula. Then, as now, Nu-fúdh land formed a sort of political island; within which more or less were exclusiveness, independence, and the migratory habit. All these facts are well established. Authentic ancient sources yield them; and in our time they have been verified from coins and inscriptions.

---

[1] In Arabic, *A'rabu l A'ribati l Ki-i-da*.
[2] Bk. xv. 4, 2.
[3] The Minæans, on the Red Sea; the *Ka-ta-bá-a*, or Catabanes; and the people of Hadh-ra-maut, whose city was Sabota.
[4] Among the industries of ancient Yemen the tanning and colouring of hides held a great place. To this day, in the towns of Arabia and 'Irák, the only article of indigenous design which at all resembles the European shoe is called a *ja-ma-ní*. Notwithstanding an increasing inflow of slop-shoes and ankle-boots from India and Europe, this is still the common wear with old-fashioned Arab folk. Bedouin as often go barefooted as otherwise. The pattern of their shoe varies; but the principle is the very ancient one of a sole attached to the foot with straps. A common kind is this :—

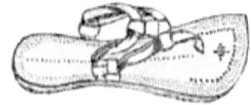

N-'l, or Shoe of the Arabs.

* *Paradise Lost*.

As just now hinted, the difficulty lies in the interpretations of them which have been invented. Whatever may have been the case

<blockquote>
" in the golden prime
Of good Haroun Alraschid,"[1]
</blockquote>

modern Baghdad affords but slight facilities for researches of this nature. It is long since an Abú 'l Fi-dá, or an El As-ma'-i, has arisen among the Arabs. So far as our acquaintance extends, the men of to-day are chiefly grammarians; without the power, even in that limited field, of going outside of Arabic into other Semitic tongues. The cultivation of their several "orthodoxies" absorbs them; and their inclination towards secular studies is even slighter than their materials. All things considered, probably the wisest of them are they who tell us that the secrets of ancient history are known to God only.

In numerous popular books, the so-called *genuine*, or *Arabian*, Arabs[2] are termed, indifferently, the *Southern*, also *Yemenite*, Arabs, from a tradition that at some infinitely remote period they entered the peninsula at its south-western angle; *African* Arabs, according to an equally nebulous theory that they came from Africa; and lastly, *Kah-tá-ni* Arabs, after a reputed ancestor, Kah-tán, a variant perhaps of Joktan, son of Eber of Genesis; though we do not know how many of these ancient names represent persons, and how many merely serve to hand down traditions.[3]

And similarly all the nations which are held to have entered Arabia later, and in whom the nomadic habit is much developed, appear in annals, now as the *Mus-ta'-ri-ba*, lit. *would-be Arabs — sc.*, foreigners who have *taken on the Arab* speech and character; now as the *Northern* Arabs, under the supposition of their having landed, not like their precursors in Yemen, but higher up, towards the isthmal

---

[1] Tennyson, in *Recollections of the Arabian Nights*.

[2] [Al] *A'raba 'l A'riba*.

[3] For example, *Eber* and Peleg. As long as European neglected Semitic learning, there were none to doubt Eber's being the great-grandson of Shem, through Arpachshad; and ancestor of Abraham's father Terah through Peleg, Serug, and Nahor (Gen. x., xi.), notwithstanding the (probably unperceived) difficulty of two separate views of him being interwoven in the genealogical lists in Genesis—one, that just stated; the other (Gen. x. 21, 25-30), bringing in no intermediate link between Shem and him, while reckoning to the "sons of Eber" not alone the descendants of Peleg (Aramaeans, Israelites, and so-called "Ishmaelite" Arabs), but the southern or Joktanic Arabs also. When, however, the name Eber was examined by etymologists, its connection with the antique Semitic root *Ebr = crossing*, was perceived. And after a time the suggestion followed, that if this *Ebr* be read in the secondary Arabic application of a *river-bank*, or *any locality thereon situated*, *Ibrî*, or *Hebrew*, may merely mean *riparian*, i.e., *dwelling*, or *encamping, on a river*. And so with Peleg, the name, as supposed, of "Eber's" son, and Joktan's brother. We owe to Sprenger the suggestion connecting this word with *Falj* or *Fa-laj*, the pl. of which, *Af-láj*, is the name of a district in central Arabia (p. 32 *ante*, in f.n.) And it is worth considering whether this view may not be carried further. *Fa-la-ja* means, in Arabic, *dividing*, especially the ground with irrigational channels; and *Peleg* may merely be a personification of settlers on irrigated and cultivated soils. There is a hamlet called Fal-lú-ja within two days of Baghdad.

extremity of the Red Sea; and perhaps oftenest of all, as the "Ishmaelite" Arabs, or "Children of Ni-zâr," after the tradition that through a real or fabulous A'd-nân, and his supposed grandson Ni-zâr, they are the descendants of Ishmael and Hagar.[1] We notice with surprise that a writer of so late a date as 1875,[2] in his haste to uproot what he terms the "Ishmaelitic mythos," would assign to both divisions of the Arabs an African origin. But this is guess-work. The few statements which its author conjoins with it, in so far as they are true, equally favour the opposite, and indeed certain, conclusion, that large portions of Africa, notably Abyssinia,[3] were colonised and Semitised from S. Arabia.[4]

The account just given of how the existing nations of Arabia are commonly classified is of course but a summary. The division rests only in part on the sure basis of facts which still admit of being tested; but it is unnecessary here to notice more than one of its many obscurities. It was just now said that the nomadic habit more showed itself in the Arabs of the later than of the earlier immigration. And much further back,[5] it will be remembered, we marked and postponed the question of whether a *race* distinction, or merely the force of circumstances, forms the basis of this divergence between the two populations. Here this topic again invites us; but instead of treating it in the abstract, let us approach it through the familiar

---

[1] Seeing that Muhammad was of the Mus-ta'-ri-ba, the several links in this pedigree are treated by many as post-Islamic inventions designed to lend new lustre to the Prophet's ancestry. This may be so: that is, the chain of connection may be the work of an eastern Debrett; but the main fact of the Mus-ta'-ri-ba having long before Muhammad's era claimed Is-mâ-îl for heroic ancestor is well established.

[2] The late Mr W. G. Palgrave, in *Ency. Brit.*, vol. ii. pp. 235-265. There never was a more useful repertory of knowledge than Messrs Black's great work in its present form. But the article on Arabia is an exception. They who refer to that article for information on Arabian topics, will on many points be misled instead of guided.

[3] "With the Ethiopians *Sa-bá* means *men*: a clear indication of their Sabæan descent."—Prof. D. H. Muller, in art. YEMEN, *Ency. Brit.*, vol. xxiv. p. 738.

[4] After crossing from Arabia (Aden) to Africa with the Abyssinian expedition, the many resemblances which we noticed between the two countries recalled the legend of the Red Sea basin having been suddenly made by an earthquake. Similar physical characteristics, such as shape and size of head, slight development of calf, and appearance of the hair, met us in the inhabitants of both coast-lines. The Shoho tribes of the passes leading from the seaboard to the Abyssinian highlands seemed almost singular in respect of the low point of physical depression, which was touched by them. But on afterwards making the acquaintance of the *Nafūd* or *'l Hasā*, as the Al Ha-sâ oasis is termed by Bedouin, we met their very brothers, in the shape of certain tribes of goat-pasturing Arabs, so desiccated of frame and inferior of aspect that a group of them squatted round a well, or sleeping on their faces with the fore-arm for a pillow, might at first sight be mistaken for weeds of the soil. Zoologically, the two countries seemed parts of one another; and even the name, *Ra-má I-rī-bīl*, of the first wild creature shot by us at Zulla, the tiny African antelope, was through and through Semitic. The floras also were similar. Lastly, several of the names for common objects were the same on both sides of the Straits of Bâbu 'l Man-dab. One such word, the most indispensable of all, viz., *mâ-i*, water, proved to be equally that of Arab, Ethiopian, and Egyptian. But on afterwards reading all the speculations to which the extended range of the words in question has contributed, from Prof. Nöldeke's "modest hypothesis" that the "primitive seat of the Semites is to be sought in Africa," to the view that Egyptian may form a relic of Semitic speech before the triliteral root development, the difficulties and dangers of aerial navigation appeared inconsiderable compared with those of philological.

[5] *V.* p. 18, *ante*.

story of Ishmael and Hagar having in a special sense *founded* the several nations of the Mus-ta'-ri-ba, or, to give them the name by which they often pass, the "Ishmaelite Arabs." Many miscellaneous gleanings on this subject are before us. We do not presume to regard them as contributions, but merely as fragments, some of which may yield suggestions to better equipped investigators. But in the first place, certain general observations are necessary.

I. From very early times the northern Arabs were mainly nomads; while Yemen, as has been seen, was the seat of settled life and civilisation. But when some European writers represent the contrast between the two groups as essentially that between nomadic and settled manners, they go too far, and are not justified by the Arabian chronicles. In point of fact, masses of the southern Arabs have the Bedouin habit. Such are nearly all the hordes of the Persian Gulf littoral—Al Mur-ra, U'j-mân, Ba-nû Yâs, and others; with notably Kah-tân in inner Arabia. Nor should the statement be omitted that from the epoch of ancient Tadmur, and before it, downward, the Mus-ta'-ri-ba have, on occasion, emulated the Yemenite settlers in obtaining a grip of towns and castles.

II. The prevalence anciently of Jewish settlements and kingdoms within the Arabian peninsula is one of those special subjects which require special reading. We do not here allude to the signs of this which Baghdad exhibits. From the ethnic standpoint, it may be of but slight significance that, in the Tigris and Euphrates valleys, not only the towns, but the most outlying places, contain Jewish traces: that on the upper Tigris, a tomb on the site of Nineveh is venerated alike by Jew, Christian, and Muslim as that of Jonah;[1] that lower down the same river, near Baghdad, the last resting-place, real or supposed, of Joshua[1] attracts the pilgrim; that lower still, not far from Bussorah, the dust of Ezra[1] occupies a conspicuous shrine. These and other kindred legends naturally connect themselves with the several deportations of the Jews from their native land by the Assyrian or Babylonian kings. Hilla, three days S.W. of Baghdad, on the site of Babylon, still contains a Jewish remnant. Modern Baghdad is understood to owe to Hilla the several thousand Israelites who are now engaged in adding farthing to farthing on

---

[1] With Arabs respectively Yû-nus, Yû-sha', U'zair, three of Is-lâm's several hundred prophets; of whom these six—Nûh (Noah), Ib-râ-hîm (Abraham), Mû-sâ (Moses), I'sâ (Jesus), and Muhammad—are dignified and distinguished above all others. As we write, the Baghdad Jews are at war with the town authorities, on the point of interment in Joshua's precincts. When cholera lately appeared, orders were issued which prevented them from carrying their dead there in any circumstances. Nevertheless, on a Rabbi dying, they took the body by night to the holy ground; and, resisting the police, interred it. Heads were broken at the time; and many of the Jews were afterwards arrested. But the ancient money-lending people, if a "feeble folk" in Pràk, are stronger in other quarters. So well has the telegraph been worked by them, that the Sublime Porte has now removed the "persecuting" Wâ-li; whose successor has, however, caused the Rabbi's body to be taken up and re-buried in another place.

the Tigris, in hopes of their children one day "sitting at meat" with European princes. But when we import into this view the larger facts that Jews at a very primitive period not only possessed districts of peninsular Arabia like Khaibar, but in towns like Mecca and Yath-rib (Medina) lived side by side with pagan Arabs, the close connection which existed when the world was younger between Arabia and Israel is well illustrated.

III. Another topic seldom coming before the general reader is, the strength and number of the attachments, to use an anatomical term, which connect Islamism with Judaism. How the Prophet of Al Islâm placed his system in the line of ideal Judaism, by carrying it back to Abraham, may elsewhere be read. At first the Jews, on learning that his theme was "the God of Abraham," hoped that it might be his mission to convert Arabia to Judaism. They soon discovered that his object was to bring out from the ancient Abrahamic stem doctrines which were new to them. Then, instead of listening to him, they hated him, and tried to kill him. At last, when he had gained the ear of Arabia, its Jews, to borrow a Kuranic expression, *entered in multitudes the religion of Allah*. The connection of these remarks is with the prominence which we are soon to see assigned to Abraham in Arabian legend. Wherever Islamism and the Arab speech have extended, the distinctive titles of *Kha-li-lu 'llah*, i.e., *Friend of God*, often shortened into THE FRIEND, and *Abû 'l Is-lâm*, or *Father of Is-lâm*, belong to him. His name, in its Arabicised form of *Ib-rû-hîm*, stands out in the Kur-ân: in one text (S. iii.) it is said that he was *not a Jew, and not a Christian, but a Ha-nîf*[1] *and Muslim*.[2]

IV. The statements last made introduce another; and that relates to the recurrence, if not invariably in the Kur-ân, at least as flotsam and jetsam of Arabian story, of much of the material which is stratified in Bible narratives. The Ishmael and Hagar episode will presently be adverted to, both in its Hebrew and Arabian forms. But first, this essential question may be anticipated, Are we justified in thinking such mixed, or common, Hebræo-Arabic elements in any true sense proper to old Arabia? Or did not the Arabs first hear of them through Islamism? We know of no modern European authorities who are of opinion that Muhammad received the prophetic impulse from other than Arabian sources. But when it comes to determining where he got the histories which appear in the Kur-ân, it is different. Most of these recitals deal with Scripture characters, from Adam downward; about whom

---

[1] V. Index I., art. HA-NIF.

[2] V. Index I., art. IS-LÂM. Not *Mahomedan*, or *Muhammedan*, but *Muslim* (Arab pl. *Mus-li-mû-na*, Persian pl. *Mus-lim-ân*) is the appellative applicable to followers of El. Is-LÂM. Considering how wide the field is of England's naval, diplomatic, and consular services, this point may at least be thought worthy of a footnote. Even the mode of transcription suggests a protest. Words formed in the mould of Senate language require, when Aryans borrow them, careful handling. Why should *Muslim*, at once proper noun, common noun, and adjective, be altered into *Mu-sul-mân*, *Mussul-man*, and, *peek-puder!* *Matsulman!*

they tell the same stories, with considerable deviations and alterations, as those in the Old and New Testaments. But others relate to ancient Arabian prophets of whom we do not elsewhere read. In respect of narratives of the former category, the supposition is reasonable, that Muhammad often heard them repeated[1] by persons not unacquainted with the "holy library" of Jews and Christians, including the gospels now regarded as "apocryphal." But this view does not reveal the sources of those other Kuranic narratives which, so far as is known, never were recorded before Muhammad's time. Of course the explanation comes ready to hand, and is not unsanctioned by European scholars, that the Arab Prophet fabricated all such "biographies,"[2] just as our own preachers "bring in for the sake of illustration" material which could hardly be verified. It is useless to appeal on these topics to learned Arabs, whose stand is on the "impregnable rock" of Gabriel. As for our own impressions, they chiefly depend on some acquaintance with oriental life, and with the methods of unlettered workers. Men naturally are speakers and hearers, not writers and readers. Gibbon said with equal truth and beauty, "The school of the Arabs was a clear firmament and a naked plain." Viewed as a Book, Al Kur-án is unique: it is the substance of Al Is-lám; and the Arab empire grew out of it, like the oak out of its acorn. But we must remember that it did not originate in any idea of book-making. After forty years or so of human contacts, the Prophet spoke out of his mind's rich stores, till he died at sixty-two, without even having caused an authentic collection of his sermonisings to be made. In the present stage of historical science, the necessary reagents are wanting for the separation of the real from the mythical in his stories of antiquity. But that does not prevent us from expressing, with great deference, the opinion, that the narratives in the Kur-án, however freely handled, are, more or less, "broad-based" on the traditions of ages lost to chronology, the diffusion of which in large classes of the Arabs before Muhammad is too probable to be reasonably doubted.

The preceding observations, it will be remembered, immediately followed the statement that the tradition of Ishmael being the eponymous father of the uncentralised Arabian nations was next to occupy us. That did not mean that we intended to restrict ourselves to the notices in Genesis of Ishmael and Hagar. The "gleanings" which we, at the same time, intimated the purpose of presenting,

---

[1] See the question of whether Muhammad could read and write slightly noticed in Index I., art. KUR-ÁN.

[2] In proof of the Kur-án's narratives being peculiar to it, and not rooted in old Arabian legend, we are sometimes reminded that the literature of the "Days of Ignorance" contains no trace of them. But nothing that could be styled a book existed in the Arabic language before Muhammad. Only the unwritten effusions of the minstrels were then in circulation; and the world of the pagan Arabs lay at an infinite remove from religious subjects. Even the god-name Allah, by which their oaths were sworn, occurs but once or twice in the seven ballads called AL MU-'AL-LA-KÁT, q. v. in Index I.

are from many quarters. Admittedly none of them are historical, if that term be strictly applied. There is nothing easier than to embellish history, unless it be to fabricate it; but if Sisyphus had been set for a change to use unhistoric tales as if they were historic, he would soon have asked for his stone again. What here suggests this remark is the subject immediately before us of Arab and Hebrew origins. The ground as to this grows very difficult as soon as we pass beyond the genuine tradition, attested in Scripture, that there was kinship between the two peoples. But writing as we do in the lands of Semites, where the common belief is that Abraham was an Arab, and through Is-mâ-i'l the father of the more typically and generally Bedouin nations, it would not be right altogether to shun this question. The following references to it fall under the four divisions, of Physical Aspect; Speech, especially Proper names; Characteristics; and Traditions. Several of the indications which present themselves are chiefly negative or neutral; while all do not point quite in the same direction: for they have not been chosen or sifted in the interests of a set conclusion. But we consider this view to run like a thin thread through them, that the Semite group, which, under a succession of great leaders, developed into Israel, came originally from that foundry of nations, Arabia.

Physical Aspect.

It is not to be disputed that the cast of countenance commonly considered typical of the Hebrew stock often appears in Arabs. And we have some idea that this facial outline more prevails in the Ishmaelite than in the Yemenite nations; though this impression perhaps depends merely on our having seen more of the former than of the latter. Thus the so-called Jewish visage often develops a high degree of feminine, yet not effeminate, beauty in the youths of the Ae-ni-za and the Sham-mar. Later in life, when sun and drought and grime, blended vacuity and vigilance, and the habit of dwelling "in the midst of alarms," have too soon brought on old age, the same features often turn large and statuesque; and the chest and bust expand. In Bedouin adhering to the Bedouin life, obesity is so rare, as rather to be taken as showing that the "cows have been in the corn" in the matter of immediate ancestry.[1] Nevertheless the tents of Shà-mi-ya and Al Ja-zi-ra con-

---

[1] Town life and Falstaffian habits (bating always the "old sack") all one's time divided between mosque and harem, and "sleeping upon benches after noon"—may give us Falstaffs even in Najd. For a Bad-u who has taken to kingcraft, and who is nothing if not a Hotspur, the keeping of his figure is essential. Amir Fai-sal (v. p. 36, awk) turned in the end corpulent; but that was after age and its infirmities, including blindness, had "tamed his force." His son and successor, Abdu'lla, was naturally obese and bovine; in which, and in the contempt engendered by it, causes of the Ibn Su-â-ds' downfall are recognisable.

tain many a powerful and formidable figure; the lineaments, when inclining to the
"Jewish," suggesting the old heroic, not the modern, stamp. We shall not soon
forget the impression received, the first time of alighting at the tents of one of the
bluest-blooded of all the septs of the Ae-ni-za. Instead of scraggy figures, in garments like night-shirts, holding on to barebacked mares, stalwart warriors in casques
and tunics of chain-armour[1] came caracoling out. At supper-time, the Shekh's *ma-
dhif*, or great guest-tent, attracted hundreds; and many a head was there which
a painter engaged on some passage of Bible history would eagerly have copied.
In the drowsy firelight, we almost felt as if we had been asleep, like Steenie in
"Wandering Willie's Tale" in *Redgauntlet*, and on awaking found ourselves with a
company fresh from witnessing the drowning of Pharaoh's army. For a moment,
this fancy conjured up many a preconceived idea; but the fallacy of confounding
resemblances, real or imaginary, with *origination*, was soon apparent. A type of
countenance approximating to the "Jewish" is even commoner in the Afghans than
in any division of the Arabs.[2]

Speech.

The view of "nations" and "languages" being convertible terms carries us
back to the description which connects the scattering of the human family with the
confounding of the Noachian language.[3] Perhaps the tendency too much to accept
differences of speech as proofs of diversity of race may be regarded as a survival of
this conception: but at all events let us not overlook the potentiality of a common
language, however formed, to weld into one, as the English tongue has done in the
United States, mixed waves of population. Speaking of the case before us: on the
one hand, no one can presume to say when the Southern, or Arabic, the Northern,
or Aramaic, and the Middle, or Hebraic, languages severally assumed their present
forms; on the other, the date of Abraham's leading his father's horde from Haran

---

[1] A modern book on the armour and weapons of Arabia is wanted. The Bedouin *dir'a*, or coat of proof, though sometimes of camel's hide, is generally of steel chain, topped with a hood or helmet, from its shape easily mistaken by others than Don Quixotes for a cap or basin - by the name for which, indeed (*this*), they call it. Modern articles of this description are chiefly the work of Persian and Frâki armourers; but among desert heirlooms are blades and shirts of proof belonging to ancient periods. To such we refer the following lines in a pre-Islamic ballad:—

Know ye not, between us and you
The squadrons charge and hurl javelins!

Ours the casques and shields of Yemen,
And the blades that curve and straighten!
Ours fell coats of shining armour;
Mark how above the swordbelts they wrinkle!
When by chance the warriors doff them,
You may see their skins black from them;
Their folds are like the surface of a lake
Ruffled by the passing breezes.
— *Antar*.

[2] Afghán chroniclers apply the name *Bä-ni Is-rä-il*, or *Children of Israel*, to their people; but evidence is wanting that they did so before Islamism.

[3] Gen. xi. 1-9.

into Palestine is undetermined, though conjecturally referred to B.C. 2000. One strongly supported view is, that the tribes of Abraham and Lot, when they settled in Canaan, spoke Aramaic, in which portions of the Bible are written: and gradually exchanged it for the kindred language of the Canaanites. The reference in Isa. xix. 18 is understood by competent scholars to indicate that the Hebrew tongue was "the language of Canaan" before it became that of Israel. In all probability our posterity will be better informed on these points than we are.[1]

It is a long step from the "children of Israel" to the British Association. We make it for the sake of saying that if the two thousand members and upwards of that body who annually take their holiday in lecturing, or hearing lectures, in the cities of the United Kingdom, would one day send a small section to Arabia—not to an English hotel in Damascus, but to the tents of Najd—to write down from men's and women's lips the words current among nomads, a very great desideratum would be supplied. Here we can only mention that although the Bedouin have the classical Arabic, they also use very many words which, if traceable to Arabic at all, neither appear in Arabic dictionaries nor are claimed by Baghdad grammarians as Arabic. This is too general a subject to be here pursued. Leaving on one side common words, let us inquire what, if any, hints on the origin of the Arabs are to be met with in their proper names. Place-names afford but few suggestions. Vast expanses, both in the peninsula and in the adjoining lands of Arabs, bear no other designation than Ha-mâd, or desert. What the word *ocean* is to sailors, *ha-mâd* is to Arab nomads: vague, boundless, undefined; yet all-sufficing, all-expressing; home-name at once of the individual and his race. Within the Ha-mâd, wells (*ab-yâr*) and springs (*u'yûn*) form the traveller's landmarks; and these may be called after men, or tribes, or wild animals. But we know of no Arabian district which is named, like so many in the New World, after native lands under other skies.

Two of the great meeting-places of the Bedouin in Shâ-mi-ya, though each larger than many an English parish, own no other name than, the one, *Al l-khai-dhar*, or *The Green*; the other, *Al Mar-ta'*, *The Pasture*. Names of persons are

---

[1] *For example.* Since the above passage was written, a happy find of upwards of 300 Cuneiform Tablets at Tell el Amarna, in Upper Egypt, has supplied philologists with new material. Among these "brick epistles" (prob. date B.C. 1500-1450) are letters from governors of towns in Palestine to Egyptian personages, written in a dialect which is held to exhibit in certain important particulars "a close affinity to the language of the Old Testament." See the edition of the Tablets, containing a bibliography, which has been published by the Trustees of the British Museum.

Lane, in the Preface of his great dictionary, thus observes: "It is evident that all the Semitic languages diverged from one form of speech; and the known history of the Arabic is sufficient, I think, to show that the mixture of the several branches of the Shemites, in different degrees, with different foreign races, was the main cause, if not of the divergence, at least of the decay, of their languages, as exemplified by the Biblical Hebrew and Chaldee, and the Christian Syriac."

more significant. We had not long sat down beside the Tigris, when it appeared that Bible names, such as Mû-sâ (Moses); Yû-suf (Joseph); Ai-yûb (Job); Dâ-ûd (David); Sal-mân or Su-lai-mân (Solomon); I'-sâ,[1] were commoner in the Yemenite than in the Ishmaelite Arabs; whereas had the latter in any *special* sense been from Abraham, it ought to have been otherwise. But the explanation was of the simplest. For we have seen how, in the first flush of Islamism, the Jews of Al Hi-jâz embraced it: not the inferior classes only—the Jew vintners, for instance, in whose hands was the wine trade, and who, when the new faith plucked down their flags,[2] thought it best to turn Muslim—but the men of culture too, the "Scribes and Pharisees" of Mecca and Medina.[3] Many of these would, sooner or later, drop their Jewish names. A Baghdad Jew informs us that when, some centuries ago, a member of his stock embraced Islamism, the family name of Obadiah bin Shalom became changed into the Islamite one of A'bdu 'llâ bin Su-lai-mân. But very many other converts have kept the old names, especially names living again in the Kur-ân. Not only the fact that names of the Hebræo-Arabic category have prevailed since Islamism among the Arabs is thus accounted for; but equally the circumstance that the frequency of such names diminishes in the several nomadic Arab nations in the ratio of separation, or remoteness, from the Islamic centres. By way of testing this, we obtained from the desert of Shâ-mî-ya a list containing forty-four tribe names, and thirty-eight personal names, of the Ae-ni-za. The roll is now before us; and, as it chances, there is not one name of the Is-mâ-î'l and Ya'-kûb[4] species in it. Also, *as it chances*—for in both cases it might as easily have been otherwise—it does not contain a single name of that brand-new series which Muslim have manufactured by the prefixing of *A'bd* (*worshipper*) to one of the "ninety-nine goodly names,"

---

[1] I'-sâ 'L Mâ-sih (*Jesus the Messiah*) having been made by Muhammad one of the six prophetic pillars of his theological structure, the name I-sâ has spread in Arab families. The Arabs have certainly confused between Jesus and Esau, and given the name of the latter to the former; but the two names have nothing to do with one another. In the Kur-ân, I'-sâ simply is a transcription of *Jesus*.

[2] We know from the ballads of the "Days of Ignorance" that wine-sellers' booths had flags for signs in ancient Arabia. A'n-tar, depicting a finished gallant, describes him as great at making the vintners *strike their flags* (in token of his having bought up their store). La-bîd in his best-known poem thus addresses the fair Na-wâ-ra:—

Perhaps thou knowest not how many a bright and pleasant night of fun and fellowship
I have spent in moonlight entertainments. And to how many a vintner's flag I have been constant, as long as it was flying, with the grape juice at a premium;

Buying up the wine, every black old skin of it, or jar smeared with pitch out of which they have ladled after breaking the seal on its mouth.
And how many a pure morning draught I have drunk off, when the glee-maiden was drawing her guitar (Arabic, *wa-toot-her*) to her, and her thumb adjusting it.

[3] One of these Jewish converts, by name A'bdu 'llah ibn Sa-bâ, closely attached himself to A'li in the stormy period of the first four Caliphs. He instituted the practice of giving allegorical meanings, or any other meanings which one pleases, to the "plain Kur-ân." In spite of A'li's anger and reprobation, he sought to teach that A'li was an incarnation of the Godhead. Thus, through a Jew of San-â', or rather perhaps of Egypt, Islamism received in Arabia, soon after the Prophet's death, a tincture of all the foreign elements of which it afterwards became the receptacle in Persia. *V.* Index I., art. SUN-NI AND SHI-I'.

[4] Ishmael and Jacob.

or attributes, supplied to Allah by the magnificent Semitic imagination of the Prophet.[1]

Not only are all the names in the list purely secular or "heathen," but all of them are regularly connected with some Arabic root; the idea wrapped up in which is now an abstract one, now a concrete. Often the name denotes prosperity, or a "flow" of pastoral wealth. One great Shekh of the Sba', Muhammadu[2] 'l Mis-rib, is content to borrow the name of the humble utensil (*mis-rib*) in which milk is set out to turn sour! Names denoting some bodily mark or peculiarity, or some trait of character, are common.[3] Equally so are those taken from plants or animals; sometimes from birds or beasts of prey; sometimes from creatures as lowly as the mouse or hedgehog. The important subject of the animal god, or *totem*—a loan word from the vocabulary of the Ojibway Indians—here crops up; but notwithstanding much patient inquiry, we can offer no new observations tending to support the view which is held by a good many European literati, that Arab stocks whose names are those of plants or animals anciently believed themselves to be the children of them. The next time that the Royal Welsh Fusiliers garrisons Hong-Kong, there is nothing to prevent a Chinese archæologist from conjecturing that the white goat marching at the head of it is its *totem*. The same savant, without going back to prehistoric ages, or citing American savages, may also find abundant material with which to build up his theory—from the British lion and American eagle down to the Scandinavian raven. And yet all of us know how far removed from sober fact his speculations would be. If any one were to suggest to Shekh Fahd, the present head of the Ibn Hadh-thál division of the Ae-ni-za, that the life of himself and his tribe mysteriously depended on the Lynx (*fahd*) species, he would be as indignant as the Plantagenets would be if consid-

---

[1] *E.g.*, A'bdu 'r Rah-mán, A'bdu 'r Ra-him, A'bdu 'l Ká-dir. In India all these names are fast coming under truncation. Thousands of A'bdu 'l Kádirs, especially those of the race-course and polo-ground, content themselves with the *Káfir*, as it were our Mr Strong. A'bdu 'l Ka-rim (*servant of the Bounteous*) tends to become in Bombay or Calcutta Mr Cream!

[2] The casual reader may think the name Muhammad not a "secular" one; but it was known, although it was not common, among the ancient pagan Arabs.

[3] The qualities personified in Bedouin names are chiefly the irascible and strong-handed; but others appear—as *Ibnu 'l wat-tad, son of the tent-peg*, own brother of our "son of a gun." Names borrowed from the tent replace with them the Halls, Rooms, Wyndowes, Kitchens, of house-building people. White and Black, Short and Long. Hand, Head, and Legge

are good desert names. The noble family of Smythes, the Carpenters, Tailleurs, Cookes, and Barbours are, of course, absent—every handicraft ranking below Leggary in the eyes of the nomads. The Semitic Ibn, Bin, or Ben, serving alike for Mac and O' of Celtic, and *s* and *son* (*Jones, Johnson*) of Welsh and English, is never wanting. Next to the obligation of transmitting the paternal name, that of publicly displaying it is felt by Arabs. Negro (*Sú-dí*) or Abyssinian (*Ha-be-shi*) slaves reared among them, and called by some such name as Mú-sá, when, as often happens, they grow wealthy, seeing that in Arabia they cannot make a pedigree, at least invent a patronymic. With no true gentile name available, poetical substitutes are fabricated—*e.g., Mú-sá ibn jú-á n, Moses, son of a hungry one*—name of evil import for one's commissariat, by which a guide once engaged by us at Ku-wait called himself.

ered under the protection of the broom; or the Clan Chattan, if held spiritually inter-related with the cat. These analogies may be considered faulty, on the ground that cognisances and heraldry are unknown to Bedouin. This may partly be so. A white-and-green banner is carried by the Wah-há-bis; and a purple one with a green border by A-mír Muhammad's musters.[1] But the uncentralised Bedouin charge in whirlwinds; with no marks to distinguish brave from brave, or friend from foe. We know a man whose face is so small and hairy, and his neck and occiput so remarkable, that his friends may meet him without being the wiser for it; while half a street off one in rear of him cannot mistake him! But this is impossible with Arabs. Their long cloaks, or otherwise long chemises,[2] make every one of them like the other; and the backs of their heads and necks are veiled by the shawl-like kerchief or *kaf-fi-ya*. In a *mêlée*, it is only by their cries that they are distinguishable.[3] Therefore if the Bad-u who has for his name one of the Rose or Lilly, Fox or Bullock, category had marked himself accordingly, it would have been but reasonable; and the learned would have had the less occasion to transfer to Semites the bestial deities of the Red Indians.

Characteristics.

If Al Is-lám have for supreme Prophet Muhammad, son of A'bdu 'llah, the figurehead of Arabism, both secular and religious, is the patriarch Abraham. So much is this so, that instead of here speaking of the characteristics of the Ishmaelite Arabs in the abstract, let us look at them through their type and father. It may be difficult to determine how much of the halo which surrounds the patriarch in Arabia is genuine and ancient; and how much depends on the ideas of later ages having been thrown back into his time by Judaism and Islamism. But we have already ventured to regard it as possible, that the memoirs of the leaders of Israel which the Kur-án contains formed the common legendary heritage of all the great divisions of the Semites long ages before they became Islamic. Credulity, we know, is apt to be carried to extremes; but so also is the opposite quality. The myth theory in historical investigation is like calomel in medicine: used scientifically it proves serviceable; in rash hands it is capable of turning all the past into a desert. In an atmosphere of pure scholar-

---

[1] On the track between I'rák and Mecca, Ibnu 'r Ra-shíd's standard, carried half-flying, half-furled, on a tall dromedary, guides the pilgrims.

[2] The long loose shirt of unbleached (and too often unwashed) linen, reaching nearly to the ankle, which, when the weather is mild, forms, night and day, the single garment of Bedouin men and women, is called, in desert speech, *ka-mís*. *Ca-mí-sa* or *camesia* was a Roman soldier's word, and the Arabs may have got it from the legionaries of the Syrian frontier.

[3] The Abyssinian in "falling on" vociferates his own name and honours; the Bedouin, the name of his sister or little daughter. The invocation of "lady-loves" is a refinement not yet attained by Semites.

ship, at Bonn or Berlin, attempts to resolve the patriarch of the Arab race into a mere oriental Theseus may meet with favour; but hardly so where we are now writing, beside the blue Euphrates.

Perhaps the question of whether Abraham should be called an Arab, or, as in Deut. xxvi. 5, a "wandering Aramæan," is not a very important one. Sprenger says with admirable brevity and directness, "All Semites are, according to my conviction, successive layers of Arabs."[1] At all events, the father of the Hebrews was essentially a nomad; a man of flocks and herds and tents (Heb. xi. 9). But beyond that, the routine of pastoral life had been varied in his case by a round of adventurous travel. Above all, he had seen the civilisation of Egypt—source of light and leading for so much of the ancient world. If traditions guaranteed by the widest acceptance may be followed, the cult of his father Terah, in which were images, was rejected by him. Perhaps from his intercourse with Egyptian sages, perhaps through other educative influences,[2] he held a more spiritual conception of the Divine than others did. In secular matters, also, he was full of experiences. He knew that an area under corn will feed far more people than it will do if kept as pasture. All round the "oaks of Mamre which are in Hebron"[3] (Gen. xiii. 18), his cultivation spread; the agricultural succeeded the nomadic stage; and the foundations were laid of that later epoch when the ideal of every Israelite was to dwell under fruit-trees of his own planting. If the fragments relating to Abraham which are pieced together in Genesis be read apart from the supernatural element, it will be perceived how much the Hebrew horde-leader had in common, both personally and in respect of what Americans call "surroundings," with the great pastoral figures of Euphrates land now. See him first in his daily life, as shown in ch. xviii. 1-8, deep in the duties of hospitality. And here it may be proper parenthetically to notice the dash of foreign colouring which is introduced into the Western copy of this picture through the *seating* of him at his *tent - door*. The very feature which distinguishes the Semite tent from the tents of all non-Arab nomads is that it has no door, or even special doorway. Instead of being round like the Turk-u-màn's, with but a churlish aperture in the centre; great or small it forms an oblong

---

[1] F. Aug. Geogr. Arabiens Bern, 1875, p. 293.
[2] The Kur-ân (S. vi.) contains the following representation: *And when the night overshadowed him (Ibrâhim), he saw a star. He said, this is my Lord: and when it disappeared, he said, I love not the constituent. And when he saw the moon uprising, he said, this is my Lord: and when it set, he said, were it not that my Lord do guide me, surely I were of the people who have lost the way. And when he saw the sun uprising, he said, this is my Lord, this is greater: and when it set, he said, O people, verily I am clear of that which ye associate [with God]: verily I have set my face towards Him who created the heavens and the earth, turning to the right way: and I am not of those who attribute to God a partner.*

[3] Hebron, situated about 20 miles S. of Jerusalem, is called to this day *Al Khal-îl*, in memory of Abraham. It is one of the few existing rivals of Damascus in antiquity.

booth, closed at the back and ends, but having its front as hospitably open as its owner's heart is. In the original the word is *petah*, which means *opening*. If another rendering than *door* could be suggested, and for *sat* something like *reclined resting on an elbow* substituted, the pose would be more lifelike. Following out this fancy, we just now turned up the text, half in hopes of finding that the youngling "tender and good" fetched by Abraham for his guests was in Arabic not a calf but a lamb — for the nomad Arab despises horned cattle as part of the estate of townsmen. But the word is *ben bakar*—in Arabic as in Hebrew, *young of a cow*: not *ra-hel*, a ewe lamb — the *rikhl* or *ra-khil* of Arabic.[1] After a foray, the Bad-u may chance to be thus provided; but the difficulty of "lifting" slow-travelling oxen is as recognised and sad a fact with him as that of marching off stacks of corn was with our own rievers of long ago. A calf of the "wild cow" or bovine antelope may, it is true, be run into by his greyhounds; but the calf which Abraham presented was from "the herd": and the colouring is by so much the less Arabian. And yet it is impossible to read the Biblical books in these Euphrates pastures, without a feeling of wonder being experienced at the permanence of oriental scenes and characters—that is, in parts of the East which have escaped the grip of Europe. The correspondence of Abraham's with modern Bedouin hospitality in the absence from both of intoxicants, was noticed in another context as a fact perhaps not devoid of significance. The chief object wanting to help the verisimilitude is the coffee-pot: but not even in Muhammad's time, far less in Abraham's, was the black juice now so dear to Arabs known among them.[2] A second tableau, that in ch. xiv., showing the patriarch's conduct

---

[1] Whence of course the name of Jacob's trans-Euphrates wife (and cousin) Rachel; whose acts and traits as given in Genesis—notably her woman-craft in concealing in her camel-saddle the *teraphim* (prob. *images of family-gods*) which she had stolen from her father Laban (ch. xxxi. 34, 35) — are typical, if we except the idols, of tent-life on the Euphrates still. Rachel's tomb near Bethlehem is one of the many other shrines elsewhere noticed, which Jews, Christians, and Muslim unite in honouring. The name *Ke-bû-rah* which is given to it in the Hebrew Scriptures, signifies in Arabic *a place of burial* generally. A modern Muslim structure of some pretensions now forms the descendant, through a long line of successive marks or pyramids, of the original gravestone set up by Jacob (Gen. xxxv. 20).

[2] The traditions about the discovery by the Arabs of their now indispensable substitute at once for food, stimulant, medicine, and occupation, are not very trustworthy. Perhaps they found the fruit or berry, by them called *bunn*, in their own country. Perhaps they had it from abroad, and afterwards introduced its cultivation. Their view of it, at all events at first, appears from their calling the decoction of it *kah-wa*—an ancient Arabic word for wine. Between this *kah-wa* and Kaffa, an Abyssinian district, the choice lies of a derivation for the world-wide name of *coffee*. Like almost every other good thing, this precious gift has generally met on its first introduction with an unkind reception. In Arabia zealots pronounced it one of the intoxicants forbidden by the Kur-ân. Somehow it became known to Bacon that " they have in Turkey a drink called coffee, . . . which comforteth the brain and heart and helpeth digestion." But the new drink did not appear in England till the middle of the 17th century. Straightway a royal proclamation was put out against it: because of the retailing of it (*i.e.*, in coffee-houses) "being used to nourish sedition, spread lies, and scandalise great men." On that failing, oppressive taxation was tried, but, thanks to smuggling, ineffectually.

as a leader, though of a less primitive stamp than the other, is in its way fraught with illustration. His nephew Lot, after entering Canaan with him from Haran (Har-rân of Arabs[1]), long a halting-place of Terah and his horde in their progress from "Ur of the Chaldees,"[2] had separated from him at Bethel, to settle down in the "cities of the Plain." When after thus turning townsman Lot was made a prisoner, in what seems to have been a tribal raid on Sodom, it will be remembered how Abraham, on hearing of it from a fugitive, started off with 318 of his following, just as a Shekh of the Sham-mar would do now; overtook the raiders; fell upon them by night and smote them; drove them before him from Dan to Hobah, north of Damascus; recovered the plunder, "and also brought again his brother Lot, and his goods, and the women also, and the people." On the same occasion, when the mysterious priest of Supreme El, "Melchizedek, King of Salem,"[3] came out to meet Lot's rescuers, Abraham acted just

---

[1] Name to this day of a well-watered district, and all but vanished town, on the Jil-likh, above its junction with the Euphrates, in the north-western corner of Al Ja-el-ra.

[2] In Gen. xi. 31, "Ur of the Chaldees" is explicitly mentioned as the locality from which Terah "went forth . . . to go into the land of Canaan." In v. 28, the same place is called the "land of nativity" of the horde. But unfortunately there is nothing written to show decisively where Ur was. Stephen, in his speech before the Sanhedrim, placed it by implication in "Mesopotamia" (Acts vii. 2); but it is not known whether he used that name in its vaguest and widest, or in its more defined, sense (v. p. 70, et f.n. 1, supra). In Dr R. Pococke's magnificent folios (Lond. 1743), *A Description of the East, and some other Countries*, vol. ii. p. 159, we find, "Many learned men, and the Jews universally, are of opinion that 'Ur of the Chaldees' is the place called Ourfa by the Arabs, to which the Turks give the name of Roi-ha, or Rou-ha; and which is generally agreed to be the antient city of Edessa;" and further, "The Jews say that this place is called in Scripture *Our-casdim*, i.e., *the fire of Chaldea*; out of which, they say, God brought Abraham; and on this account the Talmudists affirm that Abraham was here cast into the fire, and was miraculously delivered." When wandering in 1887 over the steppe land between Sinjâr and Mons Masius in which is Urfa, we felt the same sense of Abraham which one does of the "Duke" (of Buccleuch) in southern Scotland. Everywhere was Abraham's Mosque, Abraham's Well, or something that was Abraham's. If local traditions bear any evidential value, then has the mixed pastoral and agricultural land of Paddan-aram some claim to be identified with the family home of Abraham. On the other hand, modern scholars (rendering Ur, not by *fire*, but as a place-name, and guided by the suggestion which is in *K'as-dim = Chaldæans*, that Ur must be in Chaldæa) go at least 400 miles lower down for an identification—viz., to the *Uru* of the Assyrian inscriptions, where are now the ruins of Al Mu-kai-yar (commonly written Mu-gair), in the Babylonian mud-flat. The American people have spent a great many dollars in having excavations made at this site. In Gen. xxiv. a glimpse of Abraham's fatherland is opened, in connection with the fetching from it of a maiden for his son Isaac. The details therein given have been read by us, both in the Euphrates marsh land round Al Mu-kai-yar, and on the Urfa plateau. In the latter locality the verisimilitude is striking, and in the former not so. Al Mu-kai-yar, though now upwards of 100 miles from the head of the Gulf of Persia, must anciently have been a maritime town. Wells are not among its characteristic features. Even at Baghdad, where gravelly layers more or less qualify the alluvium, a well which we once caused to be dug in the hard desert collapsed the first winter.

[3] The piece introducing the Canaanite high priest whose blessing Abraham valued is relegated by modern critics to "post-exilic" times; and is declared to be quite unhistorical. The fact seems worth stating, that neither Al Kur-ân, nor, so far as we can discover, the floating lore of the Arabs, knows anything of Melchizedek.

as an *a'-kíd*,[1] or leader of Bedouin Arabs, now does to win or maintain a name for generosity, in foregoing his own portion of the recovered booty, while claiming their shares for his companions. Other parallelisms will presently be noticed between the traits displayed by modern Bedouin Arabs and the traditional character of Abraham. Here we are tempted to speak of a certain ancient vestige, much associated with the Patriarch, in which it has lately been thought that there is guidance; and that is circumcision. The quasi-sacramental character borne by this custom among the Jewish descendants of Abraham is answerable for some confusion of ideas. In the ages when criticism, itself dormant, had no materials to work on, it even was considered that the fact of the Arabs not circumcising on the eighth day after birth like the Jews, or at any other set time, but whenever convenient before man-growth, connected them in a very special manner with Ishmael—circumcised, according to Gen. xvii., *in his 13th year*. The difficulties involved in the literal reading of the Biblical narrative were not adverted to. Abraham was seen establishing in his following at Mamre on a religious basis—with primitive lawgivers a common method—a custom which may have commended itself to him on physical and hygienic grounds during his sojourn in Egypt; where its prevalence long before the Israelitish captivity is attested by monuments: and thereupon was assigned to him the authorship of a practice which existed in unrecorded times, and among the most distant members of the human family.[2] How in the progress of time all this has been sifted may elsewhere be read. No Protestant Church now refuses to sanction researches after the ordinary

---

[1] Literally *knotter* (of others) together, as for an enterprise. Under the Arabian tribal system it is not always that the Shekh is also *a'-kíd*, or *ghaz-a-*leader. The Shekhate certainly is hereditary; though a Shekh who tried to draw the bond of obedience too tight would soon lose his grip. Every tribesman retains not only his vote, but his absolute free will, in all matters save those leading up to war. An older brother may be the Shekh or Nestor, because of his experience; and a younger the a'-kíd (with the Shammar *ja-î-d*) because of his activity. No man need mount for foray unless his blood warm to it. But the owner of a mare who will lounge in the encampment when the riders are out will have a sorry time of it. So far as mere *razzia* goes, any Shekhling may have an innings as a'-kíd. A time and place of assembling are fixed by him; then according to the response given a plan is formed. Out of the booty every man gets something—one a camel, another a mare; in the making of which distribution the a'-kíd's generosity is proved. When *An-tar* boasts, in his poem, of *seeing the fight, but holding his hand from the spoils*, not merely the Najdian ideal, but equally the Abrahamic, is represented.

[2] Among the sheerest savages of the modern world are the S. African Bechwana, in whom from all accounts are no religious vestiges; yet their lads are circumcised. In the heathen hordes of Madagascar the same piece of trimming, performed amid drunken orgies, marks the inclusion of their youths among the tribe's warriors. On the Amazon, in the South Seas, and among Australian aborigines, circumcision is practised. Rising in the scale, in ancient times it formed a usage of civilised peoples of Central America. With Abyssinian Christians it is general. What has kept it out of Europe is not so much the temperate climate—to Western people shy of water its value would be even greater than to half-amphibious races—as the prejudice conceived against it owing to its association with Judaism and Islamism. Nevertheless, two military surgeons have lately stated to us that the rising generation of our countrymen show signs of taking to it.

human methods into the origin and structure of each separate writing which is contained in the Biblical literature. On points of historical, as of physical, criticism, advantage is taken of every help which science offers.[1] And thus it happens that nowhere is the inference of Abraham having come out of Arabia more led up to than in a recent monograph on circumcision by a clerical investigator. The high authority quoted[2] does not, indeed, concern himself with the origin of the Arabs. In dealing with his subject proper, he however discovers in a certain passage in Exodus[3] traces of the Arabian origin of Jewish circumcision. In gathering in this result, he brings forward indications of El, or "Jehovah," having originally formed a tribal deity *of Arabia*.[4] So that if the further we advance the greater seems the probability of Israel's having had

---

[1] The reader who has not inquired into these subjects may possibly appreciate the information that educated opinion, after centuries of disputation, now inclines to one of two extremes. Critics of the more trenchant school tell us that the narratives in our Bibles, whatever they may be, are not historical. The majority are satisfied with thinking that a copyist's note or a redactor's commentary may in divers places have become fused with the Hebrew manuscripts; none of which, we believe, are older copies than the 7th or 8th century A.D. The complexity of the issues, and the importance of the judgment pending, are against the probability of an early adjustment. To qualify any one effectively to approach the question from the literary side, not merely special training is essential, but a mastery of the Hebrew, Arabic, Aramaic, Syriac, Assyrian, Phoenician, and Moabite languages; also a knowledge of the evidence which the monuments and cuneiform tablets of Western Asia and Egypt are from time to time revealing. Therefore it is not surprising that, in hopelessness of so vast an equipment ever being available, *enfants perdus* of the secular army are in our day entering the strong place through numerous posterns.

[2] Rev. J. K. Cheyne, D.D., Oriel Prof. of Interpretation of Scripture, Oxford; in *Ency. Brit.*, vol. v, p. 790.

[3] Our reference is to the fragment in ch. iv. 25, 26, narrating how Moses' Midianitish, *i.e.* Bedouin Arab, wife, Zipporah, on a certain journey, when Jehovah sought to kill Moses, ascribed it to the neglect of circumcision in his family, hastily circumcised their son, and thereby appeased the deity. See Prof. Cheyne's rendering of this passage in the reference cited in the preceding footnote. But Wellhausen explains it more clearly, in his art. MOSES, in *Ency. Brit.*, vol. xvi. p. 861, fn. 1. What the Arab woman did with the amputated portion was, not to "*cast it at* his (Moses)

feet," as appears both in the authorised and the revised versions, but *to touch another part of his body with it*, as a sign that the circumcision of the child was substituted for that of the *khatan*, or bridegroom. In Arabic, the same word (*kha-ta-na*) which means *circumcising* also means the *making of a feast to which people are invited because of a marriage and a circumcision*. Capt. Burton (*Pilgrimage to Mecca and Medina*, vol. iii. p. 80, f.n.), Prof. Robertson Smith (Letters to *Scotsman* newspaper, 1880), and other travellers in Arabia, heard of nations in which circumcision is held over to be performed at the time of marriage. It serves as a kind of ordeal for adult youths, before they are accounted full tribesmen. The surgery which they then suffer is said to be of an aggravated description; and the bride witnesses it, and if the patient flinch, refuses to have him for her husband (Doughty, vol. i. p. 128).

Al Kur-ân nowhere mentions circumcision; but commentators so interpret certain words in it meaning *purity* or *purification*. Muhammad was content to leave the practice where he found it —a well-established national usage. In Arabian towns, and far more so in Persia, religious and symbolical conceptions have grown into it. We have even seen Indians—needless to say Shiites—before beginning to write a letter, snip off, or fold back, the upper right-hand corner of the paper, in token of its having been "purified," or for aught that we know "sacrificed." But all such "ritualism" is foreign to Arabia.

[4] To support the view of Israel having first known El in Arabia, and continued in Palestine to regard that as his habitation, out of which he "marched to fight for them on special occasions, Judg. v. 4 and Hab. iii. 3 are cited by one school of Biblicists. Seir and Edom in the former, equally with Teman and Paran in the latter passage, are Arabian places

an Arabian history before settling in Palestine, the signs of it are at least well authenticated.

In next essaying to connect the Bedouin Arabs with Abraham through certain aspects of their manners, we know that the ground will not bear too strong conclusions; nor can we here even make the most of it without anticipating surveys which are reserved for future chapters. It will appear in the sequel that Islamism is a townsman's creed or profession; and Bedouinism a desert product. But with regard to the latter, the difficulty already stated is always present of adjudging in the several traits of the Bedouin how much is percolated Islamism, and how much is really ancient material. This remark is in the fullest degree applicable to the very first Bedouin feature which it here occurs to us to mention, primitive Arabian monotheism. In how far this has come down from Abraham, and in how far it is traceable to other sources, is a very mixed question. And so in regard to perhaps the next strongest lineament of Bedouin character—the love of entertaining strangers. Or rather, there is here even a greater need of caution in respect of artificial glosses. For without the freest use of hospitality, there could be no life or movement within the Arabian desert. In England, before railways, the case was slightly similar. Nevertheless, the Bad-u's service of a guest has many special features. It is not merely that to be a Bedouin is to be hospitable—hospitable not with the idea of entertaining angels unawares, persons capable of helping on a son, or leaving one a legacy; not in the sense of gathering together people who would rather dine at home; but in that of truly ministering to the tired and hungry. However poor the inmates of a tent may be, no one is ever allowed to enter it and leave it, without eating of the best which it contains. The softest carpet, or fleeciest sheepskin, is always spread for the stranger. Born trafficker as the Bad-u is, he will not sell bread, or milk, or butter. In travelling from Baghdad southward, one of the first signs of nearing Najd is that the villages have no bread-shops. Hardware and chintzes, brought from Bombay by those who go there with horses, are exposed for sale, but not the staff of life. Now in all this the Bedouin loves to think that he follows his "Father Abraham." The stories of the "Friend of God" with which Muhammad seasoned his addresses do not come much in his way. But there is a legend of the Patriarch which is not in the Kur-ân, and not in Genesis, but in the breasts of men and women, and in secular poems —how, when the evening meal was ready, he would refuse to taste it till some "son of the road" should arrive to share it;[1] and that is one of many others

---

[1] Some may remember how, in one of his masterpieces, the "Bôstân," or Garden, Sa'di has worked up this legend into a didactic piece inculcating toleration. One day "the Friend," on receiving a stranger, and seeing him dip his hand in the dish without calling on God, angrily turned him out. Whereupon God rebuked him, saying: These hundred years have I fed and clothed him; to thee is one minute of him intolerable? What if he worship fire? wilt thou therefore draw back the hand of charity?

which passes from mouth to mouth in the black tent cities. Not only "the young ravens which cry," but every living creature, receives its food from God in the simple faith of the Bad-u: and no greater favour can be shown to him than when a brother partakes, as from him, of his appointed portion.[1]

Traditions.

On the whole, perhaps, the Kur-án is more copious in its references to Abraham than the Hebrew Scriptures are. In one Sû-ra are two important notices of him: in the first, as supernaturally receiving the command to *purify* the Ka'-ba of Mecca;[2] and in the second, as engaged in *raising the foundations* of the same structure,[2] assisted by his son Is-mâ-í'l. But the Bible episode of the banishment of Hagar[3] does not appear in the Kur-án; according to which, Ishmael, and not

---

[1] A Persian poet thus expresses this idea:—

Each has his portion allotted—his own special dole for the day:
His, not another's, the food, though it may not be laid on his tray.
But on dying. Then rejoice that with thee the provision for him has been stored;
Rendering thanks to thy guest who eats of his own at thy board.

[2] This story, in so far as it involves merely Abraham's having followed Hagar to Al Hi-jáz, offers no difficulty. But when the Patriarch is depicted as reshaping and adapting to a purer cult the Mecca temple, at least these two questions will be asked: Is not the part thus assigned to him mere Kuranic scene-painting? Is it so that the Arab Baitu 'llah at so remote an epoch underwent such transformation? To the former there is here room for only this answer, that among travelling orientalists, Burton, and among sedentary, Freytag, support the conclusion that Muhammad drew these materials from Arabian sources. The second question is more difficult. It is not in doubt that the "ancient house" when the Prophet first saw it was garnished with idols. The cult was that of "gods of nations," each protecting and dominating; but its own sept or circle; with for "God over all," and God for great occasions, Allah. A spiritual conception of this universal Allah supplied the Reformer with his starting-point. The elevation of him to a strictly monotheistic pedestal, with the degradation of all his ancient enemies and rivals, necessarily followed; and therein was Is-lâm. But whether any prophet before Muhammad had ever preached this to the Arabs is a question involving many difficulties. V. in Index I., art. Ḥᴀ-ɴɪf.

[2] *Ḳᴀ-ᴡᴀ-ɪ́-ɪᴅ.* generally rendered *foundations,* may equally mean any *supporting posts* or *pillars;* from the *two side-posts of a door,* up to the grandest columns. Therefore the text quoted does not necessarily lend a basis to the common Islamic belief connecting the *beginnings* of the Ka'-ba with Abraham. In architecture, as in poetry and history, Semites have a delightful fashion of adding part to part at any time, instead of giving themselves up to regular plans. One of Muhammad's 'Sayings' is: *Man's every work yields him a return except building.* The Prophet's own abode in Medina was in the form of a row of huts. From time to time, as is well known, he "took, like Abraham," another wife; under the system proper to the epoch when the world was emptier than now; and the idea had not grown up of leaving half the female population of every town to "wither on the virgin thorn," and assume the occupations of the other sex. On all such occasions, instead of building a new wing or story, he would merely ask his neighbour Ḥá-rith to "take ground" slightly to one flank, and so make room for another humble tenement of unburnt bricks and palm-branches. In a Kuranic passage in which it is explicitly stated that the Mecca Ka'-ba was the first *Ishᴠᴀ-ᴋ* or structure of any kind (*bait*) ever reared for mankind (to worship in)—the *standing-place* or oratory of Ib-rá-him is mentioned among the notable spots contained in it; v. S. iii.

[3] To illustrate the view now generally accepted, that the "Pentateuch," even in its narrative parts, is "a kind of mosaic," in which elements taken from two older writings are interwoven, Prof. Wellhausen thus observes: "Ishmael was fourteen years old at the birth of Isaac, and thus would be seventeen

Isaac, was the son whom Abraham was commanded to sacrifice. Al Islâm is left dependent for the story of Hagar on traditions, in which the main incidents of the description in Gen. xxi. 9 are held to have come down. Sound Muslim commentators do not find the spot where Hagar settled anywhere authoritatively indicated; and accordingly they have conjecturally looked for it in divers places. That preferred by them generally is the palmless and stony tract in the south of Al Hi-jáz, now forming part of the HA-RAM, or *Holy territory*, on which was afterwards planted the "mother of towns," Mecca. To this day the well called *Zam-zam* contained within the *Mas-jidu 'l ha-rám*, or *sacred worshipping*-place at Mecca, is supposed to be the identical spring at which Hagar and Is-mâ-i'l drank. All this framework so well serves the Arabian genealogies already glanced at, assigning the nation of Ku-raish, or Fihr, of which was Muhammad, to the "seed of Abraham,"[1] that the tendency is to deny to it the smallest fragment of substantial foundation. The strong air of Europe perhaps is needed to foster such root-and-branch conclusions. Writing where we now are, it is enough to mention that as authentic secular history contains no trace of Ishmael, it cannot possibly confirm the derivation of the Kuraish from him. Nothing is known of the disciplinary processes which first developed the Kuraish; but their position on the Red Sea in very early times gave them advantages over the nations of the interior. When the curtain rises on them—about 400 A.D.—they held in their grasp, as surely as if it had come down to them from Abraham, the Meccan Bethel; even at that early period, under the Eastern system of *ham ti-já-ra, ham zi-á-ra*, as the Persians have it, or *commerce and pilgrimage in one*, a place of cosmopolitan congress. About the same time—fifth Christian century—the independent clans of Arabia rose in revolt against the exactions of the kings of Yemen; just as they would now do if too hard pressed by Constantinople Pashas. Emboldened by success, and led by a native Jonathan called *Ku-laib*,[2] or the little

---

when, some three years later, Isaac was weaned. But how does this accord with Gen. xxi. 9 *sq.*, where Ishmael appears not as a lad of seventeen but as a child at play (*prps*. ver. 9), who is laid on his mother's shoulder (ver. 14), and when thrown down by her, in her despair (ver. 15), is quite unable to help himself?"—*Vide* art. "Pentateuch," *Ency. Brit.*, vol. xviii. p. 507. In any case, Ishmael's separation from his family cannot have been permanent, seeing that (1) he assisted at Abraham's burial, Gen. xxv. 9; (2) Esau took his daughter to wife at a time when he (Esau) dwelt in Beersheba (xxviii. 9); (3) he (Ishmael) "abode in the presence of" (more correctly, *eastward from*) "all his brethren" (xxv. 18). For a luminous view of these subjects,

at once historical and Christian, see *The Old Testament in the Jewish Church*, by Prof. W. Robertson Smith, sec. edit., 1892.

[1] *V. ante*, p. 94; *cf.* p. 99, in f.n. 1.
[2] Dim. of *kalb* = *canis*; Biblical Caleb. The fact of this Arabian Wallace figuring as *Ku-laib*, with the more important fact of *Ba-nû Kalb*, or *Race of Dog*, forming the gentile name of a Najdian nation, may seem to countenance the totem theory. But passing over the circumstance of Europe likewise having its families of Chiens, Cheynes, MacCheynes, &c.; and rejecting as too improbable Guarmani's explanation that the Ba-nû Kalb have their name from a hereditary hoarseness due to exposure, and productive of *barking;* if in Arabia, as elsewhere, the dog's own

dog, after they had thrown off the southern yoke their aims grew wider. During nearly two centuries the words of one of their poets well describes them :—

> No sooner do we carry to a people the quern (of war), than lo,
> At the first touch of it, they are flour !
> Like the skin under the mill, all eastern Najd;[1] like the handful
> Thrown into the hopper, every mother's son of the Ku-dhâ-a'.
> —'AMR.

The times must have been favourable for the development of prowess, both national and individual. Elsewhere the reader may see it chronicled how, in the great congeries of the Mus-ta'-ri-ba clans, the Kuraish came forward; till at last (*c.* 570 A.D.) a child was born to them whose destiny it was to throw into deep shadow all that had happened in Arabia before him. The Kuraish retain to this day no small portion of the prestige, or moral influence, which Muhammad and his achievements conferred upon them. When, in 1517, fate compelled them to surrender the keys of the Mecca shrine to the Osmanli Sultán, Selim I., the original scheme of Islamism must have seemed to them and others obscured beyond retrieval. But it is wonderful how, in Arabia as elsewhere, old ideals can be fitted to new facts. Successive Sultáns have treated Al Hi-jáz as tenderly as if they had been Arabs of the Prophet's lineage. A prince of the Kuraish, elected from the descendants of A'li, acts as a kind of double to the Turkish Wá-li of the "holy territory," like the Delhi emperors to the East India Company's Governor-Generals, but possessed of far more sway and influence. This is THE SHA-RIF *par excellence;* or "Grand Sherif," as Europeans say, since all the kin of the princely houses which reckon descent from the Prophet bear the title of *Sha-ríf,* or *pre-eminent.* On State occasions in Al Hi-jáz, when the Osmanli officials proper appear in gold brocades and ribbons, the Sha-rif in his Arab cloak and head-dress recalls the primitive ideal, according to which it was essential that the "Commander of the Believers," and head of the Arab empire, should belong to the Kuraish.

Our limits do not permit us to dwell on the important references to Ishmael's twelve sons which are contained in Gen. xxv. 13-17. Slight as those references are, the glimpse which they open is distinctly that of twelve main tribes of Arabs. Nor

---

better qualities have led to the adoption of his name by human beings, it is not surprising. The Arabs, it is true, will not eat the dog, and do not like to kill him. But on small enough occasion they will kick and stone him. In their towns they protect him as a kind of natural guard and scavenger. Outside, they cultivate and value him for antelope-coursing, without admitting him to intimacy. Greyhounds obtained from Tigris or Euphrates settlements, accustomed to have their food thrown to them, and to drink from the river, will not at first come near a dish even when coaxed to do so, owing to the beatings which they have received at home on that account,—not an unnecessary discipline where cooking and eating are performed on the ground.

[1] *I.e.,* all eastern Najd had been turned by them into a battle-ground. A skin or cloth is spread under the oriental handmill, to keep the flour from mingling with the sand.

is any materially different view consonant with the facts of history. The first-born was Nebaioth, or Nebajoth, patriarch, unquestionably, of a great pastoral people—if not, as seems on the whole probable, of the ancient Nabathæan nation. In the second son, Kedar, with Arabs Kai-dâr, the correspondence between the Bible description and Arabian traditions is even more conspicuous. From him, and not from the sons of Ishmael generally, Arab chroniclers, it should be stated, derive the pedigree of the Mus-ta'-ri-ba. How in Canticles the "black tents of Kedar" are used for simile, just as the black tents of the Sham-mar might be used to-day, has already been noticed: that Kedar and Nebaioth formed in Isaiah's time two typical nations of Arabia appears from a well-known passage. If here there be ground of difference, it is not on the essential facts, but on the interpretation of them. Are we to infer that Abraham and Ishmael were Arabs? Or that Ishmael, entering Arabia as a refugee or immigrant, imparted new blood, as well as new and special characteristics, to all these mighty nations? For the reasons already stated, it is probable that the veil which hangs over this subject will not soon be lifted.

It now only remains to take leave of the central question out of which so many branches have grown; are the considerable contrasts which are noticeable between the Yemenite and the Ishmaelitic Arabs consistent with ultimate race unity; or do they force us towards the supposition that the two populations own separate ethnic origins? Long ago, not much hesitation was felt on topics of this nature. Modifications superinduced by slight enough causes were made to support race classifications; just as in another branch of science misunderstood casual variations enormously contributed to the multiplication of so-called species.[1] But let us not here pursue similar lines. The pastoral tendency, or habit, in its several phases, forms, as has been seen, the chief basis of divergence between the two great divisions of the Arabian people. And so far as that goes, we see no obstacle to the assumption that both partitions, notwithstanding many fortuitous admixtures, are of one and the same stock. Having before us the substantial fact, already noted, that several of the most clannish and nomadic nations of the Arab peninsula are of those not reckoned to the Mus-ta'-ri-ba, an appeal to argument is unnecessary. Otherwise we might remind the reader how the disposition to "go forth," or wander, runs in *Homo sapiens*. Hâ-fiz the Sû-fi, at once the gravest and the gayest of the Persian sages and poets, says in Spring—

> Go fetch a book of poems, and off with thee to the country!
> Is this a time for lecture-rooms, and the arguments and expositions of the expounder?

---

[1] Darwin in *The Origin of Species*, informs us that classifiers, misled by differences of plumage, have sometimes set down the male bird as of one species, and the female, of another!

And so in Europe, the sedatest preacher from time to time must have his scamper. Or if signs like these be regarded less as *survivals* than as mere demands for relaxation, how many a slip of bookish formal folk — not dissipated, but only Bohemian—in his rooted dislike of settled ways and artificial people, turns his back on "progress," and sets off to live with kangaroos in the Australian bush. With tendencies of this description latent in the folds of our own civilisation, how much stronger must the wandering instinct be in peoples whose "environment" compels them to it! We have seen that in vast portions of Arabia man must either be nomadic or disappear entirely. The modifications of character thus produced by necessity and circumstances have become "nature." And a very hard nature is the Bedouin's; his own desert flints are soft compared with it. Some have argued that it is merely the sparseness of his hordes, and the slight temptation offered by him and his to foreigners, which have so long kept him above-ground. This should be allowed for up to a certain point. The multitudinous and ever-changing masses of the Bedouin oppose but the same kind of resistance to kingly giants as Saladin's silken cushion would have done to Cœur de Lion's sword. Their pastoral wealth does not much excite the cupidity of Governments. Nevertheless, their own stubborn temper, with the martial virtues born of the shepherd life, must have had a large share in their preservation. Every Bad-u realises that much of the strength of his untrammelled state depends on isolation. One of his stock sayings is, *Adh dhill fi-'l hadhr*, or *subjection* (is involved) *in settling down*. Houses and gardens and standing crops form hostages to "our lord the king" in a way that flocks and herds do not; and that is one reason why he will not have them. During an immensely long past, he has contrived by *his* methods to retain his nationality and independence; while all that his building, farming, sedentary congeners have got by *their* methods has been subjugation following on subjugation, by Abyssinians, Persians, Egyptians, Romans, and Turks. We have seen how for these last hundred years the Constantinople Government has been now hammering, now subsidising, the Arabian Bedouin, with the view of making them into new material both for military conscription and for the revenue officer. We have also seen that this policy has met with some success. The remarkable thing is, that that success has been so limited. For this result, as has just been observed, the hardihood of the Bedouin nature, evincing itself in dogged adherence to the ancient paths, is chiefly accountable. The Osmanli, in the teeth of their professed religion, permit the sale of perhaps the greatest known transmutative force, especially for primitive peoples, arrack.[1] But not even in I'rák has any Bedouin nation worthy of the name put

---

[1] This word is a modern importation into Europe, probably by way of India, from Arabic; in which *arák* means *juice*. Jews and Christians make *rákí* 'corruption of *a'rak*'; in Baghdad chiefly from dates; and in Mosul from *sa'lib*, or raisins.

out the hand to take it. None can say how long this conflict between traditional and modern influences will maintain itself; but, judging from appearances, the ancient Bedouin system may last long enough. So far, speaking as an eyewitness, even after all that has happened in I'rák, the Persian Gulf provinces, and Ja-bal Sham-mar, the "wild-ass" nature is but slightly affected by the strategies and enticements of the tamer.

> "Like commoners of air,
> We wander out, we know not where,"[1]

now as of yore describes the life of the Mus-ta'-ri-ba. All mankind is gregarious: the feature of peculiar interest which attaches to the Arabian Bedouin is, that while refusing to substitute the bonds of citizenship for the group-bond, they develop within their separate masses a surprising degree of humanity and organisation.

---

[1] Burns, in *Epistle to Davie*.

CHAPTER III.

OF THE BEDOUIN AS HORSE-BREEDERS.

TO make a roll of the Bedouin nations of Arabia would require many writers, and many years of work and travel. These vigorous hordes rival the scud above-head in the sky, in their tendency to change front and form. Within them, it is true, are main or central bodies which possess comparative fixity. But in respect of secondary divisions and subdivisions; swarmings off and coalescings; margins, surfaces, and projections,—such is their fluidity, now under internal, and now external, force or pressure, that a register of them would soon be obsolete. Therefore in this book but slight attempts have been made to arrange them in regular order.

When Najd was being looked at, its principal nomadic peoples were presented to the reader under the broadest stock-headings; and before proceeding further, we would do as much, and no more, for their migrated kindred, the Ae-ni-za and the Sham-mar. The main divisions and subdivisions of the former nation may thus be tabulated:—

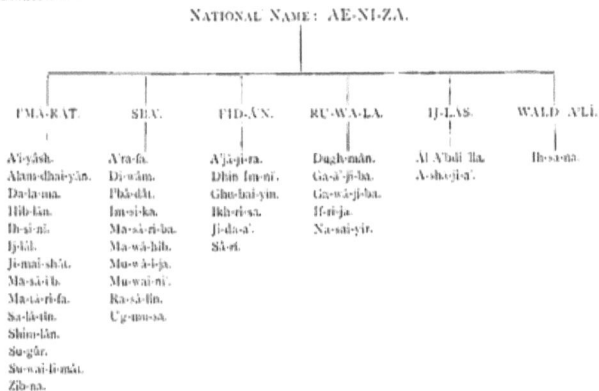

NATIONAL NAME: AE-NI-ZA.

I'MA-RAT.	SBA.	FID-ÁN.	RU-WA-LA.	IJ-LAS.	WALD ALI.
A'i-yásh.	A'ra-fa.	A'já-ji-ra.	Dugh-mán.	Al A'bdi lla.	Ih-sa-na.
Alam-dhai-yán.	Di-wám.	Dhin Im-ni.	Ga-a'-ji-ba.	A-shi-ji-a'.	
Da-la-ma.	I'bá-dat.	Ghu-bai-yin.	Ga-wá-ji-ba.		
Hib-lán.	Im-si-ka.	Ikh-ri-sa.	If-ri-ja.		
Ih-si-ni.	Ma-sá-ri-ba.	Ji-da-a'.	Na-sai-yir.		
Ij-kâl.	Ma-wá-hib.	Sá-ei.			
Ji-mai-sh'at.	Mu-w á-i-ja.				
Ma-sá-i b.	Mu-wai-ni'.				
Ma-tá-ri-fa.	Ra-sá-lin.				
Sa-lá-tin.	Ug-mu-sa.				
Shim-lán.					
Su-gúr.					
Su-n-ai-li-mát.					
Zib-na.					

Note.—In the above headings, the def. article *al* save once, where it joins itself to the name is left to be prefixed by the reader. The Al in Al A'bdi Ila is not the article, but Ál, a synonym of *Ba-nú*, *Children*.

The above table might be infinitely amplified: and like all the other contents of these pages, it is subject to correction. The names which are given in it have been received from the Arabs;[1] and most of them are traceable to roots which are in Arabic dictionaries. This has appeared in the process of transcription. The Roman forms, when they deviate from our adopted system, do so in order that the European reader may the better recognise the names on hearing them from the lips of the Arabs.

Passing to the Sham-mar, the reader will find in Lady A. Blunt's record of her own and her husband's visit to them[2] tables of their several branches, and of their allies and tributaries, drawn up, as is stated, by "a committee of Arabs," and revised by Shekh Fáris.[3]

A beginning was made by Doughty, in the face of many difficulties, towards unravelling the skein of the Sham-mar kinship. Working it out in Jabal Shammar, he found the drift of intelligent opinion about the Sham-mar to be that, instead of even theoretically or traditionally forming children of one father, they represent a comparatively modern aggregation of peoples of diverse Arab stocks; drawn together in the first instance by the ties of a common location or locations, a common cause, and common interests; and only gradually and imperfectly cemented through intermarriages. His principal informant—"a lettered nomad of the Ae-ni-za Sba' living at Há-yil"—told him, that Arabs of both the Yemenite and the Ishmaelite divisions are included in the Sham-mar nation; and that the family tree of Muhammad ibn Ra-shid himself has its roots, through the great clan A'bda, in the Yemenite stock of Kah-tán. "The other *fendis* (septs) of the Sham-mar," the same authority states,[4] "are many, *and not of one descent:* Sin-já-ra; Tú-mán; As-lam; [Ad] Du-ghai-rát; Ghai-tha; A'múd; Fad-dá-gha; Thá-bit; A'-fá-rit; Iz-mail; [Al] Him-zán; Sá-yih; Ikh-ri-sa; Zo-ba; Sham-mar To-ga."[5]

---

[1] No claim to originality is here intended. Nearly all the names are in the works of travellers. Ours has merely been to collate, arrange, and, last but not least, transliterate.

[2] *Op. cit.* in Catalog. No. 11, vol. ii. pp. 188, 189.

[3] *V. ante,* p. 72, *et fn.*

[4] *Op. cit.* in Catalog. No. 2, vol. ii. p. 41.

[5] The above names have been verified through an old henchman and genealogist of the late Shekh Farhán (*v. supra,* p. 72). Layard's classification, made in Al Ja-zi-ra, is as follows:—

"Five sorts or subdivisions of the great tribe of Sham-mar, renowned for their bravery and virtues, and supposed to be descended from the same stock, make up together the Ikh-ri-sa branch, of which the hereditary chief is Far-hán. To belong to the Ikh-ri-sa is an honourable distinction among the Sham-mar. The five septs are the Boraij, the Fad-dá-gha, the Alayian, the Ghishm, and the Hathbá. Of this last, and of the family of Al Muhammad, was the celebrated Bedouin chief Sfúk. The other clans forming the tribe of Sham-mar are the A'bda, Sá-yih (divided into As Subhi and As-lam), Thá-bit, A'múd, Theghav-gheh, Ghai-tha; Dhi-my-rie, Ghu-fay-lá, and Iz-mail. All these tribes are again divided into numerous septs. The Sá-yih have nearly all crossed the Euphrates, owing to a blood-feud with the rest of the Sham-mar, and have united with the Ae-ni-za. The Raf-fi-di, however, a large section of the Ae-ni-za, have left their kindred, and are now incorporated with the Sham-mar."—*Op. cit.* in Catalog. No. 31, p. 260, *f.n.*

OF THE BEDOUIN AS HORSE-BREEDERS.

All the divisions of the Bedouin have not the same rules as horse-breeders. Different tribes have different standards; and produce different results. This fact is widely known in Arabia. No *jam-bāz*[1] with a colt for sale will admit that he is of I'ráki breeding, if it be possible to father him on the Sham-mar. And just as "Sham-ma-ri" is thus a better show-name than "I'ráki," so is "Ae-ni-za" a better name than "Sham-ma-ri." When a mare from the Ae-ni-za passes among the Sham-mar, her new owner is proud of her because of where she comes from. But when one of the Ae-ni-za takes a Sham-mar mare in foray, it is not so. His inclination is to doubt her; and it is only after the fullest verification of her history and pedigree that he will breed from her. As a matter of precaution, this is right; but when it amounts to a prejudice against Sham-mar-bred stock, it is a mistake. All over the world, and equally in man and beast, good, bad, and indifferent are everywhere present. Especially in Arabia, where merchants and pilgrims, travellers and soldiers,

"Stained with the variation of each soil"[2]

between the Tigris and the Indian Ocean, are constantly concentrating at ports, selling their cattle, and transferring themselves to ships, the circulation of horseflesh, apart even from *Al ghaz-u* and robbery, is as brisk as that of money. Just as the shilling handed to one by the village shopkeeper may not so long ago have left the purse of Royalty, so it is possible that a horse bought even of a Baghdad Jew may be desert-bred and of noble race. This is not the poetical view, but we commend it to our readers as the practical one. Nay, where horses are concerned, the truth goes further. Arabian money is not generally taken to India or Australia: even seeds distribute themselves only within definite circles; but where is the clime to which man does not carry the animals subject to him? As we write these lines on the banks of the Tigris, there is before us a Houdàn hen hatched in Central India from an egg laid under the shadow of the Himalaya, by a bird brought all the way from France!

"O little did my mother ken,
The day she cradled me,
The lands I was to travel in,
Or the death I was to die!"[3]

is, if we except the cradling, as applicable to our domestic animals as to ourselves.

---

[1] *Jam-bāz*, in the sense of horse-dealer, will often occur in the sequel. It is a Persian word, meaning *one who plays with his life*. It is chiefly in I'rák that they say jam-bāz for horse-dealer. In Najd they use *hos-sán*, from *hi-sán*, a horse. Where horse-dealers from Najd are present, it is better not to use the name jam-bāz; for in Arabia proper it has almost the same meaning as *liar*.

[2] King Henry IV., Part I., Act i. sc. i.

[3] Ballad of *The Queen's Marie*, first published in Sir W. Scott's *Minstrelsy of the Scottish Border*.

The poor little piece of poultry, if stolen one of these nights from her roost, and sold to a steamer's cook, may travel round the world, and be made into grill in the English Channel! Nevertheless, it is good to notice which tribes of the desert do, and which do not, cling to the old traditions, under which men did not hesitate to ride a mare a month's journey, to mate her with a horse of fame. It might be going too far, to say that a falling away in Arab horse-breeders begins as soon as they issue out of Najd. Much depends on the situation of the new pastures; the facilities for leading the old life; and above all, the extent to which the pulsations of the central heart of Arabia are felt. Thus, as already hinted, the Ae-ni-za, though longer separated from Najd than the Sham-mar, are still as noted for strictness of stud-work as the latter are for laxity. We have heard that fifty years ago the Sham-mar, rather than send a mare to an inferior horse, would let her run without a foal. On the Khá-bùr and the Ja-gha-jagh, stories linger of children of Sfùk who have died in harness uttering with the latest breath the pedigree of their mares, to make their captors prize them: a trifle savage; yet infinitely higher than the Trojan champion's supreme concern about the ransom of his own dead body, after Achilles' lance had found the fatal opening. Layard relates how, in 1850, west of Mosul, on chancing to drop on an encampment of the Tai Arabs, he found them much cast down after a beating from the Sham-mar, in which forty of their mares had been captured. The while their Shekh was deep in gloomy consultation with his warriors over their misfortune, an emissary from the victorious Sham-mar, wrapped in his ragged cloak, sat listlessly among them, waiting to be informed of the pedigrees of the mares which he and his people had taken from them. Such a message, Sir Henry Layard continues, "might appear to those ignorant of the customs of the Arabs one of insult and defiance. But he was on a common errand: and although there was blood between the tribes, his person was as sacred as that of an ambassador in any civilised community. Whenever a horse falls into the hands of an Arab, his first thought is how to ascertain its descent."[1] It is not to be

---

[1] *Op. cit.* in Catalog. No. 31, p. 220. The same traveller in another work (*Nineveh and its Remains*, vol. i. ch. iv.) describes a chestnut mare belonging to the then (1843) Shekh Sfùk, of the Sham-mar, as "one of the most beautiful creatures I ever beheld. As she struggled to free herself from the spear to which she was tied she showed the lightness and elegance of the gazelle. Her limbs were in perfect symmetry; her ears long, slender, and transparent; her nostrils high, dilated, and deep red; her neck gracefully arched; and her mane and tail of the texture of silk. We all involuntarily stopped to gaze at her. 'Say *Má shá Alláh*,' exclaimed the owner, who seeing, not without pride, that I admired her, feared the effect of an evil eye. 'That I will,' answered I, 'and with pleasure, for, O Arab, you possess the jewel of the tribe.'" A few pages further on, it is added: "Sfùk was the owner of a mare of matchless beauty, called, as if the property of the tribe, *Sham-mar-ri-ya*. Her dam, who died about ten years ago, was the celebrated *Kubleh*, whose renown extended from the sources of the Khábùr to the end of the Arab promontory, and the day of whose death is the epoch from which the Arabs of Mesopotamia now date the events concerning their tribe. Muhammad Amín, Shekh of the Ju-búr, assured me that he had seen Sfùk ride down the wild ass

imagined that this first principle of desert horse-breeding has died out among the Sham-mar. But while owning to an impression that over Arabia as a whole fewer first-class horses now exist than formerly, in regard more particularly to the Bedouin of Al Ja-zi-ra, we cannot doubt that for a considerable time past they have been going downhill as horse-breeders. It is not that they have not still many noble mares. Raiding as they always are on the Ae-ni-za, there is not a mare in northern Arabia that may not any day pass from the Ae-ni-za to them. Perhaps it is that they are turning horse-dealers, and breeding recklessly for the supply of town-purchasers. Hordes of them encamp every year within a day or two of Baghdad and Mosul; and in many personal inspections of the young stock which they bring with them we have found it of a mixed description. No good comes to nomads from intercourse with towns. Of the two rival hordes of the sons of Sfúk now, as already seen, dividing between them Al Ja-zi-ra pastures, one holds to the country round Baghdad; and the other to the deserts touched by Mosul. In both alike the ties of blood or kindred find a common centre in one great family of the Sham-mar, that still retaining as its gentile name the very unpoetical one of *Al Jar-bā*, or *the scabby;* in pious memory of a female ancestor to whom the epithet was applicable, the mother of the first historical Fā-ris. But the general opinion is that the Sham-mar of the Baghdad circuit are far behind their brethren higher up the Tigris as horse-breeders. Some regard this as the natural consequence of the late Shekh of the former, Far-hân, having fallen away from the desert standards. Especially seeing that, according to the facts above stated, the Sham-mar as a whole consist of a confused mixture of different races, we would not say that this view is beside the question. But only this much is here vouched for. Outside of Najd, the stricter methods of horse-breeding are nowhere so carefully observed as among the Ae-ni-za. Although, as just now mentioned, all the great strains are in the possession of the Sham-mar, and although many of the champion Arabs of the Indian turf, especially among the big ones, have been bought as colts in Sham-mar camps towards Mosul, yet, if we wanted blood Arabians, and were not over-disposed to trust to the chapter of accidents to bestow them on us, we would go to the Ae-ni-za to look for them. Among the several subdivisions of the Ae-ni-za also, horse-breeding touches diverse levels. Certain tribes, desirous of keeping their mares always in fighting form, have other ways of mounting themselves than through breeding. For a long time past, in all the Ae-ni-za, the

---

of the Sin-jâr on her back, and the most marvellous stories are current in the desert as to her fleetness and powers of endurance. Sfúk esteemed her and her daughter above all the riches of the tribe; for her he would have forfeited all his wealth, and even Am-sha

[his wife] herself. Owing to the visit of the irregular troops, the best horses of the Shekh and his followers were concealed in a secluded ravine at some distance from the tents.'

kindreds of the Sba' and Fid-â'n bear the bell as horse-breeders, both for quality and numbers. No one who has not seen the mares of these two confederations in one of their vast encampments can adequately picture to himself what a wealth of noble horse-flesh has been given to the Arabian Bedouin. Within Shâ-mi-ya, the Sba' and Fid-â'n are spoken of, collectively, as *Al Bishr*. Judging from the little that is stated on this point by Doughty,[1] *Bishr* must form in Najd a comprehensive name for all those sections of the Ae-ni-za which still inhabit their native Nu-fûdh and deserts. In connection with these remarks, the reader will bear in mind the caution already given. Let no one fondly think that that must be perfection which comes from this, or that, division of the Bedouin. The true and only talisman is the power of knowing the Simon Pure wherever it is met with. Let us neither be taken in by the bead of glass which happens to be in the diamond-mine, nor on the other hand pass over the

"gem of purest ray serene"[2]

because it has fallen on a rubbish-heap. Given certain outward signs, and points of conformation ; and, provided that we can have the animal, any tribe may claim the pedigree. Not that pedigree is not at the root of everything; only that, at all events in the strains of Araby, the highest known degree of breeding may be inferred from the outward signs alluded to.

We do not profess in these pages fully to set before the reader the characteristic traits and manners of the Arabian Bedouin; but, mainly, to afford such glimpses of these nations as will illustrate the history of their horses. To some slight extent this has been done all along the road already travelled. It remains but to describe further the framework in which the Arabian horse is enclosed ; by which the breed is moulded ; and beyond which it cannot develop itself. First of all, then, and speaking, it will be remembered, for the present of horse-breeding *in the desert :* the Arabian essentially is a war-horse ; a knight and gentleman to the manner born ; a goer out "to meet the armed men." It might naturally be thought that the Bedouin, having no Cabinets or Foreign Ministers, would seldom find themselves set by the ears. But in reality it is not so. Edifying travesties occur within their deserts of the operations which diplomatists prepare for soldiers, in countries equipped with governments and standing armies. When one man's mastery, or a well-woven tribal confederation, too much threatens the balance of power in Najd, engagements worthy of a gazette may happen. In the extremely extended order of the desert warfare, a hundred cavaliers and camel-gunners cover the ground of a thousand ; and the parti-

---

[1] *Op. cit.* in Catalog. No. 2, vol. i. p. 331.   [2] Gray's *Elegy*.

coloured fluttering camel-trappings, like the plaids and plumes of our Highlanders, magnify size and numbers. According to ancient custom a chosen tent-beauty—her eye and voice more inspiring than the most martial music—seated in her camel litter, moves like a living standard in the front rank.[1] On great occasions of this kind, as the reader may imagine, the war-demon is usually well sated. In the old days, when no powder was burnt, the maiden was held sacred; but in these times of flying bullets her peril is greater. Outside of regular or irregular war, too, the Bad-u is full of practice. What Egypt, Afghán-istán, and India are to European nations, his wells and pastures are to him; if he have no ambassadors, he is always in his own proper person affronting or being affronted. The ordinary movements of the Bedouin resemble the Hebrew exodus from Egypt: their entire families, women, children, slaves, and cattle, march with them. Perhaps almost as many nomad infants first see the light on the line of march as under the tent's covering. When, during one of these movements, two hostile hordes cross one another's path, a collision is the natural consequence. So far from proving hindrances, the wives and daughters even of the principal Shekhs dismount at the first shot; and, their long dresses trailing behind them,[2] act the part of Plutarch's heroines. Their tears are not allowed to flow. When a wounded warrior leaves the fray, they receive him with shouts of encouragement; stop the blood with powdered charcoal; and send him back again. The Bad-u's regular *yaum*, or *day*, meaning *day of foray*, is a tamer matter. One great feature of his tribal system is, that for every friend to whom it binds him it gives him an enemy, or a friend's enemy, whom he may harry. In one of the Aryan languages, the word for *war* literally means *a desire for cows*. So in Arabic, *harb*, while serving for *battle*, includes the idea of *stripping another of his property*. To confound, or even compare, the commonwealths of Arabian Bedouin with brigands, would be to take up a wrong position; but, sooth to say, if the Bad-u must not be classed with robbers, just as little can he be called an honest fellow!

"His morning thought, his midnight dream,
His hope throughout the day" [3]

---

[1] This picturesque female is called in desert speech *Utfa*, used as we use *guidon*.

[2] Najd contains nations among whom custom requires women of condition, while freely showing their faces, to hide their feet under absurdly long dresses (compare Hor. Sat. i. 2). If the long-robed ones were excused from manual labour this would be no hardship. But among the Bedouin even Shekhs' wives are kept constantly afoot, not only in minding their children, collecting fuel, pounding corn, and such duties, but also in pitching and striking the tents, and making everything into loads for packing. Their trains must, therefore, often vex them: for example, in a tornado, when the whole body of womankind has to rush out and support the tents. According to some, the morality of a nation will always be that of its women; but be this as it may, a fine physique in a race's manhood demands a fine one in its women; see the universal difference between men sprung from vigorous mothers and those born and bred in harems.

[3] Hunting-song well known in India.

is plunder; but he goes about it jauntily. He no more desires to take another man's life than to lose his own, for in either case the result would be a perennial blood-feud. Rather than drive his long shivering lance through an enemy, he prefers to knock him off his mare and jump on her back. When he is beaten, he perceives it in a twinkling; drops his booty or gives up his property; and thinks only of living to try again. Every time that he sweeps bare a pasture, he gathers more gear in three days than he knows how to do in any honest employment in a lifetime. When instead of shearing he is shorn, he takes it calmly. He never considers his losses irreparable, any more than a gambler does. As to this, he has a saying, suggested by the up-and-down movements of a well-bucket—*The foray is a see-saw; now towards, now away from, us*.[1] His religion, such as it is, well accords with all this. The paganism of ancient Arabia had its varieties. The features of it oftenest described in books, as existing just before the Flight in places where civilisation flourished, were special, not generic. Particularly in Mecca, the Kuraishite keepers of the Ka'-ba understood the necessity of making their cult and ritual theatrical, if they would draw money into the temple coffers by means of it. But then as now the Bad-u proper lived in a different world; caring nothing about townsmen's carnivals and theologies; satisfied with a religion which he could carry about with him anywhere, and feel it no heavier than a peppercorn. To make a man a Muslim, prayer and fasting and almsgiving, with at least a smattering of doctrine, are essential. In respect of these things, visible darkness surrounds the Bedouin. In their blanket cities there is no *Mu-adh-dhin*, to sing out the prayer-call above the herdsman's whoop, and the voices of sheep and camels. When it comes to praying, they are ill provided. More than a thousand years after the reception by Al Hi-jáz of Islamism, Burckhardt noted that numerous hordes of the nomadic Arabs possessed no religion, beyond a dim traditional belief in a Supreme Being. Half a century later, Palgrave committed himself in his usual sweeping manner to the statement that the Sha-rá-rât Arabs are sun-worshippers now, as they were before Muhammad uttered his warning that the great day-star *rises from among the adherents of Satan*.[2] The desert of the Arabs is too vast for any one to say that this or that thing is not contained in it. Our own range has been too limited to furnish full conclusions. Certainly we have met with Bedouin who were unprovided with the simplest forms of prayer. But the most positive evidence would be needed

---

[1] "*Al harb si-jál; yaum la-ná; yaum a'lai-ná.*"
[2] *Op. cit.* in Catalog. No. 7, vol. i. p. 8. Palgrave, by the way, grossly mistranslates Muhammad's 'Saying.' He confounds *karn = the people*, or *following, of the Prophet*, with *kirn*, a horn. The absurdity of "the devil's horns" is thus read into it by him. Even if he had no Arabic dictionary, he should have known that Islamism sternly prohibits all such pictorial representations.

to convince us that any one in Arabia having pretensions to the name of Arab prostrates himself before, or worships, sun, moon, or star.[1] How largely in peninsular Arabia a softening of prehistoric paganism has resulted from that great aftermath, as we may call it, of Islamism, Wahabyism, will not have escaped notice. What that has done for Arabia between the seas, Constantinople formalism has done for Arabia between the rivers. Side by side with the use of firearms and other adjuncts of civilisation, praying and fast-keeping grow apace both among the Ae-ni-za and the Sham-mar. Lady A. Blunt, when staying and journalising among the latter, after writing that "prayer as an outward act of religion is not practised by the pure Bedouin," had to qualify her statement by adding that her Shekhly host Fá-ris "recites his prayers daily."[2] This subject will reappear in another chapter; when the influence of the Kuranic epoch in further knitting Arab man to Arab horse is being dealt with. Here let us regard only the grit of natural material—older than any recorded patriarch or lawgiver — which underlies and variegates Islamism, as survivals not dissimilar underlie and variegate every other developed religion. The thread of our remarks goes back, in this context, to what was said a little while ago of the Bad-u's plundering habit running in and out of his theology. The latter, as we shall soon see, may be rudimentary, and as bare of objects as the surfaces which he inhabits; but at least there is nothing bizarre or repulsive in it. The groundwork of it appears to be an extraordinary sense of the power and presence of God—a God unopposed, and unopposable, by any devil —a God to whom are ascribed every turn of fortune, and every event that happens, even when palpably due to human laziness, or worse. Thus in his meteorology Allah is everything. As if the natural, especially pastoral, life brought out under different skies the same religious type, we never hear him talk about the weather without remembering the Lothian shepherd who, on his master's disapproving of a rainy morning, pointed out how it "slockened the ewes, refreshed the trees, and was God's will." So with him : is it cloudy? it is in mercy to the calving camels. Is the heat intolerable? that is to bring on the dates. Is the season as irregular as, with us, snow at midsummer? then it is to teach him that these things do not depend on calendars. What *luck* means let them explain who understand it: many of us, from our talk, seem to believe in it

---

[1] In a paper by Dr Wallin of Finland, being *Notes of his Journey through Part of N. Arabia in 1848*, in *Journal Roy. Geog. Soc., London,* vol. xx. 1851, Part II., is the following important statement :—

"There are not, as far as I could learn, amongst the nomadic Bedouins, nor in the towns and villages in the interior of Arabia, persons professing any other religion than the Islam ; nor did I ever hear in those parts of Arabia which I visited mention made of tribes or individuals suspected to be attached in secret to another creed." P. 311.

[2] *Op. cit.* in Catalog., No. 11, vol. ii. p. 217.

more than in the Almighty. The corresponding word with the Bedouin is, *ua-sîb*. Next to Allah, no expression is more current among them; but they mean by it just what our own doctors, from Augustine downward, mean by *Providence*. Thus may, in part at least, have arisen the impression which exists in many quarters, that God's sovereignty is made by Islamism to degrade men to puppets. We cannot here pursue this subject; let us merely say, in passing, that there never was a greater error. Of course when one man submits to another for the sake of safety,[1] he obeys him; but there is no fatalism in that. Muhammad, as has been seen, was a master of eloquence, not logic. In the heated pursuit of many themes, the effect of God's absolutism on man's free-will either failed to strike him; or, like Locke after him, he was content to leave it a riddle. To express at once the finality and the immeasurable elevation of the divine supremacy, he found no words too extreme.[2] On the other hand, just as he cared not to expunge certain abrogated "revelations," so, in discoursing of men's actions and destinies, he suffered no thought of apparent inconsistency or contradiction to prevent him from depicting them as free and conditional.[3] Arabian fatalism is older than Muhammad; older even than Abraham: and the view just now presented, namely, that its strongest growth is among the Bedouin, supports this statement.[4] The Bad-u's fatalism is, however, a purely heathen feature; not a dogma, but an intuition. It is only with this life and its portions that it occupies itself; indeed it is almost certain that apart from Islamite teaching the Arabian Bedouin are still as unconscious of future rewards and punishments as the Israelites were before the Babylonian captivity. The stories of witchcraft and bedevilment which obtain varying degrees of credence among them came into the desert from towns like Bussorah and Medina. The very ancient Bedouin custom of tying a dead man's mare or camel beside his grave, to die by inches, involved only a belief in man's consisting of two portions; the body, which dissolves; and something else which is "given up," and continues to live as a ghost. It was not that the camel[5] should go to heaven, or hell, or purgatory; but that

---

[1] *V*. Index I., art. IS-LĀM.
[2] *E.g.*, in S. lxxxvi. it is said: *And truly Allah maketh to err whom He will, and directeth aright whom He will.* [Comp. Romans ix. 18.]
[3] *E.g.*, in S. xc.: *And have We not shown him* [man] *the two conspicuous ways* {of right and wrong}; *and he attempted not the difficult one.*
And in S. lii.: *Hath he* [man] *not been told that . . . truly no bearer of a heavy load* [sinner] *shall carry the burden of another? And truly there is naught for man save that for which he has striven; and surely his efforts shall be seen hereafter. Then shall he be requited with the justest recompense; and unto the Lord is the finality.*

And in S. lxxiv.: *Every soul is pledged* [with God] *for what it shall have wrought.*
[4] *Fate's arrows never miss their mark*, is a commonplace of Arabic, as of other, languages.
A'mr said—
Truly to-day, and to-morrow, and the day after to-morrow, Are deposited in pledge (with Destiny), for the bringing to pass of events of which ye have no knowledge.
And Zu-hair—
And whosoever regardeth with fear death's causes will still be reached by them,
Even were he to climb the sides of the blue vault with a scaling-ladder.
[5] In Arabic *ba-li-ya*; *q. v.* in Index I. So recently as 1781, at Treves, a charger was sacrificed outright

she should follow her master to the underground place out of which the Prophet Samuel was evoked against his will by the wise woman of Endor. To keep, however, to the upper world. As came out in another chapter, when the hospitable ways of the desert were under notice, all the world's good and evil are considered by the Arab nomad to belong to God. When in a fortunate *ghaz-u* he drives before him what a Hebrew lyrist—perhaps himself a Bad-u—graphically describes as "hills of prey," his idea is that he is but taking what God has given to him. What a very primitive religion his is will appear from this one view of it. Yet, clearly, it is the cream of faiths for populations which answer to the southern traveller's description of the Celts of Scotland : " They live like lairds, and die like loons. Hating to work, and no credit to borrow, they make depredations and rob their neighbours."[1] Whence it comes that, if netting, snaring, driving, night-shooting, have made the English poacher's wily lurcher, raiding and tilting, pursuing, fleeing, turning, twisting, have made the Bedouin courser. In a desert stave already quoted,[2] the reader may have remarked how the horseman praises, not his mare's *speed*, but her *handiness*. Of the former quality, much as he will talk of it, he can have but little true idea ; for whatever may have been the case in heathen times,[3] horse-racing is not now practised by the Arabs, at any rate till they go to India. In the Parthian warfare of the desert, two things make a mare excel : the one, endurance ; and the other, the same gift of turning and twisting which distinguishes the Arab horse in India with either a running or a charging boar in front of him. By this time, surely, the Bedouin's hatred of a master has become one of our exhausted topics. Even his own Shekhs have more of respect from him than obedience. Very few of them could make a tribesman do what he did not wish to do. If the man, in his secret heart, inclined towards an action, it might please him to say that he had been coaxed or forced to do it ; but when once his feet are firmly planted, the cudgel that will move him is still to cut. Next to this spirit of independence, as has also been shown, what helps the

---

as part of the funeral ceremony. The horse does not now follow its rider to sheol, but only to the cemetery: whence it is led back to its stable. Among the peaceful and domestic Hindus, not a man's charger, or his "weapons of war" (Tack. xxxii. 27), but his wife was sent with him : till the British power stopped the custom.

[1] Quoted by Macaulay, *Hist. of England*, ch. xiii.
[2] V. *ante*, p. 61.
[3] Races ranked among the *divertissements* of the fair held in pre-Islamic times near Mecca. The metaphor in the following ancient Najdian couplet opens a glimpse of some such Olympic contest : horses riderless — usually ten starters – each horse receiving a special name according to his place at the finish ; the winner, [*Al*] *Sâbik* – the outstripper ; the second, [*Al*] *Musalli*, or *the one of the other's back*, and so on : –

If ever one day [*i.e.*, in some high enterprise] honour's goal have to be made for,
Among us thou wilt find the first horse and the second.

But these performances were nothing more than shows. Horse-racing, properly so called, is indigenous to England.

nomad breeder is his roaming life. The Black Douglas's preference of the "lark's song to the mouse's squeak" referred only to campaigning; and if the good Lord James had been with Havelock's column, as the writer was, when it forced its way from the open fields round Lucknow into the Baillie Guard, or citadel, perhaps, for one night at least, the domestic thief's shrill chatter would have sounded like a call to rest and shelter. No such associations surround the Bedouin. In sun and rain and wind, the tent flapping in the desert blast contents them. When their mares are starving, they pass it off with one of their sayings about *plenty waiting on servitude*, and hope for better times. In towns like Há-yil, Baghdad, Kar-ba-lá, Damascus, and Aleppo, the *aóyi hoo-oo*, and other whoops, with which the desert herdsman pilots his interminable files of camels, are familiar; but every Bad-u, in passing through a city, keeps one eye behind him, like Rob Roy in Glasgow, to see that the door of the trap is not closing. The very camels go beside themselves when first the walls of a town rise up before them. The desert colt, with all his courage, requires pressing before he will bow his head to pass through the entrance of a stable. In this full development of the nomadic state we have throughout these pages been recognising perhaps the best possible conditions for the breeding of hardy serviceable horses. What Virgil says of rumour,

"Mobilitate viget, viresque acquirit eundo,"

is equally true of young horse-stock. In India, we have seen colts which if kept at home would never have proved worth their corn, take a start and grow, on a six-months' march befalling them. Nay, the same is true of men. When a campaign begins, the generals and senior staff-officers come out of the transports so broken down from sedentary work and over-living that a speedy retreat to Club-land is predicted for many of them. But the return to natural habits, with restriction more or less to commissariat rations, relieves the old fellows of their gouts and plethoras, renews their youth, and makes them weather-proof. The trait next to be referred to in the Bedouin, as affecting their breeds of horses, is their illiterate state. It is not only that the Arabian nomad cannot read or write or cipher, but that he prides himself on it. He makes it his boast that he takes in his knowledge either from the lips of the experienced or through his five senses; and that he keeps it after he has got it, not in book-stores, but at his fingers' ends.[1] This partly belongs to the phase of civilisation which is inseparable from his nomadic state. His is still the level which our countrymen

---

[1] Thus an Arab poet:
Stick you to memory, instead of collecting [knowledge] in books;
And truly as regards books, musings snake away with them:

The water drowns them; and the fire burns them;
And the thief [in Har. reed *kereeuve*] walks off with them; and the mouse makes holes in them.

occupied in the days of "Bell the Cat." Not a great many hundred years before the time of that Bishop Gawain, who

"Gave rude Scotland Virgil's page,"[1]

it had occurred in Arabia, when the Kur-ân was coming out by little and little, that the Medina Jews, many of whom were bookmen, brought their sacred writings, and pointed out to the uprising Prophet that his stories of the patriarchs differed from those in their possession; to which Muhammad answered, that though they had the books, they were "as asses laden with them," and "understood not their contents."[2] This was too good a thing to die: one of those long thoughts compressed in short clauses which the Arabs, with all their power of piling words atop of words, so excel in producing. It has become an Eastern proverb. Sa'-di, the Persian, when his day came, beat out the nugget into a quatrain as follows:—

> Nor sage nor critic grows the insensate hack
> With load of literature upon his back :
> What wots poor stupid if his loins are sore
> With food for furnaces, or lettered lore ![3]

And so the ball has rolled; and missile after missile for use against book-learning has been manufactured out of it. A Kurdish *Kochar* of Sin-jâr whose hospitality we lately experienced—a nomadic Dandie Dinmont and patriarch, rich beyond description in flocks of sheep and Angora goats [4]—*apropos* of his own and all his progeny's innocence of their letters, sarcastically said, "A man rubs a pointed reed on a bit of paper, and in a moment produces that which may prove his ruin;"—words, it struck us, not without their import for England under the modern postal system, with its half-a-dozen deliveries daily! Another reason for the Arabian Bedouin's hatred of pen-work is his identifying it with townsmen. If the sedentary Arabs look on their wandering kindred as Londoners did a century ago on Taffies, the Bad-u, we have seen, despises the Ha-dha-ri as the author of the *Noctes*

---

[1] Scott, in *Marmion*.
[2] In a recent book of Eastern travel, a copious bibliography of a certain subject is given in a footnote; while in the text the talented author affords proof of his not having read the literature which is cited by him !
[3] Similarly Pope :—
  " The bookful blockhead ignorantly read,
  With loads of learned lumber in his head."
  —*Essay on Criticism.*
A little further on is the line —
  " Most authors steal their works or buy."
Query : did Pope steal from Sa'-di ?
[4] Nothing can surpass the beauty of these creatures in their own proper pastures. "Quality" shines in every feature; their silky hair, at least eight inches long, when the morning mists have passed through it, is pearly white. Under the happy Eastern system of the flock *following* the shepherd, one or two Kurds can manœuvre an army of sheep. The duty of the canine helpers—not unlike rough Great St Bernards—is chiefly watch and ward against human and four-footed robbers. The name for the Angora goat is *mir-i'z*, which is explained in Arabic dictionaries as *the down beneath the hair of a goat*. A flock was once obtained from Mosul for export to the Cape of Good Hope; but the change from the chalky altitudes of Sin-jâr to the alluvium of Babylonia killed most of them.

did a Cockney. For one thing, he is inclined to question how far one living in a town, with all the women going where they list draped from head to foot like sheeted spectres, Eastern manners being what they are, can have any certainty who his father was. The view which is held by him, in common with Turk-u-má-ni, Kurd-i, and other tribal populations, of the absurdity of veiling honest women, is infinitely older in the countries bordering on his deserts than that which is now too much identified with Islamism.[1] In the story in Genesis (xxxviii.) of Judah's affair with Tamar, we read that when Judah saw her seated in a gateway on a certain festival occasion connected with sheep-shearing, he "thought her to be an harlot," BECAUSE "she had covered her face." And so to this day think the Bedouin; who even allow their daughters to look about them and choose, if they can manage it, husbands; instead of settling them, as is done in several Eastern countries, almost as soon as they can be taken from the mother. Next in the list of indictments brought by the Bedouin against townsmen, is the shame and reproach of living under the heels of Pàshas. Then come all their effeminacies, and the infinity of superfluous things which they accumulate,—for the desert standard of comfort mounts but little higher than that of Scott's Highland chief, who, when he saw his son pillowing his head on a snowball, pushed it away with the reproof that he should be above such luxuries! A last century traveller, in reference to the "garb of old Gaul," jumped to the conclusion that "loose clothes do make loose morals." If it be so, which we question, then the Bedouin are the least strait-laced of mankind. Desert full-dress for man and woman is little better than nakedness: the condition of a whole tribe may resemble that of Christopher Sly,—"no more doublets than backs; no more stockings than legs" (seldom even that); "and no more shoes than feet." The Bad-u who is starting on a journey will load his beast with coffee-making utensils, including perhaps a heavy mortar: but however handsomely he may, if a Shekh, dress and arm himself, he carries little clothing beyond what is on his person. At all these points there shows itself not merely his natural bareness, but his pride in being what he is—the opposite of a townsman. In so far as Islamism is Arabism, it develops simplicity of manners.

---

[1] We know from Jerome (4th cent.) and other sources that in very early times Arab townswomen concealed their faces from strangers. Hinduism forestalled Islamism in this respect in India; where, as in Persia, the custom is deeply seated in the national manners. But Al Kor-ân goes no further than in the following passage : *And say to believing women that they abridge somewhat of their look [perhaps, restrain their view from forbidden objects]; and keep in honour (or inviolate) those regions where the body parts; and display not their charms except such as show naturally; and draw their coverings over their bosoms.* [S. xxiv.] And so on through numerous details. In towns like Baghdad respectable women of all creeds, and all classes above the agricultural, when they go out muffle themselves like mummies. Only one eye is allowed a peep-hole : and the power of all the other features comes to be concentrated in it.

Sa-dí says—

Under a covering, many a form charms ;
Take off the wrapper, and behold a grandmother !

How conspicuously absent was the "pride of life," as represented by pretentious buildings, in the Prophet's own household, has been elsewhere noticed.[1] In his highest estate Muhammad was still the Arab; contented with the fare of the desert: ready to patch his own cloak, milk his goats, and take bite and sup with the poorest.[2] For 1300 years, superfluity and ostentation have been checked in Arabia proper by his single 'Saying': *Verily he who eats or drinks from a vessel of gold or silver, as it were gulps down into his belly the fire of Hell.* Commentators say that this was uttered lest the poor should be moved by the sight of such things to reproach God with having given more to others than to them. Probably it formed but an expression of the primitive Arab nature. But to continue our reference to the modern Ba-da-wi. A vein of rhetoric and poetry distinguishes him; and he is as noted for the beauty of his diction as for the purity of his blood. The very ancient practice among the Bedouin of reciting verses when they assemble outside the tents in the cool of early night, while it improves the memory, increases the natural flow of language. The minstrel lyre of Najd has slept, or given out but echoes, these thousand years and more; but the old poetry is thus kept alive. The first important series of effusions ever committed *in prose* to the Arabic language was the Kur-án; many of the most notable passages of which, though not metrical, exhibit the prevalent rhythmic form of that period.[3] When portions of it began to be publicly repeated, like Herodotus' history at the Olympic games, the Bedouin said that they were merely Muhammad's poems.[4] But even that view of the work failed to recommend it to the lovers of Im-ru 'l Kais and A'n-ta-ra. At this day no genuine Bad-u quotes it. We have never seen a Kur-ân in the desert; or indeed a scrap of writing of any kind, except in the amulets[1] which are worn as a defence against the evil eye, and in the box of the *mulla*, or "poor scholar," who is kept to perform marriages, and read, if not answer, demands for tribute, or for the restitution of "lifted" sheep.

With the above facts before him, the reader will know how to estimate at their proper value the stories which are current regarding written pedigrees of Arab horses. There is absolutely nothing of the kind in existence. The last time that we were in Paris, a fellow-countryman high in office showed us a paper which he had received with a colt from Cairo. He thought that it proved his favourite to have descended from Solomon's mares: but it was merely a charm which a groom had hung round the animal's neck to keep off the evil eye! The simple truth is this. In sales made inside a town not the most credulous would attach weight to anything stated, whether orally or in writing, about a horse's pedigree. The seller seldom knows much about it; and if he did, he would probably prefer to exercise his imagination, supposing that any one was fool enough to ask him. Just as little, though for a different reason, is it usual, when the Bedouin buy from one another, to put on paper what has never been written before, and could be sworn to in one forenoon by hundreds. But when a townsman, or perhaps a European Government, sends an agent to buy horses from the tribes of Najd or Shâ-mi-ya, nothing is commoner than to take a voucher as to pedigree with every purchase. Opposite is a *facsimile* and translation of such a paper, dabbed with the seals, or thumbs, of a round dozen Shekhs of the Su-wai-li-mât, which we once received with a colt. At the time we thought it worth less than the paper which it covered. The colt mentioned in it proved little better than a *yá-bû*.[2] Either the precious document was a town-made forgery, or some *mulla* had manufactured it in the tents of the Ae-ni-za, to promote the pious enterprise of imposing upon a European. An honest agent does not need such trumpery; scribes and seals

---

[1] For a *hi-jáb*, literally *preservative*, consisting of hieroglyphics traced on a scrap of paper by any chance visitor having the mysterious art of writing, the Arab nomad will pay money or money's worth; which is more than he will do for an honest purge, an eye-wash, or a pinch of quinine—though these also, when to be had for nothing, he will take gladly. But on the whole it is surprising how little of the supernatural mixes with Bedouin ignorance. Once it befell us to be grounded for three midsummer days in a little steamer on the Tigris. The tribesmen of the vicinity declared that it was the *Jinn* who stopped us; but a Bad-u who happened to be passing rebuked them for believing such nonsense.

[2] A Persian, or perhaps Turk-u-mân, name for the large coarse galloways used in mountainous parts. Like the Indian *tat-tû*, the *yá-bû* is mostly of nondescript race. Yet there are *breeds* of *yá-bûs* too. One breed in particular, called from its curly hair the *habashi* or African, which is common in the Candahar province, though seldom above 14 hands, comes nearest in breadth to the European cart-horse of any Eastern variety. One does not see *yá-bûs* in Arabia, except in towns and on lines of communication.

FACSIMILE OF A "HUJ-JA"

(OR ARAB CERTIFICATE OF A HORSE).

وهم خير مضبطة الاستشهاد
نحن المحرره اسماؤنا وختومنا ادناه مشايخ السويلمات من مشار عنزه واكابرها والبايات السوبايات نشهد بالله
ومحمد ابن عبداله نشهد شهاده تحقيقا من دون جبر انه محضر حصان معاشي الحشاشي السويلمي
وهو حصان احمر الذي في قصته هلال انه بلحظاه البخت ان امه ودنه خرسان وابوه كحيلان ابوجنوب
معلوم الرسن والاصل حصان ينشا وذلك في علمنا وبموجب اطلاعنا انه حمار ثمنه على خضر المعقلي
في حسابه وخمسين غازية وبموجب علمنا وحضرنا هذه الاستشهاد وما شهدنا الا بما علمنا والله
خبر الشاهدين هر وفي عى مى شنكم شهد بذلك شهد بذلك شهد بذلك شهد بذلك عن امضائكم

TRANSLATION.

This is to record :

We whose signatures and seals are below, Shekhs of the Su-wai-li-mât, a branch of the Ae-ni-za, do testify, by Allah, and by Muhammad son of Abdu 'lla, truly, without compulsion, in respect to the horse of Ma'â-shi 'l Hash-shâ-l of the Su-wai-li-mât : and he a bay, with a mark like the new moon on his forehead ; by our stars and fortune, his dam was [of the strain] Wad-na Khir-sân ; and his sire, Ku-hai-lân Abû ju-nûb—the well-known strain. He is a horse used as a sire. It is also known to us that his price has stood Khidhr, the Agel, in 550 *ghâ-zir* [about £88 sterling]. According to our knowledge and information we have written this certificate.

and oaths by Allah are never wanting to bolster up fraud and falsehood. *The unfaithful one is fearful*[1] (*e.g.*, always casting about for papers to support his falsehoods), says an Arab proverb.

Room must now be made for a remark or two on what is, after all, the cardinal feature in the Bedouin's practice of horse-breeding—the source at once of his strength and weakness—his unbounded faith in purity of blood. A large class of our countrymen, it is said, never see a sunny day without wanting to go out and shoot something. And the sight of a fine horse or mare seems naturally to suggest to many other good people the idea of crossing it with one of a different variety. Once in India we saw an Arab brought up to be admired at a regimental mess; when, because of his having won races in company of his own class, the general vote was that he ought to be sent to England and put to thoroughbred mares. As is nearly always the case with Arabs in India, no one knew how he was bred; and in point of quality he looked about fit to carry the luggage of one of the fathers of the English stud-book. If the portraits of Blair Athol and Alice Hawthorn on the wall behind us had come down with a run at the mention of such a commoner being admitted into their truly patrician family, there would have been little wonder. It is not disputed that there is a time to cross; but there is also a time to cry enough. A "happy nick" may greatly help to *originate* a breed; but it is pure breeding, aided by the selection of the fittest, that brings it to full flower. On the one hand, we know how successfully the racing greyhound was improved through a bull-dog cross, at the end of last century, by Lord Orford. On the other, the results are before us of Booth and Bakewell's triumphs with short-horn cattle and Leicester sheep respectively, while strictly following the system of close or "in" breeding. But with reference to "crossing," we must remember what a high degree of education, study, and experience is here essential. Darwin says—and who more competent to give an opinion?—that not one man in a thousand has accuracy of eye and judgment sufficient to become an eminent breeder; and that the extent of natural capacity, with years of practice added, which it takes to make even a skilful pigeon-fancier is such as few realise. This being so, what better line could the Bad-u have followed than that of holding on to a good thing when he had it—that is, on obtaining strains of horses equal to every service, keeping the blood as pure as possible? And thus, if he had been a philosopher, he could not better have avoided the rock which proves so fatal, of trying suddenly to improve a breed without considering whether the climate will favour the altered produce, and the quantity and quality of the available food will prove suitable and sufficient for it. So far nothing could

---

[1] "*Il khā-in khā-if*"—Scottice, *It is the ill doers are ill doers sair*.

be better. The fly in the pot of honey is—such a fanatic about *blood* is every desert breeder. that, in pairing his horses, he does not pay sufficient attention to *form*. Ask an Ae-ni-za Shekh whether one of his colts or fillies is *a-sîl*, and if he would maintain it, he will say, *By Allah, you may breed from it in a dark night!* Practically, this means—never mind whether the individual is shaped like a race-horse, a donkey, or a buffalo, so sovereign is the *blood*, that you may safely use it without bestowing a thought on any external feature! The mischievous effect of this purblindness on the horse-stock of Arabia—how, in consequence of it, faults of conformation spread like weeds in a neglected garden—will often appear in the sequel. But, on the whole, the Bedouin should be thankful that such lights as they possess have dawned on them. It was only right for Englishmen, with colleges of learned veterinarians and book-writers at their back, when the "wisest fool in Christendom" was pressing his Markham Arabian [1] on them, to ponder well the lines of a clerical satirist of the period,—

> "Dost thou prize
> Thy brute beasts' worth by their dams' qualities?
> Say'st thou thy colt shall prove a swift-paced steed
> Only because a jennet did him breed?
> Or say'st thou this same horse shall win the prize
> Because his dam was swiftest Trenchefice?" [2]

But it would fare ill with Najdian horse-breeders if, in their present primitive condition, they were to throw away or qualify their traditional faith in *blood*.

An important topic still remains: the desert Arab's horsemanship.

THE HORSEMAN MAKES THE HORSE has several times been stated as one of the central ideas in our volume. How certain characteristic qualities of the Arabian breed come to it by a kind of natural percolation from its human culti-vators is gradually being illustrated. Meanwhile, Bedouin equitation will repay

---

[1] The purchase by James I. in 1616 for £154 from a merchant named Markham of an Arabian stallion belonged to the shrewder side of his character. The foreign animal, it so befell, tended more to discredit than bring into favour the Arab cross. The Admiral Rous of the period, the Duke of Newcastle, did his utmost to suppress him, describing him as "a little bony horse of ordinary shape." Though his importers and others may have reckoned him an Arab, it by no means follows that he was one. The same uncertainty equally belonged, as has often been pointed out, to two of his three principal successors, the Byerly Turk, the Darley Arabian, and the Godolphin Barb, who were destined a century later to divide among them the paternity of all the thoroughbreds of England, Europe, Australia, the Cape Settlements, and America. The Darley Arabian, as we have elsewhere stated and intend further to illustrate, was a genuine one. But of the other two—one was merely a charger brought from Turkey by one of "Dutch William's" captains; while of the early history of The Barb, all that is current is, the story of his having left the shafts of a cart in Paris, in or about 1729, to become the sire of Lath; and through him of an illustrious progeny, culminating in our time in the Melbourne family.

[2] These lines, quoted during two centuries in books on racing, were first seen in Bishop Hall's imitation of the passage in Juvenal's 8th satire, in which the high-bred horse without spirit or courage is used to illustrate that performance, and not pedigree, makes the man.

separate notice. First, it should be remembered how slight and lithesome these riders are. Heavy marching order is unknown among them; the infantry of matchlockmen, with its jingling belts and ammunition, disposes itself, as has been seen, on camels: in a troop of desert prickers, but few horsemen would draw nine stone. The importance of this was impressed on us early in life, while hog-hunting with certain native officers of the Nizam's Cavalry in India. Not only were our companions light weights and fine horsemen, but they were rich enough to mount themselves, regardless of price, on Arabs powerful enough to carry two of them. In pressing the grim grey boar through one most break-neck Deccan gully in particular, what saved them was, that their horses galloped with perfect freedom. However much action may primarily be dependent on conformation, the paces of a horse accustomed to carry a heavy man soon lose their natural sprightliness.

There is very little of science in the desert horsemanship. The riding-school theory of suppling a colt's neck and haunches, and so uniting his powers in the middle of his body as to lighten the two extremities, and put them properly at the disposal of the rider, would sound mere town talk to the Bad-u. It has never struck him that his horse's natural mode of progression requires to be improved. Carried he is, but he can scarcely be said to *ride*—at any rate, at the slower paces. When anything is on hand, he makes sail with all his canvas out in this fashion—

A LA BEDOUIN.

Loose as his seat seems, he can hold with his leg-grip a reserve spear between his thigh and the saddle. When his mood is passive a walk contents him—his mare all of a sprawl under him, blundering along anyhow, and looking from side to side; with the head and neck perfectly free and unsupported. Once an Osmanli general, after an expedition against the Sham-mar, reported with military brevity that the "men had no religion; the women no drawers; and the horses no bridles." Not to go back to religion, the other two counts are still true.

Gladly as the Bad-u will pull on a pair of short breeches before mounting for a serious excursion, on other occasions he holds it but a town fashion to part the two shanks by stuffing them into separate bags or cases. A girdle of leather thongs, called *sabta*, is laced round the naked loins, to support the back: and over this falls the only garment, the *ka-mís*, or *thaub*, of calico—a decent smock: the sleeves long and wide, with bird's-wing-like endings handy for many uses; the body reaching to the heels. This is not the drapery in which "to turn and wind a fiery Pegasus." The inconvenience of it, and the absence of stirrups, may have something to do with the Bad-u's preference of the arm-chair pace of cantering to the rougher motion of trotting.

Next let us speak of the Bedouin saddlery. The following illustration exhibits the characteristic bridle:

RIDING-HALTER, or *rasán-ma*; including (1) *rasán-ma* proper, or (iron) nose chain; (2) *i-scher*, or head stall; and (3) *rasán*, the rope or rein.

The above is simplicity at its highest. When the coast is clear, it is considered sufficient; but the Bad-u carries a rusty iron at his saddle-bow, and slips it into his mare's mouth on occasions resembling those which suggest to us the tightening of the girths and the shortening of the stirrups.

The saddle, of which also we here introduce a sketch, well suits the bridle:

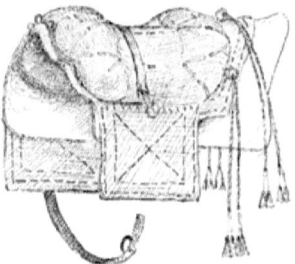

BEDOUIN PAD (*ma'-ra-ka*, also *mat-ra-ka*).

How, with the above light tackle, the Bad-u will take his mare at speed anywhere, surprises those who are accustomed only to corn-fed horses. The secret is, that she has been habituated to it from foal-hood; when, perhaps, from cold and hunger, her skin was as fast on her as the bark on a tree, and her only thought was to submit. This Arab riding-halter is useful anywhere. The traveller can feed or water his horse without disturbing it. The rope or rein, usually of camel's hair, equally serves for leading with, and for hobbling during the mid-day heat, either Australian or Bedouin fashion. It can be worn under a plain English Pelham or snaffle. We have ridden thousands of miles with it, and found it most convenient.[1] The Bedouin saddle is not so good. It is a mere

[1] While going to press, we have been favoured with the perusal of a series of journals just printed, but not published, by General Lord Mark Kerr, G.C.B. No one who has seen Lord Mark when an officer of the famous old 13th ride his own horse, or a friend's, over obstacles, needs to be informed that he was an adept in the saddle. During the Delhi Manœuvres of 1871 he made this entry: "He [Maharajah of Vizianagram] is astonished at my riding. I had the reins on one side of my horse's neck only, as I often do, and find it quite as easy as the usual way, and useful, as I often get off and walk, and thus have the reins easily in my hand to lead my horse." It further appears in the same record that another Bedouin practice, "riding without stirrups," was natural to Lord Mark; and that when a "fuss" was raised about his doing so, in the Crimea, by martinet generals and brigadiers, the only concession which he would make to the military proprieties was that he "henceforth put the stirrups on to the saddle, and crossed them over the pommel"!

Most of us lose a great deal as horsemen through over-dependence on stirrups. Once, long ago, at Hyderabad in the Deccan, an Indian who was riding in a flat race for an English patron found, about a mile from home, that his girth had given way. Instead of letting the saddle fall, and coming in short of weight, he brought it in with him in his hand, gallantly winning the race. As for bits and bitting, although steeplechases have been won bridleless, the necessity for control and guidance of this kind in the higher parts of horsemanship is evident. More than a hundred varieties of bits, we believe, could be enumerated. All but a few of them ought to be sent out of the country for sale to savages. When a horse in daily work is doing no more than carrying one, or as soldiers say, *marching*, it is absurd to overload his head with saddlery, every strap of which is an extra trouble both to him and his rider ; and to puzzle him with curb bits and curb chains. A snaffle is

make-up of felt or sacking stuffed with wool or cotton; for wood, leather, and iron are scarce in the desert. At certain seasons it is never off the mare's back night or day, except when she is swimming a river. On such occasions, her rider strips himself to the skin—as just seen, an easy matter; ties all his gear atop his saddle with the *su-mñt* or loin-strings; puts the saddle upon his head; and, rein in hand, descends into the current. Such are the only times when we have ever seen a lot of mares unsaddled; and then most of their backs were sore—not, indeed, with the terrible galls which wood or iron causes, but with skin wounds which will heal under the saddle.[1] Instead of minding these, the warlike brotherhood take the Spartan view of them: a desert poet, wishing to describe a man of ideal fortitude, likens him to *a camel under whose saddle many a wound has healed*. A Bedouin who, from having no mare, is forced to ride a stallion, hammers him with the butt of his lance when he makes a noise; or perhaps carries hanging from his wrist a thing like a dog-whip for his benefit. In his churlish thinking, the female is the better, and more patient, in all animals save Man; his gentle mare needs no other admonition than a touch on the side of the neck with the short stick called *mih-jan* (also *mish-a'b*) which is never out of the nomad's hand. Considering how vigorously, in times of warfare, the Bedouin from his first beginnings has plied the naked heel against his mare's sides, what a fact it would have been for Science if a spur like a cock's had now belonged to his anatomy! but as such is not the case, he is driven to a device of this kind:

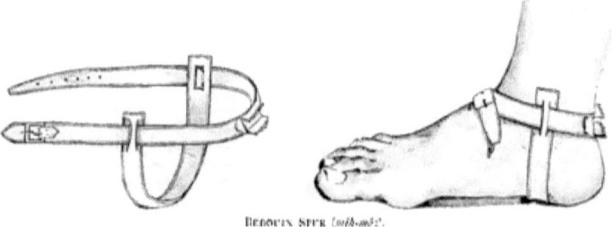

BEDOUIN SPUR (*mih-ahz*).

all that is wanted for such simple riding. As stated in the text, we have usually found a horse that is accustomed to the Arab halter march better, at all paces, when nothing is put in his mouth to exclude the fresh air, and keep him in a state of fret and irritation. If an Arab, he is pretty sure to trip and blunder, but he will not fall.

[1] The Arabic word for the *bruising* or *galling* of a beast's back is *daus*—primary meaning, *trampling*, esp. corn to *thrash* it. And the same word was once current in the British Islands—*e.g.*, "*douse the glim*" = *put out the light*, in chap. iii. of *Guy Mannering*. And in "Blind Harry's" *History of Sir William Wallace*:—

"Two supple fellows there that pressed him most,
He *doused* their doublets rarely to their cost."

Douse or *douche*; *drub* (Semitic *drb*); and many other words of the same pithy class, may have been carried our way by the gipsies.

OF THE BEDOUIN AS HORSE-BREEDERS.

Elsewhere we let an Arabian poet describe a thunderstorm;[1] and perhaps if we here introduce another piece of the same minstrelsy, and afterwards add a few explanations, this view of desert horsemanship will be well concluded :—

And often I am out betimes; when the birds are in their nests; on a sleek hunter; a shackler of wild animals:

One to him are charge and flight; advance; retreat; big as a mass of rock which the torrent has torn from a height:

A dark bay; the saddle[2] slips off the middle of his back, as slides the smooth stone in running water:

A great bounder, from high condition;[3] whose snorting, when he is excited, resembles in vehemence the boiling over of a cauldron:

Full of running when the gallopers, dead-beat, are pawing the dust in the track of his hoof-marks;

Unseating the light stripling from his back; and tossing off the cloak of the hard-riding heavy-weight:

Swift as the boy's plaything which the incessant movement of his hands sends flying round and round by the string attached to it:

Ribbed up like the antelope; with thighs like the ostrich's; lobbing along like the wolf; galloping like the fox-cub:

Great of barrel; and when you look at him from behind, he has closed his channel with a tail falling nearly to the ground, and inclined to neither side:[4]

His back as he stands in his place is like the stone on which perfumes are bruised for a bride, or the slab on which they pound colocynth:

The blood on his neck of the leaders of the herd is like the juice of the *kin-ná* on the trimmed hair of the greybeard.[5]

And there came in sight a herd, containing heifers, which were like the maidens in trailing garments that circle round the sacred stones in the temple:[6]

And they turned towards us rumps like the white shells set here and there in the necklace of a boy who has both paternal and maternal uncles:[7]

And he laid us alongside of the foremost; and behind him those that had fallen to the rear, in a lot not broken up:

And he passed, in his charge, from bull to heifer; running them down, without sweating or turning a hair:

---

[1] P. 49. *ante.*

[2] Word used is *libd, q. v.* in Index I.

[3] In the text *dhabl;* of a tree, *the drying up;* of a horse, *the being drawn fine.* It was impossible for the Arabs to follow the chase mounted without discovering the importance of *condition:* from their words for which it is to be concluded that the plan of galloping in sweaters and afterwards scraping, now fallen out of date in England, would have mightily pleased them, if there had been any one to show it to them. The old heroes and their riding cattle, whether camels or horses, are always described in verse as being lean to meagreness.

[4] To this day good judges of Arabs say that one which carries his tail askew in galloping is but middling.

[5] Naturally this suggests that the chase must have been like that of the hog in India, in which the hunters ply the spear or sabre at close quarters. But a native authority says that it is an allusion to an old Arab custom of marking the courser's throat with the blood of the game which has been run down by him. If so, bows and arrows may have been used.

[6] *I.e.,* the Ká'-ba. Whether the circumambulating virgins of the old Mecca cult were devotees of the Hindu type — daughters of song and pleasure — or ritualistic processionists, like those of the Greeks, or mere successions of worshippers, is uncertain. A special costume, at least, seems identified with them — white robes of extraordinary length. To this day the pilgrim, when he approaches Mecca, is bound to exchange the garb in which his sins have been committed for one or more clean cotton sheets through which no needle has passed. A very ancient people survives in Babylonia (v. Index I., art. Sá-bá, f.n.), whose priests, or Magi, wear a white stole, and white turban, while engaged in sacred offices.

[7] *I.e.,* who has plenty of relations to give him presents.

And the bustling cooks spent the night in boiling, broiling, roasting, stewing :
And we broke up : and one's glance went near failing by the side of him, when the eye looked him all over, up and down :
And he stood all night with his saddle [1] on him, and his bridle ; and he stood all night in front of me, not turned out.

—Im-ru 'l Kais.

Three things, according to the Eastern saying, are from God : a good wife, a good horse, and a good sword. In the horse of the foregoing verses, one of the three is exhibited. Horses in poems do not always resemble those in real life, any more than those in advertisements do. If any sanguine reader were to search Arabia for a phœnix answering to Im-ru 'l Kais' description, he would probably discover that such is rarely bestowed on any one in this life; while he who has one does not sell him. But the passage cited shows that nearly 1400 years ago, or about the time when the Romans were leaving the "abject Britons," as Hume calls them, to manage their own affairs, the Najdian sportsman, if he did not find him every day, had some experience of the stamp of horse which he should look for : a strong craving galloper ; fast enough to "put shackles on"—that is, run into the wild creatures of the desert ; as big under one as a house ; with a great back and loin, deep ribs, the propulsion from behind of a catapult, and withal perfectly in hand. The praising of a horse because of his saddle slipping off him sounds strange in European ears. But the meaning merely is, that his back was of the "double spine" pattern which Virgil also held up to admiration.[2] The primitive Arab saddle, from its softness and free and easy girthing, does not sit firm. The rider's legs help to keep it in its place ; and one reason of the Bad-u's not using stirrups is that he may freely roll off,—perhaps with his arms round his mare's neck—and be on again in a moment. The first time that an Arab horse has an English saddle properly girthed on him, he is apt to lie down with colic after going a mile or two. It is not the hind-legs alone that form the "propellers." Thighs [3] like an ostrich's, or as we say a game-cock's, running into great broad

---

[1] The word for *saddle* here is, not *lbd*, but *sarj*, *q. v.* in Index I.

[2] "At duplex agitur per lumbos spina."
— Georg., lib. iii., line 87.
A backbone along either side of which, from the fulness of the dorsal muscles, two ridges run, having a deep furrow between them, called by the Arabs a *ta-rī-ka*, or *track*.

[3] Anatomical names and those used by horsemen do not in every case coincide. The horse's thigh-bone is concealed by the muscles of the hind-quarters; as his *humerus*, or true arm, is by those of the chest. His "thigh" is our "calf"; in certain feathered bipeds, "drum-stick." His hock is the human ankle—having the Achilles tendon running into the point of it (or *cacls*) or "heel."— Man being the only animal whose heel rests on the ground. Similarly, of course, his knee (*carpus*), or part that gets "broken" when he comes down, answers to the human wrist. Above the knee is the long forearm (*radius* and scarcely traceable *ulna*); below the knee, the shank or cannon, representing the middle bone of the five metacarpals which support our palm. In the pastern, coronary, and coffin bones of the veterinarian, the joints of our middle finger are present. If we would inquire about our other digits, we must go to the anatomist. A glance at the hoof shows it to be simply a thickened and marvellously adapted nail. The Arab horseman does not apply to all fours his word for *legs*. Only the parts between the stifle and the ground receive this name from him ; what we call the *fore-legs* are with him the *hands* or *arms*.

hocks, are not so common that we can afford to pass them over. But the true-made weight-carrying runner always has a good middle-piece. Some think that the biceps muscles of the rowers send the racing boat through the water; but the trainer tells us that without the right sort of back, strength of arm is wasted. The name *Al maj-ma'* given by Arab horsemen to the place where the loins run into the hind-quarters contains the same idea as our word *coupling* or *couples*.

The identification, scientifically, of the several wild animals which are mentioned in the old Arabian poems requires more knowledge of zoology than we possess. But evidently, the game afoot in Im-ru 'l Kais' description was a troop of those ox-like antelopes, connecting links between the antelope and the ox families, of which the gnus of S. Africa, and the nyl ghau, or blue ox, of India are representatives.[1] In the verses themselves the object of the chase is merely called a *herd*; and the word which we have rendered *heifers* is applied by the Arabs to the females of numerous ruminants, both wild and tame; and figuratively even to women. Every shade and detail of meaning would be seized by the audience in a moment. There is nothing to show that hawks or hounds took part in the run; but in a contemporary poem—in which, by the way, the object of the chase receives no other name than *the untamed one*—there is a picture of how the hunters[2] slipped a couple of hounds with drop-ears and spare bodies. One of these was called Kâ-sib, or Caterer; and the other Su-khâm, or Soot. Just where the bard abruptly changes his theme, to begin a rhapsody about his camel, both dogs have been struck dead by the infuriated animal's spear-like horns.

Such is the Bedouin horseman; and such are some of the ways of the Arabian desert to which we owe the Arabian horse.

---

[1] Such were the male and female *asi-dhî-ha*, the latter "resembling a little cow," which Doughty saw in Amîr Muhammad's garden at Hâ-yil (vol. i. p. 592). He calls the *asi-dhî-ha, Antilope Beatrix;* and suggests (same vol. p. 328) that it may be the *rîm* of the Hebrew Scriptures, which is rendered in the Greek version *unicorn*. Of course it was a mistake to ascribe a single horn to a double forehead; and in Deut. xxxiii. 17, the horns, not horn, of the *rîm* are spoken of. Nevertheless the identification of the *asi-dhî-ha* with the *rîm* is doubtful. Mr C. J. Lyall, we notice, accounts the "wild kine" of early Arabian poetry, *Antilope defassa;* and the "deer" of the same literature, *Antilope leucoryx* (*Transl. of Ancient Arab. Poetry*, p. 117). A wild animal is mentioned seven times under the name of *rîm* in the Biblical books. But in Arabic and Assyrian literature also there is a *rîm*; and unless the Hebrew usage of the name differed from the Arabic, it is probable that the *rîm* of the Bible and the *rîm* of Najd are identical. Many in I'râk apply the names *rîm, gha-zâl*, and *dhaby* loosely to several different kinds of antelope; but both in speech and literature we find the cervine antelopes, of which, according to this view, is the *rîm*, well distinguished from the bovine antelopes, of which is the *asi-dhî-ha*, or *bah-tha*. Zu-hair says:—

There sweep by, troop after troop, the large-eyed ones, and the antelopes;
And their younglings rise up from every coucking-place:

in which the *large-eyed ones*—I'n (*een*)—may be the *wild kine;* while the name in the second clause is *â-râm*, pl. of *rîm*. Similarly La-bid (600 A.D.) in two succeeding lines seems first to mention the cervine, and then the bovine, antelope:

(In a certain favourite spot:—

The tops of the wild-rocks upsoar. In the two sides of the valley the antelopes [*dhab-y*] and ostriches breed:
And the *large-eyed ones* that have just brought forth lie intent on their young—their young collecting in herds on the plain.

[2] The word rendered *hunters* has a root suggestive of *archery*. The hearers would know whether the hunters were *archers* or *spear-throwers*, mounted or on foot.

CHAPTER IV.

HORSE-BREEDING AMONG THE SETTLED ARABS.

HERE again hard-and-fast lines are to be avoided. In many localities the townsman breeds from every horse or mare to which it has pleased any one to attach a pedigree. In towns like Hâ-yil, coloured through and through with Bedouin manners, or Der, a kind of house-of-call, as seen above, for the northern Ae-ni-za, the beliefs and prejudices of the desert in respect of horse-breeding are in every mouth. Partnerships in a mare between a nomad and a townsman are common, and form one of the ways in which Arabia's best blood continues itself outside of the desert. But, broadly speaking, the town and village bred division is more remarkable for diversity than quality. Little and often, is how a Turkish Pâsha likes to have his hand softened; and when no ducats offer, he will accept a mare or a colt from a candidate for his favour. Every peasant works with mare cattle; and a mare with foal at foot costs no more to keep than a barren one. Many a great horse of the Indian Turf, if we mistake not, has owed his birth to a drudge whose shoulders were sore from daily labour. From Mosul to the end of the Arab promontory, to own a "bit of blood" and breed from her, forms the ambition of multitudes. All this keeps up a great growth of horse-breeding. It is the fashion with many to express a high disdain for all horses which do not come straight from the Bedouin; but it is possible to carry this too far. We do not dispute the pre-eminence of the pure-bred desert horse. In his highest forms, he is to his half-and-half relations what our thoroughbred is to hacks and carriage cattle. But nature never gives to any breed, any more than to any individual, the combined excellences or qualities of all. The right saddle needs to be put on the right horse. It is *breeding* that makes the Clydesdale and the racer alike excel in their respective tasks; but the same illustration shows how essential it is that the work and the breeding should be conformable.

The varieties of horsemanship to be seen outside of the desert are as numerous as the differences of class and breeding in the horses. If the settled Arabs broadly represent one stratum, and the wandering another, the modern superstructure consists of the Osmanli. For the most part, these are sorry objects on a horse. But there are many exceptions, especially among soldiers. We know a commandant of artillery who is at once a finished horseman and a highly artistic coper. Colts of his training would pass muster even at Vienna. Nor should reference be omitted to countrymen of our own engaged in commerce in towns like Baghdad and Damascus, who, being light-weights and sportsmen, keep buying, or even breeding, colts and selling them. A cavalry officer in India or Egypt who chances to buy as a charger one that has passed through hands like the above may find himself to his surprise, the first time of mounting, riding a very well taught one. Tuition of a different sort is that of the numerous predatory hill-men, masters from childhood of every volt in Eastern horsemanship, who enrol themselves, with their horses, in the mounted police, to ply their natural calling in the Sultân's name. When sent hither and thither to squeeze the dues of Government out of reluctant Arabs, these worthies seldom fail to take back as their private property—often as the price of saying that they could not find the person wanted—a nice colt or filly; which, after riding it for a year or two, they turn into money. Thus they form great purveyors for the jam-bázes: and their duty takes them into places over which it would never pay professional horse-buyers to travel.

English and other European saddles, also Turkish, Circassian, and ornate Persian ones, are used in towns; but the commoner road or travelling saddle of the settled Arabs is more or less like this—

SADDLE (*serj*) OF THE ARABS AND KURDS.

The saddle on the preceding page was made at Su-lai-ma-ni-ya, a Kurdish town of eastern I'rák, which is famous for articles of this description. In some respects, perhaps, it has a hint to offer to our military saddlers. The covering is of felt, with only a few strips of leather added; so that it needs but little cleaning. It rarely sustains injury when the horse lies down and rolls while it is on his back. Owing to the wooden tree being so arched, the weight of the heaviest man fails to bring it down on the spine and withers. It straightens the rider, and throws him on his fork, thereby saving the horse's loins. The great objection to it is its weight, which is about two stone. It also too much raises the rider, and puts him out of touch with his horse's frame.

The *khur-jen*, or wallets, which hang across the saddle of our sketch, were made in Der. According to an Arab saying, the horseman's saddle-bags are his larder.

The stirrup which hangs from the saddle of our cut is of the useful, not the ornamental, pattern. They who study appearance ride out in stirrups of this shape—

STIRRUP (*ri-káb*) OF THE PERSIANS, KURDS, AND TOWN-ARABS.

On gala occasions like the *zaf-fa*, or marriage-procession, these show well. In real riding, they render unnecessary jointed stirrups or spring-bars; for the foot cannot remain in them after the seat is lost. Their sharp angles serve as spurs. *Gens d'armes* in particular have a way of feeling the horse's flank with a stirrup-corner at every step. This is said to be what makes their horses such uncommonly brisk walkers. But the property of the smart town stirrup thus to hurt a horse's sides accounts for its non-appearance in the above-sketched saddle—our seat over many an unmeasured mile of desert—the gilded shovels proper to which were exchanged with a muleteer, much to his surprise and delight, for the dingiest pair of irons in his collection. Other advantages of the quieter article are that no one mistakes it for precious metal; and when one goes among the Bedouin, it is not so suggestive as the other is of the rider's being a Beg, or official person. Arabia can have no clans so backward as those found by certain travellers on the coast of Africa who refused gold coins, and accepted gilt anchor-buttons, in payment for their cattle, because the buttons had eyes, and the guineas had not! But several times we have perceived a Bad-u scratching hard at a Whippy's stirrup, to find out whether it was silver: and once, on alighting among the Salga, a squalid, outlying sept of the Ae-ni-za, in a military cloak with gilt buttons, it looked as if we might be followed and plundered for the sake of what no one doubted was gold! Speaking of this, we are not unmindful of the objection to disguises already stated: but the professing to be what one is not[1] is one thing, and the making of one's self a gazingstock is a different thing. As far as personal safety goes, in northern Arabia, where the danger of molesting a European is realised, that plainest of all advertisements of the Frank, the stiff-brimmed helmet — so evidently not intended for prostration — forms the best passport and protection. But it has its drawbacks; and it is best for the traveller as far as possible to discard all garments and articles of equipment which too much savour of Europe. A saddle will pass, provided it be Eastern; or if European, taken from a lumber-room: for the Bedouin know that townsmen cannot mount without a half-way foothold. But as for such utensils as tubs and basins — inventions, by the way, for enabling one to perform his ablutions in polluted water— the view in the desert is, that they who carry them have too much money. Once on the Euphrates, when journeying à la Arabe, it befell us to have every article with us, except what was on the person, overhauled by a ring of Bad-us, while we were supposed to be asleep. First, the honest gelding munching his ration with the end of his rope in our hand engaged them; but the secret of him was soon talked out. Next, they

---

[1] The above view apart, it is as difficult in many localities to keep European clothes in proper trim as it is to replace them when they get worn out or stolen. Thus, in travelling once from Baghdad through Persia to Muhammara by the extremely mountainous Pusht i kûh route, we nowhere found a smoothing-iron. He who puts on a Bond Street shirt with all its particularities hanging limp, or a nicely cut white patrol jacket wrinkled and distorted past recognition by Bakht-i-â-rî washing, is apt to think that a suit of native pattern and material would be preferable. In the frontispieces of *A Pilgrimage to El Medina and Mecca* (1857 edit.); *A Pilgrimage to Najd* (1881); and *Early Adventures in Persia, Susiana, and Babylonia* (1887), three travellers so dissimilar as Captain (the late Sir) R. Burton, Lady A. Blunt, and Sir H. Layard appear before their readers in the costumes of those with whom they mixed. But of the three it was the first alone who did so with the object of escaping identification as a European; and small blame to him, considering where he went. The second did it from fancy, or convenience; and Sir H. Layard for lack of other garments. With all this, our countrymen should remember that in the East even more than in the West great men are expected to be great dressers. Especially in Persia and India, he who affects simplicity in this respect will, if unknown, be simply taken for a pauper; or, if known, for a naturally uncivilised person.

fastened on a cane of the species native to the hill-ranges of Southern India, which for hard hitting beats even our ash plant; but nothing was to be learned from an article which pilgrims and others have widely distributed. Finally, the thin hands found occupation over an enamelled iron flask, cased in a felt jacket. Cold tea, it so happened, was the strongest liquor which this had ever held; and equally its mouth and cork proved dumb witnesses. The motion that it was "a mother of brandy" seemed nevertheless on the point of being carried; when the greatest talker among them confidently asserted that it was a powder-horn; and a powder-horn it was voted.

Mares, as a rule, need nothing more to hold them when ridden than the Bedouin halter; but a bit of the kind known in Europe as the Mameluke[1] is used when necessary. The sketches which are here presented show that, while a piece of rope or string may serve for reins, the Arab townsman's bit is not a slight one.

Saddled and bridled more or less as has been shown, the colt bred in villages or oasis-homesteads makes his *début* at a fantasia, or *fan-tás*,[2]—a kind of circling exercise, with or without the flourishing, or sometimes throwing, of the *ja-ríd* or lance, in which townsmen delight, while the Bedouin, in their love of the real thing, sneer at it. A horse more for show than use, or, as we say, "a band-stand horse" or "peacock," is called by the Bedouin, and would-be Bedouin, "a horse of the *fan-tás*"; or perhaps a "horse of the *zaffa*," *i.e.*, one only fitted to carry a citizen in a marriage procession. It forms a pretty sight when, outside say of Ku-wait or Der, between the afternoon and evening prayer-call, a *fan-tás* is held. The striplings begin it, and by degrees it spreads. The greybeards poise their *bá-ká-ras*, or riding-canes, and join in it,

"In mazy motion intermingled,"[3]

charging, wheeling, shouting. The faster the pace, the more their spread-eagle style of horsemanship shows itself. Here and there, one may see a cavalier with a seat as stiff and upright as a school-rider's—perhaps from his having spent some winters in Bombay, or even ridden gallops after his own fashion on Indian coursers. But most Arabs seem to think that the further they lean forward, the more they help the horse that carries them; like a gentleman rider of former

---

[1] The introduction of this bit, name and all, into England may date from the Crusades. In the Turkish body guards which were formed in Egypt under the successors of Saladin, every man was a *mam-lúk*, or *piece of property*; and in this way the famous Mameluke Sultans and Beys passed into history. As for the bit, its proper place is a museum. Its tendency to make a horse throw up his head instead of giving to it may be the fault of the rider; but the jaws which it produces in the flesh under the lower jaw are enough to condemn it.

[2] The explanation of a word owning a common Greek root with our *fancy* thus appearing among Semites is its having spread with the Aristotelian vocabulary.

[3] Shelley, in *Queen Mab*.

CHAP. IV.   HORSE-BREEDING AMONG THE SETTLED ARABS.   131

ARAB HORSEMAN'S BIT AND BRIDLE.

days famous for his long proboscis, who, when he won on the post, as he often did, and "M—— by a nose" was the judge's verdict, used doubly to enjoy the joke. In watching a *fan-tás* of Arabs, their draperies all a-flutter, and their bodies swayed in every direction, one wonders that the mares so seldom fall, and the riders so seldom tumble off. *The horseman's grave is always open*,[1] is one of their sayings; but badly as their horses' joints, especially the hocks, fare in these exercises, accidents are rare.

Another feature of Arab life, both settled and nomadic, which bears on Arab horse history, is the royal sport of hawking. In Arabia and Persia, the ancient union between horse and hawk and greyhound is happily still unbroken. On arriving after mid-day in a Bedouin encampment, one may find that half of it is sleeping; and that the only inmate of the Shekh's coffee-tent is a *saqar*[2] or falcon. Townsmen spare no pains to procure these birds from nests in far-off mountains. When cool mornings show that the summer heats are over, the work of training begins; and the sport enlivens the short days of winter. Antelope and bustard (with Arabs *hu-bá-rá*) are the game flown at. When the gazelle is sighted, and the bird cast off, a brace of greyhounds is slipped. Behind them goes the field, over the dead level, as hard as ever it can clatter; mostly one man's friends or servants; mounted on seasoned, not to say screwed, mares, with a sprinkling of colts added. By the end of the season, these latter have either gone to pieces or galloped themselves into shapely youngsters, in which every point is developed. Such of them as suit the market are then snapped up by the jam-bázes; who, after a course of stall-feeding, with just as much exercise as will keep them from breaking their halters and kicking down the walls, take or send them to Bombay. One of the many sights savouring of antiquity in towns like Baghdad and Mosul is a Persian Agha or native Bey riding out a-hawking, followed by two or three generations of his progeny, and a tail of picturesque falconers and henchmen.

Thus the Arab horse may have a good deal of work slipped into him, apart from the Bedouin and *Al ghaz-u*. If village-bred, perhaps he will be sold when he can carry a saddle to some one who will not let him stand idle. In foal-hood he will have enjoyed his freedom round the homestead; trotting after his dam when she is ridden on a journey; developing bone and muscle; and becoming familiarised with sights and sounds when he is too young to mind them. Unfortunate exceptions are the colts dropped in towns from mares received as presents

---

[1] "*Kab-ru 'l khail-yll maftúh.*"
[2] The Semitic word *sakr*, a species of falcon, must have passed with the art of hawking from Asia into Europe. The Italians wrote it *sagro*, and we *saker*, which name also came to mean with us a small cannon.

by Pàshas, Na-kibs,[1] and other personages too exalted to care for them till it is time to turn them into money—the one thing which no one ever seems too preoccupied, or too well off, to consider. Not even in India do the collections of amateur breeders on the "cabined, cribbed, confined" system contain more light-boned or "sinew-tied" horses than may any morning be seen in Baghdad, in scions of Arabia's finest strains, when the grooms are riding a Pàsha's stud to water. Partly by this want of "timber," and partly by the skin-diseases which run riot in all such overcrowded and tainted stable-yards, the town-bred horse is recognisable.

And thus we see, not only that the climate of Arabia favours the development of a horse of the galloping type which is associated in Europe with the name of *blood*, but that the life of the people tends to stamp their stock with the characteristics proper to a saddle-horse. True, to qualify their horses for the title of *pure* saddle-horses it is wanting that they should have been bred *scientifically*—that is, through the exclusive mating, during many generations, of those individuals whose excellence in this respect had been proved. But admitting that the Arabian is not a *perfected* saddle-horse, yet he truly is a saddle-horse. He and his progenitors have been that from a very early period. However much he may be used in agriculture, or as a pack-horse, such work only comes into his life by way of interlude or accident. The horses which the Arabs employ in servile drudgery are not of one breed or class more than another. One sometimes sees harnessed to a well-rope[2] a friendless and forgotten waif, in whose skin the large full veins stand out like the fibres on a vine-leaf, and which has only to be mounted to show the Najdian mettle. Everywhere under the sweltering Eastern sun—in Egypt, Arabia, and India—where fast work, in saddle or harness, is exacted by the masses of the people from their horses, it surprises Europeans how very much better to go than to look at the commonest hacks are. Horses such as in England would pass into the kennel copper are to be seen in the East carrying their owners or their servants, perhaps a-hawking, perhaps on distant journeys; when they tumble down, rising again; and when they give in at last, needing but a few days' rest and barley to restore them. During a recent journey we bought, on an emergency, at a road-post of the military police of the Osmanli, an I'ràki Galloway, which, but for an uncommonly good

---

[1] Etymologically, the Arabic *na-kib* and Latin *quæstor* are not far apart in meaning. In the early Islamic commonwealth the *Na-kib's* functions resembled those of the Roman magistrate. Later, the same officials had for their *raison d'être* the inquiring into the pedigrees of, and superintending, all who claimed exemption, as descendants of the Prophet, from ordinary jurisdiction. Now their principal occupation seems to be the administration of lands devoted to pious uses. Thus, the Na-kib of Baghdad is hereditary warden (*mu-ta-wal-li*) of the tomb of Shekh Abdu 'l Kàdir, Gilèni; cynosure of all the Sunnite Muslim equally of Central Asia, Afghànistàn, and India.

[2] *V. ante*, p. 47.

shoulder, was by no means built for weight-carrying. Use, however, is second nature. In several respects he had suffered through carrying, before his bones were fully formed, a gendarme, whose saddle was always loaded up with property; but he was better served by his defects than many horses are by their perfections. At any rate, he proved capable of walking nearly five miles an hour, and marching all day, under fifteen stone, without tiring. European travellers in the East, when they are choosing horses for a journey, should always look out for such as have been working. Last year an officer of the Simla "Intelligence" Branch, who was leaving Baghdad for Persia, bought in the town a so-called roadster; and after the first march, one of the poor animal's fore-hoofs came off! We never could find out how it had been put on.

MOSQUE NEAR BAGHDAD.

BOOK THIRD

GENERAL VIEW OF THE ARABIAN

CHAPTER I.

THE ARAB'S LOVE OF HIS HORSE.

N old writer describes the imagination as "that forward delusive faculty ever intruding beyond its sphere; of some assistance indeed to the apprehension, but the author of all error."[1] However imperfect this view of the illumining power may be, it is one which receives frequent illustration in lands of the rising sun, whereon is the seal of antiquity; and especially in Arabia a veil of glamour frequently comes between the European traveller and real objects. They who would cut down like grass every ancient tradition which does not rest on historical evidence, may perhaps consider that in several places our "delusive faculty" has thus been captivated. But in the preceding pages on Arab men and Arab countries, it has at least been our object to separate fact from fable. And it is probable that the same process will have to be carried a great deal further in the sequel.

The fictions which content the Arabs as to how their breed of horses originated will appear in due season. Just now we would speak of the modern European idea that the Arab horse is connected with the Arab religion. Two facts are here present which must neither be overlooked nor made too prominent. One is, the demonstration of the value of cavalry which the period of the Flight afforded to the Arabs; and the other, that wherever the Kur-àn was carried it promoted the multiplication of horses. In this part of the Arabian structure layers of distinctively Jewish material or tradition are absent. According to Wellhausen, the name *Israel* means *El does battle*; and it was foreign to the ideal of Jehovah's army to trust in an animal which in Biblical times was very specially regarded as the embodiment of strength, and the "Father of Victory." In Deut. xvii. 16, the breeding and the importing of horses were equally forbidden. Moses' lieutenant and successor, Joshua, after defeating the five kings of the Amorites near Gibeon,

---

[1] Bishop Butler, in *Analogy*, Part I., ch. i.

"houghed their horses and burnt their chariots with fire" (Josh. xi. 9).[1] The Prophet and leader of the Arabs adopted the opposite policy in this respect at once in civil and military affairs. We find Cromwell, on one occasion, writing to his Auditor-general that "if a man has not good weapons, horses, and harness, he is as nought."[2] And injunctions of the same practical tenor occur both in the Prophet's 'Sayings' and in the Kur-ân. Among the former is that which occupies the place of honour on our title-page; and its meaning is, though it has many variants, *Weal is knotted in the forelocks of horses till the day of judgment*. The following three passages of Al Kur-ân will serve to show the reader how the one book used in Muslim worship—the first, and in millions of cases the last and only, text-book of Muslim children—tends to make the Arabs horsemen. Taking first a "revelation" of the militant species, we find this direction issued, in S. viii., from Medina, for the employment of cavalry to defend the rising Arabian commonwealth:—

> And set against them all that ye can of force,
> And of pickets of horse [on the frontier];
> Whereby ye shall make afraid the enemy of Allah,[3] and your own enemy;
> And others besides them, whom ye know not;—God knoweth them.

Elsewhere (S. xvi.), in an enumeration of God's works, it is brought to mind how

> "[He] hath created for you horses, mules, and asses, that ye may ride on them; and for ornature."

While in a third and more rhetorical passage, which is much admired by the Arabs, to give intensity to a denunciation of man's ingratitude, God is made thus to adjure the Horse:—

> By the hard-breathing chargers—
> The spark-compelling strikers of fire—
> The forayers at daybreak—
> When they stir up the dust,
> And charge home into a collected number—
> Verily Man is an ingrate towards his Lord:
> Ay, and he knows it!
> And truly his love of worldly weal has waxed strong.
> Wots he not, when there shall be brought forth what is in the graves;
> And made manifest what is in the breasts;
> Surely his God on that day shall know him.
> —S. c.

The first time that the writer heard the second of the above pieces quoted was in a coffee-house on the Euphrates, in which a light-hearted horse-dealer was edifying

---

[1] Nevertheless David, the second king of Israel, whose genius was imperial more than tribal, after smiting the Zoba', to this day a Euphrates nation, and capturing 1700 horsemen and 20,000 footmen, took the opportunity of equipping a small mounted force. The account of this in 2 Sam. viii. 4 (revis. vers.) indicates his having "houghed all the chariot horses, but reserved of them for an hundred chariots."

[2] Quoted by Captain Nolan in his book on Cavalry.

[3] The primary reference is to the Mecca recusants, who had not as yet submitted to the Prophet.

his friends with the interpretation, that two sorts of horses had been made— one for work, and the other for ornament; and that it was every one's own concern to see that he did not buy the wrong article. Only one or two of the people around approved of this, and a serious greybeard exhorted the speaker to "repent and fear Allah"; but what chiefly struck us was that the passage cited failed to include the Camel. When the quotation was verified, it appeared that, in the previous text, the ancient beast obtains recognition under the general name of *cattle;—carriers of your loads to cities which ye could not otherwise reach save with wearied bodies*. In the earliest times referred to in the oldest existing literature, the camel was used equally for riding;[1] in the caravan trade of the "Ishmaelites" with Egypt;[2] and in war:[3] but in antiquity, as now, its prominent function was that of travelling packman. As for the Ass, the East is not of one mind about him. Al Kur-án, while thus in one place bracketing him with the Horse, in another (S. xxxi.) divulges that *the most hideous of sounds is his braying*. The Bedouin Arab, as has been seen, despises him, and will hardly return the good-morning[4] of one who is riding him. But in numerous oriental cities, notably Damascus and Aleppo, a long-eared ambler is a favourite mount both of the religious and the mercantile classes. Steeds of this kind are so easy and amenable, that their owners are apt to form unreasonable expectations. Thus, a Muf-ti once commissioned a dealer to procure for him a brisk she-ass, which he might leave unexercised from one Friday to another, and nevertheless find, when mounted, perfectly staid and contented. The man's answer was, that if ever it should please the Almighty to transform a person of learning into a donkey, he would buy the animal for his Reverence; and his words deserve to be remembered by those of our countrymen who are always asking their friends to help them to find ideal horses. The Mule also is largely bred by the Kurds and the agricultural Arabs; but the latter prefer to sell him than to use him. One great object of Arab hatred is a Persian; and another is a Kurd: the former because he goes so dangerously near worshipping A'li; the latter, because he is held to be a savage.[5] If the elephant belong to Buddhism, and the cow to Brahmanism, similarly the Arab horse may be claimed by Sun-nite, and the mule by Shi-ite, Islamism. The stream of time has distributed among the Arabs a tradition that the Chaldeans attempted to burn Abraham;[6] that mules carried the firewood; and that their sterility forms the punishment! In the Arab biographies of the Prophet, it is men-

---

[1] Gen. xxiv. 61. [2] Gen. xxxvii. 25. [3] Isa. xxi. 7.

[4] In Arabic, *Sab-ba-ha-ka 'llah bi 'l 'khair;* lit., *May Allah morning thee with good.* It is only between Muslim that the greeting of "Sa-lám" (from the same root as Islám) mutually passes.

[5] Arabs say, *The Kurd, even if a Wáli* (Governor), *is still a bear.* Nevertheless, many of Islam's great doctors have been natives of Kurdi towns like Kar-kûk, Su-lai-má-ní-ya, and Arbil.

[6] In Hebrew *ur* means *fire*. The Rabbinic tradition that the Chaldees cast Abraham into the fire, like Shadrach and his two companions, and with the same result, for "dissent" from idol-worship, suggests the reading of *ur* in this sense, and not as a place-name, in Gen. xv. 7 (v. *note*, p. 111, in Ch. 2). The same representation is not unknown in Eastern and Abyssinian Christianity. Al Kur-án (S. xxi.) has further diffused it.

tioned that he prized and rode a white mule which he had received as tribute from the Roman Governor of Egypt. On the other hand, it is related that when a second mule was presented to him, and A'lí wished to breed another like it, he expressed the opinion that no one who possessed understanding would propose so unnatural a cross! But to return. Wherever Muhammad's words are current, a halo surrounds the Horse. In the heart of Abyssinia, among the Muslim Gallas, we have heard Mullas telling how God honoured him, by swearing an oath upon him. European readers probably think all this very trivial; and in order to understand its limits, two series of facts already glanced at must be recalled: one, that the Arabian breed was perfected long before Muhammad, so that the Arabs when they made their first grand entry into history were already horsemen and sons of horsemen; the other, that Arabia is by no means so religious a country as many imagine. As touching townsmen, Muhammad's ordinances—if we except the five daily prayer-calls, and the fast from sunrise to sunset[1] in the month Ra-ma-dhân—follow the lines of human nature. In regard to the Bedouin, it has been noted how the artificiality of the Islamic structure, its adaptations or compromises, and above all, the nodules of paganism which are embedded in it,[2] made the nomads view it as a putting of new wine into old bottles—a thing for townsmen, not for them. All this is perhaps scarcely enough allowed for by foreigners. Indian Muslim think that the city of the Ku-raish—one of the few places in the world where the only God-name that is heard is Allah—must be like a gate of Heaven; but when the pilgrim caravan deposits them there, the laxity of Meccan morals surprises them.[3] According to a well-known proverb, it is darkest under the lantern. With the important exception of the open sale of spirituous liquors being prevented, the "Holy City" is as secular as Bombay. But the nominal headquarters of the faith, and its covetous spendthrift inhabitants, are peculiar in this respect. Towns of El Islâm which do not live on the piety of pilgrims produce, as a rule, a considerable growth of sanctity of their own. The grip which the Kur-ân has of the great body of the people well supports the title which has come down with it of the "Prophet's Miracle." The volume itself, in every household fortunate enough to possess a

---

[1] The words are: *And eat and drink* (i.e., during the hours of darkness) *till, by reason of the daybreak, there be distinguished by you a white thread from a black thread: then keep the fast till night.*—S. ii.

[2] Even so the Pope's instructions to the first Archbishop of Canterbury provided that heathenism should not be abruptly broken with; and that the existing temples should be used for Christian worship. Few sensible men think the less of Christmas, as a Christian festival, because several of its customs point to the old pagan worship with which the feast was first associated. Many other, and more important, observances of Christendom represent a carrying over and adaptation of earlier usages.

[3] This reference to the corruption of manners in Mecca does not rest merely on the late Sir R. Burton's description, which is now 40 years old. At the present time, the accounts of Turkish and Indian pilgrims amply confirm it. Since the decline of the Ku-raish, the city of the Ka'ba has been growing less and less Arab. Even its more or less fixed population is full of foreign layers.

copy, is wrapped in a cover, to guard it against unworthy contact; and when not in use, reposes in honourable separation on a little wooden stand which is specially made for it. The Book is appealed to on all occasions. The shopkeeper, when he removes his shutters, sits down to pore over it, or makes his little son recite it, till the day's traffic and custom begin. The Governor of the province, when not of the reforming and absinthe school, places it near him in his divan, atop of all the newfangled codes and circulars of his Government. Old and young, rich and poor, saint and sinner, reverence and quote it as the Word of God in Heaven. Hence it follows that attachment to horses assumes for townsmen almost the character of a religious virtue. In General Daumas' work on the Arabs in Africa, it is stated that the Amír A'bdu 'l Kâ-dir, when at the height of his power in Algeria, inflicted death on every Muslim who was convicted of selling a horse to a Christian. It is likely that religious fervour, combined with oriental sentiment, had a share in this policy. But next to a full treasury and a martial population, a copious supply of horses ranks highest among the elements of a non-maritime nation's strength. At this day the Sublime Porte is too easily moved by the representations of its officials to try to stop the export of horses. But we never knew an Arab who approved of this arbitrary action; and even the Wah-hâ-bis of the central districts embark their money in the Indian horse trade.

The recurrence of the name Wah-hâ-bi, or, as we shall write it, Wahábi, suggests that it may be well to qualify the general facts of the Bedouin's coldness towards Islamism by bringing out a little further the puritanic social organisation which was founded in Arabia, ten centuries after Muhammad, by A'bdu 'l Wah-háb.[1] This too was a Muhammad, whose birthplace was in the heart of Najd. His full name was Muhammadu 'bn A'bdi 'l Wah-háb; but, according to usage, he is known by the paternal part of it. His followers bear the designation of Wahábi. In vivid personal piety, rigorous application to study, and devotion to the theocratic ideal, he was another Calvin — a Puritan, or purist, who believed that he had found the original creed and way to heaven. Yet must this name Puritan, like every other term which is transplanted from one religion to another, be applied with caution. Few now believe Puritanism to be the pure ore of Christianity. And, similarly, although the Damascus doctors have pronounced Wahabyism the true Is-lám,[2] it is best, at least for Europeans, to regard this as doubtful. Long ago, in the capital of Scotland, an eminent Hebraist used to tell his students that "Calvinism was Jehovahism." Precisely so, the Wahábí says that Wahabyism is Allahism: the un-

---

[1] *A'bdu 'l Wah-háb* means, *Servant of the Great Giver.*

[2] We cannot give chapter and verse for this decision, but learned men in Baghdad quote it: also Prof. Kuenen, of Leiden, at p. 51 of his "Hibbert Lectures" for 1882, on *National Religions and Universal Religions.*

adulterated worship of the Only One, as Muhammad preached it. Passing from this, however, among the visible features of A'bdu 'l Wah-háb's system are, antagonism to secular rule; and the putting down of saint-worship, as of every other practice which tends to approximate the created to the Creator. In Baghdad, a proverb runs that for every noble horse which neighs, a hundred asses set up their discords; and the same thing happens in religions. To make a Wahábí, it needs some approach to A'bdu 'l Wah-háb's mastery of theological learning, and some slight infusion of his rare and elevated qualities, matured by long travel. It is outside the scope of our volume to open further the slight views of Wahabite history which have appeared in other contexts.[1] In again referring to the half-religious, half-military despotism which A'bdu 'l Wah-háb, and his princely convert, the first historic Ibnu 's Su-ú'd of Du-rai-i'-ya, founded, we wish but to speak of its influences on nomad manners. It would be wrong to suppose that the essentially Arabian elements which entered into the Wahabite government made it palatable to the Bedouin nations. Its power, when at its height, was as centralised as that of the Turks; and it was supported by taxation and a standing army. The mere fact of its being a "Government" was enough to set all those against it who loved the natural manners of the desert. True, the leaders of the movement were Bedouin, mainly of the Ae-ni-za; and its fortunes depended on the prowess of Arabian Shekhs. But these were the players of the game, or their followers—the throwers-in for the spoils and prizes. The masses of the Arabian nomads clung to their traditions. Hordes of them migrated, so that Wahábí became another name for Najdian marauder, as far north as Mosul. Even then, in Najd itself, tribal jealousies brought about numerous openings in Wahabyism. Had this been otherwise, Turkish and Egyptian mercenaries, with all their hammering, would never have succeeded in breaking it. As for townsmen, except in a few districts, the Wahabite yoke sat even more uneasily on them than on their brethren in the open. A cudgelling at every lapse from strict religious practice was felt to be too high a price to pay for purity of doctrine. Owners of houses and orchards could hardly disappear like Bedouin. Their only safeguard was conformity; but very many, according to Burckhardt, sold their mares rather than follow the Ibn Su-ú'ds. The Wahabite system was as rigorous in small matters as in great. It was not enough to sack, or lay in ruins, every tomb at Mecca, Kar-ba-lá, and Medina, the Prophet's included, round which, through the offering of gifts and vows to the departed, something like polytheistic cults had formed.[2] Absolute authority, against which no appeal was possible, enforced the

---

[1] V. p. 30, ante, f.n. 2; cf Book I., chap. 3, passim.
[2] The Prophet said, Do not pray towards tombs. Following Knox's maxim that "the best way to keep the rooks from returning was to pull down their nests," in 1801 a Wahabite army not only cleared Husain's tomb at Kar-ba-lá of all "idolatrous" relics, but regularly demolished it; at the same time that the town was plundered, and its male inhabitants slain.

outward signs of piety. All amusements were tabooed. In order that the dress might be in keeping with the sanctimonious long-drawn visage, the wearing of silk, or ornaments, or gay clothing, was prohibited. In such matters as public prayer, and the observance of the yearly fast, the reins were drawn very tight. At Ri-ádh, the capital, and other towns, maintained for this purpose a machinery resembling that of Geneva. Elders[1] patrolled the streets on Fridays when the mosques[2] were full, attended by slaves for the prompt castigation of loiterers. These inquisitors entered every home, and even claimed the right of intruding on the A-mir, and advising him, as John Knox did Queen Mary. The theocratic organisation was developed to an extent unknown in Europe, where there always is a separate political administration with which the clergy, or congregation, have to reckon.[4] So far as this went, they who lived by their right hand in their own wildernesses might laugh at it when the news reached them. The desert contains no sacred edifices into which men can be driven. The features of the Bedouin are naturally grave. Even in their summer feasts, when their boys are circumcised by wandering barbers, and the chorus-chanting maidens put on feathers and bright kerchiefs, their gaiety is that of people who live on milk in various

---

[1] Called locally MUTAWA-I-AIN, or exactors.

[2] In Arabic, *masjid*; lit., place of *prostration*. Masjid is the generic term for a house of prayer. The sanctuary to which (in Arabia, chiefly in the Summer body) the people resort, *congregationally*, especially on Fridays, is called Al-Já-mi' (short for *Al Masjidu 'l Jámi'*, i.e., *Mosque which collects men*).

[3] Scotland once enjoyed similar advantages. In Chambers's *Traditions of Edinburgh* (1847 edit., p. 31) we read: "It was in those days" (about 1733) "a custom to patrol the streets during the time of divine service, and take into captivity all persons found walking abroad, and indeed make seizure of whatever could be regarded as guilty of Sabbath-breaking."

[4] "Two high points of Wahabyism, namely, "conversion" through conquest, and the repudiation of rulers who fall short of the theocratic ideal, tend to give political interest to the question of whether this is Al Islám, or a misinterpretation of it. The final authority—Al Kur-án—explicitly announces that *Allah does not lay on any man's conscience the duty of attempting that which is impossible* (S. ii.) Accordingly, all moderate authorities are of opinion that, *in certain circumstances* and *with certain important limitations*, a Muslim people may, and must, submit to a Government whose faith is not their faith. Similarly, the precept which enjoins Pilgrimage is made conditional on the possession of the necessary means

or ability. In regard to propagandism, the fact has too much escaped notice that Al Islám has, from the first, protected Christians, and other "people of the Book," on the easy terms of their ceasing to fight against it, and paying tribute. The keynote is, the noble text in S. ii., *Let there be no compelling one to do a thing in religion*. It is perfectly true that utterances apparently of a different tenor were put forth later, notably in Sú-ra ix.; but such were directed against the public enemies of the Arab empire,—those who neither had embraced Islamism nor submitted and paid tribute. Muhammad's Sú-ras cover about twenty-three years of momentous Arabian history, and in order to understand them, it is necessary to study the situations out of which they severally arose. Due allowance must also be made for the tendencies of human nature, especially under the excitement of campaigns and conquest. But, on the whole, the Muslim annals abound in bright examples of toleration. In Spain, when the success of a mere maritime *ghaz-u* from the opposite coast of Africa opened the country to Mú-sà, *ibn* Nusair, and his lieutenants (A.D. 711), the indulgence shown to Jews and Christians was, for that period, remarkable. In India, under its Muslim emperors, the Hindus held high office. At this day the Hyderabad Government builds, or helps to build, places of worship for its Christian employees; which is more than we do for our Muslim ones.

forms, or on bread dipped in melted butter; and rarely partake of animal food. But there was one thing in Wahabyism which the Bedouin hated, and that was its intolerance of tobacco; perhaps because considered an intoxicant, perhaps merely as a superfluous "fleshly indulgence."[1] If the black juice of the Mocha berry is as his life's blood to the nomadic Semite, the smoke of his pipe is as the breath of his nostrils. Truly, when one is staying with him, it looks as if, in his lazy dreamy tent-life, tobacco served him in lieu of other sustenance.[2] In vain does the strict Wahábi apply to this favourite herb the epithet of *Al Makh-zi*, or *the execrable*. No sooner is a Bad-u seated in a company, than he pulls out a little bag in which is a clay pipe-bowl; or perhaps, as he depends for that on pedlars, a substitute in wood or bone of his own carving. If no one offer to supply him, a pinch of the drug is next produced, and then a short wooden stem; though frequently the *sa-bil*[3] itself is put to the lips. What the wine-cup is in European poetry, the pipe-bowl is in the unwritten song-book of the Arabs. *Come fill up the pipe with the tobacco of*—— this locally celebrated vendor or the other, does duty in the tents of the nomads for the lyrics about "mantling cups" and "purple wine" which permeate European literature.

The fact of Wahabyism, in spite of its rigours, having so upreared itself in Arabia is as remarkable as it is apparent. At first from Du-rai-í'-ya, and afterwards, when an Egyptian general had laid that in ruins, from the new capital, Ar Ri-ádh, the light of A'bdu 'l Wah-háb's lantern spread over spaces till then unclaimed by Islamism. One consequence of this has doubtless been to place the Horse on a higher level than ever in the estimation of the Arabs, as a means of giving force and wings to armies. But more to our present purpose is the effect which, as seen already, the wars between the Osmanli and the Wahabis had, in transferring to other countries large numbers of the best mares in Najd, partly as the spoil of military officers, and partly with their emigrant owners.

Out of this view of modern Arab history there even comes an illustration of

---

[1] Here again Scottish Puritanism furnishes an analogy. Lockhart says in his *Life of Sir W. Scott* (vol. i. p. 312). As a "Presbyterian of the old school, ... Scott's father ... was habitually ascetic in his habits. I have heard his son tell that it was common with him, if any one observed that the soup was good, to taste it again and say, 'Yes, it is too good, bairns,' and dash a tumbler of cold water into his plate." In Wahabyism, the prohibition of tobacco does not stand alone, but extends, as has been seen, to other articles not less innocent than a basin of good soup.

[2] The following 17th century verses show that amid all the ups and downs of tobacco, and the fulminations and penal enactments which have been levelled against it, the sedative effect which it produces on the stomach has long been known in other countries than Arabia:—

"Much meat doth gluttony procure,
To feed men fat as swine;
But he's a frugal man indeed
That with a leaf can dine.

He needs no napkin for his hands,
His finger-ends to wipe,
That hath his kitchen in a box;
His roast-meat in a pipe."

[3] The pipe-bowl, or *sa-bil*, is called *baz* in the speech of the Bedouin.

what a small place the world is; or rather, of how the events that happen in it depend on one another. The three patriarchal and immortal horses of English Turf history, the Byerly Turk, Darley Arabian, and Godolphin,[1] were exported either before A'bdu 'l Wah-hâb was born or before he began to preach. The only one of them whose lineage has ever been established, the Darley, was bought,[2] as has been seen, in Queen Anne's reign. But without going so far back, it is easy to name valuable Arabians that have found their way to Europe in the present century, because of the troubled condition which prevailed down to a recent period in inner Arabia. Take, for example, Dervish, one of a group which is depicted in a future chapter. Sidney's *Book of the Horse* contains the following history of this genuine son of the desert, from the pen of his owner, Mr George Samuel:—

"Dervish was taken in a skirmish between the troops of A'li Pâsha of Baghdad and some of the Wahabis in the Najd country. A friend of mine, General Chzanowski, was in the affair; and A'li Pâsha made him a present of the colt, then a yearling. The General was attached to our Embassy at Constantinople. He brought Dervish and an Arabian mare of the Aeniza breed back with him. I purchased them and sent them home in 1842. Eventually I sold Dervish to Count Lavish, a German nobleman. The horse died in 1863, having been the sire of about 300 colts and fillies."

And now to bring together the results which have been arrived at. Notwithstanding the impulse given to Islamism by the Wahabite "revival," the Arabian nomad has to a great extent remained outside of the current. The mare which none can rival confers so many benefits on him, that town lore cannot add to his appreciation of her. What the cleverest collie is to the Cheviot shepherd, gives but a faint idea of what his mare is to the desert pricker. The only instance known in Scotland of a dog which helped his master to increase his flocks by transferences from those of others ended tragically — that is, at the end of a rope — both for the biped and the quadruped. In Arabia, many a one will want for milk and wool and mutton, sooner than he whose mare is always saddled. The owner of a Derby winner and first favourite for the great St Leger does not cast so great a shadow, as he does on the superiority of whose mare the safety of the flocks and herds depends. For her sake he may be asked to marry an orphan's

---

[1] *V. ante*, p. 138, f.n. 1.

[2] By Mr Thomas Darley, agent of an English mercantile firm at Aleppo. In 1705 the colt was sent from Aleppo, as a present, to John Brewster Darley, Esq., of Aldby Park, near York, a brother of the gentleman who had bought him. The letter which accompanied him expressed a modest hope that he would "not be much disliked" in England, seeing that he was "highly esteemed" at Aleppo, and such as could have been "sold at a very considerable price." The *Sporting Magazine* for December 1823 contains an account of the horse, with his portrait. To verify the latter, we had a copy made of the original painting still hanging in the hall at Aldby; and the copy thus obtained perfectly corresponds with the likeness which the *Sporting Magazine* gives. Another reproduction of the same old picture appears in *Portraits of Celebrated Race-Horses*, by T. H. Taunton, M.A.; Sampson, Low, Marston, 1887; vol. i. p. 1.

ten score camels; as, in other countries, one may marry lands and houses. If he rear a colt from her, he is everywhere received with consideration because of his horse; and his own kindred will not, if they can help it, let him leave them. Under any circumstances, the desert gallant experiences the keenest pangs when he is forced to surrender his mare as a prize to a better-mounted adversary. But if he have

"Nursed the pinion which impelled the steel,"[1]—

that is, if his own tents produced the stock which has got the better of him,—his plight is that of him who is beaten in the Derby by a castaway from his own stable. There are no hundred-guinea sires in Arabia. The prizes of the turf and sale-ring are needed for that. It is said that there exist, among the Bedouin, primitive peoples who are satisfied with a lamb as stud-fee; but wherever we have been, less Arcadian payments have been current—not large sums, but still *coin*.[2] A couple of shillings are much thought of by those who buy hardly anything beyond dates and bread-stuffs, coffee and tobacco, and, when the opportunity offers, ammunition. The Bedouin Arab is one of those who think little fishes sweet; and as no limit is set to the number of mares among the desert horse-breeders, and a colt's powers may be called on while he is still a yearling, the owner of an approved horse makes up for the smallness by the frequency of his receipts. The effect of this on the breed, and on the individual, is but little considered by the Arabs; whose opinion goes no further than that the earlier a colt begins to cover, the sooner he will be a horse! One consequence of every celebrated horse, whether young or old, sound or unsound, thus earning a little income, is that the prices which are asked and obtained in the desert for pedigree animals are apt to run high.

In regard to non-Bedouin Arabia, what we have seen is this. In the establishments of the great, horses mark their owner's rank and wealth, mount the followers, and round off the pomps and vanities. In the sheds of the humble, they reveal the irresistible bent of the Arabs to tie a mare beside them, however limited their spaces may be. Mullas praise the horse, for their Prophet's sake; travellers, because he carries them; cultivators, because he promotes their husbandry; and jam-bāzes, because the means of subsistence and foundations of wealth are "in his forehead." In a word, in settled, as in pastoral, Arabia, innumerable endearing associations of war and love, chase and journey, toil and pleasure, centre in him.

---

[1] Byron, in *English Bards and Scotch Reviewers*.
[2] The reader will understand that this statement applies exclusively to the desert. In towns, every owner of a horse of reputation feels that he can hardly refuse his services, and it would be considered a shame to receive payment.

CHAPTER II.

FOREIGN ESTIMATES OF THE ARABIAN.

UP to this point we have been chiefly occupied with the Arabian Horse in countries where he is regarded as the work and gift of Allah, which neither needs nor admits of improvement. But the time has arrived to consider another series of facts. The same breed commands almost an equal degree of admiration wherever it is known. The horse of nations with whom the world, if ever it was young, still is so, and for whom the "long results of time" are traditional and unwritten, is sought out by the most civilised Governments for the improvement of their studs and the expansion of their empire and resources. Several of the greatest generals of modern Europe have shown a strong preference for Arab horses as chargers. In the courtly circles of Persia and India, this is the horse which is prized above all others. The point is, what do these familiar facts imply? Is the Arabian abroad a genuine good thing or an illusion? Is it his merits that have thus distinguished him, or chiefly his oriental associations, and the circumstance that no one knows exactly where he comes from? Such are the questions which next await us; but first, it may be well to notice what has been said by others, both in favour of the Arabian breed and in depreciation of it.

The praises of Arabians by their owners which occur in popular books require to be received with abatement. Not only does admiration come more naturally than fault-finding, but the authors of such passages have frequently been literary persons, without any very wide experience of horses. This applies to one of the prettiest and most frequently quoted references of the class alluded to—that in which, in his *Narrative of a Journey through the Upper Provinces of India* in 1824-5, the amiable Bishop Heber commended his Arab riding-horse.[1]

No ancient or modern Church can bear comparison with the Church of England

---

[1] E. 1828 edition, in two 4to vols., of the Bishop's *Narrative*, in vol. ii. p. 319.

in the power of producing excellent preachers and parsons, who are also horsemen; but the author of "From Greenland's icy mountains" represented a different phase of clerical life. There can be no question that, for one whose seat is not well down into the saddle, the Arabian is the pleasantest and the safest of all the *chevaux de luxe* of the world. No one can be called a coachman who has never handled rougher teams than gentlemen's ones,—never worked a coach, stage after stage, and grappled with them as they came—bolters, bo-kickers, and all sorts of reprobates. And neither should one whose equestrian experiences have been confined to Arabs make too sure that he is a horseman. While noting this, we would not be thought to suggest that the *clientèle* of the Arabian is, in any considerable degree, formed of men who are not exactly centaurs. A far larger class of his admirers, in which are many of the strongest riders in the world, consists of those who, when they are in the saddle, have other things to think of than horsebreaking. An adjutant-general or an aide-de-camp, whose charger is given to "sticking up," as it is called, under the saddle, cannot perform his duty. We know as well as any one that Arabs also are sometimes difficult to ride. Even the gentlest have their little ways, especially with the timid; and we have known a few which would give any man an uneasy half hour, when it was inconvenient to treat them to all that they required to sober them—a right good gallop. But, as a rule, horses of this breed, when asked to go in one direction, do not insist on going in another direction, or fix themselves on their forelegs and curl up like hedgehogs. Their worst tantrums, compared, for example, with the sullen humours of the Australian buck-jumper, remind us of the "*Amaryllidis iras.*" If one or two of the many splendid Arabs which the late Emperor of the French collected had been reserved for his ill-starred son, the Prince Imperial, the fateful moment in Zululand would not have found him struggling with his charger.

It should also be remembered that, ever since Great Britain took charge of India, the Arabian horse has enjoyed extraordinary opportunities of shining in the public service. India has been surveyed and settled, not by the Englishman alone, but by the Englishman and his horse. Important divisions of its cavalry armament—notably the Lancers of the Nizam's country and the Central India Horse—obtain a large number of remounts from the Arab horse-marts of Bombay. In the brief but difficult campaign of 1856 in Persia, the straight swords and Arab horses of the Bombay Light Cavalry demoralised the Shah's forces. Chargers from the Euphrates have carried our soldiers to Candahar and Cabul, to Pekin and to Magdála. More recently, in Burma, where it is extremely difficult to keep foreign horses healthy, the cavalry of the Hyderabad Contingent added to the high reputation which it inherits.[1]

---

[1] An officer of the 3d Lancers, Hyderabad Contingent, informs us that in Burma ninety of his men kept constantly on the move for nearly three months "without a single sore back, and with but one or two slight girth-galls."

It would have been surprising if, in these and other ways, sentiments of admiration for Arab horses had not been produced in Englishmen. We all hold by what has served us. We may not treat or reward it properly, but at least we try to keep it. A general officer who is appointed to command an expedition forms his staff, as far as possible, of men who are known to him, and delights in seeing his batteries and regiments led by old comrades. An amusing illustration of the length to which this feeling may be carried was afforded by Horace Walpole, who believed so firmly in James's powder as to declare that, if ever his house was on fire, his first act would be to take a dose of it! A passion for Arab horses is not like that; but when it leads an Englishman to paint his Arab in colours lent by his imagination—or if, by chance, he possess a phœnix, to write as if the whole breed resembled him—then, "Save me from my friends!" may well be said for the Arabian. The principle of reaction, a great safeguard of moderation, at once comes into play. When Mr Blunt went to Newmarket, "to preach," as he relates, "at headquarters the new gospel of Arabia to the elders of the sporting world," a fine old Trojan confided to him that, if the Arab horse "had any merit, he had got it from certain thoroughbred sires imported to Arabia by Newmarket sportsmen at the time of the Crusades."[1] It is not every one who has the wit thus to turn the tables on an opponent. But many an Englishman considers that, however suitable the Arab steed may be to the half-famished Bedouin, he will sooner or later break the neck of the well-fed European; and that his value appears truly, if dolefully, at Tattersall's, when a horse which may have cost a thousand guineas fetches perhaps about the same number of shillings! The mention of Tattersall's brings before us what a despiser of Arabs the late Mr Richard Tattersall was. When the Najdi horse above referred to as taken from the Wahábis arrived in London, he would not even go to look at him. Nevertheless, on accidentally meeting him, the old man had to declare that he was "the finest blood-horse of the size he had ever seen."[2] Saul among the prophets! The diversity of opinion which prevails among practical horsemen on the subject of the Arabian will be apparent if we here insert the two following extracts. The first is from Sidney's *Book of the Horse*; and Mr Sidney informs his readers that the writer of it is "one who has been engaged in dealing in the best class of horses all his life—who has bred horses, trained them, ridden them on the road, in the field, and over the steeplechase course; driven, bought, and sold them; who is as much at home in the horse-world of Spain and France as of England." This expert states his view of the case as follows:—

---

[1] *Op. cit.* in Catalog. No. 14, p. 735.
[2] *Op. cit.* in Catalog. No. 25, p. 153, where also a famous hunting man and breeder of horses says of Dervish that "he had the most beautiful darting action that I ever saw in his trot—the knee quite straight long before the foot touched the ground."

"Do I like Arabs? No. In my opinion they have not one point to recommend them for use in England in which they are not excelled by our own thoroughbreds. They are, with very rare exceptions, very bad hacks; they cannot walk without stumbling—in fact, they are always stumbling; they have no true action in either trot or canter; they are slow in their gallop, as compared with any well-bred English blood-horse. They are too small for hunting, or for first-class harness; and cannot race with common English platers. All I ever saw were so formed, with the croup higher than the withers, that they rode *down hill*.

"When I was living in Spain, a very great personage, for whom I had procured some high-class Spanish parade-horses, presented me with two Arabs of the highest caste—purchased without limit as to price, in the neighbourhood of Damascus—a black and a grey. They were as handsome at first sight as any picture of Arabs that I ever saw; about 14 hands 3 inches high; very temperate to ride, with great power in their hind-quarters; but wanting that slope in the shoulders, and that proportionate length, breadth, and power in motion which are essential to make first-class riding action.

"I was living in Spain at that time, and had English thoroughbreds and half-breds, Spanish mares of the *carnero* or Don Carlos breed, half-breds between the English blood-horse 'Kedger' (by Colonel Anson's 'Sheet Anchor') and Spanish mares. These Arabs, which had cost, perhaps, not counting political influence, £1000 a-piece, were inferior in hack-action, and as hacks, to English or Spanish horses of one-tenth the cost. I rode the grey with a pack of harriers I kept; he was an unpleasant hack, and no hunter. I trained them both, and they were distanced by horses bred out of Spanish mares by my English blood-horse; finally, I put them to the stud, and their produce out of some twenty of my best Spanish mares were inferior in size, early maturity, and market value to the stock of my blood-horse.

"To sum up, Arabs are very bad hacks. They are too small for hunters even where, exceptionally, they have hunting conformation; too small and too devoid of elegant action for harness; and too slow for race-horses; as sires, they are inferior to the English blood-horses of power and symmetry which are to be purchased, when too slow for racing, at a less price than a high-caste Arab.

"The one quality in which Arabs excel, endurance, and which they share with Australian horses and Indian mustangs, is not required in civilised states, where travelling is either performed by railways or post-horses."[1]

As a weight for the opposite scale, the reader may take the following outburst of philo-Arabism, not by an Eastern veteran, but by a horseman at the Antipodes, whose book, *Pure Saddle-Horses*, has already been laid under contribution:[2]—

"About ten years ago," says Mr Curr, "I had many opportunities of seeing Arab horses in Syria, Turkey, the Holy Land, and Egypt; and before I saw them, I had already had some experience of the horses of England, France, and Spain, besides those of Australia and Tasmania; in none of which countries I had resided less than a year. I had also seen those of Greece, Italy, Flanders, Belgium, Switzerland, Turkey, and other places too numerous to mention; so that I may be said to have approached the examination of the Arab after having seen most of the best breeds in existence. . . . In all these countries I have ridden more or

---

[1] *Op. cit.* in Catalog. No. 25, p. 145.   [2] *Op. cit.* in Catalog. No. 39, pp. 123-130.

less; and had originally in Tasmania and Australia been so unceasingly in the saddle, that it is not to be wondered at that I acquired a habit of glancing my eye over every horse that came in my way, and involuntarily daguerreotyping his figure upon my memory. . . .

"Of Arab horses, though I have seen many belonging to Páshas and royal personages, to rich men and wandering Bedouins, I am not sure that I have ever seen one of the most esteemed castes. But, if not, I have seen many that had been purchased at respectable prices, seen many of them at work, and ridden a few of them. A gardener soon forms an opinion of a spade, and a woodcutter of an axe; and so, one who has lived in the saddle soon makes up his mind about horses. Mine, at all events, was not long in being satisfied. Instead of seeing anything to object to in the Arab as a saddle-horse—his size excepted—all that I did see, and all that I was enabled to glean concerning him in his native land, only led me the more decidedly to endorse the opinions of those numberless very competent judges who had gone before me. I never met a man who had tried him and did not like him. I found him in speed inferior to the horse of England; but in tractability, constitution, durability, soundness, abstemiousness, temper, courage, and instinct, eclipsing and surpassing all other horses that it has been my chance to meet with. In that quality so pleasing to the horseman, sagacity, I think he has no equal. Even half-breeds sprung from him are remarkable in this point. When in Syria, I bought a little horse which was no beauty, but had evidently got a good deal of Arab blood in him. He stood 14.2, and was six years off. I had him about three months, and rode him perhaps a thousand miles. He was never fed more than twice a-day under any circumstances. At sunrise his breakfast, which consisted of two double handfuls of barley, was given to him in his nose-bag. . . . Two hours after this, he was allowed about four quarts of water. Three hours before sun-down he was taken to water, and allowed to drink his fill. Two hours later ten double handfuls of barley, sometimes mixed with three or four handfuls of chaff, were given to him. Such were the habits in which he had been brought up; and such the amount of food which proved in every way sufficient for him, even when at work. . . . On this he looked as round as if he had eaten as much as our Australian horses are accustomed to do. For twenty days I rode him thirty miles a-day. He had 15 stone on his back—the country was mountainous and rocky, but he never made a false step, and I think he improved in condition. I never remember to have found him weary.

"His intelligence was quite beyond any single instance I have ever witnessed in an Australian horse. To say that he recognised his master, as one man does another, would hardly be doing justice to his sagacity; he rather seemed to recognise me as the detective does his man. If, as was sometimes the case, he was in a stable with a hundred others, where many persons would be constantly passing to and fro at all hours, he seemed to be constantly on the watch for me. My voice, of course, he knew at once. The sound of my footsteps seemed as familiar to his ear as was my appearance to his eye. He would greet me with his voice when I was several hundred yards from my tent.

. . . .

"Such is the Arabian horse. . . . I do not know where you will have to go to find such another! Such he is now, and if we may trust the accounts of old travellers, such he has long been; . . . and whilst we remember that he wants but two inches in height to be the perfection of horse-flesh (which want I firmly believe more plentiful food would radically supply in three generations), let us not forget his renown as a sire, his sure-footedness, docility, beauty, speed, abstemiousness, stoutness, and courage—where shall we find his peer? All honour to the little horse!

"Who will contradict me when I assert that no breed of saddle-horses has shone which has not possessed some strain of Arab blood? Who will show me that I am incorrect when I say that the virtues of European breeds are in exact relation to their affinity to the Arab!

"Who that has known the Arab has not preferred him to all other horses?"

The above two extracts may be said to represent the proverbial two sides of the shield. Our next undertaking will be to bring before the reader facts which may serve to illustrate those two sides respectively. But before entering on this task, let us plainly state that neither the one extreme nor the other will be upheld in the following pages. If a writer's qualifications fail to appear as he proceeds, his own recital of them will not avail him. Nevertheless, in here hazarding the opinion that the superiority of the Arabian branch of the family has been too much insisted on, our claim to practical experience may be stated. The author has spent the best hours of a long life in the saddle or on the coach-box. If all the Arabs which he has owned were to be paraded on the "further shore," a very respectable front rank and rear rank would be formed. He has marched, on horses of different breeds, from Annesley Bay to Magdála, and from Peshàwar to Cabul, as well as over large parts of India, Persia, and Arabia; having also for several years been adjutant of a cavalry regiment mounted on Arabs. If he had not found many sterling qualities in the Arabian, he would not have grown so attached to him; but that is a different thing from setting him on too high a pedestal. During the same period he has also owned many English and Australian horses. The result has been the conclusion just broadly stated; and it is proposed in the next two chapters to explain the grounds thereof.

CHAPTER III.

THE ARABIAN COMPARED WITH OTHER VARIETIES, IN RESPECT OF CONSTITUTION AND CHARACTER.

IT will facilitate the treatment of this subject if we deal with all the points in regard to which the Australian writer awards superiority to the Arabian. These points comprise, it will be noticed, every endowment, with the sole exception of racing speed, on which the horse's credit depends. They are —tractability, constitution, durability, soundness, abstemiousness, temper, courage, instinct, and sagacity; a goodly group, which, for the sake of making a division, may be classified as bodily properties, or *constitution* ; and mental qualities, or *character*.

CONSTITUTION.

This term is here used to express every quality which either helps to constitute, or is intimately connected with, soundness.

The fallacy of applying the epithet *natural*, as opposed to *artificial*, to the strains of the desert, has already appeared. In no other breed of horses is reproduction more effectually controlled and guarded by man than in the Arabian. The Arabs have no paddocks in which stud accidents may happen. The horse of unknown or unapproved pedigree which grows up among the desert folk, from never being allowed to cover, takes but little notice of the mares beside him. The stallions in use are kept so securely shackled, that stolen leaps are next to impossible. In this and other respects, the Arabian breed is broadly separated from purely natural races. But there are gradations in everything; and an unstabled variety, the native of a hot and dry climate, undoubtedly is more a product of nature than the horse of cold and rainy latitudes, which has been housed, and pampered, and physicked for many generations. As might be expected, both the respiratory and digestive organs are healthier in Asiatic than in

European breeds. Eastern horses admit of comparison with our Welsh and Exmoor ponies in this respect. The observation of ages points to hereditary predisposition as a factor in many diseases. The proof of this is rendered difficult in the human species by the action of modifying circumstances. When a *bon vivant* who loves fruity wines and French cookery declares that he has inherited gout from his grandfather, it is open to doubt whether his *chef* and butler have not more to do with it than his deceased ancestor. We know a lady who believes that a certain "churchyard cough," as she terms it, "runs in her family;" while the truth is, that, like her mother before her, she is foolish enough to be fond of an "airing" in an open carriage without sufficient covering. But in the lower animals, there is less difficulty in distinguishing between acquired and inherited unsoundness; and no practical man hesitates to affirm that, in respect of health and disease, as in so many other ways, the horse and mare live again in their progeny. It does not, however, follow that because the Arabian generally begins life with a good, sound, open-air constitution, he invariably maintains a clear health-sheet. Neglect, or mismanagement, particularly after hard riding, is apt to give him colic, which may subsequently recur from slighter causes. Coughs are perhaps even more frequent, though less hurtful, in eastern than in western horses. The Arabs say that it is lucky when the mare coughs, and the reverse when the riding-camel does so. Even when the cough is in the air-passages, permanent changes in the vocal chords rarely result from it. Wheezing, whistling, piping, roaring, are far from common sounds under the clear skies which are east of the Mediterranean. The only Arab "roarer" ever seen by us was a beautiful little horse which, owing to this infirmity, was unplaced every time he started on the turf. Professional opinion differed as to the cause. He was known to have been much used at stud in his own country; and it was conjectured that this might have affected him, as dram-drinking may affect the human larynx. But more probably the evil originated in the overstabling and over-feeding to which he was treated, directly after exchanging his own dry climate for the chilly Indian Deccan. Another colt which came with him contracted a cough that lasted till he died many years afterwards,—a stomach cough, possibly, seeing that it never did him any harm, but one with an extraordinary power of defeating the doctors. When he was picketed in the open the cough would leave him, but it always came back when he was re-stabled. Here it should be mentioned that those who take their ideas of the Arabian's soundness exclusively from what is seen of him in India, do not know the whole truth. As a rule, there is no better market than the home one for English horses. One that can both gallop and stay for two miles will fetch more money in Yorkshire than in Bengal. There never were so many races in England as now in which bad performers can be skilfully placed; and as numbers of our countrymen, honest fellows, would rather win money with a wretch at some obscure meeting, than lose it with a flyer at Epsom or Doncaster, a jade not worth its freight to a foreign port may excite keen competition at home. Abroad, the case is different. Except on rare occasions, no such prices are paid for Arabs in Arabia as those which prevail, for instance, in India; and this affords a fine field to the exporters. The disappointments which these men suffer when one after another of their selections is sent before an English veterinary surgeon in Bombay, only to be rejected for some defect unheard of by their great-grandfathers, produce a salutary effect on them. At first they blame themselves for not having offered a *bakh-shísh* to the "dochtor," as they call him; but gradually they discover that their best policy is to look for sound horses. Experiences which touch the pocket go home to every one. The tribes of Arabia also, on perceiving that the buyers who visit them object to certain defects, try to keep their rising colts as right as possible.

Returning from this slight excursion, let us search a little into the subject of the Arabian's lamenesses, beginning with *spavine*. This disease,—for a disease it truly is,—though recognised for at least two thousand years in Europe, and bearing a name in many Eastern vocabularies,[1] is unknown to the Bedouin, except at second hand, through soldiers, farriers, and jam-bázes. The natural consequence of this is that, from time immemorial, horses and mares having unsound hocks have been freely intermated in the Arabian desert. Principal Vet. Surg. Collins, in a paper read by him in 1878 before the United Service Institution of India, cites an instance in which a mare whose off fore-cannon bone had been accidentally broken, transmitted crooked fore-legs not only to her first foal, but, more or less, to every subsequent foal. But the Arabs still have much to learn on subjects of this class. They do not know that certain conformations of the hock favour the development of spavine, and that, apart from the question of whether there exist in horses taints akin to scrofula in man, having for one of their expressions the production of mischief in bone, ligament, and cartilage, unsoundnesses of the hock-joint, even when due to accident, may reappear congenitally. Their ignorance of these matters should prevent us from wondering at the prevalence of spavine in their horses. Many years ago we sent an Indian cavalry soldier to Shá-mi-ya to buy pedigree Arabians, and of the three which he brought back, two were spavined. More recently, while residing at Baghdad, we commissioned a dealer of Ku-wait to enter Najd and buy a few Arabs, or even one, of the class described by Palgrave in his book,[2] in which we then believed. The best of his selections was a desert celebrity, of many years' standing, with a large bone-spavine. Every year a considerable number of that

---

[1] In Northern India, spavine is called *cháp-ká*; and in Afghanistan, *chak-ka*.

[2] *Op. cit.* in Catalog. No. 7, ch. xii.

horse's stock had been passing into the Bombay market. This reminds us of how a fine old original, known to a past generation of sportsmen as Haj-ji A'bdu 'l Wah-háb, himself a Kurd, but the importer of very many first-class Arabians into India, used to declare that there was no such thing as a spavine, or that if there were, the seat of it was "the doctor's eye." It is true that veterinarians fresh from England, who do not understand the "roughness," as their more experienced brethren term it, of the Arabian's hocks, may see spavines merely in the natural fulness of the bony projections. But knowledge has made such progress in the coffee-houses of the town Arabs since Haj-ji A'bdu 'l Wah-háb's day, that the present race of jam-bázes, instead of disbelieving in spavine, illustrate the Persian proverb that "one who has been stung by a snake shies at a rope," or, as we say, "a scalded child fears cold water," in their anxiety not to overlook it. We have seen a Mosul dealer use a magnifying-glass to help him to compare the outlines of the two hocks, in a horse which he was examining. Baghdad possesses a family of jam-bázes, the blind and aged father of which, in his day a noted buyer, is always asked, in doubtful cases, to give his progeny the benefit of his sense of feeling. Whether the patriarch's palsied palm and fingers find out all that is expected of them is another matter, but the idea, at least, is excellent. If both hocks present to the touch the same surfaces and inequalities, then, probably, they are perfect.[1] Another oriental method of proving a hock is to hold up the limb in a flexed state, after which, if the horse halt on it when it is set down, he is pronounced to be spavined. But before the cleverest of the Arabs, even those who travel as far as Bombay or Cairo, can really know their horses' hocks, education will have to be introduced among them. In how far spavine interferes with usefulness is a question which is here foreign to us. Probably no two spavines are precisely similar in origin, situation, extent, and consequences. The celebrated Arab plater, Red Hazard, won many races while stiff from spavine. On the other hand, the spavined horse from Najd above alluded to, after galloping several thousands of miles under our 14 stone, in I'-rák, without failing, and subsequently, in India, keeping sound in the dry hot months, fell so lame from his spavine in the rainy season that he could scarcely walk. Climate or meteorological conditions may tell, it would appear, even on bony exostosis.

After spavine, one naturally speaks of that other disease of the bony framework, *splint*. All splints are not the same, any more than all spavines are. A

---

[1] The hand and the ear are as important witnesses as the eye when a horse is being examined. Once, at a fair in Northumberland, a blind gipsy was the first to discover that a horse was blind, from no sudden flutter occurring in the heart's action when one hand was laid on it, and a feint was made of hitting him with the other. The late Professor Dick of Edinburgh, when seated in his room in the Veterinary College, could often tell by the ear alone, on a horse being trotted past in the street below, not only whether he was sound or lame, but, if the latter, the peccant limb, and perhaps the cause of unsoundness.

splint close to the knee,—the *osselet* of the old farriers,—may, or may not, be perceived by the Arabs, but one which is lower down is more apparent. From Mosul to Bussorah, one may hear splint called *adhmu's sabk*—i.e., *the bone of outstripping*, or *bone of speed;* but there is no authority for this ridiculous term. Some wag of a jam-báz must have invented it, as part of a theory that a horse with a splint, or splints, is more valuable than he would be if he were sound![1] No doubt, in a horse of six years old and upwards, whose history is unknown, it is satisfactory that his fore-legs should exhibit symptoms that he has been used; but such symptoms should not be those of actual disease: and, moreover, idleness, not less than work, may be the "mother of splint." That is, when a horse has been too long in the stable, an awkward gambol may set up inflammation in the soft material which is placed, for a useful purpose, between the splint bones and the cannon, and the result may be the conversion of part of it into bone. The chief cause of splint—namely, concussion in galloping—is, of course, highly operative in the Arabian desert; but there are special causes, such as the friction of the iron shackles, and the interference of one limb with the other.[2] "Splints seldom hurt," writes Mr Day in *The Race-Horse in Training;* and similarly "Nimrod" stated, in *The Veterinarian*,[3] that he had "suffered very little from splint, and never remembered but one horse out of work from that cause." Mr Percival takes the same view in his *Hippopathology.* "The old notion," he observes, "is still very prevalent among unprofessional people, that splints often lame horses." It is maintained by him that "splint rarely produces lameness."[4] We dare say not, in England, where a tendency to throw out bony deposits is held more or less to disqualify for the stud, and where, from the first hour of a splint's history, careful notice is bestowed on it. But speaking of the horses which are bred and reared by the Arabs, we can only say that no unsoundness has caused us more disappointment than bone disease of old standing between the knee and the fetlock joints. Especially when the bony knot has been situated too near either end of the cannon, or on its posterior margin, it has proved apt to form a centre of inflammation and disturbance after fast work. Judging from the fact that the jam-bázes will not buy a horse with a splint unless they can get him very cheap, this defect must be pretty generally objected to in foreign markets.

---

[1] We have never heard the Bad-u call a splint *adhmu's sabk*. In the tents of Shá-mi-ya, they say *m'ishdāh*, a slight lengthening of the old Arabic word *m'ashdāh*, for which there is the classical authority of a verse of Al N'shá.

[2] Once, at Baghdad, a flighty Arab with turned-out toes hit one leg with the other towards the middle of the shank. A bony tumour almost immediately appeared, without lameness. This was treated for about a year, but it only grew larger. About the same time another Arab, aged, straight-limbed, and a good hack, chanced to throw out a splint. This splint, being but small, was left alone, and one day the horse knocked it clean off with the opposite fore-foot, as neatly as with a chisel.

[3] Vol. x. p. 64.

[4] Vol. iv. p. 258.

Ringbone[1] is much less common in well-bred Arab horses than in the large and fleshy legged breeds which are devoted to agriculture. The short and upright pasterns which invite it should be avoided, and the tyro must be careful not to mistake harmless rope-marks for it.

Passing from the bones to the tendons, *curb*, or *curve*, is the only unsoundness in regard to which any special features occur in the Arabian breed. It is well known that horses in which the hocks are of a certain shape are predisposed to curb. It further deserves wide publication that this class of hock, the "curby" or "sickle" hock, as it is termed, is so uncommon in Arab horses, that we comparatively seldom see in them the strain or injury of the sinew at the back of the hind-leg, below the hock-joint, which is called a curb. In 1876-77 we revisited England after a long absence, and one of the things that struck us was what a great start had been made in the United Kingdom towards breeding out those curby hocks, crooked fore-legs, and eye-diseases, which have come down as heirlooms from the days when horse-breeding was a lottery. Agricultural shows and the rejection of unsound animals had begun to connect the breeder's art with science. Perseverance on the same lines is perhaps all that is necessary for the attainment of perfection. We do not presume to say that foreign blood is wanted. Nevertheless in districts where bent hocks, combined with smallness of bone immediately below the hock-joint, are prevalent, the introduction of approved Arabian stallions for the use of the farmers would probably be found beneficial.

In pursuing our inquiry into the comparative soundness of the Arabian and other breeds, we next come to the Foot. The Arabs appropriately term all the parts of a horse from the knee downward his *a-sās*, or *foundations;* the basis of which, of course, is the foot. Different soils, we all know, produce different shapes and kinds of hoof. The ideal foot in the Arabian breed is that which strikes fire[2] from the rocky sides of Ja-bal Tu-waik, in Najd. But there are Arabian districts, such as the lower Euphrates mud-flat, in which feet of the opposite or spread-out pattern, often accompanied by very indifferent action, are prevalent. Between those two extremes, hoofs of many different forms appear; and the primitive farriery of the Arabs is also a very great factor. The shoer's art lies outside of our proper subject; but there are certain facts connected with it, as it is practised by the Arabs, which it may be as well to mention.

On the one hand, life in the open, the absence of roads and of road work, and the freedom of motion which the mares and young stock enjoy even at their pickets, are very favourable circumstances. On the other hand, Arab shoeing certainly does not tend to assist nature.

---

[1] *Ringha* of the Turkish farriers.   [2] Isa. v. 28.

At the outset a fact of some interest has to be noted, and that is, that both the nomadic and the settled Arabs, equally with their Turku-mân, Persian, and Afghân neighbours, are strongly impressed with the necessity of shoeing their horses. An Indian horseman of the old school once observed to us that an unshod horse was no better than a donkey, while a shod one was like a lion; and evidently the Arabs are of the same opinion. It is true that very many unshod mares, and very many whose shoes have been left on, without a remove, for several months, may be seen in the Bedouin nations; but this is merely a feature of the general deficiency which characterises these people. Metal, as has elsewhere been noticed, is scarce in the desert; and the Arabs do not know how to use horn as a substitute for it, like the Icelanders. No Arab of the desert will handle farrier's tools, or marry his daughter to one who does so; and the inferior people who attach themselves to the tent-cities as shoeing-smiths are often absent. None the less, the shoeing of the mares is reckoned a most important preparation for Al Ghaz-u. We know that the ancient Arabs, in passing over very rough ground, protected their horses' hoofs with leather thongs;[1] in the same way that, in similar circumstances, they still protect the soles of the riding-camel with a leathern *na'l* or sandal.

The only horse-shoe which the Arabs use is of the pattern on the following page.

A glance reveals that the oriental *na'l* is no mere rim, but a sheet of metal. Including six nails, it weighs from ten to twelve ounces. A blacksmith makes it, and a farrier buys it and puts it on cold. Thus, there is not so much as a pretence of fitting the shoe to the foot. The farrier, when he has chosen a shoe, proceeds to cut and rasp the foot before him as if it were a piece of wood, to bring it more or less to the form of the iron. There could not be stronger evidence of the natural vigour of the horse's foot, in many Eastern countries, than its power of adapting itself to this treatment. Even in the most sound-footed European horses which possess any claim to speed or breeding, but a small percentage, we rather think, could bear such shoeing. If the iron plate were to be put on tightly, with the nails close together and brought out high up the crust, lameness would follow. If it were to be lightly tacked on, it would soon fall off. The shoe of our illustration has this in its favour, that it tends to give the horse a bearing on his whole foot, and not only, or mainly, on his toe; but the process of preparing the under surface of the hoof for it involves the cutting away of vital parts. The common name with many of the Arabs for the horse's frog is *ma-ya*—an Aryan word meaning *matrix*, or *essential principle*. He who first applied this term to the part in question must have had some idea of its functions. Similar indications are not wanting in the practice of even the most ignorant of the Arabs. For instance, in the towns, all

---

[1] The authority for this statement is the third poem in the Diwân of 'Urwa. *Ibid.* F. W ard.

horses and mules which work on roads, and even the donkeys of the water-carriers, are shod: but the ponies which draw water are used with their feet in the natural state, because it is found that otherwise they slip. And in the desert, when the mare is shod, one hind-foot is always left without armature, to give it the firmer hold

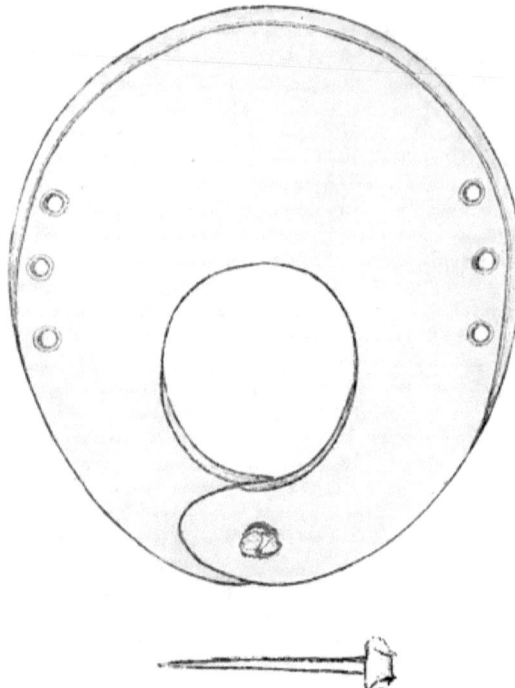

THE ASIATIC NA'L, OR HORSE-SHOE.

of the ground in the wheeling movements of the *mêlée*. With all this, the drift of the Arabs' farriery is towards the destruction of the foot's natural surface, the frog included, and the substitution of a plate of iron. Hence, when one of their horses casts a shoe, the animal goes as tender as a man who, for the first time, walks out barefoot. And when a pebble works in at the central opening in the shoe, it sets the horse a-limping, like the pilgrim with the unboiled peas.

It follows from all these facts that, notwithstanding the natural soundness both of the horny box and of its sensitive contents, in Arabian horses there is no part which demands more careful scrutiny by the intending purchaser. He who has bought an Arab colt with flat soles and a brittle crust, will derive no comfort from being informed, when cracks and vacuities ensue, that such defects are rare in Eastern horses.[1]

When a horse is lame in one fore-leg, and the cause is not apparent, stablemen commonly say that he is "shoulder-tied," or "chest-foundered." In the rare instances in which the lameness depends on rheumatism, or on accidental injury of the deeper-seated parts of the shoulder, this opinion may practically be right; but in nine cases out of ten the foot, and not the shoulder, is the seat of the evil. At least this is the case in England, but it may be doubted if it is equally so in primitive countries. The compactness of the foot in the Arabian breed seems to diminish its tendency to suffer, through sympathy, when inflammation attacks the respiratory or the digestive organs. The old school of veterinarians entered "chest-founder" or "body-founder," as distinguished from "foot-founder," in the list of horse diseases, but we do not know how far their views are now accepted. It is necessary to make allowance for the effects which different ways of treating horses, in different countries and at different periods, produce on their diseases. In Arabia, horses are still liable to be ridden till they drop, by the Bedouin and others. Very often, mares which founder—that is, tumble headlong—in Al Ghaz-u, with the lungs or some other important internal organ in a state of acute congestion, die where they fall. Those which recover generally remain, at the best, stiff in their action, with a tendency to fall lame after a longer or shorter course of fast work. This subject is so full of interest to all buyers of Arabians that, trusting to the reader's indulgence, we shall here introduce a little narrative serving to illustrate it. The facts about to be detailed relate to the bay Arabian race-horse whose portrait appears in this chapter. In 1861 the living animal became ours, as a five-year-old, soon after he had been brought from Ku-wait to Bombay by one of the jam-bāzes. His price was £300 down, with certain provisos, which subsequently increased it to £500. The cause of its being so hard to buy him was that, although he was as yet untrained and untried, many good judges considered, from his blood and his style of moving, that he might prove, as he actually did, the

---

[1] The grey Arab racer, Hermit, could not be trained during his first two years in India, owing to that fact. Another very highly bred Arabian, of the same colour, was comparatively useless all his life because his forefeet were too "shelly" to retain a shoe. The chestnut Arab, Raby, ran in many races with an iron band riveted round a fore-foot in which was a sand crack.

winner of the greatest prize of the Bombay turf the following season. When we bought him, as also when, long afterwards, his portrait was taken, he was as fat as Shrewsbury brawn, as they say in Shropshire. There was as great a difference between what he looks like in the picture and his appearance when drawn fine by training, as between the block of marble freshly lifted from the quarry and the same piece after the sculptor has chiselled it. At the same time, he was not of that very noble type of the Arabian which people take for their ideal. One consideration which induces us here to present his portrait is, that the reader may see a good game Arab of the class which may fall to the lot of any one. But to our tale. At the time of purchase he was passed sound by a veterinary surgeon. After he had been taken to the Deccan, on his shedding his winter coat, the marks of rowelling became perceptible on his off shoulder. This was startling; but it only showed that, in some unknown country, he had been considered lame in the part in question. In the course of the summer and autumn he did a sufficient amount of strong work without falling amiss; and on December 5 was to make his *début* in a two-mile race, for which a very good Arab plater was the favourite. By nature he belonged to what trainers call the craving kind, and ate the more the harder he was worked. Having had it impressed on us early in life that fleshiness is certain to stop a horse in a long race, when the pace is true, we gave him that last gallop which breaks down so many candidates, and for want of which so many others had better have been kept in the stable. He pulled up sound after it; but when he walked out in the evening—that is, less than twenty-four hours before the saddling-bell would ring—he was lame on the off fore-leg, with "nothing to be seen." The limb was kept all night in very hot water. In the morning he appeared sound, and in the afternoon won his race. In the course of the next few days he ran four times, and was only once beaten. After the meeting was over, it became necessary to determine whether he should be prepared for his great engagement, the "Dealers' Plate," in Bombay, for which seventy-three Arabs, all of the same year's importation, stood entered. Apparently he walked sound, but a few runs in hand at the trial pace of trotting showed that he was lame on the off fore. A veterinary surgeon of the Royal Artillery, after several examinations, gave the opinion that he had navicular disease; the same "sprain of the coffin-joint," in regard to which the first Englishman who wrote about it concluded by observing that "where one horse happens to be really lame in the coffin-joint" (in which the navicular joint is included), "it is mistaken a hundred times in practice."[1] The new light which has been thrown on this subject by later investigators was, of course, before us. Nevertheless, we were presumptuous enough to imagine that, even if the navicular disease was not confined

---

[1] *No Foot, No Horse*, &c. &c., by Jeremiah Bridges, Farrier and Anatomist: 1752. Quoted in Percivall's *Hippopathology*, vol. iv. p. 132.

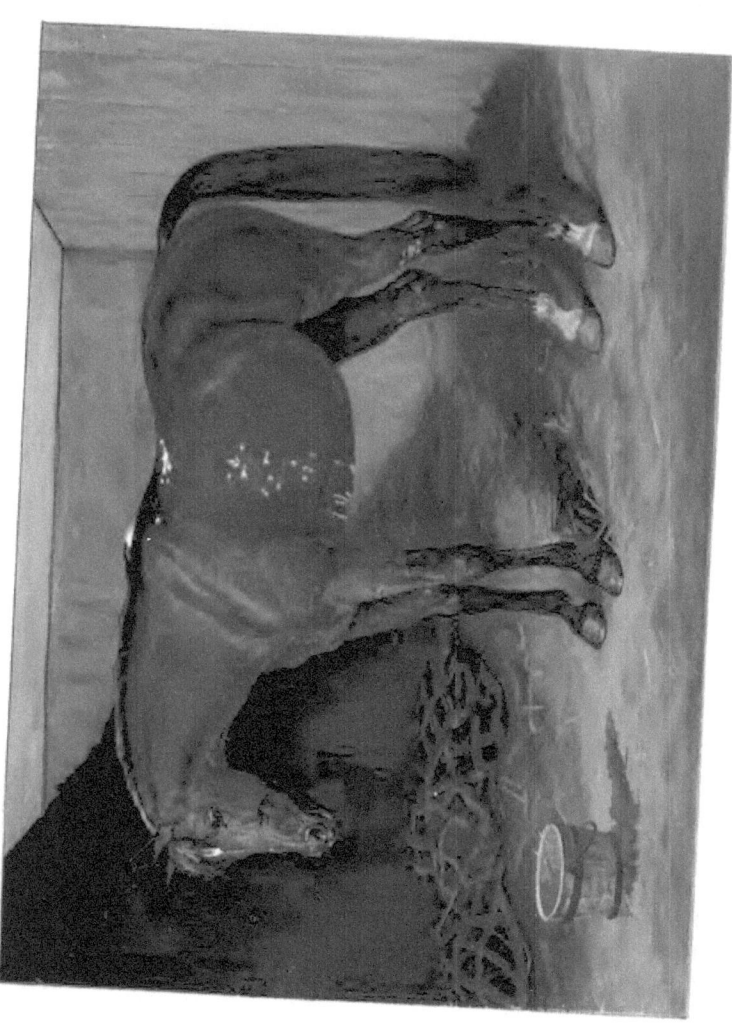

to Europe, our veterinary adviser might have made a mistake in this particular instance. Accordingly, the horse was started off to Bombay, a journey then involving a march of two hundred miles in order to reach the railway. On our following soon afterwards, we had the pleasure of seeing him win from six competitors, on the 4th of February 1862, the then blue ribbon of the Indian turf, as well as another considerable race of the same meeting. All that time his state remained just what it was at the beginning, no better and no worse. A cynic of the turf to whom we showed him said that he was "lame in his head"! For once, horseflesh had fulfilled the prophetic saying. The *palma nobilis* had been found knotted in the forelocks of a Ku-hai-lân.[1] The next thing was to get the good and true horse restored to soundness. With this object, he was taken to the most experienced veterinary surgeon then in India, whose opinion was as follows: "Lame in both fore-legs; slight ossific deposit round off pastern, with inflammation: not likely to be ring-bone, or, in other words, the result of causes generally productive of ring-bone: also has small pointed splint inside upper part of near fore-shank, probably caused by his making too much use of near fore-leg, to save lame off fore. *N.B.—Feet remarkably cool, and without a symptom of disease;* suspensory ligament and tendons of the leg perfectly sound." In the face of this record, it was impossible to entertain the idea of calling on the horse for further exertion. When he arrived at his proper home, the splint was found to have become inflamed in the course of nine days of marching. The veterinarian who had first seen him was, as it happened, absent; and a third member of the profession was therefore consulted. From him opinion number three proceeded, which was that the Arab owner who had inserted rowels in the shoulder had judged correctly; in other words, that this was a case of "chest-founder." We then sent the horse to the author of the "ossific deposit round pastern" theory; and eight months afterwards received him back, with a note intimating that, though still slightly lame, he was as well as ever he would be. For several years thereafter he led the life of a gentleman retired on an annuity. He saw no more veterinary surgeons, and seldom was asked to carry his master, owing to his "shoulder-tied" condition. At last, in the summer of 1865, having other horses in training, we took the opportunity to give the veteran a further trial. After a few weeks of steady work, he again failed in the same way as before. This time there was considerable tumefaction on the inner surface of the off fore-arm. The highly qualified, but decidedly old-fashioned, veterinary officer of the King's Dragoon Guards, then quartered at Secunderabad, when he examined him, formed substantially the same view of the case as the Arabs had done. After a time he heated an

---

[1] The generic name, as will in due time appear, of all the pure-bred strains of Arabia.

iron, and applied it across the fore-arm. We had never before seen this treatment, but had known many horses which, when brought from Arabia, bore the marks of the firing-iron in the same situation. The object in keeping the horse so long idle had partly been to reward him, and partly to give him a chance of becoming sound, and winning further honours. But evidently this was not to be. The poor animal had undergone so much medical and surgical treatment, that he had learned to recognise a doctor as a little boy does a schoolmaster, and all to no purpose. An appointment was therefore found for him in the stud department.

Long afterwards, the above particulars were recalled to memory on its appearing that, in the opinion equally of the Bedouin and of the town Arabs, the region of the chest is often the seat of acute or chronic lameness. A round course was lately laid out in the desert, near Baghdad, and several of the Osmanli Pâshas now amuse themselves by getting up races on it. Their sleek and prancing chargers are, however, invariably beaten by a certain diminutive mare, scarred on the chest and shoulders as if she had been fired with a gridiron, which a Bada-wi brings into the town the night before the event, and hurriedly takes away again, for fear of being deprived of her. This mare may have navicular disease, for though no one would call her lame when she is galloping, she walks and trots stiffly; but of course they who fired her over the fore-quarters did not suspect her feet. Referring to the frequency of marks of firing on the horses of the Bedouin, we may take this opportunity of saying that it is seldom advisable to buy a colt which has been fired. It is true that these people fire their horses, as they also do their children, rather at random. One of their saws is, *A-khiru 'd da-wi, el kai*, which means, *The last of remedies is the scoring*, or firing. When all the marks are on the flanks and belly, nothing more serious than an attack of colic may have led to the performance of the operation. In other cases, especially if the animal be aged, and the lines run equally over the trunk and the extremities, the owner may have thus blemished his property as a precaution against the covetous glances of Pâshas. But it should not be too much taken for granted that the desert Arab is a mere ignorant fellow. In many respects he is so; but no human being is cleverer than he is, at once in making the most of his own property and in transferring to himself that of others. To get up early gives one no advantage in dealing with nomads, who never, properly speaking, go to bed at all. We have three times bought from the Aeniza colts which were striped with the firing-iron from the wither downward. They all had the best of feet; but they had not been long in training when they went amiss in the same manner as the rowelled one of the foregoing history had done. In regard to one of them, we subsequently learned that at the time of the application of the iron, he lay between life and death after having been overridden. The bearing of these observations on our immediate subject is obvious. If, as is possible, the Bedouin fire their horses' chests and shoulders, when attention to the feet would be more germane to the matter, then that tends to modify the view here adopted of the exceptional soundness of the latter part in the Arabian variety. But, subject to the opinion of professional persons, we necessarily, on this point, follow the guidance of the facts which have just been stated from our own experience of Arab horses.

Durability, in the sense of wearing well and wearing long, is traceable to so many different sources, that only general statements can be made regarding it. Some horses, like some men, last long, owing to the care which they take of themselves. Even if they have the power, they have not the will to work. Others, in consequence of faults or vices, spend half of their time in being made up for the market. The sort of durability here being spoken of is a totally different quality. It depends less on where, or by what people, a horse is bred, than on *how* he is bred. Nature does not confer it, by way of privilege, on one breed more than on another. It is greatly subject to the influence of climate, habit, and mode of rearing. But, speaking broadly, the power of lasting is one of the happiest products of what is known as high breeding. Give us a horse in which the keen and generous spirit of emulation — *fier mais sensible* — animates a form perfectly adapted to the tasks demanded of it, and we will take the rest for granted. The Arabian breed remarkably illustrates this favourable combination, but it must not be imagined that it makes all competition halt behind it. Authentic cases of longevity in exported Arab horses might be multiplied till the reader's patience was exhausted.[1] But for every such record, an equally notable one might be cited from the history of our own breeds.[2] Others before us have observed that old age does not necessarily begin in horses so soon as many people imagine. An old writer says that a horse of 5 yrs. is like a man of 20; a horse of 10 like a man of 40; a horse of 15 like a man of 50; a horse of 20 like a man of 60; of 25, like

---

[1] The late brilliant Commander-in-Chief of the army in India, General Lord Roberts, now rides in the Park in London a grey Arab charger which has carried him in his campaigns and military inspections for more than sixteen years, has never been unfit for duty, and still shows himself off on parade as if he were a four-year-old. We hear of another Eastern evergreen, in the possession of General and Mrs Turnbull, formerly of Calcutta, and now of Brighton, which was brought to England eighteen years ago; is at least 24 years old, and to all appearance is as young as ever, especially when mounted.

[2] Delabere Blaine, in *Outlines of the Veterinary Art*, 4th edit., 1832, p. 30, states that, about a century ago, three monuments were to be seen at Dulwich of three horses which inhabited the same stable, and which died at 35, 37, and 39 respectively. On the same page there is a reference to a large horse of the Mersey and Irwell Navigation, which was "well known to have been in his sixty-second year when he died." Unless there be a mixing up of the stories, longevity in horses must be traditional at Dulwich. For Blaine's contemporary, Lawrence in *The Horse*, 1829, p. 105, says: "The writer, some years since, saw at Dulwich two geldings, the one 48, the other 54, years of age, both of them capable of performing some light daily labour, the property of his friend, the late E. Brown, Esq., who had both their portraits."

one of 70; of 30, like one of 80; and of 35, like one of 90. Such a scale may not be worth much, but we believe that what makes so many of us buy and use young horses is the commercial idea that a horse of 10, when we would sell him, does not readily find a purchaser.

There are two theories connected with durability in horses which it may be proper to notice. One is, that Arab horses last the longer because they are neither over-fed nor over-worked before maturity; and the other, that wearing qualities are to be looked for in foreign breeds in proportion as Arab blood is shared by them. For neither theory does the case admit of being made out. Even if it were to be conceded, for the sake of argument, that the Arabian horse surpasses other horses in hardness, the position which we have all along been maintaining is, that his virtue in this respect is much connected with the fact of his being early accustomed to the saddle. It is not work, but the abuse of it, which ruins young horses. In so far as lasting long on the turf forms a criterion, there never was an Arabian which made a better record than, for example, Fisherman, in England, and the New South Wales horse, Kingcraft. The former, we find, began his public career in 1855 as a two-year-old; and in that year and the following one faced the starter 114 times, and won sixty-five races. The latter, after being thrice defeated as a two-year-old at Sydney, crossed the sea, and came to the post seven times at Calcutta, Lucknow, and Bombay, as a three-year-old, winning every time. When he retired in 1881 he had been nine years in training, had contested sixty-eight races, and won forty-six. These hard facts deserve to be considered in connection with the proposals which are sometimes made for the abolition of the ordeal of early training. And the practice of the Arabs, though full of abuses, supports the general conclusion that colts and fillies which are bred for galloping ought to be taught their business as soon as they can carry a light weight.[1] In regard to the other point, it surely is an extraordinary assumption that because Arab blood is well fitted to fortify certain other races of horses, it

---

[1] The fact that Eclipse was not raced till five years old is quoted by John Lawrence, in *The Horse* (1829), as, in part, the secret of his vast powers. The early champions of the Australian turf, also, naturally included horses which began late and yet secured the highest honours. Take, for example, the redoubtable Jorrocks, a light bay gelding with black points, standing only 15 hands 2 inches, whose record is given by Mr Curr. Jorrocks was allowed to ripen in the sequestered township of Mudgee, in New South Wales, unruffled by whip or curry-comb. He was set in his prime to the humble drudgery of stock horse and hack alternately; and the speed and stoutness which he exhibited in his vocation, or in occasional bursts after the bounding denizens of the Australian bush, led to his being put in training. His owner was induced to exchange him for eight heifers, "equivalent to about £40 sterling," and his adventures then began. From 1840 to 1852 he remained a favourite of the public. He started eighty-seven times, and won sixty races, reckoning seven walks over. (*Op. cit.* in Catalog. No. 39, pp. 151-164.) We apprehend, however, that there is no longer much chance for amateur race-horses, so to call them, either in England or in Australia. In both countries it is now imperative that the horses which are to excel in running should be trained at an early age.

constitutes *the pre-eminent* source of stamina. Confining ourselves to well-known breeds, we may here recall as evidence those which once upon a time flourished in India, and to which a slight allusion has already been made.[1] It does not concern us here to notice the produce of the studs which the East India Company maintained for the supply of its military requirements. Those establishments, now abolished, turned out fine horses, superior in size to Arabs, and having very good constitutions;[2] but, practically, such were more English than Indian; and most of them were the results of infinite crossing and recrossing. Our reference is to the indigenous breeds on which the cavalry of the native princes and captains was mounted, throughout the long struggle for the prize of ascendancy between England and the powers and hordes of India. History contains no account of large bodies which moved more rapidly or more incessantly than the regular horse of the Mahratta armies, and the roaming legions of the Pindháris. The breeds of horses which those times encouraged died out but slowly. Indeed some may think that they are not even yet extinct, but are merely in abeyance, till the department which the modern Government of India has created for their "improvement" shall disappear in the next great Eastern tournament. But, generally speaking, they now exhibit the characters which are to be looked for in disused and neglected breeds. Those of us who knew the East India Company's "Irregular Cavalry" before the Mutiny, will recognise in the subjoined sketch a stamp of charger which was often to be seen caracoling under a swarthy troop-leader of that period.

In India there is a vague tradition that from, say, 1820 to 1857, when our best Irregular Cavalry was more or less mounted on horses of the above pattern, the finest breeds owed their lasting powers and general superiority to strains of imported Arab blood which were introduced, early in the century, by the Nizam of Hyderabad in the Deccan and his nobles. This story has a foreign ring; and even if it be authentic, it can have only a restricted application. Something is known to us of the manners and feelings of the more old-fashioned of the

---

[1] *Vide*, p. 91.
[2] The *Oriental Sport. Mag.* for October 1866 thus describes one of these "stud-bred" horses : " Bombproof, a bay stud-bred gelding, foaled in 1843, became the property of an officer of Engineers in 1848, in whose possession he remained until his death, which was caused by an accident, . . . on 20th September 1866. He was therefore twenty-four years of age. Bombproof served at the siege of Multan ; battle of Gujrát ; pursuit of the Sikhs, under Sir W. Gilbert ; battle on the Hindon (May 1857) ; Badle ka Saráí ; siege of Delhi ; capture of Lucknow ; a hot weather campaign in Oudh and Rohilcund ; and a cold weather campaign in Rohilcund and Oudh. To narrate his performances in getting over long distances, and his apparently perfect indifference to regular feeding (generally deemed so necessary to stud-breds in particular), would certainly tax the patience and belief of your readers. I will therefore only say that he commenced the Mutiny campaign in his fifteenth year, and was in constant work, as the only horse of a mounted officer, from May 1857 to February 1859, without being sick or sorry, and was in capital condition at the end of it."

populations of India, in parts which modern changes have as yet but slightly affected. And we have often perceived among the Rajpûts and the Mahrâttas the same anxiety to keep pure the blood of a breed of horses which distinguishes the Arabs. In 1859 we served with a regiment which was mounted on mares obtained from the breeders and dealers of Central India and the Deccan. These animals were the property of their riders. The British officers of the regiment rode Arab chargers. Most of the horsemen were mere rovers, who had bought their mares and arms with money advanced to them by the Government. But

there were a few who could recount their ancestors; and one, in particular, rode at the head of his troop a large dun-coloured mare which he regarded as a family heirloom. One day it was proposed to this gallant swordsman that he should mate his noble mare with an equally noble Arabian, the property of the late General W. F. Beatson, of Báshi-bázouk celebrity—a part of whose special command the regiment formed. At the risk of affronting a singularly irascible General officer, by whom the offer was meant as an act of condescension and favour, the Rajpût evaded coming to the point, and the matter dropped. About twenty years afterwards we found ourselves in political charge of the western states of Rajputâna. One of these is Mâr-wâr, a part of which, the arid district of Ma-lâ-ni, is directly under British management. Nominally, Ma-lâ-ni is watered by the river Lû-ni, but its physical features are almost as severe as those of Shà-mî-ya. As the saying is, blades of steel grow better in it than blades of corn; and its camel-pasturing clans, of Aryan stock, have traits in common with the Bedouin Arabs. The mares which they breed, and of which they are most tenacious, display the clean muscle, lean head, thin nostril, and large dark eye of the race of Najd. We were, however, assured that the breed owed nothing to crossing, but, on the contrary, had been preserved and handed down unaltered in these pure-blooded Rajpût families through centuries of warfare. One or more of our predecessors, it was further stated, had recommended the use of Arabian stallions; but by means of that passive resistance which now forms the sole defence of the people of India, the unwelcome proposal had been put aside. Such at least were the representations which the Ma-lâ-ni horse-breeders made to us when we marched over their desert pasture-lands in 1880. Of course it is possible that they were romancing, and that, after all, the beauty and energy of their mares are derived from Arabs. If any reader know that the case is so, we are only too ready to be corrected.

CHARACTER.

Tractability is intimately bound up with temper, than which there is no more important element of character. It would not be easy to find another breed of horses which is so uniformly distinguished by evenness of temper, gentleness, and willingness, as the Arabian; and the explanation is easy. The force of human companionship in forming the characters of inferior animals has been recognised from antiquity downward. The story of the Seven Sleepers of Ephesus receives in Persian literature the embellishment, that the dog which shared their three hundred and nine years[1] of cave life became a man! With the Arabs and their horses serving to illustrate this influence, it is unnecessary to fall back on legend. The common representation that the Bedouin and their mares dwell together under one tent-roof belongs to the domain of poetry, but the groundwork of it may be accepted. In the desert, the mares and foals and stallions stand day and night before their masters. There are no grooms in our sense. Black slaves keep the ground clean, and the wives and daughters of the tent-folk wait upon the mares. Woman, heaven be praised! is everywhere merciful and compassionate; and romance becomes reality when a drooping mare, or a motherless foal, is taken into the best part of the tent to be nursed. In villages the mare's

---

[1] E. Al. Kur-ān, S. xviii. 24.

shed is close to the habitation in which the family life proceeds. The result is, that food and fellowship are among the first ideas which are associated in the minds of Arab horses with the human figure. The mares turn as kindly to those around them as "Gustavus" did to Dugald Dalgetty. The youngling takes its cue from the dam, and is not afraid of that with which they are all familiar. The colt which is handled by every one from the first, and ridden as soon as he is strong enough, is sure to prove docile and obedient. It is thus that "nature" forms itself. We all know to our cost how prone horses are to practise that which they have learned. One that has run away with his rider only a few times, whether through fear or frolic, or kicked in harness because a strap or a fly fretted him, may escape falling into the habit of doing so; but the horse which has often done a thing will always do it. The best systems have weak places. It must be admitted that the Arabian breed suffers, among the Bedouin, from over-galloping, and among the agricultural classes, from over-weighting, before the bones and joints are set. In this way, probably, is produced the ungraceful, but not necessarily detrimental, turning in of the hocks,[1] with or without deviation of the fore-legs also from their proper relative position, which is so prevalent. But almost anything is better than letting a young horse grow up unmastered, so that he must be what is called "broken" on the wheel of the "rough-rider," after he has become strong and wilful. Even when full allowance is made for the advantages of early tuition, Arab men deserve some credit for the fine temper of Arab horses. The most patient colt may learn to resist his rider, if either his anger be excited or too much of his own way be given to him. A little incident which we lately witnessed in a crowded thoroughfare in Baghdad may here be worth introducing. An awkward groom had tumbled off the back of a playful filly, and left her free to career hither and thither. Among the spectators there was nobody who blamed the filly. A red-bearded Persian, whose book-stall was kicked into the Tigris by her, had the sense to curse the biped and not the quadruped. When she was caught, and the end of her halter-rope was put into the groom's hand by a bystander, the man merely jumped on her back and rode quietly away. The Arabs lose their temper with one another, and are both rude and violent; but they think it absurd to burst into a passion with irrational creatures. One of the few so-called vicious horses ever owned by us was an Arab plater, which had been cruelly flogged in his races. At first it was impossible to please him; and if any one who was dressed like his late Persian jockey came in sight, he would rush open-mouthed at him. After about a year, notwithstanding his being kept in training, the evil spirit left him, apart from any special treatment beyond the potent magic of kindness. If the other method had been continued, it might

---

[1] When the horse is said to be "cow-hocked."

have made him into what is called a "born devil." And then, if he had gone to stud, very likely the same crooked temper would have "run in his blood." The hereditary fault of buck-jumping—that is, making both the rider and the saddle fly like shuttlecocks—which forms a great objection to the common kinds of Australian horses, is understood to originate in a certain violent process of "breaking" to which they are subjected. Perhaps it is scarcely too much to say that there never was what is called a vicious horse without there being a vicious, or, at all events, uncivilised and reckless, man more or less connected with it. When we see any one beating, or roaring at, a horse, every time that he shies or stumbles, or unmercifully punishing him in a race, we always wish that he could be changed into a Yahoo.

Tractability and temper having thus been taken together, let us pass to "abstemiousness"; alongside of which the same writer might have mentioned fortitude. Both these virtues are made in the same mould. One is, the power of *going without*; and the other, the power of *never minding*. The reader has seen how the Arab of the desert can both feast and fast, and how his mare can do so with him. Sa'-di says, that *to heat the oven of the stomach every minute, is to suffer for it in the day of want;* but such an idea is too literary for the Arabs. Since beginning this chapter, we have been present at a supper among the Bedouin, when the leader of a successful foray was feasting his companions. There was only one dish, a vast wooden trencher, as black, from never being washed, as the mouth of a coal-pit. In it was served a camel, hacked in pieces, boiled to rags, and piled on a heap of dingy rice.[1] The "heads of families," a phrase which among the Arabs does not include women, were gathered round this, three or four deep. The mess was smoking hot, but the Bedouin manners do not permit any one to hesitate on this account. The same desert code which binds the host to fill the platter, obliges the guest to do immediate justice to it. Certainly no delay occurred on this occasion. Rows of brawny right arms, bared to above the elbow, kept making play into and out of the layers of rice and camel. As one man after another retired wiping his fingers[2] on his cloak or on the tent wall, others succeeded. In a short time only the *débris* remained in the platter, which was then carried out by the African servants. For a long time previously, nothing more substantial than dates and dried milk, or wheat porridge, had come in the way of these people. Whether a healthy man shall require one meal a-day, or three meals, more or less depends on habit. It is said very truly that "half the good of a horse goes in at his mouth;" but then we must remember that "forcing" disturbs nature's balance. In order to send a horse to the three-year-old

---

[1] The Bedouin term for this *pièce de résistance* is, *talla 'l lahm*, or *mound of flesh*.

[2] The Arabs call the fingers of the right hand *Al Khums-a*—i.e., *par excellence*, THE FIVE, by means of which the food is conveyed to the mouth. The first time that a Ba-da-wi sees a Frank dining, he wonders if he have a leprosy in his fingers, so that he cannot eat with them?

starting-post as fully furnished as colts of that age are in England, as much "forcing" is requisite as for the bringing out of a John Stuart Mill in our species. The point here is, that horses which have lived luxuriously in racing-stables, no matter what their breed is, cannot, as a rule, be expected to endure privations, as well as those do which have experienced hard times from foalhood upward, owing to the poor circumstances of their owners.

On the march to Magdála six horses stood before our bell-tent. One was a daughter of Kingston, which had won races both in England and India. Another was the Bengal-bred plater Verdant Green,[1] whose sire was an Arab, and his dam an imported thoroughbred English mare. Two were Arabs; and two were ponies, one Indian and the other Abyssinian. The two last lived on what the others left, or on what they would not eat, and performed far more than their own share of work. The Indian pony, in particular, whose scarred back and turned-in hocks betokened early familiarity with the burden, carried us many a march lasting from sunrise to sunset, and improved in condition all the time. Fortitude is as marked a characteristic of the Arabian breed as frugality. In the days when most veterinary surgeons were partial to strong measures, we have seen many a poor broken-down Arab racer fired and blistered on both fore-legs at once, but never one which refused his nose-bag after the operation. Horses of European breeding are generally less patient. We know of a case in India in which a thoroughbred English colt so banged himself about from mingled rage and pain, after being blistered, that it became necessary to destroy him. The way in which the Arabian will pass through strangles, or catarrh and influenza, without losing his natural spirit and gaiety, is one of his characteristics. As a racer he is indomitable. Heats are his forte; and he will run two or more races in one afternoon. On the 13th of February 1862, in a two-mile cup race at Calcutta, the grey Arab Hermit, though defeated by the thoroughbred English mare Voltige, gave Voltigeur's daughter such a stretching, that the following day, when the two were to have met again in a two-mile race, the mare had to be kept at home, and the Arab proved the winner, in the excellent time of 3 minutes and 51 seconds. Many a staunch Arab plater could be mentioned whose doughty deeds have been performed after he has more or less broken down. It is but seldom that a horse can be kept in training when the flexor tendons are permanently damaged; but many an Arab racer has continued, year after year, to add to his laurels, in spite of a thickened

---

[1] When the expedition broke up at Zulla, a Yorkshireman bought Verdant. Afterwards, merely on the ground that he had "come from some place far abroad," they exhibited him at Islington as an Arabian. We wonder how many, besides him, of the so-called Arabs which have at different periods been used by our countrymen for stud purposes, owed their superiority to English ancestry. Verdant's show-name in England was Magdála.

suspensory ligament. Not to speak too exclusively of racing, fifty-three years ago Captain Horne, of the Horse Artillery, undertook to ride his grey Arab horse, Jumping Jimmy, 400 miles in 5 days, and accomplished the feat on the Bangalore race-course, before crowds of spectators, with 3 hours and 5 minutes in hand. Detailed accounts of this performance may be read in the *Bengal Sporting Magazine* of 1840. The feature which distinguishes it from the recent trials of equine endurance in Germany is, that Jumping Jimmy showed no signs of distress either during or after his exertions. At the end of the final lap of 79 miles, 5 furlongs, and 30 yards, which was done in 19 hours and 55 minutes, the gallant grey was as ready as ever for his corn. Any strong man can override a horse, and in so doing make a record which at first sight shall seem extraordinary. To constitute a true test, it ought to be provided that the horses shall be so selected, and so brought to condition, as well as so ridden and cared for during the trial, as that they shall neither suffer misery nor be rendered inefficient. Horsemanship should always be associated with humanity.

Some are of opinion that the rough usages of the desert life serve to harden the desert horse. This view pleasantly or unpleasantly revives the traditions of the methods by which ancient Sparta made her young men into heroes. There is, at least, no lack of facts behind it. The Arabian Bedouin are accustomed patiently to endure all the aches which life inflicts on them. So far as can be judged in the absence of statistics, death at a comparatively early age awaits most of them. Nobody can expect them to have more pity on their mares than on themselves. As long as a mare can gallop, it little matters whether she is lame or sound. When she breaks down, she is fired. The ragged-coated cripples which we have seen in winter in the Bedouin tent-cities have made us think of the "young noblemen" in Dotheboys Hall. We remember an old mare which had broken down so badly that both her fore-fetlocks touched the ground, and she hobbled along, perfectly happy, on the half-raw surfaces, with a foal at foot. In London she would have fetched just what the cat's-meat-man or the sausage-maker would have bidden for her. On the Euphrates her wrecked condition did not greatly lessen her value. She belonged to a strain of established reputation, and it would have been difficult to buy her. We do not presume to ignore the possibility of all these circumstances helping to develop fortitude in the Arabian breed—just as the rigorous winters of Europe tend to bring out stubborn endurance and other useful qualities in mankind. But, on the whole, according to our experience, at two years old the desert colt may safely be considered to have had enough of his native element.

"Courage, instinct, and sagacity" are allied virtues. When it is said that a horse has high courage, what is commonly meant is that he is a free-goer, and full of fire and mettle. But here we shall understand by *courage* the partly natural and partly acquired character of fearlessness of objects and noises. In every considerable number of well-bred yearlings, even if they are all from the same sire and dam, some will be found which are naturally courageous, and others which are naturally timid. One of the former class can easily be persuaded to go up to new and threatening objects. One of the latter kind will struggle hard to keep clear of everything which is strange to him. But while this essential difference in different horses is admitted, the influence of education also claims recognition. Timidity arising from defective vision belongs to the province of the veterinary surgeon. The horse which is apprehensive merely through ignorance will show his courage as he grows in knowledge. The constitutionally nervous one will more or less continue to be so, though he will improve with every year of gentle treatment. Following the manner of story-books, we shall here illustrate our remarks by means of a few histories drawn from real life. Of all our horses, the one most deserving to be named for courage was equally pre-eminent in sagacity. He was not an Arabian, and still less one of the inanimate kind, fearing nothing because feeling nothing, but one in whom the flutter of a sparrow's wing sufficed to kindle the fire of equine energy which he inherited from Voltigeur. Captain White, as his name was, had not been long in India when one day he chanced to meet, on a bridge, the largest of all surviving terrestrial animals, bowling along with a howdah on its back. He was so far from showing any signs of alarm, that he actually tucked up a hind-leg to keep it out of the elephant's way in passing. Shortly after that occurrence, the honest yokel who had brought him out from Yorkshire obtained leave to go to a race-meeting. The horse then quickly realised that he was master of the situation. On finding himself regarded by the Indians as a kind of Sâ-hib,[1] or imperial foreigner, he was seized with the humour of keeping the dusky stablemen at a respectful distance. He carried out this little play so perfectly, without, however, doing any one the smallest injury, that nobody could take him out of his box. His friend the Yorkshireman had therefore to be recalled. His first act, after his return, was to march up to his favourite with a bamboo in his hand, lay hold of him by the tail, and give him a couple of whacks along the ribs. This discipline was received with every sign of penitence, and the next minute any little boy might have put a bridle on him. He who thinks that there is no virtue in the stick should come and reside for a time in the land where these pages are written. To make it descend, like the rain, on the just and the unjust, is good neither for the giver nor the receiver. But applied at the right time, in the right quantity, and in the right cases, the bamboo corrects the transgressor as nothing else does, and the weight of it falls exclusively on the proper person. Next let us give

---

[1] V. Index I.

two instances in which courage, when at first deficient, was developed through experience. A few months ago we received two colts for both of which Baghdad contained many new objects. One of them, a son of the great Chester, was bred in the Sydney district, and the other in Najd. The former, when he saw a camel, especially one that was couchant and braying, would bound to one side, and place a good many yards of the desert between him and it. The latter, while meeting the splay-footed ruminant as an old messmate, would jump like a deer rather than put his foot in the shallowest rill or glittering piece of water. Both these animals gradually ceased to be frightened at objects which did not injure them. The first experience which made the son of Chester look a camel in the face, was when he observed one of his own species eating from the same manger as the long-necked monster. After some time he would do the same thing himself. The second example is brought in to illustrate constitutional nervousness. It relates to a horse from Najd which, after beginning life in India as a cavalry charger, made his mark as a racer. The sound of a piece of paper being opened by the man on his back would set him all in a flutter. He was most apprehensive of strangers; and if even his master tried to mount him in an unfamiliar uniform, he would struggle to get away from him. His suspicions generally were unfounded. It was no easy matter to make him face a harmless carriage; but when firmly handled, and pressed with both spurs at the right moment and in the right place,[1] he would bring his rider handsomely alongside of a running boar.

The only conclusion we can come to, in view of all these facts, is, that Arab horses possess no advantages over other horses in the qualities now under notice.[2]

---

[1] A remark is suggested by this casual reference to spurs and spurring. The best modern authorities justly protest against the abuse of the last resource of horsemen. It is pitiful to see a man who cannot ride, and whose feats are necessarily confined to a beaten track, appear in spurs. If he were going for a walk, it would not matter, for then he would only cut his boots. But it is to be dreaded that, before his return, he will have lacerated his horse, and, if he should chance to tumble off, scored his brand-new saddle. It may be doubted how far it is advisable, even for first-rate riders, to arm their heels, as a mere point of dress, on all occasions. A good horse will do his best without having his sides wounded. When he flinches, either he is not properly asked or he distrusts himself. Nevertheless, the spur has many uses, of which he who understands them certainly ought to avail himself.

[2] If a graduated scale were to be made, showing approximately the order in which our more or less educated fellow-animals rank in point of intellectual capabilities, the horse would not stand at the top of it. His head is large, but its characteristic form is due to the development of the masticating apparatus at the expense of the brain-case, which, with the brain itself, is extremely reduced in size. A number of horses will contentedly remain confined in a field; but if a donkey be introduced, he will probably open the gate and march out, with the whole party in rear of him! Could anything be more stupid than the habit which horses have, when in camp, of rolling on the ground, no matter how cold the night may be, till their clothing is stripped off? Contrast with this the good sense of the elephant, which, when standing at his pickets, may be seen pulling branches from a tree and driving off the flies with them. It is just now going the round of the Indian newspapers, that a Commissariat elephant which was accustomed to receive its supper in twelve cakes, on one occasion when only eleven cakes were produced, refused to touch them till the proper number was brought! We cannot vouch for the truth of this anecdote. But in campaigns in

In respect of sagacity, and of the courage which is derived from it, the desert breed has kept pace, within its own limits, with the intelligence of the people who have made it—and that is all. It may be that the Arabs are behind several other Asiatic peoples as teachers of young horses; but their quiet and rational way of managing them goes far to make up for this. They talk to their four-footed servants as if they were human beings.[1] They lead their flocks and herds, more than they drive them. Even their laden camels are left free to march in droves, instead of being tied, every one by its nose-rope, to the tail of another, according to the practice, which causes so many wounds, and adds so much to the mortality, in Indian transport-trains. The traveller between Baghdad and the Caspian straps his two portmanteaus across the back of a galloping post-horse, which, without being led or ridden, instantly sets off with them; and but for an occasional tumble, necessitating his being pulled out by the tail from under them, gallantly shows the way to the next station.

So far, the bat of description, as the Persians say, has, on the whole, been hitting the ball of superiority towards the goal of the Arabian breed, and away from that of its European rivals. More strokes remain to be given; but this is a good place to break off.

India, when elephants were used to level deserted villages, they were always most careful not to apply the skull to a piece of wall without first ascertaining that no living object was behind it. Students of the development theory should observe the fact, that of the two species of animals the tuition of which dates from the remotest ages—namely, the elephant and the camel—the former is perhaps the wisest, and the latter one of the silliest, of beasts.

[1] In India we adopted this practice to the extent of teaching every coach-horse to come to the walk or the halt at the word of command. Long ago English coachmen freely used the voice, but now even a whistle from the box is disapproved of. Nevertheless, considering how commonly the propensity to run away proceeds from fear, it is a great advantage, when only one or two horses in a team are seized with a panic, to be able thus to stop the others.

CHAPTER IV.

DEFECTS OF THE ARABIAN.

THE fault which is most commonly found with Arab horses is that they are too small.

In one sense size is but a secondary character. The town Arabs admire large animals, and the Turks think that a Pâsha ought to be like an elephant. But the Bedouin Arab knows better, and when he sees a Goliath, will want to know if he have a great heart.

As a matter of course, inferiority in size bears against a breed of horses. On the race-course a first-class little one may defeat a second-rate big one;[1] but the horse of full and symmetrical development, whose heart or courage is true, easily strides away from an equally good little one. For ordinary riding, burly long-limbed men prefer horses which can not only carry them, but which look and step and feel as if they could do so.

Admiral Rous, in support of the contention that in 170 years the thoroughbred English horse has been improved one-eighth in power, speed, and stature, cited Stockwell, Knowsley, Rataplan, Thormanby, and King Tom as horses which could have carried 16 stone to hounds, and could stand up under more weight than any London dray-horse. The latter fact, if, as we assume it to be, fully verified, is very remarkable; and the power which the compact little Arabian possesses to carry a heavy man both far and fast is equally so. Her Majesty's 17th Lancers rode Arab horses in the Indian Mutiny campaign. We imagine that there are few of the survivors, from the gallant Sir W. Gordon downward, who, if they had to perform the same work again, would not desire to receive back from shadowland the well-bred thick-set horses of medium stature which then carried them. The

---

[1] In India horses under 14 hands may often be seen finishing in front of Walers and others a hand or more taller.

late Captain Nolan's book on cavalry contains an account of a Persian[1] troop-horse which, though only 14 hands and 3 inches high, was ridden throughout an 800-mile march in India by a private of the 18th Hussars, who weighed, with his accoutrements, 22½ stone! At the crossing of the Kistna—a broad, rapid, and dangerous river—his rider, it is stated, scorned the ferry-boat; and, declaring that "a hussar and his horse should never part company"—what the latter said to that is not narrated—gallantly stemmed the current in heavy marching order.

Sometimes it is said that the Arabian horse cannot or will not trot, and sometimes that he does not jump; but these are random statements. Trotting tends to uncover, or perhaps even to rub off, the brown skin of the unbreeched Bedouin horseman. It forms, we know, one of the three natural paces of the horse, but the Arabs do not cultivate it. The desert mare springs all at once from the halt or walk into a free-and-easy hand-gallop, which is too disconnected to be properly called a canter.

As for leaping, one may cross many a league of the pathless desert without the crystal stream, far less walls or rails, or even a dry ditch, appearing. When, however, the Arab horse is taken elsewhere and schooled, his thorough willingness may carry him over fences which larger animals are refusing through roguery or stubbornness. In India we once saw a field of Australian horses in a steeplechase completely stopped by what they had to encounter. Some fell; others would only jump what they thought proper; and not one ever passed the judge's box. Afterwards, when their owners were protesting against the course, a battery sergeant-major of the Hyderabad Contingent, who happened to be present on his regimental horse, an Arab Galloway, rode him over every obstacle.

It is less easy to defend the Arabian from the charge of being a careless walker, and therefore not a good hack. His more thoroughgoing admirers undertake to do so, but they are in the minority. Of course, the exceptions are not infrequent. Thus Colonel Bower, who owned the famous racing Arab, Child of the Islands, says that, although he was a "daisy-cutter," he had been ridden over the roughest ground, and had never been detected in a trip. "A pleasanter, safer hack," it is added, "could not be."[2] But occasional instances like this only bear on individual horses.

To perceive the difference between the movements of an Arab horse's fore-feet and those of an approved English pleasure-horse, one should first stand behind

---

[1] Persia possesses, so far as we can see, no well-established breed of the blood-horse, except, possibly, in a few princely families; and then, too generally, the owner's death is followed by the dispersion or the neglect of his brood-mares. A "Persian horse" may be by sire or dam, or both, an Arabian; or he may be a Turku-mâ-ni. Far more commonly he merely is a *ku-dísh* or a *yá-bú*.

[2] Quoted in Stonehenge's *Book of the Horse*, p. 21. The Child of the Islands (1846-49) was a dark bay, with black points, slight but muscular in figure—that is, possessing good substance without weight. He stood 14 hands 2½ inches.

the two animals while they are carrying their riders at a walk over a dusty road. The scientifically bred one, it will be noticed, disturbs the surface no more in setting down than in picking up a foot. The Arab, on the contrary, stirs up the dust with his fore-feet. His fore-hand, instead of being carried well forward, appears to find a difficulty in getting out of the way of his hind-quarters. Next observe the Arab horse while he is trotting. However well he may have been taught, his action at this pace has an undeveloped character. His is not the musical trot of the accomplished English stepper, the very sound of which goes bail for him that he will not fall. It is not that Arab horses are unsafe. Apart from accidents, we owe them only about six falls in thirty years. Their power of righting themselves in a twinkling after a false step, so as not to make a downright stumble, commands admiration. It depends partly on constant practice, and partly on their pluck and springiness. But there are worse things than falls. Many a time when an Arab hack has been sprawling along, and scraping the road at every rough place with a fore-foot, so that occasionally the reins would be jerked over his ears, we have wished that he would fall and be done with it.[1] If it had merely been that the Arabian abroad, shod after a novel fashion, and played on, like Hamlet, by those who "do not know his stops," was addicted to tripping, who could have wondered? But it must be admitted that in his native country also he trips at a walk—the pace of all others at which a horse ridden for health or pleasure should be faultless. At first sight it seems extraordinary that a whole race of horses should thus be characterised by an unmethodical style of marching; but the facts which have been stated in other contexts [2] about the shortcomings of the Bedouin, equally as horse-breeders and as riders, sufficiently explain it.

If any one were to ask a dog why, before he lay down, he turned round and round, he might think it enough to answer, with a faulty logic not unknown in higher circles, that he always did so. Perhaps the Arab horse might offer the same explanation of his habit of tripping. But, according to some authorities, a transmitted cause is to be recognised in both cases,—in the dog, the instinct of making a place for himself, and clearing it of roughness; and in the horse, peculiarities which are bred in him. Not to mention such obvious causes as want of condition, a saddle-horse may be an awkward walker, because naturally a sluggard; or because he is badly shaped, or has chronic disease of the feet or shoulders, or is overweighted, or has not been properly educated. If the bodily framework be the machinery, temperament is the steam. Many splendid Arabs, as well as many thoroughbred English horses,[3] while showing their high breeding by a distinguished

---

[1] It is not meant that this description is applicable to most Arabs, far less to all of them. It puts the case at the strongest, and we have owned but one of the breed which it fitted.
[2] Vide, pp. 138 et 139.
[3] For example, Touchstone "was very lazy at exer-

style of walking, have been sleepy movers till their blood was warmed. Such never can be clever hacks. When not born racers, their proper part is to gallop as leaders in a pleasure-coach. Conformation carries us back to what has been stated on the subject of the Arab's thinking so much more of *blood* than of figure.[1] When a horse that turns out his toes walks clumsily, the fault lies with the people who will use a sire or a mare with twisted ankles. We shall speak further on of the Arabian's shoulders. But having mentioned crooked fore-legs, let us here say that this malformation is perhaps spreading in the horse-stock of the Arabs. In the days when almost the only Arab horses seen by us were those which the dealers brought to India, the prevalence among them of twisted fore-legs seemed surprising. Subsequently, on becoming acquainted with the Arabs, and observing how many crooked-legged horses they rear, we were more inclined to compliment the importers on their being able to find so many straight ones. Among the *élite* of the desert stallions, one may meet with horses whose fore-legs are like this:—

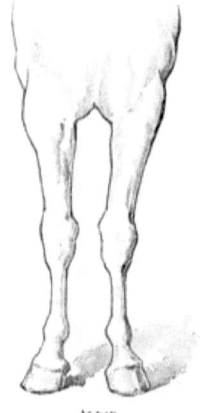

AS-DAF.

In twenty years we have not seen as many "pigeon-toed" Arab horses—that is, those having the fore-feet, one or both, twisted *inward*—as we have seen in one year of the opposite or "dancing-master" variety. Opinions differ as to which fault the more interferes with true action. The proper way to settle the question

---

cise, and could hardly be kicked along."—*Portraits of Celebrated Race-Horses*, by T. H. Taunton, M.A., vol. iii. p. 158.

[1] *V. ante*, p. 138.

CHAP. IV.   *DEFECTS OF THE ARABIAN.*   201

is to buy only straight-limbed ones. When a horse is a proved racer, or a brilliant and accomplished hunter, his "points" may be disregarded. But we would here say to every young horseman, and especially every soldier, If you will make it a rule never to choose, as a charger or a remount, a horse that turns out, or in, his toes, or one of them, in any considerable degree, many griefs will be saved to you; unless, indeed, you resemble the Bedouin in their indifference to all such trifles as stumbling and interfering, or are content to have your horses look like posters, with boots strapped round their fetlocks, to save them from coming in after a march raw and bloody from cutting.

SHOE TURNED UP AT TOE.   (Ground surface.)

In India, our best cavalry officers, both of the combatant and veterinary branches, have sought for means of improving the defective action of the forehand in the Arabian. Their efforts have chiefly resulted in the invention of new kinds of horse-shoes. Many years ago, Lieut.-Col., now General Sir F., Fitzwygram, when commanding the Inniskilling Dragoons at Poona, recommended a shoe of the above form.[1]

---

[1] *V. Notes on Shoeing Horses*, by Lieut.-Col. Fitzwygram. London: Smith, Elder & Co. 1861.

The "turned-up shoe" was closely connected with the idea that the straight toe causes horses to trip. It proceeded on the principle that new fore-shoes ought to be shaped like the old and worn ones, so as to make the wear and tear nearly even all over the foot. Twenty years or so later, Veterinary Lieut.-Col. Hallen, C.I.E., now Inspector-General of the Civil Veterinary Department in India, invented a shoe to which he gave the name of "Central."[1] Its *rationale* was, that as only the "quarters" require protection, the toe, frog, bars, and heel may be safely left to shape themselves through friction with the ground. Its design will appear from the following diagram :—

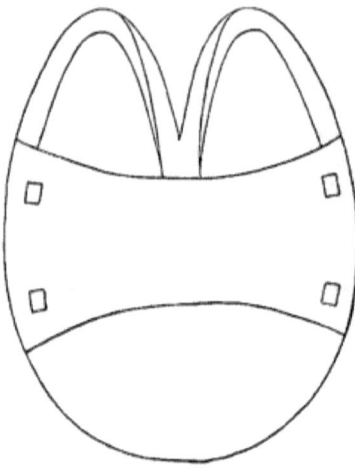

"CENTRAL" HORSE-SHOE.

About two years after the birth of the "Central Shoe," an anonymous inventor recommended, as a "great improvement on the ordinary shoe, and also on the 'Central Shoe' advocated by Mr Hallen," one which is depicted opposite.[2]

We have tried the above novelties on Arab horses which were addicted to "toeing." A great objection to all such contrivances is that ordinary workmen cannot do justice to them. In India, where the European method of shoeing is estab-

---

[1] *V.* "Notes regarding a New Horse-Shoe," by J. H. B. Hallen, Esq., in *Journal of the United Service Institute of India*, September 1880.
[2] *V. Asian Newspaper*, Calcutta, January 16, 1883.

lished, and every Englishman is a ruler, the horseman who is himself an expert may succeed, with personal supervision, in having effect given to his ideas. But in other oriental lands, every workman regards the traditions of his craft as a part of himself. For a long time we endeavoured, at Baghdad, to have our horses shod in the usual English fashion, instead of in the manner described in the preceding chapter. With that object, horse-shoes and nails [1] were procured from

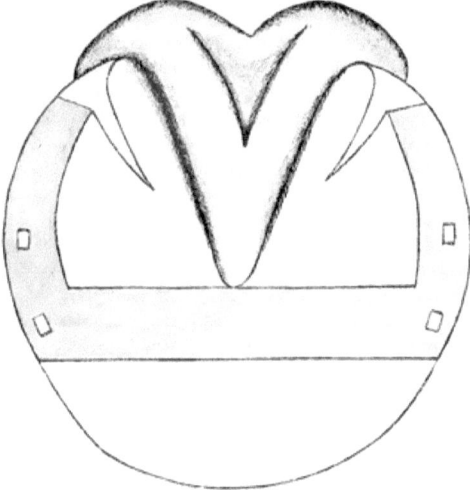

A MODIFICATION OF THE "CENTRAL" HORSE-SHOE.

Bombay; but the result clearly showed the uselessness of casual efforts to disturb modes of shoeing which prevail in any country. Fancy shoes are at best but palliatives. Flat-footed horses, and those having "castle-hoofs" or "road-scrapers," will always be difficult to shoe. New inventions are unnecessary for hoofs which are made of good material, and are properly shaped and properly set on. It may

---

[1] In Irâk, the horse-shoe nails are too brittle to admit of their ends being split and "clinched" after they have come through the crust. The hammered-down parts form clumsy projections, which are always hitting the opposite fetlock. Foreign cavalry and artillery would need to bring with them not only farriers but shoes and nails. The bony enlargements resembling small filberts which many Arab horses have at the inner and posterior corner of the fetlock joint, and which often are congenital, attest the prevalence of *cutting*, or *brushing*, in the Arabian variety.

be said that, outside of Arabia, the European buyers of Arab horses have to take them as the jam-bázes bring them. This is true, but it is subject to a limitation. There has long been a demand for large Arabs at Bombay, Constantinople, and other centres; and to meet this call, upstanding horses, which are more or less Arabs, are now collected in considerable numbers. A similar result would probably be witnessed if foreign buyers, instead of listening to the talk of the Arab dealers, would follow the same general principles as they do at Tattersall's. Straight shoulders, a bull neck, and crooked fore-legs, are surely as objectionable in Arabs as in other kinds of horses. More will be seen of this view in the sequel. There is just one other point which has to be mentioned in connection with the defects of the Arabian. The purchaser who takes care to buy only properly-shaped colts will find that their faults of action are susceptible of improvement. After he has made his purchase, let him, if he have the necessary leisure, patience, seat, and hands, not begrudge the trouble of teaching that which is to form, perhaps for many years, a part of himself, to play the same tune with all four legs, at the walk, trot, and canter. Above all things, let him be as gentle as he will find his pupil to be. If it be hard on him to have a raw horse under him, it is harder on the horse to be suddenly taken from a nation of light weights, and set to carry perhaps a cavalry major whose riding weight, thanks to a good mess and Indian allowances, exceeds that of two desert Arabs. For the Arabian horse, the "blessings of civilisation" generally consist of over-bitting, over-weighting, and hands of iron. The wonder is, not that the change perplexes him, but that he does not rebel and fall to kicking, or, like a horse of which we lately read, lie down in despair.[1]

---

[1] *A History of the Horse*, by W. C. L. Martin (1845), contains the following anecdote, which, although it can hardly be altogether true, may be partly so: "The late General Pater, a remarkably fat man, purchased a charger, which all at once betook itself to lying down whenever the General prepared to get upon his back. Every expedient was tried without success to cure him of the trick; and the laugh was so much indulged against the General's corpulency, that he found it convenient to dispose of his horse. Upwards of two years had subsequently passed, when General Pater left Madras to inspect one of the frontier cantonments. The morning after his arrival, the troops were drawn out; and as he had brought no horses, it was proper to provide for his being suitably mounted, though it was not easy to find a charger equal to his weight. At length an officer resigned to him a powerful horse for the occasion, which was brought out duly caparisoned in front of the line. The General came forth from his tent, and proceeded to mount, but the instant the horse saw him advance he flung himself flat upon the sand, and neither blows nor entreaties could induce him to rise. It was the General's old charger, who from the moment of quitting his service had never once practised the artifice until this second meeting!"

CHAPTER V.

A SUMMARY.

THE comparison of the Arab's horse with other people's horses from which we are now passing, at least bears out the conclusion that in certain circumstances, and for certain uses, the Arabian horse stands unrivalled. With all his faults, he is such a horse as can never be produced again. When the ever-widening margin of European unrest and civilisation shall have extended over the deserts of the Bedouin, and the breeds of Najd are as extinct as those which furnished the fields at Olympia and Delphi, the world of soldiers, travellers, and sportsmen will be the poorer.

The safe position thus attained brings into prominence two familiar questions:—

Do not the merits of the Arabian breed warrant the anticipation that "a further cross" with it would improve our English blood-stock?

And, apart from crossing, is it not a perfectly natural course to transplant Bedouin mares and horses to other countries, with a view to the production of an unmixed Eastern race, under the favouring influence of new conditions, aided by methodical selection?

The object proposed in this chapter is to collect and review the salient facts which bear on the above two questions.

I.—OF THE ARAB CROSS.

In previous passages we have spoken with some reserve of the beneficial effects of crossing. On the one hand, it has been noticed how, by means of a judicious cross, a new breed, combining more or less the good qualities of several breeds, may be founded. On the other hand, the practice of the Arabs has been held to confirm the conclusion that our choice breeds of cattle or of poultry, our wonderful race-horses, and our endless varieties of high-bred dogs, have been obtained less by crossing and feeding than by pure breeding and the repeated selection of superior specimens. This view will be further illustrated in future chapters. Here we offer but one remark, the soundness of which is little likely to be questioned— viz., that a higher breed can rarely be improved by crosses with an inferior one. No one knows from what quarter Captain Byerly of the Boyne obtained the Eastern horse destined, after King William's Irish wars (1689), to become from a regimental charger the direct ancestor of Herod, Highflyer, Woodpecker, Selim, Sir Peter, Filho da Puta, Bay Middleton, and others ; but it is probable that the foreigner excelled our island mares of that period in those qualities which purity of race develops. In the previous chapter it was held to be possible that there still remained in remote parts of the British Islands neglected kinds of half-hackney, half-agricultural cattle, for the improvement of which it might be advisable to try well-chosen Arabian stallions. Going further, we readily grant that if ever any one bring forward, whether from Asia or Africa, a sufficiently well-bred horse or mare more excellent in any considerable number of those points on which the superiority of a race or of an individual depends than the best specimens of the same class now in our possession, then by all means the stranger should be bred from. As, however, most practical men would stop at this point— that is, refuse to mate a noble mare with a stallion of doubtful origin—the utility of the Arab cross in Europe must be held to be dependent on the circumstances in which it is resorted to. Now as to this, let us first state that never in India, Arabia, or any other country, have we seen an Eastern horse which suggested the idea that he was capable of improving the perfected and established breeds of race-horses, hunters, or pleasure-hacks of our islands. No one who knows anything about it claims for the Arabian equality in speed or racing form with the descendants of Eclipse. Some indeed go further than the facts justify in the way of disparaging the Arabian as a race-horse. His performances on the Turf have even been spoken of as "wretched exhibitions." Mr Blunt, in one of his writings,[1] quotes this description, without rebutting it as decidedly and completely as a reference to the Indian racing calendars would have enabled him to do. He admits that "no *Ku-hai-lán* purchased of the Aeniza, and imported into England, would be likely to run with success against English thoroughbreds, even at the 2 stone 4 lb. allowed him in the Goodwood Cup, and over a two-and-a-half-mile course." He would not "recommend speculators to invest their money on him at greater weights, and over a longer distance." In the next sentence he maintains that the

---

[1] "The Thoroughbred Horse," in *Nineteenth Century*, September 1880, pp. 416 and 419.

Arabian " nevertheless is essentially a race-horse, the sire of race-horses, and that his produce, bred in England for a few generations, will be able to hold their own upon the English Turf—perhaps more than their own." Further on in the same article he argues that the explanation of the Arabian horse now proving but little fitted for the arena of the Turf, lies in " the circumstances of his desert breeding." [1]

In so far as this means that the desert breed would have yielded swifter race-horses if it had been cultivated by Englishmen for racing, instead of, as is actually the case, by the Bedouin Arabs for Al Ghaz-u, it is incontestable. But if the facts be examined, it will be found that, taking public running in India as the criterion, the Arabian is, *for his size*, a true race-horse, equally in speed, endurance, and power of carrying weight. It is not that the stock of Najd is not fast, but that the New-market breed is incomparably faster. Over the well-turfed course of Calcutta, Arab horses have, in a few rare instances, accomplished two miles, under about 9 stone, in three minutes and forty-five seconds—*i.e.*, at the rate of fifty-six and a quarter seconds for each half mile. To speak of an earlier period, we find the grey Arab Crab, "a large, powerful, but rather coarse horse," and the bay Arab Oranmore, " a handsome, small, slight of make, and very blood-like " one, contesting with one another no fewer than five heats of two miles, carrying 8 stone and 7 lb.

---

[1] Mr Blunt thus describes these circumstances : "The desert-bred Arab has had everything from the first against him. Starved before birth, he is generally a pony foal, but is nevertheless weaned at a month old, according to the invariable Bedouin practice. Even during the first month he is not allowed to run with his dam, being kept at the tent-ropes, tied by the near hind-leg above the hock ; nor has he any exercise, unless the tribe be on the march. During the next few months he is fed by the hand on camels' milk, or on such refuse dates as the owner can spare him, or on gathered pasture, if pasture there be. Then in his first autumn he is turned out to shift for himself, shackled, to prevent his being stolen, with heavy iron handcuffs. As a yearling he is like a little half-starved cat, and he only begins to grow in his third spring. Then—it will be in his second if he has been foaled in the autumn—he is mounted, I do not say broke, for he needs no breaking, and, unless he is to be kept as a stallion for the tribe, is sold to the village dealers on the edge of the desert. These put him into their close and filthy stables, where he generally sickens for a while, but then grows fat and sleek, when, after a sufficient training in such circus tricks as the Turks delight in, he is resold at an immense profit to some Pasha, Kâim-makâm, or Ulema, as the case may be, from whom he finds his way into Frank hands. During all this time he has probably had not one fair gallop in his life, and has hardly stretched his legs even in a loose-box, for he is kept hobbled day and night. At six, seven, or eight years old, when all his bones are set to short paces, and he has served maybe some seasons at the stud, he is suddenly put by his new owner into training, and disappoints him because he cannot win a common country race against English thoroughbreds. . . . It is therefore, I say, difficult to judge, by such perform-ances as we have seen, of all that the Arab is capable of as a race-horse." The fault of all this is, that it includes all the horses of all the Arabs in one de-scription. It has already been shown, and will further appear hereafter, that prior to export almost every Arab horse has a different history. There may be cases in which well-bred horses which have never been galloped are sent to India. Such ani-mals, even when they possess racing form, evince their lack of early advantages by disappointing their admirers for the first year or two of training, and ultimately winning a good race. But these are the exceptions. Most of the Arab horses which have run well in India have come to the post as colts, and must previously have done plenty of work in their native places. The "village dealers on the edge of the desert" are not Turks, and they im-part no "circus tricks" to the horses which they purchase.

each, in the Bengal Cup, on the 9th of January 1845. The bay won the first heat, and the grey the third and fifth heats, while the second and the fourth were dead heats. In the first heat, strong running was made only for the mile home; and it was run in one minute and fifty-two seconds, and won by a head. In the second heat, again, they made play only for a mile; and the heat was run in half a second less than the previous one. The third heat, which was won by a neck, was run in three minutes and fifty-six seconds. In the fourth heat, the real racing was confined to the last half mile, which was accomplished in fifty-four seconds. The deciding heat was won by the larger horse—Heenan wearing out Tom Sayers. Many similar instances might be given tending to exhibit the racing qualifications of the Arabian in a very favourable light. It is only when such records are compared with modern Newmarket form [1] that the difference is evident between a comparatively diminutive horse and one which, owing to his more lengthy stroke, derived from his superior size, is able, while galloping within his rate, to keep the other stretched at the extremity of his stride. Long ago, when our countrymen in India lived more than is now the case in a world of their own—which was, on the whole, a very pleasant world—the idea of winning the Goodwood Cup with an Arab horse grew and ripened in many an old-fashioned head. In 1847, when that great race was won by The Hero, carrying 9 stone 6 lb., the best Arab horse of his time in India, the blue-grey Monarch, though "turned loose" at 5 stone 4 lb., was among those which, "panting, toiled after him." Again, in 1861, one of the stoutest and bravest of the desert lineage—Dr Campbell's bay horse Copenhagen, a winner twenty-two times in India—was trained at Newmarket for the same severe two-and-a-half-mile ordeal. An officer of the Indian Irregular Cavalry, who at that time happened to be in England, thus described, in the *Oriental Sporting Magazine* for September 1870, a glimpse which he obtained of this Eastern candidate:—

"As Copenhagen was then well forward in his preparation, we determined to have a trial, so that I might be able to tell Dr Campbell what I saw. So I got on the filly Farfalla, riding about 10 st. 7 lb., and the lightest of the Sharps on Copenhagen—the latter getting at least 4 st. the best of the weights, not to mention allowance for age. We went the two middle miles; and the filly, then, I think, only a three-year-old, and by no means a first-class animal, lost him. He could not live with her from the first hundred yards, and the further we went the further the filly cantered away from him. . . . Had Copenhagen started for the Cup, he would have reached the T.Y.C. start-post about the time Tim Whiffler caught the judge's eye."

If in our day any one were to propose to enter an Arab at Goodwood, his friends would give him their vote and interest for Hanwell.

---

[1] *E.g.*, two miles and five furlongs in four minutes and ten seconds; two miles in three minutes and twenty-seven seconds; one and a half mile (Robert the Devil and Bend Or) in two minutes and thirty-nine and a half seconds; one mile (Brag, in the Brighton Cup) in one minute and thirty-seven and four-fifth seconds.

The claim of the Arabian to be accepted as a sire for hunters, pleasure-hacks, and coach-horses may be dealt with in a similar manner. It is well known how specialised these several groups of horses now are in the British Islands. There are men among us who will write a cheque in four figures for a perfectly satisfactory hunter or park horse, and never ask the former to serve as a hack, or the latter to go out of a walk. No such demand, it is needless to observe, exists within reach of the Arabs, nor do they know anything of these distinctions. What, we would inquire, has produced the difference, in looks, action, and manners, between the winners of prizes in the blood riding-horse class at our great shows this last half century, and the herds of semi-feral horses which, in Australasia and South America, are boiled down for the sake of their hides and tallow? Why, what but the selection, generation after generation, of those specimens which most nearly approach an accepted model. And it appears problematical how far kinds which are without a rival in their special business of topping fences and galloping through plough-lands under welter weights, or other kinds which, in harness, suggest the " wings of the winds," admit of being made better, through admixture with strains in which those qualifications are less developed. An old-fashioned Yorkshireman once observed, in India, of our team of Arabs, that they were all very well as toys, but that when he should take to bantam-cock-fighting he would ride and drive Arabs. And truly, who can challenge the abstract superiority of long and free-actioned horses over short ones? It is indisputable that week after week there are sold at Tattersall's so-called hunters which are more likely than many an Arab pony to hang up their riders in the first big place. But, speaking of the type of hunter which is to be seen in the Shires and elsewhere, something extraordinary must happen before the start-to-finish hunting men of England exchange their great-striding, long-shouldered weight-carriers, whether thoroughbred or what is technically called half-bred, for Arabs or the produce of Arabs.[1]

---

[1] These observations are wholly general. They are not intended to discredit the records concerning the feats of Arabs, and the produce of Arabs, in English hunting-fields, which have been published. It is needless to say that a great deal depends on the rider. There are men, and women too, who can put steam into a donkey, especially when the hounds are running. Apart from all that, the question is very much one of big horses *versus* little horses. According to "The Druid," one of the past generation of the Clibbles, of Kinlet, in Shropshire, contrived to beat all Leicestershire on a half-bred Arab. In such cases there is room for doubt on two points. How much of the superiority of the half-bred hunter depended on his Eastern, and how much of it on his English, ancestry? And further, will the oriental part of the pedigree stand the test of investigation? Many years ago, when the fame of Mr C. Davis's reputed half-bred Arab hunter, Hermit, was more talked of in England, over the mahogany, than is probably now the case, a portrait of his dam, the supposed Arabian, was shown to us. To our eye, she was an Indian stud-bred—*i.e.*, practically of English, and possibly thoroughbred English, stock. The account which was given of her, that she had carried a regimental trumpeter in India, hardly bore out the idea that she was an Arab. India is as great a mine of horse-flesh as it is a museum of human races; and English cavalry regiments, when serving in it, obtain remounts from many different quarters.

A question here occurs. Notwithstanding the wide diffusion of Arab horses, or so-called Arab horses, in I'rāk and Syria, India, Egypt, and the Western hemisphere, is there not some reason to believe that the pure ore of the breed is inaccessible to foreigners? Obviously it is idle to compare the Arabian with other varieties, if it be left open for any one who pleases to say that the authentic Ku-hai-lân is as unknown, outside of certain inner circles, as the fabled breed of volant Pegasus. Such an idea fascinates minds of the imaginative order, and some of those who have visited Central Arabia have played up to it. So many vague impressions exist on this subject, that it is necessary here to consider it. The chief supporter of the theory that he who has not entered Najd is but little likely to have seen the genuine Najdi horse is Mr W. G. Palgrave, whose book has more than once been quoted in the preceding pages. Several of his own descriptions bear against the position which he takes up on this point. For instance, in Chapter V. he mentions that, when he and his companions were approaching the township of Bu-rai-da, in Najd, they were overtaken by a band of travellers, in which was a "runaway negro conducting four horses destined to pass the whole breadth of Arabia, and to be shipped off at Ku-wait, on the Persian Gulf, for Indian sale." The reader is not left to imagine that the man had stolen the horses, though thefts of this nature are not infrequent. The following page discloses that "a rich artisan of [Jabal] Shammar had entrusted them to him;" in connection with which statement the author explains that, although "more than half the export of Arab horses to Bombay passes by the seaport of Ku-wait, . . . the animals themselves are generally from the north of Arabia or the Syrian desert, and of real Arab, though not of Najdian, breed." As to this, we do not know what "real Arab" means, if it do not denote the "Najdian" breed. The same writer makes the following ill-weighed statements in his article "Arabia" in the *Encyclopædia Britannica*, vol. ii. p. 241 :—

"Nor is a horse—or, *a fortiori*, a mare—ever disposed of [in Najd itself] by sale; gift, war-capture, or legacy being the only recognised methods of transfer where a genuine full-blood is concerned. Consequently, no commercial export of Najdi horses has ever been established ; and whoever professes to sell, or boasts of having bought, one, may be unhesitatingly set down as either deceived or deceiving. In three manners, however—two occasional merely, and one customary—has the Najdi breed been to a certain extent transplanted beyond the actual limits of Arabia. The first of the occasional or chance means . . . is, the fortune of war. . . . Secondly, a few thoroughbred Najdis have crossed the frontier as presents; . . . but mares are never given away thus, only stallions. The third, and customary, method is, by the admixture of the race. Najdi stallions are yearly hired out by their owners, and sent into the pastures of Jabal Shammar, of Syria, and even of Mesopotamia, there to breed with the mares of those countries belonging to the Arabs of Shammar, or the Aeniza, or the Ru-wal-la tribes of Syria and the like. These mares are themselves of Arab though not of Najdi stock, the proportion of good blood varying in them from a half up to three-fourths nearly; but none are of absolutely pure race.... These are the breeds from which European stables, even regal and imperial, have often obtained a supply of noble, but never absolutely pure-blooded, animals; frequently at prices proportioned to the imagined difficulties of the purchase, or the affected unwillingness of the cunning owner (Arabs are very cunning) to part with his beast. The best market for these mixed breeds is at Baghdad; the second is in the neighbourhood of the town of Hâma, in Syria; inferior animals are sent to the port of Ku-wait on the Persian Gulf, whence they are shipped for India."

All this is very misleading. Najd contains too many traders for even the smallest of its valuable products to be tabooed. If there had been no commercial outlet for the several thousands of colts which are foaled every year in the Arab peninsula, their owners would not have known what to do with them. Restricting the view for the moment, with Palgrave, to "chiefs and individuals of considerable wealth and rank," we may fairly allow to Muhammad ibnn 'r Ra-shîd, of Jabal Sham-mar, at least five hundred head of mares, for himself and his retinue. Let it be estimated that in every year one hundred of these run empty, while two hundred bear colts and two hundred bear fillies. In ten years that would burden him with two thousand consumers of harvests, each more or less requiring attendance, seeing that the *ri-jâ-jîl*, or MEN, who mount with him, are mare-riders. There is plenty of evidence as to the manner in which overstocking is obviated. Thus it has already appeared how freely both the colts and fillies are utilised in the gift-making process.[1] And we can confirm from actual observation the fact stated by Doughty, that the Hâ-yil chief is not above recovering a part of the expenses of his establishments by sending batches of colts to India, to be sold there, or perhaps exchanged for Martini-Henry rifles. It is not asserted that the younglings which he thus distributes invariably are of the highest class; but a few of them must be so, were it only through accident. In the Bombay sale-stables we have seen better colts of the Amir's forwarding than the best of those which have been sent by him in our time as presents to Baghdad Pâshas. Not to take further note of personages, it is impossible to approach Najd without perceiving that its horse-stock passes out of it through numerous channels. Here, as everywhere, the force of trade acts like a colossal pump. All the nomads in Central Arabia find it as convenient as the Shekh of Jabal Sham-mar does to sell the colts which they do not require. The buying of these, when very young, from the desert-scourers, is a favourite speculation of the oasis-dwellers; and the best of them ultimately go to India or Egypt. The mares and fillies, as is well known, do not fall into these trade courses,

[1] *V. ante*, p. 47.

as the colts do. But it is quite another thing to leap to the conclusions that Najdi mares "are never given away as presents," and that the pastures of Mesopotamia contain no mares which are "of absolutely pure race." Such statements involve an ignoring of the plainest facts; for example, the fact that hordes of the Bedouin are continually passing between Middle and Northern Arabia. Goers and comers of this description may frequently leave their mares in Najd, but it is impossible to suppose that they invariably do so. And nothing is more certain than that the mare of perfect pedigree, when, with her rider, or as a gift, a booty, or a marriage portion, she is taken out of Najd into Shá-mi-ya, may there find many of her own true kindred which have gone before her. The trade statistics, so to call them, which appear in the above-quoted passage are only fitted to produce wrong impressions. A dozen other places are equally entitled with Baghdad and Háma to be considered "the best markets for mixed breeds" of Arabian horses. Every considerable town, from the Armenian mountains to the Gulf of Persia, attracts to itself the saleable colts, mixed and pure, good, bad, and middling, of the adjacent districts, as surely as it does other rural produce. And similarly, the representation that "inferior animals are sent to the port of Ku-wait on the Persian Gulf, whence they are shipped to India," is true as far as it goes, and, at the same time, very inadequate. Ku-wait, or Grane, is the chief port of Najd, at all events for horses. It is only nine desert marches from Há-yil. Its inhabitants preserve, in spite of the Turks, much of the Arab character. The collecting of colts from inner Arabia, and from the Ae-ni-za nation of Shá-mi-ya, perhaps ranks as their principal industry. Admittedly, many of these animals are "inferior." But every year a certain number come forward which are of the flower of the stock of Najd. Indeed, we do not know of an easier method in which a European might see and buy Najdi horses prior to export than by stationing himself, from June to September, in the well-oasis of Bar-ja-si-a, a three days' journey out of Ku-wait. He would there be on the caravan route which leads from Najd to the sea-coast. Larger and smaller batches of Bedouin horses would be led or ridden past the spot in which he was ruralising. But even there he would have to be careful, as these caravaners buy colts as they proceed; and not every horse which comes from Najd is a Najdi, or even an Arabian.

A view akin to Palgrave's has been recorded by another of our countrymen. The late Mr Skene, her Majesty's Consul at Aleppo, writing more than thirty years ago, advised a correspondent that there was "blood and stride in the desert which has never been seen out of it."[1] What does that mean? For example,

---

[1] See his letter published in *Sporting Review* for March 1864.

are we to believe that Mr Darley's treasure-trove,[1] the progenitor in the female line of Herod, was inferior to other members of the same family which were to be found in Najd or on the Euphrates? Let no one imagine that it was so. In order to understand the Consul's statement, it is necessary to go behind it and take note of the circumstances which account for it. Mr Skene was a devoted admirer equally of the Arabs and of their horses. The lore of the black tents filled his head in the same ratio in which it emptied his pocket. He wound up his letter by intimating that, through helping the Arabs in their business with the Turkish Pàshas, preventing oppression, and enabling them to trade in safety with English exporters of wool, he was "perhaps the only one who had succeeded" in getting them to sell at long prices[2] a first-class horse or mare. It is unnecessary to say more on the subject of these representations than what may be safely said generally of assertions on the part of any one, that he is able to accomplish what perhaps no other person has ever accomplished. Misled in some measure by printed pages, and in some measure by the imagination, we have been trying, for thirty years, to call from the desert's "vasty deep" not spirits but peerless coursers; and, so far, the mere pursuit has had to satisfy us. Not only do all the facts refute the argument that Arabia contains better colts than those which she distributes, but they go further. They show that every desert of which we have any knowledge is so extensively stripped of its best bloodhorses, that not many likely colts of from three to five years old remain in the hands

---

[1] Major Upton has stated, in his *Gleanings from the Desert of Arabia* (p. 42), that there are documents in the Aleppo Consulate relating to the Darley Arabian; but our Aleppo colleague informs us, after a diligent search in his archives, that such is not the case. This is not here alluded to as if it threw any doubt on the Darley's history (*v. ante*, pp. 138 *et* 165, and f.n. 2), but merely to show the precariousness of hearsay. Among the Arabs all things are told by word of mouth; a statement has but to be heard or an incident witnessed in order to be bruited from Dan to Beersheba; and the horizon of men's imaginations is, besides, illimitable. Another illustration of this presents itself in connection with the Darley. Both Major Upton and Mr Blunt have passed it on to us that he belonged to the strain which is called *Rìsm'l Fi-dáwi*; whereas Mr Darley wrote of him that he was "of the most esteemed race among the Arabs, both by sire and dam, and the name is called Maanicka" (*v. supra*, p. 165 in f.n. 2). *Mi'-ni-ki*, or *Ma'-na-kì* (from a root meaning *long-necked*, whence also "Sons of Anak"), is known to every dabbler in desert pedigrees. In the case of Arabians of established lineage, a distinctive adjunct, like the second name in plants, always follows stock names of the class of *Mi'-ni-ki*. But either this escaped Mr Darley, or his Yorkshire senses were but little exercised over the Bedouin nomenclature. The name, as well as the strain, of Mi'-ni-ki found its way into our stud-book with the Darley. A "Manica," foaled in 1707, figured among his immediate progeny, side by side with Aleppo (1711), Almanzor (1713), and Flying Childers, in that not always to be relied on record.

[2] The prices which Mr Skene quoted as those at which he would undertake to procure really first-class Arabians from the Bedouin were £300 a-head for mares and £200 a-head for horses. A European gentleman in Bombay took advantage of his readiness thus to oblige his friends. About 1862 a number of Mr Skene's selections passed through Baghdad on the way to India. There were no mares among them; and although mares afterwards followed, such were probably intended more for breeding than for racing. At all events, no fillies ever distinguished themselves in the importer's colours on Indian courses. Several colts did so; but the stride which they exhibited was not superior to that of hundreds of other Arab horses which have reached India through the usual trade channels.

of their breeders. If England possesses too many stud-horses, Arabia retains too few. One may visit a considerable encampment of the Ae-ni-za and see no unweaned colts, except a few reserved ones, and those which the dealers will not buy. The stock which these people always have with them chiefly consists of well-tried mares, aged stallions, and the rising fillies.

The mention of fillies suggests a different line of inquiry. Many hold the opinion that if the Arabian blood is fitted further to improve the established breeds of Europe, the desert mare should be sought for in preference to the desert stallion. About twenty years ago a demand for Arab horses as sires prevailed in the Australasian colonies. The idea of obtaining a second Satellite, the Darley Arabian of the Antipodes, excited the imagination of the horse-breeders and sportsmen of New South Wales and Victoria. At the request of a much-esteemed friend in the former colony—the late Mr James White of Sydney—we procured for him at different times between 1869 and 1875 four carefully chosen Arabian horses. One of these made a good mark, under the name of A-mir, in stud-book annals. In 1881 Mr White wrote that A-mir's stock "had proved unequalled" as light harness-horses; and that a pair of them had elicited "the praises of one of the greatest authorities in England on the horse-supply question, who, when he saw them being driven by a lady in Sydney, said that they would readily bring a thousand guineas in London." But A-mir, who, by the way, was closely inbred, never sired a race-horse, or a really good hack, in spite of the excellent opportunities of doing so which Mr White afforded to him. Nevertheless, Arabs claiming high character continued to make their appearance in Australia. The local horse-dealers who went to India brought back several of those which had run well at Calcutta; and at least one pastoral Crœsus spared no expense to obtain specimens which had been specially selected in Shá-mi-ya. But it does not appear that any improvement was thus effected in the thoroughbred strains of the colonies. Public opinion in that quarter would appear to have now undergone a change. In 1885 one of the leading horse-breeders in New South Wales wrote to us saying that the great strides made by his adopted country in the production of blood-stock [1] discouraged the idea that there were now any better sires in Arabia than the descendants of Whisker and Satellite, but that perhaps room existed for a further trial of really first-class Bedouin mares. In the same letter he expressed his readiness to pay a thousand guineas, or more if necessary, for one such mare. His impression was that the

---

[1] A little more than a century ago the rich virgin prairies of Australasia did not support a single horse. When the first fleet sailed into Sydney harbour, in January 1788, there were landed one stallion, three mares, and three colts. It was not till 1825 that the Australasian colonies received their first thoroughbred mare, Manto, though before her several thoroughbred stallions had been imported. Thus the Australian blood-horse cannot be said to date back for as much as eighty years.

desert practice of selling the colts and keeping the fillies resulted in the Arabian mare generally being superior in size and swiftness to the Arabian horse. At Baghdad many indications of the acceptance of this view present themselves; but it would be vain to build on it till some adventurous Englishman, sated with the Riviera and Monte Carlo, shall enter the desert and purchase a few of its choicest mares—not such as have been used for breeding, but fillies fit for cup races. In regard to our friend's application, during several years we took a great deal of trouble to find an animal worthy of being forwarded to him. But accident vouchsafed no assistance; indirect means, as usual, proved worse than useless; it was impossible personally to go and hunt up the pearl in the black-tent cities; and consequently, his desire remained unfulfilled.

Before the subject of the Arab cross is passed from, an attempt may be made to sift the common impression that the desert Arab will not sell his mare. At the outset, it has to be admitted that this belief is not groundless. Stories of priceless mares, dearer to the owner than his life, are widely circulated. It seems always to be assumed in the literature of the Arabs that, apart from the foray, there is but one way of acquiring a filly which is the property of a stranger, and that is by stealing her! To illustrate this, room may here be found for the following translation from the well-known Arabic book entitled *Naf-ha-tu 'l Yemen*.[1]

A respectable person relates that one day he saw a man of the Agel,[2] on whose back were marks like those of cupping, and asked for an explanation of them, and received this answer:—

"The state of the case is, that I loved a fair cousin, and sought her in marriage, and her kindred said, 'We will not give her to thee unless thou makest *Sha-ba-ka* the wedding-gift.' And Sha-ba-ka was a mare, the fleetest of all, and she belonged to one of the Ba-nû Bakr. And on that I married my cousin. And I went out to effect by stratagem the taking of the mare from her owner, that I might be able to make good the bridal dower. In the guise of a camel-butcher I visited the tribe in which the mare was, and kept going in among them till I learned to distinguish her place from the tent in which her master was. And I saw that she had a filly. And I contrived to enter the tent and conceal myself under a heap of wool carded for washing. And when night came, and the master of the tent appeared, and his wife had dressed supper for him, and they both began to eat, and the gloom had deepened, and they had no lamp, and I was hungry, I put out my hand and stretched it towards the platter, and ate with them. And the man became conscious of my hand, and did not know what it was, and he gripped it; and I laid hold of the woman's hand with my other hand, and she said to him, 'What do you want with my hand?' And he supposed the case to be that he was

---

[1] A collection of biographical and moral pieces, of date about 150 years ago, by Shekh Ahmad of Yemen.

[2] The Agel, or more correctly *U-kail*, are a nation of Arabia. Their roots are in Najd, but they flourish in every locality to which the trade of the Arabs is extended by means of camels. Like the *chârans*, or reciting bards, of India, they are privileged to pass everywhere, irrespectively of tribal feuds and enmities.

holding his wife's hand, and let go my hand, and I released the woman's hand, and we ate. . . . And the meal came to an end; and the man stretched himself on his back and slept. And while he slept I watched them, and the mare was shackled beside the tent, and her filly was unshackled in the tent, and the key of the mare's fetter was under the woman's head. After a little time a black slave arrived and threw a small pebble. And the woman awoke and rose to him, and left the key in its place, and went out of the tent to the back of it, and I crept and took the key, and unlocked with it the mare's shackles. And I had a hair bridle with me, and I bridled the mare and mounted her, and went off on her from the tent. And the woman came back and entered the tent. Then she called out, and the tribe caught the alarm and became aware of me, and mounted in pursuit. And I put the mare to her speed, with a troop of them after me. And I entered on the time of morning, and did not see save one horseman, armed with a lance, and he overtook me, and the sun had risen, and the man began to thrust at me, and could not get his spear-point any nearer to me than sufficed to make these traces on my back. Neither did his mare come up to me, so that he might have me in his power, nor did my mare carry me away, so that the spear should not touch me. And we came to a stream, and I shouted to the mare, and she jumped it; and the horseman shouted to his mare, and she did not jump. And when I saw that she could not cross, I got off my mare to rest myself and her. And the man called to me, and I said, 'What is it?' and he answered, 'I am the owner of the mare that is under thee, and this is her filly, and as you have got her, take care of her; and truly, by God, I never asked anything of her without attaining to it; and she was like a fisherman's net (*shabaka*) in the matter of taking.'"

There is no sure way of distinguishing the facts which lie at the foundation of tales like the above. Such elopements certainly hold a place among the usages of the desert; but perhaps they are confined to those who have no money, or money's worth, to offer. On the other hand, it is an easy inference, from all that has been stated regarding the value of the mare to the Bedouin Arabs, that their natural inclination is to keep her. According to their saying, her back is the seat of riches, and her womb's produce their year's harvest. In face of the enormous sums which we will pay for retiring turf heroes,[1] and even for untried yearlings,[2] there is nothing incredible in the stories which are current of very large offers having occasionally failed to tempt the Bad-u to transfer his treasure to a stranger. It is not a very simple matter to determine what, if any, share mere sentiment or affection has in hardening this bond of union. Each separate case requires to be experimented on with a heap of gold or a string of camels. Sometimes a report reaches Baghdad that one of the Ae-ni-za possesses a mare for which he has refused fabulous offers. We never have taken steps to test such representations, because, for one thing, a mare may be worth a great deal to the Bedouin, and be almost valueless to the

---

[1] *E.g.*, twelve thousand guineas for Blair-Athol, fourteen thousand guineas for St Gatien, and the same amount for Ormonde. At the Antipodes Mr Cox of Sydney refused ten thousand guineas for Yattendon.

[2] As we write this, we hear of a daughter of St Simon and Quiver fetching five thousand five hundred guineas, at her Majesty's sale of yearlings; also of a yearling colt by Chester realising four thousand six hundred guineas at Sydney.

European.[1] It is easy to be cynical on the subject of sentiment; but even when the Bedouin Arab agrees to sell his mare, it is not improbable that he does so with sorrow in his heart. A well-known writer relates a story of a Northumberland gipsy who was employed to kill down the otters in a nobleman's fish-pond, and was so ably assisted by a terrier of his own breeding, which he called Charlie, that his lordship tried to buy the dog, but to no good purpose; the sturdy "Egyptian's" answer being, "By the winds, his whole estate canna buy Charlie!"[2] There are many analogies between the Arabian Bedouin and the Aryan gipsies. And it is but reasonable to concede to the desert Arabs the same high degree of attachment to their mares which the "Ishmaelites" of Europe display towards useful pets of other descriptions. A salient feature of the Arab horse-trade appears to indicate that not only Arab public opinion, but oriental public opinion at large, is adverse to the removal of mares to foreign countries. The feature alluded to is, that the dealers who ship Arab horses to India include but few mares in their collections. Many of these men are not Arabs, but Persians who have more or less assumed the Arab speech and manner, and their code of law is flexible. Nevertheless, as a rule, they only take horses. Of course, a mare costs more money, all things being equal, than a horse does; but this explanation is inadequate. It occasionally happens that a dealer receives, when he is in India, a commission, backed by an advance of money, from a millionaire Rajah, to purchase race-horses for him after his return to Arabia. In these favourable circumstances, one would expect him to buy desert fillies, regardless of price, for his employer; but he does not do so. Or, to keep to the ordinary trade level, any dealer might bring together a string of useful and more or less well-bred Arabian mares, at prices varying from £5 to £200 a-head, in and around Baghdad or Bussorah. Animals of this description would find a ready market in India. The Indians would buy them for breeding, and for processional occasions; and our countrymen would appreciate them as pleasure-hacks, especially for ladies. It is true that the Ottoman authorities would oppose their exportation; but all the measures which they might adopt to prevent it would prove as futile as their periodical embargoes on the exit of horses generally.

It is established by many witnesses that mares of high quality and reputation have been sold to strangers by the Bedouin Arabs. Thus Mr Skene, in letters

---

[1] For example: a mare, originally from the nation of Harb, in Najd, lately fell into the hands of the Bussorah Government, after she had made a great name for herself among the Ae-ni-za. When she was sold, a townsman bought her for about £30. Her general appearance was worthy of her reputation. She was a magnificent specimen of the Arabian blood-horse. But she was far too unsound to be fit for breeding, and she could not walk without stumbling. One day we tried her for a mile against a hack, and the winged one of desert hyperbole was beaten in the wretched time of two minutes and eleven seconds!

[2] *V.* "Our Dogs," in *Horæ Subsecivæ*, by John Brown, M.D., 1862, p. 207.

which subsequently found their way into print, described several first-class mares which he had bought, at prices running up to £400, from the tribes of Shâ-mî-ya and Al Ja-zî-ra. Captain Upton mentions "six horses and mares" which he and his companions obtained from the Ae-ni-za, in 1874-75.[1] In *Bedouin Tribes of the Euphrates* it is not disclosed how, where, and at what prices the Crabbet Park stud matrons were procured; but Mr Blunt says, in a later essay, that "good Arabian mares of the best blood may be purchased in the desert at from £200 to £250" each, and that he got many of his for less.[2]

The truth is, that it all depends on circumstances. The mares of the Arabs, though not in the first instance intended for the market, do nevertheless drift towards it. If accident may bestow a first-class mare on an English consul, it may equally do so on others.[3]

Perhaps it will be thought that all these observations on "a further cross" with Arabs follow a wrong direction. No practical person, it may be said, now supposes that if the best mare in England were to visit the best Arab that ever trod the desert, the immediate issue would excel, or even equal, its progenitors on the dam's side. But apart from all idea of producing *improvement* or increased superiority, is it not necessary, at certain intervals, to return to Eastern blood, with the object of *warding off decline* in the modern English race-horse, and in all the secondary kinds which derive their virtue from him? Owing, perhaps, to long residence among the Arabs, we fail to understand how any one can advocate such a piece of retrogression. It would be presumption to hazard an opinion on the moot-point of whether the heroic line of Voltigeur and the Dutchman, Hampton and Rosicrucian, is now undergoing deterioration. Any one may see, in the course of a few visits to the training-grounds of England, that far too many leggy weeds and flat-sided, five-furlong wretches exist among us. Our island breeders must look to this, if they would continue to supply Europe and America, as well as Egypt, India, China, Australasia, New Zealand, and South Africa, with thoroughbred horses, while retaining a sufficient number with which to challenge the world. But other saving measures are at their disposal than crosses with horses of unverified pedigree. It may be taken for granted that the Darley Arabian, besides being, in all

---

[1] *Op. cit.* in Catalog. No. 5, p. 402.

[2] "The Forthcoming Arab Race at Newmarket," in *Nineteenth Century*, May 1884, p. 763.

[3] *Par exemple*, while this is being printed we hear from Baghdad of a Russian nobleman who has just returned from a long and difficult journey in Central Arabia. Naturally so distinguished a traveller did not fail to visit Amir Muhammad, the prince of Ja-bal Sham-mar. Presents worthy of the occasion were of course not omitted; and the Amir's return gift to the Baron consisted of three mares "on which was Allah's blessing." One of these mares, as we are informed, is being taken to Constantinople, for presentation to H.I. Majesty the Sultan; while the other two have passed into the possession of a French gentleman, who, after the annexation of his native province by the Germans, transferred himself, with much of his property, to the City of the Caliphs.

probability, pretty closely inbred, was a model both in respect of make and soundness. But if he possessed as good a set of legs as those of the only Derby winner which we have ever had an opportunity of looking over, then he was fortunate.

Here we pass to the second of the two divisions of this chapter—

ON THE NATURALISATION ABROAD OF THE ARABIAN BREED.

Our century has seen a considerable number of experiments made with this object, but the results are not encouraging. His Majesty the late King of Würtemberg (1817-1864) was an enthusiastic admirer of the Arabian horse. Altogether, he was able to obtain for his stud near Stuttgart thirty-eight horses and thirty-six mares of Arabian blood and birth. His object was to breed pure Arabs. During his reign, when an Arab was in all strictness a royal hobby, the four-year-old Arabs which his Majesty distributed by means of annual sales brought an average of £125 each as chargers. After his death the average fell to £67.[1]

Another pre-eminent name in this connection is A'b-bás Pásha, from 1848 to 1854 Viceroy of Egypt. Many accounts exist of the lavish manner in which this prince dealt out the good things of Egypt to the Arabs. Palgrave assigns to him a set policy of buying the allegiance equally of the Wahabite confederacy and of the disunited clans of the desert, so that he might rule in Egypt less as the Porte's vassal than as sovereign of the Arabian peninsula.[2] But to understand the character of his administration, it is perhaps only necessary to remember that, in his childhood, he had lived in the desert; that as a Muslim he naturally preferred Arab to European alliances; and that he was not a great man, but one who followed the bent of his inclination. At any rate, there never was a more zealous collector of Arabian mares and horses. His stud contained upwards of a thousand animals of the purest strains of blood; and to this day the mouths of the Bedouin water when they think of the prices which his agents would pay for one colt or filly.[3] Perhaps the most important feature in the record is the remark which his Highness the Pásha made to Freiherr von Hugel, chief of the stud of the King of Würtemberg, when he was describing the pure Arabs in the royal stables at Stuttgart: " Even if you succeed in getting hold of genuine Arabs, you will never breed real Arabs from

---

[1] "The Breeding of Horses," in *Edinburgh Review*, October 1873, pp. 444-446.
[2] *Op. cit.* in Catalog. No. 7, vol. i. pp. 189-194.
[3] *E.g.*, according to Mr Skene, £800 for one stallion. A'b-bás Pásha's stud was but little cared for by his successor. In 1860 the remains of it came under the hammer at Cairo. By that time only about three hundred and fifty animals were left. The sale was spread over three weeks. On one day twenty-six horses fetched five thousand guineas. Mares twenty years old were sold at from one hundred and eighty to two hundred and fifty guineas. Colts and fillies realised from three hundred to seven hundred guineas each.

them; for an Arab horse is no longer an Arab when he ceases to breathe the air of the desert." Probably A'b-bás Pásha had brought himself to think that Egypt was Arabia; and compared with the South-German plateau, it is so. Nevertheless, climate is irresistible. A well-watered country, lying near the sea, cannot fail to exert other influences on animal life than those which belong to the grassy limestone uplands of Najd. If the finest known specimens of the Barb, or African Arab, lack the perfect balance of the parent type, climate, probably, is at the bottom of it. In the same way, it is not impossible that A'b-bás Pásha's shrewd observation about the Stuttgart Arabs admitted of extension to his own Egyptian Arabs, in the second or third generation.

At the mention of transplanting the Arabian breed to Europe, all must naturally think of Mr Wilfrid Blunt. Here respect must temper criticism. The British public is much indebted to Mr Blunt. Without having the smallest personal object, he worked hard, and freely expended his money, in order to bring about a reconsideration of the basis on which our thoroughbred stock is established. But how can any one be expected seriously to consider an argument which proceeds on the assumption that the Arabian horse "*is the descendant of* a single race kept pure *since its first domestication*"?[1] As to this we may be allowed to say that if Mr Blunt, before giving way to such a fancy, had taken the trouble to think clearly, his views would have been modified. If the necessity of examining the foundations of his theory failed to impress him, at least he had the courage of it. He imported eighteen Arabian mares and two Arabian stallions, confessedly as an experiment, but not without the sanguine hope of their one day bestowing on the English turf, to quote his words, "*a new race of thoroughbreds, this time really thoroughbred;*" and on the stud, "*a more perfect animal than any that England has yet possessed.*"[2] After an interval of four years, he reported progress in an exceedingly interesting paper,[3] in which he gave measurements showing that, "with, of course, a few exceptions," the general run of the young Arabs bred in England from the imported animals had been increased in size by the action of the English climate, combined with good feeding. The only wonder is that, in this nineteenth century, any one should have considered it necessary to demonstrate over again a fact which everybody knows, or ought to know. Without going beyond the limits of Arabia, one may notice how the breeds of camels vary in bulk and stature in different districts, according to the climate.

If only character or manners be in question, perhaps there is a way in which

---

[1] F. Mr Blunt's article, "The Thoroughbred Horse," in *Nineteenth Century*, September 1880, p. 423.
[2] The same article, p. 422.
[3] *Nineteenth Century*, May 1884.

European horses might be brought to resemble those of the Arabs, and that is, through our coming to closer terms with them. Admittedly there must always remain, like a priestly caste, between us and them, those consequential persons who keep the key of the stable door; but the modern system of education may be trusted to improve these people. The *bon camarado* feeling with which the Bedouin regard the equine sharer of their adventures would well become all of us. That true-toned moralist of the realm of sport, Whyte Melville, showed the way in this direction, when he impressed it on his readers that the hunter which has carried one in a fast run deserves the same solicitude, both then and afterwards, as does the beautiful and gentle partner in a waltz! The desert horseman's treatment of his mare is unique in several features. He does not "spare for spoiling" of her: we have seen how he will ride her to death in urgent circumstances. But he exalts her above the level to which the inferior animals are necessarily restricted in the lands of commerce and high pressure. One of the heroic tales of Najd contains a battlepiece in which the reciter describes how he *rode at the hauberk-wearers till his charger seemed clad in a shirt of blood*; and the dumb animal is no sooner mentioned than the following sympathetic reference is brought in by way of climax:—

> And he swerved from the thrusts of the spears in his breast;
> And made moan to me with tear and *ham-ha-ma*;[1]
> Had he known how to confabulate, he would have complained;
> And if speech had been given to him, he would have addressed me.
> —A'NTAR.

In our country, sentiment of this description may seem exclusively to belong to the domain of poetry. We can no longer say with Spenser—

> "Chiefly skill to ride
> Seems a science proper to gentle blood."

The squire of Cowper's *Task*—

> "Who always, ere he mounted, kissed his horse,"—

represents a type which is vanishing. The creation of a new equestrian class in the British Islands has formed a great commercial feature of this century; but it may be doubted whether the increase in numbers of horses and horsemen has, on the whole, been attended with improvement in the horse's status. The use of such a

---

[1] A word of the same class as *neav*, *bow-wow*, &c. Derivatives from natural sounds are frequent in Arabic. *Ghar-ghar-ra*, gargling; *ma-kha-ra* [our "nicher"], snorting; *na-ma*, *ya-in-ma*, whining, or moaning; *i'ts*, sneezing; *kahh*, coughing; *hiss*, a low sound,—are examples.

term as status in this connection may excite a smile in those whose thoughts about their horses always work round to money. But there are others of our countrymen who will perhaps concur in the opinion, that the more considerate we are of our horses' happiness and feelings, the less reason we shall have to draw unfavourable comparisons between them and those of the Bedouin Arabs. The "gentleman" is "gentle," not only towards his fellows, but also towards the inferior animals.

A BIT ON THE TIGRIS.

BOOK FOURTH

THE ARABIAN AT HOME

CHAPTER I.

ON THE ORIGIN OF THE ARABIAN BREED.

HAT branch of geology which is more particularly occupied with fossil remains traces back the "creation" of the Horse, as now known, through numerous progressive forms or stages, to an absolutely prehistoric period; but they who would pursue this subject must consult special books.[1] It is at the point where the discourse of the naturalist ceases that that of the breeder or "fancier" begins. When the zoologist has ticketed off, in genus *Equus*, the so-called "species" of (1) *Equus caballus*, or horse; (2) *Equus asinus*, or domestic ass; (3) the rufous wild asses of Asia; and, lastly, the striped quaggas, dauws, and zebras of South Africa,—he leaves it to the horseman to register the following, among other, varieties of *Equus caballus*:—

The English Thoroughbred;
The various established strains of trotting, coaching, and agricultural horses of the British Islands;
Other European breeds—*e.g.*, the Flanders or Flemish breed;
The Arabian;
The Barb;
The Turku-mâ-ní;
The Dongola, and other African breeds;
All the races of ponies, from the Shetland Isles to Burmah.

Lovers of the æsthetic may expect from us a different treatment of our subject than that we should begin by labelling as a mere variety of *Equus caballus*, the horse which is held to be the prototype of his species, the rosy-coated[2] Arabian courser;

---

[1] *E.g.*, *The Horse* in "Modern Science" series, by W. H. Flower, C.B., LL.D., D.C.L. London, 1891.

[2] *V.*, in table of colours, p. 263, *wa-ṣaw-rad*, or roseate, as a colour of Arab horses.

of whom an I'ráki poet of the artificial school imagined that the pure air satisfied his hunger,[1] and the smoke uprising from sun-scorched plains his thirst. But as a good deal more of this moonshine falls on the track which awaits us, it is the more necessary to take preliminary note of the Arabian's place in Natural History.

The reappearance among the Arabs of the ancient fable about the condensation of the south wind to form the Horse was glanced at in another place;[2] and the wonderful stories which prevail in towns like Bussorah regarding the origin of the specialised Arabian breed look like embellishments of the same conception. In a very old recital of this class, the sea foam takes the place of the wind as the procreant element. Solomon, King of Israel, it is stated, had a horse of matchless excellence. One day he made the genii toss this animal into the sea, and push him back every time that he tried to swim ashore. Seven colts, each destined to sire a noble lineage, proceeded out of the foam which marked his sinking.[3] Orientals do not believe these stories, any more than we do certain similar legends which we nevertheless repeat to our children; but they do not seem to look much further than them. The above representation possesses but one feature which is of interest here, and that is, its allusion to King Solomon. To this day the three grandest, truest, and most original figures in Semite story, as it appears to many, are Abraham, Solomon, and Muhammad. The David of the Books of Samuel holds the highest place among the rulers and judges of Israel. But all over Western Asia, the renown of him whose military genius made Jerusalem an imperial capital is lost in that of his successor—the grand monarch, at whose bidding temples and palaces arose; whose commercial policy extended the circle of his prestige; and for whose magnificent acts, and insights into Nature's Kingdom,[4] tradition could only account by supposing him invested with sovereignty over demons. In another context,[5] familiar passages of Scripture were cited to illustrate how the collection and distribution of horses ranked among the many sensational features of Solomon's reign. A daughter of a Pharaoh was

---

[1] Similarly, Ariosto—
"East Angalia's courser, which was born
From a close union of the wind and flame,
And nourished not by hay or heartening corn,
Fed on pure air."
—*Orlan. Fur.*, c. xv.

[2] *V.* p. 4, *ante.* In the same way, Homer, to account for the hurricane-like course of the horses in Achilles' chariot, assigns to them the pedigree, "by Zephyrus out of the harpy Podarge" (*Il.*, xvi. 148). And according to Tasso—
"This jennet was by Tagus bred; for oft
The breeder of these beasts to war assignede,
When first on trees hangen the blossoms soft,

Pricks forward with the sting of fertile kinde,
Against the aire cast up her hand aloft;
And gath'reth seed so from the fruitfull winde,
And thus conceiving of the gentle blast
(A wonder straunge and rare) she foales at last."
—*Jerus. Freed*, Bk. vii. (Fairfax's translation).

[3] This story also, as the reader will notice, admits of being traced to many sources. In Greek mythology, a horse was created by the sea-god Poseidon's striking the ground, in Thessaly, with his fish-spear. And the sacred Indian horse Uccaihsrawas was produced at the churning of ocean.

[4] 1 Kings iv. 33. [5] *V. ante*, p. 27.

one of his 700 wives.¹ At that time (10th century B.C.) the Nile kingdom was rich in horses.² Hence it naturally followed that "the horses which Solomon had were brought out of Egypt; and the king's merchants received them in droves, each drove at a price."³ Now the connection of these facts with our present theme lies in this, that the masses of the Arabs, for whom the Kur-án is the beginning and end of all history and geography, hold Solomon, King of Israel, to have been an Arab. Before Muhammad,⁴ Arabian tradition was not less charged than Hebrew with floating and fragmentary notices of the "man of peace";⁵ and very many of these afterwards found a place in the Kur-án. At the risk of overtaxing the reader's patience, one such reference must here be quoted, because of the way in which modern fabulists interweave it with their own veracious pieces of horse history. Gabriel's words, very literally rendered, are—

And We [Allah] gave to Dá-úd, Su-lai-mán, the best of God's servants—truly a constant turner [Godward].
When, at eventide, the standers on three legs, touching the ground with the tip of the fourth foot—the outstrippers—were ranged before him,
Then he said, Truly I have loved the love of worldly weal, more than the remembrance of my Master, until is hidden [the Sun] behind the curtain [of Night];
Bring them back to me. And he began to smite them neck and thigh.
—Sú-ra xxxviii.

In this quotation, the Prophet, to admonish those who heard him, brought in a fragment narrating how, once upon a time, the pious king and patriarch, absorbed in admiration of his stud, omitted the evening prayer; and afterwards, on his conscience pricking him, sacrificed the four-footed idols. The historical starting-point of this merely was the extraordinary pains which the traditional Solomon took to improve the horse-supply of his kingdom. But mark the use which is now made of it. If we should here inform the general reader, solely on our own authority, that there are numerous persons of considerable knowledge and understanding who hold that in our day every genuine Arabian derives his pedigree from strains preserved by Solomon, the statement might exceed the bounds of credibility. But evidence to that effect is about to be cited in the words of one of the principal recent figures in

---

¹ 1 Kings iii. 1; cf xi. 3.
² The horse begins to appear in the Egyptian monuments so far back as the 18th century B.C., and tradition points to Egypt as one of the first places in which the breeding and management of horses received full attention from settled people.
³ 1 Kings x. 28, revised version. But from 2 Chron. ix. 28, it further appears that "they brought horses for Solomon . . . out of all lands."
⁴ Ná-bi-gha. 1. 22.
⁵ The Biblical form, Shelōmō, for Sh lōmōn, is now

thus rendered. In the Kur-an it is written Su-lai-mán. The Arab grammarians reckon this a regularly derived form (diminutive) from Sal-mán, at this day a much esteemed proper name throughout Arabia. European scholars hold "Su-lai-mán" to be an Arab deformation, or adaptation, of She-lō-mō. In any case, the root of Shē-lō-mōn is also that of Sal-mán, equally in Arabic and Hebrew. The same root appears in sa-lám, ís-lám, Salem, Jerusalem, Absolom, and many other words.

the Arab horse trade, the late Esau bin Curtas,[1] of Bussorah and Calcutta. Esau was not a reading man or a writing one; but he was a very shrewd one, as his success, not only with horses but in other branches of Arabian commerce, showed. Even book knowledge reached him indirectly, in the modern *Arabian Nights' Entertainments*, or conversaziones, of Zubair and Bussorah. If he could not write himself, he had those who could both write and read for him; and the editors of a Calcutta magazine, in the number for October 1869, allowed him to enlighten English readers regarding the history of the Arabian breed. The groundwork of his ideas is thus described by him:—

"Solomon, it appears, was a great lover of horses; in fact, he spent the greatest part of his day, and devoted much of his time, in admiration of them. This great patriarch, a devoted and humble servant of God, one day, engrossed by the company of, and perfection of the beauty of, his horses, omitted to say his prayers; for which reason, on reflecting on his neglect to God for worldly pleasure, he took an extreme hatred to his horses, and turned them all loose, all over the country: on which occasion, let it well be noticed, six of the *élite* of known mares were selected from the loose and abandoned lot, and kept especially for breeding purposes by an equal number of individuals.

"From that date the names of those six individual owners were given to the six mares respectively, and which can be traced to the present day. From these six mares have descended a long list of names which have no end. The produce, unlimited, from the above six mares is to a degree astonishing; and unless the blood of the foals can be traced back to one of them, they are scorned by the Bedouins, who will have nothing to say to them. The Bedouins of the present day have not, as is supposed, relaxed in the slightest degree their search or trace back to their six renowned dams; and their minuteness in their inquiries is extremely correct."[2]

Now it must not be imagined that Esau fabricated this account. It simply is, as the reader will perceive, a garbled version of the passage in the Kur-ân about Solomon and his mares which has just been quoted. The fact of its owning such a source is enough to separate it from the genuine—that is, Bedouin—Arabs, who no more occupy themselves with material of this description than the pure Romany blood does with church history in Europe. The proper way to regard it is as a piece of lore of the Arab horse-dealers, who find it a valuable aid to business when they go to India. Strange as it may sound, they frequently succeed in impressing the essential part of it on the minds of educated Europeans. For example, the late Major Upton, in *Gleanings from the Desert of Arabia*, takes up the wondrous tale where Esau left it. He finds no difficulty in believing that a breed which existed when the throne of Israel was at its highest glory has been continued

---

[1] Correctly, Îsâ dou 'l Kir-tas, or *Îsâ, son of the paper*; but we write the name as it is commonly known. "Bin," for "ibn," is not Arabic. "I-sâ" no doubt is a corruption of "Esau"; but the Arabs themselves, in naming a boy "I-sâ," are naming him after "the Prophet Jesus," whom by a strange confusion they call by the Jewish distortion of his true name; *v. ante*, p. 106, in fn. 1.

[2] *Op. cit.* in Catalog. No. 38, vol. ii. p. 670.

down to our day. So far he agrees with Esau; but he goes further. In his opinion it is "unwarrantable to suppose that the great King of Israel is intended," by the "genuine Arabs," when they trace back, as he says they do, the first five (Esau writes *six*) Arabian mares to the stud of Solomon. He says that this is "a misconception." The Arabs, he continues, "unpretending and thoroughly truthful, have simply mentioned a fact in their history connected with their own direct ancestors"—that is, of course, in naming a Solomon as their heroic horse-breeder.[1] An appeal is then made to what is called Arab "history." And the result is the discovery that the Solomon to whom the "genuine Arabs" hold themselves indebted for their horses was "an Arabian patriarch" of that name who "lived some six centuries before the time of Solomon, King of Israel," and was "only fourth in descent from Ismail." The work in which this is stated is less known than the same author's *Newmarket and Arabia*, of which it forms a fitting continuation. The only important fact which we can discover in it is, that Major Upton lived and died believing it to be "recorded in history" that "an authentic family of horses has been preserved in Arabia for 3500 years." If all the accumulations of antiquity concerning the old world were history, even in the restricted sense of relating to men that have lived, or events that have happened, this statement might be worth sifting; but as the facts are, the *Arabian Nights* contains nothing which is more unsubstantial. At the same time, however, it should not be left unstated that Major Upton has Mr Blunt more or less with him. Both these authorities are entitled to respect in matters of opinion. But there are also such things as facts; and where facts are wanting, various degrees of probability and improbability require to be considered. They who have reached this chapter by the skipping process may here go back, if so inclined, to the pages which were devoted to showing that Arabia, as now known, never can have supported wild horses.[2] And in regard to the knotty question of when its famous breed originated, he who is content to imagine, without any real evidence, that the Arabs of King Solomon's time possessed the very stock of which was the Darley, must continue to be of that opinion. In due season we shall again refer to the ancient Arabian poetry in connection with this subject, but first it is necessary to escape out of fable-land. The sober-minded reader may marvel at any European pausing before the pile of artificial horse-lore of which Solomon, and next to him Muhammad, are made the pillars. The two fragments of it which we have quoted are merely specimens. One of them—that which introduces seven mysterious colts of Solomon's—is, of course, a pure piece of myth-growth. The other, wherein six *mares* are mentioned, is not even a legend. We have just seen that it is merely a modern perversion, by illiterate

---

[1] *Op. cit.* in Catalog. No. 4, pp. 289-291.   [2] *V. ante*, pp. 7 et 74.

townsmen, of a passage in one of Muhammad's homilies. No better foundation is assignable to the cycle of stories which represents the Arabian breed as descended from mares identified with the Arab Prophet. Such tales are kept for travellers. If they possess any significance, it is but to illustrate how, when once a nation has found its hero, everything is made to connect itself with him. The direct and indirect influence of the Muslim era in increasing the importance of horse-soldiery has been fully noticed; but it has also been observed that Arabia before the Flight nursed the breeds which mounted the cavalry of the first four Caliphs. Love of horses runs in the blood of the Arabs, and Muhammad was not an exception. Nevertheless, in so far as he was a martial man, he represented the Cromwell more than the Rupert type. Tradition relates that he never struck any one in his life except in defence of the Faith.[1] His biographers give him at least three chargers;[2] but less is heard of his horses than of his she-camels, especially AL KAS-WÁ, from whose back he addressed 40,000 people on a solemn and memorable occasion; his mule, DUL-DUL; and his ass, U'FAIR.

The fiction that the Arabian breed came in with the Kur-án finds congenial soil in coffee-houses, but the desert does not know it. There are, however, two points in the current stories on this subject which deserve to be attentively considered. One point is, that according to a concert of Arab representation, the pure-bred stock of the desert descends in the female line. The other is, that the mothers of the breed are now arranged in five collateral branches.

In the towns of Syria, I'rák, and Persia, there is a widespread notion that the male parent transmits the qualities of the breed—in other words, that the foal follows the stallion. The idea of the horse being the maker, and the mare "only a sack," may attract those who habitually look down on females, and who have no experience of horse-breeding on a large scale. The much-travelled and cosmopolitan Guarmani builds on the same assumption, in his memoir on the pure-blood Arab horse in Syria, Palestine, Egypt, and the Arabian deserts;[3] but then, he was a horse-buyer, not a horse-breeder, and had made it his profession to seek for commissions from foreign Governments for the purchase of Arab stallions. Nobody who knows the difficulty of this question will be too sure about it. Of course, one horse may yield a greater progeny in a year than a shipload of mares will do in ten; but this is the only light in which it is safe to regard the sire as the more valuable. European authorities in the science of breeding now reckon it one of

---

[1] The Prophet said, *Let not the Kádhi judge when he is angry*. And again, *When one who is standing waxes angry, let him sit down; if his anger abide, let him sleep; and if angry still, let him perform the ablutions*. And once again, *Forgive thy servant seventy times in one day*.

[2] Their names were; SAKB=*running like water*; SAH-BAH=*a great swimmer*—i.e., galloper; and MUR-TA-JIZ=*Thunderer*, or perhaps *Neigher*.

[3] *Op. cit.* in Catalog. No. 18, *passim*.

the methods of nature that a well-bred animal will mark his, or her, stock more surely and considerably than an under-bred one. They even quote instances showing that, when both parents strongly exhibit a given character, the offspring do not inherit it so surely as when only one parent is so characterised. Accordingly, Governments having possessions in which the horse stock is degenerate, incur the enormous expense of collecting foreign stallions, of various classes, for its improvement; but the results are seldom published. At all events, these are not matters on which evidence need be looked for among the Arabs. Not the improvement, but the preservation, of a breed occupies them; and their ideal method of accomplishing their object is by the pairing of animals of equal purity.

How then comes it, the reader may here inquire, that, in telling the pedigrees of their horses, they give the mare pre-eminence; exactly as if we should describe a foal by Melbourne, out of Queen Mary, as a "Queen Mary" colt or filly, instead of, as we do, a "Melbourne" one?

The masses who liken the mare to a vase, out of which only what is put into it can be taken, are more given to talking about subjects than considering them. Guarmani is one of the few exceptions to this statement. In bringing out his theory that the regeneration of the equine breeds of the world depends on crossing them with Arabian stallions, he rejects the common account that desert pedigrees begin with mares. He says that the youngling is reckoned to its dam's family only when strain has been mixed with strain, and the dam is held to be inferior to the sire. It is right to take his word for it, that in his wide peregrinations he saw or heard of people who did so. But in regard to the genuine Arabs, it would be affectation to attach importance to a view so much in conflict with all the information which comes from other sources. The only animals that we have ever heard called by their sire's family name in the desert have been those which the Bedouin describe as "not horses" but "sons of horses"—that is, got by a first-class sire out of an inferior mare.

It has been seen that the tent-dwelling Arabs, in arranging their marriages, attach equal importance to purity of blood on both sides. The head of one of our "oldest" families may wed a girl of unknown origin, without the supposed soundness of his line being thereby affected. But if a Bedouin Arab were to do so, the offspring would not be considered genuine representatives of his stock. Precisely the same view, neither more nor less, underlies the desert rule of horse-breeding; and it is quite unjustifiable to infer from the Arabs reckoning their horses to dams and grand-dams, that they attribute a greater part in reproduction to one parent than to the other. The reader who has followed us thus far, does not need to be reminded of the reasons which make the nomad hold to his mare as others do to a field or garden, and object to sell her to persons who will carry her off altogether, even when he will sell what he calls "a leg of her"—that is, a certain share in her produce—to a neighbour. The Hi-sàn, or horse, he who "swalloweth the ground with fierceness and rage,"[1] is in his element in pitched battles; but the mare's gentler qualities make her the more suitable in desert hurly-burly. She neighs but little, and possesses other advantages which are important to the rider. When Chivalry married the horse to Knighthood in Europe, horse-breeding was favoured by the assignment of the mares to peaceful labour.[2] In the same way in Arabia, the use of mares in preference to horses checks their being sold for export. But, like all one-sided systems, both methods have drawbacks. If the one imparted to the mares of feudal England too much of the farm-stable character, the other gives less than fair-play to the colt division of the Arabs' horse-stock. In modern times we know better. For every Sir Hugo which is made known by the Derby, a La Flèche is brought into notice by the Oaks. If our prize-winners be not the off-spring of "good fathers and good mothers," it is not for want of highly-tried material equally on both sides.

The real explanation of the dams always standing first in the pedigrees of desert horses is writ large in the preceding sentences. Seeing that the mares do all the ghaz-u work, it naturally follows that it is they, and not their brothers, who, through the display of superiority, as we say, "found families."

The chief object, so far, has been to separate the protean stories of the townsmen from the lore of the tent-folk about Arabian horses. Many may consider the one class of material not less unprofitable than the other; but, with due deference, we cannot in our own mind bring down the relations of the Bedouin to the same level with the confused mixtures of the jam-bázes. At any rate, it is impossible faithfully to echo the voices of the desert concerning the Arabian horse, while shunning all paths where the light is dubious.

It was seen just now how the Bedouin, when they recite a pedigree, set out with the dam. But this is only half of the story. It is a desert tenet that all the stock of approved lineage now existing has for its common root the mare of a certain, or rather very uncertain, *a'-jûz*, or old woman. We have never seen a Bedouin Arab who pretended to know either the old woman's name or when she flourished. The legend-spinners have been at work on both points, but their tales are not worth repeating. Of course, it is open to any one who pleases to relegate the crone and her mare to the same prolific region out of which Old Mother Hubbard and her dog proceeded. But if the concurrent belief of all the Bedouin nations count for anything, this would be going a stage too far.

---

[1] Job xxxix. 24.
[2] Bede (born c. 673), to whom we owe the most and the best of our knowledge of early English history, states that, in 630, when the bishops, who until then were wont to go on foot, took to riding, they used mares as a mark of humility.

Here it is essential that we should gain some idea of the two very common terms of desert tradition, KU-HAI-LA and AL KHAMSA.

KU-HAI-LA.

Arabic has the epithet *ku-hai-lán*, the feminine of which is *ku-hai-la*, in construction, *ku-hai-lat*. The mare just now brought up from the limbo of antiquity is immortal in desert legend, under the name of *Ku-hai-la-tu 'l a'-júz*, or the *Kuhaila of the old woman*. And all the authentic stock of Najd, which is supposed to be descended from her, bears the appellative, at once comprehensive and distinctive, of KU-HAI-LÁN.

Now KU-HAI-LÁN is an epithet from *ku-hail*, diminutive of *kuhl*, which appears in Europe as the name of the prince of antiseptics, al-cohol.[1] Among the simpler meanings of *kuhl* is *blackness*,[2] or *blueness*, as of the eye or heavens; and we think it so probable as to be almost certain that "KU-HAI-LÁN," as applied to the Arabian blood-horse, is an example of names derived from colour. In this breed, and especially in white and grey horses, the skin is characterised by a dark-blue tinge, which appears through the hairy covering. The large expressive eye, standing out from its socket, suggests, in its lustrous blackness, a body intermediate between jet and diamond. Hairless surfaces, not unlike blue or black velvet, encircle the eyes, and overspread the face and muzzle. No doubt it is possible to propose different explanations of "Ku-hai-lán." Among the concrete meanings of *kuhl* and *ku-hail* are (1) antimony, (2) tar. The coffee-house story that the eyes and eyebrows of the "*Ku-hai-la-tu 'l a'-júz*" were beautified with antimony, after a common Eastern fashion, is too trivial to be worth considering. But if it pleases any one to associate the Arab mare of very early times with *ku-hail*, in the sense of wood-tar, there is nothing absurd in such a supposition. We know how dependent pastoral nations are on this product. It is stated by Lord Macaulay of his Celtic ancestors, that their "hair and skin would have put to the proof the philosophy of any one visiting them;" and that some of them would have been found "covered with cutaneous eruptions, and others would have been smeared with tar like sheep."[3] There is no authority to justify the application of this

---

[1] Similarly, in *alchemy*, *algebra*, *cipher*, *assay*, *alkali*, *alembic*, and other survivals, there are traces of the sojourn with the Arabs of sciences which they no longer cultivate.

[2] Whether *coal*, the *kol* (in German, *kohle*) of the Teutonic nations, likewise *houille*, in France and Belgium mineral coal, admit of identification with *kohl*

of Semites, is a question for philologists.

[3] *History of England*, ch. xii., where this doggerel, by one Cleland, is quoted as authority:—

"The reason is, they're smeared with tar,
Which doth defend their head and neck,
Just as it doth their sheep protect."

description to the Arabian Bedouin. These certainly have their own share of skin diseases. During visits to them, we have been shocked by the unsalved sores which the falling aside of a vest has uncovered in the apparently robust. They may also be found redolent enough of unguents, after a bout of dressing over mangy camels; but we never saw one of them who had himself been rubbed. Not to pursue this subject, it appears from references in the old poetry that the primitive Arabs obtained tar by a rude process of wood distillation. A'n-tar compares the sweat which exuded from his riding-camel's *dhif-rá*, or part behind the ear, first with "*rubb*," or inspissated juice,[1] and then with "*ku-hail*," or liquid pitch bubbling in a caldron. Another and contemporary *rá-wi-a*[2] depicts himself as shunned by all his clan, so that he was as solitary as a *camel besmeared with pitch*. The "rosy-coated" Ku-hai-la of the modern period may rarely need a tarry dressing; but the early mothers of the breed cannot have approached the ideal so closely. The objection to all this is, that it makes too great a demand on the imagination. In our opinion it is best to consider that the stock of Ku-hail owes its name to certain characteristics of colouring which it possesses.

Al Kham-sa.

In Arabic, THE FIVE. This term has already met us, as denoting *the fingers of the right hand*.[3] Another use of it is, *The Five* essential plenishings, of carpet, nose-ring, neck-chain, bracelets, and travelling-bag,[4] which every nomad wooer presents to his betrothed. Here it means, THE FIVE primary ramifications of the central stem of Ku-hai-lán. During a long residence in El I'rák, and on many journeys, we have made constant inquiry on this subject from the Bedouin. One undeviating answer has been given on two points: first, that every noble strain in the Arabian desert goes back to the " Ku-hai-la of the old woman"; and further, that it does so *through one or other of the lines which constitute* AL KHAM-SA. The five main compartments, so to call them, of the great consolidation which the Arabs call Ku-hai-lán are not the same in all narrations. The table opposite shows them as they are usually recounted. No Ba-da-wi ever by any chance omits Ku-hai-lán. This, as has been seen, is the parent trunk. The four great branches, as considerable as itself, which have grown

---

[1] It may have been in Spain that the Arabic *rubb*, English rob, first became in Europe a name for fruit-syrups.
[2] Ta-ra-fa.
[3] *V. ante*, p. 191, f.n. 2.
[4] Not the complicated case so well known to civilisation; but a hold-all, which they suspend from the *gha-bít*, or camel-pillion.

A TABLE OF
THE FIVE (AL KHAM-SA) MAIN DIVISIONS OF AL. KU-HAI-LÂN,
OR STOCK OF KU-HAIL,
SHOWING UNDER EACH DIVISION ITS BEST-KNOWN BRANCHES.

I. KU-HAI-LÂN.	II. SAK-LÂWÎ.	III. U-BAI-YÂN.	IV. HAM-DÂ-NI.[1]	V. HAD-BÂN.	VI. OTHER ISSUES OF THE STOCK OF KU-HAI-LÂN.
					[The following strains and sub-strains might equally have been placed in Column I.; but in arranging them separately we follow the desert usage.]
K. [Al] Khars	S. Al Abd	U. Mel-hi-hi	H. Jel-fi	H. Fa-ras	Abû U'-kân, { Al Ab-dah / Su-wah
„ Abû-ta-fa	„ Ar-ta-bi	„ Ho-rish	„ Sim-ri	„ In-zi-hi	
„ Abû-sam	„ Aa-zi.	„ Ha-sul		„ Mu-shai-ri.	Dah-min, { Abû (or Umm) A'-mir / Kho-mai-yis / Shi-o-ir.
„ A'-nâd	„ Ibn Su-bai-ni	„ Ja-fan		„ [Az] Zai-ti	
„ A'nus 'el dar-wish	„ Jul-d-i-mi	„ Kha-rish			Jil-fan, { Dal-wa / Si-i-atu 'l tol-lul.
„ At-na-bi	„ Jir-bak	„ La-di			
„ Ar-fa-wi	„ Najma-tu 's subh	„ Mu-an-jiz			Ku-hai-shân-u 't Umair.
„ Bi-i-zi	„ Shi-a'-fi	„ Shor-ak			Mi'-ni-zi, { Had-ra-ji / Sc-id-ni, or Sla-gi / Shâ-fi,or M. Binti s Su-hail. / Sâ-fi.
„ Ba-de-ya	„ U-bai-ri-ya	„ Su-hai-an			
„ Du-r		„ Tan-dur.			
„ Dej-ji-ni		„ U-hail			
„ Dhib-yân		„ U'ri-ji-ya.			Mu-s-ib Sha-rân.
„ Di-khi					Ma'-aj Hum-mâd.
„ [Ad] Du-mân					Rab-Ab-, { [Abû] Shai-bi / Zal-ti
„ [Al] Gha-ci-la					
„ Ha-da-li					Ri-shân, { A'-ra-n / Shâ-r-bi.
„ Hai-fi					
„ Ha-li-wi					Sa'-dân, { Hush, / Tan-kin or Tan-gin.
„ Ha-lij					
„ Ha-ra-ka					Sam-hân, { [Al] Go-mi-ja / [Al] Hi-fi.
„ Ho-mat					
„ [Al] Fuhr					Sha-wi-mân, { Sab-bâh / Zi-bu.
„ Ja-i					
„ jem-ba-ra					Tu-wai-sân, { Al Ki-an / Ki-al.
„ Ju-mân-u 't mir					
„ Ki-ki					Wah-iān Kha-man.
„ Kaw-a-i-ki					
„ Khun-zi.					

[1] The research made in the text that Five First primary branches of Al. KHAM-SA may be differently connected, especially appears to HAM-DÂ-NI, in place of which some of the Bedouin put MU-NI-KI.

out of it, are not held to render it undistinguishable, far less to dwarf it. Perhaps it is proper to mention Palgrave's dissent from this representation. According to his view, the uncontaminated Arabian stock has never known subdivision. He stoutly asserts that partitions of it are but modern and degenerate features, which are met with in the deserts round Baghdad and Mosul, " almost, often wholly, unknown even by name in Najd."[1] It would, however, have been no more than just to himself if he had produced the evidence leading up to this conclusion. The well-known tendency of all breeds to split into varieties, like languages into dialects, weighs heavily against it. It is incredible that any breed should have run on for ages without breaking into strains. And, moreover, it has been seen how all the nations now occupying Shá-mi-ya and Al Ja-zí-ra originally issued from the immense native land of nomads, Najd, freighted with their desert stock and lore. Unquestionably many new ramifications of AL KHAM-SA are due to these migrations ; but that is a different matter. For the ordinary reader, the names in our table can be no more than foreign curiosities ; but points are involved in them which buyers of Arab horses should notice. The key to the table is, to understand by its radical groupname, KU-HAI-LĀN, what we express by *Thoroughbred;* to compare its five *secondary* lines with the three stocks which are called in our Stud-book after the Darley Arabian, the Byerly Turk, and the Godolphin Arabian respectively; and then to consider all the minor ramifications as corresponding with the Waxy, Orville, Buzzard, Blacklock, Tramp, and other strains of our racing calendar. Thus KU-HAIL, or KU-HAI-LĀN, denotes the *breed,* in Arabic *nis-ba,* or *nasl ;* and every other name, a greater or smaller *offshoot* of it, with Arabs a *ra-san* (lit. *rope*), also *mar-bat.* All these terms float in the breath of Bedouin, and it is chiefly foreigners who put them on paper. Jam-bázes and other townsmen, little as they know about them, make much use of them when they are recommending or selling horses. It greatly impresses an Englishman to hear a high-sounding epithet which is unintelligible to him reverently given for pedigree, to a patrician-like animal, by men as strange of garb and aspect as any of those in Fenimore Cooper's novels. But he who would buy a horse, and not a name, needs a word of warning as to this. In the first place, the common representation that the Arabs do not romance about a horse's pedigree does not apply to the jam-bázes. And next, even supposing the pedigree which is given to be authentic, it guarantees no more than that the subject of it is fitted for Al ghaz-u. It is perfectly true that, within the desert, the names referred to constitute at once the proofs and the subdivisions of the term *a-síl ;* and so far they are important—to those who understand them. Of course, in the Arabian stock, as in that of Herod, Eclipse, and Matchem, a horse may be, and indeed is *sure to be,*

---

[1] *Op. cit.* in Catalog. No. 19, vol. ii. p. 241.

mixed of *strain*, while not outside of the *breed* or *blood*. The desert horseman is not satisfied with the information that a colt or filly is, for example, a Sak-lā-wī, but insists on ascertaining *what his strain is in the Sak-lā-wī family*. Not even *Ku-hai-lān*, though in a sense generic—*i.e.*, of itself descriptive of the genuine Arabian—is sufficiently explicit for him. It is taken for granted that if the animal be of good repute, more must be known of his breeding than that; and he will not be accepted till every detail is satisfactorily established.

In regard to the words which fill our table, practically they are proper names. Nevertheless, they are sound Arabic forms. In so far as their derivations are apparent, they show that, just as very many of the names of the Bedouin depict their lives and qualities, so do those of their strains of horses embody the ideal characteristics of their coursers. Here it may be mentioned that the Arabs, with a fine respect for humanity, do not give men's or women's names to the lower animals. If they had their sporting newspapers, the reader would be spared such items as that some famous living preacher, or party leader, had "turned a roarer," or undergone some other alteration. With them, as with us, men's fancies or caprices, traits or peculiarities of appearance, or, as in Eclipse's case, events which happened about the time of foaling, have suggested names for mares, and these names have become traditional. When a mare's name is clearly an epithet, like *Mī-ni-kī*, meaning *long-necked*, it is sometimes an open question whether the long neck or other feature belonged to her or to her owner. A'n-tar's charger has come down as Abjar, or *big-bellied;* for Arab horsemen know how much depends on the digestive organs. At the present time, one of the most renowned mares in Arabia is A-mir Muhammad's Mu-nī-ra, a name very like the Lantern of the Australasian stud-book.

The problem of whether a colt which is truly of Al Kham-sa necessarily surpasses, in practical qualities, one which is not, will in due course be considered. In passing from the two great terms of desert nomenclature, KU-HAI-LĀN and AL KHAM-SA, it may be worth while here to repeat that all the merit which is derivable from considerable antiquity and from wide recognition unquestionably belongs to THE FIVE *par excellence*, and to the *hu-dūd*, or *approved*, strains and sub-strains into which they now branch out.

It is next proposed to look for a rational view of the derivation of the Arabian stock. The results of the discussions which appear in sporting journals about the origins of comparatively recent breeds are so uncertain, that it may seem absurd to attempt to go too far back, in regard to the breed of horses standing first in seniority of all the high-bred coursers of the world. Nevertheless, if we cannot expect to find full information, there are at least traces to which attention may be drawn. The question of when Arabia first received the Horse has already occurred. The other day a cavalry officer of the Osmanli recalled it, on happening to notice this picture in a book which was on the table :—

Out of respect to his religious teachers, he believed in the *Jinn* and other marvels, but he could not accept the Centaur. His reason was the practical one, that if Allah had created so superior an animal, the biped race of Adam would have been exterminated. And truly, the most sensible account of this particular representation of mythology is that which connects it with some historic episode involving the subjugation of peasants by barbaric riders.[1] It is known that, from the earliest down to comparatively modern times, hordes of equestrian warriors and archers, pouring westward, have formed dynasties in many parts of the world; but there is no proof that Arabia proper ever felt the tread of Mongol horses. Nineteenth-century research finds evidence in philology that the horse was known to the Aryans before they separated; but in regard to the Semites, the words for horse which appear in their several languages[2]

---

[1] The Scyths, or Caucasian nations of ancient Asia, whose march was from beyond the Jaxartes, down the Oxus and the Indus, and across the Tigris and the Euphrates to the Bosphorus and the Nile, are thus alluded to by Herodotus (B.C. 484-443) :—

"Having neither cities nor forts, and carrying their dwellings with them wherever they go; *accustomed, moreover, one and all, to shoot from horseback;* and living, not by husbandry, but on their cattle,— how can they fail of being unconquerable?"

What were the Boer marksmen who hit so hard at Majuba Hill but fighting centaurs, trained to arms of precision instead of bows and arrows?

[2] For instance, in Arabic, the current terms for mares and horses, *hi-zān, fa-ras, khaïl,* and, with the Bedouin (as in Esther viii. 10), *ra-mak,* are less names than epithets.

have not been held to justify a similar inference. The allusions to "horse-hoofs" in Judges v. 22, and to "horses very many" in Joshua xi. 4, are accounted the earliest notices of this animal which are contained in Semite literature. On these and other grounds, it has been suggested that the Semitic peoples, as a whole, were indebted for the horse to the Iranian upland which comprises Persia; but this is only a conjecture.[1] Restricting the view to Arabia, Sprenger considers that the Arabs possessed but few horses down to the period of the Flight.[2] The tradition that A'lí's[3] charger, Mai-mûn, was of Egyptian breeding, is sometimes used to support this opinion; but if the fact that so many of our own princes ride Arabs were hereafter to be cited as proof that, in the nineteenth century, Europe was poor in horses, the cases would be parallel. In A'lí's time, Egypt held the same high place as a school for cavalry which she did at the date of the 31st chapter of Isaiah. It is observed by a recent authority that "literature affords no trace of the horse, as indigenous to Arabia, prior to about the beginning of the fifth century A.D."[4] Without repeating what has been stated on this point in another connection,[5] it may just be said that the period at which an animal first gets into a literature is not necessarily that of its first appearance on the actual stage. When, as has happened in most countries, compositions of the pre-literary epoch are delivered to penmen who come later, it is impossible to tell how many similar treasures have lived and died in remoter ages. Evidence drawn from the earliest known Arabian poems is already before the reader, showing how familiar the sportsmen of Najd were with the points of a good horse at the beginning of our sixth century. The

---

[1] There is at least no lack of evidence that the horse was highly esteemed in Persia in early times. For example, the custom still traceable, of granting the rights of sanctuary to all who take refuge at the foot of a horse, or in a stable, must be very ancient. The Persians are excelled by many as horse-breeders, but by none in the art of caring for horses, and obtaining from them a full amount of work. Their stable management takes no account of many things which we consider important. But at least feeding, clothing, and working are well understood in Persia.

[2] *Leb. Moh.*, iii. 139, 140. Compare Ignazio Guidi's paper, "Della sede primitiva dei popoli Semitici," in the *Transactions* of the Accademia dei Lincei, 1878-79.

[3] A reference to the actual A'lí will be found in art. SUNNI AND SHI'I, Ind. I. The A'lí of romance is not so easily represented. Religionists style him,

the last and worthiest of primitive Muslim; him who attained to where the flood of El Islâm collects; and reached the first springs thereof; and tasted the purest of it. Bookmen ascribe to him every sententious, didactic saying, especially those in verse, the authorship of which is unknown. As a military leader, he is held to personify the force and passion of early Islamism. El. KARRÂR, or *The Returner again and again to the charge*, is one of his epithets. His exploits are magnified in numerous Arthurian legends. His good horse fills the place in Eastern story and pictorial representation which the marvellous steed Bayard does in the Charlemagne cycle of fiction; and his two-edged sword, "*Dhû 'l Fakâr*"—a trophy and favourite weapon of the Prophet—is the Excalibur of Arabian and Persian romance.

[4] *Ency. Brit.*, vol. xii. p. 181 in f.n. 1.

[5] V. *ante*, p. 27.

following passage from the same source, and of about the same period, is even more significant :—

> And on morn of raid and mêlée,
> Comrades true, the mares we rear;
> Never lost we yet a filly,
> But a rescuer was near.
> Like an heirloom long descended,
> In our tents their lineage runs;
> And when time for us is ended,
> We shall leave it to our sons.
> . . . . . .
> When they lead the mares to pasture,
> Ye may hear our white ones[1] say,
> Not for us the lord and master,[2]
> Who is fearful of the fray!
> —'AMR.

That is, not only did Najd possess highly cultivated strains of horses some 1400 years ago, but then, as now, such had been handed down by many generations of horsemen. Modern scholarship is so far from doubting the authenticity of the pre-Islamic ballads, that it undertakes the task of editing them.[3] Thus, in addition to brushing aside numerous phantasmal structures about the origin of the Arabian breed, we arrive at firm ground in regard to its antiquity. Next, in the absence of actual knowledge or records, analogy may be asked for suggestions on the point of how the race of Ku-hai-lân may be supposed to have been produced. The first words on the first page of a recent book on the Dandie Dinmont terrier[4] are, that the "exact origin" of the breed "is practically unknown"; in spite of its being no farther back than "the first Sabbath of the year 1820" that James Davidson, of Hindlee in Roxburghshire, the original, in some respects, of the immortal Dinmont, was gathered to his fathers.[5] Now, it is not known whether Davidson, like the late Rev. John Russell,[6] and many others, made his breed of terriers out of the materials round him, or received it from the Border gipsies. The facts, so far as they can be traced, best fit the latter view—that is, that the ochre, or "Mustard," and the greyish black, or "Pepper," terriers of Liddesdale were as essentially the products of nomad life as the Ku-hai-lâns of Araby. But whether the breed was made by basket-weaving, otter-hunting, and poaching fortune-tellers, or by mountain farmers, is immaterial.

---

[1] *I.e.*, the fair-skinned Arab women, of honourable lineage, as distinct from those of mixed blood.
[2] In the original, *ba'l* (or "Baal"), *v.* Ind. I.
[3] *Op. cit.* in Catalog. No. 35.
[4] By Chas. Cook, Edin.; David Douglas, 1885.
[5] *Vide* Note C to ch. xxiii. of *Guy Mannering*.
[6] *V. The Outdoor Life of the Rev. John Russell:* London, 1883. A point worth noticing is, that both Mr Russell's breed of terriers and the still more famous "Mustards" and "Peppers" derived their pedigrees, like the Ku-hails of Araby, from a mother, not a father; *v.* book just cited, p. 61; *et Horæ Subsecivæ*, by Dr J. Brown, 1862 edit., p. 200.

Clearly, necessity was the mother of it, and use helped to shape it. That is, the inhabitants of a wild country, abounding in hill-foxes and badgers, bred a race of terriers which, when properly entered, excelled in the rough sports depicted in the 25th and 26th chapters of *Guy Mannering*. The case now under consideration is not dissimilar. At an early time the Bedouin Arab must gradually have formed his breed of horses in accordance with the sure decree, "*Boni et fortes bonis et fortibus creantur*." If special and exclusive breeding, directed to a certain object, explain our English race-horse, there is no need to go further for the secret of the Arab's foray-mare. This view is not in conflict with that which has elsewhere been presented of the Bad-u's weak points as a horse-breeder. One may exercise much skill in choosing the parents of each fresh generation out of the preceding one, without possessing a full idea of the more important questions which are here involved. Darwin cites it as an illustration of the natural tendency to preserve the useful, that the savages of Terra del Fuego in times of famine save their cattle and kill off their old women. And so with nations living by the chase, the first rude kind of "selection" is to keep the likeliest puppies in a litter when they will not rear all of them. To do this with the idea of "breeding" comes much later; but the Arabs must very early have given their adherence to "heredity." During a great many generations, as was just now seen, it has formed a part of their system that a mare of renown may add a new strain, called by her name, to one of the sub-groups of AL KHAM-SA. This kind of selection may not be, in the full scientific sense, "methodical," but it is tolerably practical. In applying it, the Bedouin are aided by considerable powers of perception. Their code about *blood* forms a gathering up, it should be remembered, of the results of their experience. A mare's "standing pretty," as the late Sir Tatton Sykes used to call it, is one of many other points which are beyond them; for galloping, not standing, is what they would breed up to. But a short and upright pastern is an eyesore to them; and equally so too long a one, especially when it is either too oblique or too upright. The greyhound girth, well spread ribs, and breadth behind the saddle, all delight them. Coffee-house Arabs, when they look over the half-brother of Kirkham and Narellan[1] which is now with us in Baghdad, are very uncomplimentary. A Turkish Pásha lately said that he more resembled a she-camel than a horse. But no son of the desert ever sees him without perceiving that, though of unknown and unaccountable pedigree, he is other than a commoner. A leader of the Aeniza, on noticing his unsexed state, declared that he was as good as a mare; and that, if he were his, he would sweep the board—that is, an enemy's pastures—with him! In truth, however, the colt referred to would be as

---

[1] *V. ante*, p. 195. The two sons of Chester, which the late Mr White of Sydney sent to Epsom to con- test the classic race of 1890, were named by him Kirkham and Narellan.

out of his element in Shà-mi-ya as Gulliver was in Lilliput and Dr Johnson in the Hebrides. Supposing him to be ridden out in the bloom of condition, the ghaz-u would go one way and he another, with or without his rider, as the Fates might rule. If he survived the first drought, he would never be the same animal afterwards.[1]
But to resume. If the pairing of superior animals in successive generations have made the Bedouin Arab's breed of horses, a favourable result has been promoted by the circumstance that, instead of having many points to aim at, his one idea is AL GHAZ-U. What gives the Arabian his speed, length of stride, and staying power? Whence the gamecock throttle; flat, well-laid, muscular shoulder; straight-dropped hind-leg, with great thighs and hocks; powerful ligaments; symmetrical back; and admirable length, in proportion, between the elbow and stifle-joints? BREEDING, we all know, is the answer; but then, what does that mean? Not so very long ago it would have been said that "breeding" partly represents the summation, in succeeding generations, of all the characters which have been produced, in individual animals, by use or effort. Darwin thought that "acquired characters," in the limited sense of the effects of use and disuse of parts and organs, are *in some cases* thus inherited; but later investigators otherwise explain the facts which our forefathers accepted as evidence of such transmission.[2] We do not here presume to discuss this complex question, which has still to be brought to the test of experimental researches. Of course every one admits that, for example, sinewy fore-legs are due, *in the individual*, in some measure at least, to the influence of work. One has but to take his stand of a morning near the gate of an Arab town, and observe those who ride in from the desert, to be able to form a shrewd guess, from the proportions of their horses' legs, whether they and their nags are "sons of the road" or idlers. The conclusion which is assailed by some recent writers is, that this greatness of limb, and other similar characters, *after having been acquired in an animal's lifetime*, tend to reappear in the progeny. The traditional belief that the case is so pervades these pages; and until science shall finally certify her conclusions, it is best for ordinary people not to be too scientific.

There is another assumption on which the foregoing remarks have a bearing,

---

[1] Since the above passage was written, the subject of it has become well known on the Calcutta race-course as Ivo.

[2] *E.g.*, the refinement of the tushes in the wild boar's domesticated descendants; and the different characters of the breast, wing, and leg-bones in the goose that cleaves the heavens and the farmyard waddler respectively. India affords special opportunities for observations of this kind in the human species, owing to the prevalent custom, particularly in caste-bound communities, of the son pursuing the paternal handicraft or occupation. Those who accept Professor Weismann's theory, according to which the transmission of acquired characters is impossible, argue that if the case had been otherwise, the sinewy arms of the village blacksmith, equally with the clever fingers of the watchmaker, would be inherited by the younger offspring in a higher degree than by the older.

and that is, that a way of galloping with straight fore-legs characterises the coursers of Al ghaz-u. Certainly a considerable number of the desert mares exhibit this peculiar action. It is an interesting question how far it depends on every animal's "points"; and how far on the youngling's forming its faster paces in the grip of a desert horseman, and over level spaces, instead of being allowed, like the village-bred one, to gallop, cow fashion, without a rider. But the impression which many buyers of Arab horses have that this is, *par excellence*, the gallop of the race-course,[1] does not stand scrutiny. For neither is this style of movement restricted to the Kuhailans, nor does it necessarily indicate pace. It is on record that Touchstone, for example, "went with a perfectly straight knee." In India, many Arabian horses of good racing reputation have displayed this form of action. Such have seemed to cover the ground with but slight effort, while their rivals ploughed the dust behind them.[2] But we have known and tried several Bedouin "swimmers," which put out their fore-legs like stilts in galloping, and, for want of the racing-like sweep of the haunches, or for other reasons, could not get away from the commonest hack. In the same way, very many Arabs having what is called "round" action, have astonished people equally by their speed and staying power. A celebrated trainer said, that there were only two essential points in the race-horse—legs to carry him the pace, and a heart[3] to make him use his legs. This, however, is one of the many good things which are true as parables, without being true literally. Balance is better than *prettiness;* and a horse may bend his knees, without being either a clambering or a labouring goer.

So far, only casual references have occurred to in-and-in-breeding as a factor in

---

[1] An Indian who lately came our way in quest of true-bred colts, either brought with him, or picked up in coffee-houses, the piece of innocence, that the straight knee action of the Bedouins' horses depended on the desert custom of shackling the stock with iron fetters (*kaid*; round the pasterns). Accordingly, after making his selections, he hobbled them, pastoral fashion. On riding out to see him and them, we found each colt not only fettered, but tethered to a pole with fathoms of rope, to keep him from playing the fool with his fellows. The fresh desert breezes and the growing barley had so raised the animals' spirits, that they were plunging round and round, with both fore feet off the ground,—the very opposite kind of action from that which it was intended to produce in them. The weight and friction of the irons had caused the formation of splints. Methods which do no harm to famished Bedouin cattle may prove the ruin of corn-fed and idle horses.

[2] I. Imru 'l Kais' description of this, in line 5 of the passage from his poem which is translated *ante,* p. 143.

[3] Notwithstanding the late Admiral Rous's "philosophic doubts," we do believe Eclipse to have been the greatest galloper and stayer that ever was saddled; and in addition to being a big horse in every sense —tall of stature, broad of frame, and long in the right places—he had a heart which, when weighed after his death, drew 14 lb. (*V. A History of the British Turf,* by J. C. Whyte (1840), vol. i. p. 250.) Many good judges have been of opinion that Eclipse's unbeaten record, or rather, the power which he exhibited of passing every rival, like a shot out of a gun, when and where he pleased, depended on the exceptionally full development of the central organ. Somewhat similarly it is affirmed in an old work on cocking, that what was called a bird's "athletic weight"—*i.e.,* the weight at which he would display his greatest courage, strength, and activity, *and at which it was considered impossible to keep him for more than twenty-four hours* —was that under which the proportion of the weight of the heart to the weight of the body was greatest.

the several strains of AL KHAM-SA. With every stud-horse in England standing near a line of railway, it is not surprising that all our thoroughbreds are either closely or distantly related. If it be otherwise in the case of the stock of Najd, its diffusion from the Khâ-bûr river to the Indian Ocean affords an easy explanation. People whose marriage system is as close as that of the Arabs, are little likely to make a bugbear of interbreeding in the mating of their cattle. Nevertheless, common use prescribes a limit. Thus the Aeniza freely bring together colts and fillies by the same sire, out of different mares; but they do not approve of pairing a colt with his own sister, or a mare with one of her immediate progeny. It may safely be assumed that this restriction, however founded, is beneficial. Several European authorities are of opinion that it is not the inbreeding *per se* which is injurious, but its tendency, when not guarded by rigid selection, to fix and perpetuate constitutional taints and other bad points.[1] Considering how rare perfect soundness is, this distinction does not seem a very practical one. At any rate, not all the wise men of Babylon, and far less the Arabian Bedouin, are qualified to breed horses on the in-and-in principle, without the evil results preponderating.

---

[1] *The Marriage of Near Kin*, by Mr A. H. Huth.

CHAPTER II.

THE TYPICAL ARABIAN.

AT this late stage it is superfluous to repeat that the typical Arabian is the horse of the Bedouin nations of Najd. Necessarily the blood-horse, or horse of speed, approaches everywhere more or less to one and the same type ; but the best judges will be the most guarded in drawing an ideal pattern, and then declaring that every genuine specimen must resemble it. The variability of animal forms, even in the natural state, is now, thanks to Darwin, well apprehended. The popular generalisation that "like begets like" is accepted with due reference to the fact behind it, that if the offspring were in all cases exact copies of their parents, new breeds would be impossible. And, of course, in artificial varieties the causes of divergence are even more numerous and influential.

There are two points as to which we wish to be on clear ground, before proceeding to search for a "type" of the thoroughbred Najdi horse. These are, the use of our term "thoroughbred" in connection with the Arabian blood-horse, and the standard by which, in Arab horses, "thorough-breeding" is to be determined.

I. IN WHAT SENSE IS THE ARABIAN VARIETY THOROUGHBRED ?

It has been seen that the Arab's word for "thorough-breeding" is *a-sá-lat*, or the state of *being firmly founded*.[1] The *a-síl* stock of the desert, though now rising, like certain classes of plants, on innumerable stems, instead of on a central one, is theoretically of one breed, which, according to the Arabs, is perfected and established. It seems a waste of time to notice again the hazy ideas on this subject which several of our countrymen have committed to writing.[2] In a pedigree table

---

[1] V. ante, p. 94.   [2] V. ante, pp. 7 et seq., et 220.

of the Arabian thoroughbred stock in *Bedouin Tribes of the Euphrates*, Mr Blunt brings in the Newmarket breed in two places—once as a derivation, in the male line only, from the Darley, and again as a side-get of the Godolphin's.[1] In the same book the English race-horse is figuratively styled the "bastard cousin" of the Arabian.[2] This is pretty well; but it is eclipsed by Major Upton's great discovery, that when the waters of the Flood subsided, a pair of horses not unlike the Darley Arabian descended the sides of Ararat.[3]

It is a relief to turn from such glaring absurdities to the technical term "Thoroughbred" of our Stud-book. Among us the meaning of this word is perfectly definite. Its range of application is wide. Not only the blood-horse,[4] and other equine breeds, but highly bred animals of every kind, may be denoted by it. This fact, however, gives rise to no confusion of ideas. In every case alike, the essential condition of "thorough-breeding" is, that the pedigree shall be traceable, without break or flaw, to certain approved *and recorded* progenitors. The modern British race-horse is the product of about two hundred years of exclusive breeding. If any one consider that period all too short for the development of a thoroughly established, or in Arab parlance *a-sīl*, breed of horses, the field of discussion is open to him. Here it may be said, and truly, that although it was in the beginning of the eighteenth century that our countrymen made their greatest start in horse-breeding, it was not till about a hundred years later that they began systematically to record the pedigrees of the horses and mares from which they bred. When this fact is examined, it is found strongly to bear on the point which is now being made for. The English Stud-book was first regularly started in 1808; and in the preface it was stated that, "with a view to correct the then increasing evil of false and inaccurate pedigrees, the author was in the year 1791 prevailed upon to publish an *Introduction to a general Stud-book*, consisting of a small collection of pedigrees, which he had extracted from racing calendars and sale papers." That means, that the compiler had to go back for about a century, and glean and piece together such items of information as existed. Mark the result. He was near enough the starting-point to discover with tolerable certainty the names and histories of most of the early fathers of the line. The dates which occupied him seldom went further back than the eighteenth century, and he was free from the necessity of romancing. In 1791, many must have been alive who remembered Lord Godolphin's so-called Arabian. Only about one

---

[1] *Op. cit.* in Catalog. No. 11, vol. i. p. 276.
[2] *Ibid.*, vol. ii. p. 247.
[3] *Op. cit.* in Catalog. No. vi.
[4] The term "blood-horse" may be merely a vestige of the primitive notion, that there is an essential difference between the red corpuscles of the "quality" and the commonalty respectively. But the name also points to that beautiful swelling out of the veins after a gallop, in the racer and his descendants, by means of which the heart and lungs obtain relief.

hundred and twenty years had passed since the second Charles's Master of the Horse, who was sent to purchase Eastern stock, brought over the "royal mares," upon which, and upon the many proved mares already in the island, were grafted the imported Anatolian, Barb, and Arab elements of the English breed. Nevertheless, the comparative shortness of the misty period did not prevent errors. Many doubtful animals were entered in the Stud-book. Many others which ought to have been registered were omitted. There are even grounds for thinking that several of the pedigrees which have come down to us are inaccurate.[1]

A confirmation of the position now reached will be found in connection with the next question also :

II. On what Evidence does the point of "Thorough-breeding" depend in the Arabian variety?

The tree of *a-sâ-lat* is known by its fruits. The Bedouin Arabs hold that a mare which is not *a-sîl* cannot take care of her rider in AL GHAZ-U. It may be assumed that they are right in this belief. If they had not discovered that purity of blood was an essential qualification, they would not have been so careful to produce it and maintain it. But obviously we have here a test which lies outside of the European's world. Nobody but a Bad-a-wi appreciates the ideal with which it is connected, or possesses the means of proving that ideal.

Another form of evidence by means of which *a-sâ-lat* may be certified is the general testimony of the Bedouin. Particular stress must here be laid, however, on the condition that all such witnesses shall be of the Bad-u, and that they shall be actually before one. The difficulties which confront foreigners when they would thus personally and directly appeal to desert folk will be further considered in the sequel. The European who is an honest gentleman runs some risk of being befooled when he attempts to do so; while the European of the jam-báz school is more interested in making money than in observing facts. This, however, is not the point which is at present under consideration. It has elsewhere been stated that the Bedouin, when approached in their own deserts, declare truly all that they know about a horse's pedigree. The question is, What intrinsic value are we to attribute to what they tell us on this subject? Here it is necessary to recall what has elsewhere appeared regarding the illiterate state of the Arabs.[2]

---

[1] In the Stud-book, Eclipse (1764-89) is credited to Marske. But see in *The Horse* (1829), by quaint John Lawrence, who remembered the morning that he was foaled, a different story.

[2] V. ante, p. 132.

Among them knowledge is not an affair of writing. Several of our countrymen have persuaded themselves that, where the Arabs are concerned, Stud records are unnecessary. We would go as far as any one in allowing for the fact that the conditions of life are different in Eastern and Western countries respectively. But miracles do not happen in Arabia, any more than in Europe; and it is everywhere incumbent to keep within the bounds of probability. If any one imagine that strains of horses can be strictly and perfectly preserved, apart from the registration of matings and foalings, let him refer the question to the great English, Continental, and Australian Stud masters. If it were an affair of memory, who would not rather trust to that of an educated Englishman than to that of desert herdsmen, who cannot even say how many camel-riders are in a troop in front of them, without multiplying the number by about ten? It is an evident fact that the Bedouin Arabs, aided by the isolation of their deserts, by their well-developed power of orally handing down pedigrees, and by other circumstances, have to a surprising degree succeeded in preserving the approved character of their Ku-hai-lâns. But in our opinion the floating accounts of the purity of even their best strains require to be received with some allowance. It may be conceded, though actual proof is wanting, that tribes or families have at different times preserved a mare's lineage for perhaps even a few hundred years,—a pretty liberal allowance, considering all the circumstances. But this is a different matter from assigning to an ancient and widely distributed breed, in which the main guardian of the pedigrees is oral transmission, as high a degree of thorough-breeding as that possessed by our own stock of this St Simon and Ormonde period. We almost hesitate to mention performances on the turf as a guarantee of *blood* in Arab horses, seeing that the Bedouin do not resort to trials of this kind. As, however, all the jam-bâzes lay stress on this view,[1] it seems to call for notice. Unquestionably, a high degree of *blood* is demanded to make a horse in any proper sense a racer. Nobody now thinks of entering a "cocktail," any more than an Arab, for a good race in England. Al ghaz-u calls for a fine turn of speed, and for other qualities which can only be developed through special breeding; but it does not do so up to the point which racing does. A less perfected type suffices for pursuit and flight, and for galloping from morning

---

[1] Thus the late Esau bin Curtas (*ante*, p. 228), in the *Oriental Sporting Magazine* (Calcutta) for March 1870, p. 968, writes as follows:—

"Gentlemen, before purchasing, ought to make searching inquiry regarding the blood. This important precaution should never be neglected. *It is quite a different thing when a horse has won races; . . . the fact of winning races is proof positive of blood.*" The italics are ours. Considering what Arab racing is in India, there never was a rasher statement.

to night at a moderate pace, than for crucial tests like those of the Beacon course. Many—perhaps the majority—of the famous Arabs of Indian turf annals have borne the stamp of thorough-breeding. But many other great winners of the same series, judged by their appearance, must have belonged to the secondary division from which the Bedouin Arab will not breed; nay, if one of which should by accident approach a *Ku-hai-la*, the indignant owner will bare the arm, and by the rudest conceivable piece of surgery remove the newly vivified ovum. A letter, written in 1887, is before us, from her Majesty's late Consul at Aleppo, Mr Henderson, who states that at first he was an enthusiast for Arab horses and mares, and bought some very good ones. After mentioning that A-sil, the winner of Mr Blunt's races at Newmarket and Sandown, was of his breeding, Mr Henderson gives it as the result of his experience that "half-bred horses are much more reliable and useful" than those which the Bedouin account to AL KHAM-SA. He further says that for his part he had long ago stopped buying "pure-bred ones." *Non nostrum est tantas componere lites.* On the one hand, who can surrender his innate faith in *blood?* On the other, it is contrary to the observed facts to imagine that turf performance is a full or conclusive test of pure breeding in Arab horses.

Another form of evidence on the point before us remains to be mentioned, and that is the indications which are evident to the eyesight. The Arab of the desert does not trust to these external features, any more than we do in the case of our own blood-horses. That which is called in England a "half-bred" may have nineteen-twentieths of Stud-book blood. In good looks, and in every point of physique, he may resemble a true-bred son of Saunterer or Sweetmeat. On the other hand, there have been dams of St Leger winners whose appearance was far from thoroughbred, especially when wearing their winter coat. Apart from Ruff, and the inflexible standard of the winning-post, we possess no means of separating our pure blood-horses from those of less than sixteen quarterings. The Arabs are in the same position, except that, instead of a connected family history, or Stud-book, the chief evidence which they have to guide them is oral tradition. Foreigners may think that there is as manifest a difference between a *ka-dish* and a *Ku-hai-lán* as between a "twinkling star and a celestial sun"; but the Ba-da-wi does not attempt to discriminate between them by the eye alone. When a horse which he has never before seen is shown to him, he asks about his dam and sire. If satisfied on both points, he looks him over; but he neither assumes the pedigree from the appearance, nor attaches importance to the latter apart from the former. When in foray or otherwise he obtains possession of a mare which is only "the daughter of" an *a-sil* one—*i.e.*, "half-bred"—he does not continue her line. Living and moving in his own narrow world, he contemptuously affixes the label of *ku-dish*[1] to all horse-stock of which he does not know the parentage. This exclusiveness is entirely bound up with his system of horse-breeding. In India and other countries we occasionally see a flaring *ka-dish* from I'râk or Syria, which some one has fitted with an Ananias pedigree, employed to regenerate fallen-away breeds, with the usual result that the produce turns out worse than himself. The Bedouin nations are safe at least from this danger.

In the preceding remarks we claim to have reduced to order these two subjects—viz., the sense in which the Arabian, as compared with the English, blood-horse is "thoroughbred"; and the point up to which memory and oral recital are safely to be trusted as respectively the depositary and the transmitting medium of horses' pedigrees.

An important practical question next invites us. Among all the strains of blood-horses which the Arabian deserts nurture, is there no pre-eminent strain? Can we, or can we not, discover one "precious porcelain" of equine clay, every piece of which, while readily distinguishable from counterfeits, closely resembles the other?

"Facies non omnibus una,
Nec diversa tamen; qualem decet sororum."[2]

Palgrave has led people to suppose that there is such a breed. His book of travels contains a description of about three hundred "most consummate" specimens of it, which he says he saw in A-mir Fai-sal's stables at Ar Ri-âdh in 1861. The passage referred to has been quoted by numerous writers, but it is necessary again to cite it. The words are:—

"Never had I seen or imagined so lovely a collection. Their stature was indeed somewhat low; I do not think that any came fully up to fifteen hands—fourteen appeared to me about their average; but they were so exquisitely well shaped that want of greater size seemed hardly, if at all, a defect. Remarkably full in the haunches, with the shoulder of a slope so elegant as to make one, in the words of an Arab poet, 'go raving mad about it'; a little, a very little saddle-backed, just the curve which indicates springiness without any weakness; a head broad above, and tapering down to a nose fine enough to verify the phrase of 'drinking from a pint-pot,' did pint-pots exist in Nejed; a most intelligent and yet a singularly gentle look, full eye, sharp, thorn-like, little ear; legs, fore and hind, that seemed as if made of

---

[1] Pl. of *kwdish*, q.v., p. 47, ante, ct Cn. 3. This word is so current among the Arabs that Niebuhr, and after him other writers, make "Kochlani" (*Ku-hai-lân*) and "Kadeschi" (*kwdish*) their two leading subdivisions of the Arabian breed. If we understand by the two terms no more than *a-sîl* and *less than a-sîl*, respectively, we shall have a useful enough rough classification. Ibn "Kadeschi" must not be mistaken for a strain name. The *kwdish* merely is the pariah of horse-flesh.

[2] Not all featured alike; And yet not different—such likeness as sisters ought to have.
— Ovid: *Metam.*, Lib. ii.

hammered iron, so clean and yet so well twisted with sinew; a neat round hoof, just the requisite for hard ground, the tail set on, or rather thrown out, at a perfect arch; coats smooth, shining, and light; the mane long, but not overgrown nor heavy; and an air and step that seemed to say, 'Look at me; am I not pretty?' their appearance justified all reputation, all value, all poetry. The prevailing colour was chestnut or grey; a light bay, an iron colour, white, or black, were less common; full bay, flea-bitten, or piebald, none. But if asked what are, after all, the specially distinctive points of the Najdee horse, I should reply, the slope of the shoulder, the extreme cleanness of the shank, and the full, rounded haunch, though every other part, too, has a perfection and a harmony unwitnessed (at least by my eyes) anywhere else."[1]

A poet of the modern school says, or sings:—

> "When Nebuchadnezzar went out to grass,
> With the horned cattle and the patient ass,
> He said, as he tasted the unwonted food,
> This may be wholesome, but it is not good."

And in the same manner Palgrave's delineation may be pretty, but it is not true. It is the work of a penman, not of a horseman. Who ever saw a "perfect arch," whether circular or pointed, formed by a horse's tail? It is the case that a flag-like carriage of this part is characteristic of the Arabian blood-horse. That is, it helps to distinguish him from horses of other classes. The Bedouin, when a foal is dropped, raise and press back its tail with the hand or with a stick; and they say that the stylish manner in which their horses carry the tail out from the quarters is owing to the set thus given to it. Another equally innocent desert operation will be noticed afterwards, but we are not yet done with Palgrave. It is a matter of fact in England, where the astutest of mankind, from Prime Ministers down to betting-list keepers, are always trying to breed up to models, that even half-a-dozen level-bred animals are seldom, if ever, shown in any one class. And we would like to know how a stud of three hundred, all with the same curve of "saddle-back," and, except in height and colour, as like one another as so many Geneva watches, can have been collected in Arabia. If they were obtained by breeding, an incredible number, of which they formed the pick, must have been produced in the Amir's own pastures. If purchasing agents brought them in from every quarter, the men who served Amir Fai-sal must have been of no common kind. Under any circumstances, Palgrave's account relates to a period to which it is needless to go back. The collapse of the Wahabite Empire has been incidentally noticed. Its capital, Ar Ri-àdh, is a *ba-lad mát*, or *died-out place*; and its secular state is transferred to Amir Muhammad's city, Hà-yil. Comparatively few travellers now spread their carpets, and hang their belts and arms, in the guest-hall of the Ibnu 's Su-ò'd family. The mangers in the palace-yards are choked with weeds. The

---

[1] *Op. cit.* in Catalog. No. 7, vol. ii. pps 93, 94.

imperial mares of Palgrave's story are as much things of the past as is the collection which the Messrs Tattersall dispersed at the sale at Hampton Court on the death of King William IV.[1]

In this book no attempt will be made to draw up a regular description of the typical Arabian. The aim is, less to define an ideal than to exhibit approved animals that have existed; and pictorial representation is indispensable for that purpose. The seven horses which form the subjects of our seven full-size illustrations have this in common, that they were brought from the Arabian ports to India through the ordinary trade channels. At first the only real vouchers for them were their good looks. To this day their "records" are simply the proofs which they afforded on Indian race-courses of speed and stoutness, heart and honesty. On the point of long ancestry, every reader must draw his own conclusions, in regard to each of them, from the presumptive evidence which their several figures supply. To us they do not all appear to touch the same high level in respect of pedigree. Nevertheless, the reader may, if he will, accept all the seven as "typical"; and the three whose portraits appear in the present chapter are designed respectively to serve for examples of the medium-sized Arabian, the large Arabian, and the dwarf Arabian. We shall presently come back to these three models, with the object of further illustrating through them the breed which they adorned. But in view of the fact just stated, that the history, in Arabia, of the series represented by them is, at the most, a matter of hearsay, let us first exhibit another group belonging to a different category. None of the horses which are figured in the opposite picture ever heard the saddling-bell. Not the jam-bâzes, but persons as distinguished as an I-mâm of Muscat, and others, selected them as worthy representatives of the race of Ku-hai-lân. They have every appearance of being of one breed, if not precisely of one type. In the line of Eclipse the several leading strains or admixtures are not less remarkable for their differences than for their general inter-resemblances, and any one can distinguish, for example, a Blacklock from a Venison. Of course, the same thing is to be looked for in AL KHAM-SA. The group which is placed opposite brings together some of the very cream of the stock of Najd. We consider Nos. 1 and 6 pre-eminently typical. Sultân Su-û'd, for fifty-two years the I-mâm of Muscat, and master of all the

"banks of pearl, and palmy isles"[2]

---

[1] At the sale alluded to the two Arabian mares from Muscat fetched but fifty guineas and one hundred and fifty guineas respectively, though stinted to The Colonel, winner of the Doncaster St. Leger, for which his Majesty George IV. had given four thousand guineas. The two stallions from the same quarter, the Black Arabian and the Bay Arabian, figured more creditably in the sale-ring. The former, the very much admired Sultân, was taken, for five hundred and eighty guineas, by an agent of the King of Wurtemberg; and the latter for four hundred and ten guineas.

[2] Moore, in *Lalla Rookh*.

(1) Grey Mare, from Indus of Mewar.

(2) "Maroufa."

(3) "Dervish."

of Oman, would not have sent to a king of England anything short of the best. He whose eye retains the images of the "grey mare" and "black Arabian" will never want for authentic models of the Ku-hai-lân. Youatt chose the head and *madh-bah*[1] of the latter for the frontispiece of his well-known book. He describes the head as "inimitable in the broadness and squareness of the forehead; the smallness of the ears;[2] the prominence and brilliancy of the eye; the shortness and fineness of the muzzle; the width of the nostril; the thinness of the lower jaw; and the beautifully developed course of the veins."[3] He might also have called attention to another feature of the breed which the same head exhibits,—namely, the fossa-like depression,[4] as in the antelopes, across the face, between the forehead and the muzzle. No. 2 in the group, a *Ham-dá-ni-ya Sim-rí*, is also characteristic. No. 3 is the Najdian skirmisher, Dervish, whose history was given at p. 165, *ante*. Not much is known of Nos. 4 and 5. The originals of both appear in Lt.-Col. Ham. Smith's standard work on the *Natural History of the Horse*. The one forms a representation of an Eastern charger much associated with the fame of the first Napoleon.[5] The other illustrates a breed[6] "shaped like greyhounds, and destitute of flesh, but of high spirit and prodigious endurance," which is preserved by the Arabs on the sandy plains south of Atlas, in the north-west part of Africa. The remaining figure in the group is copied from Stonehenge's book on the Horse. The original of it was Sha'-bân, the property of H.M. the King of Würtemberg.

---

[1] Lit., *place to which the knife is put*. In all perfect Arabians the windpipe runs exquisitely into the throat.

[2] *V. post*, p. 255.

[3] *The Horse*, by W. Youatt (1855), p. 22.

[4] Called by the Arabs *af-nas*, for *af-las*.

[5] Lt.-Col. Ham. Smith omits to give any explanation of the illustration which is entitled by him "Marengo, Bonaparte's Arab." His work was published in 1843. Perhaps it may be assumed that his engraving of Marengo follows one of the portraits made by various artists of a horse which, after Napoleon's last battle, came into the possession of Lord Petre, and subsequently of the late General Angerstein. The General believed the horse to be "Marengo, barb-charger of Napoleon, ridden by him at Marengo, Austerlitz, Jena, Wagram, in the campaign of Russia, and finally at Waterloo." Many have doubted General Angerstein's favourite, which he kept and bred from near Ely, ever having been at Waterloo at all. And naturally such sceptics are even more incredulous of the story that one and the same horse carried Bonaparte in the Marengo campaign (1800), and, fifteen years later, in the final act of his marvellous military career. It is pretty certain that Napoleon brought over from Egypt, in 1799, after the battle of Abû-Kir, a light-grey barb, which he rode at Marengo. Either this animal, or another of the same colour called A'li, taken at the battle of the Pyramids, in Egypt, in 1798, may have been the "small horse" which Delaberre Blaine, whose working period was in the first half of our century, delineated in his *Rural Sports* (p. 245), with the explanation that he saw it in the *Jardin des Plantes*, where, owing to Bonaparte being "so fond of it," they usually kept it. In twenty years, nineteen chargers were killed under Napoleon in sixty general engagements; and the chronicler is unborn who can unfold the histories and services of his Marengo, Marie, Austerlitz, A'li, and Jaffa, all of which were either grey or white in colour. All that can be certainly said on this point is, that a white Arab became part of the Napoleonic legend. When, during the Second Empire, Meissonnier broke upon the artistic world with a series of pictures illustrative of Bonaparte's campaigns, he necessarily set the hero on an Eastern charger of this royal colour.

[6] Locally designated *Shu-ra-ba-tu 'r rih*, or *Drinker of the wind*.

A horse of Sha'-bân's appearance is, in his way, as great a triumph of breeding as are our own successful racers, champion shorthorns, and Waterloo Cup winners.

And now to speak of the three full-page illustrations of this chapter.

The desert Arab's natural perception of the essential points of a blood-horse has already been noticed. For horse-talk, and betting on horses, our island is beyond the reach of competition; and there is no horseman like the Englishman when he is a horseman. But in the martial clans of Arabia a knowledge of horses, be it great or small, is truly national. That is, it forms the common possession of every man, woman, and stripling. Not merely a class, or a profession, but thousands of deeply interested breeders, generation after generation, are to be credited with the production of a stamp of horse like Greyleg. The author's memory unfortunately carries him back to Greyleg's time, and he can vouch for the truth of the likeness of him which is here given. The original of it is a water-colour portrait, from the life, which we bought of W. Brewty, the rider of him in all but seven of his eighty races. The horse was brought to India, from Ku-wait or Bussorah, in a dealer's string. Judging from the very moderate price which sufficed to buy him at Mysore, his importer must have had him on easy terms from the Arabs. We saw him, at Bombay in 1864, walk to the starting-post for the Forbes Stakes in company with a T. B. E. mare, a daughter of Harkaway, to whom, in the race which followed, he gave a complete go-by; and he never so much as saluted her. Twenty-five years later, we were informed by Brewty that the horse was put to stud in his green old age, and grew very troublesome and unmanageable. Perhaps it may be inferred from this, and from the smallness of his original price, that his Arab breeders, owing to some objection to his pedigree, refused him the opportunity of transmitting his form and qualities. But, on the other hand, he may have been a stolen treasure; or his people may have sold him because of his strain being fully represented among them. It is best to keep clear of comparisons, and not claim for any horse superiority to all his kind. Like many a good horse in England, from Gimcrack down to Little Wonder, Greyleg was of comparatively small size, and did not exceed fourteen hands and one inch at the withers. Perhaps there have been faster ones, though, for an Arab, he possessed a rare turn of speed. In a race he was lazy, and needed to be wakened up in the middle of it. Several of the few defeats which he suffered were caused by his being over-indulged in the first part of the journey, so that some rival, which he could easily have beaten, instead of receiving his quietus early in the race, was left to come with a rush, and catch him on the winning-post. In every point of outward form, Greyleg was typically Arabian. No one who has seen him is likely to live long enough to see another equal to him. It is not, however, as a "high-mettled racer" that he is here depicted. If he had been the slowest of the slow, he would equally have been chosen to represent his family in these

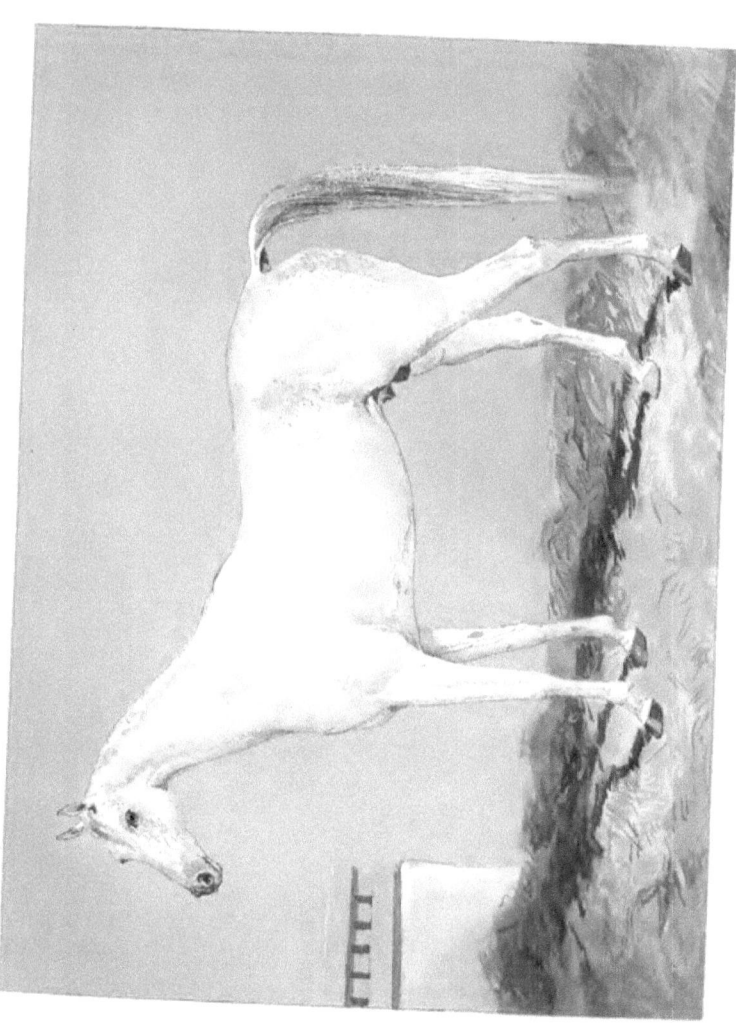

pages. From head to heel he is a Ku-hai-lân. Those who believe pure blood to be the secret at once of racing form, durability, symmetry, and beauty, may appeal to him for proof; but this view is not just now before us. Our immediate object is to trace in "the little grey horse," as far as possible, the essential features of the desert breed. It will be seen hereafter, when the colours of the Arabian are spoken of, that Greyleg's colour is one of the praised ones. His skin was of the traditional *ku-hail* colour, which an Arab poet says is "blacker than charcoal." When in his prime, his silver-grey coat was more interspersed with nutmeg roan than perhaps the picture indicates; and the red spots in it resembled those on the speckled shoulders of a sea-trout. Beginning with the *tout ensemble*, or general appearance, what superb *quality* meets us; what length and depth and substance; and what unison of form, from the elastic and capacious nostril to the tail as light and airy as falling water! The outlines present no abrupt transitions; the junction of the neck and shoulder forms a plane and only slightly undulating surface; the ribs come out from the spine barrel fashion; he is beautiful alike behind the saddle and before it. What shape and finish are in the head and throat! The ears are not short and not long—though long ears may be seen in Arabians of the highest class—but loose and slender, and pointed like a well-cut pen.[1] There is none of that narrowness between the eyes which in several of our own strains denotes a most undesirable form of "cuteness": the forehead is very broad; and the eye is large and prominent, and brimful of honesty, courage, and gentleness. Then see the neck! To enable a horse "to run with the stout or wait with the speedy," a strong, deep, broad neck is essential; and Greyleg's neck was a true model, equally removed from the weak and tapering and from the *bellator equus* or equestrian statue types; having its great muscle (*splenius*) as sharply cut as the blade of a Damascus scimitar, and the windpipe full of play and freedom. Mark next the chest and arms; the depth from the withers to the shoulder-points; the greyhound dip to hold a powerful heart, and lungs of sufficient volume; the long forearms; square bony knee; short cannon, with tendons behind it bigger than itself; and large, strong, elastic pasterns. It takes a great deal of breeding to get the middle-piece as true-made as it was in Greyleg, who, with all his *general* length, as shown by the reach of ground which he stood over, had a model back and loins. The importance of the last-mentioned parts has elsewhere been noticed. But a shoulder running far into the back is so essential that, instead of "loins and hind-quarters," "loins, back, and shoulder" sounds more like the real conjunction. It will be perceived that Greyleg had not the "straight-dropped" hind-leg, like a camel's, which is often

---

[1] The poet Ta-ra-fa describes his riding-camel's ears as *pointed*, or *sharpened*; and mentions this as a mark of her nobility of breed.

seen in racers. He had wide hips, and a broad pelvis. We have never seen a horse of his class better to stand behind or follow. If there was anything angular or projecting about him, it was his haunch-bones. In breadth across the quarter from the stifle backwards, he was very good. The chief point noticeable in his hind-legs was their muscularity, and the extraordinary play which he made with them in his faster paces. In his time horses were galloped in clothing, and Brewty loved to be out before daylight; but Greyleg's friends could always recognise him, when he was set in motion, by the rapidity with which he threw forward his hind-legs.

Another Arabian race-horse of the same period, Hermit, well deserves to stand before the reader by the side of Greyleg. Hermit measured fifteen hands at the withers, and all his points were in due proportion; but not the most fastidious eye could find fault with him on the score of quality. On the Bengal turf he was, among Arabs, the Eclipse of his day. It is true that on one occasion he sustained a defeat from Greyleg. At that time the Indian railway system was in the early stage, and a Calcutta horse rarely had an opportunity of meeting a Mysore one. For once, however, fate so arranged, and Hermit's owner, with the instinct of a true sportsman, sent him out, like a knight-errant, to challenge and encounter Greyleg. The result was that which is so often witnessed when one horse is running on his own ground, and the other is away from home. No horse is the same every day, and over all courses. The fact that Greyleg lowered Hermit's flag at the Mysore meeting proved no more than that, on the day, over the course, and as the race was run, the Calcutta champion was somehow at a disadvantage. The likeness of Hermit which is here given is reproduced from an oil-painting in the possession of his owner, General M. J. Turnbull. One of the truest friends that man or horse ever had, Mrs M. Turnbull, did us the honour of painting a copy of the picture expressly for this volume. The eye which is set on picture-book ideals will perhaps dwell with greater pleasure on Greyleg than on Hermit; but the more of substance united with quality which the Ku-hai-lân exhibits, the more valuable is he. It is possible that not a few of our countrymen who have seen good Arabs may say of our portraits of Greyleg and Hermit, that they never came across flesh-and-blood animals which agreed with them. The reason is not far to seek. Horses of this stamp are extremely uncommon. In the palmy days of cocking we know what innumerable broods of black-reds and duck-wings the hero of the main represented. And in the same way the Arabs breed a countless number of plain animals for every distinguished specimen.

Our third illustration, Rex, is partly chosen because of the opportunity which he offers of speaking of size as a feature of the "typical" Arabian. A horse's general size is not to be confounded with his mere height at the withers. Once,

HERMIT

in a dispute about the comparative dimensions of England and Scotland, the northener clinched the argument by requiring that before the measurement was taken, all the mountains in the latter country should be flattened! And in the same way, many a pony contains sufficient material to make into a sixteen-hand horse, good enough for riding-school purposes; while many of the lathy sort, if compressed into "little big" ones, would do more credit to their owners. A leggy horse may suit a long and lanky rider, or serve to elevate as a pair of high-heeled boots does a general officer above his aides-de-camp; but in order to make a "great-sized" steed, a deep and broad body, and not a set of stilts, is wanted. The tape conveys more useful information as to a horse's measurements than the standard does, and the latter, after having been held over the withers, should always be used over the couplings also.[1] Many of our countrymen are under the impression that no horse which exceeds about fourteen hands and two

---

[1] Eclipse "rose very little on his withers," and was "higher behind than before;" v. Stubbs' engraving, on p. 177 of Sidney's *Book of the Horse*. In the Arabian, also, the hind-quarters are frequently higher than the fore-hand; and in picking Arabs for racing, it is not a bad plan to take Eclipse for a model. The subjoined likeness (from the *Oriental Sporting Magazine*, June 1870) of the Hon. A. Stewart's famous Arab, Akbar, shows a horse among whose measurements were "fourteen hands and half an inch at the withers, and fourteen hands two and a half inches over the loins; girth, five feet and six inches."

B. A. H., AKBAR.

Akbar's owner wrote that he was "an excellent charger, hunter, and pig-sticker." The Newmarket lad who rode him in Calcutta said that he was one of the only two "real good movers" which he had seen in India. The honest bay had "largish ears," a zebra stripe down the back, and a slightly mulish look. At first he was more laughed at than admired. After he had shown his quality, all the self-styled judges, as usual, merely said that no one could form an opinion of an Arab. If they had carefully looked him over, perhaps they would have learned a lesson.

inches in height can be a genuine Arabian; but this is a mistake. Without doubt, the taller a horse is, especially if he be met with towards the Tigris and the Euphrates, the more care is necessary in making sure that he is true bred. But if a stature of from thirteen to fifteen hands be given to the horse of Najd, we shall not be chargeable with founding on exceptions. Food, *per se*, has a direct influence on this point. The workhouse boy does not usually grow into a man of the farmer build; and it has been seen how, as a rule, the Arabs treat their mares and horses. Apart from special causes, the small fry enormously outnumber their larger kindred in most classes of animals. In the Ku-hai-lân family, the proportion of Galloways to horses of superior size and substance must be as several hundreds to one unit.

Rex affords a beautiful illustration of the dwarf Arabian. For many years he was a prominent figure on the turf in India. He ran brilliantly, not only in pony and Galloway races, but over the longest courses, and in races for all Arabs. At last a sort of Indian Ibnu 'r Ra-shîd, H.H. the Maharâjah of Jodhpore, in Rajputâna, added him, at a princely price, to his vast stud of English, Australian, Arab, and other celebrities. His appearance here is due to H.H. the Maharâjah's kindness in supplying a life-like sketch in oil of him. Rex's height varied from thirteen hands and two inches to slightly over it, at different times and places of measurement. His importer was the horse and camel merchant, Â'-id bin Ta-mi-mî of Najd, who, from his home in U'-nai-za, a township of the Ka-sîm province, collects colts for India. There is no worthier or honester man of his class than Â'-id, and most winters see him and his red cloak in Bombay with horses. He and many others have related how Rex was bought as a weanling from his breeders for the easy equivalent of about £8 of English money. As usually happens, his merits escaped notice. Even after his arrival in India his merits remained unnoticed until his performances revealed them. Miniature Arabians of his stamp just now possess a special interest for sportsmen, owing to the prevalence of Galloway-racing, pony-racing, and polo, particularly in India. It is a misnomer to call horses like him ponies. The little ones for which our island, Australasia, and Arabia are now so diligently searched by dealers, are in reality blood-horses which, from whatever cause or causes, fall short of the ordinary standard. Arabia, as has been already noticed, yields no breed resembling our Shetlanders; and of course the production, systematically, of pedigree ponies, such as are to be seen at Rigmaden Park in Westmoreland, and in a few other places, is beyond the range of the Bedouin. The Najdi horse, when he is undersized, too often is small-framed, light-boned, and narrow; and one like Rex is perhaps even harder to find than one like Hermit. A diminutive Ku-hai-lân is called by the Bedouin *hi-sân ka-sîr*—i.e., *a short horse*—which is exactly what he is; but the

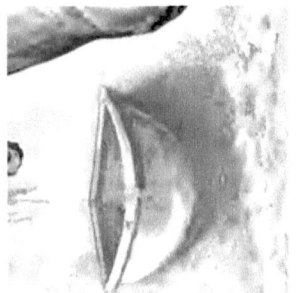

jam-bázes borrow the Indian word for pony, *tat-tû*.[1] Every time that an unusual price is obtained in India for a small Arabian, the Bedouin of Shá-mi-ya and Al Ja-zí-ra hear of it. A Shekh of the Ae-ni-za lately sent to beg of us a thirteen hands and two inches measuring standard. A piece of thin brass wire, fifty-four inches long, was accordingly sent to him, but he will not know how to use it. Jam-bázes who would be very clever carry measuring-rods; but most members of the fraternity buy every animal which looks like "keeping the money together," and trust to "luck" on the day of measurement. Many good sportsmen look coldly on pony-racing, on the ground that it interferes with the "legitimate" game. A more serious objection is, that it encourages the practice of paring horses' hoofs to the quick just before the official measurement, and keeping the poor animals without food and sleep, so that they shall droop under the standard. At the principal racing centres in India there are farriers and others who profess to be experts in the nefarious art of thus "cutting down" horses. Another effect of pony-racing in India is to promote the influx of counterfeit Arab horses. In the year of writing, we chanced to reach Mu-ham-ma-ra, after a long march through Persia, just when the jam-bázes were assembling at the sea-coast, like the swallows about the same season in England, before taking flight with their year's purchases to India. There happened to be a good-looking ka-dish, young and under "pony height," among our baggage-horses, and a dealer bought him as soon as he was unsaddled. A month later we saw the same animal standing in the corner box of a Bombay commission-stable. At first this appeared to be the height of audacity on his owner's part, but the fellow had not miscalculated. In a short time a highly placed and highly paid official of the Government accepted the late carrier of our pots and pans as of the "breed of Solomon," paid a ridiculous price for him, and despatched him to Calcutta. "Am

---

[1] Among the few indigenous Indian things which British rule has spared is the common *tat-tû*, of from nine to thirteen hands. Now, as in Akbar's time, this active creature is to be seen on every road, carrying an "undivided Hindu family." That is, a "senior" and a "junior" wife, the latter probably with babies, are seated on him, atop of many a bag of household stuff, with innumerable sundries, not forgetting the parrot's cage, tied, or hung, around them. The proud possessor of all this happiness trudges at the tail, to apply the stick where wanted. The tat-tû's place in agriculture is to take produce to the market. In certain localities he comes out in harness. When the Bengali needs something faster than his "cow-cart," he mounts a one-horse vehicle called an *ek-ka*, in connection with which whole provinces are famous for what truly are blood-tat-tûs. The tat-tûs of Western India have been increased in size by the superior climate and by freer crossing. In his military capacity, the tat-tû is now losing ground before the mule, but no army moves without him. His hardness is astonishing. After the longest day, a fight with one of his companions seems to reinvigorate him. If he is borne on the strength of a regiment, a corn ration is issued for him; but his attendant generally saves him the trouble of eating it. If the property of a camp-follower, his fore-legs are tied together after his burden is taken off, and he is left to hop about in quest of what will serve him. Nevertheless, many a gallant boar has been laid low from the back of a tat-tû which has had a little good keep.

I not thine own ass?" the honest quadruped seemed to say to us, as he was being galloped up and down before his new owner. Inside of a yard, after a long course of eating and sleeping, with a couple of horse-keepers to polish him, the I'rā-kí mongrel will look as if the place could not contain him; but on the open plain he draws in his horns. If he be put in training, the clumsy neck and long flat barrel will not long remain hidden. These remarks are not directed at the jam-bāzes. As long as people in India continue to buy I'rā-kí cattle, at prices not unaffected by turf and polo honours in prospect, they may depend on a full supply of the article. And, moreover, there is no reason to suppose that the dealers whose homes are in Najd often bring round ka-dishes. Ā'-id bin Ta-mī-mi, and many of his associates, shun both Bussorah and Muhammara. Such men march their horses straight to Ku-wait, and, in their Semitic love of cheapness, as well as to escape Persian contacts, ship them in Arab *baghlas*, or sailing-boats, instead of steamers, at the risk of losing several animals during the protracted and uncertain voyage.

The next aspect of the typical Arabian which has to be presented to the reader is his colour. No question is more frequently put to us on the subject of Arab horses than what is the correct or the best colour? In England an antiquated idea lingers that the authentic Arab must be grey. A most distinguished predecessor in this consulate, General Sir H. C. Rawlinson, exhibited in 1864 a bay Arabian, stated "to have a pedigree of four hundred years"; and London actually objected to him on the score of his being a bay, and not a grey. This illusion is sanctioned by Palgrave, who says in his article "Arabia" in the *Ency. Brit.*[1] that "dark bay never" occurs in the "genuine Nejdee." If by "dark bay" he meant dark brown or *quasi* black, the statement might be received, subject to qualification.[2] But speaking of "dark bay" as understood by horsemen, every Arab prizes it. In rhapsodies about horses by desert riders, we have twice seen the bay colour set above every other.[3] In one such passage the descriptive used is *ah-mar*, meaning *red*.[4] Perhaps *ah-mar* includes chestnut. And perhaps the same word denotes in strictness the bright or golden bay. But unquestionably the ancient Arabic word *ku-mait* which Im-ru 'l Kais uses signifies *dark bay*. *Ku-mait* is explained in dictionaries as the *dark red hue, verging towards black, of the fresh ripe date*. A classical Arabian poet, in telling his audience that his hunter was *ku-mait*, says that the colour was not an uncertain one, such as a man would have to be put to his oath about, but that of the herb with which the hide that has been dyed is dyed a second time. The reader may depend upon it that bay is now as well established a colour

---

[1] Vol. ii. p. 241.
[2] See, however, *ante*, p. 57.
[3] *V. ante*, pp. 61 and 143.
[4] The feminine form of *ah-mar*, with the def. article, lingers in Europe in the name of the historical hill-fortress, and palace of the Moorish kings of Granada.

in AL KHAM-SA as it was before the Arabs possessed written compositions. It would be impossible to quote a higher authority on the colours of Arabian horses than the late A-mir Fai-sal of Najd. His Highness informed Colonel Pelly that the finest Arabian horses may be of any colour; that the prevalent colour among the first blood was various shades of grey; that, as a rule, the foal received its colour from its sire; that, on the whole, colour went for little, and height for nothing, and that blood was everything.[1] Further information regarding the colours of Arabian horses is presented in a convenient form in the Table which is included in this chapter.

Lieut.-Col. Ham. Smith, whose classic work on horses is that of an accomplished naturalist, describes the Arabian breed as one of "great admixture";[2] and this view is illustrated by the diversity of the colours which are displayed by it. At the same time, the diversity has its limits. Thus, the dun colour is most unusual in Arabian horses. Sooty blacks prevail in the vulgar stock of the pastoral and agricultural Kurds round Kar-kûk and Mosul, whose oxen also show a great deal of the same colour. There are, however, many different classes of black horses, and those of the Kurds can have no real relationship with the black Arabians, one of which was taken by Youatt as a model. Not half-a-dozen Arabians of this colour have made footprints on the turf in India. Occasionally we hear of a noble black which is the boast of the Ae-ni-za; but such of the colour as come our way too much resemble the dismal quadrupeds which in Europe are reserved for the last scene of all. Practically, the Ku-hai-lân colours are bay and chestnut, and the numerous different shades of grey and roan. Nobody can pretend to say of any one of these colours that it is more "typical" than another.

It is well known that there are several knotty points concerning colour which the most eminent investigators of Europe and America are still discussing. Such questions do not bear more directly on Arab horses than on horses generally; and the results of horse-breeding among the Arabs offer little, if any, guidance in regard to them. But before passing from colour, we wish just to indicate some of the various questions which are connected with it.

First, then, is there any warrant for the common impression that a horse's character may be inferred from the colour of his hairy covering? We have all heard of "temperaments"—the nervous, the bilious, the sanguine, and the lymphatic—and their combinations, and of the indications of them which the colour of the hair is supposed to furnish in human beings. It is certain that the leading peculiarities of these temperaments, denoting differences in brain and muscle, circulation and digestion, are characteristic in horses also not merely of the different breeds, but, in a

---

[1] *Op. cit.* in Catalog. No. 28, p. 55; *et re ante*, p. 36. | [2] *Op. cit.* in Catalog. No. 22, p. 210.

TABLE OF THE COLOURS

A.—COLOURS AKIN TO BAY.

Arabic Names.		Explanations.	Remarks.
Horse.	Mare.		
Ku-mait		Dark bay	"Bay with black points" is As-dá.
Ah-mar	Ham-rá	Bay. As applied to horses, *Ku-mait* and *ah-mar* are the same	The Arabs use "Al Ah-mar" to denote a European.
Ash-kar	Shak-rá	Chestnut	In Ku-mait or Ah-mar the mane and tail are black; in Ash-kar, red or sorrel. Chestnut of a dark copper colour, called by Indian horsemen after the fruit of the mahúá tree (*Bassia latifolia*), is not very common in Arabian blood-horses.
Ad-ham	Dah-má	Equally "coal-black" and dark brown. If not black, so black as to pass for black	Rare in Al Kham-sa.
As-wad	Sau-dá	Black	Ad-ham and As-wad are synonymous; but horsemen say *ad-ham*; just as we do not speak of a *red* horse, but of a "bay" or a "chestnut." The old poets call a dark-coloured, or pitch-black, horse *jaun*; and this colour was evidently much esteemed.

PROPER TO ARABIAN HORSES.

B.—THE WHITE, GREY, AND ROAN COLOURS.

Arabic Names.		Explanations.	Remarks.
Horse.	Mare.		
As-far	Saf-rá	(1) White, with a saffron or sorrel infusion, which is chiefly apparent in the mane and tail (2) Milk-white	The Bedouin include all whites and light greys as *as-far*. The "ἵππος χλωρός," or "pale horse," of the Apocalypse, must have been of this colour. In Arabic and Persian respectively, the exact equivalents of χλωρός are *akh-dhar* and *sabza*—meaning, 1st, and generally, the green of new verdure; 2d, and specially, the grey colour in horses.
As-hab	Sah-bá	*Ut supra.*	
Ash-hab	Shah-bá	*Ut supra;* except that the infusion into the white is blackish, not yellowish.	
Am-lah	Mal-há	Of the colour of *milh* = (1) milk; (2) crude salt—*i.e.*, practically, "silver-grey"	Applied to all the vaguer shades of grey.
Ash-a'l	Sha'-lá	Much as above	Strictly (in El I'rák), when there is much white on the face and tail.
Ni-li		The colour of *nil*, indigo. Blue-grey	Opener, and with less of black, than our "iron-grey," which is more of a ka-dish than a Ku-hai-lán colour. [*Nil*, indigo, is a loan word in Arabic, and has nothing to do with the name of the great river of Africa.]
Az-rak	Zar-ká	A lighter variety of the above. A blue or blue-grey colour, which is common in Nature—*e.g.*, in the eye	Much prized. Even further from "iron-grey" than is the *nl-li*. Dappling is not very common in Ku-hai-láns. Of greys, perhaps the az-rak most inclines to a light fleecy grey.
Rum-má-ni	Rum-má-ni-ya	From *rum-mán*, the pomegranate. "Nutmeg-grey"	The "Mu-war-rad," or "rose" colour of Najd. Within its range, this, like all the greys, admits of different proportions of white, red, and black. The desert contains no vulgar, patchy, or mealy roans; and no flesh-coloured muzzles and pink orifices. The true "nutmeg roan" or "nutmeg grey" runs the bay colour close for the prize of excellence in the Arabian breed. However white in the course of years a rum-má-ni turns, his "strawberry" spots remain.
Ab-rash	Bar-shá	Marked with flecks differing from the main colour. "Flea-bitten grey"	Bay or black pencils which come out of a white, or a grey, coat. The true "flea-bitten" generally grows more and more so with age. Some say that there never is a sorry horse of this marking. It may be so; but though the colour undoubtedly runs in Ku-hai-láns, yet it is also common in ka-dishes. The Persians and Indians call it *ma-ga-si*—from *magas*, a fly.

minor degree, of different individuals. Why, then, may not a horse's colour help us to draw conclusions as to his temper in the sense of "manners,"—that is, whether he is more inclined to knock one's brains out, or cheerfully to do what is required of him? As to this, the Arabs are ready with the theory that the testimony of colour is important. One of their sayings is, *The kings of horse-kind are those which are of a dark colour.*[1] If this mean that whatever the colour may be, the intenser or more pronounced it is, the better the horse will be, then it is worth considering. Another Eastern saying is, that one should be slow to buy a chestnut horse, and still slower to sell one of that colour which has turned out well; but the same maxim applies to the buying and selling of horses of all colours. On this, as on so many other subjects, the lore of the Arabs, at any rate in towns and villages, has a good deal of superstition engrained in it. An example of this is, their absurd notions about "lucky and unlucky" markings. Many millions of Eastern people still think that life, or wealth, or conjugal honour may be connected with, for instance, in a "white-stockinged"[2] horse, the number of limbs thus marked, and the height to which the colour rises![3] Another branch of the same oriental goose-lore draws its presages from whorls in the hair. Curly places, or "feathers," of certain shapes and in certain situations, are taken for omens that he who owns or mounts the horse will rue it; and similar arrangements of the hair on other spots, for assurances of prosperity. Ridiculous as all this is, it occasionally proves useful. When the owner of a long purse wishes to refuse a horse which an obliging friend would foist on him, convenient objections are to be found in these markings. And, moreover, "feathers" on a horse's neck or body no more indicate high breeding than a twist in the beard does in man. Horses in whose coats the hair thus disports itself are commoner among the Sham-mar than among the Ae-ni-za. And thus may superstition, perhaps but half believed in, supply the place of knowledge in saving men from bad bargains. Europe also keeps its little idols on the point of colour. "A good horse is never of a bad colour," is one of those truisms which mean little. When a horse is before us of which we know not whether he is good or bad, the question is whether any clue to this may be found in his colour? We often hear all the chestnuts in the world included in one condemnation, as hot-tempered, or "washy," or something else; and it is not to be denied that there are grounds for this opinion. There have been a great many

---

[1] "*Mu-lū-ku 'l khail duh-mu-hā.*" *Dukn*, pl. of *ad-ham—q. v.* in Part A. of *Table of the Colours proper to Arabian Horses.*

[2] Stockings enter less into Arab life than riding through rivers does. Accordingly, a horse with "all four white" to above the knees and hocks is, in Arabic, *mu-khew-wadh*, because his appearance suggests that he has just *passed through a ford.* A horse which has one, two, or three white pasterns, is called *mu-haj-jal*—lit., *ankleted*, or *shackled*.

[3] The importance which the old Arabs attached to a dash of white on the mare's face was noticed at p. 61, *ante.*

chestnuts which, owing to their essential bad qualities, have been worse than useless. But, on the other hand, stud statistics attest the pre-eminence of the chestnut colour. Was not this the uniform of Eclipse and Plenipotentiary, Stockwell, and his blaze-faced son, Blair Athol? Some of the best Arabs that ever trod the turf in India have been of this colour. Long ago, when it was permitted us to drive a coach, we always drove chestnuts, because of the beautiful manner in which the Eastern sun lights up their jackets. Many chestnut horses, both Arabians and Australians, have thus received their schooling from us. Some of them, when first taken up, brought little credit on their colour—one minute gaily trying to pull the whole coach, and the next minute jibbing without either sense or reason. But many others were not to be surpassed in natural sweetness of temper. The devil does not dress all his servants in jackets of the same colour. Our advice to the reader is, by all means to consider colour, but to understand that it is only one of many other points which require to be weighed in the scales of knowledge and experience before a sound opinion can be formed. Above all things, it is necessary not to hamper ourselves with "notions," if we would buy the best horses.[1]

Another set of facts relating to colour are those which seem to invest it with significance as an indication of breed, or breeding. Before Darwin, colour passed for a mere piece of natural ornamentation, designed to give pleasure to mankind. A pastoral passage in Genesis was much quoted in this connection.[2] Numerous facts of common observation, notably those turning on the relations between locality and colouration, seemed at first sight to involve the view that colour is a trivial character which is prone to vary. In certain parts of Najd, the tawny hue gives place to the black one in camels. In our island the mountain-hare becomes white in September, to resume its russet coat in May. Alterations of bodily state or structure in the individual are frequently followed by changes in the colour of the hair. A horse now in our possession, which when cut in 1882, as a five-year-old, was a sound bay, among other deviations from the male type has turned more of a weak chestnut. The hair which grows after a wound is white. Darwin's speculations on the origin and uses of colour in animals may be read in other books. We have now only to say that the old naturalists who held colour to be an unim-

---

[1] The Government of India, in its operations for the improvement of native breeds, now taboos grey stallions. Not knowing the grounds or objects of the desired exclusion of horses of this colour from regiments and batteries, we can but assume this restriction to be well founded. But it every year puts on one side, in a not too well supplied market, horses which otherwise would be most eligible. In the unfixed state of colour in the Arabian breed, many a grey Arab has on both sides bay or chestnut parents.

[2] "And Jacob took him rods of fresh poplar, and of the almond and of the plane tree; and peeled white strakes in them, and made the white appear which was in the rods. And he set the rods which he had peeled over against the flocks in the gutters in the watering-troughs where the flocks came to drink; and they conceived when they came to drink. And the flocks conceived before the rods, and the flocks brought forth ringstraked, speckled, and spotted."—Chap. xxx. 37-39 (revis. vers.)

portant character had many facts not very consistent with that opinion before them. As a rule, colour is constant in each species of wild animal; and variegation waits on domestication. A white elephant is as rare as a white Hindu.[1] The slight differences of colour in a sounder of wild hog, or herd of deer, or shoal of perch, chiefly follow sex or period of life. The breeder of domestic animals modifies colour, as just stated, in the same way that he does most other characters; but he cannot get rid of the old grit. In the Leicester breed of sheep, after a century of cultivation, grey-faced, black-spotted, or wholly black lambs still occur. In horses certain markings seem indelible—for example, the dark patch on one hind-quarter which is so common in the descendants of Eclipse, though we have also seen it in mongrel I'râkis; and the spinal stripe which Darwin used to support the view of the horse being a co-descendant with the ass, the quagga, and the zebra, of some striped and extinct progenitor.[2] But further, if the immediate effect of domestication on colour be to variegate it, most of our pure and valued artificial breeds are characterised by definite colours which constitute one of their distinctive marks. In the "Pepper and Mustard" terriers, for instance, it is seldom that pied puppies, or puppies which are not either slaty-blue or sand colour, appear. One reason of this is, that when irregularly marked specimens occur, they are promptly drowned; but perhaps the two colours in question are the more easily fixed because natural to the dog. On the other hand, who can deny that the modern English greyhound is very highly bred? and yet, see how diverse his colours are. Antiquity abounds in references to breeds of horses all of one colour, especially white—the colour with respect to which the erroneous view is prevalent that it is not natural or original, but the result of old age. Marco Polo, in describing "the city of Chandu," mentions that the sovereign of the Tatars, "Cublay by name," kept "an immense stud of white horses and mares, in fact, more than ten thousand of them, and all pure white without a speck," the milk of which was drunk by the Kaan and his family, and by none else, except one great tribe, on whom the privilege had been conferred by his grandsire Jenghis Kaan.[3] Sir W. Scott, in chapter xl. of *The Antiquary*, following, as may be

---

[1] The colour of the Hindu's hair is even more fixed than that of his skin. This fact receives illustration in the offspring, in India, of European fathers and dusky mothers. Even when both parents are Eurasians, and very dark, several of their children may be white-skinned. But fair hair is never seen in the most European-looking Eurasian. If even the great-grandmother have been Indian, and her husband, with all the intervening steps of descent, pure European, the hair will be black. In the races which inhabit El I'râk, the black colour of the hair seems less firmly fixed than in Indians.

[2] Darwin should have seen the comparatively uncrossed breeds of horses, mostly dun or slate-coloured, and remarkable for their hardy constitutions, power of endurance, and indomitable tempers, which still exist in several remote provinces of India, especially Kâthiâwâr. Not only the spinal stripe, but with it the asinine bars on the forearm and shoulder, are scarcely more conspicuous in the zebra than in these equines, among whose characteristics are long ears, having the points much turned inward.

[3] *Marco Polo*, Sir H. Yule's edit. (1875), vol. i. p. 291.

assumed, some sound tradition, makes an aged woman croon the following fragment, having reference to the Earl of Mar's cavalry of the time of the battle of Harlaw (1411):—

> "They saddled a hundred milk-white steeds,
> They hae bridled a hundred black,
> With a chafron of steel on each horse's head,
> And a good knight upon his back."

And, to name no more, Lord Beaconsfield, in *Alroy*, introduces another race of white horses—the white Anatolian, to which, and not to the Arabian, he assigns pre-eminence in equine history. So far, all is in the ordinary course. The production by man, through "methodical selection," of breeds of horses of one colour, is as intelligible as the distribution by Nature of troops of wild horses, every individual of which resembles the surface of the ground. But another fact here presents itself which seems still to await explanation. Except in so far as statistics show that there have been more winners of one colour than of another colour, English breeders for the turf may safely be acquitted of all preference, or fancy, respecting colour. And yet, equally in our islands and at the antipodes, the long course of scientific breeding of which our racing stock is the product has practically resulted in its becoming a family of bays and chestnuts—two colours essentially one. In olden times, when England was full of fresh Eastern blood, greys were as often seen at the starting-post as they were down to a much later period in New South Wales and Victoria. In a book published in 1866,[1] it is "estimated" that the Derby had been won during the previous thirty years by 7 chestnuts, 7 browns, and 16 bays; the St Leger by 5 chestnuts, 8 browns, and 17 bays; and the Oaks in like proportion. Of course, there are exceptions. The Greyfriars of our day may have been as good a horse, though he was not so successful, as the Grey Momus of that of our grandfathers. But cases like this—in all probability reversions—are merely those that prove the rule; and apparently the conclusion confronts us, that the tendency of the highest breeding, in latitudes far separated, is to wipe out in horses all colours save bay and chestnut.

So far we have confined ourselves to the outer aspect of the typical Arabian. In point of personal character, the subject of our description merely carries us, as it were, into the inner circle of AL KHAMSA. With the tide now running so strongly in Europe towards *education*, it is interesting to notice how firmly the Arabs still believe in *breeding*. *Generosus nascitur non fit* is a principle to which they do not attach any limitation. When they perceive a colt sulking under the spur, and displaying other mulish symptoms, what instantly strikes them is, not that he

---

[1] *The Turf and the Race Horse*, by R. H. Copperthwaite, 2d edition (Day & Son), p. 144.

requires tuition, but that he is, as we should say, "bad from the egg." It is necessary, however, to protest against the idea that the Najdi horse is wanting in resolution. The instinct of *noli me tangere* is well developed in him. It is not for nothing that his head, instead of being small and meaningless like a sheep's, is broad and full in the frontal part. His admirable self-command habitually subdues the fire of his highly nervous temperament ; but if any one would fight him, he will fight. A yahoo of a rider may exhaust his patience. Even the noble mare, which the Arabs compare to the high-born lady on whom it is meet that all maidens should attend, frequently shows her aversion when those whom she does not know approach her. The stallion picketed beside the tent is as good as a sentinel. The first sound of an intruder brings him to attention. Generally he will stamp with one fore-foot, and challenge ; not braying like a ka-dish, but sounding one or two short and sharp notes, to intimate that he will make no terms. On the open plain, his strong character is even more exhibited. He seems to increase in size when moved from his standing-place. After a gallop, every joint and sinew and useful part stand out, as if made by work and for work. There is very little of the mere "pet" about him. When his glance is not fixed on some object near him, in which he imagines that there is danger, he is always scanning the horizon. His gentle salutations of passing mares are widely different sounds from the bagpipe-like squeals of the I'rāki stallion. At the sight of a crowd he neighs out musically, like one who is delighted to meet others of his species. Most of all, a whoop excites him. In a moment his thoughts appear to revert to Al ghaz-u ; and if a townsman be on his back, and he be fresh, he will require a great deal of steadying. It is said that the Bedouin wake up their horses' ears for life by shouting into them, at the top of their voices, as soon as possible after the foal is dropped.

CHAPTER III.

THE ARABIAN IN SHÁ-MI-YA AND AL JA-ZI-RA.

A SALIENT fact much insisted on in what precedes has here to be carried forward. That is, that the description of the *a-síl* Arabian which has been attempted is equally applicable in Najd and outside of it. At least it is *essentially* so, seeing that he is the horse of nomads; though the modifying influences of food, work, soil, air, and water have also to be remembered. In so far as data are available, the view may reasonably be adopted that the Ku-hai-lân tends on the Euphrates, through the power of barley, to excel in physique his brother in Nu-fûdh-land. It is recorded of the Darley, that as a four-year-old he was "about 15 hands high." The authority for this is his owner's letter which was quoted at p. 165 *ante*. There is no means of ascertaining whether the great-great-grandfather of Eclipse, as pedigree tables represent him, first beheld the world in which he was to obtain such distinction from some valley thick with *un-si* and the feathery *ithl* in the heart of the peninsula; or in the deserts west of the Euphrates, where Mr Darley bought him. But we know of many other scions of Al Kham-sa more or less resembling him, that never were out of Shà-mi-ya or Al Ja-zi-ra, from the date of foaling to that of export. Such were most, if not all, of the invincibles which made the Agha Khan cap and jacket the terror of Western India race-courses, from about 1850 to 1880. One of these furnishes our frontispiece. All the time that the "Agha Khan" who first took refuge in India "kept his court in grand and noble style" in Bombay and Poona, as did his ancestor, "The Old One" of Marco Polo's *Travels*, in the fortress of Alamût in Persia, his influence at Karbalâ enabled him annually to procure, through a private channel, selections from the best blood-colts of the Aeniza. His stable management was a curious mixture of the Persian and the Newmarket systems; but the horses were so superior that an uncommon power of winning races was accounted among the miraculous gifts of the "Old Man of the Mountain."[1]

---

[1] V. art. ALAMÛT, in Ind. I.

Both Mr Blunt and Major Upton chose their stud Arabians from the stocks which drink of the Euphrates. Several of the animals selected by the latter were sent to New South Wales. According to an advertisement sheet now before us, dated 1888, from Rochester, New York, one of them became the *prima donna* of a breeding establishment in the New World. We all know that Mr Blunt's favourites, notwithstanding the collapse of Arab racing at Newmarket, continue to multiply in Sussex.

Many years before the Crabbet Park stud was formed, a merchant of Bombay took to England a genuine Arab horse named Venus. This may seem a strange name for a horse; but the explanation is that his importer, a not too reverent A'jami, or Persian, called him after the Prophet Yû-nus, out of which "Venus" was evolved by the Secretary of the Turf Club. We never saw this modern "Bay Arabian" during his stud career in our island, and do not know what chances were allowed him; but he was a true-made one. He belonged to the horse, not the Galloway, series; and the only fault which the most critical judges could find in him—over-slackness at the couples—did not prevent him from carrying ten stone to victory, on at least one occasion, in a two-mile contest. We have lately had the good fortune to find evidence that Venus and the Darley, with an interval of about a century and a half between them, passed in the same deserts, and out of the hands of the same nation, from nomad to ha-dha-rī ownership. Since beginning this chapter, we have lost the chance of purchasing a four-year-old colt of the same strain as Venus in the following of a Shekh of the Sba'. While we were offering money, a messenger from the Mun-ta-fik bought him with thirty camels.[1] In the same desert £55 and three riding-camels were offered for another colt, to the dire offence of his breeder. These experiences show what considerable prices are often demanded by the Bedouin of Shâ-mī-ya. In every country a good horse, or one which from his breeding is likely to prove such, excites competition.

We have only space to notice here two of the many approved Arabians which Euphrates land has more recently yielded.

About twenty years ago, Esau bin Curtas, of Bussorah, bought a large bay colt from the Bedouin of Shâ-mī-ya. He first offered him to the Government of India; but his fore-legs were pronounced unsatisfactory. Ultimately the colt was sold, for Rs. 10,000, to one of our countrymen, in whose hands he became the conquering Revenge.[2]

---

[1] In Arabia the purchasing power of camels so varies in different years, at different seasons, and in different localities, that it is impossible to express a given number of them in £ s. d. He who works with a camel currency quickly realises the first principle of commerce, that what is called *money* bears a very indeterminate value.

[2] Not to be confounded with his namesake of later date, Young Revenge, of whom we have failed to discover whether he came from Najd, Shâ-mī-ya, or Al Ja-zī-ra.

Our second instance will also be taken from India, where the running of the bay Arab horse Euphrates is still remembered. Euphrates was one of the most commanding Arabs that have ever appeared, and he was taller even than the Darley. His exporter, A'li bin Khu-dhai-ri, whose home is in Baghdad, bought him in the neighbourhood of Aleppo, from the Aeniza. Some of our readers may have seen Euphrates cut down his fields like a second Eclipse. There is a laudable tendency in Englishmen to claim for old England everything that is very superior. As often as a "Triton of the minnows" like Revenge and Euphrates comes out in India, many who should know better assert that he is partly English. The point to observe is, that nothing would induce the breeders of the pure Arabian to use an English stallion, even if the opportunity of doing so existed. A brother of the Shekh of the Ma-sâ-ri-ba division of the Sba' Aeniza married an Englishwoman, with whom he is said to live in much happiness, at certain seasons of the year in a Damascus chateau, and at others in tents in the desert. Lady A. Blunt states that the Ma-sâ-ri-ba take advantage of this connection for the importation of guns, revolvers, and ammunition;[1] and some may think it probable that English stallions also reach them through the same channel. Perhaps this might be so if anybody were to convince them that mixed blood would prove as superior to pure blood in Al ghaz-u as carbines do to lances; but experience has fortified them against such an idea. Many of the finest Ku-hai-lâns, especially those of the bay colour, more or less resemble Newmarket three-year-olds; but the relationship between the two varieties explains this, taken in connection with the fact that both alike are bred for galloping. In the same way, the type of remote oriental ancestors is occasionally reproduced in our blood-horses—for example, in Touchstone, and his very Arab-like son Motley.

We now come to the important feature of Shâ-mi-ya and Al Ja-zi-ra—that is to say, the endless series of adulterated breeds of horses, more or less founded on Arab blood, which they contain. There should be no blind buying of horses anywhere, and least of all towards the Tigris and Euphrates. History narrates how the country between El I'râk and Egypt has from time immemorial formed one of the world's caravan routes and battle-fields. When it received the Aeniza and the Shammar, it was already tenanted not only by many nations of Arabs, such as the Ba-nû Sakhr and Ma-wâ-li, now called collectively *Ahlu 'sh Shi-mâl*, or *Northerners*,[2] but also by multitudes of other kindreds. In Burckhardt's time, hordes of Turku-mâns were prominent elements in its population.[3] Nearer our day, a British remount officer explored the Aeniza encampments round Damascus, and wrote in 'Blackwood's

---

[1] *Op. cit.* in Catalog. No. 12, vol. i. p. 10.
[2] To distinguish them from the Aeniza, who are spoken of as *A'rabu 'l Kibli*, or Southerners.
[3] *Op. cit.* in Catalog. No. 13, vol. i. p. 12, *et passim*.

Magazine' a delightfully matter-of-fact account of his adventures. His reference to the Turku-mâns is as follows :—

"Besides the Arabs, there was another race whose tents might be found in our neighbourhood; the wandering Turcomans, a nomadic people very similar, both in manner of life and in dress, to the sedentary Arabs. Their history, as it was related to me, is this: They belong to the great Turcoman race from which the Osmanlis sprang, and which still exists towards the north of Persia. Their forefathers came into Syria to help to resist the Crusaders, and have remained there ever since; and the language which they to this day speak is not, as with the other people of Syria, Arabic, but Turkish.

"They possess camels, goats, cattle, and horses. The latter are very poor. They are not, I think, superior in height to the Arab, and in every other point are so inferior that, seen by his side, they seem fit for little else than pack-horses. They are heavy and clumsy, with coarse heads, staring coats, very drooping hind-quarters, legs long in the shank, and coarse, draggling, ill-carried tails. In temper they are very shy; and although almost all geldings, are commonly obstinate and vicious when mounted. The mares, by reason of finer coats and greater age (for both Arabs and Turcomans sell their horses very young), are better looking, but are still coarse and Flemish."[1]

The Bedouin Arabs of Najd, when they overflowed into Shâ-mi-ya and Al Ja-zi-ra, neither expelled nor subjugated the peoples whom they found there. The spaces were ample, and the new-comers took only what they wanted. Their boast is that they have preserved from Shi-mâ-li admixture[2] the strains of horses which they brought with them; but this account exceeds the bounds of credibility. In these northern pastures, the best Najdi blood is that which is the most frequently revivified by fresh supplies from Najd.

The granges and hamlets on the Euphrates produce innumerable horses which it would be an abuse of language to call Arabians.

Where the Bi-likh fertilises north-western Al Ja-zi-ra, the Ba-râ-zi-ya, as we have already seen,[3] drive the plough and raise cattle. These are not Al ghaz-u folk, and their mares are mostly Shi-mâ-li. They are, however, skilful horse-breeders, and they have access to the stallions of the Bedouin. They specially aim at breeding large horses. A considerable number of charger-like upstanding colts of all shades of blood are annually collected from them by the Mosul and Ur-fa dealers. When a horse of the coarse or "carty" stamp appears in India, and strides away by sheer force of bone and muscle from cleaner bred ones, he may be the product of these pastures. Horses of this class occasionally make a *coup*, but they do not train on. There is no instance of one of them winning races in his

---

[1] *Op. cit.* in Catalog. No. 20, p. 273.
[2] Shi-mâ-li literally means *northern*, or *north-western*. Here it denotes the horse stock which existed on the Euphrates before the coming of the Aeniza and the Shammar. The term *bi-ri-di-tu 'l jauf*, lit. *cold-hearted*, is given by the Bedouin to the produce of Shi-mâ-li mares by *ku-dhd*, *i.e.* pure-bred, stallions.
[3] *V. ante*, p. 75.

teens, like little Greyleg. The old story of "English Arabs" is reproduced in connection with them, but it is wide of the mark. It may be the case that the Ba-rá-zi-ya, unlike the Aeniza, would send their mares to any large horse of good character which might come their way; but they could neither procure an English sire nor take care of him if they had him. One summer we kept an Australian thoroughbred beside us in Baghdad.[1] He was a patient gelding, which had experienced the climate of India, and he had a cool stable, with ample attendance. But one afternoon in August a wasp attacked him. Contrary to orders, the native grooms had fastened him with head and heel ropes, to keep him from rubbing himself. The attachment of the head-rope was to a solid square of wood firmly planted in the stable floor, and that of the heel-ropes to an iron peg; but the affrighted animal kicked and plunged till both pieces started. He then set off through the town, with his plucked-up anchors dangling both before him and behind him, and banging him. When he was brought back, the blood was streaming from him, and it was several weeks before he recovered. Even in India, European horses are difficult charges. One of the best that ever was shipped from Cape Colony, Sir Benjamin, was so excited by the ordeal of being taken through the surf at Madras in a native boat, that the first thing which he did on landing was to "knock over a black fellow."[2] A high veterinary authority declared that he was mad, and recommended, for the sake of the public safety, that he should be destroyed. We once saw two superb English hunters arrive in the capital of a Hindû State in Rajputâna. A young Rajpût was ordered to mount one of them; and he had no sooner done so than the noble quadruped, with a slight lift of his hind-quarters, sent the youngster rolling down the road like a cricket-ball.

When a medical man writes us a prescription consisting of half-a-dozen ingredients, nobody can venture to say which of them is the one that shall cure us. And in the same way the Shi-mâ-lî horse stock of Shâ-mi-ya and Al Ja-zi-ra is so curiously compounded, that it is impossible to give an exact account of it. One of its elements is the deteriorated Turku-mâ-ni mass, which is described in the above extract from 'Blackwood.' There is evidence to show that blood relationship exists between the Turku-mâ-ni horse which is bred to the east of the Caspian and the Ku-hai-lân of the Arabs. One of the good deeds of A'b-bâs I. of Persia, whose dominions at his death (1628) stretched from the Tigris to the Indus, was to collect and distribute a large number of Arabian mares and stallions. The new breed thus founded was well cared for by the northern nomadic Kurds, and it flourished greatly in certain localities which now belong to Russia. We have heard it stated by those who know "Turk-

---

[1] *P. ante*, pp. 193 *et* 241. [2] *Op. cit.* in Catalog. No. 26 (Aug. 1837), p. 118.

menia," that the best variety of the Turku-mâ-ni horse, that known in Central Asia as the Argamak, essentially is a modified Arabian. Our first introduction to the Argamak occurred in India. At Hyderabad, in the Deccan, a bay horse was offered to Sir Sâlâr Jung at an enormous price by a Hirâti dealer, who said that he had brought him from the steppe-land north of Khurâsân and Afghânistân. It so happened that a couple of years previously we had received from Sydney a thoroughbred Waler, the grandsire of which was an Arab, and finding him unsound, had sold him by auction. Sir Sâlâr Jung had often seen him, and when the Turku-mâ-ni horse was taken to him he sent him to us, with a letter asking if he was not our late property. And really the two were so similar that it was difficult to distinguish them, except from the Waler being a gelding and the other a horse. Afterwards, in Afghânistân, we saw many Argamaks of the same Anglo-Arabian stamp,—not at Cabul, whence the true sabreurs had fled, but at Jalâl-â-bâd, in the possession of Sher A'li's governor.[1] Pilgrims and other travellers from kingdoms as distant as Bukhâra frequently pace over the routes of Shâ-mi-ya and Al Ja-zi-ra on Turku-mâ-ni horses. The best specimens which have come our way have been long, and if anything rather narrow, animals, with straight back and croup; long, fine, and well-raised neck; head "dry," as the Russians say—that is, bony and fleshless—and the eyes as lively as a game-cock's. Bay, grey, and dark brown are the established colours. As a rule, these horses are of greater height and scope than Arabs. Their fore-legs are of the "brass-wire" kind, and the fore pasterns incline to be too long and straight.

We have thus dwelt on the subject of Turku-mâ-ni horses, partly because the breed is an interesting one, and partly in connection with the well-attested and evident fact, above alluded to, of this blood, in a debased form, being spread over Shâ-mi-ya and Al Ja-zi-ra. In a batch of horses which lately reached us from the Aleppo quarter, a dark bay colt with black points greatly took the eye. Although only two off, he stood 14 hands 3 inches, and was long, low, and level. His head was not good. It appears in the illustration on p. 140, where it is used

---

[1] A son of the historical Amir Dost Muhammad Khan of Cabul, resided till he died at Baghdad. He has often told us that, according to his experience, the Argamak is even a better traveller and campaigner than the Arabian. His view was that no sane person will sell a proved good horse unless he has turned useless, the only way to obtain a sound and genuine Argamak is to buy him as a yearling from the nomads. Russian posts are now established in the country of the Akhal Tekkes, i.e., in "Turkmenia," as distinct from Turkistân. Probably either Yeok Tepe or Ask-âbâd would be the best centre to work from if one desired to buy Argamaks. But it would be necessary to go in person, as Count de Mailling did about fifteen years ago. An agent would bring back animals which he had bought from peasants; or perhaps half-wild Kirghiz Galloways, the hardy creatures with the aid of which Kokand, Bokhâra, and Khiva have lately been "civilised" by Russia.

as a block on which to exhibit the Bedouin bridle. His length from hip to hock was extraordinary, but the quarters were as close and narrow as if they had been pressed together. When roused, he was a dashing galloper, but he was a slug at all other paces. The man who exercised him called him *Al ká-rúk*, or *The cradle*,[1] from his ponderous rocking motion at the walk. His manners raised a strong suspicion that he was not a true Arabian. The desert colt carries his feeding-bag with him, and knows that if he would reach his halting-place he must march straight ahead. "Sticking up" under the saddle and all the other signs of stubbornness indicate town breeding. This one, if Balaam's ass had been his grandfather, could scarcely have had a more inveterate habit of stopping when the humour seized him, standing like a statue, and resisting every intimation to proceed. The usual excuses were made for these symptoms of worthlessness. It was thought that time and work would perhaps develop Bedouin manners. Eclipse, when he was a colt, was so full of vagaries that they thought of castrating him; and it was only through his being hacked about all day by an Epsom rough-rider, who often kept him out all night, that his strong character was mastered. Bumble's theory that "meat will raise an artificial soul and spirit," was perhaps in this case applicable, for truly a boy's, or a colt's, worst enemies are idleness and over-feeding. At all events, it was decided to keep the colt, in the hope that he would improve. In Baghdad it is difficult to do justice to young horses. In winter the desert is soaked with rain, and in summer its surface resembles brick-work. As has elsewhere been noticed, there is also constant trouble about shoeing. A civilised riding-boy can scarcely be made from the existing materials; and practised lads are unwilling to leave India for a country in which there are no race-meetings. The sight of a rising colt being hauled about by a Turk or Arab who holds on by the bridle, and whose seat is wherever he can find it, is as painful to a horseman as that of an Errard's harp in the hands of a kitchen-maid would be to a musician. It so befell, however, that the best thing which can happen to any horse happened to this one; that is, in his third and fourth years he saw less of his stable than of desert marching. The practice of making horses which are intended for contests of speed cover long distances of ground every day, like mere baggage animals, is not perhaps the best promotive of racing form; but it is an excellent discipline and preparation. In this instance it worked wonders. The colt grew as muscular as a prize-fighter; and after a time it seemed that he had learned the lesson of obedience. But event-

---

[1] In the classical Arabic, *the place in which the babe is first laid* is called *mahd*—lit. a *flat surface*. The *swinging cradle* is a town invention, and the word for it, *káráck*, is apparently of the same coinage as *crack*, *croak*, *creek*, &c.

ually he yielded another illustration of the words of Sa'-di, that *no one can make a good sword out of bad metal;* and that *careful upbringing, in the case of the worthless, is like a walnut on a dome;* or, as our proverb runs, *water on a duck's back.* He was trained in India as a five-year-old, under every advantage; but the more he was galloped, the more he resembled a ka-dish. It was afterwards ascertained that he came from a village near Aleppo, and that his dam was not an Arabian, but a Turku-má-ní mongrel. Some say that according to the contour of the head in foalhood will be the mature horse's outward form; and we are inclined to think that every youngling, whatever its early promise may be, will the more confess its origin the older it grows.

CHAPTER IV.

THE ARABIAN IN EL I'RÁK AND EAST THE TIGRIS.

THE general features of I'rák A'ra-bi have been elsewhere shown.[1] Every reader knows the importance of this region to investigators, owing to the antiquity of its annals,[2] especially those tablets of burnt clay which are excavated and deciphered by Assyriologists. The first Semitic settlers among its primitive population are believed to have come as traders. The career of these people, under their historic name of Assyrians, is compared by Professor Sayce with the development of the British power in India.[3] The disappearance in due time (B.C. 539) of Nebuchadnezzar's empire before an invasion of Aryans led by Cyrus, is among the outstanding facts of history. A thousand years afterwards, El I'rák received another irruption of Semites. This time they were Arabs, and the spirit which moved them was national and religious. Islâm had set out to conquer, and these were its soldiers. At that period the western limits of Persia included the ancient Parthian capital of Ctesiphon on the Tigris, about twenty-five miles below modern Baghdad. Ctesiphon had suffered with varying fortunes many attacks by Roman emperors and others; but in A.D. 637 it surrendered to Sa-â'd, the Arabian general. After that the political centre of Islâm gradually shifted from El Hi-jâz to El I'rák. The "Eastern Caliphate" lasted 626 years from the death of Muhammad. In A.D. 1258 Hulagu and his Mongols extinguished it. From that date to ours, Tatars, Turks, and Persians have kept wresting

---

[1] V. ante, pp. 78-86.
[2] Even supposing the calculation which fixes Adam's date no further back than B.C. 4004 to be accepted, the references in Genesis to Phrat and "Hiddekel"—i.e., the Euphrates and the Tigris—as coeval with Eden, assert for the present Babylonian plain an antiquity of 6000 years. But according to Professor Huxley, "another kind of evidence," v. geological, "tends to show that the age of the great rivers must be carried back to a date earlier than that at which our ingenuous youth is instructed that the earth came into existence;" v. "Hasisadra's Adventure," in Nineteenth Century, June 1891.
[3] In art. "Babylonia," in Ency. Brit., vol. iii. p. 192.

from one another the mastery of the Tigris. To-day, as all the world knows, the ball is with the Turk, as it has been for the last 250 years; but there is no saying when it may be turned in a new direction. "Sublime Porte" is even a more complex expression than "Government of India." The motive-power on the Bosphorus resides in cliques of inflated Secretaries and "advisers"; but the Sultan's personality also constitutes a factor as formidable as it is uncertain. The political conditions of El I'râk of course take their colour from those of Constantinople. Fifty years ago the Pâsha of Baghdad was a kind of sovereign. When the Porte desired to oust him, a force had sometimes to be sent to accomplish that object. In our day his enemies undermine him, and his masters displace him, by telegraph. A bad system is administered by a worse executive; he who has place or money has nothing to fear save its being taken from him; while the poor have only their poverty to protect them. The Porte does not depute its best officials to provinces which are considered places of banishment.

After the above rapid sketch, but slight explanation is needed of the disadvantages which press on the urban and rural population of El I'râk as horse-breeders. There is no want of inclination; the commercial incentive is considerable; and the country, as has been seen, affords rare natural facilities. Wherever the Tigris, the Euphrates, or the Dhi-á-la passes, or irrigational channels run, the man who ploughs but an acre turns out a hobbled mare. The upas-tree is the Government. Agricultural shows and horse-fairs are impossible; for the Pâsha who should start them would be credited with the intention of annexing, for himself or for the military department, all the exhibits. The practice of periodically prohibiting the export of horses harasses numerous classes. It turns honest merchants into smugglers. The public treasury loses its custom's dues on exported horses. The young stock of the country is hurried out of it without the wealthy classes having had an opportunity of buying it.

All of us are familiar with the story of a colossal structure having once upon a time been begun at Bâb-il, or Babel, on the plains of El I'râk. It is not clear whether some catastrophal incident of the prehistoric world makes its appearance in this description; or whether the purpose of the writer merely was to bring the existing diversity of human speech into agreement with the fragment imbedded in the same writing,[1] to the effect that "the whole earth was of one language and of one speech," at an antecedent period. But however this may be, if a tower and city fallen to wreck and ruin were used to typify the character of the I'râki horse-stock, it might not be inappropriate. It has already been stated that a large proportion of the so-called Arabians which appear in foreign markets are produced in El I'râk. A competent

---

[1] Gen. xi.

judge of horses has recorded that, in the course of his professional career in India, he had "scarcely seen," in the Arab breed, "the perfectly formed symmetrical creature that is to be found in her Majesty's possession at home."[1] It is not surprising that he should have formed this conclusion. The case of the Arabian is not the only one in which the genuine article suffers in reputation through counterfeits being mistaken for it. Sometimes, in El I'râk, when a home-bred colt is being shown, the owner says that a ghaz-u of the Bedouin left it with him as an unweaned foal, because its dam had been taken from them in foray. Such a tale is not impossible. The intending purchaser need not receive it with a face of incredulity, but he should be sceptical. In the rare instances in which the account is true, a pertinent question is, What effect does the "water and air" of El I'râk produce on younglings which, after having been foaled say in Najd, are thus expatriated? but facts bearing on this point are wanting. Occasionally a governor or a military commander brings to El I'râk from Arabia proper a notable Ku-hai-lân, and lets the breeders use him. The result is, the appearance of superior stock round his headquarters for many years afterwards. Gradually, however, the stamp dies out, and the long backs and coarseness again prevail. It is scarcely possible to fix a type of the I'râki horse. They say of Scotland that all its people get a sip of learning, and none of them a full draught. And so in the Tigris valley, every horse has more or less of *blood* or breeding, and no horse the full quantity. The only comprehensive description applicable is, that they are all saddle-horses. Those that are bred in towns like Baghdad have no true pedigrees. Light-framed colts grow up weedy, more like slices of horses than horses. Bulky colts turn out coarse and beefy, with "pig's eyes"—which the Arabs, by the way, call "locusts' eyes"—a thick skin, a throaty jowl, and a neck entering the chest below the shoulder points. A touch of the comical is often imparted to these soft town products, through the fashion of keeping the tail close-clipped, or shaven, during colthood, to promote the growth of the hinder parts! Sad to relate, they are very generally suffered to be fruitful and multiply. Owing to this cause, and through over-feeding, their manners resemble those of Persian horses. From not being shut up, they are seldom pugnacious in company; but most of them possess a trick of neighing till their sides shake when they see a mare. No amount of cudgelling will serve to conquer this habit. The more they are belaboured the more they squeal, especially when they breathe the air of the desert. The only alternative is, to bear with the noise that they make, or to castrate them. Many oriental peoples entertain a prejudice against castration. This question is still a more or less open one; but having for thirty years advocated the emasculation of horses not required

---

[1] *A Glimpse at Horse-breeding*, by Principal Vet. Surg. F. F. Collins; read before the United Services Institution of India, 20th August 1878.

and not suited for propagation, especially cavalry and artillery cattle, we may as well record that the only cases in which we have known the patient to be lowered in strength or useful courage by this operation are those in which it has been badly performed, or resorted to in animals that were too old, or were otherwise disqualified. It is not impossible that, especially in the coarser breeds, there are horses which, if unsexed, will lose a portion of their natural briskness; but after all that can be said, it is certain that agricultural communities which tie up their yearling colts labour under a great disadvantage, when compared with others who castrate them and turn them out. A slight practical lead in the latter direction is being given in El I'râk by the Osmanli. Mounted soldiers naturally prefer geldings, to screamers which they may have to rise and mind several times in the course of a night if they would find them in the morning. Besides its military farriers, Baghdad possesses at least one private practitioner of this useful art—who, although but a cobbler, is a very skilful operator. First, he casts the patient, partly with a hobble improvised from any odd piece of rope, and partly by pressure against the buttocks. After that, an old penknife, with a couple of twigs from the nearest tree and a few inches of twine for clams, sees him through the business. A pinch of sulphate of copper is then rubbed in, and the moment that the animal rises, as well as twice a-day afterwards, he is mounted and cantered round the stable-yard, to keep the wound from swelling. Only a drop of blood escapes. In eight years we have never heard of any of this man's cases going on otherwise than favourably. Occasionally he travels as far from home as the Euphrates, but his special qualifications are not utilised, except on mules, by any Arabs. The substance of this digression is, that the first thing wanted for the town-bred horse-stock of the country of the Tigris is castration.

In El I'râk, as in other places, the further we recede from cities, the more the horse improves. Thus the horse of the mixed pastoral and cultivating Arabs of Al Ha-wî-ja serves as a useful substitute for the genuine Arabian, when only a small price can be given. The U'baid, his breeders, have barley; and many of their colts touch 15 hands and upwards. Good specimens, when not too suggestive of the gun wheel, after a month of town polish, pass with the inexperienced for Arabians of the picture-book type. Once at Kar-kûk we bought one of this class for £15. Though only a four-year-old, he was already grown into a weight-carrying charger, with good trotting action. For a long time he had been at grass, and yet he carried us, in nearly a month of daily marching, over a most rugged country, without ever having a sore back or making a bad stumble. If he had been true-bred, instead of but a happy blend, he would have been very valuable. As it was, the dealer who bought him when our journey was over, sold him in Bombay to a racing confederacy for about twelve times his Kar-kûk price! One might as well take a horse out of the first passing Oxford Street omnibus and enter him for the Grand National, as put one of his kind in training. In another place it was stated that the Sâ-yih families of the Sham-mar now pitch their tents in Al Ha-wi-ja, owing to feuds with their kindred between the two great rivers. The Sâ-yih do not possess more than about a thousand mares. These are generally undersized; but they show a good deal of type and quality. The local dealers, when they cannot just say that they obtained a horse from the Aeniza, are fond of tracing him to the Sâ-yih. A pair of Galloways from this quarter, picked up for less than £20 each in the open lands round Tak-rit, may bring Rs. 1500 in Bombay, and prove well worth it for light harness. A considerable number of the small blood Arabs which are so much sought after for Indian pony-racing may be bought young, for very moderate prices from the Sâ-yih.

Next let us speak of the Kurds of El I'rák and their horses. Most readers know that vast mountain-ranges shut off the Porte's Asiatic provinces from Persia. The several masses, as they ascend and descend over one another, from the junction of the two arms of the Euphrates, by Lake Van, to Su-lai-mâ-ni-ya, present a stupendous picture of confusion. Here and there a summit rises, white with snow, to perhaps even 15,000 feet. But the usual elevation is much lower; and the mountain-slopes and undulating uplands are clothed in summer with rich herbage. Rivers and innumerable streams flow through the landscapes; a temperate, or in winter rigorous, climate hardens the people for labour; and cereals are produced in the valleys in extraordinary abundance. A very great, but not the only, element in the population of this region consists of Kurds.[1] In certain localities these are claimed by Persia, and in others by the Porte; but, as far as possible, they preserve the tribal organisation. Although not Persians they are Aryans; and this appears in the numerous superstitions with which they variegate Islamism. Both in Persia and Turkey the great body of them are Sun-nis; but highly as they esteem their patriarchal chiefs, they pay even greater reverence to "holy men" or Sai-yids.[2] In this respect they resemble the Afghâns. Six words of the Kur-ân, detached from the context and misinterpreted, will outweigh with them every earthly consideration, subsidies not excepted after the money has been pocketed. The Persian and Osmanli Governments are greatly troubled by them. At the

---

[1] At the dawn of history, as now, a nation named *Gutu* (*warrior*), which the Assyrians rendered by the synonym of *Gardu* or *Kurdu*, occupied these mountains; and Cyrus found it necessary to curb them before he descended upon Babylon.

[2] The greatest personage in the Kurdi town of Su-lai-mâ-ni-ya, where this footnote is added, is a certain Kâ-ka Ah-mad, of patriarchal age but not ascetic habit, to kiss whose hand thousands of people congregate. As he receives only his disciples, it is impossible to ascertain his tenets; but the secret meetings which he holds are probably traceable to times before Is-lâm. The title *Kâ-ka* means *elder brother*. The word reappears in India as *châ-châ = uncle*. In Hungary, the leader of a band of gipsies is their "*Ga-ka*."

present time the country crossed by the Him-rin[1] barrier, through which the Tigris the U'dhaim, and the Dhi-á-la find their several openings into the Babylonian plain, is harassed by one small Kurdish clan called the Ha-má-wands, or Ah-mad-á-wands. This tribe musters no more than five hundred fighting men; and yet it keeps up a sharp, if unequal, conflict with two great Governments, which are supposed to be acting in concert, sometimes for its pacification, and at other times for its destruction. We lately rode a march with a Bey of the Ha-má-wands, who had made terms with the Turks and stopped in his castle, doubtless to watch the authorities. The blood-mare which he rode looked as if she had been bred in Najd. He and his retainers exhibited feats of horsemanship in the most rugged places; and their expertness in loading and firing their Martinis at speed explained the difficulty of reducing such centaurs to obedience. The first European Power which shall acquire a cantonment in the lands inhabited by the Kurds should find it easy, by means of regular pay and discipline adapted to the national temper, to raise a formidable army.[2] After what has preceded, it is superfluous to observe that in the area now being glanced at, which is roughly calculated at 60,000 square miles, local circumstances strongly conduce to horse-breeding. The nomadic Kurds ride mares, not camels, and love to be well mounted. Their settled kindred raise colts for sale to dealers, and rear the young stock cheaply. The drawback is want of system, and the scarcity of good stallions. Now, as in the time of the Crusades, every Kurd assigns the highest place to ancestry. It is probable that certain Kurdish families which still flourish can each show a pedigree of at least five hundred years. Nevertheless the practice of these people as horse-breeders seems to aim at nothing higher than the obtaining of foals out of such mares as they possess by any horses which may strike their fancy. Hence it is wrong to assign to the term "Kurdî horse" any other meaning than that of a horse bred by the Kurds. In this sense, many so-called Arabian horses are more correctly Kurdî ones. If Arab blood form the basis of the Kurdish horse-stock, admixture is its prevailing feature. We have only once seen in El I'râk a horse that reminded us of the thoroughbred, or nearly thoroughbred, weight-carriers of the Shires. This was an aged grey which the Baghdad troops had taken in a skirmish with the Ha-má-wands near the Persian frontier. Nobody knew his history except his owner, whose split

---

[1] The Him-rin range leaves the main series of the Zagros near Man-da-li, and runs S.E. to N.W., to within a short distance of the ruins of Al Hadhr (*q. v.* in Index I.) Not its height, which rarely exceeds 500 feet, but its length, about 200 miles, and breadth make this rocky barrier formidable. More or less elevated ridges of sandstone and pebbles run parallel with it, enclosing gorges and oases, and serving as outer defences to the central recesses.

[2] General Sir H. C. Rawlinson, in 1882, computed the Kurds under Turkey at 15,000,000, and those under Persia at 750,000.—(*Ency. Brit.*, vol. xiv. p. 156.) The term *Kurdistân*, or *Kurd country*, is more convenient than scientific. The Kurds are distributed from about 39 N. lat. and 39 E. long. to about 34 N. lat. and 47 E. long.

skull had swung for a day's march at the saddle-bow of an Osmanli Rustam. After figuring for a time under the bulky form of a military Pásha, the horse was sold for the stud of a Persian governor. He had plenty of blood for himself; but whether he had enough to transmit to others was doubtful. Probably he was one of those with respect to which it is necessary, in order to breed others like them, to go back to the sire and dam.

There is no evidence that European blood has ever been used by the horse-breeders of El I'rák. The case might easily have been otherwise, for these people are very different from the Bedouin Arabs. St Petersburg imports a considerable number of English horses, the progeny of which, in the form of Russian carriage cattle, may be seen as far eastward as Kirmánsháh in Persia, only ten days' march from Baghdad. If a Consul, or a merchant, residing on the Tigris, or on the Shattu 'l A'rab, were to bring out for his own riding a foreign stallion, and the natives liked him, they would bribe the grooms and obtain his services. But a thing may be possible, or even probable, and yet may never have actually happened; and such would appear to be the case in this instance. An Anglo-Arabian, or "English-Arab," bred on the Tigris, is still in the future. Supposing a series of colts of this description to begin to appear in the Bombay market, it is likely that the local Turf-Clubs would find it necessary to frame a new rule, with the object of excluding them from the many valuable races which in Western India are still reserved for Arabs. Even in moist Bengal the produce of the English thoroughbred horse, not always from the best mares, has often given weight and a beating to champion Arabs.

The I'rákí cultivators are fully aware that if they could breed better horses they would obtain better prices from the wandering dealers; but there is no one to give them the lead. Their mares are inferior, but they are better than the horses to which they are sent. The so-called Arab horse-stock of El I'rák thus dwindles more and more. Signs of this appear in the prevailing colours. The silver, nutmeg, and sky-blue greys of the desert are lost on the Tigris in a series of debased roans, sorrels, and russets. Chestnuts turn pale or washy, and put on blazes or white stockings. Bay to a great extent disappears. While residing at Baghdad we have obtained from the Bedouin horses of all the good colours; but no breeder has ever asked for the services of one of them which was not a bay. The reason of this is, that buyers will give a better price for a bay I'rákí than for an I'rákí of any other colour. We know what an extraordinary aptitude England possesses for changing waste lands and pastures into granaries and cities, not only in the British Isles, excepting Ireland, but in every country which she occupies. The drawback is that the supply of horses fit for military purposes decreases in like proportion wherever her foot is planted, so that it becomes necessary to look abroad for remounts. Naturally El I'râk, owing to its nearness to Bombay and Karáchi, is full of interest from this point of view. The worst I'râki is at least inured to a burning sun in summer, and to more of cold and wet in winter than he will ever see in India. The better bred ones, especially those of Kurds like the Dâ-û-di-ya, abound in useful qualities. Very commonly they grow to 14 hands and 2 inches at the withers. They are good marchers, and very hardy, and have strong legs and feet. The Kurd's horse never refuses to thrust his head into his feeding-bag, no matter how severe a day's work he may have done. A large number of colts which more or less answer to this description are always coming forward on both sides of the Tigris. It has, however, to be remembered that horses adapted for high-class cavalry cannot be bought in lots, but require to be collected in the course of long miles of travel. It would be very difficult for remount agents, especially if Europeans, successfully to compete in this work with the jam-bâzes. When the military authorities of an Indian Presidency send officers to buy remounts in countries already well opened, they defeat their own ends; for the supply of horses through the established channels is thereby checked.

The deputing of experts for the purchase of *stud* horses rests on a different basis, as it cannot be said that the regular exporters specially address themselves to this task. If we wished to breed race-horses, whether in India or in any other country, we should use none but the best Newmarket blood on both sides. The improvement of Eastern stocks, so as to bring them up to the mark of military service, is, however, a different matter; and all who realise the necessity of avoiding extremes in breeding, question the utility, from this point of view, of the over-sized and over-developed horses of Europe. Accordingly, the Government of India for many years endeavoured to procure compact and well-bred Arabians through its Political establishment in El I'râk, or "Turkish Arabia"; but the system of ordering "per indent" a dozen or more horses, all of the same pattern, did not invariably yield satisfactory results; and it is now considered preferable to select, in India, Arabian, or oftener, it may be feared, I'râki, stallions from the strings of the jam-bâzes. A combination of strong points, with a freedom from defects, such as is rarely met with in Eastern countries, is required to make a good stallion of any description; and in purchasing horses which are intended to contribute through their near and remote descendants to the defence of the empire, it is impossible to maintain too high a standard, provided that it is a practical one. The horses suitable for this purpose which we have seen in a decade's residence in Baghdad, might all be tied with one rope. India is not the only foreign country that draws on El I'râk for stud-horses. The Shâh of Persia, and still more frequently the tribal magnates who live by spear and spur in the Bakht-I-â-ri and Lû-ri mountains, despatch agents in the same direction. A few years ago, a Russian cavalry officer riding a weight-carrying and very charger-like Turku-má-ni, visited Baghdad on duty of this kind; but he did not see a horse which he reckoned worth buying. If he had been a novice instead of, as the case actually was, an old campaigner, he would have found no difficulty in collecting a boat-load. A decade or two later the proper bureau of the Czar's Government would most likely have had occasion to pass an order on reports submitted to it, that "the Arabian stallion had been tried and found wanting;" the truth perhaps all the time being, that not one of the horses which had been forwarded could claim other than a chance connection with the stock of Kʻ-hail.

AN INTERIOR IN BAGHDAD.

CONCLUSION

CONCLUSION.

MANY may think that the full stop at the end of the preceding chapter would have made the best conclusion; but it might then have been said that everything had been told about the Arabian horse except where and how to find him. We therefore propose to consider now the various methods in which horses of this breed are procurable—without, of course, approaching the too wide subject of horse-buying generally. And so many of our countrymen are interested in promoting and extending the use of Arabs in the British Isles and Empire, that a few observations on the requirements of Eastern horses during and after exportation will also perhaps be appreciated.

It may be as well at the outset again to protest against the idea that any royal road to success lies open to the buyers of Arabian horses. Before all things, as has been seen, it is needful that he who searches shall possess the power of recognising the genuine animal in all places and circumstances. He must also be able to decide, in doubtful cases, whether a horse is *perhaps* pure-bred, or too far outside the pale to be worth considering. Another necessary endowment is the faculty of brushing aside random stories and exaggerations. In some countries, if not in all, it is a positive advantage to be a little hard of hearing. Persons are to be found in our islands, both in the breeder and the dealer classes, who, for the sake of their reputations, will honestly give one the benefit of their knowledge and experience. But in the East this resource is not so fully available, for the Bedouin Arabs are not horse-dealers, and *Caveat emptor* is the motto of the jam-bazes. A man may have taken the highest degree in a veterinary college, and yet be wanting in the power of obtaining information on points of horse-history. Do not then imagine, O youthful reader, that the perusal of the following, or of any other pages, will qualify you to go through a collection of Eastern horses, and separate the true metal from the counterfeit. Written descriptions, especially when accompanied by authentic portraits, are useful; but experience is the great schoolmaster. Horsemen, at least, will not quarrel with that portion of Mr Squeers' system of education which, when a boy had learned what a horse was, sent him to work out the remainder of the lesson by practical methods.

One other prefatory remark of a general nature will perhaps prove useful—namely, that he who desires to buy an Arab should have a clear knowledge of the proposed object. The method which he ought to follow depends more or less on that. When merely a charger, a hunter, or a pleasure-horse is wanted, it is seldom advisable to go behind the regular exporters, and try to approach the breeders. To find a colt which shall win a name in racing story is a far more serious undertaking. And when the design is to obtain an Arabian good enough in points and pedigree to improve the character of other breeds, special opportunities have to be awaited.

Section I.—Of buying straight from the Bedouin.

We say "straight," because the European who deputes an Arab, or an I'râki, messenger, or agent, to go and buy horses for him in the Arabian desert, can scarcely lay claim to a sound understanding.

"Let every eye negotiate for itself,
And trust no agents,"[1]

should be written in large letters, and kept before the eyes of every one whose situation exposes him to this temptation. As for him who is sent on such an errand, his courage mounts with the occasion. His employer may be in Europe, or in India, or, at the nearest, in a town of El I'râk or Syria. In order to join the Bedouin, he must necessarily enter spaces where there are no posts and telegraphs. He must also carry the requisite cash, in gold if he go towards Damascus, or in dollars in Arabia proper, for the wandering Arabs laugh at paper money. The reader may be more inclined to wonder at a messenger in these circumstances ever returning, than at his doing so after unfaithful service; but the latter is the Eastern method. Usually the man makes a compromise with his conscience. While serving himself first, he also tries to obtain some return for his employer. One great question with him, naturally, is how to avoid the danger of falling among thieves. If he is a native of El I'râk or Syria, he settles perhaps for a year on the Euphrates, and utilises the money which has so foolishly been intrusted to him in setting up a little cultivation. Or, if ambitious of connecting himself with the Bedouin, he may enter the desert, claim a Shekh's hospitality, and sue for the hand of a tent-maiden—as is needless to

---

[1] "Much Ado about Nothing," Act ii. sc. 1.

say, unsuccessfully. At last, when he thinks that it is time to return, he buys a number of "peacocky" horses in towns like Der or wherever he sees them, and unblushingly delivers them to his employer.

A Persian poet says—

> If thou art single on the pack,
> Ride where thou hast a mind;
> But with another at thy back,
> 'Tis best to be resigned![1]

This may apply to Orientals. But as regards our countrymen, we fail to perceive that even the bliss of matrimony in any sensible degree restrains the tendency to travel. Taking no account of family parties, or of cases in which the explorer is a spinster or a widow, it may be depended on that for the traveller, as for the soldier and the sailor, no pole-star is so full of guidance as the "*placens uxor*" who is waiting for him in England. Nevertheless it is too true that none of our countrymen, or countrywomen, whose steps have trod Arabia proper, have ever yet tested the hospitality of nations like Kah-tân, with the view of discovering the extent to which they practise horse-breeding. The circumstances which account for this have been described in an earlier chapter.[2] It has also been unreservedly stated that Najd is the source of sources; and that it becomes us to be guarded in all conclusions relative to the richness of Arabia in horses, till the innermost pastures of the peninsula shall be examined. We therefore wait for the appearance in the rising generation of a Mr Blunt and a Mr Doughty rolled into one, before whose spirit of adventure and force of character the guardian genii of the Nu-fûdh will vanish. Our regret is that, unless we should quit the safe ground of personal knowledge, we cannot, as regards Najd, afford to such traveller of the future any very useful hints or itinerary. The programme which is about to be offered to the buyer of Arabian horses of authentic pedigree will not conduct him into middle Arabia. The starting-point may be either Aleppo or Damascus at his pleasure. The ground marked out includes all the spaces into which the tribes of Najd have kept issuing, ever since the overthrow of the ancient nationalities of Syria by the Chaldæan empire. Numerous facts bearing on our present subject have already been cited; for example, that the Darley was bought in the deserts touched by the Euphrates;[3] and that Burckhardt recommended Damascus as a good position for the establishment of persons employed to purchase high-class Arabians.[4] It has further appeared how easy, and to one possessing Bohemian habits and a sound digestion how delightful, it is for the European to visit the camps, or rather cities of camps, which form the only hospitable features of the

---

[1] Sa'di, in the "Gulistân."
[2] Vide, p. 33 sq pp. 44, 45.
[3] Vide, p. 26).
[4] Vide, p. 64.

barren land between the middle course of the Euphrates and El I'rák. Occasionally people write to us, both from Europe and India, asking to be informed how to procure Arab horses, taller, or faster, or handsomer, or cheaper, or of surer pedigrees, than those exported by the jam-bázes. It is always difficult to answer such letters, either from knowing too little of the writer, or because he evidently expects to receive, through some *deus ex machiná*, and without risk or trouble on his part, specimens of the best colts or fillies, or brood mares, in Arabia. But if we imagine ourselves speaking here to one of our countrymen whose enthusiasm prompts him to see with his own eyes the Aeniza horse-stock, the following is what occurs to us. It is taken for granted that you are a judge of horses, not self-styled, but made by experience. If not a specialist on Arabs, it may be all the better. Your mind will be the opener; you will not go to worship, any more than to cavil, but will take things soberly as you find them. First of all, it is necessary to acquire some knowledge of Arabic. Do not all at once run off on this errand to Arabia. A layer of book-work[1] forms the proper foundation; and that is better laid wherever one may be in a tolerable climate, and with a competent person to assist, than amid the distractions of travel. Beware of outfitters and outfits. Nothing that requires to be whitened, or blackened, or starched, or ironed, is suitable for the Arabian desert. The best material for shoes is the deer-skin which in India is called *sám-bar*. The ideal dress for Eastern travel is that which, while draping the "forked radish" aspect of humanity, shall be equally comfortable to walk, ride, and sleep in; having nothing tight about it except the *hi-zám*, or belt, which girds the loins. An inside-pocket should hold a trusty stop-watch. The best route is by Bombay, where it is not impossible to engage a couple of Indian riding-lads. Among the Arabs there is no lack of youths who can "ride like fiends," as the saying is; but that is precisely what is not wanted here. The biggest box, or only big box, in your baggage should hold a couple of 5 lb. saddles, a few snaffle bridles, and an eighth of a mile steel chain to measure off a trial-ground. *Tentes d'abris*, common saddles, and other travelling requisites, are best bought in El I'rák. By way of "sinews," £1000 should prove sufficient. Brains will improve a slender capital; while one effect of too much money often is to make us unduly depend on others. Thus prepared, you would find Bussorah a good starting-point. Half of your money should be sent from there, through a

---

[1] Phrase-books in the Roman character may fulfil all the requirements of Cook's tourists; but the key to a country is its language; and the Arabic alphabet, which is also that of the Turks, the Persians, and the Muslim Indians, need frighten no one. The excellent Arabic grammar by the late Professor Wright of Cambridge is unfortunately out of print. A good substitute for it is that by Dr A. Socin (1885), Professor in the University of Tübingen. A very small grammar is that by Fá-ris El Shidiac, of Beyrouth.

Consulate, to Damascus. The next step would be to buy riding-camels, and engage three followers of the liberated slave class, which would cost about £100. With the remaining £400 in your waist-belt you should then join a party of Agelis who are going to Al Ha-sá to purchase camels. If you should choose the easy Arab cloak and tunic, remember that, in Northern Arabia, disguise is as impolitic, and indeed ridiculous, as it is unnecessary. Poetry never uttered a sounder warning through any of her prophets than Scott's in " Marmion " :—

> " O what a tangled web we weave,
> When first we practise to deceive ! "

However dressed, be known for an Englishman and a Christian. Outside of the Peninsula religion counts for little, and no one has a right to pretend to believe in another's faith, or to go through forms of worship as a kind of play-acting. Short of that, the company manners of the Arabs should be studied, and more or less adopted. At first these do not attract us, but by degrees we perceive their advantages. Even the oriental mode of eating proceeds upon the sound principle that every man can rinse his fingers, whereas the cleaning of a knife and fork is an undeveloped art in backward countries. A well-washed hand is better than an unrubbed iron, or, as is daily seen in India, a spoon freshly wiped with the end of a scullion's turban. Between the Mediterranean and the Sea of Persia men's complexions are too diverse for mere colour to attract particular attention. As for speech, the Aeniza and the Shammar are accustomed to hear the pure language of the Ku-raish infinitely confused and deformed by strangers. Well-worn garments are not only the most comfortable, but also least excite the covetous thoughts of the Bedouin. Above all things, keep clear of the style and manners of a Pásha. Rather be one whose estate needs mending, and who would improve it by Arab methods. Thus it will be the easier for you, while moving about in Al Ha-sá, to suit yourself from among your Ageli friends with a *ra-fík* or partner. *Aw-wal ra-fík, thum-ma ta-rík*, or, *First, a companion, then the road*, is a maxim among the Arabs. An associate of this kind, to whom a small money interest in the enterprise has been given, is essential to success ; but he should not be a townsman, or one who has seen the world. After collecting camels in Arabia Proper, and moving with them, still under Ageli pilotage, to Damascus, you would there find such a brisk demand for camel cattle, that you might sell a part of the drove for the cost price of the whole; or, otherwise, you might retain all your camels, with the view of bartering them for colts and fillies. Elsewhere it has been seen that camels represent more money in Shá-mi-ya than in Najd; and, irrespectively of commercial value, a beautiful dromedary exercises an extraordinary power over the hearts of the Bedouin. Once we chanced to be in an encampment of the Sham-mar when a southerner arrived with a string of camels. It did not appear whether he was a horse-dealer and a camel-dealer combined, or only the latter. The first thing which struck us was how comfortably he progressed, with camels' milk to sup on, unlimited transport, and a family party of stalwart brethren to assist him. His camels were in an exhausted state. Through over-travel their humps cleaved to their bellies, as the Arabs say.[1] All their beauty depended on their breeding, and that produced a great impression. As the news of their arrival spread, groups of Bedouin horsemen, with their long spears over their shoulders, repaired to the spot from considerable distances. Merchant-buyers like those of Ku-wait, who will take colts as they are offered, good and middling all in a lot, without minding how long their strings may grow, certainly find it more advantageous to buy with camels than with money. We shall, however, suppose you to sell off the shuffle-footed cargo which you brought with you from Al Ha-sâ, except a few head retained as riding-camels and milchers. It would be well to leave those with two of your black servants among the *quasi* Bedouin round Damascus, while you yourself set off to the fertile Syrian district of Al Hau-rân. It would be necessary there to set up a regular horse nursery—on which, however, no buildings would have to be erected, as booths of black blanketing are sufficient in that Arcadian climate. £100 laid out on cultivation would bring your crops well forward. Protected by the Druses, your property would be safe. Your labourers would be paid in produce, and the customary rate is one-fourth of every harvest. Intrusting the depot to your third slave-servant, you and your companion would then have to join a caravan of merchants trading with the Bedouin proper.[2] A couple of hundred pounds

---

[1] The camel is said to *feed on the fat of his own hump*, and this is proverbial in Arabia. What the paunch is in man, and the top of the tail in sheep, the *sa-nâm*, or hump, is in the camel,—his provision for a time of leanness.

[2] Such of the Bedouin people as periodically approach towns are much attracted by the shops. We lately saw at Kar-ba-lâ a brisk trade going on with the Aeniza in metal saucer-baths from Birmingham; and on inquiry it appeared that these utensils are now, within certain circuits, replacing the ancient wooden trenchers from which the Arab of the desert eats his motum. *V. ante*, p. 191. The remoter Bedouin nations depend on pedlars. Articles of dress, swords, powder and ball, horse-shoes, nails, iron, leather, coffee, tobacco, and spices thus reach them. Damascus is a great starting-place of the pedlars. The travelling merchants possess their own tents and camels. When they have joined a camp they move about with it, and they will barter their goods for sheep and butter. Another town from which they set out is Ku-bai-sa, situated at the I'râk entrance of Shâ-mi-ya. In summer and autumn Ku-bai-sa is half empty, while its inhabitants are out with merchandise among the Aeniza. Burckhardt says of the traders who in his day had their homes in Damascus, that they were "men of probity, and in good esteem among the Bedouin"; that half of them were Christians; and that "should a European traveller wish to visit the interior of the desert between Damascus and the Persian Gulf, he may best contrive to accomplish his design through their assistance" (*op. cit.* in Catalog. No. 15, vol. i. p. 195).

invested in cloth and other merchandise would furnish you with the best introduction to the nomadic nations of the Euphrates. Thus in a short time you would find yourself among the real Arabs of the desert. The advantages of the unostentatious style of travelling would then be apparent. Several of our countrymen have paid such high prices for Arab horses, and exhibited such enthusiasm, that to this day Shâ-mî-ya and Al Ja-zî-râ long for the coming of others like them. We have grown chary of those of the Bedouin who cultivate what in Europe would be called *a stud*. A simple fellow who owns but one mare, and rides her, is more likely to tie a genuine colt or filly beside his tent than the Shekh who boasts a wide connection with Pâshas, Consuls, and jam-bâzes. But when one is travelling as a Beg, or European of position, it is almost impossible to enter a Bedouin encampment without being conducted straight to the Shekh's *ma-dhîf* or guest-tent. Even when the stranger is permitted to set up his own little tent, the Bedouin will be attracted by it, as schoolboys are by the monkey-house in the Zoological Gardens. Sticks may not be pushed through its openings, but it will be intruded on in every possible manner. If he offer a price for a colt—no nomad will condescend to name a sum himself—the result will be that the owner will jump on its back and ride out of sight in a huff,[1] perhaps to return, perhaps not. Under no circumstances are the Aeniza easy to deal with; but the more quietly you approach them, the less impracticable you will find them. The proper class of stock to purchase would be two-year-olds which had suffered no unfair usage. The very flower of the race should be taken,—the broad-hipped, large-jointed, darting-actioned colts and fillies, of assured AL KKAM-SA lineage, but not necessarily of "fancy strains." These selections should be sent to drink milk and grow to three-year-olds among the Damascus Arabs, while you waited to pick a second lot from the following season's two-year-olds. By the time that you had accomplished this task, your first year's purchases would have ripened. It would then be proper to transfer these first-fruits from the neighbourhood of Damascus to the Hau-rân farm, where there would be plenty of barley. In a few months' time, with the help of your riding-lads, you would know more about them than mere looking at them would ever tell you. The Arabs say that *the horse is in the foal, as the flower is in the bud;* but then the bud cannot be seen into. Such of your selections as did not look as well after a course of steady work as when only standing, could be sold to the jam-bâzes. Season after season it would be necessary to follow the same course of buying, feeding, trying, and drafting. In two or three years' time you would find yourself possessed of a

---

[1] Arabic also contains the imitative word *huff*, in the sense of *blowing*, as the wind does. What we call a fun, and the Indians a *pank-hâ*, is *mu-hay-ya* in Arabic.

collection of the very best stock which Northern Arabia has to offer,—of Najdi race; proved runners, supposing the *gaudia certaminis* to form your object; young, sound, and of ascertained pedigrees.

SECTION II.— OF BUYING IN ARABIAN AND I'RÁKÍ TOWNS.

So much has been said on this subject, that the merest summary of the chief facts will now suffice.

In towns like Há-yil, where Arab, not Osmanli, rule prevails, the European stranger is allowed but little liberty of action. A mare can hardly be moved from her pickets for his inspection without the A-mír's order. Instead of quietly marking such animals as he would like to purchase, and afterwards tempting their owners to part with them, he has to take those which are offered to him, and express his obligations at the same time that he pays the money.

In parts like Bussorah, where Turkish officials fill the chief places, the field is opener. A late Governor-General of El I'rák was so fond of horses, or rather of the money which they represented, that he never went on tour without bringing back both colts and fillies which he had collected from the Bedouin. At that period, chiefly at the instance of that very Pásha, the Sultan's Government persistently obstructed the export of horses. But an easy way of getting round this difficulty was open to the wealthier dealers. When one of them had a string of horses which he desired to take to India, all that he had to do was, to buy two or three colts from the Pásha, in the price of which a pass for all the others was tacitly understood to be included. To our certain knowledge, several very high-class Najdi horses have, in the course of the last ten years, thus been taken from Baghdad to India. And apart from officials, there are many Persian and Indian residents of Baghdad and Kar-ba-lá who are great collectors of Arab mares and horses from the Bedouin nations. It is true that such people do not, as a rule, sell their property; but many a horse and other object which is "not for sale," may nevertheless be bought. Outside of the trafficking classes, all Easterns like to call that with which they part a gift, and the price which they receive the return present. Self-respect is thus maintained, while mutual kindly feeling is strengthened. Before any European founds on these facts the conclusion that towns like Baghdad are good places to visit in search of Arab horses, it will be well for him to consider all that has been stated about the activity of the jam-bázes. While he is sleeping, or dining, or writing letters, these people will be on the watch. No sooner does a horde of the Bedouin encamp within a two or three days' journey of a town, than a stream of professional buyers begins to flow in their direction. At such times, one may also notice long-haired and barefooted figures leading colts into the town. This may seem to contradict the commonly accepted statement that the Bedouin will not bring their colts to market. But all such rules are subject to exceptions; and, besides, it is not always that these hawkers of colts are true Bedouin. Under most circumstances, when a horse of note is brought into a town, the jam-bázes are sure to see him before any word of him reaches the European quarter. It is the case that the Englishman may afterwards buy the animal from the jam-báz who has been beforehand with him; but in order to play this card, he must be a resident, not a visitor, as such chances do not often happen. Moreover, the price that he will have to pay will represent not only the animal's value in the distant market for which he is intended, but the sum which his owner *hopes*, or *imagines*, that he will there obtain for him.

SECTION III.—OF PROCURING THROUGH CONSULATES OR CONSULS.

Travellers, especially those of position, expect a great deal of assistance from Consuls. The Government mint-mark is supposed to instil information into these officials; and in some situations they are regarded as co-ordinate with Divine Providence. But in order to sift this, it is necessary to know the Consul, and also the dragoman, or other member of his establishment, through whose filmy eyes he chiefly sees things. The situation of the Consulate also requires to be considered. From the point of view which now concerns us, the Damascus, Aleppo, and Bussorah Consulates are more advantageous positions than the Baghdad one. The British flag, unfortunately, no longer flies at Mosul.

The influence of the foreign Consulates in Asiatic Turkey is, at the best, a very variable quantity. The local people who are the most forward to cultivate a connection with them do not invariably belong to the most respectable classes. The Shekhs of the Arabs will freely give their friendship in exchange for Martinis, telescopes, and revolvers; but when a service is proposed to them in return, they only "ask for more." They reserve their own offerings for Turkish Pashas. The sentiment of clannishness produces the same effects in tribal bodies which nationality does in Europe. No British tradesman ever seriously quarrelled with himself for overcharging a Frenchman. And in the case of the Arabs, honesty, and even generosity, inside the *gens*, are not incompatible with cunning and rapacity for all who are outside of it.

It should further be observed that a Consulate cannot cultivate the friendship of the Bedouin Arabs, without the susceptibilities of the Ottoman Government being thereby offended. The reason of this is obvious. Jealousy of European influence forms a marked feature in the policy and attitude of the Porte, especially in its outlying provinces. When a Consul quits his flag-town, the authorities are careful to send an escort with him. Even if he were to obtain regular leave of absence, it is probable that he would experience greater difficulty than a private person in forming the acquaintance of the Bedouin nations. It is true that, if he cannot easily go out himself, he has those whom he can send; but the warning above given against buying through agents is here applicable. To borrow an Arab figure, those who cultivate this field will always be thin. We write these words feelingly. A few autumns ago, when the dates were turning golden, and the Aeniza, according to their habit, were swarming into El I'rák to buy them, rumour said that in one of their camps there was a dark-grey colt, of the Had-bán In-ze-hí strain, which was bound to grow into A HORSE. Everybody talked about this colt, and his services were in great request among horse-breeders on the Tigris. For official reasons, it was impossible to set out after him. It was to be feared that, if a professional buyer were to be paid for going to see him, he would contrive to get him for himself, and keep him, if he liked him; while if a greenhorn were sent, he would take him as a cock does a gooseberry. The messenger chosen was "respectable," but he was inexperienced. In due time he returned, proudly leading, in lieu of the fifty honest liras which we had given him, a spidery object, whose fore-legs looked as if they grew out of one hole; too light for draught; straight-shouldered; very pinched in the girthing-place; and with wretched walking action. The jam-bázes were busy buying for India, but £15 was the highest offer which any of them would make for him! A plain-spoken friend was of opinion that A'-ji-lu 'l Fu-gu-gi, the Shekh of the Di-wám division of the Sba', into whose Tartarean pouch our sovereigns had descended, must have "lifted" him from some tribe of cow-keepers; but it was not so. For one thing, he had the true Arabian head, with a large and bold *jtó-ha*, or forehead, covering the brain-cavity. His skin was very fine; and every hair in the mane and tail was separate and silky. His back and loins were beautifully formed, and by the power of them he "lost," one morning in a mile trial, an I'rá-kí mare bulky enough to carry him. Unless there exist some fatality which suspends, where the Arabs are concerned, the common rules of evidence, both his sire and dam belonged to one of the great strains of Najd, and the former had been bought at a large price by a Consul for a stud in Europe, during the northward migration in the year before of the Di-wám Aeniza. Nevertheless, after two years' keep, he appeared only fit to carry a desert urchin. When a colt is shaped like him, why should we concern ourselves with his pedigree?

SECTION IV.—OF BUYING ARABIANS WHICH HAVE BEEN EXPORTED.

This means, taking advantage in distant markets, chiefly or wholly the Indian and the Egyptian, of the labours and experience of the professional buyers. We cannot speak of Egypt from recent personal knowledge. Perhaps, if the British occupation continue, the jam-bâzes of Upper I'râk and Syria will more and more look for a market in Cairo, especially in the present fallen state of the Indian rupee. But it may safely be asserted that, in our day, as for the last hundred years or so, Bombay is the best and greatest market in the world for Arabian horses.[1] It has been seen how, during several months of every year, the draught of a vast drag-net, which has been passed more or less over all the country of the Arabian horse, discharges itself into India. There is not a colt in Arabia which may not one day be seen at Byculla. On several occasions we have recognised in the Bombay sale-stables a pedigree horse which we had known, a year or two previously, in Shâ-mi-ya. In the saddling paddock at Poona, on the Governor's Cup day, a larger number of first-class Arabians are annually assembled than may easily be seen in any one spot in Arabia, if the brood-mares and fillies be excepted. All credit, then, to the jam-bâzes of Najd, the "Flanks of Najd," I'râk A'rabi, and Mosul. If, thus far, we have done less than justice to these hard-working and far-travelled traders, we would here make up for it. There is an Eastern proverb that when a stranger offers you curdled milk, two measures are water and one spoonful is whey. It has been seen how completely this description applies to the jam-bâzes; but it would be impossible for them to carry on their useful calling on any other principle. They do not leave their homes, and wives and families, for the greater part of every year, merely that they may enjoy a change of climate. When, by chance, they obtain a true specimen of the Arabian, they expect, to borrow their own expression, that a number of inferior ones will "go down as broth to him"—that is, sell because of him. The spirit of speculation which is born in the Arab race gains in energy by not having too many outlets. Israel, we know, while forbidden to "lend upon usury" to a "brother," was permitted to do so "unto a foreigner."[2] But the Arab lawgiver condemned, and cursed, the "eating of usury," without making any reservation or distinction.[3] The consequence is,

---

[1] We lately wintered in Bombay. In five or six months, about 3000 horses were received from the ports on the Persian Gulf. Out of that number, stud-horses were selected for the whole of India; and for Queensland, Germany, the United States of America, and other countries. Every day witnessed the diffusion of horses; and when the season closed, the unsold residue was inconsiderable.

[2] Deuteronomy xxiii. 19, 20.

[3] AL KUR-AN: Sú-ras ii. iv iii.

that every true Arab who would increase his store is compelled to do so either by his personal labour or through the direct agency of a partner or a servant. From hearing a jam-báz talk, one would think that every trip which he performed brought him the nearer to beggary. *Horse-flesh*, he says, *is a very mother of teeth as merchandise*—that is, "eats its head off." Nevertheless, thousands of Arabs thrive by it, and add house to house, wife to wife, and progeny to progeny. No one can pass through Bombay without remarking, in its motley tide of nationalities, the yearly influx of Arab horse-dealers. The long cloaks and particoloured head-dresses of these people are characteristically Arab; but it is the acme of absurdity to imagine that they are of the Bedouin. Each man retains the charge of his horses as long as they stand unsold. About half-a-dozen commission-stables divide the business among them. The keeping of one of these repositories is a safe and profitable speculation, in order to embark in which it is only necessary to acquire a piece of ground, put up a few sheds, and engage a book-keeper. Every importer feeds his own horses, and if he have enough of English or Hindustani, deals more or less directly with buyers. The owner of the place is generally a native of India. Our countrymen do not appear to have much inclination for this essentially oriental form of horse traffic. At every deal, a fixed fee from the purchaser, and an equal sum from the vendor, pass into the stable-keeper's pocket, by way of rent, commission, and all other charges.

The foregoing observations are meant to introduce the picture which is here exhibited of an Arab horse-mart. The Indian elements of the tableau may be dismissed without further remark. For us the interest centres in the kerchiefed figures round whom is the air of the Semitic world. It is not to be supposed that all these Arab horse-dealers belong to the same category. Those of them whose homes are in Najd form one group; which, however, is composed of diverse members, from the well-to-do merchant, down to the black slaves of Muhammad ibnu 'r Ra-shid. The men from El I'rák are too mixed for description; and their buying-grounds extend from Zu-bair and Bussorah, by Súku 'sh Shu-yúkh, Hilla, Baghdad, Der, and even Tadmur, to Aleppo and Damascus; or otherwise, by Kar-kúk and the Persian frontier to Mosul and Urfa. And last, but not least, there is the great company settled in Ku-wait, the members of which pride themselves, not without justice, on their Arab exclusiveness, and on bringing round only Arab horses. It should not be imagined that all this army, when absent from India, disperses itself over the Arabian deserts in search of horses. Here, as elsewhere, the principle of the division of labour comes into action. There are numerous thin fellows of small capital who travel from camp to camp of the Bedouin, but such men are slow to assume the *rôle* of exporters. Either the sight of the sea at Bussorah, or dread of the

AN ARAB HORSE-MART AT BYCULLA, BOMBAY.

expenses, inclines them to transfer their purchases *en bloc* to one of the established merchants. Many of the latter are fat men and Hajjis, who prefer the coffee-house bench to the *shi-dàd*, or camel-saddle. When they return to their homes in summer, after two sea-voyages and many months of angling for purchasers in the Bombay stables, they like to take life quietly. Day after day they may be seen seated in some convenient market-place, where every horse that is brought into the town will pass before them. They thoroughly understand that a horse when well bought is already half sold, and the one point which they keep before them in making their selections is the point of *profit*. The more enterprising of their number will give a hundred lirs for a colt which appears likely to bring twice that sum in the land of promise, India; but the members of the sure and safe division prefer to buy half-a-dozen horses with the same money. Freight from Hussorah to Bombay is about £3 a horse; and the cost of keep in the commission-stables seldom falls short of £2 a head *per mensem*. According to the jam-bâzes' creed, Allah never made a horse without making a man to buy him; and he who has fed an unsaleable animal for a twelvemonth, still retains his faith that the appointed day when he shall be sold will come round. Nevertheless, a colt must be very superior, in order to fetch even £100 in Bombay, unless his owner be one of those whose recommendations are implicitly believed in throughout a wide connection. Many a good horse, after standing for a long time at some such price, is sold for half the sum. Others are put back time after time by veterinary surgeons; while others die. With the risks and expenses thus certain, and the prizes not too many, there is little wonder that the jam-bâzes are cautious buyers. If the small prices at which they frequently pick up good horses are surprising, the readiness of some of them to take the merest castaways is equally so. Thus we lately sold to a Baghdad dealer for about £2. under a guarantee that he should be taken out of the country, a fine upstanding Arab, which was twelve years old, a gelding, and broken down beyond the hope of recovery or concealment. His was a case for the merciful bullet, but oriental public opinion is strongly opposed to such dismissals; and besides, he was the property of Government, and a rule required that a price should be brought to book for him. When the honest Sai-yid who bought him was gently rallied on the copiousness of language which it would be necessary for him to use in Bombay in order to make the rounded leg pass for the result of an accident, he replied, with a face which Gammon might have copied, that although on many subjects a lie might be advisable, only a reprobate would utter one about a horse!

We come back, however, to the illustration. A glance will show how superior are the facilities for having a look round which the Arab horse-mart in Bombay presents. The scene is an open-air one, and the Eastern sun or sky illuminates it. There are no closed doors or dark places; one may ramble for hours among the rows of horses; and at the slightest signal an Indian groom will lead out any animal for inspection. Riding-boys are in waiting to trot, canter, and gallop; and in most cases the buyer will be permitted, before concluding the bargain, to mount his selection and test him. On the other hand, unfavourable circumstances are not wanting. One fact of this kind soon confronts the new-comer, and that is, the number of brokers, so to call them, who are constantly waiting on the market. Some of the best judges of Arab horses that we have ever known have belonged to this mixed company of Persians, Arabs, Pârsis, Indians, and others. These people are not infallible; but the ring which they form is a recognised difficulty in the way of the casual buyer. It is true that any one who pleases may obtain their services; but he who does so without possessing an adequate stock of experience on his own part, is sure to rue it.

Nobody who would undertake to buy the exported Arabian for stud purposes is likely to require assistance from us in his enterprise. There are, however, two other classes of purchasers to whom a few hints may prove acceptable—those who only desire a good Arab for common use, and those whose affections are bound up in the contests of the turf.

We shall first speak—

OF BUYING ARABIANS FOR ORDINARY PURPOSES IN THE BOMBAY STABLES.

Every one desirous of possessing an Arabian should take care that he does not choose a horse which is not an Arabian. In "famous London town" one may buy the "smallest toy-terrier in the world"; and the pigmy, when carried home and set down, may surprise its new owner by turning out to be a rat, and running up the bell-rope. In the East, the union of art with nature has not yet been perfected to the same extent. When an Arab dealer leads out a horse, we can at least feel certain that it is not a disguised camel. This is good; but it stops short of assuring us that the steed is an Arabian. The Bombay stables generally contain many so-called Arabs which have never seen the sea, except perhaps in transit from one Indian port to another. Some of these may be from Sindh, and others from Hirât or Cabul. When Amîr Sher A'lî ruled Afghânistân, he received as presents from H.H. Agha Khan of Bombay and others a goodly number of first-class Arabians. In the Afghan war we saw many horses and ponies which had been sired by these; and the best of them might have been ticketed as Arabs, not only at Islington but at Poona. A supposed Arab Galloway which twenty years ago shone on the turf in Western India, was ascertained to be what several of his "points" suggested, the produce of one of the thoroughbred English stallions of the Government stud department in the Bombay Presidency. Many years ago, a young officer fresh from Eton bought in Bombay, as an Arab, a thoroughbred Australian, which after a ten or twelve years' career on the Madras turf had been artistically "bishopped."[1] There is, however, a certain *something* in the look of every horse of full Arabian lineage and nurture which it is next to impossible to mistake.

It is well known what a sealed volume the horse is to most men. Nobody can see more in him than that which the eye from previous education possesses the power of seeing. Therefore, till one become familiarised with the "points" of Arabian horses, it is highly necessary, before entering the Bombay commission-stables, to seek the assistance of an adept who is not a dealer, but a trusty friend and an honest gentleman. Moreover, in the East the law of warranty is still uncertain; and the precaution of obtaining a veterinary surgeon's report on a horse before his price is paid should never be omitted. A veterinary surgeon who is also a horse-dealer had better be regarded by the public strictly in the latter character. Honest Speed's maxim, "If you love her, you cannot see her," is frequently illustrated in the Bombay horse-mart. He who buys a colt merely because he is smitten by his fine coat and manners, will probably repent it. As long as he keeps him chiefly to be fed, and groomed, and looked at, he will more and more admire him; but the proof is in actual trial. The hint which Horace gives to horse-buyers will be remembered — namely, to throw a rug over the intended purchase, so that the eye may not be drawn off defective legs by a handsome head and topping. Without presuming to enter a protest against a practice which boasts such high sanction, we cannot help recalling to mind that we owe to it a distinctly unkind cut from Fortune. In 1862, we had bought a large grey colt, for a moderate price, on the very day of his landing in Bombay from Arabia. In taking him to our place of abode, we sent him, during a break in the railway journey, to a certain forge; and on going there soon afterwards, we found him under the critical eye of one of the most eminent professional judges of horses then in India. The hocks were the suspected parts; and when the Horatian test was applied, the hind-legs from the gaskins downward certainly presented a mean appearance. Our mentor then turned prophet, and assured us that the hocks would not stand much galloping. Under this opinion the colt was returned to his importer; and after a great career on the turf as Jar-ham, finished by winning, when about twenty years old, the principal hog-hunters' stakes of Northern India. One experience of this kind is sufficient. No more covering up of horses for us when they are being

---

[1] Some of our readers may never have heard of the operation of "bishopping," which is called after a knave of the name of Bishop. In horses of from eight to twelve years' old, a small cavity is scooped in the wearing surface of two or more of the teeth, and coloured black by means of a hot iron. Animals which have been thus treated are palmed off on the inexperienced as six or seven. The Bedouin are guiltless of all such practices; but not so the Syrian, Iráki, and Persian jam-bázes.

inspected. It is highly necessary to observe not only the several parts, but the proportion which all the parts bear to one another. To sum up: a well-bred horse, such as good judges would approve of if he were not an Arab, is the sort to look for. He must be sound, and not one which other people have ridden to a stump. It is useless for a 12-stone man to buy a horse which can never be master of more than 10 stone. *Au reste*, if the fore-legs are straight, the feet of the proper form, and the action bold and free, he will not be a bad one. Plenty of horses of this description are to be found. In the East it is the good judges of horses who are scarce, and not the good horses.

Let us next survey the more difficult subject—

OF BUYING ARABIANS FOR THE TURF IN THE BOMBAY STABLES.

Few pastimes prove more attractive to Englishmen in India than the training of Arabs. For a century and a half, the black coat and the red, the bench and the bar, the commercial establishment and the editor's sanctum, have here found common ground. Some one has said of children that they are "very certain cares and very uncertain pleasures"; and it must be admitted that this is equally true of horses in training, though perhaps less so in the case of Arabs than of other breeds. But in spite of philosophers, the owner of a good horse loves the excitement of matching him against another. Racing in India has undergone great changes in the last twenty years. The railways have produced an unfavourable effect on the smaller meetings, in which, formerly, local animals were the chief competitors. They have also stopped the supplies of Arabs which the travelling dealers used to keep in circulation. Bombay is now the only place in India where fresh Arabs are to be bought, except casually; and racing draws more and more to certain centres. It is also said that the number of those who like to see a good race for its own sake is decreasing. The large sum of more than Rs. 90,000 of added money, exclusive of numerous valuable trophies, which is advertised in the programme of the Calcutta Races for 1891-92,[1] certainly looks like business. But we have never heard of any one who made a fortune, whether by a *coup* or gradually, on the turf in India. Even at Calcutta, the betting-ring is cast in a different mould from that of Epsom. The steamer companies now take out annually a small flight of book-makers; but there are no welshers, and the ring-men are more of the rook kind than the vulture. The real beak-whetters do not drop down on a country where, for them at least, there is less of flesh than feathers. Men of high position among the native

---

[1] The Rs. 90,000 (equal, at the exchange of the day, to about £7000 sterling) is spread over eight days of racing, including two days' steeplechasing.

Indians do not gamble away their patrimonies. Englishmen who have ancestral homes to mortgage, and who are ready to risk them on a horse and jockey, have no occasion to cross the sea in order to do so. But, passing from these painful features, every one who pursues a manly sport loves to excel in it; and this leads us to draw attention to the difficulty which our countrymen in India experience in obtaining untried Arabs such as will not discredit them when brought to the starting-post. In spite of the circumstance that the common run of the jam-bázes' horses are three years old and upwards, he who essays to pick a racer from among them is as likely to suffer disappointment as the purchaser of yearlings is in England. Or rather, he is more likely to do so. Every colt and filly that steps into the sale-ring at Doncaster or Newmarket possesses at least an undeniable pedigree. The collections of the Arab dealers, on the contrary, always contain a large number of animals which, as far as racing is concerned, might as well be mules. There are many persons who, through attentive study, have more or less acquired the power of recognising, by the eye alone, in the Bombay stables, that this colt from his breeding, build, and action, may prove a race-horse, and that it is impossible for that other colt to do so. Of course this is a step, and an important step; but nothing short of actual trial can convert the *may* into a certainty. Even the specialised racing-stock of England yields, according to Admiral Rous's calculation, only about three remarkable runners out of two thousand. From one and the same mare, a Bay Middleton will one year get a Flying Dutchman, and another year a mediocrity like Vanderdecken. That is to say, many of the best-bred and best-looking horses are foaled without the gift of speed; and no time or training can impart what Nature has denied. Every man who buys young horses experiences the truth of this.

> "Oft expectation fails, and most oft there
> Where most it promises; and oft it hits
> Where hope is coldest, and despair most sits."[1]

Our present argument does not depend on mere chance occurrences; and we shall not lay stress on cases in which the best Arab horse of the season has been thrust by fortune on a novice. Sa'-dí says that *Sometimes a good result does not proceed from the clear-sighted expert; and sometimes the ignorant boy hits the mark with an arrow by mistake.*[2] Accordingly, a youth whose self-assurance pushes him through thick places, as his budding horns do the billy-goat, may step off a troopship, walk into a dealer's yard, and purchase the conquering hero of the coming season. Many years ago, an artillery subaltern, fired with a "noble rage" to play the great game, went to Bombay to buy a couple of Arabs. Of the two which he selected, one was said to be a scion of the "Ishmaelite," or pre-Ishmaelite, strain

---

[1] "All's Well that ends Well." Act ii. sc. 1.   [2] "Gul-istán."

called *Banâtu 'l a'wâj*, or *Daughters of the Deformed*; and several of the jambâzes declared that they knew his foster-camel! The other was merely taken along with him, like the cat with the dromedary in the Arabian tale. The result was, that the highly esteemed one never earned a feed of corn; while his stable companion, after having been in vain offered for sale at a small price, made a great turf record as Red Hazard. Instances of this kind, if they stood alone, would hardly be worth citing; for there is no branch of sport or business in which what are called "flukes" do not happen. It will better serve to illustrate our immediate subject if we here adduce a few typical cases, in which the most experienced judges of Arab horses have been concerned.

The two Arabs, Minuet and Child of the Islands, still represent the Castor and Pollux of Anglo-Indian racing story. At all weights not exceeding 9 st. 7 lb. the "terrible Child" was indisputably the best Arab which had appeared up to that date on the Indian turf. Lieut.-Col. Bower[1] was the first purchaser of those two horses after their arrival in India; and the following is his description of the circumstances in which they became his property:—

"In 1845 an emergent indent from the Government of India on Madras for six hundred horses to replace vacancies in the Army on the Sutlej, cleared the dealers' lots of everything fit for a trooper, and saved those poor people from bankruptcy; but there was no sale for their high-priced cattle, and it was with the market in that disordered state that I offered fourteen hundred rupees for a sturdy three-year-old, whom, from his smooth easy style of moving, I named Minuet.

"In another lot there stood a very blood-like colt of the same age, but with such peculiar action that several good judges doubted his soundness, and indeed a veterinary surgeon thought him weak in the loins. I offered one thousand rupees for the *cripple*, for better or for worse! My offer was then refused, but, after a lapse of three months, the dealer came to me and said he had sold all his horses except the colt I had offered for, and as nobody would buy him, he would gladly take whatever I pleased to give him, as he was anxious to get rid of the animal, that he might return to Bombay. My answer was that I would adhere to my original offer of a thousand rupees, which was at last accepted; and as I happened to be reading Mrs Norton's pretty little poem at the time the colt arrived, I named him The Child of the Islands."[2]

Few Europeans have enjoyed better opportunities of becoming judges of the Arabian horse than the late Dr Campbell of Mysore, the owner of Greyleg.[3] In 1856 or 1857 he received, as one of a lot, from A'bdu 'l Wah-háb of Bombay, a rich bay colt, about 14 hands and 1 inch at the withers, which, the longer he looked at him, the less he liked. He considered the head plain, the neck thick, and the shoulder straight, and was inclined to cast him. When A'bdu 'l Wah-háb heard of this, he wrote to the doctor asking him for his sake to put the colt in training. After a few

---

[1] *V. ante*, p. 198 cf f.n. 2.
[2] *Op. cit.* in Catalog. No. 26, pp. 111 et 112.
[3] *V. ante*, pp. 254-256.

gallops, the denounced one, in a trial, covered a mile in 1 minute and 54 seconds. There was no longer any talk of the "bull neck" and "Roman nose," but of the "strong loin and quarter," "good eyes," "brave look," and "easy creeping style of action."[1] A present of £500 was sent to the old dealer, in reward for his advice; and in due time all India heard of the performances of Copenhagen.[2]

Another brilliant Arab which at first had few admirers was Honeysuckle. For two years people looked upon the little grey as "mean in his hind-quarters," and "not a taking goer to the eye, in any of his paces." When he was beaten in the Calcutta Derby of 1846-47, the race-goers never expected to see him again. It is, however, interesting to notice that, while such was the general opinion, an old Arab horse-dealer, by name Shekh Ib-râ-hîm, protested against it like a prophet. On hearing his favourite disparaged, the veteran would say, "Very well, gentlemen, you will see what a horse he will prove;" and when, in the course of a year or two, Honeysuckle became the pride of Indian racing circles, there never was a fairer "I told you so" than the Shekh's.

Some may infer from the two last-cited cases that the Arab dealers are better judges of their merchandise than their European customers are; but the facts scarcely warrant so sweeping a conclusion. Both A'bdu 'l Wah-hâb and Shekh Ib-râ-hîm were, in their way, celebrities. After making a little money, they had, more or less, settled down—the former in Bombay and the latter in Calcutta. They received their horses from agents, or relations, in Arabia. They did not confine themselves to dealing, but added racing to it. Their natural faith in *blood* doubtless prevented them from too lightly condemning those horses which they knew to be of high lineage. But for once that this system proves advantageous to the Oriental, it twenty times leads him to persevere with worthless animals. The Arab dealers, when they engage in racing, certainly make as many misses as hits. Sportsmen who have been in India may remember the late A'bdu 'r Rah-mân and Esau bin Curtas,[3] the former of whom, by birth a townsman of Najd, was for many years quite at the top of the Arab horse-trade in Bombay. Both these men were devoted to racing, and trained and tried as many as possible of the inmates of their several stables before letting other people have them. Their natural wits were sharpened by intercourse with Europeans; and, apart from their too fixed ideas about *blood*, they really were uncommonly good judges. And yet, if they were still living, they would have much to confess on the side of the present argument. The best racing Arab that A'bdu 'r Rah-mân ever owned was Young Revenge; and what did he do with him?

---

[1] *Op. cit.* in Catalog. No. 38, vol. iii. pp. 13-24. [2] *V. ante*, pp. 226, 248, 270.
[3] *V. ante*, p. 208.

Why, despatched him, untried, to a military officer in a distant cantonment, who, when he saw him, returned him! Similarly, Esau bin Curtas, a few years ago, allowed another uncut diamond to escape him—in this case for ever. One day there was offered to him at Bussorah a rough colt, which an Arab had brought in from the Mun-ta-fik. Esau bought him cheap, for he was but a pony, and sent him to Bombay. He stood there for several months, with all the wise men looking him over and refusing him, till at last a subaltern bought him for about £70. Not to be tedious, behold, as the hero of our story, BLITZ, twice the winner of the richest turf prize in Northern India, the Civil Service Cup, for ponies! He all but won the same race a third time, and was only just beaten for it by the English pony Mike, to whom he gave 2 stone 8 lb. of weight. After the latter performance Blitz changed ownership for the substantial equivalent of Rs. 20,000. Facts like these are greatly dwelt on by the jam-bâzes. It stands to reason that if these people knew the merits of all their horses, nobody would ever get a Young Revenge or a Blitz from them. With little or no book-learning, they possess a fine natural eloquence, which many of their number have acquired the power of expressing in persuasive English. It is a part of their business to uphold the idea that every fresh colt in their possession may be a winning ticket in the lottery of the turf. In leading out, for instance, a muleteer's baggage-pony, if any one should call him "coarse," they have the answer ready that Copenhagen was "fiddle-headed," or that some other distinguished runner was either bought out of a buggy, or was pronounced by the best judges, before his real quality was ascertained, only fit to carry boxes. It is all very well for Arab horse-dealers thus to build castles on the sandy foundation of sheer accident; but when an Englishman does so, it is a symptom that his power of calculating chances has become impaired.

The foregoing remarks, it will be observed, apply to the selection of *fresh*, that is, newly imported, Arabians. There is a charm in unstrung pearls which appeals to every one; and in the olden time in India, many sportsmen disdained to buy horses that had carried other men's colours. To race on these terms implies a long purse and an open hand—two things which are not always conjoined. It is said that barbers, when they want two or three razors for use, purchase a score, and after trying them, keep the superior ones and sell the rest at cost price. Sportsmen in India who aim at winning the maiden Arab races, adopt more or less the same practice; but their discarded horses are not so easily sold at cost price as razors are. A member of the Melbourne turf, who, up to about ten years ago, devoted half his time to India, grew so tired of year after year selecting fresh Arabs which won no races, that he would buy no more except after a trial against a stop-watch. In the days when the Arab

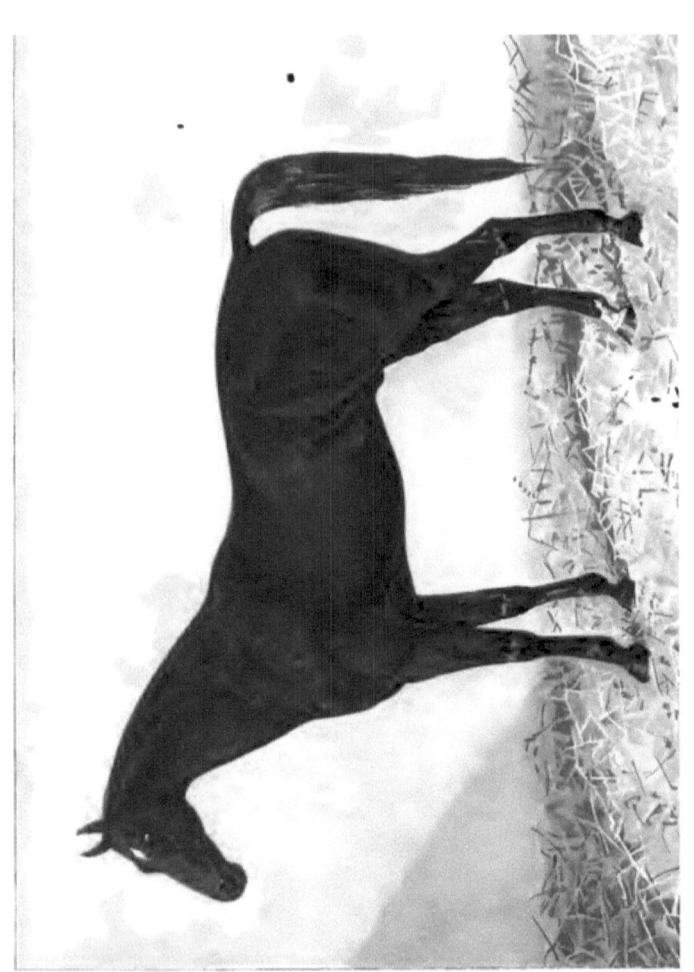

horses were brought to Bombay in sailing-vessels, and took several months to recover their strength after the voyage, this practice could not be carried to any great extent; but the jam-bâzes of the present time readily lend themselves to it. Every morning they take out their raw colts, which ought to be at walking exercise, and gallop them. When a purchaser comes forward, they offer to try one or more of them for a mile, or even a mile and a half. A large price is mutually agreed on beforehand, subject to the chronometer's verdict, and many a deal is thus effected. In a purely business aspect, this arrangement may possess advantages; but it is unfair to the horses, and it savours more of the "sporting man" than of the sportsman. Side by side with the admitted difficulty of choosing, apart from trial, Arabs which will show racing form, the fact should be kept in view that many of our countrymen and others have learned to do so—not of course invariably, or without risk of error, but in a higher degree than it is possible to ascribe to mere "luck" or accident.

Through the kindness of a well-known sportsman, Major Elliot of the 1st Bombay Lancers, we are enabled to introduce here a couple of portraits which bear witness to the correctness of the foregoing statement. The fame of Euclid and Lanercost is still fresh. The former is now at stud in Hungary, and the latter is in the possession of that prince of straight riders, H.H. the Maharájah of Dholepore, in Central India. Major Elliot bought both colts in two successive seasons, immediately after they had been brought to Bombay from Ku-wait by their importer, Ha-san bin Badr. The prices which he paid for them were, Rs. 1200 for Euclid, and Rs. 1000 for Lanercost. At that time they were but raw colts, and each in his own year won, as a three-year-old, a severe two-mile race. While truly forming a *par nobile fratrum*, they are not, so far as is known, related to one another. Hasan had no other history to give of them than that he had obtained them from the Aeniza. He and many others of his class are worthy men, and good judges of horses; but it is absurd to suppose that they can foretell the racing qualifications of an untried colt. Questions of this kind should always be addressed through the eye to the animal itself, and not through the tongue to its importer.

For the sportsman who possesses neither a large bank balance nor twenty years of experience, there is a way in which the taste for training and running Arabs may be gratified without the risks being formidable; and that is, by leaving on one side the "maiden," or weight-for-age, races, and beginning with a proved cup-horse. He who is still in his novitiate may find it a surer plan to give Rs. 3000, or even more, for one Arab which has fought his way to fame, without being "done to a turn," as the phrase is, in the process, than to expend an equal sum in the purchase of untried colts. The author can here speak from experience. When he was a beginner, and stationed at Hyderabad, a purse of £150 was presented by H.H. Agha Khan, to be run for at the local meeting. The Agha sent several of his best Arabs to contend for this and the other prizes; and along with them, a number of castaways to be sold. One of the latter—a good old plater—became ours at an easy price. Two months afterwards he won for us his late owner's gift-money, beating the champion horse of the Agha's stable! It may be said that this is mere "leather-plating"; but there is nothing derogatory in a man playing in a humble way, when his means do not permit him to do more. Those who have their place "on the mountain-tops of existence," whose wealth is ample, and who consider it a part of their proper state to maintain a racing stud, may care little about financial considerations. But speaking of ordinary gentlemen, they cannot, on the one hand, follow this amusement on a scale which *necessitates* their winning money, without imminent risk of assuming the characteristics of a different class of people altogether; while, on the other hand, it is only natural for them to appreciate their winnings, were it but as proofs of good judgment, and, above all, of that perfect self-command, apart from which the harmless stretch of green turf is apt to prove the broad road to ruin. The pace can gradually be increased. But even when it is contemplated to enter for the valuable prizes reserved in Western India for maiden Arabs, one may choose between buying the raw material from the importers, and looking out for one or two horses which, although they have failed, so far, to secure a winning number, have run well in good company. The advantage of the latter plan is, that it follows public form—in horses, as in men, the soundest test of merit. Some may say that it proceeds on the idea of one man being able to do that which others have failed to do. Admittedly this objection would carry weight in England. A colt which one of our great trainers has discarded is not very likely to turn out well in other hands. But the case is different in India. It is more than half a century since the art of training took there a great start in advance, and it has been kept well abreast of modern changes. Nevertheless, it is very unequal. In most fields there will be one or two candidates as well prepared for the contest as if Mr Day were answerable for them, and there will be others which are less so. Hence, in India, condition first, and riding second, win between them more races, perhaps, than intrinsic form does. Far more frequently than in England, a Stockwell may there be seen finishing behind a Daniel O'Rourke, as in our 1852 Derby. No doubt, this increases the opportunities of making what are termed "lucky" purchases of beaten horses—though the luck consists in one's having the power of combining circumstances, and seeing behind mere appearances. It is, however, most necessary to remember that there are Arabs which, the longer that they are persevered with, grow the slower; as well as others which, for want of finish-

ing powers, or perhaps through fear of punishment, cannot, or will not, run up into the first place. A horse that is always finishing second is anything but a blessing in disguise.

We shall conclude this section with a reference to certain indications, to be seen in exported Arabians, in which there is guidance for those who understand them; while others either pass them over or invest them with absurd meanings.

Occasionally, then, there will be a gelding in a lot of exports. It is impossible to make this condition support an inference in regard to the animal's history. First, caution is necessary before accepting it as certain that he is a fresh arrival, and not an old buggy-horse, for which a jam-bâz has consented to stand sponsor! Such things happen. But perhaps he is a rejection from the establishment of a European Consul in El I'râk or Syria; and if so, he may be anything. Or, if his back is scarred from the withers to the croup, and if he is a clean-bred one, he may have been carrying the iron hobbles (*ha-dîd*), and other gear, of a party of horse-dealers, who have altered him to admit of his being turned out to feed when they halted. In that case he is probably a "has-been." Racing form is not promoted by a course of drudgery and load-carrying, any more than, in men, the labours of a heavy porter tend to make a Deerfoot. Nevertheless, a horse of his description may prove a treasure to those who, like Chaucer's knight, would have a nag "good, albeit not gay"; for work has hardened him, and, if not too old, he will improve. Or, lastly, the unsexed one may have come from the desert. A ghaz-u rider may have taken him in foray, and treated him thus, either because unable to ascertain his pedigree, or because he has lost his mare and would mount himself in this manner. Such a history, supposing it to be well established, is satisfactory; but to agree with it, the back must not be scarred all over, like a mule's. The whitening of the hair must follow, more or less, the outline of the Bedouin saddle. A gelding is easier to train than a horse, and is less apt to jump about and injure his legs at walking exercise.

Enough has been said in another place of the marks of firing. The dealers encourage the notion that such are distinctive of the Bedouin horses; but their talk rests upon air. One of the secrets of the Arab and Persian muleteers is to use mare mules which will follow their owner's riding-horse. The caravaner's hack is generally a good one. When the object is to earn the day's hire easily, he is loaded up with chopped straw or barley, and allowed to fall behind. No amount of driving will then make the she-mules in front of him step out. But when the muleteer really desires to get over the ground, he mounts his hack and pushes on ahead. The caravan, or *ki-fi-la*, will then flit across the desert, almost like a ghaz-u. Notwithstanding the mule's having but a jack's leg from the knee down, we have never seen one with a splint. At other points, also, this animal either escapes unsoundnesses which afflict the horse, or, owing to his lower sensibility, takes them more lightly. But when a horse is set to lead a string of mules, he soon requires the firing-iron. Hence, even apart from questions of soundness, he who buys in India or Egypt a horse which has been fired is, so far as this sign goes, as likely to have chosen a Persian ka-dish as an Arabian.

Sometimes the strings of the jam-bázes contain full-mouthed horses on which there is no scar or blemish. Such may be very nice young gentlemen, but the traces of a public school, so to speak, are wanting in them. When we find them, at the same time, light below the knee, and happiest when their heads are turned homeward, we need not wonder.

Nine Arab horses out of ten will, at the very least, show a couple of scars at the roots of the ears. Our countrymen value these marks; and we daresay that the jam-bázes make them when they chance to be absent. But nearly all Arab, Kurdi, and Persian horses have them. They indicate no more than that a horse is not English, or Australian, or Indian. One of the points which Eastern horsemen cannot be brought to admire in European horses is the excessive spread of the ears. When the milk-selling Arabs of El I'rák are pasturing their sheep round Baghdad in spring, the donkey-foals may be seen running about with their long ears drawn together, both at the roots and tips, with pack-thread stitches, to give them the desired set. Many of the Bedouin nations of the Euphrates apply the same treatment to the roots at least, if not also to the tips, of the ears in newly dropped colts and fillies.[1] Nevertheless, our Aleppo colleague informs us that marked ears are comparatively rare in the best desert horses of the upper Euphrates; and that, when they occur, they merely signify that the parts have been slightly cauterised in early colthood as a cure for a cold in the head, or for strangles.

The fact should be remembered that every vendor of an unknown Arabian will, if possible, represent him as coming from the desert. In markets outside of Arabia it is comparatively easy to put forward this description. In proof of it, some casual blemish will be paraded as a spear-wound. Even the collar-marks on the shoulders of a ka-dish fresh from the tram-cars which run between Baghdad and Kâ-dhi-main are occasionally made the basis of a romantic story. In the same way, when little lines like lancet marks have been produced on the flanks of the commonest hack by the sharp corners of the townsman's stirrup, they are apt to be described as traces of spurring in Al ghaz-u!

---

[1] Burckhardt says, in *Notes on the Bedouin and Wahábys*, vol. i. p. 209: "Immediately after the birth of a colt, the Arabs tie its ears together over its head with a thread, that they may assume a fine pointed direction; at the same time they press the tail of the colt upwards, and take other measures whereby it may be carried high." *V. ante*, p. 251.

Another series of skin and hair marks depend on the various modes of tying horses, in countries where hobbling is more in vogue than stabling. In Persia different tribes follow different usages in this matter. Marks of tying round both forearms, or fore-pasterns, or from a fore to a hind pastern, or from a forearm to a gaskin, suggest localities in which the Arab *rash-ma*, or riding-halter, is not prevalent. For the desert Arab invariably ties his mare, and the traveller in Arabia his riding nag, during short halts, by bringing the halter-rope from the head, between the fore-legs, to above the near hock, and knotting it there. In this way raws are established, first across the near gaskin, and then perhaps across the off one also—for the latter takes its turn of the knot when its fellow is too much cut to bear it. The more or less permanent scar which is thus caused is termed by the Arabs a *shgir*. The extraordinary thing is, that these traces above one or both hocks, though merely due to a particular mode of tying, are regarded in India as cabalistic signs of turf promise! So far back as 1831, they were known in Bombay as "the Fort Adjutant's marks," because a certain officer of the garrison who held that appointment, and who was noted for his power of selecting Arabs which proved winners, attached the highest importance to them! In the above-mentioned year a local writer, possessed of an inquiring mind, drew attention to this blemish in the pages of the *Oriental Sporting Magazine*.[1] He scoffed at the idea of a mere rope-mark bearing any significance; and to make good his point, produced a roll of thirty-eight famous Arab race-horses, nineteen of which had, and nineteen had not, this coat of arms. Some may think that this common-sense criticism must have accomplished the desired object, but the case is otherwise. Although the name "Fort Adjutant's mark" is now forgotten, the mark itself is as highly esteemed as ever. Indeed, it is more so, for the jam-bázes of our day manufacture it. We cannot say how the case is towards Najd; but in the country of the Tigris, when a horse which does not show these marks of tying has been bought for the Indian market, it is a common practice to bind a strip of fresh intestine (*mis-ráu*) round one or both gaskins, a little above the hock-joint, so that as it dries it shall cut into the flesh. At the period of the year when the jam-bázes' yards are full, one may see in Baghdad and Mosul rows of horses which are undergoing this villainous piece of preparation. By the time that these animals reach Bombay the wounds are healed, and more or less covered with white hair. The practised eye can generally distinguish between a town-made *shgir* and a natural one. But, after all, what does it signify? Even the *shgir* which has been produced by hobbling is more likely to indicate the gendarme's horse than the desert courser; for the Bedouin, as has been seen, seldom ride their colts. Long ago this mark may have possessed

---

[1] *Op. cit.* in Catalog. No. 36, vol. ii. p. 84.

some slight value, as showing that the bearer had at least not been an idler. But it is now chiefly a reflection on the judgment or the sanity of buyers in India.

SECTION V.—ON THE PROPER TREATMENT OF THE EXPORTED ARABIAN.

In reference to what is termed "naturalisation," there is at least a series of admitted facts to set out with. It is known that certain kinds of animals possess, and that other kinds do not possess, the power of flourishing in new homes. Thus, the horse can increase and multiply, without special protection, in almost every inhabited region of the globe. The common brown rat, which is supposed to be a native of Central Asia, has not only spread to all parts of the world, but proved stronger in many countries than the indigenous species. On the other hand, the yak cannot live to the south of the Himalayas beyond the immediate neighbourhood of the snow; it is extremely difficult to keep European dogs healthy in the plains of India; snakes, which are so abundant in warm climates, diminish as we go north, and wholly cease at lat. 62°. A totally different question is, whether it is possible for races which are removed to uncongenial climates to grow inured to them. This is still an open subject; but it is safest to consider that the natural habit, or constitution, can be but slightly, if at all, altered in this direction. Thus, it does not appear that there is any such thing as "acclimatisation" for the unmixed offspring of Europeans in the plains of India. And we know of a family from Hi-rát which settled upwards of sixty years ago in the Madras Presidency, which in the intervening period has obtained wives exclusively from the country of its origin, and which, owing to the number of premature deaths among its members, is now dying out in India. To confine our illustrations to Arab horses, there exists in India a peculiar disease called *ka-ma-rí*, or loin-ill, which tends to paralyse the hind-quarters.[1] This disorder is most prevalent in the province of Bengal, where the climate is as humid as that of Arabia is the opposite. In the hot and rainy months it attacks the Arabian horse in Bengal inevitably, the English horse less surely, the Australian horse but casually, and the native horse rarely. On questions of this nature, artificially protected animals do not supply perfect data; and the fact that in Bengal proper Arab horses can by no means be saved from *ka-ma-rí* is therefore all the more telling. When, after a time, a horse hardens in a climate which at first appeared injurious to him, the improvement is

---

[1] Much has been written in India, and a little in England also, on the subject of *ka-ma-rí*, and its usual accompaniment, *worm in the eye*—e.g., in a series of papers on "Indian Horse Diseases," which appeared in the *Asian Sporting Newspaper*, Calcutta, between May and October 1879.

probably more connected with his natural growth, and with good stable management, than with supposed "acclimatisation."

In regard to the importation of Arabian horses into India, there are two facts which will not be disputed. Owing to the inferiority of its breeds, "England's miracle," as our Indian Empire is styled in Turkish circles, has need of every serviceable foreign remount which can be procured. And India, outside of certain districts, possesses a climate in which the Arabian may live as healthily, and with as little care, as in his native one. In more than thirty years we have lost but five Arabians, three of which would not have come to harm if they had been better cared for.[1] In the preceding pages, the facilities which now exist for the transport of Arab horses from Bussorah to India have been noticed. The steam-companies will not ship horses in the season when rough weather is to be expected. Boxes are not thought necessary; and the horses are ranged as close as they can stand, on both sides of the upper deck. At first they are inclined to be troublesome, especially at feeding and watering times. When the spray dashes against their hind-quarters, it sets some of them a-kicking, so that they hit their hocks against the iron railings of the ship's side. But, on the whole, they are landed in excellent health and spirits. The temptation which this offers to their Arab owners to try them before they have been a month in India has already been glanced at. The annual Bombay race-meeting takes place in February. To encourage the dealers, several prizes *for horses landed between that month and the previous September* are included in the race programme. At that time of the year, the climate of Bombay is a curious blend of heat and cold.[2] The nights and mornings are damp and chilly, and by day the temperature mounts to sweating-point. Horses fresh from Najd, and even those from high up the Euphrates, feel this more than horses from El I'râk do. But all imported animals are apt to suffer; and it is noticed that Arab horses which, after a hurried preparation, win races at Byculla in the season of landing, rarely distinguish themselves afterwards. The proper course with valuable Arabians is to remove them, as soon as possible after they reach India, from the sea-shore districts to a plateau like Mysore or Poona. An open-air, or, at any rate, a very airy billet, will best agree with them there. Necessarily, they must experience a change of

---

[1] One fatal case was that alluded to at p. 33, *supra*, in f.n. 2. A better fence would have kept out the mad dog. Hæmorrhage after castration was the immediate cause of death in another case; but the *real* cause was the employment of an unqualified operator. The third victim of preventible causes was a beautiful little mare from Najd, which, when found to be in foal, and put out of training, was allowed to fill her stomach with the dry harsh grass of a compound at Ahmednagar, and died from rupture of the intestine. About the same time, and at the same place, a thoroughbred stallion which the Government had just imported from England died in his box of snake-bite. This means that the horse-keepers failed to keep down the rank weeds of the monsoon season in his stable-yard, and that their superiors failed to make them do so. Genuine accidents will certainly happen, but the results of carelessness are not accidents.

[2] *Sard-garm*—i.e., *cold-warm*—is the expressive Indian descriptive.

water; but they should be gradually introduced to grains which are new to them. Barley is the horse-corn of Arabia, and it is cultivated in India. Cooked food and sloppy messes are approved of by many, owing to their filling appearance; but horses do not relish them, and it is to be assumed that they know what suits them. The value of bran is admitted by all. Every horse should be brought to eat it, both dry and mashed, when he is in health. But saliva is essential to digestion, and this fluid is secreted in the proper quantity only when the grinders are at work on hard dry corn.

The climate of the British Islands is even more favourable than that of India to the Arabian horse. It prepares for him no special diseases. He can do at least as much work in it as in his own. His natural soundness, hardness, cheerfulness, and longevity continue to display themselves. The only property which suffers impairment is that of fecundity. How far it is worth while to take a foreign horse to a country so well supplied is a different question. Sentiment apart, it depends on the rider's weight, and on his wants as a horseman. The man whose riding is restricted to metalled roads, and to the stony streets of great cities, hardly knows what to do with a galloping hack like the Arabian. The mounted officer who has the prospect of serving in the United Kingdom after his return from Egypt or India will save his purse, and perhaps his neck, if he take home with him his trusty Arab charger. In another place the Arab's qualifications for crossing a country were considered. But after passing from that subject we received a letter from a sportsman in England, an extract from which may prove acceptable. Referring to an Arab horse which he had bought in Bombay, our correspondent thus describes a day's work in Northamptonshire:—

"Leaving his stable yesterday at 10.30, he carried me nine miles to cover; and we had an hour's run in the morning, and two and a half hours in the afternoon, over a very big country. He carried me all day, with only one fall (not his fault); and when we finished, was fresher than many of the second horses. He came home ten miles, arriving at 7.10 P.M., having covered about sixty miles, ate up everything, and seems fairly fresh, indeed quite fresh, to-day—a performance that, I am sure, has never been equalled in the Shires before by a 14.1 horse, carrying nearly, if not quite, twelve stone."

In our day the transport of Arab horses to England offers no difficulties. In European waters a crib, or horse-box, cannot be dispensed with. The shipping-agents' yards at the several seaports usually contain a collection of boxes which have seen service. These require to be carefully refitted[1] before being again

---

[1] For one thing, if the inside lining be merely tacked on, the weight of the padding which is put between it and the wood will soon cause the tacks or nails to give. A greater evil is the *milling down* of the matting or other material which is laid in the box to lessen the jar. Nails in such a situation are sure to work out; and parts of them will perhaps be found, at the end of the voyage, lodged in the poor animal's unshod and softened hoofs.

used; but for Arab horses they can scarcely be too open.[1] Before embarkation, the horse should be made familiar with the structure that is to form his cabin. The last Arab horse which we took to England had so recently left pastoral Arabia, that when he had to be shipped at Bombay he had only been a few times in a stable. When his travelling carriage was shown to him, he stubbornly refused to enter it. We then had it carted to his stable, and set down like a little porch, with both ends open, in front of his loose-box. Still, he would not go into it, although he must have seen his bed and corn awaiting him beyond it. After standing for at least an hour tied to it, with no one near him, he began to hammer it with his fore-feet. Thus he gradually felt his way through it, and never afterwards mistrusted it. The advantage of this was, that during the voyage he could be led out of his box in fine weather, exercised, hand-rubbed, and put back again. There is this to be said in favour of having a horse's travelling-box made movable, that it can then be shifted from one part of the vessel to another to suit changes of wind and climate. As the ship's officers, however, may not always take the trouble to do this, or may even remove the box from a bad site to a worse one, perhaps it is a better plan to arrange that a regular berth shall be knocked up for the animal by the ship's carpenter, in a good situation. Two divisions can then be made, in one of which the horse may be allowed his liberty in favourable weather. As a rule, horses will not lie down and rest on an iron deck as readily as on a wooden one.

In every foreign country to which the Arabian is carried, the salient features of the method in which he must have been reared in his native land should be remembered. It is absurd to imagine that because he has cost a large sum he ought to be shut up in a grand stable. We are no advocates of over-exposure. It is true that Eastern horses, if well fed, will keep in good condition when picketed on the bare plain, with the sun beating on them by day, and, perhaps, rain or snow at night. Even in these circumstances, any little protection that can be afforded is repaid by the results. The horses which work in the tram-cars of Bombay and Calcutta last the longer, if padded sun-protectors are placed over their polls and back-bones. In camps in India and Afghanistan, it has been found beneficial to line the horses' blankets with cotton cloth, and put them on white side uppermost when the sun is powerful. In cold nights, a slight enough screen of earth or snow between a horse's standing-place and the blast helps to preserve him. Stabling is as essentially a phase of civilisation as house-building is. If any breed of horses requires air and light more than another, it is the Arabian one. Every

---

[1] It is unnecessary to roof in the horse-box. Three removable iron hoops, to support a tarpaulin, are far better. A broad canvas sling should be hung at night below the animal's belly, so that he may rest on it, and as a stay in rough weather.

318   CONCLUSION.

stabled horse, when a window is within reach, turns to it as naturally as plants do to the light. Solitary imprisonment in the most palatial loose-box cannot be agreeable to the horse which, in his native land, was never out of sight and sound of his fellows. Every country has its own usages, which are commonly based on good reasons. At all events, the usages are not to be altered, and it is whimsical to attempt to do so. The Arab horse in India does not, as a rule, experience any very startling change in his mode of life — though perhaps he wonders at the amount of grooming which he receives. But when he is taken to Europe, many things must puzzle him. After having, all his days, fed from the ground, or, at the most, from a nose-bag,[1] he now has his hay presented to him high up towards the ceiling, as if he were a giraffe. The stable-men and stable-gear are equally novel. The human hand, with its thumb and fingers, its palm, nails, and convenient articulations, forms a perfect tool-chest, and the oriental groom knows how to use it.[2] But, with us, the body-brush and the curry-comb, the sponge, the wisp, and the rubber, not to mention the broom and the pitchfork, are considered indispensable adjuncts. What with flicks from the towel or leather, too much stable language, and too energetic brushing or wisping, the sensitive and glossy-coated Ku-hai-lân is in some danger of being made "vicious." There are stable-men who, even at the risk of having their crowns cracked, delight in seeing a horse "lively" when he is being dressed over — that is, in tickling him till he kicks again; but it is assumed that no one who is likely to import an Arabian would permit this practice.[3] The horse of Najd can seldom, if ever, need clipping;

---

[1] Feeding-bags preserve the corn, or chaff, from being lost; but they impede respiration, favour too rapid eating, and are not always taken off at the proper time. They should not be made of leather or of canvas, but of light and porous stuff. The Arab feeding-bag, of goat's or camel's hair, resembles a sieve in texture, is very cheap, and can almost be carried in the pocket. Hempen feeding-sheets, about 3 ft. square, and heavy enough to lie flat, do well in horse-lines, but not where high winds may be expected.

[2] In an old English work on Farriery, entitled *The Perfect Horseman; or, The Experienced Secrets of Mr Markham's Fifty Years' Practice*, 1684, the groom is directed "to rub down a horse's legs with wisps, or with a clean cloth, or *with your bare hands, which is best of all.*" On another page, he is told "to go over all parts" with his wet hands; and further, that "what his hands did wet, his hands must rub dry again." The sponge is not mentioned; but we do not know whether to infer from this, that sponges were not generally imported into England at that date, or that Gervase Markham disapproved of their use in stables. If he really meant to say that the "bare hands" were better than sponges, then his ideas were in advance not only of his own time but of our time. Even the well-cared-for bath-sponge soon becomes coated, in its countless pores or cells, with sedimentary animal matter, which, when the structure is wetted, issues again in liquid form. It is stated that soap-suds form a richer manure than even poudrette does; and if so, it can easily be imagined what the contents of a used sponge are.

[3] Persian muleteers, when they remove the *pâl-lân* or pack-saddle, on halting days, curry their beasts with an iron instrument; but the only article which we have ever seen the Arabs thus use is the mare's *mikh-lât*, or feeding-bag. This, when rolled up, resembles the glove of cocoa-nut fibre with which the Indian grooms dry-rub their horses. Even in Baghdad, the shops will be searched in vain for a horse-brush. In India, the fashion of picketing horses with head-ropes and heel-ropes facilitates grooming; and native horsemen put a bit in the horse's mouth at "stable-hours,"

but his natural coat, even when in our climate it grows thicker, generally requires the addition of a blanket. The happy mean has to be observed here. It is true that animal warmth proceeds from the food, but the surface also demands care. A stable, provided that it be dry, may be comfortable without being at summer heat; and it is better to increase the clothing than to light the fire. We mention this here, because in England many people think that the Arabian, as the native of a warm climate, requires hothouse treatment. This, however, is a mistake. As low down on the Euphrates as Kar-ba-lâ, thick ice may form night after night in February. Taking into account the absence of stables, the Bedouin horse in Shâ-mi-ya experiences annually greater changes of climate, cold included, than any highly-bred horse in England does. What the former is *not* accustomed to—not at least till townsmen buy him—is smells. To insist that a stable shall not smell of a stable is nonsense. The inoffensiveness, within due limits, of horses, compared with most other kinds of domestic animals, is rather remarkable. The Irishman does not object to allow pigs and poultry to live in the same room with him, but that is an exceptional bias; whereas no reasonable mortal should quarrel with his quarters, if lodged in a spare loose-box in a well-kept stable. This circumstance enhances the risk of cleanliness being neglected. Accumulations in a stable do not greatly offend the senses; but the inhaling over and over again of air which is thus contaminated ranks among the causes of weakness and illness in stabled horses.

The Arabian, as we have seen, possesses the best of constitutions. If lodging suited to his habit, and to the climate and season, judicious feeding, scrupulous cleanliness, sufficient grooming, and last, but not least, plenty of work or exercise, fail to keep him healthy in foreign countries, purgatives and tonics will not do so. Of course we do not mean that the most perfect stable economy will altogether ward off disease from the exported Arabian any more than from other horses, however much it may abate it. If ever the Arab horse hang his head, and refuse to pick so much as a blade of green grass, it may be concluded that the diagnosis and prescriptions of an experienced veterinary surgeon are demanded. We say *experienced*, because not every man who holds a diploma can tell what ails a horse. The juniors have their way to open, their rivers to set on fire, and their

---

and pass the bridle of it under his tail like a crupper, to keep him from biting, and at the same time improve his carriage. Of course, the grooms like this method, and no man can master an animal of which he is afraid; but a horse is the better of being allowed some play while he is being "dressed." A good way to fix a horse which is being groomed in a loose-box is, to stand him with his head towards one corner of it and his tail towards another corner, and tie him by two ropes passing from his head-stall to staples in the wall on either side. There will then neither be dead wall nor bars in front of him, for him to grab at. A bit will seldom be necessary, and as for a "dressing muzzle," it is worse than useless. A horse which is very ticklish had better be groomed in knee-caps; and if he stamp and jaw with his fore-feet, an old mattress should be thrown down in front of him.

paper-kites of theories for which to find, or make, materials. Give us the old man who has passed his period of experimenting, and whose views of what will kill and what may cure are fixed on the basis of practice. When competent professional advice cannot be obtained, and the seat of the ailment is unknown, it is better that the poor animal should merely be made comfortable, and allowed to die of the disease which has seized him, than that medicines should be rashly administered. We know of a case in which a horse, after having been thus surrendered to his fate, unexpectedly began to recover. One advantage which the Arabian enjoys in India is that his Hindû groom does not give him slow poisons, under the name of condition-balls or powders. In the East every horse-master has himself to blame if this mischievous practice is followed; but the desert horse which has never tasted physic is in danger, when taken to England, of having his constitution tampered with by groom-doctors as ignorant of the nature and effects of the various compounds employed by them as they are of the animal economy. In many cases a distemper tends to pass off naturally, either through running its course or on the removal of its cause. And illnesses which will not yield to artificial medicines may do so under changes of air and diet, comfortable warmth, rest, work or exercise, hot or cold fomentations, hand-rubbing,[1] and, above all things, patience.

In buying Arabians in Arabia, it is impossible to obtain a professional man's verdict as to soundness. But this is no reason for pursuing an ostrich-like course towards such purchases, after they have been brought to a civilised country. On the contrary, they should all be submitted to a thorough veterinary examination, after they have recovered from their "sea-sorrows" or injuries of transport. Not many Bedouin horses which have been kept till five years' old in the desert will pass this test satisfactorily. One which does so must be a very straight-made and superior piece of workmanship. When the practised eye and hand of the veterinarian have ascertained that there are no external traces of unsoundness, that is final. But the case is different with the majority of "used" horses. At one or more points, trivial or serious alterations indicate where certain parts have proved unequal to the tasks which have been exacted from them. It is then that the judgment of the qualified practitioner enables him to form an opinion of how far the injury has proceeded, and what limitations it imposes on usefulness.

---

[1] Hand-rubbing is not exactly counter-irritation; but in many of the cases in which parts are blistered, this simple stimulant and form of pressure would prove better treatment. Its value as a help to the circulation, especially when exercise cannot be given, is very considerable. Acting locally on the absorbing and repairing power of nature, it promotes the disappearance of non-inflammatory effusions round the joints, and in the sheaths of tendons. Even bony matter, when recent, tends to yield to it. With hand-rubbing, a horse's legs will stand more work than they will do without it. The bandaged leg looks dull and flabby, while the hand-rubbed one shines like silver.

Not to mention old horses which have left the desert as such, and are so unmistakably broken down that no one would ever think of galloping them, there is many a fresh-looking colt which may seem to ordinary people uninjured, but in reality has been well started on the road to unsoundness by his Bedouin rider. If such a one be hurriedly put in training, he may astonish his owner by "breaking down badly," as it is called, after very moderate work. If, as a preliminary step, he had been submitted to an able veterinarian, perhaps it would have been pointed out that one of his suspensory ligaments was thicker than the other, or that there was a thickening of its lower and sheath-like portion on one side of the fetlock joint, or on both, and that an interval of at least a year was essential to recovery. A hasty preparation may ruin the soundest horse; and, even apart from the dictates of humanity, it is a sad thing when a noble colt, which might have proved a treasure to his owner for half a lifetime, is permanently injured through incautious treatment in his first year in a new country.

THE BEDOUIN HAUDAJ.

INDEXES

NOTE.

ON several grounds this Index requires to be introduced with something not unlike an apology. First, the fact is evident that it contains a good deal of material of a kind which is not usually committed to a table of reference. What opened the way for this irregularity, if such it should be considered, was the adoption of the method of relegating all foreign terms to a separate Index, instead of intermixing them with our own English words in the columns of a general catalogue. From this it formed but a small step to proceed to the task which has been undertaken, of adding under the more important headings a little special information. In how far that information will be appreciated is a different question. According to our experience, those who, as travellers or otherwise, are interested in Asiatic Turkey and Arabia, do not soon tire of fresh notes on the topography of those countries. It also appears probable that the general reader, when he encounters references to oriental worthies of antiquity, such as El Asma'-I and Abû 'l Fi-dâ, will gladly find at the end of the volume slight notices of those people. And lastly, with so many of our countrymen serving officially in parts like India and Egypt, the few articles which are devoted to the elucidation of certain Arabic words bearing the closest relationship to Islamism will, we venture to hope, be received with indulgence.

In regard to the attempts which are made in the Index to interpret Semitic names, we are conscious that such explanations demand a fuller conversance than ours with linguistic science. In Arabic, as in every other language, there are countless words the first meanings of which cannot be discovered. The Arabic lexicographers did not know the origins of very many of the terms which they collected; and the etymologies given in Lane's great Arabic-English dictionary are wholly Eastern in character. As for the Bedouin, they are still too hard pressed in the struggle for existence to bestow much thought on the names which are handed down among them. If the reader ask why, in the face of such difficulties, etymological material is admitted into the Index, good reasons are not wanting. In the first place, it cannot be altogether uninteresting to notice, even approximately, the lines which, from prehistoric times, the Arabs of the desert have followed in bestowing names on their national or tribal subdivisions, and on their breeds of horses and camels. And, secondly, some of the European travellers who pass our way exhibit a kind of instinctive tendency to investigate the meanings of proper names. As the result in part of their researches, a plentiful crop of "popular etymologies" has arisen;[1] and the word-meanings which are offered in this Index, however open to correction, are at least improvements on those that are arrived at through a process of guessing.

---

[1] For example, a writer so learned as the late Dean Stanley, in Sinai and Palestine (App., pp. 503 et 508) identifies "Peleg" with vilayet—which is as if we should derive the name of the N. American river Potomac from verasis. The number of articulate sounds is not unlimited; and the European traveller in Semitic lands should always remember that two words may be similar both in appearance and meaning, without being akin to one another.

INDEX I.

BEING A GLOSSARIAL INDEX AND SUPPLEMENT TO ALL REFERENCES
TO ARABIC AND OTHER FOREIGN WORDS.

A

A'B-BÁS. An Arabic proper name. The Prophet's paternal uncle was A'B-BÁS *ibn* MUT-TA-LIB, one of whose descendants, nearly a century after the Flight, supplanted the U-may-yad dynasty by the still more brilliant

A'B-BÁ-sí. or "Abbaside," line of thirty-seven princes; with which the historical Arab Caliphate terminated. *V.* arts. BAGHDAD, *et* HULAGU, *infra*.

A'B-BÁS I. King of Persia (1585-1628), introduction of Arabian stallions into Persia by, p. 273.

A'B-BÁS PÁSHA. Viceroy of Egypt (1848-54), collection of Arabian horses by, p. 219 *et* f.n. 3. His view on this subject, *ibidem*.

A'B-BÚD. [A man's name.] The name of a strain in AL KHAM-SA, Table p. 235 col. i.

A'BD. [*Worshipper, slave*.] P. 106. *Et v.* art. A'BDU 'LLA, *infra*.

A'B-DA. A subdivis. of the Sham-mar Bedouin, represented both in AL JA-ZÍ-RA and (through Muhammad *ibnu* 'r Ra-shid) in peninsular Arabia, p. 122 *et* f.n. 5.

A'BDU 'L A'ZÍZ. One of the (Islamic) proper names of the Arabs which are described at p. 107 *et* f.n. 1. It has been given to an inconsiderable mountain-range in N.W. AL JA-ZÍ-RA, p. 73.

A'BDU 'L KÁ-DIR. A proper name of the class described at p. 107 *et* f.n. 1.
A-MÍR A'BDU 'L KÁ-DIR, Prince of Maskara, and champion of Arab independence in Algeria, quoted, pp. 60, 161.
At p. 153 f.n. 1, SHEKH A'BDU 'L KÁ-DIR, *Gí-lá-ní*, whose mausoleum adorns Baghdad. The Shekh was a Sai-yid of the 12th Christian century. GÍ-LÁN, or GÍL, the Persian province on the Caspian in which is Rasht, is believed to

A'BDU 'L KÁ-DIR—*continued*. have been his birthplace. He is now regarded as a great *Pír*, or saint, through whose intercession both spiritual and mundane blessings are to be obtained. A hereditary NA-KÍB (*v*. p. 153 *et* f.n. 1), or warden, holds possession of his tomb, and of the broad domains which are attached to it. Many generations of pilgrims have enriched the Nakibate. The azure dome which surmounts the Shekh's resting-place is one of the chief features of Baghdad. Spacious bázárs, and the residences of the Na-kib's relatives, give a good appearance to this quarter. In religions, not only extremes, but also lines of separation, tend towards one another. The Wahábi, as he passes through this region, reviles the "associators of saints with Allah"; but many millions of the Sun-níte Muslim find in A'bdu 'l Ká-dir all the comfort which their Shí-ite brethren do in A'lí.

A'BDU 'L KA-RÍM . One of the proper names described at p. 107 *et* f.n. 1.

A'BDU 'L WAH-HÁB A very great figure in Arabian history. Born 1691; died 1787. Pp. 161 *et* f.n. 1, 164. (For page references to the school which he founded, *v*. under WAHABYISM in Index ii.)

A'BDU 'L WAH-HÁB, HAJ-JI . The Arab horse-dealer, pp. 176, 306, 307.

A'BDU 'LLA An extremely prevalent proper name among the Arabs. The Prophet's father bore it. (The accusative and the vocative forms are A'bda 'lla; and the genitive, A'bdi 'lla. *V*. arts. A'BD, *et* ALLAH.)

———— Prince of Jabal Shammar, p. 40.

———— . . . Grandson of Fai-sal, Sultán of Najd, p. 42.

———— *ibn* SA-BÁ P. 106 f.n. 3.

A'BDU 'R RAH-MÁN The Arab horse-dealer, p. 307.

AB-JAR . . A'ntar's charger, p. 237.

AB-RA-HA One of the Ethiopian kings of Yemen, p. 28.

AB-KASH . One of the colours of Arabian horses, Table p. 263.

ABÚ, or AB One of those ancient Semitic words which, we may assume, existed before Hebrew was Hebrew, before Syriac was Syriac, and before Arabic was Arabic: *v*. p. 34 f.n. 1. As far back as the beginning of literary Arabic, *a-bú* conveyed the idea of *physical paternity*; for AL KUR-ÁN uses it in this sense—*e.g.*, in S. xxiv. If this be the *primary* meaning of *a-bú*, then such phrases as *abú-zau-ja, possessor of a wife*—*i.e.*, husband; *abú-'l-husain, constructor of the little fortress*—*i.e.*, the fox; and the like, are rightly regarded as *figurative*; and this is the common view. But see, in Professor Robertson Smith's *Kinship and Marriage in Early Arabia*, an argument that the idea of *possession* which is so frequently conveyed by *a-bú* forms the *primary*, not the *secondary*, meaning; that in prehistoric Arabia fatherhood did not necessarily imply procreation; and that the family was held together by the rule that the head of it was the *father*, merely in the sense of *possessor*, of all the children born on his bed.

ABŪ A'MIR	The name of a sub-strain of the stock of KU-ḤAI-LĀN, Table p. 235 col. vi.
ABŪ JU-NŪB	[*Possessor of flanks—i.e.*, large-barrelled, and well ribbed up.] The name of a strain in AL KHAM-SA, Table p. 235 col. i., and in pedigree facing p. 136.
ABŪ 'L FI-DĀ. Pp. 20, 79, 98.	[*Father of ransom, heroism, devotion.*] The epithet of a Saracen leader, born at Damascus in the time of the Crusades, who, when his inherited but disputed princedom of HĀ-MA (*q. v.*) had been confirmed to him, as the reward of prowess, by the Egyptian Sultān, divided the remaining 20 years of his life between the duties of government, the encouragement of scholars, and the gratification of his literary bent. Abū 'l Fi-dā's epitome of Arabian history was fully drawn on by Gibbon, and only the most recent European writers have opened up new material.
ABŪ 'L IS-LĀM	A title of the patriarch Abraham, p. 101.
ABŪ 'L KHASHM	V. p. 34 f.n. 1.
ABŪ MA'-RA-FA	[*Possessor of a mane.*] The name of a strain in AL KHAM-SA, Table p. 235 col. i.
ABŪ RU-WAIS.	The name of a leader of the Sham-mar, p. 64.
ABŪ SAUR	[*Having impetuosity.*] The name of a strain in AL KHAM-SA, Table p. 235 col. i.
ABŪ U'R-KŪB.	[*Possessed of large hocks.*] The name of a sub-strain of the stock of KU-ḤAI-LĀN, Table p. 235 col. vi.
AB-YĀR	[Pl. of *bīr*.] Wells, p. 105.
ĀB WA HA-WĀ	In Persian, *water and air*; idiomatically, *climate*, p. 3.
ADEN	In Arabic, *a'dn* means *abiding*; and in AL KUR-ĀN, *Jan-na-tu 'l a'dn* means Heaven. The Hebrew "Eden" is the same word as the Arabic *a'dn*; but the idea of a *terrestrial* Paradise, though not untraceable in ancient Arab legend, is absent from Islamism. The seaport of Aden or A'dn, in Yemen, early became a great entrepot of the trade between Europe and Asia; but the identification of it with the "Eden" mentioned in Ezek. xxvii. 23 is erroneous. The "Eden" with which the merchant princes of Tyre trafficked, almost certainly was a place on the Upper Euphrates, near Bā-lis. The history of the modern Aden—pp. 20, 26—is that of the Red Sea route to India. The capture of the town, in 1839, was the first addition made to the British empire in the reign of Queen Victoria.
ADH DHILL ḤI 'L ḤADHR	The Bedouin saying, p. 119.
AD-HAM	One of the colours of Arabian horses, Table p. 262.
ADHMU 'S SĀIK	A name which Arab horse-dealers facetiously give to splint, p. 177 *et* f.n. 1.
A'D-NĀN.	An important step or figure (said to be the 21st before Muhammad) in the genealogical ladder by which Arabian pedigree-makers connect the "Ishmaelite" Arabs with Abraham, p. 99.

ADK . [Correctly *idh-khír.*] The Lemon grass [*Andropogon schœnanthus*], p. 38.

A'D-WÁN . [*Chargers.*] A Bedouin horde whose pastures are in the north-western parts of Al Ja-zí-ra, p. 75.

AE-NI-ZA . The greatest, perhaps, of the Bedouin nations of Arabia. [The connection of the name with *a'nz*, the she-goat, is too probable not to have been noticed both by Arab and European scholars.] Pp. 23, 42, 51, 65, 69, 73, 75, 83, 84, 85, 103, 104, 106, 122 *et* f.n. 5, 123, 129, 138, 146, 149, 184, 210, 214, 218, 241, 244, 264, 269, 292, 293, 294 f.n. 2, 298.

A'FÁ-RIT . [Pl. of *ifrit ; q. v.* in art. OPHIR.] A subdivis. of the Sham-mar, p. 122.

AF-DHA-HÍ The name of a strain in AL KHAM-SA, Table p. 235 col. iii.

AF-NAS [For *af-tas, having the nasal bones depressed and expanded.*] A characteristic feature of the face in the Arabian breed, p. 253 *et* f.n. 4.

AGEL [Correctly *U'kail ;* from the same root as *i'-kál ; v.* MA'-GIL.] A body of the Arabian people, pp. 215 *et* f.n. 2, 293.

AGHA KHÁN Or more formally, in official documents, "His Highness Agha Khán, Meheláti," is the title familiarly borne by each succeeding head of the distinguished Persian family which is mentioned on the frontispiece of our volume, at pp. 269, 310, and more fully in art. ALAMÚT, *infra*. (Agha, Aga, *et* Akà, and Khân or Kaan, are Tatar words of the same meaning as BEY or BEG, *q. v.* In Persia and Central Asia, *khán* is also a common name for the caravansary, a merchant's store or place of business, and the like.]

AH-DAB or AL AH-DAB . [Co-derivative with HAD-BÂN, *q. v.*] The name of a sub-strain of the stock of KU-HAI-LÂN, Table p. 235 col. vi.

AHL . *All those of one house, race, or religion ;* like our *people* in "one's own people."

AHLU 'L BAIT . *Tent-folk*, another term for the Bedouin, p. 91.
AHLU 'L HA-YIT *People of boundaries*, such as villagers and townsmen, p. 91.
AHLU 'L MA-DAR . Peasants, p. 48 *et* f.n. 1.
AHLU 'L WA-BAR . A descriptive given to the Bedouin, p. 48 f.n. 1.
AHLU 'SH SHI-MÂL *Nations* (more or less nomadic) *of the North*, p. 271.
AHLU 'T TÎN . Another epithet of peasants, p. 15.
AH-MAR . . . A colour in horses, p. 260 *et* f.n. 4 ; Table p. 262.
A'-ID BIN TA-MI-MÍ The Arabian horse-exporter, pp. 258, 260. [The root of *á'-id* is that of *I'd ;* sc., *returning time after time,* as a *holiday* does.] The Ba-nû Ta-mîm are chiefly cultivators. The town of Hûta in Najd is their centre.

[AL] A'ITH . . . [*Plain of sand.*] A segment of AL HA-WI-JA, pp. 82, 83.
AI-YÂMU 'L JÁ-HI-LI-YA [*Days of Ignorance.*] The pre-Islamic ages in Arabia, p. 52 *et* f.n. 7.

A'I-YÁSH . [*Having much of the means of life.*] A subdivis. of the Ae-ní-za, Table p. 121.

AI-YÛB P. 106.	The Arabs thus render the proper name which in the Biblical literature is Iyyob ["Job"]. It is impossible to say whether the name originated in the speech which is now called Hebrew, or in Arabic. A certain man named Ai-yûb is cited in AL KUR-ÂN as an example at once of firm piety under affliction, and of the great reward thereof. Of course, if it be considered that the "Iyyob" of the Hebrew poem was *ab origine* a poetic creation, or an allegoric figure like Bunyan's Greatheart, then the "Ai-yûb" of the Arabs must have been borrowed; and the traditions about him which commentators on the Kur-ân relate, seeing that "The Book of Job" does not contain them, cannot be really ancient. But if the hero of the poem was more or less a historic person, then it is highly probable that he was an Arab. "The Book of Job" is adjudged to be "a genuine outcome of the religious life and thought of Israel;" but its anonymous author may have taken his materials from the traditions of the Arabs; and this supposition supplies an easy explanation of the Arabian characteristics of the poem.
AJÂ or JA-BAL AJÂ	A mountain-chain over against HÂ-YIL, *q. v. infra*. P. 39.
A'JÂ-JI-RA	A subdivis. of the Ae-ni-za, Table p. 121.
A'JAM	The Arabs thus designate Irân or Persia; and a Persian is with them *A'jamî* (p. 270), to which they attach the sense of *barbarus*—*i.e.*, strange or foreign in origin, speech, and aspect.
A'JÛZ	Etymologically, the *stump* or *rump of anything*; or the *being behind-hand*, or *incapacitated, in respect of a thing*; whence *an aged woman*, pp. 232, 233.
A'KA-BA	The name usually given by the Arabs to a pass over mountains, pp. 23, 25, 29.
AKH-DHAR	One of the colours of Arabian horses, Table p. 263.
Á-KHIRU 'D DA-WÂ, LL KAI	Arab saying as to *firing*, p. 184.
A'KID	The organiser and leader of an expedition, p. 112 *et* fn. 1.
AL	The Arabic def. article. [Before certain letters of the alphabet,—"dentals," "sibilants," and "liquids,"—the *l* of the def. art., though expressed in writing, is passed over in pronunciation, and assimilated to the following consonant.]
ÂL	Often mistaken for the foregoing. Used as prefix of that part of an Arab's name which indicates his *family*. Perhaps a variant of AHL, *q. v.*
[AL] A'BD	The name of a strain in *Al Kham-sa*, Table p. 235 col. ii.
ÂL A'BDI 'LLA	[*Race of A'bdu 'lla.*] A subdivis. of the Ij-lâs Ae-ni-za, Table p. 121.
ALAM-DHAI-YÂN	The name of a horde of the Ae-ni-za, Table p. 121.
ALAMÛT	In fn. 1 p. 30, "Ismailism" was mentioned. In this connection the "Ismailians" are those among the Shi-i' who hold Ismâ'îl, the seventh in descent from A'li, to have been the last of the revealed I-mâms. Out of the Ismailians there

ALAMÛT—*continued*.

proceeded, in our 11th century, the secret military and religious sect which in 'The Book of Ser Marco Polo' is designated the "Ashishin," and which is known in Europe as "The Assassins."[1] One of the numerous mountain strongholds of "The Assassins" was Alamût (p. 269), on the Elburz range, in Persia. It has been generally assumed, though without much warrant, that that was the site of the Elysium to which the following passages in Marco Polo relate: "The Old Man"[2]—*i.e.*, the head of the Assassins—". . . had caused a certain valley between two mountains to be inclosed, and had turned it into a garden . . . running with conduits of wine and milk and honey and water, and full of lovely women for the delectation of all its inmates. And sure enough the Saracens of those parts believed that it *was* Paradise! . . . He kept at his Court a number of the youths of the country, from twelve to twenty years of age, such as had a taste for soldiering; and these . . . he would introduce into his garden, some four, or six, or ten, at a time, having first made them drink a certain potion which cast them into a deep sleep. . . . So when they awoke, they found themselves in the garden. . . . And the ladies and damsels dallied with them to their hearts' content, so that they had what young men would have. . . . And when he [the Prince whom we call the Old One] wanted one of his *Ashishin* to send on any mission, he would cause that potion whereof I spoke to be given to one of the youths in the garden, and then had him carried into his Palace. So when the young man awoke, he found himself in the Castle, and no longer in that Paradise, whereat he was not over well pleased. . . . So when the Old Man would have any Prince slain, he would say to such a youth, 'Go thou, and slay so and so'; and when thou returnest, my Angels shall bear thee into Paradise. And shouldest thou die, natheless even so will I send my Angels to carry thee back into Paradise. So he caused them to believe; and thus there was no order of his that they would not affront any peril to execute, for the great desire they had to get back into that Paradise of his." [*V.* Marco Polo, Bk. I. chs. xxiii., xxiv., *et* xxv.]

In our 13th century, Hulagu, the Tatar, completely broke the power of the "Assassins" in Persia, slaying about 12,000

---

[1] Sir H. Yule sanctions the interpretation that the *Hashishin*, or *Hashshin* (*Assassin*), of the "Old One's" Paradise were called *Hashishin* from their use of the drug *hashish*, and that the modern application of the word "Assassin" thus originated.

[2] In the time of the Crusades an offshoot of the "Assassins" of Persia flourished in Syria. The Crusaders called the chief of these Lebanon sectaries "The Old Man of the Mountain," a translation of his popular Arabic title, *Shaikhu 'l jabal*. It has not been ascertained, but it is probable, that the same title was borne by the prince of the Alamût "Assassins" also.

ALAMÚT—*continued*.	of them. A few years afterwards, the Syrian branch was nearly extirpated by Bibars, the Mameluke Sultán of Egypt. How times change is strikingly illustrated by the circumstance that the lineal descendants of Ha-san *ibn* Sa-bá, the founder of the "Assassins," have for three generations lived quietly at Poona, Bombay, or Bangalore. The title of "Agha Khan" is that by which the family is now best known. An ex-Governor of Bombay, writing when the Agha Khan who first sought refuge in India was still alive, thus remarked : "His sons, popularly known as the 'Persian Princes,' are active sportsmen, and age has not dulled the Agha's enjoyment of horse-racing. Some of the best blood of Arabia is always to be found in his stables. He spares no expense on his racers; and no prejudice of race or religion prevents his availing himself of the science and skill of an English trainer or jockey when the races come round. Lads who learned to ride on Epsom Downs may be seen carrying his colours to the front on horses bred in the stony valleys of Najd. The Agha is always present, eyeing the contest with as keen an interest as forty years ago he would have watched a charge of horse on the plains of Khurásán or Kandahár." [*V.* two papers on *The Khojas : The Disciples of the Old Man of the Mountains*, by the late Sir H. B. E. Frere, in 'Macmillan's Magazine,' vol. xxxiv. pp. 342-350 *et* 430-438.]
AL BÚ MUHAMMAD [BÚ for ABÚ].	An I'ráki horde, p. 84 f.n. 1.
AL HAMDU L' ILLAH . .	The common expression of the Arabs, p. 38 *et* f.n. 3.
AL HARB SI-JÁL; YAUM LA-NÁ : YAUM A'LAI-NÁ.	A saying of the Arabs, p. 128.
AL HIM-ZÁN .	[*Children of Him-zán.*] A subdivis. of the Sham-mar, p. 122.
AL KÁ-MI	The name of a strain of the stock of KU-HAI-LÁN, Table p. 235 col. vi.
AL KHÁ-IN KHÁ-IF . .	A saying of the Arabs, p. 137.
AL KHAIR MA'-KÚD FI NA-WÁ-SI 'L KHAIL, I-LÁ YAU-MI 'L KI-YÁ-MA.	Thus may be written the "Saying" of the Prophet which in the original Arabic letters adorns our title-page. At p. 158 the "Saying" is translated.
AL KHAM-SA .	[THE FIVE.] *Sc.*, the five great central and parallel lines of blood in which the Bedouin Arabs consider all their *established* strains of horses now to run, pp. 233. 234, 236, 237, 241, 252, 261, 267, 269, 293. Table of AL KHAM-SA, p. 235.
——————— .	The five fingers of the right hand, p. 191 *et* f.n 2, 293.
——————— .	The five plenishings of an Arab bride, p. 234.
A'LI .	A very old proper name. The best known bearer of it was A'li *ibn* Abi Tá-lib, the fourth Arabian Caliph : for references to whom *v.* pp. 106 f.n. 3, 159, 160, 239 *et* f.n. 3 ; and in art. SUN-NÍ AND SHI-Í', *infra*.
A'LÍ BIN KHU-DHAI-RI .	The Baghdad horse-dealer, p. 271.

332   GLOSSARIAL INDEX AND SUPPLEMENT.

ALLAH   [*Al*, the def. article, et *i-lâh*, an *object of awe, reverence, or worship*.] The Arabic form, ALLAH (*passim*), is thus a development of the very ancient god-name *El*, out of which, in every Semitic speech, the name expressive of the unspecialised deity has proceeded. Max Müller thus observes, in *Introduction to the Science of Religion*, p. 179, "In Arabic, ... Allah becomes the name of the God of Muhammad, as it was the name of the God of Abraham and of Moses."

[AL] A'MIR .   In the sense of king (synonyms, *Malik*, and, less usually,
[PL U-MA-RA]   *Sultân*), pp. 17, 39 f.n. 2, 40-48 *passim*.
A'MIR . .   [*Living long*.] A Bedouin proper name; after a bearer of which is called a sub-strain of the stock of KU-HAI-LÂN, Table p. 235 col. vi.

AM-LAH .   One of the colours of Arabian horses, Table p. 263.
A'MR   .   One of the Seven poets of THE MU-A'L-LA-KÂT, *q. v. infra*; Translations from A'MR's poem, pp. 42, 104 f.n. 1, 117, 130 f.n. 4, 240.

A'MÛD   [*Supports*, esp. *tent-poles*.] A subdivis. of the Sham-mar, p. 122 et f.n. 3.

A'NA   A town on W. bank of the Euphrates, 160 miles N.W. of Baghdad, pp. 12, 67.

AN-SÂB .   [Pl. of *nusb*.] *Settings up* of the class described in Gen. xxxv., the primitive type of all later "altars," p. 54 f.n. 2. *Et v.* art. BAITU 'LLAH, *infra*.

A'N-TAR . . .   A renowned warrior and *raconteur* of pagan Arabia, whose
[For A'N-TA-RA.] classic poem is included in the MU-A'L-LA-KÂT, *q. v. infra*. There also exists a romantic account of A'NTAR's adventures, in rhythmic prose interspersed with verses, which, after being printed at Alexandria and Beyrout, has been translated into English. Translation from ANTAR's poem, p. 221. Other references to, pp. 56, 106 f.n. 2, 112 f.n. 1, 136, 234, 237.

A'N-ZU 'D DAR-WÎSH [*Goat, or wild goat, of the dervise*.] The name of a strain in AL KHAM-SA, Table p. 235 col. i.

[AL] A'RABU 'L A'RIBA .   The so-called *Arabian, i.e.* (comparatively) indigenous, inhabitants of the Arab peninsula, p. 98 f.n. 2.

A'RABU 'L A'RIBATI 'L BÂ-I-   A collective name for the prehistoric inhabitants of
DA.   Arabia, p. 97 f.n. 1.

A'RABU 'L KIB-LI .   [*Arabs of the South*.] Comprehensive appellation of certain great masses of the Bedouin, or *quasi* Bedouin, Arabs, p. 271 f.n. 2.

A'-RA-FA .   Name of a subdivis. of the Sba' Ae-ni-za, Table p. 121.
A'RAK   As origin of naturalised word *arrack*, p. 119 f.n. 1.
AR-BÎL.   One of the many dwindled Assyrian cities which the Porte now possesses. Its situation between the two Zâb (or Di-âb) rivers, near the mountain barriers of Persia, makes it a good military post. Near it the empire of Asia transferred itself (331 B.C.) from Darius to Alexander. Once again (A.D. 749) the same locality witnessed a decisive battle, when the

GLOSSARIAL INDEX AND SUPPLEMENT. 333

	last prince of the Damascus dynasty received his quietus from the soldier of fortune, Abû Mus-lim, and Syria was overrun by Persians. Pp. 62 f.n. 2, 159 f.n. 5.
A'-RIDH .	[*Presenting itself.*] Name of a province in Najd, pp. 32 f.n. 1, 43.
AR-JA-SÍ .	The name of a strain of the stock of KU-HAI-LÁN, Table p. 235 col. vi.
AR-KA-BÍ	[*Having large knees.*] The name of a strain in AL KHAM-SA, Table p. 235 col. ii.
AR-NA-BÍ .	[From *ar-nab*, a hare.] The name of a strain in AL KHAM-SA, Table p. 235 col. i.
AS-A'Y	The name of a strain in AL KHAM-SA, Table p. 235 col. ii.
A-SÁ-LAT	"Thorough-breeding." pp. 94, 245 *et seq*.
A-SÁS	The parts of a horse from the knee downward, p. 178.
AS-DÁ	One of the colours of Arabian horses, Table p. 262.
AS-DAF	[*Turning away from.*] Said of a horse whose fore-legs incline outward, p. 200.
AS-FAR .	One of the colours of Arabian horses, Table p. 263.
[AL.] A'-SHÁ . P. 177 f.n. 1.	Mai-mûn, Al A'-shá, was an Arabian poet of the Prophet's era. Some authorities would have included his masterpiece in the MU-A'L-LA-KÁT, *q. v. infra*.
AS-HAB .	One of the colours of Arabian horses, Table p. 263.
A-SHÁ-JI-A'	Name of a horde of the Ij-lás Ae-ni-za, Table p. 121.
ASH-A'L .	One of the colours of Arabian horses, Table p. 263.
ASH-HAB .	" " Table p. 263.
ASH-KAR .	" " Table p. 262.
A-SÍL .	As applied to breed or pedigree, pp. 94, 138, 236, 245 *et seq*.
ASK-ÁBÁD	A settlement, now a Russian post and railway station, within 400 miles of Hirát, in the great oasis called Atok of the Turcoman desert, p. 274 f.n. 1.
AS-LAM	[*Sound.*] A subdivis. of the Sham-mar Bedouin, p. 122 *et* f.n. 5.
[AL.] AS-MA'-Í, ABÚ SA-Í'D A'BDI 'L MALIK, *ibn* KU-RAIB. P. 98.	One of the authorities quoted in the romance of A'n-tar; but not, as is sometimes represented, the author of the poem, which belongs to a much later period. "El As-ma'i" was born at Bussorah, *c*. 740 A.D. In the palmy days of Há-rûnu 'r Ra-shíd he formed one of the principal attractions of Baghdad. A European writer has described him as "the almost perfect type of those nomadic devotees of literature who, after they had grown pale on the benches of Bussorah or Kûfa, went to complete their education in the desert, in the possession of boundless stores of learning, and yet animated by an enthusiasm for further acquisition which made them willing to travel across the sands for hundreds of leagues, if only they might preserve an ancient tradition, or pick up the fragments of an ancient song."
AS-WAD .	One of the colours of Arabian horses, Table p. 262.
A'T-FA	[*Inclining, esp. towards.*] The Bedouin girl who, on great occasions, leads the tribesmen towards the enemy, p. 127 *et* f.n. 1.

AU-SÁM . . . . . Specimens of ———, or camel brands, p. 67 f.n. 3.
AW-WAL RA-FÍK, THUM-MA A saying of the Arabs, p. 293.
TA-RÍK.
AZ-BA-RÍ . [*Large between the shoulders.*] The name of a strain in AL KHAM-SA, Table p. 235 col. i.
AZ-LÁM . . [*Arrows.*] The rods by means of which the Arabs, in the time of Ignorance, sought to know what was allotted to them. They did so by making certain marks on the arrows, placing them in a receptacle, and then drawing them. This practice put down by Muhammad, p. 54 f.n. 2. [From Ezek. xxi. 21, we know that the Semite Babylonians used divining arrows, at the same time that they inspected entrails, as a means of guidance. For divination in Israel, *v.* Zech. x. 2. A very late survival of the "praying and drawing lots" usage is depicted in *Silas Marner*, ch. i.]
[Pl. of *za-lam*.]
AZ-RAK One of the colours of Arabian horses, Table p. 263.

B

BÁB . A doorway, or entrance.
BÁB I Á'LI [*Lofty entrance.*] The Osmanlis' name for the Prime Minister's official residence; whence "Sublime Porte" has come to signify H. I. Majesty the Sultân's Government, p. 78.
BÁB-IL, BÁB-ILI, BÁB-EL. [*Gate of God.*] In the language of the ancient Sumirian and Akkadian inhabitants of Assyria and Babylonia, the name of the capital was Ka-di-mir-ra (by some written "Ka-dingira"); and the Semitic rendering of this word is BÁB-EL, or BÁB-ILI. P. 78.
[Gr. form Babylon.]
BÁBU 'L MAN-DAB . Straits of ———, which connect the Red Sea and the Indian Ocean, pp. 23, 99 f.n. 4. [*Man-dab* equally means *place of weeping*, and *place of summons*. Either interpretation may connect the site with the geographical legend that the existing separation between Arabia and Africa was here effected; according to one account, through a natural catastrophe, and according to another account, through the labours of workmen whom a king or a god assembled.]
BÁ-DI-A . . . The desert, p. 18.
BÁ-DI-ATU 'L 'IRÁK *V.* arts. BAD-W, *et* 'IRÁK, *infra*. P. 65.
BÁ-DI-ATU 'L JAZÍRA *V.* arts. BAD-W, *et* JAZÍRA, *infra*. P. 65.
BÁ-DI-ATU 'SH SHÁM *V.* arts. BAD-W, *et* SHÁM, *infra*. P. 65.
BADR, BADAR, BEDR [*The full round moon.*] At p. 40 f.n. 1, Badr, the son of Ti-lâl, prince of Ja-bal Sham-mar.
BAD-W [*The being plain, or open.*] From this root come *ba-di*, et *bâ-di-a*, the desert; and *ba-da-wi*, of or belonging to the desert. The pl. of *ba-da-wi* is *ba-da-wi-yi-na*, and, in the oblique cases, *ba-da-wi-yi-na*, ex quo, our form "Bedouin," *q. v.*, for page references, in Index ii.

BA-GHA. Ringbone, p. 178 et f.n. 1.

BAGHDAD. The well-known city on the Tigris, about 500 miles inland
[For page references v. In- from the sea. Not long ago, all the country from Mosul to
dex ii.] the Sea of Persia constituted one large Ottoman Pashalik,
which was administered from Baghdad. The same districts
are now arranged in the three governorships of Mosul,
Baghdad, and Bussorah.

The modern Baghdad is near, but not on, the site of the
capital of the Abbaside princes—the Baghdad of Ha-rûnu 'r
Ra-shíd (A.D. 786-809), the Barmecide family, and *The Thousand and One Nights.*

A city of Babylonia named *Bak'dadu*, or *Pak'dadu* (possibly
Khudadu), has recently been traced in the Assyrian geographical catalogues of the time of Assur-bani-pal, the "Sar-
danapalus" of the Greeks. This cannot be the Baghdad
which we know; but the name may have descended from the
one city to the other.

The Baghdad of our day is little better than a heap of
relics, wrapped in a bright but tattered covering.

BAGH-LA. [*A female mule.*] Name given by the Arabs to one of
their largest kinds of sailing craft, p. 260.

[AL] BAI-ÁT Peasant squatters of N.E. I'rák, p. 84 f.n. 1.
BAI-DÁ. Synonym of bá-di-a, p. 18.
BÁ-I-RI. The name of a strain in AL KHAM-SA, Table p. 235 col. i.
BAIT Perhaps the simplest, or *radical,* meaning of this word is,
P. 115 f.n. 3. the *being in a place, whether in the night-time or the day-time.*
But practically, *bait* signifies a tent, or even a more permanent
habitation, as in Gen. xxxiii. 17.

BAITU 'LLAH. [*V.* arts. BAIT, *et* KA'-BA.] Etymologically, *Baitu 'llah*
and *Beth-el* are, of course, but slightly different forms of one
Pp. 54 f.n. 2, 115 f.n. 2. name. The Semitic "Baitulia" of antiquity, we know, were
not *houses.* Acts of worship consecrated them; but the
Deity was not supposed to *inhabit* them. And at this day
the same remark is applicable to the "Baitu 'llah" of Mecca.

BAKH-SHÍSH. A Persian word, meaning a present or gratuity, p. 175.
[It may be very true that, in the East, the thirst for *bakh-
shísh* savours of beggary. But those of our countrymen
whose duties lie in Asia or Africa should remember that the
best kinds of dependants value an occasional "little present"
from a master, more highly than they do their regular wages.]

BAKHT-I-Á-RI. The name of the great mountain series which separates the
lower Tigris from the Ispahán plain. The strongholds and
Pp. 149 f.n. 1, 284. pastures of the Bakht-i-á-ri nation are contained within these
rugged spaces. The Bakht-i-á-ri are absolutely lawless;
but a considerable degree of nobility and elevation characterises them. They are divided into greater and smaller
clans. They boast that they are of the old Lú-ri blood; and
they look down on the Sháh and his nobles as foreigners.

BÁ-KI-LA   The tall spring bean of El I'rák, p. 82 f.n. 1.
BÁ-KÚ-RA   The short stick, often of almond, having a crook at the thicker end, with which the Arab seizes his camel's nose-ring and his mare's halter, p. 130. [A more classical name for the *bá-kú-ra* is *mik-jan*. It is also called the *mish-a'b* and the *mugh-án*.]
BA'L. [Biblical "Baal"]   Equally in Arabic and in other cognate speeches, *be'l* means *master*, or *owner*; and it has been seen, p. 240 *et* f.n. 2, that at least as far back as A.D. *c*. 550, the Arab women spoke of their husbands under this name. From remote ages, successful expeditions have meant for Semites a fresh supply of wives. The tradition existed in ancient Arabia that the strongest children were those born of reluctant mothers. The Arab bridal procession still presents the semblance of raiders bringing back a maiden. The poet A'mr mentioned *distribution, sc.* by captors, as among the dangers against which the desert gallants were bound to defend the free-born Arab spouses who accompanied them in their migrations.
BA-LAD   Any tract comprehended within certain limits, p. 5. [Professor Nöldeke considers *ba-lad* to be the Latin *Palatium*.] *Ba-lad mit*, a dead, or deserted, town, p. 251.
BÁ-LIS   Ruins on the Euphrates which are held to mark the spot where the river issues into "Northern Arabia," p. 65.
BA-LI-YA .   [*Worn out, as with travel, or starvation*.] The mare, or she-camel, tied beside the dead man's grave, according to the ancient Bedouin usage, which is mentioned at p. 130 *et* f.n. 5. [We have diligently sought for evidence showing that any of the Bedouin still tie up the *ba-li-ya*. Every townsman, and every desert Arab, has heard of this custom; and several people have informed us that they, or others whom they knew, had seen it practised; but such statements are not to be trusted. The pastoral Todas who inhabit the mountains of Southern India, when one of their number dies, slaughter buffaloes, under the belief that the deceased will drink their milk in the place to which he has departed.]
BA-NÁ-TU 'L. Á'-WAJ   The name, according to tradition, of a very ancient race of Arabian horses, p. 306.
BAN-DAR .   Eldest son, and, after his uncle Mut-a'b, successor, of Amír Ti-lál of Ja-bal Sham-mar, p. 40 *et* f.n. 1.
BA-NÚ HIJR .   A Bedouin nation of the Persian Gulf littoral, p. 59 f.n. 2.
BA-NÚ IS-RÁ-IL   [*Race of Israel*, p. 104 *et* f.n. 2.] The name of an African antelope, p. 99 f.n. 4.
BA-NÚ KALB .   [*Race of Dog*.] Nomad hordes which spread from Yemen northward, p. 116 f.n. 2.
BA-NÚ KHÁ-LID   A considerable Bedouin nation, pp. 29, 58, 59 f.n. 2.
BA-NÚ LÁM .   A confederation of tribes, partly settled and partly nomadic, p. 84 f.n. 1.

GLOSSARIAL INDEX AND SUPPLEMENT.   337

BA-NÚ SAKHR
P. 271.
An important division of the AHLU 'SH SHI-MÁL (q. v.) Burckhardt says: "The manly persons, broad features, and thick beards of the Ba-nû Sakhr are no proofs of Bedouin origin; yet they pride themselves on being the only descendants of Ba-nû A'bs, an ancient Najd tribe, famous in Bedouin history." (*Op. cit.* in *Catalog.* No. 15, vol. i. p. 23.)

BA-NÚ YÁS
[*Race of Yás.*] A seaboard people of Oman, p. 100. [In Arabic the myrtle is *Ás*. Our jasmine, or jessamine, is in Arabic and Persian *yá-sin*, *yá-sa-man*, et *yá-sa-min*.]

BA-RÁ-ZI-YA
Horse-breeders of N.W. AL JAZÎRA, pp. 75, 272, 273.

BÁ-RI-DA-TU 'L JAUI
A Bedouin term for what we should call *half-bred* horses, p. 272 f.n. 2.

BAR-JA-SÍ-YA
A well-oasis, near Zu-bair, p. 212.

BASHI-BAZOUK
[In the Turkish army, the "*Báshi-bázuk*" soldiery are those whose dress and equipments are not uniform.] P. 188.

BA-TÍN
A term of the Arab, and especially of the Bedouin, geography, p. 75 f.n. 1.

BEG .
[Fem. *Begum*.] A Tatar word for *lord*, which the Mongols, or Mughals, carried into India, and the Osmanlis into Arabia. In the latter country, in towns, as Beg, and in the desert, as Bej, it supplies a title of respect for Europeans. In Africa, it is softened into Bey. Pp. 149, 295.

BEY .
Pp. 152, 282.

BI-LÍKH
A sister affluent with the Khá-bûr, (on the left) of the Euphrates, in N. Al Ja-zi-ra, pp. 75, 82, 111 f.n. 1, 272.

BIL-KÍS
The name of a Queen of the kingdom of Sa-bá, p. 27.

BINT
[*A daughter.*] *V.* IBN. As entering into epithets, p. 34 f.n. 1.

BINTU A'MM
Daughter of a paternal uncle, p. 94.

BIR .
[A *pit,* usually one at the bottom of which there is water.] The name of a very old town on the eastern bank of the Upper Euphrates, p. 74.

BISHR
A collective name for certain divisions of the Aeniza, pp. 39 f.n. 1, 126.

BUH-THA
Bovine antelope of Najd, p. 145 f.n. 1.

BU-KHÁ-RÍ
The celebrated Muslim jurist ——, quoted, p. xii of prefixes of volume, f.n. 2.

BUNN
[*An aromatic odour, as of a sheepfold or a cattle-pen.*] The coffee-plant, and berry, p. 110 f.n. 2.

BU-RAI-DA
One of the two great clay townships of Middle Najd. The population may be 5000; comprising merchants and caravaners (*v.* AGEL) to whom every town and trade-route equally in peninsular and N. Arabia are known, pp. 32 f.n. 1, 210.

BUSSORAH, for *Bas-ra* [Sinbad's "*Bulsorah*"]. For page references *v.* Index ii.
[*Soft ground,* esp. such as *glistens* with gypsum, or other *whiteness.*] The well-known open port, about seventy miles above the Persian Gulf, on the Ottoman (western) bank of the SHATTU 'L A'RAB (q. v.) A considerable emporium of commerce, and a date-garden both of Europe and America.

2 U

BUSSORAH—*continued*.	The present city is modern. The old city (founded A.D. 636 by the Caliph O'mar) stood on a canal S.W. from the present site. Bussorah must not be confounded with Bostra, Bozra, or Buzra, Trajan's capital of Roman Arabia (now a ruin), on the Damascus Hajj road.
BÚ-STÁN .	[*Place of fragrance, i.e.* a garden.] The title of a classical Persian poem, quoted p. 114 f.n. 1.
BUT-LI-YA	The name of a strain in AL KHAM-SA, Table p. 235 col. i.

C

CAIRO . . . . . For page references *v*. Index ii.	A very ancient name for Egypt and for its capital city is *Misr* ; and the title of the capital is *Al Ká-hi-ra* (meaning, *Victrix, Augusta,* and the like), which Europeans have shortened into CAIRO.
CHÁR-DÁK	[Persian, *Chár ták, four pillars.*] The name, with the Osmanli and the Persians, of the summer kiosks, supported on pillars, and open towards the cool quarters, in which the sultry hours are spent, p. 81.
CHOL	[*Not Arabic.*] Used in El I'-rák as "jungle" is in India, p. 19.

D

DAH-MÁN	The name of a strain in the stock of KU-HAI-LÁN, Table p. 235 col. vi, *et v.* Table of Colours, p. 262.
[AD] DAH-NÁ .	The great southern desert of the Arabian peninsula, pp. 25, 34, 37.
DAH-WA .	The name of a sub-strain of the stock of KU-HAI-LÁN, Table p. 235 col. vi.
DÁ-I'R .	The name of a strain in AL KHAM-SA, Table p. 235 col. i.
DAJ-JÁ-NI	[*Keeping to the tent, familiar.*] (A *rá-wi-a* uses the word for *trained* or *domestic* hounds.) The name of a strain in AL KHAM-SA, Table p. 235 col. i.
DA-KHIL. . . Pp. 36, 37 f.n. 3.	*Guest* is but an inadequate rendering of this essentially Arabian word. Lit., it means, *one who enters* ; and specially, *one who enters into the protection of another.* There are various acts by the doing of which, according to the ancient law of the desert, a fugitive or a captive may render himself entitled to the protection and hospitality of a tent or a tribe of the Bedouin. It is interesting to notice how similar conditions of life breed similar manners. Thus Dr Johnson saw, in a castle wall in the Hebrides, an inscription intimating that "if one of the clan Maclonich shall come at midnight with a man's head in his hand, he shall there find safety and protection against all but the king."

DA-LA-MA	[*Multitude*.] Name of a subdivis. of the Aeniza, Table p. 121.
DAL-LÂL .	An agent between two parties, p. 69 *et* f.n. 1.
DÂ-MA . P. 54. f.n. 2.	Draughts. The Arabian history of this game is unknown. In Baghdad they play it with sixteen pieces a side, on a board or table like that of chess. The pieces are larger than those used in backgammon; and they are not moved diagonally, but straight to the front, and laterally. In Spain, about the fifteenth century, chess was called *Axedres de la Dama*. In the old classic speech of Scotland, the word for draughts was "DÂM."
DÂ-ÛD .	The Arabic form of the proper name "David," p. 106.
DÂ-Û-DÎ-YA	About 400 square miles of El I'râk, between Kif-ri and Su-lai-mâ-nî-ya, are occupied by a clan of Kurds, calling themselves Dâ-û-di-ya, after a legendary Kuraishite leader named Dâ-ûd *ibn* Su-lai-mân. The wheat which these Kurds produce is favourably known in the Baghdad market. At the same time, they are far from peaceful; and good colts may be found among them. P. 284.
DAUS .	A saddle-gall, p. 142 f.n. 1.
DAU-SAR .	A grass of El I'râk, p. 82 f.n. 1.
DÂ-WAR .	The name of a horde of El I'râk, p. 84 f.n. 1.
DA-WÂ-SIR	As the name of a region, p. 32 f.n. 1; as that of a people, p. 59 f.n. 2.
DEM or DAIM .	[From *di-ma*, a *lasting rain*.] P. 80 *et* f.n. 1.
DER . .	[*Daur, dâr, du-wâr, der*, all mean in Arabic any *place where people have alighted and tarried*. In this sense the word has travelled to India—*e.g.*, "Dera Is-mâ-î'l Khan," the name of a station; and *dera*, a tent. Before Islâm, the *râ-hib*—lit. *fearer, i.e.* of God—lighted his taper in sequestered places throughout Arabia,[1] and *dair* was one of the names given to his hermitage. See art. HA-NIF, *infra*.] The Der of these pages (pp. 68, 69, 72 f.n. 1, 146, 150, 291, 300) is a settlement of the Arabs, and a military post of the Osmanlî (under Aleppo), on the upper portion of the Euphrates.
DERVISH, DERVISE . P. 45.	Many different meanings, none of which are Arabian, cluster round this word. The root idea is said to be *begging from door to door*. Turkey abounds in Dervishes. In Persia also, and Egypt, Central Asia, and India, there are many varieties of this order; "Pir," "Murshid," "Fa-kîr," "Shekh," and the like. The crowds who now visit Cairo make a point of seeing its "Dancing Dervishes." The gyrations of these votaries are in some schools held to represent or follow the circling movement of the spheres; and in others, the centrifugal vibrations of hearts acted on by strong religious

---

[1] V. translation at p. 49, couplet 2.

DERVISH, DERVISE—*continued*.	influences. But our countrymen should remember that all such hare-brained cultivators of *kaif*, or religious quiescence, passing into ecstasy or worse, and all pretenders to supernatural powers and endowments, borrow most of their doctrines from Gnostic and other Aryan sources.
"DERVISH"	The Arabian horse, portrait in group facing p. 252; other references, pp. 165, 169 *et* f.n. 2.
DHABL	*Fitness*, or *condition*, in a horse, p. 143 f.n. 3.
DHAB-Y	One of the Antelope group, p. 145 f.n. 1.
DHA-FÎR	A Bedouin nation of the Lower Euphrates, pp. 59 f.n. 2, 83.
DHA-LÛL	A "dromedary," or swift camel, one-humped, deep-chested, large-quartered, and highly bred, pp. 36, 57. Cantata of the Arabs about their *dha-lûl*, p. 61, *et v.* f.n. 3 same page.
DHI-Á-LA	A river of El I'-râk; about 400 miles long, from its rise in Persia to its junction with the Tigris below Baghdad, pp. 79, 81, 82, 84 f.n. 1, 278, 282.
DHIB-YÁN	The name of a strain in AL KHAM-SA, Table p. 235 col. i.
DHIF-RÁ	The place in the back of the camel's neck from which sweat first exudes when the beast is working, p. 234.
DHIN IM-NI'	The name of a subdivis. of the Aeniza, Table p. 121.
DHÛ 'L FA-KÂR	[*Possessor of vertebræ*.] A'li's famous sword was so named; possibly from its high temper and flexibility; but more probably because scolloped at the edges, p. 239 f.n. 3.
DHÛ NU'ÁS	The Himyarite king, p. 28.
DHÛ 'R RUM-MA	[*Endowed with wealth or fertility*.] Name of a town in Najd, p. 32 f.n. 1.
DI-ÁR BAKR	A town of the Upper Tigris; on the western bank of the river, N.E. from Aleppo. [The ancient Amida.] P. 63.
DI-FÁ-FA'	A horde of Lower I'râk, p. 84 f.n. 1.
[AD] DIJ-LA. For page references *v.* TIGRIS in Index ii.	This is the only name which we have ever heard given to the Tigris by the people now dwelling on its banks. Etymologists explain that the "Hiddekel" of Genesis, and the form "*Dij-la,*" are variants of one and the same name. For *Hid* is but a prefix, meaning in the pre-Semitic language, *river;* and the Akkadian and Assyro-Babylonian forms are *Idigna*, and *Idiklat* (or Diklat), respectively. In the Medo-Persic language, *Tig-ra* means an arrow.
DI-MISHKU 'SH SHÁM: or, shortly, SHÁM. For page references *v.* DAMASCUS in Index ii.	The well-known capital of Shám or Syria [Gen. xv. 2]. Since A.D. 634, the city of Saladin has occupied a unique place in El Islám, equally under the Caliphs, the Egyptian Sultans, and the Turks.
DÍN	An old word, denoting in EL IS-LÁM, Religion, in the widest sense of the term, practical and doctrinal. *V.* art. IS-LÁM, *infra*.
DÍ-RA	[*V.* DER, *supra*.] Most of the divisions of the Bedouin have certain recognised wells and pastures which are proper to them; and such constitute the tribe's *dí-ra*, pp. 16, 21, 59.

GLOSSARIAL INDEX AND SUPPLEMENT.   341

DIR-A' A warrior's jerkin, of mail or leather, p. 104 f.n. 1. [The first meaning of *dir-a'* is the long shirt which the Arab women wear. Im-ra-u 'l Kais depicts a growing maiden as "between the *dir-a'* and the *mij-wal*." The latter is the shorter garment, in which the little girls run about. Thus the Arab poet expresses the same idea as that conveyed in the lines by Longfellow—

"Standing with reluctant feet
Where the brook and river meet,
Womanhood and childhood fleet."]

DI-WÁM . [Root-idea, *stability*.] The name of a subdivis. of the Sba', Table p. 121, 298.

DÍ-WÁN [or *Dí-ván*] An Aryan word, which is now diffused over Central Asia and Persia, Turkey, India, Arabia, and parts of Africa. The following are some of its meanings :—A *list* or *roll*. An *imperial council. President of such*, whence *vizier* or *minister*. A *hall of audience* or *assembly*. In India, under the E.I. Co., the *body of superior native officers*; whence *the revenue* and *financial administration*. Still more curiously, a *rotatory dance of sun-worshippers*. Out of the first of these senses there comes that in which the word occurs at pp. 49 f.n. 1, 179 f.n. 1—viz., a *series of poems*; while at p. 161 it signifies a Turkish official's *room*. In Europe it often means a *café*.

DRAGOMAN Some identify this word with *tar-ju-mân*, which, though post-classical, is included in Arabic dictionaries, with the meaning of *translator*, p. 297.

[AD] DU-GHAI-RÁT [Pl. of *du-ghair, one who rushes*, esp. *to snatch a thing*.] A subdivis. of the Sham-mar, p. 122.

DUGH-MÁN The name of a horde of the Ru-wa-la Aeniza, Table p. 121.
DÚ-KHI . The name of a strain of AL KHAM-SA, Table p. 235 col. i.
DU-LAIM . A Bedouin nation of the Euphrates, whose pastures begin about three days N.W. of Baghdad, pp. 84 f.n. 1, 85.

DUL-DUL . The name of one of the Prophet's riding-mules, p. 230.
DU-NAIS . [*Grimy*.] The sobriquet of a well-known family in the Aeniza, from whom the name has passed to a strain of AL KHAM-SA for which their tents are noted, Table p. 235 col. i.

DU-RAI-Í-YA [From DIR-A', *q. v. supra*.] The first capital of the Wahabite empire, pp. 58, 162, 164. [Instead of rebuilding the city of A'bdu 'l Wah-háb's preaching after its demolition (1818) by Egyptian soldiers, the inhabitants transferred themselves to AR RI-ÁDH (*q. v.*), four miles off. Only soil-bound cultivators remained behind in date-gardens amid the broken walls and fortifications.]

DÚZ KHUR-MÁ-TÚ . A small town on the post-road between Baghdad and Mosul, p. 84 f.n. 1.

F

FAD-DÁ-GHA. [Root-meaning, *pounding*, or *mauling*.] A subdivis. of the Sham-mar, p. 122 *et* f.n. 5.

FAHD. The Lynx. Shekh Fahd, of the Ibn Hadh-dhâl Arabs, p. 83. Remarks on the use of *fahd* as a proper name by the Bedouin Arabs, p. 107.

FAI-SAL. [One who *divides, adjudicates, governs*.] Amir Fai-sal of Najd, pp. 36, 40, 42, 103 f.n. 1, 250, 251, 261.

FÁL. An omen, p. 54 f.n. 2. [In the East, it is chiefly among educated Arab Muslim of the strict Kuranic school that exceptional persons who absolutely repudiate omens are met with. The masses of the people are still liable, after overcoming every moral and prudential consideration against an undertaking, to be turned back from it by the cry of a night-bird, the braying of an ass, or the advice of a mulla.]

FA-LAJ [pl. AF-LÁJ]. A labyrinthine and fertile tract in Najd, pp. 32 f.n. 1, 98 f.n. 3.

FA-LÁT. The empty desert, p. 19.

FAL-LÁH [pl. *Fal-lâ-hîn*]. [Root-meaning, *ploughing*.] Peasantry, p. 15.

FAL-LÛ-JA. As a name for peasant settlements, p. 98 f.n. 3.

FAN-TÁS. P. 150 *et* f.n. 2, 152.

FA-RAS. Generically, the horse; in El I'rák, restricted to the mare, p. 238 f.n. 2.

FA-RAT. [*Outstripping*.] The name of a strain in AL KHAM-SA, Table p. 235 col. v.

FAR-HÁN. [*Joyous*.] A name much given by the Bedouin equally to their boys and to their colts. The late Shekh Far-hân, of the Sham-mar, pp. 72, 122 f.n. 5, 125.

FÁ-RIS. [*Horseman*.] A proper name among the Bedouin. References to the present Shekh Fâ-ris of the Sham-mar, pp. 72 *et* f.n. 1, 122, 125, 129. [The idea in *fâ-ris* corresponds with that of *cavalier*. The title is only applicable to a *hur*, i.e. a *gentleman* and *armiger*.]

FENDI. Has the same meaning as *fa-khidh*, i.e., a *limb*, branch, or family group, within a horde or clan, p. 122.

FEZ.
[For *fes*.] The red, or white, round woollen cap which the Osmanli wear. The Arabs, when they assume the fez, wind a turban round it. The European employees of the Porte wear the fez at official receptions. As a head-dress for horsemen, when solar heat and glare are not in question, the fez is as superior to most kinds of hats and helmets, as it is to the desert Arab's kerchief and rope-twist. It seldom falls off, except when the rider does so. P. 71.

FID-Á'N. [*Distorted, or deformed, at the wrist, or ankle-joint, or at both*.] The name of an important divis. of the Aeniza. Table p. 121; pp. 126.

Fihr	The Ku-raish (*q. v.*) are also called "Al Fihr" (p. 116); but the latter name particularly designates those of the Ku-raish who, instead of being settled in Mecca, occupied the surrounding country.
[AL] Furát For page references *v.* Eu- phrates in Index ii.	The prestige and beauty of this river are most impressive. Reckoning the two-branched upper part, it is about 1600 miles long, from Erzeroum and Lake Van, to where, after meeting the Tigris, it falls into the Persian Sea. In parts of its course, inhabited islands, not unstudded with ancient ruined castles, rise out of its bed. The Arabs think that no other river contains such wholesome water. In Al Kur-ân, *fu-rât* is used (S. xxxv.), not as the name of a river, but, epithetically, to distinguish potable from salt or brackish water.[1]

G

Ga-á'-ji-ba	The name of a horde of the Ru-wa-la Aeniza, Table p. 121.
Gal-la P. 160.	The Gallas constitute an important part of the population of Abyssinia and Eastern Africa. Above all things they are warriors, and they are infinitely divided into hostile tribal nations. Their cults are full of interest to the student of religions. During many centuries, both Italian priests and Arabian teachers have lived among them, and they now exhibit variegated layers of Paganism, Christianity, and Islamism. The Wollo Gallas to the north of Magdâla who lent their services to our Abyssinian expedition, save in that they lived under a female sovereign, resembled Sunnite Arabs.[2]
Gan-ji-fa	Cards, p. 54 f.n. 2. These are probably of Asiatic origin. Strict Muslim condemn them, because of the Prophet's prohibition of gaming. But the crowd is not so nice. From the China Sea to the Mediterranean the "devil's picture-books" make life's wheels move faster.
Gan-ta-ra Khaz-ga	The name of a spot on the Euphrates, p. 67 *et* f.n. 2.
Ga-sá-ib . [For *ka-sâ-ib*.]	[Pl. of *ka-st-ba*, anything *cut*, or *jointed*, *e.g.* a reed.] The plaited locks of the Bedouin, which hang free like whiplashes, p. 29. [The Abyssinian ties back the hair in ridges and furrows, and walks out with no other covering on the crown than a pat of butter [Psal. cxxxiii. 2]. The Arab omits the butter; but he divides his hair crossways, and twists it into four spiral tresses.]

---

[1] When the Assyrians first saw "the great water," it was called, in the older Akkadian language, "*Bu-rit*," or "*Pu-rât*;" which they made into *Pu-rat-tu*. The Persians modified this form into "Ufratu," whence the Gr. "Euphrates." Exceptionally, queens also succeeded to the sceptre. Much as the Arab Prophet did to improve the status of women, the principle on which his commonwealth was founded excluded the idea of female sovereignty. Tradition even ascribes to him the "Saying," *That people never prospered whose affairs were ordered by a woman.*

[2] Long before Islâm, in the hereditary monarchies of South Arabia, as a rule the son followed the father; but

GA-SÍR	V. art. KA-SÍR.
GA-WÁ-JI-BA	The name of a horde of the Ru-wa-la Aeniza, Table p. 121.
GHA-BÍT	At p. 49 *et* f.n. 3, a place-name. At p. 234 f.n. 4, the lower part of the camel-saddle.
GHA-DHÁ	A camel-shrub of the *genus* Euphorbia, p. 36.
GHAI-LÁN	A wind of the desert, p. 67 *et* f.n. 1.
GHAI-THA	[*Rain.*] The name of a subdivis. of the Sham-mar, p. 122.
GHA-ZÁL	The Arabian and Persian antelope [*Gazella*]. The *Antilope Dorcas* of naturalists, p. 145 f.n. 1.
GHA-ZÁ-I-A	The name of a strain in AL KHAM-SA, Table p. 235 col. i.
GHÁ-ZI	One who takes part in the GHAZ-U, *q. v.* A small gold coin is so called, after Mah-mûd II. (styled Ghâ-zi), one of the few modern Osmanli Sultans (1808-1839) who have displayed ruler-like qualities. Illustration facing p. 136.
[AL] GHAZ-U . For page references *v.* RAID-ING in Index ii.	[*Aiming at a thing.*] A plundering expedition. The "*ba-ran-ta*" of the Turkumâns. In some Muslim countries, the epithet GHÁ-ZI has been specialised, in the sense of *fighter in the cause of religion*; but this meaning is foreign to the Arabian Bedouin. In El Islâm the first war adventures were expeditions against caravans, *e.g.* the "RAID OF BIDR," A.H. 2.
GHU-BAI-VIN	[*Overreaching* another *in a bargain.*] The name of a subdivis. of the Fid-a'n Aeniza, Table p. 121.
GHUR-RA	A "blaze" on a horse's forehead, p. 61 *et* f.n. 2.
GO-MI-YA	[*Belonging to an enemy.*] The name of a strain of the stock of KU-HAI-LÁN, Table p. 235 col. vi.
GRANE	V. KU-WAIT.
GURNA [Correctly *Kurna.*]	[From a root which means *connecting*, or *conjoining.*] The name of the place, about forty miles above Bussorah, where the Tigris and the Euphrates unite their waters, pp. 20, 84 f.n. 1, 85.

H

HA-BA-SHÍ	Abyssinian, p. 107 f.n. 3. [The Semitic root of Abyssinia, or Habessinia, is said to imply *admixture* or *collection*. A large number of kidnapped Abyssinians of both sexes, chiefly Gallas (*q. v.*), pass through Jedda, Suez, and Muscat, into all the countries of Asia, where, in thousands of families, they become happily domesticated. Their brown complexions and straight and regular Caucasian features render them incomparably more pleasant inmates than their woolly-pated and bituminous black congeners.] The breed of ponies called the Habashi, p. 136 f.n. 2.
HA-DA-LI	The name of a strain in AL KHAM-SA, Table p. 235 col. i.

HAD-BĀN	The name of one of the Five primary divisions of the stock of AL KHAMSA, Table p. 235 col. v., *et* p. 298. [In a simile in Im-ra-u 'l Kais' poem, comparing the tit-bits of camel's fat on which a party of gallants feasted to the unwoven ends of a piece of Damascus silk, the word used for the silky filaments is from the same root as *had-bán*. As a name for a line of horses, HAD-BĀN perhaps has reference to some such feature as *long forelocks*, or *long eyelashes*.]
HA-DHA-RI	[Belonging to the *hadhr*, *i.e.*, the demarcated, and more or less cultivated, country.] The opposite of BA-DA-WI. Pp. 15, 16, 52, 97, 133, 270.
HADH-DHĀL	The name of a horde of the Aeniza, pp. 83, 107.
[AL] HADHR	[Apparently a survival among the Arabs of the Roman proper name Hatra, Atra, or Atræ.] The ruins of "Al Hadhr," in AL JAZĪRA, prepare a surprise for travellers. An imposing panorama of tolerably well-preserved palaces, temples, tombs, and reservoirs, now presents itself on the site of a city believed to have been the capital, down to our fourth century, of an Aramæan principality of the Palmyra type which was tributary to the Parthian empire. Hatra repulsed Trajan (A.D. 116), and eighty-two years later, Severus. The wild animals of the desert now pass freely over it. P. 75, 282 f.n. 1.
HADH-RA-MAUT	[*Death's presence*: from the severity of the climate.] The southern coast district of Arabia, pp. 25, 29, 32, 97 f.n. 3.
HA-DĪD	Iron. At p. 311, the iron shackles which the Arabs put round their horses' fore-pasterns.
HA-DĪTH . [Pl. *A-há-díth*.]	Literally, tidings, or traditional information. Then, *specially*, a tradition of what the Prophet said or did, handed down by word of mouth, as distinguished from the written KUR-ĀN. The HA-DĪTH, or "Saying," which adorns our title-page is translated, p. 158. Other references to "Sayings," pp. 20 *et* f.n. 3, 38, 81 f.n. 1, 93 *et* f.n. 1, 115 f.n. 3, 128 *et* f.n. 2, 135 *et* f.n. 2, 162 f.n. 2, 230 f.n. 1.
HAD-RA-JĪ [For the mare, *Had-ra-jía*.]	The name of a strain of the stock of KU-HAI-LĀN, Table p. 235 col. vi.
HĀ-FI	[*Uushod*.] The name of a strain of the stock of KU-HAI-LĀN, Table p. 235 col. vi.
HĀ-FIR	[*Digger*.] The horny box in which the horse's foot is enclosed, p. 11. [In Saxon, *hóf* et *hófe*; Dutch, *hoef*; Norw. and Dan. *hov*; Gr. *hoph'*. In the Icelandic language, which of all the existing Teutonic dialects has retained the greatest number of old forms with the least alteration, the word for hoof is *hofr*.] [1]

---

[1] Those who are bent on discovering a "language of Eden," or one primeval linguistic stem of which equally the Indo-European and the Semitic groups of languages are offshoots, may add "*hafr*" to their list of illustrations. A stock example of the same kind is *corb* (German, *erde*), which is *arf* in Arabic; and many other examples might be

HÁ-FIZ Pp. 54 f.n. 2, 118.	[*Keeper*, or *preserver*.] The sobriquet, which passes for name, of the famous Persian poet, Muhammad Shamsu 'd din, of our 14th century. In Persia and India, one who has *committed* AL KUR-AN *to memory* (a feat discountenanced by the stricter Arabian Muslim as savouring of formalism) receives the title of "Há-fiz."
HAGAR	[From a Semitic root meaning *separation*, as from one's home and country.] The Egyptian girl (the Arabian traditionalists write her name *Há-jar*) of whom was born Ishmael, pp. 100, 115, 116.
HAI	The name of a small branch of the Tigris, in Lower I'rák, pp. 84 f.n. 1, 85.
HAI-DAR (*Hyder*) A'LI	[*c.* 1702-82.] The son of a petty officer of the native Hindú government of Mysore, who, through innate aptitude for war, and the utmost energy, raised himself to sovereignty, and, aided by his son Tippoo, contested with us the mastery of India. P. 95.
HAI-FI	[*Drawn fine*, from work.] The name of a strain in AL KHAM-SA, Table p. 235 col. i.
HA-JA-RAT KHAZ-GA	A place-name, p. 67 f.n. 2.
HAJJ	The pilgrimage to Mecca, p. 37. One who performs the Hajj is designated a HÁJ, which is softened into HAJ-JI, pp. 176, 301. [The Turks, Persians, and Indians change *Haj-ji* into *Há-ji*.
HA-LAB	[*Milk*.] The Arabs thus write the place-name which we write ALEPPO ; *sub quo, v.* page references in Index ii.
HA-LÁ-WI	The name of a strain in AL KHAM-SA, Table p. 235 col. i.
HA-LÚ J	[*Flashing*, as lightning does.] The name of a strain in AL KHAM-SA, Table p. 235 col. i.
HÁ-MA	[Hamath of the Bible.] One of the oldest cities of Syria, on the Orontes, about 100 miles north of Damascus, pp. 211, 212.
HA-MÁD	The desert, pp. 19, 65, 67, 83, 105. [*Ham-ma-da* is the name used to designate the flintier segments of the great African Sahara [*v.* art. SAH-RÁ], the vastness of which, even when the view is not carried east of the Nile, is estimated at between three and four millions of square miles—nearly equal to all Europe, minus the Scandinavian peninsula and Iceland.]

---

cited. Of course, words which are imitations of sounds must be more or less similar wherever they occur. It is also easy to trace how the gipsies, the crusaders, the Moorish conquerors of Spain, and the Greek philosophy have contributed to the process of word-diffusion. But there is no connection between these facts and the endeavour to derive Aryan and Semitic from a common source. Until the secret of the Semitic root shall have been discovered, all such attempts rest upon air. The mystery of the Semitic language is that, with comparatively few exceptions, every word either consists of, or proceeds out of, three letters (consonants), neither more nor less. The Jews and the Arabs of ten centuries ago made a good deal of grammar, but they did not make the triliteral root. A Sanscrit root may consist of a single vowel, or of consonants and vowels in varied combinations; but the tri-consonantal root of Semitic language, as historically known, is as firmly moulded as if it had been created out of moist earth, at the same time with the camel. The science of comparative philology is still in its infancy ; and a sure means of retarding it is to compare words and lexicons, when we ought to be comparing structural and grammatical characters.

[Al.] Ha-má-sa	[Literally, *firmness* as against an enemy; and figuratively, *poetic genius*.] A collection of 884 poetical pieces, chiefly pre-Islamic or early Islamic, which was brought together, about two centuries after Muhammad, by Ha-bíb *ibn* Ausi 't Tá-i, commonly called Abû Tam-mám, himself a practised lyrist. As a storehouse of ancient legend, and mirror of Arabian life and manners, the Ha-má-sa ranks with the Mu-a'l-la-kát (*q. v.*) Verses by a poet of Al. Ha-má-sa translated, p. 43.
Ha-má-wand	The name of a small horde of Kurds, p. 282.
Ham-dá-ni [For mare, *Ham-dá-ní-ya*.]	The name of one of the five primary divisions of the stock of Al. Kham-sa, Table p. 235 col. iv.
Ham-ha-ma	In a translation from A'n-tar's poem, at p. 221, a whinnying sound, softer than neighing, which horses make.
Ham Ti-já-ra, Ham Zi-á-ra.	A Persian proverb: as we should say, *The making of a bargain at the church door*, p. 116.
Ha-níf P. 101.	The importance of this word to students of Arabian topics depends on the following facts. Professor Max Müller says of El Is-lâm that it "springs, as far as its most vital doctrines are concerned, from the ancient fountain-head of the religion of Abraham, the worshipper and friend of the one true God."[1] Now, Al Kur-án six times styles Abraham a "Ha-níf." In five other passages the same epithet is applied to the Patriarch's religious attitude, in turning from idols to the "Allahu 'k Rahmánu 'k ra-hím" of Islamism. And it is needless to observe that the Arab Prophet, in calling Abraham a "Ha-níf," called himself one. Out of all this, a plentiful crop of questions issues. *Ha-níf*, we know, was an established word in Semitic language long before Muhammad. It occurs in the Talmud, with the meaning of "hypocrite." Clearly, Muhammad cannot have used it in that sense. But, first, did he "bring it in" as a weird expression, borrowed from a foreign source; or was it current among the Arabs, before his period, with a special religious application? As far as this point is concerned, the best authorities are now agreed that the Arabian Ha-nífs are historical; that is, that before Muhammad, and especially towards his era, there lived, in Medina and elsewhere, Arabs who, because of their religious earnestness and their rejection of polytheism, were called by others, if they did not call themselves, "Ha-nífs." But this does not inform us who these "private judgment" people were; or in how far the representation is justifiable, that a traditional "faith of Abraham" had been preserved by them during the pagan ages. Without professing to solve these difficulties, we are tempted to place them alongside of a familiar passage of history. It is not unusual for Protestant writers to describe

[1] *Introduction to the Science of Religion*, p. 105.

HA-NIF—*continued*.
the Mystics of Germany and Holland as precursors of the Reformation. Perhaps they were so; but not in the sense that they saw any glimmering of the light which afterwards dawned on Luther. And so in regard to the Ha-nifs. However helpful some of them may have been to Muhammad when his own mental life was at its crisis, and however considerably the body of the Ha-nifs ("*Al Hu-na-fâ*") may in the course of time have given their adherence to his formulated system, established facts are opposed to the conclusion that the source of Islâm was among them. The European reader must not imagine that the Hu-na-fâ composed a regular "Sect." Many divergent types both of thought and action may be traced among them. For example, the Arabian anchoret, or "râ-hib," to whom a slight reference occurred in art. DER, *supra*, if he was not a "Ha-nif," was at least tinctured with Hanifite ideas. Muhammad himself, according to unanimous tradition, as part of the ordeal through which he passed before he assumed his mission, was wont to spend the truce month, Ra-jab, in solitary devotional meditation (*ta-han-nuth*)[1] in the clefts of Mount Har-râ over against Mecca. Before his time, many of the Hu-na-fâ had even carried asceticism far enough to lead the populace to associate them with those Christian monks[2] who exalted celibacy from a mere feature of the hermit life to the rank of a religious virtue (Matt. xix. 12; 1 Cor. vii.)

HA-RA-KA
The name of a strain in AL KHAM-SA, Table p. 235, col. i.

HA-RAM . . . . .
For the European form, "harem," *v.* pp. 17 f.n. 1, 47 f.n. 2, 103 f.n. 1. For "*Ha-ram*," in the sense of *holy*, *v.* p. 116: also a slightly different form of the same epithet, in art. MAS-JIDU 'L HA-RÂM, *infra*.
This word is much used to denote *the precincts which, under the polygamous system, are in the exclusive occupancy of the female division of the household*. In Persia the corresponding term is *zan-â-na*; and in Europe, *scraglio*. By metonymy, the same words mean *the inmates of those precincts*. The root-idea in *hrm* is, *prohibited*; but it yields many other meanings, ranging between that of *sacred, inviolable, holy*, and that of *a thing to be abstained from*, as is, *e.g.*, swine's flesh under Judaism and Islamism. Thus does *ha-ram* contain two seemingly divergent ideas—that of *holy*, and that of *tabooed* (popularly, "*abominable*," *v.* Isaiah

---

[1] There is good old Arabic authority to support the view that *ha-nif* and *ta-han-nuth* claim a common root. Some Eastern scholars derive *ha-nif* from *ha-na-fa*, which is purely Arabic, and means to *incline*, or *deviate*. The proper name Ha-nî-fa existed in pagan Arabia. A nation so called held, we know, the mountainous heart of Najd, till a soldier of Islam broke them in a sanguinary battle. The name of the same people still lives in "Wâ-di Ha-ni-fa," one of the winding passes which lead to the Wahabite capital. But these facts do not affect the explanation that the Ha-nifs of Arabia took their appellation from *ta-han-nuth*, which occurs in the Bible in the sense of Prayers.

[2] The friar, or celibate ecclesiastic, of pre-Reformation times, is termed in AL KUR-ÂN a "*râ-hib*." The Arab Prophet perceived only the worst features of monachism. He held strongly, like Bacon after him, that "wife and children are a discipline in humanity; bachelors are morose and austere." It is unnecessary to quote the severe animadversions on the state of being a Râ-hib, and on the Râ-hibs themselves, which AL KUR-ÂN contains, as in Sû-ras ix. *et* lvii. "Râ-hib" is pure Arabic, and is now confined to literature. A Christian "priest," or cleric of ordinary rank, is called by the modern Arabs a *kass*, or *kis-sîs*, a Syriac word signifying Elder.

HA-RAM—*continued*. (Lev. 4); but the explanation is simple. The word translated "unclean" of the Levitical prohibition here, as elsewhere, produces a confusion of ideas. In the pig's case, for example, it is generally assumed that his disgusting habits caused the eating of him to be interdicted by primitive lawgivers. It appears more probable that the prohibition in question points to the time when numerous animals were exclusively appropriated to the gods. Interesting facts bearing on this subject are to be observed in El 'Irák. At Mosul, where we are at this moment writing, the Osmanli cavalry soldiers allow a pet pig to run about their barrack-yard, under the superstition that evil spirits will enter it, and not the horses.[1] Again, the name for whooping-cough in Arabic is *khi-uni-zi-ra*, sc. *pig's cough;* for which distemper water from a pig's drinking-trough is held to be a sound prescription. An English resident of Baghdad keeps a pig-stye in his garden. On our asking him whether his Muslim neighbours did not object to his doing so, his answer was, that, on the contrary, he found it difficult to exclude those of them who desired to procure cupfuls of the water for patients in their harems! And lastly, in the country of the Tigris, not only Shi-ites, but even Sun-nis of the less educated classes, adorn the necks of their mares with amulets made of boars' tushes. Such facts as these deserve to be considered in connection with Muhammad's prohibition of swine's flesh. In none of the passages of AL KUR-ÁN which lay down the law on this point is any reason given. The Prophet, in certain of his "Sayings," affixed to the pig the word which is used to denote the "impurity" of the dog. But we know that the dog also was treated as an object of worship by many nations of antiquity. A Muslim merchant from Egypt lately described to us with horror, and, it may be hoped, not without exaggeration, how the ancestral canine guards of Cairo are now being done to death by "scientific" methods.

HARB The name of a great confederation of the Bedouin, whose *dí-ras* extend from about Medina eastward, pp. 39 f.n. 1, 59 f.n. 2, 127, 217 f.n. 1.

HA-RÍK The name of a large oasis, on the borders of the great southern desert of Najd, p. 32 f.n. 1.

HA-RISH . The name of a strain in AL KHAM-SA, Table p. 235 col. iii.

---

[1] A familiar Gospel story has for its basis the special eligibility of the pig to form the receptacle of devils. Among the many kind things which the Sun of rays of the Shí-'í in El 'Irák is, that when they die they are changed into pigs, and sent back to their old haunts. To illustrate the value of testimony in such matters, it may be mentioned that in Baghdad, in the present year of grace, any one who is not an official could, we feel assured, find witnesses who, without having a set purpose to deceive, should make affirmation that, to the certain knowledge of themselves or others, well-known Shí-ite townsmen have shortly after their death and burial been seen reposing in porcine form in their recently vacated summer-houses, or perhaps grubbing for roots in the garden?

HA-RISH—*continued*.	[A camel-master of Mosul says that *ha-rish* means *having the lips excoriated*. The camel's gullet can pass down thorns from which the horny sole of the same animal flinches. But both in the mare and the camel the upper lip is apt to be wounded in cropping the acacias of the desert.]
HAR-MA .	The name of a strain in AL KHAM-SA, Table p. 235 col. iii.
HAR-RAN	The "Haran" of Genesis; and see Ezek. xxvii. 23. P. 111 *et* f.n. 1. [In Assyro-Babylonian, Har-rân means *road*, and the city of Har-rân is often mentioned in the cuneiform literature.]
HA-RÚNU 'K RA-SHÍD	Hâ-rûn, the Kuranic transcription of Aaron; *ra-shîd*, *v*. in this Index. The "Haroun Alraschid," 5th Abbaside Caliph of Baghdad (last quarter of 8th Christian century), whose strolls incognito through his capital are immortalised in the *Arabian Nights*. P. 98.
[AL] HA-SA [Pl. *Ah-sá*.]	The well-known Arabian province on the Persian Gulf, pp. 29, 30 *et* f.n. 2, 31, 48, 99 f.n. 4, 293, 294. [The name denotes, *Ground on which water collects; or, accumulated sand beneath which is hard ground, so that when the sand is scraped away, the water that has rained on it is found.*]
HA-SAN	[*Beautiful*.] An exceedingly common proper name among the Arabs. A'li's eldest son, and nominal successor in the Caliphate, bore it.
HA-SAN BIN BADR .	The Arab horse-dealer, p. 309.
HA-SHISH	Fodder. The same word yields a name (in Baghdad, "ha-shí-sha") for an intoxicant obtained from the hemp-plant, the Indian preparations of which are *bháng*, *gánjá*, and *charas*. P. 82 f.n. 1. *Et v*. art. ALAMÚT, *supra*.
HAS-SAN .	A horse-dealer [lit., *one who is constantly occupied with the hisán*, or horse], p. 123 f.n. 1.
HA-TIM	A name or title in which is the idea of *judging*. In Arabia the fountain of power is still that of judgment, or justice. Accordingly, Hâtim is the equivalent of Amir, or Shekh. *V*. p. 62 f.n. 2, a reference to the famous Arabian Hâtim.
HAUB	Many words, especially those of the chiding category, have either been made by the Arab camel-drivers, or borrowed from the guttural speech of their cattle; and one such is *haub*. A strain of the stock of KU-HAI-LAN is also thus designated, Table p. 235 col. vi.
HAU-DAJ .	It forms the ambition of every desert lady, when she mounts her camel, to have the *raht*, or saddle, fitted with the exceedingly picturesque sedan, which they call a *hau-daj*, p. 321. Doughty saw the daughters of the Harb nation (vol. ii. p. 304 of his *Travels*) seated in "crated frames, trapped with the wavering tongues of coloured cloths, and long lappets of camel leather." The hau-daj depicted in our volume is from a sketch by Layard. The same distinguished traveller and writer thus describes the structure:—

HAU-DAJ—*continued*. "A light framework, varying from sixteen to twenty feet in length, stretches across the hump of the camel. It is brought to a point at each end, and the outer rods are joined by distended parchments; two pouches of gigantic pelicans seem to spring from the sides of the animal. In the centre, and over the hump, rises a small pavilion, under which is seated a lady. The whole machine, as well as the neck and body of the camel, is ornamented with tassels and fringes of worsted of every hue, and with strings of glass beads and shells. It sways from side to side as the beast labours under the unwieldy burthen; looking, as it appears above the horizon, like some stupendous butterfly skimming slowly over the plain."[1]

Beyond the limits of the desert, the hau-daj is called a *mah-mil*, lit. *vehicle*. The "Mah-mil" which accompanies the annual pilgrim caravan from Cairo to Mecca is an example. Like a royal carriage in a procession, the Egyptian Mah-mil represents the Sultan and the Viceroy of Egypt. In thirty-seven days of marching, it serves as the venerated guide of the swollen concourse: *v.* Lane's *Modern Egyptians*, ch. xxiv.

HAUR or HOR A marsh; and especially a space which, after having been under water, has dried up through evaporation, p. 82.

[AL] HAU-RÁN The remarkable district east of the Jordan, south and south-
Pp. 294, 295. east of Damascus, which is now much identified with the Druses. The Haurán formed a part of the ancient kingdom of Bashan. It was here that "the Midianites and the Amalekites and all the children of the east lay along in the valley like grasshoppers for multitude; and their camels were without number, as the sand by the sea-side for multitude" (Judges vii. 12). In our day this description is applicable to the Aeniza, when they swarm into the Haurán in early summer. According to Arab tradition, it was here that Job increased in sheep and camels, oxen and she-asses. The name Haurán occurs in Ezek. xlvii. 16-18. If the standing interpretation of it by *cave-land* be uncertain, nothing better has been offered. Porter's *Five Years in Damascus* is the book most quoted by European travellers in Al Haurán who pass our way. But the accounts therein given are very unsatisfactory from the archæological point of view; and the cities described as "pre-Mosaic" are mostly of the Roman period.

[AL] HA-WI-JA A term of Arabian topography, pp. 82, 83, 280, 281, 283.
HÁ-YIL [*Situated between, i.e.* between AJÁ and SAL-MÁ.] The principal settlement in Ja-bal Sham-mar, pp. 37-48 *passim*, 58, 72, 122, 132, 146, 251, 296.

HIB-LÁN [*Irefal.*] The name of a great horde of the Aeniza, Table p. 121.

---

[1] Cf. *ib.* in Catalog. No. 30, vol. i. ch. iv.

352 GLOSSARIAL INDEX AND SUPPLEMENT.

HID . [*V*. in art. DIJ-LA, *supra*.] The river of Lower I'rák which is called the Ilíd, after forming many intricate ramifications (navigable only for the *tar-rí-da*, or canoe), loses itself, as is believed, in a sheet of water marked on maps as *Ha-wí-ja*. Pp. 84 f.n. 1, 85.

HI-JÁB . A charm or amulet, p. 136 f.n. 1.

[AL] HI-JÁZ The mountain-land which separates the lowlands on the Red Sea coast from the upland plain of the Arab peninsula, pp. 26, 28, 29, 30, 34, 47 f.n. 2, 49, 106, 116, 117, 128.

HIL-LA [*A company alighting*.] The name of a small town on the Euphrates, pp. 100, 300.

HIM-RI A natural grass of the Arabian steppe-land, p. 73.

HIM-RÍN [*Red*] . . . . Name of a range of mountains, pp. 84 f.n. 1, 282 *et* f.n. 1.

HIM-YAR, HIMYARITES, HO- The name of a people whose hegemony followed on that of
MERITES. the old Sabæan kings of Yemen, pp. 27, 28.

[AL] HIN-NA . The name of the plant which is incorrectly rendered, in the authorised version of Cant. i. 14 *et* iv. 13, "camphire." Botanists name it *Lawsonia alba*; and the Indians, *menh-dí*. Many oriental nations prize the hinna for its vulnerary and beautifying properties. The Persians, and the Shi-ite Indians, make its leaves into a paste, with which they impart an orange-red colour to the beard, the palms, the soles, the finger-tips, and other parts. We know from Im-ra-u 'l Kais' poem that this practice prevailed among the pagan Arabs: *v*. line 11 in the translated passage at p. 143. Some traditions are held to show that the Prophet habitually stained his beard in this manner. From other traditions it is inferred that he did so only once.

HIR-FÁ A name signifying *active*, which the Bedouin give to their daughters, p. 51.

HI-SÁN THE HORSE. The root-idea in *hí-sán* is *inaccessibility*. That is, the horse's back is a tower of strength, or fortress. When an Arab, in looking over a horse, exclaims, *Hí-sán!* he would say that he is "a *horse, and no mistake*," or as he sometimes expresses himself, "two horses." Pp. 123 f.n. 1; 232, 238 f.n. 2.

HI-SÁN KA-SÍR A Galloway or pony, p. 258.

HIT . A small town on the west bank of the Euphrates, about 100 miles W.N.W. of Baghdad, pp. 73, 75, 78 f.n. 3, 84.

[AL] HI-TAIM . Certain inferior hordes of the Arabian peninsula, p. 59 f.n. 2.

HI-ZÁM A man's *girdle*, p. 292 ; a beast's *girth*, and the like. The *part* of the horse *round which the girth passes* is *mah-zim* ; for which they commonly say *hí-zám*. Arab horsemen understand the importance of depth and capacity in this region. So long ago as our sixth century, a desert "makar" described his courser as large-limbed, full-flanked, and great in the girthing-place.

GLOSSARIAL INDEX AND SUPPLEMENT. 353

HU-BÁ-RÁ	An Arabian bustard, the affinities of which are with the cranes in one direction and the plovers in another, p. 152.
[AL] HU-DHAIL	A shepherd nation of Central Arabia, p. 39 f.n. 2.
HU-DÚD . .	An Arab scholar says that *hu-dúd* means pre-eminent. As a term of horse-breeding (pp. 237, 272 f.n. 2), it practically expresses the same idea as *a-síl*, *sa-híh* (genuine), *madh-búh* (firm), and many other words.
HUF-HUF .	The name of the chief settlement in AL HA-SA, pp. 30, 31. [The etymological meaning perhaps is, *encompassed*, as with palms.]
HUJ-JA	[*Convincing evidence.*] A written pedigree of a horse is called by the Arabs a "huj-ja"; of which *v.* an illustration, with remarks, pp. 136 *et* 137.
HULAGU . . Pp. 30 f.n. 1, 277.	[Marco Polo relates how "Alau" (Hulagu) gave up to fire and slaughter "Baudas" (Baghdad with the gutturals slurred, Mongol-fashion), "the great city, which used to be the seat of the Calif of all the Saracens in the world, just as Rome is the seat of the Pope of all the Christians." This merciless pillager of Western Asia is now all but forgotten in the Tigris valley, which in the 13th century he overspread with terror.]
HU-MÁT .	[*Protectors.*] The name of a strain in AL KHAM-SA, Table p. 235 col. i.
HUR-TU-MÁN .	A kind of pulse, p. 82 f.n. 1.
HU-SAIN . .	[*The little Ha-san*, or younger brother of Ha-san.] Ali's second son; he who, when marching to Kú-fa, to head a revolt against the Caliph Yazid's government, was intercepted by a force of horsemen, and with all his followers butchered, on the plain of KAR-BA-LÁ, *q. v. infra.* P. 162 f.n. 2.
HÚ-TA . .	A town in Najd, p. 32 f.n. 1.
HU-WAI-TÁT .	These people are met with by travellers in the region of the Dead Sea. They also occupy parts of Egypt. If they can claim a headquarters, perhaps it is in the cultivated lands of the very ancient oasis which was known to the Greek traders as Petra. P. 59 f.n. 2.

I

I'-BÁ-DÁT .	The name of an important subdivis. of the Sba' Aeniza, Table p. 121.
IB-IL	Camels; a collective noun; synonyms, *ba'-ir*, pl. *a-bá-i'r*; *ri-káb*, *q. v. infra*; and other words. P. 57 f.n. 5.
IBN .	[*Building*, or *raising up*, sc. by the father or ancestor.] A son; son's son; and remoter descendants. The fem. forms are *ib-na*, *ab-na*, et *bint*, a daughter. In many shapes the word is familiar in Europe : *e.g.*, *Ben*, as Benjamin, prob. *son of right hand*; *Bin*, or *Ibn*, as Ibnu 'r Ra-shíd; and BA-NÚ, or *Be-ni*, as B. Is-rá-il. Pp. 34 f.n. 1, 107 f.n 3.

2 Y

IBNU Á-WÍ	[*Son of a howler.*] The jackal, p. 34 f.n. 1.
IBNU 'L WA-TAD	As an illustration of Bedouin names, p. 107 f.n. 3.
IB-RÁ-HÍM	Abraham, pp. 100 f.n. 1, 101. V. Abraham in Index ii.
——— SHEKH	The late, Arab horse-dealer, of Calcutta, p. 307.
I'DHÁR	The part of the Arab riding-halter which lies upon the animal's *cheek*. Illustration on p. 140.
IF-RI-JA	The name of a subdivis. of the Aeniza, Table p. 121.
IH-SA-NA	A section of the Wald A'li Aeniza, Table p. 121.
IH-SI-NI	The name of a horde of the Aeniza, Table p. 121.
IJ-LÁL	*Ut supra.*
IJ-LÁS	The name of one of the great confederations into which the Aeniza nation is divided, Table p. 121.
[AL] I-KHAI-DHÁR	A generic name for pastures, p. 105.
IKH-RI-SA	[*Dumb.*] The name of a horde of the Fid-A'n Aeniza, Table p. 121, 122 *et* f.n. 5.
I'K-RISH	[*Pungency.*] The name of a grass, p. 82 f.n. 2.
I-MÁM	The simplest meaning of this word is, a *model*. Al Kur-án six times uses it. In S. ii. it is said of Abraham, *Truly I am making thee an I-mám for men.* In two texts, the same word denotes an inanimate tablet. Accordingly, the title I-mám, as borne by a Muslim ruler, signifies that he is, before all things, an *exemplar*, as well as an establisher, of the Faith. Among the developments of this theory there are two which have important political bearings—viz., the people must determine whether the head of the State is "orthodox";[1] and a principality which is thus compacted like a sect or a congregation, the more it expands, grows the weaker through dissensions. Not to dwell on these aspects, the "I-mám" is he who, when two or three of the Muslim pray together, posts himself in front of the others. Leaders of public devotion (" I-máms "), as well as lecturers, or preachers (" kha-tíbs "), may be appointed by authority—*e.g.*, by the Sultán of Turkey; but such officials do not perform religious acts on behalf of others. The one great sacrifice of the Muslim is that in which a camel, a cow, a sheep, or a goat is annually presented, in commemoration of Abraham's willingness to offer up his son. The leading idea in this ceremony is that of a thank-offering, and a benevolence to the poor.[2] The Arabs do not read into it any mystical meaning; as an act of religion it partakes of the general simplicity of desert life. This is noticed here because confusion follows when terms like *I-mám* and *Muj-ta-hid* are rendered, as they very often are, by *Priest* and *High Priest*. No doubt the Persian *Muj-ta-hids*,[3] the Turkish
Pp. 39 f.n. 2, 252.	

---

[1] A "saying" of the Prophet is, *Obey your rulers up to the point (or the *hadd*) that they obey Allah.*

[2] The same remark applies to the a'-*kí*-*ka*, or slaughtered kid, with which the Muslim, following the example of the Prophet's wife Khá-dí-ja, do honour to every birth in the family. For a boy two kids, and for a girl one, are thus devoted.

[3] Under the present dynasty of Persia, the Mujtahids, or theological doctors of the highest degree of learning, have more and more felt the weight of the secular government. But their position is still that of spiritual Páshas of the most formidable type; and their interference in public affairs is, on the whole, a great source of mischief.

I-MÁM—*continued.*	*U'-lu-má*, or *Knowers* (*i.e.*, of theology), and all the Asiatic army of dervishes, fa-kirs, and mullas, represent orders which may be called "religious." It is equally certain that these privileged persons tremendously impress the uninstructed masses. People who consider "holiness" to be associated with special kinds of learning naturally tend to exalt their "mullas" over the rest of mankind. But if either "Levitical" or "apostolic" succession, or even the simplest process of "ordination," essentially enter into the idea of "clericalism," then is Islamism as remarkable among the higher religions for the non-development of this thought as for the absence of ritual in its worship. Beyond the One God's existence, and His gift of a Prophet and a Kur-án, there is nothing very abstruse in the Arabian theology. Worship is the affair of the individual. With "sacramental" ideas wholly absent, there is no room for "priestly" services. The fulfiller of the patriarchal law of circumcision is merely the village barber. Any one who can read or recite a few sentences of Al Kur-án is competent to confirm the mutual contract between the bride and the bridegroom.
I'-MÁ-RÁT [Pl. of *I'-má-rá*.]	[Root-ideas, *firmly holding a land, being populous*, and the like.] (1) A *quasi*-Bedouin people of El I'rák, p. 84 f.n. 1. (2) A primary subdivis. of the Aeniza, Table p. 121.
IMRU 'L KAIS. [For IM-RA-U 'L KAIS.]	[Either man (*vir*) of the *tribe* of Kais, or man, in the sense of devotee, of the tribe's tutelary deity, *Kais*.] Translations from his poem, pp. 49, 143. Other references, pp. 50, 56, 97, 136, 144, 145, 243 f.n 2, 260.
IM-SI-KA .	[Root-idea, *seizing*.] The name of a subdivis. of the Sba' Aeniza, Table p. 121.
IM-TAIR .	[From *matr, rain*.] The name of an important Bedouin nation of Central Arabia, pp. 10, 58, 59 f.n. 2.
I'N (*cen*) .	[Pl. of an adjective meaning *large-eyed*, from *a'in, the eye*.] Bovine antelope, p. 145 f.n. 1.
IN SHÁ ALLAH	A favourite expression of the Arabs, and of all the Muslim, p. 38 f.n. 3.
IN-ZI-HI .	The name of a strain in AL KHAM-SA, pp. 235 col. v. *et* 298. [One who lives near us understands from the name *In-zi-hi* that the "Had-bâ" mare from which this strain proceeded belonged to a Badawi who had *quitted his own people*, and become KA-SIR (*q. v.*) among strangers.]
[AL.] I'RÁK	The well-known province on the Tigris, pp. 23, 65, 67, 78-86, 119, 120, 148, 203, 210, 230, 234, 271, 277-285, 298, 312, 315.
I'-SÁ .	The Arabs thus write "*Jesus*," pp. 100 f.n. 1, 106 *et* f.n. 1, 228 f.n. 1.
I'-SÁ *bin* KIR-TÁS .	The late "Esau bin Curtas," Arab horse-dealer of Bussorah, Calcutta, and Bombay, pp. 238, 248 f.n. 1, 270, 307, 308.
I'SHB	Spring grasses, p. 82 f.n. 1.

356   GLOSSARIAL INDEX AND SUPPLEMENT.

[AL] ISHR   The name of a strain in AL KHAM-SA, Table p. 235
                     col. i.
[AL] IS-LÁM .   [The Semitic root *slm*[1] (v. p. 227 f.n. 5) yields, among
                     other forms, the form *is-lâm*, and *is-lâm* means *surrender*,
                     scil., in its religious application, *surrender to the Almighty*: v.
                     as to the distinction between this "surrender" and "fatalism,"
                     p. 130 *et* f.n. 2.] For references to the "Dínu 'l Is-lâm," or
                     monotheistic faith of Arabia, v. Preface, *et* pp. 4 f.n. 1, 101,
                     108, 160 *et* f.n. 1, 161, 163 f.n. 3, 277, 281 *et* f.n. 2.
IS-MÁ-Í'L .   [*El heard*.] The Arabian form of "Ishmael," *q. v.* in
                     Index ii.
IS-RÁ-ÍL . . . .   [*El fought* or *strove*.] "Israel," *q. v.* in Index ii.
ITHL or ETHEL (correctly *Athl*) A tree of the *Tar-fâ*, or Tamarisk order, p. 269.
IZ-MAIL . . . .   [Diminutive of *zi-mâl*, the ass.] The name of a subdivis. of
                     the Sham-mar, p. 122.

J

JA-BAL   A mountain, pp. 39, 178. [The cosmogony given in AL
                     KUR-ÁN is highly pictorial. The earth is of course repre-
                     sented as an immovable expanse, or flattened body, with the
                     vault of heaven for a canopy. The stars are supposed
                     to be the lamps; and the mountains are described as the
                     "*au-tâd*," or tent-pegs, which keep down the margins: v.
                     S. lxxviii.]
JA-BAL SHAM-MAR .   The name of a territory in pen. Arabia, pp. 37-48, 120, 122,
                     210.
JA-BAL SHA-RÁ   The "Mount Seir," and the adjacent parts which are
                     defined in Deut. ii. 1-8, and are referred to in Judges v. 4. *V.*
                     p. 113 f.n. 4. [The plateau of Seir, the highest elevation of
                     which is about 4000 feet, is called by the Arabs *Ar-dhu 's saw-
                     wân*, or *flint-land*. It overlooks the Dead Sea and Wâ-diu 'l
                     A'raba, and in some respects forms a barrier between Syria
                     and Arabia.]
JA-BAL TÚR .   The mountains which form the chief feature of the "Sina-
                     itic peninsula," p. 25. [The mountain from whose top, ac-
                     cording to an account which is embodied in both the Hebrew
                     and the Arabian Scriptures, the Deity entered into special
                     relations with mankind, no more admits of identification than
                     the site of the Garden of Eden does. The Jewish nation,
                     never knew where "Tor Sina" was. The Arabs have taken

---

[1] The radical idea in *slm* is *peace, security, salvation*; such as those enjoy who escape from evil through the fulfilment of an obligation. Practically, the word *Is-lâm* signifies, *the conforming with the essentials ("er-kân") of God's law; and the undertaking to do, or say, as the Prophet has done or said*. The Muslim's salutation to his brother Muslim is, "*As sa-lâm-u a'-lai-kum*, or *The Peace* (*i.e.*, God's Peace, the peace of *believers*) *be on you*. And the answer is, "*A'-lai-kum-u 's sa-lâm*," *On you be the peace*: with perhaps the addition of "*wa rah-ma-tu 'l'lâ-hi wa ba-ra-ki-tu-hu*" *wand the mercy of God and His blessings*.

GLOSSARIAL INDEX AND SUPPLEMENT.   357

	"*Túr*" from the Aramaic, in which language it means *mountain*.]
JA-BAL TU-WAIK P. 178.	The name of a mountain-range, running almost due south, which is described by Palgrave as "the backbone" of the Arab peninsula. According to the same traveller, it forms "a broad limestone table-land, at no point exceeding, so far as has been roughly estimated, the limit of 5000 feet in height, covering an extent of 100 and more miles in width; its upper ledges clothed with excellent pasturage, its narrow valleys sheltering in their shade rich gardens and plantations, usually irrigated from wells, but occasionally traversed for some short distance by running streams."[1] (*Op. cit.* in Catalog. No. 7, vol. ii. p. 239.) [*Tu-waik* is a *diminutive* from *tauk*, which means, *anything that surrounds another thing*, e.g., *a yoke*.]
JAB-RÁ-IL. [*et* JAB-KIL.]	The Biblical "Gabriel," p. 4 *et* f.n. 2.
JA-DÁ-IL. . . .	Synonym of *ga-sd-ib*, q. v. P. 29 f.n. 2.
JA-GHA-JAGH .	An eastern arm of the Khá-búr, in N.W. AL JA-ZÍ-RA, pp. 74, 124. The "Gozan" of 1 Chron. v. 26 is the Ja-gha-jagh. The Greeks knew the same stream as the "Hirmás." It is often described as the "rivulet of Ni-si-bis" (the modern hamlet of Na-si-bin). In writing the name as we do, we follow the pronunciation of the natives; but others make it *Jagh-ja-gha*. The form "*Jerujar*" which Layard uses is merely an approximation. In one of Kiepert's maps the word is spelt *Djakhdjakha*; and in another, *Dschachdschacha*. Four consonants and three vowel marks suffice in Arabic.
JAIS, for KAIS .	The name of a horde in N.W. AL JA-ZÍ-RA, p. 75.
JAI-SI, for KAI-SI	The name of a strain in AL KHAM-SA, Table p. 235 col. i.
JA-LÁL-ÁBÁD .	The historic Afghan town, midway between Peshawar and Cábul, p. 274.
JA-LAM .	[Another name for the *tais*, or he-goat.] A strain in AL KHAM-SA, Table p. 235 col. iii.
JA-MAL	The Camel, *sub quo v.* Index ii. *Sed v.* NOTE ON TRANSCRIPTION, in prefixes of the volume, p. ix f.n. 1; *et* text, pp. 55 f.n. 1, 57 f.n. 1.
JAM-BÁZ .	A horse-dealer, p. 123 in f.n. 1. *V.* HORSE-DEALER in Index ii.
JAM-BI-YA	The *skean*,[2] or "slaughtering steel" of the Arabs, p. 46 f.n. 1.
JÁ-MI'	The place of congregational worship among the Sunnite Muslim, p. 163 f.n. 2.
JA-RÁD .	[*Stripper*.] The locust, pp. 12-14. A good illustration of

---

[1] The flora of the range is thus touched on by the same writer: "Except the date-palm, the *ithil* or *athel*, the *markh*, a large-leaved spreading tree, the wood of which is too brittle for constructive purposes, and some varieties of acacia, the plateau produces no trees of considerable size; but of aromatic herbs and bright flowers, among which the red anemone, or *shakark*, is conspicuous, this region is wonderfully productive, so much so that Arabic writers justly praise the sweet scent, no less than the purity and conduces of its breezes."

[2] In Arabic a knife is "*sik-kin*."

JA-RĀD—*continued*.	the flexibility of the Arabic language is afforded by the way in which word after word, each containing the idea of *denuding*, is formed from the same root as *ja-rād*. E.g., *ja-rīd*, originally a palm-branch with its leaves stripped off—the "Djerid" of Moorish ballad poetry—p. 150. Other derivatives severally mean the *bare* parts of the body, like the face; one who is *stripped*, in the sense of being reduced to poverty or to solitude; and, to name no more, a portion selected or *severed* from a larger set or body, whether as a detachment of Horse, or a pamphlet or newspaper.
[AL] JAR-BĀ.	The name of a great clan of the Sham-mar, p. 125.
JAR-JAR.	[Probably a word taken from a sound.] One meaning of *jar-jar* is, the bray which the camel *reiterates* in the windpipe; akin to which sense is that of *chewing the cud*. The spiked cylinder with which they break up the sheaves of corn is also called a *jar-jar*, p. 80. In Isaiah xli. 15, *mô-rag* (equally in Hebrew and Arabic a *roller*) is used for *jar-jar*.
JAT, for KAT.	Lucerne, p. 31. Towards the Persian Gulf this crop grows luxuriantly, but it seems to find Baghdad less congenial. In Persia, "jat" is called *yun-ja*.
[AL] JAUF	[A *cavity*.] Topographically, any depressed tract of country, especially one of *basin* form. Arabia contains many surfaces of this description. P. 37.
JAU-HA-RA	The name of a strain in AL KHAM-SA, Table p. 235 col. i.
[AL] JA-ZĀ-IR.	The name of a people on the Lower Euphrates, p. 84 f.n. 1.
[AL] JA-ZI-RA.	The country east of the middle part of the Euphrates, pp. 63, 64, 65, 70-77, 78, 79, 103, 125, 218, 236, 269-276, 295.
JENGHIS KAAN [In Chinese, "*Ching-sze*," or *perfect warrior*]. P. 89 f.n. 1.	This son of a minor Mongolian prince died (1227) the master of an empire which stretched far into Northern China. He also created, through his warlike descendants, Mongol, Mogul, or *Mughal* dynasties all over Asia. An incredibly large sum of human misery must be written down to Jenghis. One of his armies is said to have massacred in one week, at Hi-rât, more than a million and a half. The formidable offshoot from his house, HULAGU, in the seven days following his seizure of Baghdad (15th February 1263), permitted 800,000 to be butchered. But if we except the presence of the Turks on the Bosphorus, and the existence, in Southern India, of the Nizam's Hyderabad—founded (1712) by Ching Kulich Khan, better known as Nizāmu 'l Mulk, Ā-saf Jāh— the vestiges which maps now retain of the terrible empire of the Mongols are inconsiderable.
JIB-HA, for JAB-HA.	In a horse, the part that is below the ears and above the eyes, p. 298.
JI-DA-N'.	[The root-idea is *maiming*.] The name of a subdivis. of the Aeniza, Table p. 121.
JID-RĀ-NĪ	The name of a strain in AL KHAM-SA, which is called after a certain *jid-rān*. This is the fancy lineage of the horse-

JID-RÁ-NI—*continued*.	breeders of the Euphrates. It is said to be extinct, except in offshoots transplanted to Europe and Egypt by royal personages. But, judging from the statements of the dealers, every other horse in whose strings is a "*Sak-lá-wī Jid-rá-nī*," this must be an error. The name has even become proverbial. The donkey-boys of Baghdad and Hilla, when one of their steeds is seized with a fit of galloping, dub him on the spot a "Sak-lá-wi Jid-rá-ni"! Even so should every reader, before assigning too much value to these desert stud terms, wait till the bearer of it shall have given proof of superiority. Table p. 235 col. ii.
JIF-LÍ	The name of a strain in AL KHAM-SA, Table p. 235 col. iv.
JIL . .	Straw, p. 80 f.n. 3.
JIL-FÁN .	The name of a strain of the stock of KU-HAI-LÁN, Table p. 235 col. vi.
JI-MAI-SILÁT	[*Shorten* or *shorn*.] The name of a subdivis. of the Aeniza, Table p. 121.
JI-NÁ-HU 'T TAIR .	[*Wing of the bird*.] The name of a strain in AL KHAM-SA, Table p. 235 col. i.
JINN *et* JÁN [*Inglice*, genii] . Pp. 136 f.n. 1, 238.	This generic name is connected with several words in other Semitic dialects, but the root-sense is obscure. The more educated of the Arabs are beginning to fight shy of demonology; but the JINN stand on the firm basis of Al Kur-án. According to one view, the Order includes all incorporeal beings, from THE DEVIL, *par excellence*, or "Satan" (*Shai-tán*), down to the puniest elf. Others assign three divisions to the unseen kingdom: the good, or angelic; the intermediary—*i.e.*, the JINN; and the absolutely wicked, whose leader is IB-LÍS.[1] A curious belief exists in El I'rák, that the wolves hunt down the Jinn and eat them!
JIR-BÍ-Á .	The name of a strain in AL KHAM-SA, Table p. 235 col. ii.
JU-BÚR	The name of a people of El I'rák, p. 84 f.n. 1.
JU-NÚ B . . [Pl. of *jmb*.]	[*Sides*.] (1) The skirts of a country, p. 33; (2) the flanks, or *barrel*, of a horse. [Not to be confounded with *ja-núb*, the S. wind, from the same root.]

K

KA'B [commonly pronounced Cha'b]. P. 85.	A people of El I'rák. They now overspread Khûz-istán (*q. v.*) in Persia; and their camps and villages are distributed on both banks of the Ká-rún river, from Ahwáz to the SHATTU 'L A'RAB. Change of water and air, and intermixture with other nations, have altered them in manners, religion, costume,

---

[1] In the Kur-án *Shai-tán* and *Ib-lís* (*Iblees*) are interchangeable terms. The former is said by European scholars to be one of the few words in the Kur-án which are of Christian origin. It is held to have been acquired by Arabs from the Abyssinian, although introduced before Muhammad's time.

KA'B—*continued.*

and character. They are now more Persian than Arab. Their country is much interspersed with arid desert, but where there is water they are cultivators. Fa-lá-hí-ya is their principal settlement. Their Shekh lives at Fai-li-ya, on the Shattu 'l Arab, a few miles above Mu-ham-ma-ra, in a well-built chateau. He also possesses a castle on the opposite, or Ottoman, bank of the river. In this way he is enabled to be "not at home" to the officials of either Government. As a third refuge, he keeps an armed iron steamer on the surface of the river. Old-fashioned territorial people of his class obstruct the path of centralisation. Rights which they regard as their ancestral property are apt to be sold at Teherán to the agents of European Companies, or perhaps given away as "concessions." The "Shekh of Muhammara" lives in a constant state of apprehension lest he should be seized by a Persian Governor or Commander, and forwarded as a little present to his not too much loved master the Sháh.

KA'-BA .
Pp. 38, 115 *et* f.ns. 1 and 2, 128, 143 f.n. 6.

In the first instance this is a name given to bones having certain characters, and to bones used as dice. *Specially,* the "KA'-BA" or "*Ka'-batu 'l bait*," is the great building which stands towards the middle of the precincts known as the "MAS-JIDU 'L HA-RÁM" of Mecca. The KA'-BA was last rebuilt in A.D. 1627. It resembles a colossal astragalus of about 40 ft. The "black stone" which the pilgrims kiss is let into the wall, inside, about 4 ft. above the ground. This stone exhibits the traces of having at least once felt the spoiler's fury; but its pieces have been cemented together, and a rim or frame of silver encircles the stone.[1] The relic is the sole survivor of the 360 fetishes which were lodged in the same spot, before the Arab Prophet did for the Ka'-ba of Mecca what Joshua did for Jeroboam's chapel at Bethel—2 Kings xxiii. 15.

KA-BAR . . . . . The name of a plant, p. 81 *et* f.n. 4.
KABR [in Hebrew, *kebûrah*] . [*Burying.*] A grave or sepulchre, pp. 110 f.n. 1, 152 *et* f.n. 1.
KABRU 'L KHAI-YÁL MAF-TÚH The saying of the Arabs, p. 152 *et* f.n. 1.
KÁ-DHI [in Eur. books, *Cadi ;* and in Anglo-Indian, *Kazee*]. The Caliph's chief justiciary officer under El Is-lám's earlier organisation, pp. 43 f.n. 3, 230 f.n. 1. [The Ká-dhi deals executively with *cases*, and the Muf-ti with abstract references.]

KÁ-DHI-MAIN . [For MAK-BA-RA-TU 'L KÁ-DHI-MAIN, or burial-place of the two Ká-dhims.] The name of a town near Baghdad which the Persians, and all Shi-ites, greatly venerate, p. 312.

---

[1] Compare the following record, in Dr Johnson's Journal of his Tour in the Hebrides : "The place is said to be known " (in the convent churches of Icolmkill) "where the black stones lie concealed on which the old Highland chiefs, when they made contracts and alliances, used to take the oath which was considered as more sacred than any other obligation, and which could not be violated without the blackest infamy. . . . They would not have recourse to the black stones upon small or common occasions ; and when they had established their faith by this tremendous sanction, inconstancy and treachery were no longer feared."

[AL.] KÁ-DIR .   [*The Powerful One.*] An attribute, used as name, of Allah, pp. 106, 107 *et* f.n. 1.

KA-DISH . .
[Pl. KU-DUSH.]
[*Working for a livelihood;* but it is doubtful if the root be classical Arabic.] The name which the Bedouin bestow on all horses of which they cannot tell the pedigrees, pp. 22, 47 *et* f.n. 3, 249, 250 *et* f.n. 1, 259, 260, 263.

KAF-FI-YA *et* CHAF-FI-YA
[For KU-FI-YA.]
Ku-fi-ya is a loan-word in Arabic. It is the Italian *cuffia*, the Spanish *cofia*, and our *coif*. The Arabs apply it to any kerchief [in Turkish, *char-chaf*], but chiefly to the shawl-like covering which, with a rope (*'kâl*) twisted round it, forms their head-dress, p. 108. [The *kaf-fi-ya* covers the poll, shades the eyes, and falls over the neck and shoulders. But, like most picturesque objects, it is untidy.]

KÁ-FI-LA .
The train of travellers [perhaps but half a dozen, perhaps a host] which the Persians call a *kâr-vân* [our "caravan"] is termed by the Arabs a *ká-fi-la*, p. 311.

KÁ-FIR
P. 6.
The simplest meaning of this word is, *one who covers up* an object. This is the sense in which, in S. lvii. of Al. KUR-ÁN, it is applied to *cultivators*—*i.e.*, those who *bury the seed in the ground*. In EL ISLÁM, a "Ká-fir" is one who disallows, rejects, denies, Muhammad's mission and message. Logically, nobody who professedly does so should object to pass by this description; but practically, "Ká-fir" is used, like "infidel," offensively. Among the Muslim it is before all things necessary to be a believer. Just as in Israel David's misdeeds did not weigh very heavily against him; so, in Arabia, the due discharge of religious obligations condones mere offences against men.

Ká-fir is too technical a word for the primitive Bedouin. In place of it they use *a'dû*, or *enemy*—*i.e.*, *enemy of Allah*. The thought that any one exists who is in so monstrous a condition shocks them. And seeing that Allah does not slay his enemies, some of them are apt to do so for him.

It is only natural that the Muslim Afghans should assign the name " Káfir-istán " to the " unconverted " tracts on their borders. But the use of " Kaffre," or " Cafire," first by the Portuguese, then by the Dutch, and now by ourselves, to designate numerous tribes of Africa, is a curious instance of the extension of language.

KAH .
KAH-TÁN .
V. p. 80 f.n. 3.

(1) The Arabian form (as is supposed) of the " Joktan " of Gen. x., p. 98. (2) The name of a Bed. nation of Central Arabia, pp. 59 f.n. 2, 62, 94, 100, 122, 291.

KAH-WA .
The decoction which we call *coffee*, p. 110 f.n. 2. The coffee-house, whether covered or al fresco, is also called *kah-wi*, pl. *ka-há-wi*. What the public-houses are in Europe, the ka-há-wi are in the towns of the Arabs. Homes of the humbler order are so tightly packed with inmates, that their

	masters, when they get up in the morning, hasten to quit them for the coffee-houses.
KAID	The iron shackles with which the Arabs secure their horses. p. 243 f.n. 1.
KAI-DÁK . . . [Biblical "Kedar."]	The Arabs thus pronounce the name of Abraham's second son, pp. 49 f.n. 3, 118.
KAIDII . .	Summer, p. 50 f.n. 2.
KAI-LÚ-LA . .	The Arab's word for his mid-day nap, p. 81 *et* f.n. 1.
KÁ-IM MA-KÁM	A minor official of the Osmanli, p. 207 f.n. 1.
KAIS .	*V.* in art. IM-RA-U 'L KAIS, *supra*.
KÁ-KÁ .	The name of a strain in AL KHAM-SA, Table p. 235 col. i. *Et v.* p. 281 f.n. 2.
KAL-A' SHER-GÁT[1]	A series of grass-covered mounds extending for about two miles along the W. bank of the Tigris, some 55 miles S. of the site of Nineveh. The principal mound rises in some places nearly 100 feet. Dr Budge, of the British Museum, informs us that these remains are as old as B.C. 1820; that cuneiform inscriptions of the time of the Assyrian King Tiglath Pileser I. (B.C. 1130) have been found in them; that they represent the "city of Assur" (Ellasar of Gen. X. 11); and that, in all probability, long before the date (1820 B.C.) of Assyria's becoming an independent kingdom, the Akkadians and Babylonians had a fortress there, the name of which resembled that now given to these ruins by the Arabs.
	V. at p. 72 a reference to a futile attempt which a late Governor-General of Baghdad made to restore Kal-a' Sher-gát, by bribing a section of the Sham-mar to settle near it and cultivate; so that the Mosul trade might again, as of old, pass along the right bank of the river, instead of making, as now, a great detour by Ar-bil and Kar-kúk.
KA-MA-RI	Hindûstáni name for the disease called *paraplegia* in horses, p. 314 *et* f.n. 1.
KA-MIS .	The long cotton shirt which, worn under the cloak or *a'bá*, forms the dress of the primitive Arabs, pp. 108 f.n. 2, 140.
KA-RÁ-MI-TA . [Pl. of Kar-mat.]	The followers of Ham-dán, *ibnu* 'l Ash-a'th (*c.* 887 A.D.) [Ham-dán, from a disfigurement of the face, was called, in the local Aramaic dialect, *Kar-má-ta*; which the Arabs made into *Kar-mat*. *V.* a reference to the "Carmathians," p. 30 f.n. 1.]
KAR-BA-LÁ . . . Pp. 83, 132, 162, 294, 319.	Also called MASH-HAD HU-SAIN, or *place where Hu-sain was martyred.* The plain of Kar-ba-lá is about 60 miles S.W. of Baghdad. The town which has here grown up, though of modest size, is one of the most flourishing in the

---

[1] This spelling proceeds upon the assumption that *Kal-a' Sher-gát* is a name of the semitic period. If so, it may equally signify, *Fort of the eastern parts,* or fort which marked the Babylonian limits; and *fort commanding the middle* (or perhaps the *bifurcation*) *of the road.* It is, however, possible that either or both parts of the compound name in question may represent some still more ancient proper name, such as the Kal-hu or "Calah" of Gen. x. 11.

GLOSSARIAL INDEX AND SUPPLEMENT.   363

KAR-BY-LÁ—*continued.*   Turkish empire. A'li's own tomb is at Na-jaf, about 50 miles further south. Pilgrims from all parts of Islám annually assemble in Kar-ba-lá and Na-jaf, to recall to mind and bewail the scenes there enacted in the month *Mu-har-ram*, A.H. 61. [*V. supra*, in art. HU-SAIN.]

KARD   The name of the apparatus with which, in El I'rák, they draw up water, p. 47 f.n. 3.

KAR-KHA.   A river of S.-Western Persia, p. 5 f.n. 1.

KAR-KÚK   A town of the Kurds, about 140 miles N. of Baghdad, pp. 84 f.n. 1, 159 f.n. 5, 261, 280, 300.

[AL] KAR-RÁR   An epithet of A'li, p. 239 f.n. 3.

KÁ-SIB   The name of a hound, p. 145.

KA-SÍM   [According to the old philologists, *sandy ground producing gha-dhá bushes.*] A part of Najd, pp. 32 f.n. 1, 39, 258.

KA-SÍR   [Vulg. "*Ga-sir.*"]   Said of a body of the Bedouin who have joined themselves to another than their own people, p. 83 f.n. 1. [*Ka-sír* may mean one whose steps are *shortened*, as if by fetters; and an Arab says that it is in this sense that the word is applied to those who dwell with strangers. In all countries it is difficult to attain the perfect mean between neglecting a guest and *hampering* him. The Persian says, *Á-ma-dan, ba i-rá-da; raf-tan, ba i-já-za*—i.e., *To come, is at thy pleasure; to depart, depends on thy host's permission.* Theodore of Abyssinia, it will be remembered, literally shackled his English visitors to prevent their abrupt departure.]

[AL.] KAS-WÁ .   [*Slit-eared.*] The name of one of the Prophet's riding-camels, p. 230.

KA-TA-BÁN   A people of ancient Yemen, p. 97 f.n. 3.

KA-TÍF   An ancient Arabian town on the Persian Gulf, p. 20. [Ka-tíf, U'kair, and Ku-wait are the principal outlets for the products of Central Arabia.]

KAU-KAB.   *Kau-kab* means a star; and TALL KAU-KAB, or MOUNT KAU-KAB, is the name of a solitary volcanic projection, about 300 ft. high, which rises abruptly from the plain, in N.W. Al Ja-zi-ra. P. 73.

KA-WÁ-I'D   At p. 115 f.n. 3, see this word considered in connection with the Arabian tradition that Abraham founded the KA'-BA of Mecca.

KAW-WÁ-LÍ   The name of a strain in AL KHAM-SA, Table p. 235 col. i.

KHÁ-BÚR.   A river of N.W. AL JA-ZI-RA, pp. 72 f.n. 1, 74, 75, 82, 124, 244. The Greek geographers noted the Khá-búr as the "Habor" *et* "Chaboras." Rising in the fountains of RÁSU 'L A'IN (*q. v.*), it enters the Euphrates near Kar-ki-si-yá (Circesium). The name Khá-búr is traceable for at least thirty centuries. The Tigris also owns a tributary of the same name.

KHA-DÍ-JA   The name of the Prophet Muhammad's first wife, in whose lifetime he married no other, p. 17. [Said to mean, (1) *one prematurely born*; (2) small or delicate.]

[Al.] KHAI-BAR p. 101.	An important palm oasis in the debatable land between Al Hi-jáz and Najd. Before Is-lám, its mountain-sides and dark-green valleys formed Jewish townships. At the present time its principal inhabitants are Osmanli soldiers, and the black or bronzed cultivators of African race who represent the absent Bedouin soil-owners. The Aeniza nation hold inalienable land-rights in the old Jew country, which probably ranked among their earliest lordships over settled parts. Every year, in the date harvest, they gather round it, to reckon with their village partners. Even those divisions of them which have passed far away have left their traces in the nomenclature of its localities. In settlements on the Euphrates, it is only the townsman's mare that we find owned in part by a nomad. But in the seven Khai-bar valleys, every palm-stem, and even the houses of the villagers, more or less belong to the Bedouin. In the economy of the Arabs, it is more general for the open country to command the towns than for the towns to protect the open country. The village is considered to belong to some tribe of the surrounding wilderness. The men of the cloak and spear are its "*khu-fa-rá*," or protectors; and it is exclusively under their escort that caravans approach it and set out from it.
KHAIL . . . . . . Arabic motto on title-page, pp. 57 f.n. 5, 264 f.n. 1.	Horses collectively, as in a stud or a squadron. [According to certain Arab scholars, the word implies the idea of *pride*; and the generous elation with which the well-bred and healthy horse carries himself is a characteristic feature. A forgotten versifier thus describes a cavalry march in one of Cæsar's triumphs:—
	"And their chargers stepped as if they felt that they were Romans too."]
	A horseman is *khai-yíl*, p. 152 f.n. 1.
[Al.] KHA-LÁ .	A name for the desert, p. 18.
KHA-LÍL . .	A friend. Al. KUR-ÁN says, in S. iv. 124, *And Allah took Abraham for His friend*. Hence the Patriarch's title of "KHALÍLU 'LLAH," p. 101, *et v.* p. 109 f.n. 3.
KHAMR .	*Fermented liquor*, and generally, every description of "strong water," pp. 52-55.
KHÁM-SÍ .	The name of a strain in Al. KHAM-SA, Table p. 235 col. i.
KHA-RISH	*Ut supra*, col. iii.
KHARK . . . [Vulg. "Kharj."]	[*Place where the wind blows*.] The principal town of Ya-má-ma, in Najd, pp. 32 f.n. 1, 42.
KHASHM .	The nose. As a term of topography, p. 75 f.n. 1.
KHATN . .	Circumcising, pp. 112-114 *et* f.ns.
KHÁ-TÚ-NÍ-YA.	The name of a small lake between Sinjár and the Euphrates, p. 74. A hamlet has grown up beside it. Many houses stand on a promontory which stretches athwart the water. When we visited the spot in 1887, the people showed the usual signs of friendship, but they had no chopped straw or barley,

KHÁ-TÚ-NI-YA —continued.	Their lake was covered with wild-fowl, which they declared that they were without the means of shooting or snaring. Its fish were said to have poisoned themselves with putrid locusts.
[Al.] KHA-WÁ-RIJ P. 30 f.n. 1.	[*The goers out from*, or *against*.] In order to understand the distinctive position of the "Kharijites," both in the Prophet's lifetime and afterwards under the U-may-yad Caliphs, it is essential to remember that El Is-lám, in its first conception, was a theocracy. One of Muhammad's Companions said, *There never was a Prophetic dispensation which was not succeeded by a kingdom of force*. The truth of this was soon illustrated in the case of Islamism. Almost from the first start, reasons of State were allowed to outweigh loftier aims and motives. The tide of worldliness rose higher and higher; enthusiasm gave place to "orthodoxy"; the great spiritual movement resulted in the setting up of a secular Arab empire. The Kharijites obstinately resisted this process. They formed one of many other unbending militant sects, which, for the sake of abstract principles, threatened to involve El Islám in anarchy. When they were put down in Asia, they broke new ground in Africa.
[Al.] KHA-ZÁ-'I'L	A people of El I'rák, p. 84 f.n. 1.
KHIRR	The back-flow from a river into a natural channel, pp. 81, 82. [The name is probably imitative, like "*whir*," from the *susurrus*, or murmur of the water. In the same way, both murmur (*mar-mar*) and *susurrus* (*sar-sar*) may perhaps claim to be of native growth in Arabic. Several kinds of vociferous creatures, both birds and insects, are called by the Arabs *sar-sar*. The name *búm* for the owl—in Hindústáni, *ul-lú*—is common to them and to the Persians.]
KHIR-SÁN	[*Dumb.*] The name of a strain of the stock of KU-HAI-LÁN, Table p. 235 col. vi.
KHU-MAI-VIS	[From *kham-sa*, five.] A proper name of the Arabs. The name of a strain of the stock of KU-HAI-LÁN, Table p. 235 col. vi.
KHURJ-ÍN	A pair of saddle-bags. Reference, with illustration, p. 148. [A Persian word which the Arabs claim, and write *khur-jain*.]
[Al.] KHURS	[Another form of *khir-sán*.] The name of a strain in AL KHAM-SA, Table p. 235 col. i.
KHÚZ-ISTÁN [The Biblical Elam and the classical Susiana.] P. 79.	The seaboard province of Western Persia, the port of which is MU-HAM-MA-RA. Evidently the name is a later form of KHÚZ, a geographical term of the Sasanian (corresponding with the early Christian) period of Persian history. Some identify the word *Khúz* with "Uwaja," which occurs in the Persian cuneiform inscriptions, and perhaps means *Aborigines*. If such be the history of the name, the prevailing feature of the modern province of "Khúz-istán" agrees

KHÚZ-ISTÁN—*continued*.	with it. For, while its southern and champaign division is overspread by alien immigrants (*v.* art. KA'B), the mountain-ranges which traverse its northern part shelter a nation (*v.* art. BAKHT-I-Á-RÍ) pre-eminently aboriginal. The former tract is now loosely called "A'rabistán," or *place of Arabs*; and there is a growing tendency to bring the Bakht-i-á-ri territory also under the same official designation.
KI-ÁD	[*Easy to lead*.] The name of a sub-strain in the stock of KU-HAI-LÁN, Table p. 235 col. vi.
KID-DÁ-MI-YA.	[From *kud-dám, in front*.] A kind of dagger, p. 46 *et* f.n. 1.
KIF-RÍ	The name of a small town which the Turks call SA-LÁ-HI-YA, N.E. of Baghdad, on the post-road to Mosul, p. 84 f.n. 1.
KIN-DA	The name of an ancient Arabian monarchy, p. 50. [Before the Prophet's birth Kin-da had lost its hold on Eastern and Central Arabia, and contracted to its original seat in HADH-RA-MAUT.]
KIN-VÁN.	[*Clusters of dates*.] The name of a strain in AL KHAM-SA, Table p. 235 col. i.
KIR-MÁN-SHÁH	This is a very well-known division of Western Persia; but a few notes made on the spot itself may be acceptable. One feature of the whole region is, the amenity of the climate. The flag-town, which is of the same name with the province, is 4760 feet above the sea. In winter it receives a great deal of snow, but the summer is temperate. The Kara Sû, or *black water*, which washed the walls of the ancient city, passes within two or three miles of the modern one. Commercial activity constitutes another feature. Wheat and gums are the chief exports; the caravansaries teem with merchants and pilgrims; and the settled population of about 50,000, though rigorously governed, are in no wise oppressed by poverty. Those of them who send produce to London have long desired to connect the Kara Sû with the head streams of the Ká-rûn, so as to obtain a continuous water-way to Mu-ham-ma-ra, in lieu of the present trade-route, which goes by Baghdad, and thence down the Tigris. In this part of Persia, fertile tracts—covered with corn-fields, avenues of trees, summer-houses, and gardens—are intersected by rugged and precipitous, but not very lofty, mountains. Some of our readers may appreciate a slight allusion to an antique custom which prevails in Kirmánsháh. In the same moment that an important traveller alights at his host's threshold, a sheep, or a steer, is slaughtered before him. And when, for example, the proprietor of a village rides up to visit it, or passes it on a journey, the principal inhabitants meet him and perform the same ceremony. This usage is not exactly the same as the hospitable Arab practice of preparing a lamb on the arrival of a stranger; for the meat

KIR-MÁN-SHÁH—*continued.*	is not served to the visitor, but is given in his name to others. The Mullas say that this action is purely an expression of respect—a view which is borne out by the fact that the guest frequently stays the performance of it; just as officials in India "remit," or return, the "offerings" that are made to them. But the inhabitants of Kirmánsháh retain many marks of their Aryan origin. The Persians to this day begin their letters with the formula, *May I be thy sacrifice.* And we shall probably not be mistaken if we regard the Kurdish observance now noticed as a vestige of the very ancient conception that calamities, and even sins, admit of being transferred to others.[1]
KO-CHAR	[Probably from the Tatar word *köch*, to move from place to place.] [The name *Ko-char* (p. 133) indicates the nomadic habit, apart from nationality. For example, Afghánistán contains many groups of different races who move about with their camels, and are known as Kúch-ís.]
KO-DA	The tax which the Osmanli take from sheep-owners, p. 84 f.n. 2.
KU-BAI-SA	[*Plastering*, or *building.*] The name of a small settlement, of about 300 houses, in Shá-mi-ya. Many generations of pedlar life have imparted to its inhabitants a volubility of language which renders a "Ku-bai-si" easily recognisable. P. 294 f.n. 2.
KU-BAI-SHÁN . [Fem. *ku-bai-sha.*]	[From *kabsh*, a ram ; figuratively, a leader.] The name of a strain in the stock of KU-HAI-LÁN, Table p. 235 col. vi.
KU-DHÁ-A'	A noble Bedouin nation, of the stock of Kah-tán, which is often mentioned in the early Arabian poetry, p. 117.
KU-HAI-LÁN . [From KU-HAIL.]	A comprehensive term for all the "thoroughbred" horses of the Arabs. The derivation of the word considered, pp. 233, 234. Table of the stock of KU-HAIL, or KU-HAI-LÁN, p. 235. Other references, pp. 183, 206, 210, 240, 248, 249, 253, 255, 256, 258, 269, 271, 279.
KU-HAI-LA-TU 'L A'JÚZ .	The traditional epithet of the parent mare of all the stock of KU-HAI-LÁN. Pp. 232, 233, 234.
KU-LAIB .	The William Tell of Arabian legendary history, p. 116 *et* f.n. 2.
KU-MAIT .	The dark bay colour, Table p. 262. Other references, pp. 4, 260. [*Ku-mait* is also a very old Arab word for wine.]
KUMIS	The drink of the Mongols, p. 60 *et* f.n. 1.
[AL] KU-RAISH	The best-known name of the branch of Ki-ná-na settled in and about Mecca, of which, in the "Ba-nú Há-shim," or House of Há-shim, the Arab Prophet was born. Pp. 17, 116, 117, 128, 160, 293.
[AL] KUR-ÁN .	The "Message," or "Admonition," which now forms the

---

[1] In old-fashioned Indian households the crones crack their knuckles and make passes with their arms, above the heads of young persons, under the idea of thereby taking upon themselves the misfortunes that are hanging over them.

[AL] KUR-ÁN—*continued*. sacred Book of the Muslim, was described by him who preached it as a "plain Kur-án," S. xxxvi. Much discussion has arisen as to the signification of the word *kur-án*. It comes from *ka-ra-á = legere*; and the accepted meaning of a *reading*, and equally a *recitation*, seems perfectly adequate and satisfactory. This opinion is expressed with due deference to the view on the same point which the eminent Oriental scholar Deutsch proposed in his famous article on "Islám" in the *Quarterly Review* for October 1869, p. 306. According to Deutsch *kur-án* means, not a "reading," but a "cry." His argument is, that the text which begins with "IK-RÁ!"—the imperative of *ka-ra-á*—though placed by the redactors in Sú-ra xcvi, stands first in point of date of the prophetic utterances; that in "*ik-rá*" there "lies hidden" one of those "very few onomatopoetic words" (sc. *cry*, *schrei*, &c.) which are "still common to both Semitic and Indo-European;" and lastly, that "Muhammad distinctly denied being a scholar."[1] Our only reason for noticing this speculation is, that several recent writers have appropriated it. The philological part of it is purely imaginative. The residue breaks down before the simple fact that oral recitation was the primitive Arab's method of reading. The "Ik-rá!" of Gabriel merely means, RECITE ALOUD!

V. as to the *rationale* of AL KUR-ÁN'S "down-sending," or "revelation," p. 4 f.n. 2; and on the point of its *literary* history, a note, under KUR-ÁN, p. xii. of prefixes of this volume.

Translations from AL KUR-ÁN occur at pp. 21 f.n. 1, 50, 54, 109 f.n. 2, 130 f.ns. 2 *et* 3, 134 f.n. 1, 135 f.ns. 3 *et* 4, 158, 139, 160 f.n. 1, 163 f.n. 4, 227.

Other references will be found at p. vii of prefixes of volume, pp. 12 f.n. 3, 17 f.n. 1, 20 f.n. 3, 27, 28, 44, 52, 53, 96 *et* f.n. 1, 101, 102 *et* f.n. 2, 106 f.n. 1, 110 f.n. 2, 111 f.n. 3, 113, 115, 133, 135, 136, 137, 159 f.n. 6, 160, 161, 189, 227 f.n. 5, 230, 281, 299.

KURD The name of an important Asiatic nation, pp. 5, 6 *et* f.n. 1, 16, 70, 133 *et* f.n. 4, 134, 159 *et* f.n. 5, 261, 281 *et* f.ns. 1 and 2, 282 *et* f.n. 2, 283, 284, 312. [In Arab parlance a Kurd, or anything "Curdish," is "Kur-di"; out of which they form the plural "Ak-rád," the Kurds.]

KÚT [officially, *Kátu 'l Imá-ra*, *v*. art. KU-WAIT, *infra*.] An Ottoman station on the east bank of the Tigris, about half-way between Baghdad and Bussorah, in the country of the Ba-nú Lám Arabs, p. 84 f.n. 1.

---

[1] In S. xxix. it is adduced as a miraculous sign that, *before it* (*i.e.*, before AL KUR-ÁN) *thou* [Muhammad] *didst not recite any book; nor didst thou write thy right hand write* (transcribe) *one*. In another Sú-ra [62], it is noticed that the Prophet belonged to the "pagan," or "gentile," section of the Arabs, whose natural condition of course was that of the unlearned. Nevertheless, evidence is wanting to decide the moot-point of whether Muhammad was acquainted with writing. All that can be safely said is, that, so far as is known, he employed some one else when he had anything to write.

KU-WAIT. Pp. 32 f.n. 1, 36, 150, 175, 181, 210, 211, 212, 254, 260, 300.

[A diminutive, formed by the Arabs from the Aryan word *kût*, our cot. *Kût* has spread over the East in the sense of a *fort*, or other substantial building.] The bay, harbour, and Arab town of Ku-wait, at the head of the Persian Gulf, form for all who know them ideal places—because of the salubrity of the air, the briskness of the commerce, the hardihood of the sailors, the success with which ship-building on a small scale is practised, and the remoteness of the Ottoman Government. Ku-wait is also called *Karn* [1]—in European maps written "Grane"—from the bay being *horn*-shaped.

KUW-WA. A town in Najd, p. 32 f.n. 1.

L

LA-BID [One meaning of *la-bid* in Arabic is, a horse's *mikh-lât* or fodder-bag.] The lives of the seven poets of the *Mu-a'l-la-kât* (*q. v.*), extended over upwards of a century. La-bíd was the latest of the series, and the only one who embraced Islamism. He is said to have lived till A.D. 661, or even later.

Translations from his poem, pp. 106 f.n. 2, 145 f.n. 1.

Other references, pp. 49 f.n. 1, 61 f.n. 4.

LIBD The felt which they who do not know how to weave make by beating, or *compacting*, wool into a fabric. The Kurds of both sexes cover themselves in winter with seamless and ungraceful cloaks of this material. Among the Arabs *libd* is a very old name for a saddle, p. 143 *et* f.n. 2. The Persian word for *libd* is *nî-mâd*, *ex quo* the Anglo-Indian form "numdah," meaning the piece of felt which in warm climates they place between the horse's back and the saddle. When saddles can be properly dried, and from time to time re-stuffed, the advantages of the "numdah" [*nam-da*] are doubtful. At all events, it should never be made of dyed material. Even a red or yellow binding will on a warm day discolour the horse's coat. It is better to vandyke the edges of a saddle-cloth, as the Kurds do, than to bind them.

LIB-DI The name of a strain in AL KHAM-SA, Table p. 235 col. iii.

LÔ-BIA [Gr. λοβός.] A species of bean, which in El I'râk bears in autumn. It does not stand up, like its congener the *bâ-kil-lâ*, but covers the surface of the ground with its dark-green leaves and woody branches, p. 82.

LÛ-RI Of or belonging to the Lûr nation, p. 284.

---

[1] In f.n. 2 p. 128, it is said that *the parts of the head where the horns grow* are "karn"; while the people of a particular religion are "karn." But at Bussorah, where this note is added, scholars denote both these words by "karn."

3 A

M

MĀ . . . [Pronounced *mā-i*.] Water, pp. 3, 99 f.n. 4.
MADH-BAH The throat, or throttle, p. 253 *et* f.n. 1.
MA-DHIF . [Post-classical.] The *place in which guests are received*, pp. 104, 295.

MA-DI-NA . . . . [Sound authorities hold that this word is not Arabic, but
For page references *v*. Me- a loan-word from the Aramaic; in which language it means
dina in Index ii. *sphere of authority*, or *province*, and then a city.] The Medina
["*Ma-dî-na-tu'r Ra-sûli 'llah*"] of AL KUR-ĀN [S. xxxiii.]
dates but from the Flight. From that time onward, till the
U-may-yads removed the seat of empire from it to Damascus, it was a place of the first importance. But long before
Is-lâm, the oasis of Yath-rib, about 200 miles north of Mecca,
in which the modern Medina is situated, witnessed events of
no small magnitude; now, unhappily, too much confused by
fable to be intelligible. Enough to notice, that the oasis,
when it comes into the light of history, was held by Jews.

MA'-GIL . . Any halting-ground of camels, where they are hobbled
[For *Ma'-kil*.] with the rope called *al i'-kâl*, p. 17.
MAHD . . . A child's resting-place, or cradle, p. 275 f.n. 1.
MAH-MŪD OF GHAZ-NĪ . The Afghân town of Ghaz-ni, the name of which was
carried a generation ago into our peerage by a British General,
stands associated from a much earlier period (A.D. 1000) with
one of the great figures of Eastern history. Rapid ascents
and rapid falls have always been common in the vast ter-
ritories washed by the Oxus and the Jaxartes. Mah-mûd's
father, Su-bak-ta-gin, the son of a Turk-i slave, was the first
of a new family, by which were founded the illustrious "Ghaz-
navî" dynasty, and the Muslim empire of India. Mah-mûd
nine times invaded India. From the Punjâb to Guzerât he
demolished the idols in the Hindû temples. He collected
at Ghaz-ni the spoils of innumerable cities. But after all
he was essentially a plunderer. The eloquent old woman
who reproved him for taking more countries than he could
govern (p. 43) was perfectly right. The opposite in this
respect of Alexander, he made no attempt to tame the
nations which submitted to him. It is only his kindness to
the poet Fir-dû-si, and to other men of letters, that serves
to mitigate Time's judgment on him.

MAH-RA . A maritime district of Arabia; the climate of which is very
unfavourable to the development of the human family, p. 32.
MAI-MŪN . [*Fortunate*, from the same root as YEMEN.] The name
of Ali's charger, p. 239.

MAI-SĀN . [Said to describe the characteristic walk of the high-bred
Arabian.] The name of a strain in AL KHAM-SA, Table p.
235 col. i.

GLOSSARIAL INDEX AND SUPPLEMENT.

[AL] MAI-SIR . A game of chance of ancient Arabia, p. 54 f.n. 2.
[AL] MAJ-MA'. [*Place of junction.*] The name of a town in Najd, p. 32 f.n. 1. One of the "points" of a horse, p. 145.
MAKH-zí . [*Execrable.*] Applied by the Wahábis to tobacco, p. 164.
[AL] MA-LIKU 'DH DHA-LIL . [*The erring prince.*] A sobriquet of Im-ra-u 'l Kais, p. 50.
MAM-LÚK ["Mameluke."] P. 150 et f.n. 1.
MAN-DA-LI The name of a pastoral town, of about 1500 houses, three days' journey E. by N. of Baghdad, p. 282 f.n. 1. [Vague, though not unrecorded, traditions indicate the probability that if excavations were made at Man-da-li, traces throwing light on the history of Christianity in ancient Persia would be discovered.]
MA'-RA-KA A name for the Bedouin saddle, p. 141. [If *ma'-ra-ka* be derived from *a'rk, sweat*, then the word corresponds with the Persian name for a saddle, *kho-gîr*.]
MAR-BAT . [Lit., *place where a beast is tied*.] Used by the Bedouin, like *rasn* (*q. v.*), for what we call a "strain" of horses, p. 236.
MÁR-DÍN . A historical city, picturesquely seated on a summit of Mount Masius, about 4000 ft. above the sea, in the Di-ár-bakr Pashálik, p. 74.
MÁ-RIB One of the ancient cities of Arabia, to the miraculous destruction of which AL KUR-ÁN alludes in S. xxxiv. P. 97.
MAR-KAZ . *The spot where* the Shekh *strikes his spear in the ground*, to form the centre of the encampment. The word bears many secondary meanings from, in geometry, the centre of a circle, up to the widest extensions.
[AL] MAR-TA'. A general name for desert pasture, p. 105.
MA-SÁ-I'B . [Pl. of *mas-a'b, untamed*.] The name of a subdivis. of the Aeniza, Table p. 121.
MA-SÁ-RI-BA [From *mis-rib, q. v.* p. 107.] The name of a subdivis. of the Sba' Aeniza, Table p. 121 ; p. 271.
MÁSH The name of a vetch, p. 82 f.n. 1.
MÁ SHÁ ALLAH An expression of the Arabs, pp. 38 f.n. 3, 124 f.n. 1.
MA-SHÁ-HÍF [Pl. of *mash-hûf*.] Canoes, p. 84 f.n. 1.
[AL] MA-SIH . The form in which the title "Messiah" is written in AL KUR-ÁN. P. 106 et f.n. 1.
MAS-JID . The Arabic word which in English is written "mosque," and in Spanish "*mezquita*." P. 163 f.n. 2.
MASJIDU 'L HA-RÁM Thus is designated the whole space (an oblong square, 250 paces long and 200 broad) which contains the KA'-BA (*q. v.*) of Mecca, with many other buildings and standing places, p 116.
MA-TÁ-RI-FA [From *mat-raf*, a certain garment having coloured or figured borders.] The name of a subdivis. of the Aeniza, Table p. 121.
MAT-RA-HA [*That upon which one throws himself.*] A name for the Bedouin saddle, p. 141. [In some Bedouin nations they distinguish between the *ma'-ra-ka* and the *mat-ra-ha* ; restrict-

372   GLOSSARIAL INDEX AND SUPPLEMENT.

MA-WÁ-HIB
ing the former name to the saddle proper, and the latter to the cloth or felt which is placed under it.]
[Root-idea, that of *giving*.] The name of a subdivis. of the Sba' Aeniza, Table p. 121.

MA-WÁ-LÍ
[*Defenders, allies*, and so forth.] A horse-breeding people of the country round Aleppo and Há-ma, p. 271.

MÁ-YA
The horse's frog, p. 179.

MA'Z
A nation of Najd, p. 59 f.n. 2.

MECCA.
[For *Mak-ka*.] *V.* Index ii.

MI'-DÁN.
The name of a nation of the Babylonian marsh-land, p. 84 f.n. 1.

MIH-JAN.
Et MISH-A'B: *v.* p. 142.

MIH-MÁZ.
[Root meaning, *kicking*.] The spur, p. 142 (illustration).

MIJ-WAL.
Shekh —— of the Sham-mar, p. 72. [*V. mij-wal* in art. DIR-A', *supra*.]

MIKH-LÁT
The feeding-bag, p. 318 f.n. 3.

MIL-WÁH.
[Large in the *al-wdh, i.e.* any of the *spread-out* bones, especially the shoulder-blades.] The name of a strain of the stock of KU-HAI-LÁN, Table p. 235 col. vi.

MIN-DA-KIH
The name of a strain in AL KHAM-SA, Table p. 235 col. i.

MIN-DAL.
[*Hard steel.*] *Ut supra*, same column.

MI'-NI-KÍ.
The name of the strain in the stock of KU-HAI-LÁN to which the Darley Arabian was reckoned, Table p. 235 col. vi. *et* f.n. to Table; also pp. 213 f.n. 1, *et* 237.

MIR-I'Z
The name, in Sin-jár, of the breed of Angora goats which is there much cultivated, p. 133 *et* f.n. 4.

MIR-KA.
The name of a strain in AL KHAM-SA, Table p. 235 col. i.

MI-SHÁSH
Splint, p. 177 f.n. 1.

MIS-RÁN.
Gut, or *intestine*, use of, by the horse-exporters, to produce a certain blemish, p. 313.

MOKHA
The well-known, but now utterly dwindled, town of Yemen, on the Red Sea coast, p. 20. [Mokha, or "Mocha," never produced coffee. The surrounding country is sterile. The European name of "Mocha coffee" is out of date. It originated in the days when the port of Mocha enjoyed a short-lived prosperity in connection with the coffee trade.]

MOSUL, ...
For page references *v.* Index ii.
In Arabic, *Al Man-sil* means *the place of junction*; and El Ja-zi-ra and El I'rák touch one another near the town of Mosul, on the Upper Tigris, over against the site of Nineveh. [Marco Polo saw Mosul in the 13th century, and with his usual touch of exaggeration described it as "the very great kingdom of Mawsal." He also noted that "all the cloths of gold and silk that are called Mosolins are made in this country"—Marco Polo, Bk. 1. ch. v.] European imports have long ago killed the old manufactures of Mosul. Except for students of antiquity, and in particular for those desirous of investigating ancient Eastern Christianity, the town now offers but few attractions.

MÓTH	The Indian word, p. 47 f.n. 3.
MU-ADH-DHIN	This word is now established in English dictionaries in the form "muezzin." It is one of a series of words in which are á-dhán, a sound, and u-dhun, the ear. In El Is-lám, the Á-dhán is the Call to Prayer; and he whose office it is to raise it, from the Mosque minaret or other elevated station, is the MU-ADH-DHIN, p. 128. [The Á-dhán was never, so far as is known, dictated in precise terms by the Prophet. It accordingly admits of slight variations; but the following is the prevailing formula:—

ALLÁHU ÁK-BÁR[1]! ALLÁHU ÁK-BÁR! ALLÁHU ÁK-BÁR! ALLÁHU ÁK-BÁR!
I DECLARE THAT THERE IS NO OBJECT OF WORSHIP SAVE ALLAH! (*twice*.)
I DECLARE THAT, OF A TRUTH, MUHAMMAD IS THE APOSTLE OF ALLAH! (*twice*.)
HIE[2] TO PRAYER! HIE TO PRAYER!
HIE TO THE MEANS OF THE ATTAINMENT OF PARADISE! (*twice*.)
PRAYER IS BETTER THAN SLEEP![3] PRAYER IS BETTER THAN SLEEP!
ALLÁHU ÁK-BÁR! ALLÁHU ÁK-BÁR!
LÁ I-LÁ-HA IL-LA 'LLÁH![4]

The Jews, we know, used the trumpet for the purpose of calling people together; while the bell and the gong were identified with numerous cults. The Arab Prophet lost nothing from being thus led to prefer the human voice.]

[AL] MU-A'L-LA-KÁT*	THE SEVEN MU-A'L-LA-KÁT are seven recitative poems of the pre-Islamic Arabs. They were committed to writing soon after Muhammad. A little later, some Scott or Ritson —probably Ham-mád of our 8th century—included them in one collection. At least, the view now generally accepted is that, although other pieces existed, the Seven which are contained in the standard collection at a very early period
Translations from (or references to):—	received the preference. The names of the seven poets are Im-ra-u 'l Kais, Ta-ra-fa, Zu-hair, La-bid, A'n-ta-ra, A'nr ibn
IM-RA-U 'L KAIS, pp. 49, 143.	Kul-thúm, and Há-rith *ibn* Hil-li-za. It is impossible for
TA-RA-FA, pp. 57, 234, 255 f.n. 1.	any one who has sojourned in the Arabian desert to read these heirlooms of antiquity without feeling their fascinations.

---

[1] Meaning *Allah is greatest*.

[2] The word rendered "hie" is *hai-ya* in Arabic. It resembles an interjection; but the Arab grammarians explain it as "between a verb and a noun." They include in the same group with it *Á-min*, a word which is used in Muslim much as in Christian prayer. Of course the Arabs hold that *Á-min* is Arabic; and they say that it means *respond*.

[3] It is only in the Á-dhán of early morning that this clause is uttered.

[4] Meaning, *There is no object of worship save Allah*. In this, with the companion clause, *Muhammad* [*is*] *the apostle of Allah*—in Arabic nine words in all—consists the formula by the utterance of which the Muslim declares himself to be such. The remark which these words suggested to Gibbon is too familiar to need quotation.

* In the days when "general belief" was held to render research unnecessary, the title "MU-A'L-LA-KÁT" was interpreted in its most literal sense of *suspended*; to correspond with which the story was fabricated, that these productions were *hung up* by the Arabs on, or in, the KA'-BA at Mecca. But Arabic is not so poor as to afford only one meaning for *mu-a'l-la-ka*. If each poem bore this name from the earliest period, the root-idea may have been that of *preciousness*. If the title only originated when the Seven Pieces were *strung together* by an editor, then the word equally admits of this interpretation.

374 GLOSSARIAL INDEX AND SUPPLEMENT.

Zu-HAIR, pp. 130 f.n. 4, 145 f.n. 1.
LA-BID, pp. 49 f.n. 1, 61 f.n. 4, 106 f.n. 2, 145 f.n. 1.
A'N-TA-RA, pp. 112 f.n. 1, 221.
A'MR, pp. 42, 104 f.n. 1, 117, 130 f.n. 4, 240.

They are far removed from all conventional models. To say that they reflect the desert and its inhabitants, as a lake does the heavens, is inadequate. Their authors made history before they made verses. Warriors and hunters, passionate lovers and knight-errants, seem to speak to us. Picture follows picture, like the movements of the mirage. In one line it is the scud of the wild ass or the ostrich which we see before us; in the next, a train of tent-ladies in their camel-litters.

MUD-DA-I'-YIN.

A spoken form (for *mud-da-ä'na*), which is current in Najd as the title of certain office-bearers, p. 163 *et* f.n. 1.

MUF-TI.
P. 159.

[*Surpassing*, primarily through *youthful vigour*.] Under the Osmanli, an officer, chosen from among the U'-la-má, whose duty it is to issue judgments on such points of faith and law as are officially referred to him.

MU-HAF-FA.
MU-HÁ-FIDH.

A fan, p. 295 f.n. 1.
[From the same root as HÁ-FIZ, *q. v. supra*.] A title of dignity among the Arabs, like our "Lord Keeper," p. 17.

MU-HAJ-JAL.
MU-HAM-MAD.

Explained at p. 264 f.n. 2.
[*One who is highly*, or *repeatedly, praised*.] For the *form* of this name, *v.* NOTE ON METHOD OF TRANSCRIPTION, p. x of prefixes of volume. For its antiquity, *v.* p. 107 f.n. 2.

MUHAMMAD, *ibn* A'BDI 'LLAH.

The Prophet of Arabia. Born *c.* 570. Fled from Mecca to Medina, with only one companion, April 622, which was chosen as the epoch of the Muslim era. Died on Monday, 8th June 632. Pp. 4 *et* f.n. 1, 17 *et* f.n. 1, 20 *et* f.n. 3, 28, 54 *et* f.n. 2, 93 f.n. 1, 96 *et* f.n. 1, 99 f.n. 1, 100 f.n. 1, 101, 102 *et* f.n. 1, 106 f.n. 1, 108, 115 f.ns. 2 and 3, 117, 130, 135 *et* f.ns., 158, 160, 229, 230 *et* f.ns., 299.

MUHAMMAD, *ibn* SU-U'D
MUHAMMAD *ibnu 'r* RA-SHID.

The grandson of Amir Fai-sal of Najd, p. 42.
A-mír of Ja-bal Sham-mar, pp. 40-48, 122, 145 f.n. 1, 211, 237, 251.

MU-HAM-MA-RA.

[*Reduced, v.* p. 260 f.n. 4.] The Persian port on the SHATTU 'L A'RAB. The town does not contain more than about 2000 inhabitants. It is a mile from the river, on the right bank of an artificial canal, or "*hafr*." Pp. 82, 259.

MU-HÁ-WIT.

[*Protector*.] The name of a strain in AL KHAM-SA, Table p. 235 col. i.

MU-HID.
MU-JAL-LI.

[*Nonpareil*.] *Ut supra*.
The name of a strain in the stock of KU-HAI-LÁN, Table p. 235 col. vi.

MU-KHAL-LA-DI-YA.

[*Adorned with bracelets*, or *with little bells*.] The name of a strain in AL KHAM-SA, Table p. 235 col. i.

MU-KHAW-WADH.
[AL] MU-KAI-YAR.

"All four white," p. 264 f.n. 2.
[From *kīr*, bitumen or mineral pitch.] *V.* p. 111 f.n. 2, a reference to the city of "Mugair." [Naphtha, in Arabic *naft*, is still yielded by the soil of Babylonia. It supplies the cement or plaster of aqueducts. The round boat called

GLOSSARIAL INDEX AND SUPPLEMENT. 375

[Al.] MU-KAI-YAR—*continued.*   *kuf-fa*, or "*guf-fa*,"[1] is paid both inside and outside with it, as in the days when Hasisadra dwelt in the city of Surippak, and weathered a seven days' deluge in a vessel thus rendered water-tight.²]

MUL-LA.   [*According to most authorities, a loan-word in Arabic.*] In the Arabian desert, *any one who can read*, pp. 13, 136. Generally, *a scholar*; more specially, (1) a master and expounder of the Kur-ân and Sun-na, and of the body of jurisprudence which is thereon founded; (2) a schoolmaster.

MU-LŮKU 'L KHAIL DUH-MU-HÁ.   A saying of the Arabs as to horses' colours, p. 264 f.n. 1.

MU-NAI-JIZ   The name of a strain in AL KHAM-SA, Table p. 235 col. iii.

MU-NÍ-RA   [*Brilliant.*] The name of Muhammad *ibnu 'r* Ra-shid's favourite *ghaz-u* mare, p. 237. [We have the word in *minaret*, in Arabic *mí-nár*, the place on which a light, *nár* or *núr*, is displayed.]

MUN-TA-FIK   The name of a Bedouin nation of the Lower Euphrates, pp. 84 f.n. 1, 85, 86, 270, 308.

MURR   [*Bitter.*] Doctors sometimes give Arabic names to home-made stuffs; but the myrrhs and the basil are among the herbs which, on reaching Europe from Asia, have retained their native names, p. 19. [In one of A'n-tar's verses, both *murr* and *bá-sil* are used as epithets of a bitter and terrible combatant.]

[Al.] MUR-RA.   The name of a Bedouin nation, pp. 29, 59 f.n. 2, 100.

MUR-TA-JIZ   The name of one of the Prophet's chargers, p. 230 f.n. 2.

MÚ-SÁ   [The Arabic transcription of the Hebrew name "*Mosheh*," which is known to us (through the Greek translation of the Old Testament) as "Moses," pp. 100 f.n. 1, 106.

MÚ-SÁ, *ibn* NU-SAIR   The "Moorish," *i.e.* Muslim Arab, governor of Africa through whose energy the West Gothic, or Visigothic, kingdom in Spain was subverted, p. 163 f.n. 4. [Mú-sá's lieutenant, Tá-rik, was the first to plant a fortress on "The Rock," or *ja-bal*, which was called after him, *Ja-bal Tá-rik*, our "Gibraltar."]

MU-SAI-LI-MA. P. 30 f.n. 1.   [Diminutive (of derision) of *Muslim*, meaning *false Muslim*.] One of the Ba-nû Ha-ní-fa, of Ya-mâ-ma, in Najd, who set up prophetic pretensions, in opposition to Muhammad. His cause received support, and it was not till the Caliphate of

---

[1] The basket-boat of El I'râk is made of *an osy*, or osiers, plaited over uprights of stout material. The section shews a gentle curve at the bottom, and a deep one above forming the side. The ordinary *kuffa* is about 3½ feet in diameter and 2½ feet deep. One man can work it, by using a paddle on the two sides alternately. Camels are ferried across rivers in craft of this description; and the horses and mules of the country all know the kuf-fa. The Persian poet An-va-ri, in a description of the Tigris at Baghdad, says, that a thousand moon-shaped *coracles* on its surface resembled the stars in the clear blue firmament. Less poetically, the whirling kuf-fas suggest the idea of huge black Bird-nests which are being washed down by the current.

[2] V. in Professor Huxley's *Essay upon some Controverted Subjects*, pp. 585-625, a critical examination of "Hasisadra's Adventure," as set forth in certain recently obtained Assyrian tablets.

[AL] MU-SAL-LI	Abu Bakr that, after the defeat and death of the pretender in a sanguinary battle, Is-lâm was freed from this danger. *V.* p. 131 f.n. 3.
MUSCAT .	The Gibraltar of the Persian Gulf, and capital of Oman, pp. 20, 252 *et* f.n. 1. [In the Arabian ballad literature, *mas-kat* means, *the place where* the sandy ridge *subsides* into the plain.]
MU-SHAI-TIB .	[*A palm-branch drawn forth from its skin.*] The name of a strain in AL KHAM-SA, Table p. 235 col. v. [An Arab says that the name, as applied to a courser, means, long, and level, and light of flesh.]
MU-SIN-NA	The name of a strain in AL KHAM-SA, Table p. 235 col. i.
MUS-LIM .	A follower of the DÎNU 'L IS-LÂM. *Passim, et v.* p. 101 f.n. 2. [The name *Mus-lim* is probably as old as its Semitic root *slm*. It occurs in the Talmud, where it is held to mean *a righteous man.*]
[A'RABU 'L] MUS-TA'-RI-BA .	[*Naturalised Arabs.*] According to the Arab chroniclers, immigrants who entered Arabia, at a less remote period than the "Himyarite" Arabs, pp. 98, 99 *et* f.n. 1, 100, 117, 118, 120. [*Mus-ta'-ri-ba* appears in Spanish as "Mozáribe." The Arab conquerors of Spain thus designated the Christian communities which they tolerated in Cordova, Seville, Toledo, and other cities.]
MUT-A'B .	[*One whose arm, or leg, has been broken, and imperfectly reset.*] The name of a prince of Ja-bal Sham-mar, p. 40 f.n. 1.
MU-TA-WAL-LI	One who administers trusts for a religious purpose, p. 153 f.n. 1.
MU-WÂ-I-JA	The name of a subdivis. of the Sba' Aeniza, Table p. 121.
MU-WAI-NI' . .	[*Repelling.*] *Ut supra.*
MU'-WAJ HAM-MÂD	[*Mu'-waj*, inclining *now to this side and now to that*, in galloping; *Ham-mâd*, a man's name.] The name of a strain in the stock of KU-HAI-LÂN, Table p. 235 col. vi.
MU-WAR-RAD .	One of the colours of Arabian horses, p. 225 *et* f.n. 2, and in Table p. 263.
MU'-YIL .	The name of a strain in AL KHAM-SA, Table p. 235 col. i.

N

NA-BI	A "Prophet," in the sense described at p. 4 f.n. 1. [Every RA-SÛL or *messenger* is a "*na-bî*"; but every "*na-bî*" is not a "*ra-sûl.*"]
[AN] NÂ-BI-GHA P. 227 f.n. 4.	[Said to mean *one who, not having been born a poet, becomes one.*] Epithet serving for name of Zi-yâd, of the tribe Dhub-yân, a distinguished Arabian poet, whose fame was established in the half-century before Muhammad.

NAF-HA-TU'L YA-MAN	[*Odour or breath of Yemen.*] The title of an Arabic tale-book, a piece from which is translated, pp. 215, 216.
NAGA [for *na-ka*]	The cow-camel, p. 56.
NÁ-I'J	[*A white camel.*] The name of a strain in AL KHAM-SA, Table p. 235 col. i.
NA-JAF	A town of El I'rák, the chief feature of which is the mausoleum of A'li, p. 44.
NAJD	[*A plateau.*] The well-known name of the elevated central portion of the Arabian peninsula, pp. 8, 9, 16, 19, 21, 22, 23, 25-64 *passim*, 121, 124, 125, 126, 127 f.n. 2, 135, 136, 145 f.n. 1, 153, 164, 175, 205, 210, 211, 212, 220, 236, 244, 245, 260, 293, 300, 315. [Of or belonging to Najd is "Naj-di."]
NAJ-MA-TU 'S SUBH	[*Morning star.*] The name of a strain in AL KHAM-SA, Table p. 235 col. ii.
NA-KIB	[*One who searches into.*] P. 153 *et* f.n. 1. *V.* art. A'BDU 'L KÁ-DIR, *supra.*
NA'L	The ancient Semitic sandal, described and illustrated p. 97 f.n. 4. In Persia, Afghánistán, and India, *na'l* (p. 179) now generally means a horse-shoe, *v.* illustration p. 180.
NA'MÁN	A proper name, p. 4 *et* f.n. 3.
NARD	[In Baghdad, *tâ-li*, or *long.*] Backgammon, trick-track, or tables, p. 54 f.n. 2. [*Nard* is considered Persian. In Baghdad the Persians call dice *zár*; and the Arabs, *fus*, pl. *fu-sûs.*]
NA-SAI-YIR	[*Aiding.*] The name of a subdivis. of the Ru-wa-la Aeniza, Table p. 121.
NA-SIB	A man's *lot* or *portion*, p. 130.
NA-SI-BIN	In the Assyrian, early Armenian, Roman, Parthian, and later periods, Na-si-bin, in the north of AL JA-ZI-RA, was an important military and commercial station. The residences of emperors, viceroys, and generals, adorned it. The name may either imply the idea of *military posts*, or of *columned edifices and palaces*. At the present day, ruins, in which are a hamlet, form its principal features, pp. 63, 74.
NAU-FA-LI	[*Nau-fal*, in its commonest use, is the name of a certain wild flower; and it is also a favourite proper name among the Arabs.] A strain in AL KHAM-SA is called *Nau-fa-li*, Table p. 235 col. i.
NÁ-U'R	The large vertical water-wheel, which is described p. 81 f.n. 2.
NAW-WÁK [*Vulg.* NAW-WÁG.]	[Same as *dha-lûl*, *q. v.* p. 61 f.n. 3.] The name of a strain in AL KHAM-SA, Table p. 235 col. i.
NÍ-LI	One of the colours of Arabian horses, Table p. 263.
NIS-BA	[Lit., *relationship.*] Used by the Bedouin in the sense of a breed of horses or other animals, p. 236.
NI-ZÁR	According to the Arab genealogists, a patriarch of the "Ishmaelite" Arabs, p. 99.
NU-FÚDH	A term of Arabian physical geography, pp. 34-38, 97, 126, 269.

3 B

NUK-RA .	Any depressed tract. A common name for oases. P. 99 f.n. 4.
NÛH	"Noah," p. 100 f.n. 1.
NU-SI	A natural grass of Najd, pp. 51, 82, 269.

O

OMAN	[In Arabic, *U'-mán*, the root-idea in which is *abiding*.] The name of the Arabian kingdom, the capital of which is Muscat, pp. 25, 32, 253.
OPHIR . . Pp. 12 f.n. 3, 27.	In one treatise, not older than 1848, 80 pages are occupied with the different theories which have been propounded respecting the site of Ophir. A later authority thus, in our opinion, conclusively settles the point:—

"It is quite plain from Gen. x. 29, that Ophir belonged to Southern Arabia, from which the Phœnicians still derived gold and precious stones in the time of Ezekiel (xxvii. 22). All attempts to place Ophir in India, or on the east coast of Africa (Sofâla), are at variance with Gen. x. It is true that Indian products were also brought to Solomon (1 Kings x. 22); but these are not said to have come from Ophir, and therefore we cannot even be sure that Ophir was the emporium where the Indian trade and the Western met, as they did in Southern Arabia in later times."[1]

Niebuhr, in *Description de l'Arabe*, arrives at the conclusion that Ophir probably was situated somewhere between Aden and Dha-far. In Baron von Brede's learned paper in the Journal of the Royal Geographical Society, vol. xiv. p. 110, the name Ophir is interpreted *red;* and it is also stated that certain tribes of Hadh-ra-maut call themselves men of *the red country*, and the Red Sea, *Bahru 'l ophir*. The fact that the name "Ophir" has for its first letter a different symbol in the Biblical and in Arabic writings respectively, does not necessarily preclude the explanation of it from the latter language, in which names derived from colour are extremely prevalent. The Arabs of the desert call the wild pig *i'fr*, probably because his colour resembles that of the ground. The JINN have for one of their designations *i'f-rît*. La-bîd bestows on the calf of a wild cow which a lion had seized, the epithet *mu-a'f-far*, meaning either *The dust-coloured*, or *The one that has been rolled in the dust*. The only permanent settlement between Mosul and Sinjâr is TALL A'-FAR—*i.e., the hill of a reddish colour.*

OTTOMAN . . . . For page references *v.* Index ii.	The English form of the descriptive which the Arabs write "U'th-mâ-ni," and the Turks, "Osmanli"; meaning anything belonging to the race or dynasty of *U'th-mán*, or "Osman," the founder of the present "Turkish" empire.

---

[1] *Ency. Brit.*, vol. xvii. p. 780.

P

PÁ-LÁN . . . . . . The Persian pack-saddle, p. 318 f.n. 3.

PÁ-SHA, BÁ-SHA ; PÁD-SHA, BÁD-SHA. An Aryan word. The Constantinople Government bestows it as a title, like our " Lord." Under the Muslim rulers of India, the Emperor of Delhi was the " Pádsha " ; while each great feudatory of the empire was styled a " Naw-wáb," or Viceroy. Pp. 44, 134, 146, 153.

PUSHT I KÚH P. 149 f.n 1. [In Persian, *Back of the mountain*.] The mountains which separate " Lûr-istân " from Asiatic Turkey are collectively known by this name. Numerous rich valleys, and some of the best pasture-grounds in Persia, here present themselves. A semi-nomad people, of the Lûr, or Lûri, branch of the old Iranian stock called Fai-li, maintain their independence within the limits of Pusht i Kûh. A native chief, on whom the Sháh of Persia confers the title of Wáli, exercises patriarchal authority over them. Nominally, they are Muslim of the Shi a' ; but in religion as in other respects they more resemble the pagan Kurds than the Persians. A *kû-la*, or booth, woven of leafy branches, is preferred by them to the tent, and every *kû-la* is defended by a separate inclosure of thorny fencing. In summer they live in the mountains, and in winter in the plains. These lines are written at Dih-bá-la, or High-town, the summer-quarters of Hu-sain Ku-li Khán, chief of the Lûrs. With the aid of an enterprising Swiss merchant, who in his last journey fell from his horse and was killed, a demesne and palace recalling some of Marco Polo's descriptions have uprisen at Dih-bá-la ; but this modern " old man of the mountain " prefers to occupy a booth in the open, where all his clan and progeny can see him. His hospitality leaves nothing to be desired ; and yet it is not without a peculiar feeling that one receives the daily tray of fruit or game, by the hands of the herculean Lûri whose hereditary functions include that of hewing off the head of any one who has flinched in the foray, or otherwise incurred the Wáli's anger. A figurative rather than positive regiment of about 200 ragged musketeers is hutted and rationed at Dih-bá-la. The older men relate that they saw the English gunboats in vain bombard Mu-ham-ma-ra in 1857 ; " in vain," seeing that although our countrymen took the town they did not retain it ! The only trophy which Pusht i Kûh has yielded to us is a head of the BUZ KÚ-HI, or mountain-goat of Persia—the BA-DA-NA of Central Arabia, and Steinboc (*Capra ibex*) of Europe. In the Lûri mountains it is not uncommon to see the horns of these wary creatures rising against the sky-line, at elevations to which only a chamois-hunter could climb ; but the solitary males descend at night

PUSHT I KŪH—*continued.*	to easier regions. Hu-sain Ku-li Khan's country is famed for its mules. The only really first-class riding-mule that we have ever ridden is one which belongs to his principal henchman, but it is the pick of many hundreds. The Lūrī chief trusts to Arabian mares and Martini-Henrys in his raids on the Ba-nū Lām and other Arab flock-masters. He captures the mares of the Arabs in foray, and keeps his followers well mounted by means of buying, taking, and breeding. Almost every winter he and a merchant of Kirmān-shāh despatch in partnership a number of horses to the Bombay market.

R

RAB-DĀN .	[*Ash-coloured*, whence, the ostrich.] The name of a strain in the stock of KU-HAI-LĀN, Table p. 235 col. vi.
RA-BĪ	Spring, p. 50 f.n. 2.
RĀ-DHĪ .	[*One who is satisfied.*] A guide's name, p. 38.
RA-DĪF .	One who rides behind another, on the back of the same beast, pp. 36 f.n. 3, 61. [In the Ottoman service, the "Reserves" are termed the "Ra-dīf."]
RAH-HĀ-LI-YA .	[*Saddling of camels.*] The name of a palm oasis, and ancient settlement, in the desert west of Kar-ba-lā, p. 42. The inhabitants occupy two townships, which are at some distance apart. Apparently they cultivate little else than dates, with, under the palm-trees, lucerne.
RAH-MĀN	Of which RA-HĪM is a synonymous form, meaning *compassionate*, as a part of men's names, p. 107 *et* f.n. 1.
RAK-KA .	An ancient settlement [Alexander's Nicephorium] on the Euphrates, in N. AL JAZĪRA, at the mouth of the Bi-likh, p. 63.
RA-MA-DHĀN . . . . [In Turkey, Persia, and India, "Ramzān."]	[*Vehemence of heat.*] The ninth lunar month in the Muslim calendar, which is set apart for fasting, p. 160 *et* f.n. 1. [In the year in which the pagan Arabs re-named their months, the month which received this name chanced to fall in the season of heat.]
RA-MAK .	Some Bedouin nations use this word as a synonym of FA-RAS, *q. v.* P. 238 f.n. 2.
RĀS . .	A town in Najd, p. 32 f.n. 1.
RA-SĀ-LĪN	[Root-idea, *rivalry.*] The name of a subdivis. of the Sba' Aeniza, Table p. 121.
RA-SAN	*V.* illustration, p. 140. In the sense of a "strain" of horses, p. 236.
RA-SHĪD .	[Root-idea, *straightness.*] An epithet much used in names and titles among the Arabs. "Hā-rūnu 'r Ra-shīd," or Aaron the Just (or Orthodox), is an example, p. 98.
RASH-MA .	[A *mark*, or *impression*, *e.g.* of a seal or chain.] The Bedouin riding-halter, described and illustrated, p. 140, *et v.* p. 313.
RA-SŪL	[Root-idea, *sending.*] An apostle. [*V.* art. NA-BĪ, *supra.*] P. 4 f.n. 1.

GLOSSARIAL INDEX AND SUPPLEMENT. 381

RÁSU 'L 'AIN . [*Head of the spring.*] In N.W. AL JA-ZI-RA, the sources of the Khá-búr river [p. 75], where long ago the city of Ra-si-na flourished.

RÁSU 'L FI-DÁ-WÍ . [*Leader of the* "enfants perdus," *v.* in art. ALAMÚT, *supra.*] The name of a strain in AL KHAM-SA, Table p. 235 col. i., *et* p. 213 f.n. 1.

RÁSU 'L HADD [*Head or point of the boundary.*] The extreme eastern shoulder of the Arabian peninsula at the entrance of the Gulf of Oman, p. 26.

RAU-Á' [Fem. of *ar-wa'*, *strong-hearted.*] The name of a strain in AL KHAM-SA, Table p. 235 col. i.

RÁ-WI-A . [*The pouring out of water.*] The primitive Arabs called the maker and reciter of verses a *rá-wi-a*, precisely as the orator is sometimes called among us a "spouter." P. 234.

RAZ-ZÁ-ZA A small oasis in Shá-mi-ya, S.W. of KAR-BA-LÁ, p. 83.

[AR] RI-ÁDH . [*The watered lands or gardens.*] The name of the second
 [Pl. of RAU-DHA.] Wahabite capital of Najd, pp. 32 f.n. 1, 36, 42, 44, 45, 58, 164, 250, 251.

RI-JÁ-JIL . [Pl. of a plural; singular, *ra-jul* = *vir*.] "Manly men," pp. 42, 211.

RI-KÁB . A stirrup, *v.* illustration, p. 148. *Rikáb* means, as does
 [Common pronunciation, *ri-* *mar-kab* [although the latter is much specialised in the sense
 chab.] of a *ship*], *that on which one rides*, particularly camels. The desert Arab, like the ancient Grecian hero, trusts to his agility, with or without the aid of his spear-shaft, in mounting and dismounting. It is not known when the Arabs first saw a stirrup; but from their naming it *rikáb* they would appear to regard it as a *means of mounting*. The ordinary I'ráki horseman seems to consider that the main use of his stirrups is to enable him to double up his legs half-way to his mouth, and by putting himself to bed as it were on his horse, the sooner give him a sore back.

RIKHL A ewe-lamb, p. 110.

RIM . The name of an antelope, the identification of which is disputed, *v.* p. 145 f.n. 1. [To support the suggestion that the "rim" of Arab poetry is cervine, not bovine, a verse of Im-ra-u 'l Kais might be quoted, in which it is said that the ground, in a certain favourite spot, owing to the droppings of the *a-rám* [plural of *rím*], *appeared to be covered with black pepper berries.*]

RÍ-SHÁN . [*Feathered.*] The name, in the sense of winged or volant, of a strain in the stock of KU-HAI-LÁN, Table p. 235 col. vi.

RUBB . . . . Fruit-juice, inspissated, p. 234 *et* f.n. 1.
[AR] RUB-U' 'L KHÁ-LÍ . *V.* pp. 25, 26.
RÚ-DÁN . . [*Easy-paced.*] The name of a strain in AL KHAM-SA, Table p. 235 col. i.

RÚM The Arabs thus pronounce "Rome," p. 44. The name Rome has been differently applied by them at different periods. Sometimes they have understood by it Europe at

RÚM—*continued*.	large. Another of its meanings has been "all the lands of the Romans"; and another, the Byzantine empire. In our day they mean by "Rûm" the Osmanli empire. In the Orthodox Greek Church, "New Rome" still lingers as the official designation of Constantinople, which the Turks call Istamboul or Stamboul.
RUMH	The long Bedouin spear, p. 75.
RUS-TAM	The son of Zâl, a Goliath of the old Iranian kingdom, whom the Persian Homer Fir-dû-sí chose as the hero of his great national epic, the SHÂH NÁ-MAH, or *Book of Kings*, p. 283.
RU-WA-LA	[Root-idea said to be *saliva*.] The name of a great divis. of the Aeniza, Table pp. 59, 63 f.n. 1. 68, 121, 210.

S

SA-Á'D	Murder of ———, a grandson of Amir Fai-sal of Najd, p. 42.
SA-BÁ	The inscriptions which have been discovered in south-western Arabia throw new light on the reference in Gen. x. 29 to a people whose name was Sa-bá ("Sheba"). Pp. 27, 28, 97, 99 f.n. 3. [Under the interpretation that *sa-bá* means *to make a trading journey*, it is conjectured that at the period referred to in Genesis the Sabæans[1] occupied a

---

[1] It is mentioned in the text, p. 28 f.n. 2, that the "Sabæans," or ancient Yemenites, are no longer confused with the sect of the "Sá-bí-û-na." The former name is now but a term of history. The latter belongs to certain descendants of the ancient Semitic population of Chaldæa who still exist as a small community of artisans and cultivators in lower Babylonia. The first time that we entered El I'rák, a deputation of these people came on board the steamer at Bussorah, bearing a petition which they requested us to forward to England. The honest mariner in command of the vessel was one of those who keep varied stores of information on Eastern topics for the benefit of travellers. The account which he gave of the "Sabians" was, that they were "Christians of St John," who built no churches, married only one wife, and considered themselves under the protection of the Archbishop of Canterbury. It afterwards appeared, from a considerable literature which exists on this subject (v. 'Edinburgh Review,' July 1880), that most of these statements were erroneous. The question of whether the "Sá-bí-û-na" possess churches depends on what is understood by a church. They erect edifices which they consecrate with a singular ritual; but only priestly persons may enter them, and the congregation responds from outside. They are so far from being Christians, that both Judaism and Christianity are abhorrent to them. All the Biblical personages, from Adam to John and Jesus, appear as false prophets in their theology or mythology. Their burial or ablutionary ceremonies (whence "Sabians," from *sá-bí*, in Syria a *washer*) tend to group them with those disciples of John, or "Yah-yá," who held aloof from Christianity; but that does not justify us in connecting them with "John the Baptist" of our Gospels. Whether they shall marry one wife, or several, is regulated by their circumstances. At KUR-ÁN commends them to toleration under the name of *Sá-bí-û-na* (Sâ-ra v.) More properly they are "Mandæans," *lit.* Gnostics. In truth theirs is an exceedingly ancient religion, in the light of which nearly all other well-developed religions may profitably be studied. Æons, or emanations, from an origin of all things, compose the groundwork; and the greatest figure in the system of the Mandæans, from whom they take their name, is the "Messenger of Life," MANDÁ D' HAYYE, who is also called the "primal man." Even such scholarship as Dr Nöldeke's confesses itself unable to fathom the profundities which are contained in the Scriptures of the Mandæans. Their "priests" are more of magic-men, devil-exorcisers, and astrologers, than teachers. When a house is being designed, a priest is fetched to mark out the lines, and fix the position of the doors. In sickness the sovereign medicine is a priest's amulet. Apparently, however, the "holy men" themselves prefer natural to divine assistance. A priest of the Sabians has just come to Baghdád in a Lynch's steamer, to ask the surgeon of the British Consulate to cure him of a sore leg. Attempts to obtain from this old man an account of his sect's theology are always frustrated by his bringing the conversation round to the subject of a possible subsidy from Lambeth. He wears blue stones as ornaments. This may refer to the Mandæan conception that a turquoise mountain separates earth from paradise. But the Turks also, and the Sikhs of India, esteem the blue colour; and the Sín-jás YA-zí-rís (*q. v. infra*), while attracted by blue objects, think blue clothes too sacred to be worn. The old man now referred to stoutly testifies against celibacy. He also repudiates fasting; but, like his Muslim neighbours, has obligatory prayers, and kills meat in the name of the Divine.

SA-BÁ—*continued*. subordinate position in Yemen, and did not rise to prominence till later. Owing to the great place which the heavenly bodies held in the religion of ancient Yemen, Sabæanism is often used as another name for astral worship.]

SÁ-BÁT   The "summer-house" of the desert Arabs, p. 81.

SAB-BÁH .   The name of a strain in the stock of KU-HAI-LÁN, Table p. 235 col. vi. The name of one of the Prophet Muhammad's chargers, p. 230 f.n. 2.

SAB-BA-HA-KA 'LLAH BI 'L KHAIR.   The "Good morning" of the Arabs, p. 159 f.n. 4.

SA-BIL   The little bowl of clay, or wood, or bone, in which the Arab smokes tobacco, p. 164 f.n. 3. To make the "chi-búk" of the Turks and Turco-Arabs, an ornamented wooden stem, at least a yard long, which is called a *sha-tub* (lit. *palm-branch*) is fitted to the *su-bil*. In the "kal-li-ân," or "nâr-jîl" (*coco-nut*), of the Shâh's dominions, the smoke passes through water. The Persian "water-pipe" is much relished in Turkey also, where its name is modified into "nargila."

[As] SÁ-BIK   *V.* p. 131 f.n. 3.

SAB-KHA .   Marshy land, which yields salt, p. 82.

SAB-TA .   The leather plaits which the Bedouin of both sexes bind round the naked loins, p. 140. [Other names are *brim*; and in classic Najd, *hag-ga*, for *lut-ku*, from a word for the loins.]

SAB-ZA (Persian)   One of the colours of Arabian horses, Table p. 263, col. of remarks.

SA'-DÁN .   The name of a strain in the stock of KU-HAI-LÁN, suggested by the desert shrub, *sa'-dân*, Table p. 235 col. vi.

SA'-DI .   This name was assumed in honour of a royal patron, by
[Another form of Su-û'd, *q. v.*, and of many other derivatives.]   one who was destined to make it shine for ever with no borrowed lustre, MU-SHAR-RAFU 'D DÍN, the son of MUS-LI-HU 'D DÍN, of Shi-râz. The great poet-teacher of the Eastern world was born at Shi-râz, about A.D. 1184. He was a travelling, not a sedentary, student. His schools included El I'râk and Central Asia, Syria and India, Yemen and Abyssinia. In his old age he returned to his native Persia, to meditate on all that he had seen, and learned, and written; and it was not till his 110th lunar year that death summoned him away from his pleasant rose-gardens in Shi-râz. *V.* quotations or translations from his works, pp. 12, 45, 114 f.n. 1, 133, 134 f.n. 1, 191, 276, 291, 305.

SA-DIR . .   The name of a province of Najd, pp. 32 f.n. 1, 43.

SA-FA-RI . .   A season of the year, p. 50 f.n. 2.

SA-GAR [for *sakr*]   A hunting hawk, or falcon, p. 152 *et* f.n. 2.

SÁ-HIB . .   [Primarily a *companion*, whence a *protector*, also *possessor*, *e.g.* of a quality.] In India, "Sá-hib" is used as a title of respect, like "Beg" in Turkey, p. 194.

SAH-RA   The Arabic word which in our maps appears as "Sahara," or desert, pp. 18, 60.

SAI-YID Pp. 281, 301.	Lord, or Master, especially applied to the Prophet Muhammad. Those of the race of Muhammad, through Husain's son Zainu 'l A'-bi-din, the sole male survivor of the slaughter at Kar-ba-lâ, are distinguished in Arabia by the title of "Sai-yid," or collectively, "Sâ-dât." In India, "Sai-yid" is merely a component part of the name of those who bear it.
SAKAR Pp. 53 cf f.n. 2, 54 f.n. 1.	The primary idea contained in this word is *inebriation*, and it occurs in AL KUR-ÂN in the generic sense of *wine*. [In numerous languages the same word signifies those saccharine principles in vegetable and animal juices, from which intoxicating beverages are produced by spontaneous fermentation.]
SAKB	The name of one of the Prophet Muhammad's chargers, p. 230 f.n. 2.
SAK-LÂ-WÎ	The name (it is said with the meaning of *long*, or *great, of flank*) of one of the primary divisions of AL KHAM-SA, Table p. 235 col. ii. It is a matter of tradition among the desert Arabs that long ago a Shekh named Jid-rân (*v*. art. JID-RÂ-NI, *supro*) possessed three famous mares. One of the trio, that called after him is held to have transmitted her blood down to our day. The second was given, or bequeathed, to Jid-rân's slave; and she and her descendants are now spoken of as the SAK-LÂ-WÎ-YA 'L A'BD (*v*. Table p. 235 col. ii.), or "Saklâwiya of the slave." The third mare suffered a misalliance, and her owner would have cut her throat, had not his brother Û-bair begged her from him, and obtained her, under the stipulation that her descendants should be called by the name of Û-bair, not by that of Jid-rân.
SAK-LÂ-WÎ-YA .	A revenue outpost of the Baghdad Government, on the east bank of the Euphrates, three days west of Baghdad, p. 84 f.n. 1.
[As] SA-LÂ-TÎN [Pl. of *Sul-tân*.]	[*The masterful*.] The name of a horde of the Aeniza, Table p. 121.
SAL-GA .	The Aeniza group of the ―――――, p. 149.
SA-LÎ-LA .	The name of a part of Najd, p. 32 f.n. 1.
SAL-MÂ	[From the same root as IS-LÂM, *q. v.*] A "long bluish chain" of N. Central Arabia, which is part of the TÂ-I, or Sham-mar, mountains, p. 39.
SA-LÛ-KI .	The name of a strain under MI'-NI-KI, in the stock of KU-HAI-LÂN, Table p. 235 col. vi. [Either the progeny of a mare which resembled the Arab *slû-gi*, or greyhound; or the progeny of a mare belonging to a man who was so characterised, or named.]
SÂ-MAR-RÂ	A tomb hamlet, and place of Shi-ite pilgrimage on the site of a historic city, on the east bank of the Tigris, below Takrit, p. 78 f.n. 3.
SA-MÂ-WA	A small permanent settlement of the Lower Euphrates marsh-land, pp. 84 f.n. 1, 85.
SAM-HÂN .	The name of a strain in the stock of KU-HAI-LÂN, Table p. 235 col. vi.

ṢAN-Á'	[Root-idea, *manufacturing*, or *constructing*.] The capital of Yemen, and the centre of a large district which takes its name from the city, pp. 28, 97.
SA-NÁM	The *highest part*, or hump, of the camel's back, p. 294 f.n. 1.
SA-RÁB	[*Running*.] The mirage,[1] p. 81 *et* f.n. 5.
SARD-ÁB	[Persian.] The depressed, but not subterranean, apartment or cellar in which they spend the hot hours of the day in El 'Irak and other countries, p. 81.
SARD-GARM	A term of the Indians for a certain phase of climate, p. 315 f.n. 2.
SÁ-RI	[*Going along*, or *journeying*, especially by *night*.] The name of a subdivis. of the Fid-á'n Aeniza, Table p. 121.
SARJ	[By some said to be Persian.] A saddle, pp. 144 f.n. 1, 147 with illustration.
SAR-RÁ-E .	The name of a horde of El 'Irák, p. 84 f.n. 1.
SA-WÁ-KIN	[Pl. of *sá-kin* = *settled*, or *stationary*.] The well-known port of the *Bi-lá-du 's Sú-dán*, or *Country of the Blacks* (the "Soudan"), on the Red Sea, p. 27.
SÁ-WÁ-NÍ . . [Pl. of *Sá-ni-a*.]	The camel which works the well in Central Arabia; also the whole irrigational apparatus, p. 47 f.n. 3.
SÁ-YIH	[*Shouter*, as in Al Ghaz-u.] The name of a sept of the Sham-mar, pp. 83, 122 f.n. 5, 281.
SBA' .	[From *sa-bu'*, the lion.] The name of one of the primary divisions of the Aeniza, pp. 63 f.n. 1, 107, 121 in Table, 122, 125, 270, 271.
SHAM-LI	The name of a strain under MI'-NI-KI, in the stock of KU-HAI-LÁN, Table p. 235 col. vi.
SFUK	The patronymic of each succeeding Shekh of the division of the Sham-mar which now possesses AL JAZIRA. [The local explanation of the name is that it signifies *bloodshed*; and that the first "Sfúk" received this sobriquet because of a war which happened in his time between his people and the Wahábis.] Pp. 122 f.n. 5, 124 *et* f.n. 1.
SHA-BA-KA	[*The infixing of part to part, as in a lattice*.] At p. 215, the name of an Arabian mare.
SHA'-BÁN .	The name of a horse, illustration, and reference, pp. 253 and 254.
"SHÁH-RUKH"	[*Shah's countenance*.] The name of the Arabian horse depicted in frontispiece; a namesake of SHÁH-RUKH, the son of TI-MÚR I LANG, or "Tamerlane."

---

[1] Al Ku-s-ÁN, in comparing the works of unbelievers with the mirage [S. xxiv.], uses the word *sa-ráb*. The same term occurs in Isaiah xxxv. 7. The authors of the Revis. Vers. translate it "glowing sand," and place "mirage" in the margin. The poetic desert figure of the evanescent delusive vapour being changed into running water is thus put on one side. In Arabic, *sa-ráb* cannot mean "glowing sand." The idea which the ancient Arabs attached to this word is known from a passage in La-bíd's MU-AL-LA-KA. A party of ladies proceeding in their camel-litters, are described as separated from a lover's gaze by the "*sa-ráb*," under the effects of which they appeared *lit. the tamarisks and stony brows of the valley of Biesha*. In Arabic poetry another name is the *sa-ráb*, especially that of the morning and evening, is *ál*.

SHAH-WÁN	The name of a strain in the stock of KU-HAI-LÁN, Table p. 235 col. vi.
SHAI-BÍ	[*Hoary.*] *Ut supra.*
SHA-I'R	Barley, p. 80 f.n. 3.
SHAK-RÁ .	A town of Najd, p. 32 f.n. 1. Fem. of *ash-kar*—*i.e.*, a chesnut mare, Table p. 262.
SHAL-FA .	A variety of the Bedouin *rumh*, or spear, in which the iron head, or *si-nân*, is very broad, p. 75.
SHÁM	The country so named, p. 65.
SHÁ-MÍ-YA	The well-known desert tract on the Upper Euphrates, pp. 20, 23, 42, 58, 63, 65-69, 79, 103, 105, 136, 175, 213, 214, 218, 236, 242, 259, 269-276, 293, 319.
SHAM-MAR	The great Bedouin nation so named, pp. 23, 39 f.n. 1, 63 f.n. 1, 64, 70-77, 85, 103, 122, 123, 124, 125, 129, 139, 210, 264, 293, 294. [Numerous etymologies of this word have been extracted from lexicons, or from the imagination, but it is useless to discuss them.]
SHAM-MAR TOGA	A people of El I'rák, pp. 84 f.n. 1, 122. [The root of " Toga " is that of *ta-wáik, q. v.* art. JA-BAL TU-WAIK, *supra*. The " Sham-mar Toga," perhaps, received their designation, because *subjugated* by the Sham-mar.]
SHA-NÍN .	[Probably from the same root as *sha-ní-na*, butter-milk.] The name of a strain in AL KHAM-SA, Table p. 235 col. i.
SHA-RÁ-BÍ	The name of a strain under RI-SHÁN, in the stock of KU-HAI-LÁN, Table p. 235 col. vi.
SHA-RÁ-RÁT .	A migratory people, whose *dí-ras* are situated in, and near, WÁ-DI SIR-HÁN towards Central Arabia, pp. 16, 39 f.n. 1, 52, 59 f.n. 2, 128.
SHAR-BÁN	The name of a strain in the stock of KU-HAI-LÁN, Table p. 235 col. vi. [An Arab says that "shar-bán" means an animal which, *without having drunk, is as though it had done so.*]
SHA-RÍ-A'.	A way of access to a river, *i.e.* a cutting made through its bank, for the use of men and cattle, p. 73.
SHA-RÍF .	[*Elevated.*] In Arabia, the " SHU-RA-FÁ," pl. of *sha-ríf*, are the descendants of the Prophet *through the two sons of Hasan*. The " Shu-ra-fa " devote themselves to war and government, and leave theology and letters to the " SÁ-DÁT," pl. of SAI-YID, *q. v. supra*. Pre-eminent among the SHU-RA-FÁ is "THE SHA-RÍF" who forms the modern counterpart of the ancient Amirs of Mecca, pp. 29, 117. [*V.* in Table p. 235 col. i. *sha-ríf* used in its ordinary sense, to distinguish a strain in AL KHAM-SA.]
SHAR-KI .	[From *shark*, lit. *parting* or *breaking*, whence, the *rising of the sun*, the *eastern quarter*, and the like.] At p. 80 f.n. 2, *v.* a description of the *shar-ki* or "sharji," wind of El I'rák.
SHAR-RÁK	An Arab's name which has come down as that of a well-known strain in AL KHAM-SA, Table p. 235 col. iii.

SHATTU 'L A'RAB .	[*River of the Arabs.*] The united Tigris and Euphrates, from Gurna to the Gulf of Persia, pp. 20, 74, 78 f.n. 3, 85, 283. [Only a first-class river receives the name of *shatt*. The Arabs call a minor stream *nahr*; a brook, *jadwal*; and a rill, *sb-ki-a*.]
SHEKH . [For SHAIKH.]	This widely-known title of respect corresponds with our "elder." The superiority which is indicated by it may be that of birth, or of years, or of prowess, or of learning, according to the ideals of different communities. In India, the use of the word as a part of men's names has all but effaced its distinctiveness. In Persia and the towns of El I'râk, any one who possesses a large turban may play the Shekh. Pp. 52, 61, 71, 72, 76, 83, 85, 104, 107, 112 f.n. 1, 124, 125, 131, 134, 136, 138.
SHGÂR	A certain blemish in Arabian horses, p. 313.
SHI-ÂH	[Pl. of *shât, wild creatures*.] The name of a strain in AL KHAMSA, Table p. 235 col. i.
SHI-A'I-YI	[*Smeared* or *smearing with tar*.] Ut supra, col. ii.
SHIB-RÎ-YA	A kind of knife or dagger, p. 46 f.n. 1.
SHI-DÂD .	[*That which is made fast on a beast's back*.] Another name for the *raḥl* or camel-saddle, p. 301.
SHIL-U	[*Light of flesh*.] The name of a strain in AL KHAMSA. Table p. 235 col. i.
SHI-MÂL . [For *Sha-mâl* or *Sham-al*.]	The north or north-west wind. In most regions this is the wind for which the Arabs pray, p. 80.
SHI-MÂ-LI	[*From the quarter of the north wind*.] Shi-mâ-li horses, pp. 272 et f.n. 2, 273.
SHIM-LÂN	The name of a horde of the I'ma-rât Aeniza, Table p. 121.
SHI-TÂ .	Winter, p. 50 f.n. 2.
SHI-THÂ-THA . P. 42.	A very great "mother of dates" in Shâ-ini-ya, a day's journey west of Kar-ba-lâ. Belts of palm cultivation, extending for several miles, embrace a natural spring, which fills an open pond or pool with tepid and fetid mineral water. Our visit to Shi-thâ-tha took place in winter, when the ordinary streams were more or less frozen; but the water in the central pond maintained its high temperature. The inhabitants are of the Shi-I'. The only Sun-nis are the Osmanli officials. It would appear that the Jews once possessed this oasis, as they did Yath-rib. It contains many imposing, though ruinous, chateaux, some of which still bear the names of otherwise forgotten Jew owners.
SHIT-RANJ	Chess, p. 54 f.n. 2. [*Shit-ranj* is considered to be a Persian corruption of *chatu-ranga*, in Sanscrit, the *four angas—i.e., four members*, of an army; *scil.*, elephants, horses, chariots, and foot-soldiers. The "king" and "queen" of the English game play corresponding parts in the Eastern one also. Our "knight," "bishop," "castle," and "pawn" respectively, are the "horse," "camel," "elephant," and "foot-soldier" of the Asiatic chess-board.]

Shu-a'i-la	The name of a strain in Al. Kham-sa, Table p. 235 col. i.
Shu-ka-ba-tu 'r kih	The name of an African race of Arabian horses, p. 253 et f.n. 6.
Shu-wai-man	[Diminutive of *shá-ma*, a *mole*, also one of the markings in horse's coats which are referred to at p. 264.] The name of a strain in the stock of Ku-hai-lán, Table p. 235 col. vi.
Si-di	[From *as-wad, black*.] The negro, p. 107 f.n. 3.
Sid-li	The name of a strain under Mi'-ni-ki, in the stock of Ku-hai-lán, Table p. 235 col. vi.
Sim-ri	[*Tawny*.] The name of a strain in Al. Kham-sa, Table p. 235 col. iv.
Sin-jár	The name of a mountain-range, and of an ancient settlement, between Mosul and Der, pp. 5, 6 et f.n. 3, 73, 74, 75, 77 in illustration, 124 f.n. 1, 133.
Sin-já-ra	The name of a subdivis. of the Sham-mar, p. 122.
Sir-hán	[*Meandering*.] Wá-di Sir-hán [pp. 37, 52, 75] is the name of a long and sinuous depression "bearing, in the main, from north-west to south-east, or nearly so," which extends across half the northern desert, from Al Hau-rân, to Al. Jauf. [The *dheb*, or wolf, is poetically designated *Abú sir-hán*, or *Father of prowling*, because of his circuitous gait; and probably "Wádi Sir-hán" owes the epithet which serves as its name to the same feature.]
Si-támu 'l Eú-lád	[*Sinews of steel or iron*.] The name of a strain under Ji-lfán, in the stock of Ku-hai-lán, Table p. 235 col. vi.
Sleb, or Slebí [More correctly, Su-la'-bi, collectively, As Su-la-bá.]	A people of high antiquity in Arabia, whose origin is unknown, p. 74. In many respects the Su-la-bá, or "Sleb," are the counterpart of our gipsies. Asses are their only cattle. Wherever they wander, from Syria to Najd, their skill as joiners, Tubal Cains, and implement-makers gains them a welcome. They are also the herbalists and horse-surgeons of the desert. They display the true gipsy light-heartedness; and their songs and musical instruments would repay investigation. Before all things they excel in hunting. The Bedouin do not regard them as Arabs. "Ki-lâbu 'l kha-lâ," or wild dogs, is one of the contemptuous names which they give to them; but they also say that all the game of the desert belongs to them. When the Bedouin are starving, the Su-la-bá will be gathered round messes of venison. [The word which in literary Arabic denotes "the Cross," is "Sa-lib," and this has given rise to the conjecture that the "Sleb" may have a Christian history. But the primary meaning of the Arabic root *slb* is simply *strength*, or *stiffness*. The word for the backbone is *su-lub*. The Bedouin call the two small pieces of wood which they place crossways in the mouth of the leathern well-bucket to keep it open, *sa-li-bán*. In Persia and India, *sa-lá-bat*, with the sense of *firmness*, has entered into many high-sounding titles.]

SU-BAI-NI, or *ibn* SUBAINI   The name of a family of Bedouin, after which is called a strain in At. KHAM-SA, Table p. 235 col. ii.

SUEZ   The well-known Egyptian port on the Red Sea, p. 20. [The only reasonable conjecture on the point of etymology which we have seen is, that "*Su-wais*" may have originated in an old word, which the Greeks Hellenised into oasis—*i.e.*, an inhabited spot in the desert.]

SU-FI   The nearest English equivalent of this term perhaps is "Theosophist."[1] A full account of Súf-ism would necessarily include a review of all the appearances of "Mysticism," from the days when the sages of ancient India were absorbed in the problem of extrication from self, and assimilation to the "Ultimate Unity," down to our time. But the Sú-fis of El Islám took their rise in Persia. From very ancient times the Iranian soil has been the fruitful mother of new religions. Accordingly, there is little wonder that, when a "plain Kur-án" was summarily imposed upon it, a reactionary outburst of the old pantheistic ideas followed. Thus began Persian Súf-ism, in the first century after Muhammad; and it still flourishes in El 'Irák and Persia, Syria, Turkey, Central Asia, and India. From the standpoint of the Arab Prophet's teaching, Súf-ism is simply "*Kufr*," or "infidelity"; but the Sú-fi masses, in leaving the paths of "sound doctrine" for those of metaphysical speculation, keep hold at least of the skirts of Shi-ite Islamism.

Most of us know how deeply Persian literature after the Flight[2] is indebted to Sufite elements, but looked at from the practical side, Súf-ism is probably not unconnected with the weakness of Persia as a nation. The foundations of energy and effort are more or less sapped by it. Háfiz in one of his Odes describes his mental state as so ecstatic, that every object which he beheld set him a-weeping. Another poetic inculcator of passivity compares the soul of the perfected Sú-fi to the surface of a pellucid lake on which not a mote can fall unnoticed. It is all very well for "emancipated persons" to surrender themselves to conditions of this description; but when a whole nation more or less inclines in the same direction, the elements of strength are evidently wanting.

SUF-RA   A traveller's provisions, whence, the receptacle thereof, and as it is customary to spread this out, at meal-times, *anything off which one eats*, p. 93 f.n. 1.

---

[1] It is possible that "Sú-fi" is from σοφός; but Eastern scholars derive the name from *súf*, wool; under the explanation that one of the early leaders of the movement, a certain Abú Sa'íd, *Ibn* Abú 'l Khair, and his disciples, wore a distinctive garb of woollen stuff.

[2] Especially the works of Sa'adí and Háfiz; and the MASNAVI MA-NA-VI, or Spiritual Collection, of "Mau-lá-ná" (meaning our Master) Ja-lálu 'd din, Rú-mí, of our 13th century. The Mas-na-vi contains between 30,000 and 40,000 double-rhymed verses. A European scholar describes its author as "soaring on the wings of a genuine enthusiasm high above earth and heaven, up to the throne of Almighty God," and the poem, as a "production of the highest poetical and religious intuition."

390   GLOSSARIAL INDEX AND SUPPLEMENT.

SU-GUR   [Pl. of *sakr*, or "sagar," any game-catching hawk.] The name of a horde of the Aeniza. Table p. 121.
SU-HAIL   Canopus, in constellation A. Argus. P. 50 f.n. 2. [This brilliant star crosses the meridian of Baghdad, in Lat. 33° 21′ N., at 6 h. 13 m. A.M., 20th September; and rises at 9 h. 57 m. P.M.]
SU-HAI-NI   The name of a strain in AL KHAM-SA, Table p. 235 col. iii.
SU-KHÁM .   .   .   The name of a hound, p. 145.
SÚKU 'SH SHU-YÚKH   A settlement of the Arabs, near the mouth of the Euphrates, pp. 83, 85, 300.
SU-LAI-MÁN .   The Arabic proper name, pp. 106, 227 *et* f.n. 5.
SU-LAI-MÁ-NI-YA   A town on the Turco-Persian frontier, 200 miles east of Baghdad. It is about 100 years old, and is named after a Governor-General of the Baghdad Pashalik. Pp. 148, 159 f.n. 5, 281 f.n. 2.
SUL-TÁN .   [In Arabic, *an absolute ruler*.] For page references to H.I.M. the Sultan, *v.* Index ii.
SU-MM-SÁT *et* SAM-SÁT. [The ancient Samosata.] A site on the Euphrates (about 1200 miles above its embouchure) near which the river is considered to enter the Syrian plain, p. 71.
SU-MÚT [pl. of *simt*] [*Any suspended things*.] The Bedouin give this name to the cords, often of variegated worsted, which they attach to the cantle of the saddle, pp. 141 (in illustration) *et* 142.

SUN-NÍ AND SHÍ-Í'   Without overlooking the well-known fact that the etymo-
 [*Anglicè*, "Sun-nite" and   logical root of a word is not a safe guide to its signification,
 "Shi-ite."]   we would just mention that, in the bare root-sense, *Sun-ní*
Pp. 113 f.n. 2, 159, 281.   means one who follows the *regular path*, or *customary law*
                    (*sun-na*); and *Shí-í'*, one who makes, or joins, a *separate party* or *sect* (*shí-a*').[1]

The Shi-a', *par excellence—i.e.*, the greatest schism which the history of El Islám exhibits—is intimately associated with the career of A'li; so much so, that it is often called by his name. In the lifetime of A'li, "the party of A'li" was, however, a political, not a theological, body; and A'li himself was not a "Shi-ite," but is often quoted as an authority in the books of the Ha-dith. For the elucidation of this subject, the fact must first be recalled that the commonwealth which Muhammad founded was essentially a religious democracy. The Prophet died sonless, and without explicitly indicating a successor (*Khalífa*, or "Caliph"). The elective, as opposed to the dynastic, principle was thus left all the freer; and every reader knows how Abû-bakr was chosen Caliph. Among the disappointed candidates of course was the Prophet's son-in-law and near kinsman, A'li. During all the time that the

---

[1] In India, a member of the Shi-a' is called a "Shi-a'"; but in Arabia and El I'rák, they correctly say "Shí-í'" for the sect, and "Shí-í'" for the adherent of it.

SUN-NÎ AND SHI-Î—*continued*. Arab empire was being spread abroad, A'li persistently opposed the Government. His efforts, we know, so far prevailed, that, in succession to U'th-mān, he was nominated the fourth Caliph; but his capacity proved unequal to his ambition. After a series of reverses, he was assassinated at Kû-fa, in El I'râk, by one of those puritanic soldiers and genuine zealots who are described in article KHA-WÂ-RIJ, *supra*. After his death he was elevated to the rank of a national hero;[1] and the tragic fate which subsequently befell his son Hu-sain, with many other members of the AHLU 'L-BAIT, or family of the Prophet, at Karbalâ, further contributed to render permanent the breach between the Sun-nî and the Shi-î. On the whole, it is open to doubt whether the historical A'li possesses much in common with any of the divisions of Islamism which have used his name. A'li's aim, as has just appeared, was to press his own claims to the Caliphate,[2] chiefly on the grounds of his relationship to the Prophet. From this point of view his cause was favoured by the Persians, in whom the idea of hereditary monarchy is firmly rooted. But Persia is also the ancient home (*v.* art. SÛ-FI, *supra*) of conceptions diametrically opposed to Arabian monotheism; and the Shi-a', or "*party* of A'li," no sooner became the national party of the Persian race than doctrines which A'li would have been the first to repudiate were brought out as part of the true Is-lâm, and spread by means of emissaries over the Muslim world.

The Sunnites, including the Wahâbis, are at least five times as numerous as all the other divisions of Islamism put together—that is, the Shi-ites ("*Ithnâ a'-sha-rî-ya*,"[3] "*Is-mâ-î-lî-ya*," and others), and the unconditional predestinarian sect of A'bdu 'lla *ibn* I-bâdh, the headquarters of which is in Oman. It is sometimes represented that the Sunnites stand in that relation to the other divisions of El

---

[1] The common representation that the Sun-nîs "hold A'li's memory in abhorrence" is altogether erroneous. It is true that the Sun-nî rabble, when they hear those of the Shî-a' claiming for A'li more than human dignity, are apt, in a spirit of sectarian protest, to disparage him; but this means nothing. After the massacre at Karbalâ, they cut off the head of Husain, the son of A'li, and forwarded it to Damascus. According to the historian Tabrarî (ii. 282), the Caliph Ya-zîd, when he received the trophy, struck with his cane the senseless features. This action caused a profound sensation; and a bystander exclaimed, "*Put up thy cane! By Allah! how often have I seen the Prophet of God kiss those lips!*" It is superfluous to add that the same sympathy with the Prophet's kindred is still prevalent. From A'bbasside times at least, all the Muslim have regarded A'li and Husain as martyrs and heroes. No Arab, and no Muslim who is above the level of the *canaille*, needs to learn from Persians how to reverence A'li's memory. *V.* p. 239 f.n. 2.

[2] If proof were wanting that A'li, according to contemporary opinion, merely fought for himself, the rejection of his cause by the Kha-wâ-rij would supply it. These "soldiers of the Faith" unquestionably constituted the only great party which was in earnest in opposing the secularisation of El Islâm. At first they ranked among the numerous malcontents who made common cause with A'li; but at a later period they stubbornly refused to fight for him. Ultimately, one of their number slew him.

[3] Literally, *Twelvers—i.e.*, votaries of the twelve "I-mâms," and *de jure* Caliphs, A'li and his eleven immediate heirs through I'á-ti-ma. A tenet of the great mass of Shi-ites is, that the last of these Imâms was one Muhammadu 'l Mahdî, of the 3d Islamic century. At Baghdâd a general belief pervades the Shi-a', that this Muhammad, of whose death there is no record, is all this time lying *perdu*, probably near Sâ-mar-râ on the Tigris, biding the time when he shall reappear to fill the world with righteousness.

SUN-NI AND SHI-Í—*continued.*	Islám in which the Roman Catholic Church stands to the Reformed sects of Christendom. The basis of this comparison of course is, that the Sun-nis trace back their authoritative canon, both religious and political, *without any interruption*, to the Prophet; while the Shi-a' ignores in every possible manner the first three Caliphs.[1] Up to a certain point some such parallelism may be sustained; but when we have regard to the numerous superstitious beliefs and embellishments which now form an integral part of the Shi-a', we are more reminded of the Roman than of the Protestant phase of Christianity. The term "worship" is too ambiguous to be used rashly; but the commemorative scenes which are enacted every year at Karbalá and Najaf, and at the other great seats of the Shi-ite theology in El I'rák and Persia, attest the fullest possible development of the idea that A'li and his descendants are veritable deities.
SÚ-RA	The designation of the individual Pieces of AL KUR-ÁN, *v.* p. xiv of prefixes of vol., in f.n. 1.
SU-Ú'D *et* SA-A'D	Co-derivative proper names, implying the idea of *good fortune*, which often occur in the annals of the Wahabite monarchy, pp. 39 f.n. 2, 42, 43, 51, 162, 253.
SU-WAH	The name of a strain in the stock of KU-HAI-LÁN, Table p. 235 col. vi.
SU-WAI-LI-MÁT	[Plural of *su-wai-li-ma*, diminutive of *sâ-li-na, souad*.] The name of a horde of the Aeniza, Table pp. 121, 136.
SU-WAI-TI	(*The strain belonging to the man with the little whip.*) Table p. 235 col. i.

T

TA-BA-RI .	Abû Ja'-far Muhammad, *ibn* Ja-ri-ri 't Ta-ba-ri (*i.e.*, of Tabaristán), was one of the ornaments of Baghdad in our 9th century. His two chief works are a great commentary on the Kur-án, and his Annals. Books of Arabian history and biography began to be written in Arabic in the 2d century after the Flight; but all these histories are more or less thrown into the shade by the great work of Tabari. P. 28 f.n. 4.
TAD-MUR .	The well-known place-name, pp. 66 *et* f.n. 1, 100, 300.
TAI .	A nation of the Bedouin, pp. 62 *et* f.n. 2, 75, 124.
TÁ-IF	An ancient town in the high land above Mecca, p. 59, f.n. 2.
TAI-MÁ	The name of an oasis in AL HI-JÁZ, p. 49. ["Tema" appears in a genealogical table in Gen. xxv. 15. In Isaiah

---

[1] It followed logically from this disavowment by the Shi-a' of A'li's three predecessors that, on the failure of A'li's visible descendants, the Caliphate, according to Shi-ite dogma, fell into abeyance. In Sun-nite Turkey, the Sultán is regarded as *ex officio* the successor and representative of the Prophet. But in Shi-ite Persia the Shah is looked upon merely as the deputy of the "Hidden Prince" of A'li's race, whose title is Al Mahdi, or *The divinely guided*.

	xxi. 14, we see the inhabitants of the land of Tema bringing water unto him that was thirsty, and meeting the fugitives with their bread.]
TÁ-JÍ	In El Îrâk, p. 84 f.n. 1.
TAK-RÍT .	A town on the west bank of the Tigris, 120 miles above Baghdad, pp. 73, 75, 281. [From Mosul to Baghdad it is 250 miles by river, and Tak-rît is the only permanent settlement which one passes. Ordinary river steamers cannot ascend the Tigris much higher than Tak-rît, without the risk of being stranded, and perhaps having to lie in the desert till the river rise in the following spring.]
TAL-A'T MIL-HIM	A spot in Shâ-mi-ya, p. 63 f.n. 2. [If some traveller between Baghdad and Aleppo, by the Euphrates route, would make a careful sketch of the "Tal-a't of Shekh Milhim," it would help to settle the question of whether the desert term "*tal-a't*" denotes an *elevated spot*, or a *corrie*, or the *tail of detritus which is washed down from the corrie*.]
TALL . .	Any natural or artificial eminence, p. 84 f.n. 1.
—— - GÛSH .	Name of a mound near Baghdad, *ibid.*
TALLU 'L LAHM	The Bedouin dish, p. 191 f.n. 1.
TAM-BUR. .	Name of a strain in AL KHAM-SA. Table p. 235 col. iii.
TAMR .	The fruit of the date-palm tree. Dates, p. 66 f.n. 1. [As "tamarind," or *Indian tamr*, we have this word in Europe.] The proper name Tamar, p. 134.
TAM-RÍ	[*Date-coloured.*] Name of a strain in AL KHAM-SA, Table p. 235 col. i.
TA-RA-FA .	A single tamarisk tree. The generic name is *Tar-fá.* References to Ta-ra-fa, one of the poets of THE MU-'AL-LA-KÁT, pp. 57, 234, 255 f.n. 1.
TA-RÍ-KA .	At the root of this word is the idea of *beating*. The Arabs and Persians use it in several senses, p. 144 f.n. 2.
TÁS .	A drinking-cup; also the cap, or cup, which protects the head in a suit of armour, p. 104 f.n. 1.
TATAR, TÁTÁR, TATTAR Pp. 74, 89, f.n. 1, 266.	A high authority identifies this name with that of the "Ta-ta" Mongols, who in our 5th century inhabited the great sandy desert of Gobi, in Central Asia. It is now generally applied to all the Mongol hordes who followed Jenghis Kaan and his successors. [One of the impressive foreign words occurring in AL KUR-ÁN is "*tat-rá,*" which is used (S. xxiii.) to convey an idea of the *spreading abroad* of Allah's prophets before Muhammad.]
TAT-TÚ .	The Indian pony, p. 259 *et* f.n. 1.
TAU-KÁN .	Name of a strain of the stock of KU-HAI-LÁN, Table p. 235 col. vi.
TA-WÍL	*Long*, p. 75 f.n. 1.
THÁ-BIT .	[*Established.*] The name of a subdivis. of the Sham-mar, p. 122.
THAI-YIL .	*Agrestis linearis*, p. 82 f.n. 1.

THAR-THÁR	A cleft extending from the Sin-jár range to south of Tak-rít, p. 73. In some years, and in some places, Thar-thár may contain, up to May, a current fifty yards broad. It keeps varying between that condition and sheer dryness. Only the Arabs can drink its brackish waters.
THAUB	The long Arab shirt, p. 140.
TIBN WA SHA-ÍR	The horse provender of El I'rák and Arabia, p. 80 f.n. 3.
[AT̤̤ TI-HÁ-MA P. 26.	A very hot region, which, as the name is now generally applied, forms the sea-shore strip of Yemen; although many of the Arabs follow El Asma'-i in reckoning Mecca, and all the low-lying region round it, not to El Hi-jáz, but to the Ti-há-ma.
TI-LÁL	[*Light refreshing rain.*] The name of a prince of Jabal Sham-mar, p. 40.
TIPPOO SÁHIB	Sultán of Mysore (1749-1799), p. 95.
TOBBA'	The hereditary title of the ancient kings of Yemen, p. 27 *et* f.n. 6.
TÚ-MÁN	A subdivis. of the Sham-mar, p. 122.
TUR-KÍ	The personal name, or distinguishing epithet, of a gallant prince of the Ibnu 's Su-úd family, who, from 1824 to his death ten years later, successfully headed a revolt of the Arab tribes against the Turkish power in Central Arabia, p. 40.
TURK-U-MÁN or TURCOMÁN. [Correctly *Turk-mán.*] For page references *v.* Index ii.	The term "Turk," meaning one of the "Osmanli," is more of a political and conventional than of an ethnic definition. Between the 11th and 13th Christian centuries hordes of Tatars continually passed westward out of Central Asia, owing to the rise of the Mongol power. Many of these immigrants settled in Persia, where they received the name of "Turk-mán." In our day the Shah's so-called Turkish "Ili-yát," or nomads, are thus designated. But the "Turk-máns" proper consist of all those formidable horse-riding nations of Tekkes, Sáryks, and very many others, who possess, under Russia, the steppe-land east of the Caspian. According to Marco Polo, "excellent horses, called Turquans, existed among the Muslim hordes of Turcomania." (Bk. l., ch. ii.)
TÚ-WAI-SÁN	[Diminutive from *tá-ús*, a peacock.] The name of a strain in the stock of KU-HAI-LÁN, Table p. 235 col. vi.

U

U'-BAID	[Diminutive from *a'bd.*] (1) The name of a Bedouin nation of El I'rák, pp. 82, 83, 84 f.n. 1. The horses of the U'baid, p. 280. (2) The name of a strain in AL KHAM-SA, Table p. 235 col. iii.
U-BAI-RI-YA	The name of a strain in AL KHAM-SA, Table p. 235 col. ii.

GLOSSARIAL INDEX AND SUPPLEMENT. 395

U'-BAI-YÁN [From *a'ba*, the Arab cloak.] Tradition narrates that a desert Arab who was being pursued threw off his cloak, because it caught the wind, and afterwards found it hanging over his mare's tail, so high did she carry it. And the mare of the story is held to have originated the "U'-bai-yán" branch of AL KHAM-SA, Table p. 235 col. iii.

U'-DHAIM [*Greatness*.] The name of a tributary of the Tigris, pp. 82, 282.

U'FAIR [*V*. art. OPHIR, *supra*.] The name of a riding-ass of the Prophet's, p. 230.

UG-MU-SA [Prob. from KA-MIS, *q. v. supra*.] A great confederation of the Sba' Aeniza, Table p. 121, 68.

U'J-MÁN Bedouin Arabs of the peninsula, who are held to be of Persian (*a'-ja-mi*) origin, pp. 29, 59 f.n. 2, 100.

U'-LA-MÁ [pl. of *a'-lim*] Men of knowledge and learning, p. 207 f.n. 1.

U"MAIR [Diminutive of U'mr.] The name of a strain in AL KHAM-SA, Table p. 235 col. i.; and of a strain which is shown in col. vi. of the same Table.

UMM Mother, *i.e.*, originator, cause, origin, or principle of a thing, pp. 34 f.n. 1, 57 f.n. 5.

UMMU 'L IB-IL An epithet of Najd, p. 57 f.n. 5.

U'-NAI-ZA At p. 56, a girl's name. The town of U'-nai-za, in Najd, pp. 32 f.n. 1, 258. [A recent writer says, "The horse-dealers of Onaiza procure young horses from the nomads round the town, even as far as Yemen, and ship these (known in India as Onaiza horses) at Ku-wait for Bombay."[1] This account requires correction. Neither in India nor anywhere else does the term "Aeniza horse" denote a horse which has been bought by an inhabitant of Onaiza. An "Aeniza horse" is one which has been bred by the Aeniza Bedouin in the Arabian desert, irrespectively of locality.]

UR-DÚ The Aryan term ——, p. 59.

UR-FA The well-known town of the Turkish empire, in Al Jazira, on the Daisun, a left-hand tributary of the Euphrates, seventy-five miles west of Diár-bakr, pp. 63, 111 f.n. 2, 272, 300.

U'-RÚ-JI-YA The name of a strain in AL KHAM-SA, Table p. 235 col. ii.

U'R-WA *ibnu* 'L WARD The Di-wán of ——, p. 179 f.n. 1.

U'-TAI-BA [Root idea, *anger*.] The name of a great Bedouin nation, pp. 10, 59 f.n. 1, 62. Guarmani is responsible for the statement that the horses of the U'tai-ba are esteemed the best of all the horses of the deserts of Najd.

U'-YÚN [Plural of *a'in*, the primary meaning of which is said to be *the eye*.] With the meaning of springs, p. 105.

U'-ZAIR The Biblical name "Ezra" is thus written in AL KUR-ÁN, P. 100 *et* f.n. 1.

---
[1] *Encyc. Brit.*, vol. xvii. p. 773.

W

WA-DIHI-HA   The ox-like antelope, or "wild cow," of the Arabian wilderness, p. 145 f.n. 1.

WÁ-DI   This word, now naturalised in Europe, has a wide range of meaning, from the great strath or valley down to the merest gully, or "fiumara," pp. 37, 52, 65, 68, 73, 75.

WÁ-DI DA-WÁ-SIR   The name of a strip of Najd, p. 32 f.n. 1. The inhabitants thereof, p. 39 f.n. 2.

WA-DI   The government tax on camels in El I'rák, p. 84 f.n. 2.

WAD-NÁN   [*Puny of birth.*] The name of a strain in the stock of KU-HAI-LÁN, Table p. 335 col. vi.

[AL] WAH-HÁB   In the theology of the Muslim, an attribute of the Divine, p. 107 f.n. 1.

WAH-HÁ-BI   An epithet formed from the second part of the name of A'bdu 'l Wah-háb, of Najd, the resolute enemy of "saint-worship," relics, and pilgrimages. A "Wah-há-bi" is one who recognises in A'bdu 'l Wah-háb's teaching the latest great exposition of the Prophet Muhammad's testimony. The Government of Turkey, and the Turks themselves, yielding to practical considerations and to natural laxity, have so considerably watered down the peculiar leaven of Islamism, that even the more moderate of the Wahábis who are residents of Ottoman cities find it advisable to screen themselves from notice behind the name of one of the four schools of "cold orthodoxy," usually that called after AH-MAD *ibn* HAN-BAL (*c.* A.D. 800) of Baghdad.

For page references *v.* Wahabyism in Index ii.

In India, where the circle of sound Arabic scholarship grows narrower every year, the Wahabite element is broadly divisible into three classes. First, we find adventurers from parts like Bussorah who possess just sufficient scholarship to mislead the Indians. Then come Indian townsmen, equally ignorant and fanatical, who from various motives desire to upset the Government under which they have thriven. Lastly, rustic youths are never wanting, whose untutored minds it is easy to inflame with visions of "Holy War" and Paradise, so that they shall attempt impossibilities in the name of Allah.

WALD A'LI   The name of a subdivis. of the Aeniza, pp. 63 f.n. 1, 68, Table p. 121.

WÁ-LI   In the Ottoman empire, the Governor of a province, pp. 100 f.n. 1, 159 f.n. 5. [The territorial jurisdiction of a Wá-li is called a "Wi-lá-i-at."]

WASHM   A province of Najd, p. 32 f.n. 1. [*Washm*, meaning tattooing, is a well-known word; and some say that *washm* in this

WASM	sense, and the proper name Washm, mean, in the first instance, *spreading*, as *e.g.* verdure does.]
WA-TI	*V.* AU-SĀM.
	[*Accustomed to the saddle.*] The name of a strain in AL KHAMSA, Table p. 235 col. i.

Y

YA-BÚ	A kind of horse, p. 136 *et* f.n. 2.
YA'-KŪB	"Jacob," p. 106.
YA-MĀ-MA	A province of Najd, pp. 32 f.n. 1, 42, 43.
YA-MĀ-NĪ	A Yemenite, or native of Yemen, p. 97.
YA-MA-NĪ	The Arab shoe, p. 97 f.n. 4.
YAM-BŪ'	[*The welling up of water.*] The port and harbour, connected with an inland group of villages (the old "Yan-bú'"), where steamers touch for Medina, pp. 10, 29. From Yam-bú' to Medina, it is about ten days for caravans.
YAR-BŪ'	The jerboa, p. 95. [Up to the year of writing, considerable numbers of these rodents burrowed in the desert round Baghdad. Their principal feeding time was after sunrise. Owing to their power of jumping and doubling, they were safe on the open plain from the smartest terriers. A recent overflow of the Tigris has apparently destroyed them.]
YATH-RIB	The oasis of ——, p. 101.
YAUM	Day, or a day, p. 127.
YA-ZI-DĪ	Travellers in the Mosul district hear with surprise of a certain sect of "Devil-worshippers," but such designations should not be taken for more than they are worth. The "Yazidis" of Sin-jâr (p. 6) are pagan Kurds of the mountains, among whom, naturally, there are traces of the old Persian religion, and especially of the Persian dualism. Approved books, by men still living, exist in Europe, in which the power of Satan is depicted as rivalling that of the Almighty; and the same conception comes forth into distinct shape among the Yazidis. The ancient Iranian name "Yazd" represents for them the "good god," while their clear recognition of the devil is evidently a shred from the system of Zoroaster. They worship the principle of Good through several of the appearances of Nature, notably the Sun, or light, and water. We write this note in the midst of these primitive people; and one of them who is with us never fails, on observing the sun rise, to prostrate himself on the spot where the first rays fall. In India we have seen Rajpût princes perform the same act of reverence to a common reading-lamp when it chanced to be carried into the room. The Yazidis of Sin-jâr consist of about 2000 families, distributed in extremely sequestered hamlets. Their

YA-ZI-DI—*continued.*

speech is one of the numerous dialects of Kurdi. Other bodies of Yazidis are scattered over Syria. The "A-mir" of the community resides at the village of Ba-adh-ra, a day's ride from Mosul. Near Ba-adh-ra is the "sacred valley" which contains the shrine, or perhaps tomb, of "Shekh A'di." If this be a "temple," it is the only "house of God" which the sect possesses. The ceremonies performed at the annual festival there have been described by Layard, *v.* his *Nineveh and Babylon*, ch. iv. We cannot pretend to add anything to so full and graphic an account. The Yazidis are in the habit of informing both the Osmanli officials and European travellers that they possess a revealed book resembling Al Kur-ân; but we have not been able to verify this statement.[1] Their chief religious treasure is the brass image of a bird, called "Malik Tâ-ûs,"[2] which Layard saw and sketched. Four of these objects are in their possession. Layard says that they do not look upon the image "as an idol, but as a symbol or banner." However this may be, "Malik Tâ-ûs" is greatly honoured by them—not the only instance of a bird-figure appearing where those of quadrupeds and reptiles are absent.

The Yazidis, like the Nepalese Gurkhas, are natural soldiers, mountain-made, and endowed with the hardy habits of a temperate climate. Down to about 50 years ago the Porte enforced its conscription among them, on the grounds that, as they belonged to no recognised non-Muslim sect, they must be of the Muslim. With a fine inconsistency, their children were, however, held to be "Kâ-firs," and therefore lawful objects of sale.[3] These wrongs were not righted till after the Sin-jâr range had witnessed scenes of bloodshed. At the present time (1891) the Yazidis are prosperous and contented; but their safety from Turkish persecution chiefly depends on England, and on the power and inclination of Her Majesty's Embassy at Constantinople to cover them unofficially with the shield of its protection.

---

[1] Since the above was written, the traveller Mr Parry, we learn, has brought to England extracts from a sacred book, entitled "THE JAL-WA," found by him in the possession of the Yazidis.

[2] "Malik" apparently is the ancient title familiar to us as "Moloch"; while "tâ-ûs" is an Aryan name for the peacock. Layard says that the image of "King Peacock" (on which he "could see no traces of inscription") is "more like an Indian or Mexican idol than a cock or a peacock."

[3] As determining, in theory at least, the attitude of IS-LÂM towards slavery, two authoritative passages may be quoted. One is the text in S. xlix. of AL KUR-ÂN, meaning,
Truly believers alone are brothers.
And the other is the "Saying,"
The Muslim shall not be sold; shall not be bought.
In considering the spread of Islamism, it is right to assign all due prominence to conquest; but we must not overlook the effects resulting from the brotherhood tenet. The "four ayers of the morning" appear on the scene only occasionally; the fact that "conversion" generally involves social elevation is an energetic agent which is always operating. There is, however, another side to the account. It follows from the equalisation before Allah of all the Muslim, (1) that there are many inferior kinds of service which no "believer" will exact from a "brother believer"; and (2) that outside of Islâm there is neither law nor safety. In towns like Baghdad, there are plenty of non-Muslim natives to open what required the public and private cesspools. The Arabs of the desert, of course, have no such work to perform; and yet even they spare no pains to procure African drudges. If ever India should fail to yield men which devote themselves, hereditarily, to conservancy duties, our countrymen there will have the question of imported labour forced upon them in a new and serious aspect.

YEMEN	The "Arabia Felix" of Ptolemy and other ancients. Pp. 19, 26-30 *passim*, 97 *et* f.n. 4. "Arabia Felix" was a mere mistranslation. The primary idea contained in *Yemen* is *the right*, or *the right hand*; and the meaning of *auspiciousness* is secondary and figurative. In Im-ra-u 'l Kais' poem, *ya-mín* is used, as it is still in Arabic, to express *an oath*, perhaps from the part which the right hand performs in making it.[1] In all probability the idea anciently enwrapped in the name Yemen had something to do with the right or the right hand in sun and moon worship, or in the offering of sacrifice and incense.
YÚ-NUS	"Jonah." Often alluded to in AL KUR-ÁN. Pp. 100 f.n. 1, 270.
YÚ-SHA'	"Joshua," p. 100 *et* f.n. 1.
YÚ-SUF	"Joseph," p. 106.

Z

ZAB	The Tigris in its passage through north-eastern El I'rák receives the snows of the Kurd mountains from two considerable affluents, respectively called, in books and maps, the Greater and the Lesser Záb or Di-âb (p. 82). The people living on the banks of the rivers bestow, as usual, their own local names on different portions of them.
ZA-BÍB	Dried grapes or raisins, p. 119 f.n. 1.
ZAF-FA	The procession which accompanies a bride to her husband's tent or dwelling, pp. 148, 150.
ZA-GROS	The west Persian frontier Highlands are sometimes collectively termed the "Zagros mountains" (pp. 79, 282 f.n. 1); but this Greek appellation applies properly only to the range skirting the plains of I'-rák A'-ra-bi, and separated by the Kar-kha river-valley from the more easterly Lûr-istân and Khûz-istân systems.
ZÁ-HI	The name of a strain of the stock of KU-HAI-LÁN, Table p. 235 col. vi.
ZAID	[*Increase.*] Name of the Prophet's favourite amanuensis, *v.* Note to AL KUR-ÁN, in *List of Works Consulted*, p. xiv of prefixes of the volume.
[Az] ZAI-TÍ	[From *zait*, the oil, or essential parts, of the *zai-tûn* or olive-tree.] The name of a strain in AL KHAM-SA, Table p. 235 col. v.

---

[1] We have failed to discover in Arabia any traces of the practice described in Gen. xxiv. 9, whereby Abraham's servant put his hand under his master's thigh, and sware to him; but in divers other ways the Arab's right hand performs the same function. In his marriage ceremony, in which, by the way, the presence of the principals is dispensed with, the proxies of the bride and bridegroom come forward at the proper moment, and place the right hand of the one on that of the other, in ratification for their respective principals of the obligations which are then contracted.

ZAL-LA   The name of a strain in the stock of KU-HAI-LĀN, Table p. 235 col. vi.
ZAM-ZAM . The well within the sacred precincts at Mecca ; the deep shaft of which is inclosed in a marble-paved building, p. 116.
ZI-Ā-DA . [*Excess*, as of speed, or beauty.] The name of a strain in AL KHAM-SA, Table p. 235 col. i.
ZIB-NA [*Pushing out.*] The name of a horde of the Aeniza, Table p. 121.
ZIPPORAH P. 113 f.n. 3. [On the principle that all words which occur in the Biblical literature are to be interpreted from Hebrew, this name means *little bird*,[1] lit. *whistling, twittering*. In our day "Dha-fī-ra" is a common name among the Arab women ; but the comparative philology of the two names is a complex matter.]
ZO-BA'   The name of a confederation of tribes in El I'rāk, which claim kindred with the Sham-mar, pp. 122, 158 f.n. 1.
ZU-BAID . A nation of Babylonia, p. 84 f.n. 1.
ZU-BAIR . [*Strength, cleverness.*] A modern Arab town which refugees from Najd planted, in the troublous times of Wahabyism, on the site of ancient Bussorah. Most of the inhabitants of Zubair are engaged directly or indirectly in the horse trade. Pp. 32, 83, 228, 300.
ZU-HAIR . [Diminutive of *zahr*, a flower or blossom.] The name of one of the poets of the SEVEN MU-A'L-LA-KĀT. Translations from his poem, pp. 130 f.n. 4, 145 f.n. 1.
ZULLA
[For ZU-LA.] A village near the head of Annesley Bay, on the African coast of the Red Sea, pp. 99 f.n. 4, 192 f.n. 1.

---

[1] "U's-fūr," the common Arabic word for a sparrow, comes from the same root as "Zipporah."

INDEX II.

INDEX OF SUBJECTS.

A

Abraham, his setting no wine before the angels who visited him quoted in connection with the abstinence of the desert Arabs from intoxicants, 52; holds an important place in Arabian story, 101; common belief among the Arabs that he was one of them, 103; the history of, noticed, 108 et seq.; legends regarding his hospitality, 114 et f.n. 1; references to, in AL KUR-ÁN, more copious than in the Hebrew Scriptures, 115; his connection with the Ka'ba of Mecca, ib. et f.ns. 2 and 3; according to AL KUR-ÁN, Ishmael, and not Isaac, the son whom he was commanded to sacrifice, 115, 116; tradition that the Chaldeans attempted to burn, 159 et f.n. 6.

Abstemiousness, the, of the Arabian horse, 191.

Abyssinia, horses left in, by the British expedition, 28 et f.n. 1; large portions of, colonised from S. Arabia, 99 et f.ns. 3, 4.

Abyssinians, the, have lost the art of training the elephant, 28 f.n. 3.

Acquired characters, latest theories regarding, 242 et f.n. 2.

Adulterated breeds of horses, the, in Shá-mi-ya and Al Ja-zí-ra, 271.

Africa, points of resemblance between Arabia and, 99 f.n. 4.

African elephant, the, carried into Yemen, 28.

Ages of horses, the, compared with ages of men, 185.

Agriculture in El I'rák, 79, 80 et f.n. 3, 85.

"Akbar," the Arab race-horse (with illustration), 257 f.n. 1.

Aleppo, carrying of Arabia as far north as, by a fourteenth-century geographer, 20; the Darley Arabian bought by a resident of, 165 et f.n. 2; Mr Skene consul at, 212; Mr Henderson consul at, 249; as a starting-point for the horse-purchaser, 291.

Amulets, use of, among the desert Arabs, 136 et f.n. 1.

Angora flocks of Sin-jár, the, 133 et f.n. 4.

Animals, comparative degrees of intelligence in the different kinds of domesticated, 195 f.n. 2.

Antelope, the, of Arabia, 8, 74, 145 et f.n. 1, 152.

Arab horses, collections of, made by Muhammad ibnu 'r Ra-shíd of Ja-bal Sham-mar, 45; by the King of Würtemberg, 219; by A'b-bás Páshá, Viceroy of Egypt, ib. et f.n. 3; by Mr W. S. Blunt, 220; by A-mír Fai-sal of Najd, 250.

Arabia, the intensity of its climate, and the effects thereof, 6; characteristics of the surface of, 8, 9; its capabilities as a nursery of horses, 8 et seq.; Burckhardt quoted on this point, 9; Lane's suggestion regarding etymology of the name, 19 f.n. 2; delimitation of, 19 et seq.; maps of, 22 et f.ns. 1 and 2; sketch of peninsular, 25-64; the treatment of travellers in, 33 et f.n. 2; extract from old Arabian poet illustrative of climate of, 49; list of the nomadic races of Arabia proper, 50 f.n. 2; from very early times, occupied by two more or less distinct peoples, 97; the central portion of, was but slightly affected by the historical vicissitudes of the empire of Yemen, ib.; the prevailing classification of the existing nations of, 98, 99; article in Ency. Brit. on, 99 f.n. 2, 210-212; points of resemblance between, and Africa, 99 f.n. 4; and between the Arabs and numerous African peoples, ib.; prevalence anciently of Jewish settlements and kingdoms within, 100, 101; hints to travellers in, 149 et f.n. 1, 292-295.

Arabian horse, the. See Horse, the Arabian.

Arabic and other foreign words, glossarial index and supplement to all references to, used in this work, 325-400.

Arabic language, method of transcribing Arabic words used throughout this work, is, x of prefixes of volume; its love of personification illustrated, 34 f.n. 1; antiquity of, 104, 105; Lane's view on this point, 105 f.n. 1; currency among the desert Arabs of many words unknown to grammarians, ib.; place-names and names of persons among the

3 E

INDEX OF SUBJECTS.

Arabs considered, 103-108; hints on the study of, 292 et f.n. 1; words imitative of sounds, 221 f.n. 1, 295; words lent to, and words borrowed by, Index i., 345-346 f.n.

Arabs, the, broadly divisible into the Bedouin or nomadic and the settled Arabs, 15; from earliest ages have had an instinct for emigration, 20; their skill and enterprise as navigators, 21 et f.n. 1; cannot on the whole claim to rank as scientific breeders of animals, 22; their origin, 92 et seq.; their claim to "purity" of blood, 93 et seq.; extreme importance attached to this view by, 94; inter-resemblance of, 95; traces of "breeding" in their pose and figure, ib.; their blood seems to possess a special virtue, ib.; the northern are mainly nomads, 100; but masses of the southern also display the wandering habit, ib.; the connection, anciently, between the Jews and, ib., 101; and between their respective religions, 101; their physical aspect, 103, 104; their speech, 104-108; the epithets "Yemenite" and "Ishmaelite," considered from the racial view-point, 118 et seq.; horse-racing not practised among, 131 et f.n. 3. 248 f.n. 1; illiterate condition of, 132, 247; the condition of women among, 134 et f.n. 1; the sport of hawking among, 152 et f.n. 2; their love for their horses, 157-166; how the influence of AL KUR-ĀN tends to develop this sentiment, 158 et seq.; recognise the necessity of shoeing their horses, 179; management of their horses, 196; how they name their horses, 237.

Arabs, the Bedouin. See Bedouin Arabs.

Arabs, the settled, of El Frâk, 83, 84 et f.n. 1, 85; horse-breeding among, 146-154; their saddle and stirrup, 147, 148; the place of the horse among, 166.

Arabs, the town-dwelling, why despised by the Bedouin, 133, 134; as horse-breeders, 146 et seq.; their fantasia described, 150; influence of AL KUR-ĀN upon, 160, 161; how they were affected by the Puritanical rigour of the Wahabite system, 162-164; admire large horses, 197; remarks on the theory that the stallion, more than the mare, transmits the qualities of the breed, 230.

Argamak horse, the, 274 et f.n. 1.

Armour and weapons of, 104 f.n. 1.

Armck, the sale of, permitted by the Ottoman Government, 119; origin of the word, ib. f.n. 1.

Aryan and Semitic languages, error of deriving one from the other, Index i., 345-346 f.n.

"A-sil," the winner of certain races for Arab horses at Newmarket and Sandown, 249.

Ass, the domestic, of Arabia, 22; the white, of Al Ha-sā, 31; merits of the, variously estimated in the East, 159; the wild, 8, 74, 75.

Australasia, an Australian writer quoted on the importance of flowing water to horse-breeders in, 9 f.n. 1; the horses of, will perform long journeys on a grass diet, 11; maritime districts of, found unsuitable for horse-breeding, 26; Arabian stallions in, 214; the blood-horse of, quite modern, ib. f.n. 1; large sums paid for race-horses in, 216 f.ns. 1, 2.

Australian horses, "Kingcraft," 186; "Jorrocks," ib. f.n. 1; the origin of their habit of "buck-jumping," 191; their uncertain temper, 198; an Australian colt by "Chester," 195. 241, 242, 273; occasionally mistaken for Arabians, 303.

B

Baghdad, 13; immunity of, from rabies and hydrophobia, 35 f.n. 2; the learned men of, 98; the Jews of, 100; horse-breeding in and around, 127; as a horse-mart, 211, 296; the difficulty of exercising race-horses in, 275; horses bred in, have no true pedigrees, 279.

Bathing, method of, practised by the Kurdish women of Sin-jār, 5.

Beatson, the late Gen. W. F., and "Beatson's Horse," alluded to, 188.

Bedouin Arabs, the, etymology and definition of the name, 15 et seq.; are of composite origin, 16; delight in trading enterprises, ib. 17; a strict demarcation of their limits impossible, 18; their love of Najd, 32, 38; have sound reasons for their exclusiveness, 33; how they contend against the want of water, 48 et seq.; the four seasons recognised by, 50 f.n. 2; the question of their abstinence from wine considered, 52 et seq., 119; exoduses of, out of Najd, 62-64; hints afforded as to the history of, by their proper names, 105 et seq.; qualities personified in their names, 107 f.n. 3; their hospitality, 114; how they have preserved their independence, 119; as horse-breeders, 121-145; table of the divisions of the Ae-ni-za nation of, 121; the divisions of the Sham-mar nation, 122 et f.n. 5; different septs of, have different standards of horse-breeding, 123 et seq.; their method of conducting warfare and foray, 126-128; their condition as regards religion, 128, 129, 160; Dr Wallin quoted on this point, 129 f.n. 1; their fatalism, nature of, 129, 130 et f.ns. 2-4; their very ancient custom of tying a dead man's mare or camel beside his grave, 130; despise book-learning, 132, 133; desert costume, 134; the poetical temperament of, 135 et f.n. 4; the chief feature of their practice of horse-breeding is faith in blood, 137, 231, 267; their fanaticism on this point renders them too unmindful of form, 138; their horsemanship, 138-140; their riding-halter, 140, 141; saddle, 141, 144; spur, 142; a poet's description of their horses and horsemanship, 143; their natural gravity, 163; but slightly affected by Wahabyism, ib.; their love of tobacco, 164 et f.n. 2; how the possession of a mare raises the nomad's social position, 165; their acuteness, 184; their consideration for their horses, 189, 221; their manner of feasting, 191 et f.n. 2; are generally short-lived, 193; their reluctance to part with a mare, 215 et seq.; instances of their nevertheless selling their best mares to strangers, 217, 218; in pedigrees they give the mare pre-eminence, 230 et seq.; how they name their horses, 237; how they preserve the purity of the strains, 241, 242, 248; in their own deserts, will truly declare all they know of a horse's pedigree, 247, 248; their horse knowledge a national possession, 254; their superstitions regarding colour and markings, 264; their trade with pedlars, 294 f.n. 2.

INDEX OF SUBJECTS.

Bedouin supper, description of a, 191.
Bedouin women, their duties and their dress, 127 *et f.n.* 2; the measure of liberty allowed to, 134; the tending of the mares by, 189.
Bengal Cup, running of the Arab horses "Crab" and "Oranmore" in the, 207, 208.
Bible narratives, recurrence of very many of the, in AL KURʾÂN, 101.
BIBLE, THE, references to, 27 *et* f.n. 3, 41, 43 f.n. 1, 44 *et* f.n. 1, 49 f.n. 4, 52 *et* f.ns. 4 and 5, 64 *et* f.n. 2, 65 *et* f.ns. 1 and 2, 66 f.n. 1, 70, 74 *et* f.n. 1, 78 *et* f.n. 1, 80 f.n. 3, 92 f.n. 2, 94 f.n. 1, 98 f.n. 3, 104 f.n. 3, 109, 110 f.n. 1, 111 *et* f.n. 2, 112, 113 f.ns. 3 and 4, 115 f.n. 4, 117, 130 f.ns. 2 and 5, 134, 157, 158 *et* f.n. 1, 159 *et* f.ns. 1, 2, 3, and 6, 178 f.n. 2, 226 f.n. 4, 227 *et* f.ns. 1 and 3, 232 *et* f.n. 2, 238 f.n. 2, 265 *et* f.n. 2, 278 *et* f.n. 1, 299 *et* f.n. 2.
"Bishopping," 303 f.n. 1.
Bishops, in early times in England, rode mares, 232 f.n. 2.
Bits and bitting, 141 f.n. 1, 150, 151 (with illustrations); the Mameluke bit, 150 *et* f.n. 1.
Blackwood's Magazine, reference to observations of an early English traveller in Mid-Lothian in, 6 f.n. 2; quotation from an article in, on the Turkû-mâns and their horses, 272.
Blaine, Delaberre, quoted regarding longevity in horses, 184 f.n. 2.
"Blitz," the Arab race-horse, 308.
Blood-horse, meaning of term, 246 f.n. 4.
Blood, purity of, faith of the Bedouin Arabs in, 137, 231; the winning of races not an infallible proof of, 248 *et* f.n. 1; the tendency of the Arab horse-dealers, when they engage in racing in India, to persevere with worthless animals which are of fancy strains of blood, 307.
Blunt, Lady Anne, 8, 39, 149 f.n. 1; her *Pilgrimage to Najd*, 37; her description of the Nu-fûdh, 38; her remarks on the scarcity of horses in Najd considered, 58; her estimate of the numbers of the Ae-ni-za and the Sham-mar, 63 *et* f.n. 1; on the effect of the spring rains in Shâ-mi-ya, 68; on Der as a horse-market, 68, 69; her visit to Shekh Fâ-ris, 72 f.n. 1; on the religion of the Bedouin, 129.
Blunt, Mr W. S., favours the theory that Arabia was the primeval home of the horse, 7, 8; praise of the Arabian horse by, at Newmarket, 169; on the Arabian as a race-horse, 206, 207; remarks on his description of desert horse-breeding, 207 f.n. 1; on the purchase of Arabian mares, 218; his experiments in the naturalisation of Arabians in England, 220; quotation from a pedigree table in *Bedouin Tribes of the Euphrates*, 246; chose his mares and horses from the Bedouin tribes in Shâ-mi-ya, 270.
Bombay, the best and largest market in the world for Arabian horses, 299 *et* f.n. 1; the Arab horse-mart of, described (illustration), 300-302; purchasing Arabian horses in, 302-314; its climate, 315.
"Bombproof," the Indian stud-bred horse, record of, 187 f.n. 2.
Bones of the horse, the, anatomical and horseman's names for, contrasted, 114 f.n. 3.
Bower, Colonel, owner of "Child of the Islands," quoted, 198, 306.

Breeders of animals, the Arabs cannot claim title of scientific, 22.
Bridle, the, of the Bedouin Arabs (with illustration), 140, 141.
British Association, a suggestion to the, 105.
British Isles, the climate of, favours the Arabian horse, 316.
"Bucephalas," reference to, p. vi of prefixes of volume *et* f.n. 3.
Buck-jumping, origin of the habit of, in Australian horses, 191.
Budge, Dr E. A. W., British Museum, his visit to Sin-jâr, 6 f.n. 3.
Buffon cited on the point of wild horses in Arabia, 7.
Burckhardt, references to, 5 f.n. 1, 26, 29, 291, 312 f.n. 1; on the horse-yield of Arabia, 9; the extent of his travels in Arabia, 10; on the climate of Yemen, 26, 27; on the horses of Yemen, 26, 27, 29; and of Al Hi-jâz, 29; on the numbers of the Ae-ni-za, 63 f.n. 1; on the religion of the Bedouin, 128; on the traders who enter the desert, 294 f.n. 2.
Burton, the late Sir R., cited, 115, 160 f.n. 3; translation of S. *Al Fâ-ti-ha* by, 135 f.n. 3; his costume on pilgrimage to Mecca, 149 f.n. 1.
Bussorah, its fertility as a date-garden, 74; a good starting-point for the horse-purchaser, 292; facilities for transport of Arab horses from, to India, 315.
Buyer of horses, qualifications of a successful, 35 *et* f.n. 2, 289, 290.
Buying horses. See under Horse, the Arabian.
"Byerly Turk," the, 138 f.n. 1, 165, 206.

C

Cairo, sale of A'b-bâs Pâsha's stud of Arabians at, 219 f.n. 1; may become a considerable market for Arabians, 299.
Camel, the, Huf-huf in Al Ha-sa as a market for, 31; in Oman, 32; Arab life impossible without, 55; a high authority cited on the primeval home of, *ib.* f.n. 1; the Arab's love for, 56, 57, 294; its money value in Najd, 57; its part in desert warfare, 60, 61; only true beast of travel in the desert, 76; its uses in early times, 159; limited intelligence of, 195 f.n. 2; its money value in Shâ-mi-ya, 270; the purchasing power of, varies, *ib.* f.n. 1; Damascus a good market for, 293, 294.
Camel-brands, the, used by the Arabs (with illustration), 67 *et* f.n. 3. See also AT-SÂM, in Index i.
Campbell, the late Dr, of Mysore, 306.
Canine madness unknown in Baghdad, 33 f.n. 2; prevalence of, in India, *ib.*
Cape, the, purchasing of horses at, 35 f.n. 2.
"Captain White" (the name of a horse), sagacity of, 194.
Castration of horses, remarks on the, 279 *et seq.*
Cavalry, the uses of, indicated by AL KURʾÂN, 158; Egypt as a school for, 239.
Centaur, myth of the, used as an illustration, 238 *et* f.n. 1.
Chaldeans, tradition regarding attempted burning of Abraham by the, 139 *et* f.n. 6.
Character of the Arabian horse. See under Horse, the Arabian.

Chargers, the Prophet Muhammad's, 230 f.n. 2.
Chess among the Arabs, 54 f.n. 2.
"Chest-founder" *v.* "foot-founder," the question of, 181 *et seq.*
Chestnut colour, in horses, 264, 265; English racing-stock practically become bay and, 267.
Cheyne, the Rev. Dr, quoted on Jewish circumcision, 113.
"Child of the Islands," the Arabian race-horse, 198 *et* f.n. 2, 306.
Chivalry, the influence of, on horse-breeding in England, 232.
Circumcision, practice of, among the early Arabs, 112; prevalence of, among many savage and some civilised peoples, *ib.* f.n. 2; reference to, by Rev. Dr Cheyne, 113 *et* f.n. 2; other authorities cited with regard to its practice among the Arabs, *ib.* f.n. 3; not mentioned in AL KUR-ÂN, *ib.* f.n. 3.
Cities, the perished, of the Euphrates valley, 65, 66.
"Claverhouse," author's Arabian horse, history and career of (with full-page illustration), 181-184; his lameness considered in reference to "chest-founder" and "foot-founder," 182-184.
Climate, as an element of the general "environment," regarded throughout these pages as a most important factor, 1-6, 89; intensity and effect of that of Arabia, 6; extract from old Arabian poet illustrative of, 49; of British Islands, suitability of, to the Arabian horse, 316.
Coach-horses in olden times spoken to from the coach-box, 196 f.n. 1.
Coffee, comparatively modern introduction of, into Arabia, 110; traditions regarding the discovery of the plant by the Arabs, *ib.* f.n. 2; derivation of the name, *ib.*; royal proclamation against, on its introduction into England, *ib.*
Collins, Vet.-Surgeon, quoted, 175, 279.
Colour of the "typical" Arabian horse, question of the, considered, 260 *et seq.*; colour as an indication of character, *ib.*; and as an indication of breed, and breeding, 263-267.
Colours, the, of the Arabian horse, Table of, 262, 263.
Constitution of the Arabian horse. See under Horse, the Arabian.
Consuls, the variable influence of, in Asiatic Turkey and Arabia, 297, 298.
"Copenhagen," the Arab race-horse, 208, 307.
Coughs in the Arabian horse, 174.
Courage, the, of the Arabian horse, 193 *et seq.*
Cox, Mr, of Sydney, and his horse "Yattendon," 216 f.n. 1.
"Crab," the Arab race-horse, his race with "Orranmore," 207, 208.
Crooked fore-legs, prevalence of, in Arab horses (with illustration), 200.
Crossing the Arabian with other breeds. See under Horse, the Arabian.
Cuneiform Tablets, the, of Tell el Amarna, 105 f.n. 1.
Cup-horses, or platers, the buying of, 309 *et seq.*
Curb an unsoundness seldom seen in Arab horses, 178.
Curr, Mr, on Australian horse-pastures, 9 f.n. 1; extract from his *Pure Saddle-Horses*, 170-72; his account of "Jorrocks," 186 f.n. 1.

D

Damascus, recommended by Burckhardt as a market for Arabians, 64, 291; the Arab's name for, 65; horse-buying in the deserts round, 271, 272; a starting-point for the horse-purchaser, 291; a good market for camels, 293, 294.
Dandie Dinmont terrier, history of the, used to illustrate difficulty of ascertaining origin of breeds of animals, 240; this breed said to trace back *to a mother*, *ib.* f.n. 6; the colours of, more or less fixed, 266.
"Darley Arabian," the, came from the Ae-ni-za, 65; from whom bought, in Queen Anne's reign, by Mr Darley of Aleppo, 165 *et* f.n. 2, 269, 291; a certain account of him shown to be unsupported, 213 f.n. 1; probably a model in respect of make and soundness, 219; locality in which foaled unknown, 269.
Darwin cited, 118 f.n. 1, 137, 241, 242, 245, 266 *et* f.n. 2.
Date, value of the, as food for men and horses, 12 *et* f.n. 1.
Date-groves of Bussorah, the, 74; of El I'râk, 79.
Daumas, Gen., work by, on the Arabs in Africa, referred to, 161.
Day, Mr, his *Race-horse in Training* quoted, 177.
Defects of the Arabian horse. See under Horse, the Arabian.
"Dervish," the Arabian horse. See Index i.
Desert, etymology and definition of the word, 18, 19.
Desert horsemanship, characteristic features of, 138-140; an Arabian poet's description of, 143 *et* f.ns. 2-7, 144 *et* f.n. 1.
Desert horses, the trade in, 211; the desert is continually being stripped of its blood-horses, 213.
Desert travelling, importance of the camel in, 76.
Desert warfare, 61, 108 f.n. 3, 124, 126-128; the place of the women in, 127.
Dick, Professor, of Edinburgh, able to detect lameness in a horse by ear alone, 176 f.n. 1.
Diseases, special, of the Arabian. See Horse, Arabian, *Constitution of*, also *Treatment of, when exported.*
Dods, Prof. Marcus, quotation from *Muhammad, Buddha, and Christ* by, as to sense in which Muhammad was a Prophet, 4 f.n. 1.
Dog, the, how treated by the Arabs, 116 f.n. 2.
Doughty, Mr, his experiences in Najd, 33 f.n. 2; his estimate of the population of Ja-bal Sham-mar, 39 f.n. 1; his account of Prince Ban-dar's accession to Chiefship of Ja-bal Sham-mar, 40 f.n. 1; on the administration of justice by Amîr Muhammad, in the same province, 43 *et* f.n. 3; his description of the same Amîr's stud, 45; his experience of the scarcity of water in Western Arabia, 51; on the numbers of the U'rai-ba Bedouin, 59 *et* f.n. 2; the subdivisions of the Sham-mar nation according to, 122.
Dress, the, of the Arabs, 108 *et* f.n. 2, 127 f.n. 2.
Drinking-bouts of the ancient Arabs, legendary lore regarding, 53 f.n. 1.
Dromedary. See Camel.
Durability, the, of the Arabian horse, more or less a product of high breeding, 185; qualified by method of rearing, 186 *et* f.n. 1.

INDEX OF SUBJECTS.   403

E

Ears of Arab horses; frequent presence of marks on, 312; spread of, methods of obviating practised by the Bedouin and other breeders, *ib.*
East India Company, quality of horses bred by the, 187.
"Eclipse," Lawrence's explanation, in *The Horse*, of his vast powers, 186 f.n. 1; size of his heart, when weighed after death, referred to, 243 f.n. 3; possible inaccuracy of his pedigree, 247 f.n. 1; his conformation, as shown in engraving in Sidney's *Book of the Horse*, recommended as a model to buyers of Arabians for racing, 257 f.n. 1; marking in descendants of, 266; his character as a colt, 275.
Egypt, monumental and traditional evidence as to the breeding of horses in ancient, 227 *et* f.n. 2; in A'li's time, a school for cavalry, 239; as a market for Arabian horses, 299.
Elephant, the, imported into Yemen from Africa, 28; the art of training, lost by the Abyssinians, *ib.* f.n. 3; the Indian, instances of its intelligence, 195 f.n. 2.
Elliot, Major, owner of the Arab race-horses "Euclid" and "Lanercost," 309.
Emigration, instinct of the Arabs for, 20.
Encyclopædia Britannica, references to, 6 f.n. 1, 26 f.n. 3, 30 f.n. 1, 54 *et* f.n. 3, 99 f.ns. 2 and 3, 113 *et* f.ns. 2 and 3, 115 f.n. 4, 210, 239 *et* f.n. 4, 277 *et* f.n. 3, 282 f.n. 2.
English Stud-book, the, its beginning and history, 246; probable inaccuracies in, 247 *et* f.n. 1.
Esau bin Curtas, his account of the history of the Arabian breed, 228; colt afterwards famous as "Revenge" sold by him, 270; circumstances in which "Blitz" was bought and sold by him, 308.
Etymologies, Eastern grammarians not generally qualified to consider, 98; "popular etymologies" illustrated, prefatory note to Index i., 324 *et* f.n.
"Euclid," the Arab race-horse (with full-page illustration), 309.
"Euphrates," the Arab race-horse, 271.
Euphrates, the river, mixed population in the valley of, 16; deserts west the, 65-69; numerous perished cities near, 65; husbandry in the valley of, 66; its importance to horse-breeders, *ib.*; dominated by the nomads, 67; deserts east the, 70-77; water-wheels on, 81 f.n. 2; the horses of the settled Arabs on, are of adulterated blood, 271.
European clothes, difficulty of keeping in proper order, or of replacing, when travelling in the East, 149 f.n. 1.

F

Farriery, no true Arab will handle farrier's tools, 179.
Fatalism, true character of, in El Islâm, 130.
Fauna of Arabia, grace and beauty of the, 95.
Feasting, the Bedouin's manner of, 191 *et* f.n. 2.
Feeding-bags, horses', 318 f.n. 1.
Firing horses, the Arab practice in respect of, 184, 185, 311, 312.
Fish as food of horses, 12.
"Fisherman," the English race-horse, his record, 186.
Fitzwygram, Lieut.-Col., the horse-shoe recommended by, 201.

Flags, use of, in ancient Arabia, as signs for wine-sellers' booths, 106 f.n. 2.
Flight to Medina, Muhammad's, epoch-making nature of, 52 f.n. 7.
Foot, the, of the Arabian horse, significant Arabic name of, 11; different shapes of, produced by different soils, 178; circumstances affecting it, *ib.*; its natural soundness shown by its power of resisting those circumstances, 179; is cut to fit the shoe, *ib.*; demands most careful scrutiny from the intending purchaser, 181 *et* f.n. 1.
"Foot-founder" *v.* "chest-founder," the question of, 182 *et seq.*
Forsyth, Sir Douglas, the late, quoted on question of wild horses, 89 f.n. 1.
"Fort Adjutant's mark," meaning of the, in Arabian horses, 313.
Fortitude as a feature of character in the Arabian horse, 192, 193.

G

Gabriel, the Angel, his place in Muslim story, 4 f.n. 2.
Games, prohibition of certain, by the Prophet Muhammad, 54 f.n. 2.
Geldings in freshly landed batches of Arabian horses, 311.
"Godolphin," the, 138 f.n. 1, 165.
Goodwood Cup, the, cases connected with, cited to demonstrate the futility of entering the best Arabian racers for races in England, 208.
Grass, importance of, as food for horses, 9, 11.
Grasses of El Irâk, 82 *et* f.ns. 1, 2.
Greyhound, the Arab, high "quality" of, 96.
"Greyley," the Arab race-horse, description of (with full-page illustration), 254-256.
Grooming horses, Eastern and Western methods of, 318 *et* f.ns. 2, 3, 320.
Guarmani, the Italian traveller and horse-buyer, 52, 59; his experiences in Najd, 57; supports the theory that the stallion, more than the mare, transmits the qualities of the breed, 230, 231.
"Gulf Arabs," remarks on this descriptive term, as used in India, 31.

H

Hagar and Ishmael, the "Ishmaelite" Arabs claim to be descendants of, 99, 100; the banishment of, by Abraham, not mentioned in AL KUR-ÂN, 115; Professor Wellhausen's observations on the Bible narrative of, *ib.* f.n. 4; place of Hagar's settlement according to the Muslim commentators, 116.
Hair of the head, the exuberance of, among uncivilised peoples, 6 f.n. 1; the decadence of, follows the advance of civilisation, *ib.*; the Hindu's hair invariably black, 266 f.n. 1.
Hallen, Vet. Lieut.-Col., and the "turned-up" horse-shoe, 202.
Hampton Court, sale of Arabian horses at, on death of King William IV., 252 *et* f.n. 1.
Hand-rubbing of horses, value of, 320 f.n. 1.

INDEX OF SUBJECTS.

Harems, Georgian and Circassian girls in Turkish, 47 f.n. 2.
Hasan bin Bade, the Arab horse-dealer, 309.
Hawking among the Arabs, 152 *et* f.n. 2.
Heart, a large, said to be essential to a race-horse, 243; example of, as regards "Eclipse," *ib.* f.n. 3.
Heber, Bishop, and his Arab riding-horse, 167.
Hebron, a rival to Damascus in antiquity, 109 f.n. 3.
Henderson, Mr, late Consul at Aleppo, letter from, to the Author quoted, 249.
"Hermit," the Arab race-horse, 181 f.n. 1; cited as an example of the indomitable qualities of the Arabian race-horse, 192; his career in India, and his great race with "Greyleg" (with full-page illustration), 256.
"Hermit," Mr C. Davis's reputed half-bred Arab hunter, 209 f.n. 1.
Hobbling, marks caused by, in El Frâk or in Arabia, mistaken, in India, for proofs of superiority, 313.
"Honeysuckle," the Arab race-horse, his career, 307.
Hoof of the Arabian horse. See Foot.
Hoopoe, the, fable of Solomon and, 12 *et* f.n. 3.
Horace, his advice to horse-buyers, 303; an unfortunate application of the same, *ib.*
Horne's, Capt., distance ride, on his Arab horse "Jumping Jimmy," 193.
Horse, the, copiousness of existing literature on subject of, v, vi *et* f.n. 1 of prefixes of volume; traditions regarding the origin of, 4; his power of adapting himself to new foods, 10 *et seq.*; his herbivorous habit, 10, 11; when first imported into Yemen? 27, 28; the horseman makes the, 88-91; lost breeds of, 90, 91; anatomical names for the bones of, compared with those used by horsemen, 144 f.n. 3; in Eastern countries the commonest varieties of, are generally much better to go than to look at, 153, 154; the breeding and importing of, forbidden to the Israelites, 157 *et* f.n. 1; the standard of intelligence possessed by, considered, 193 f.n. 2; examples of the large sums paid for, 216 f.ns. 1 and 2, 219 f.n. 3; varieties of, 225; adulterated breeds of, towards the Tigris and Euphrates, 271.
Horse, the Arabian, where bred? 19-22, 225-244 *passim*; what is an Arabian horse? 22 *et seq.*; the degree in which the breed shows diversity of form and size, 22, 23, 62 f.n. 1; in Yemen, 26, 27; in Al Hi-jâz, 28, 29; in Al Ha-sâ, 29-31; in Oman, 32; the numbers and use of in Najd, 57-61; Mr Palgrave's and Lady A. Blunt's observations on this point, 57-59; large numbers of, bred in El Frâk, 78; essentially a war-horse, 126; written pedigrees of, 136; is a true saddle-horse, 153, 168; honoured wherever the Arab Prophet's teachings are received, 158 *et seq.*; foreign estimates of his qualities, 167-172; his tractability, 168; his services in India, Afghanistan, and other countries, *ib. et* f.n. 1; conflicting pronouncements upon, 169 *et seq.*; Mr Sidney's *Book of the Horse* quoted, 170; Mr Carr's *Pure Saddle-Horses* quoted, *ib. et seq.*; compared with other varieties as regards constitution and character, 173-196; the breed artificial, 173; defects of, 197-204; the theory that the cream of the breed is inaccessible to foreigners discussed, 210 *et seq.*; origin of, 225-244; galloping with straight fore-legs, 243 *et* f.n. 1; in-and-in breeding of, 243, 244; the typical, 245-266; in Shâ-mî-ya and Al Ja-zî-ra, 269-276; in El Frâk and east the Tigris, 277-285; buying, from the Bedouin, 290-295; and in Arabian and Frâki towns, 296; procuring, through consulates or consuls, 297, 298; buying exported Arabians, 299-313; proper treatment of the same, 314-321.

As a hunter: various estimates of, 209 *et* f.n. 1, 316.

As a race-horse: Mr Blunt quoted on, 206, 207 *et* f.n. 1; some performances on the turf in India cited, 207, 208.

Character of: rationale of the Arabian's tractability, 189; treatment as determining character 190; "abstemiousness," 191; fortitude and staying power, 192, 193; courage, instinct, and sagacity illustrated and discussed, 193 *et seq.*

Constitution, &c., of: coughs, 174; spavins, 175, 176; splint, 176, 177; ringbone, 178; curb, *ib.*; various shapes of foot, *ib.*; necessity of shoeing recognised by the Arabs, 179; their method of shoeing and its results, *ib.*, 180; "chest-founder" v. "foot-founder," 181 *et seq.*; firing, 184; longevity, 185 *et* f.ns. 1, 2; durability, 185, 186 *et* f.n. 1 *et seq.*

Cross, the Arab, the question of, considered, 137; the circumstances in which crossing is of value, 206; is the Arab cross now calculated to improve the English race-horse? *ib. et seq.*; or the hunter? 209 *et* f.n. 1; tried in Australia, 214; might it not tend to strengthen the modern English race-horse? 218.

Defects of: small stature, 197, 198; trotting and jumping, 198; a careless walker, and therefore not a perfect hack, *ib.*, 199; rationale of this, 199; prevalence of twisted fore-legs, 200, 201; attempts to cure "toeing" by means of novelties in horse-shoes, 202, 203; effect of over-weighting on action, 204 *et* f.n. 1.

Diseases of. See *Constitution of, and Treatment of, when exported.*

In El Frâk and east the Tigris: Government opposes obstacles to horse-breeding in, 278; the animals bred are not generally of pure race, 279; their manners, *ib.*; need for castration, *ib.*, 280; the horses of the U'baid and Sâ-yih Bedouin, 280, 281; the Kurds and their horses, 281-283; no evidence that European blood is used, 283; the stock is deteriorating, *ib.*; possesses useful qualities, 284; El Frâk as a country from which to procure stud-horses, *ib.*, 285.

In Shâ-mî-ya and Al Ja-zî-ra: the pure-bred Arabian is essentially the same in and out of Najd, 269; the horse of the Euphrates Bedouin often has the advantage in physique, *ib.*; considerable prices asked and obtained for their horses by the Bedouin of Shâ-mî-ya, 270; two famous racers of Shâ-mî-ya, *ib.*, 271; many adulterated kinds of horses found in the same localities, 271; the Ba-râ-zî-ya as horse-breeders, 272, 273; the Turku-mâ-ni horses, 272 *et seq.*; the horse stock here is composed of diverse elements, 273 *et seq.*

INDEX OF SUBJECTS. 407

Naturalisation of, abroad, 219 et f.n. 3, 220.
Origin of: some poetic accounts of, 226 et f.n. 3; the myth of Solomon's colts, 226 et seq.; every genuine Arabian believed by enthusiasts to be descended from strains preserved by Solomon, 227 et seq.; theory that the male parent transmits the qualities of the breed, 230, 231; the opposite opinion held by the Bedouin, 231, 232; the desert tradition of the KU-HAI-LA-TU 'L A'-JŪZ, 233; and of AL KHAM-SA, ib. et seq.; historical testimony regarding, discussed, 238 et seq.; literary evidence of antiquity of the Arabian breed, 239, 240; suggestions on this question, 241 et seq.
Purchasing, methods of :—
(1.) From the Bedouin, 290-296; folly of employing agents, 290; the intending purchaser's starting-point, 291; preparations and outfit, 292, 293; route, 292 et seq.; how far to adopt Arab usages, 293; camel-dealing, ib., 294; establishment of a horse-nursery, 294; the selection and purchase, 295.
(2.) In Arabian and I'rāki towns, difficulties of buying in, 69, 296, 297; the activity of the professional buyers, 297.
(3.) Through Consulates or Consuls, 297, 298; the influence of Consuls in the country, 297; obstacles in the way of their approaching the Bedouin, 298.
(4.) In the Bombay stables: (a) Buying horses for ordinary purposes, 302-304; the genuineness of every so-called Arabian should be carefully ascertained, 302; instances of horses of other breeds being mistaken for Arabians, ib., 303; the points to be looked for, 304. (b) Buying for the turf, 304-308; the difficulty of selecting apart from actual trial, 305; the chances of picking a hero by accident, ib., 306; some rejected horses which became famous, 306-308; use of the time test, 308, 309; buying tried horses, 309, 310; some indications as to the qualities of exported Arabians, 311-314; geldings, 311; fired horses, ib., 312; scars at the roots of the ears, 312; every horse is represented as having come from the desert, ib.; marks caused by hobbling, 313.
Treatment of, when exported: is there 'such a thing as "acclimatisation"? 314; management of, in India, 315, 316; suitability of the British climate, ib.; method of stabling, 317-319; and grooming, 318 et f.ns. 2, 3; treatment of disease, 319, 320 et f.n. 1; advisability of obtaining veterinary surgeon's opinion as to soundness, 320, 321.
Typical Arabian, the: sense in which the Arabian is "thoroughbred," 245-247; how is proof of "thorough-breeding" to be obtained? 247; on this point oral tradition is not infallible, 248; while turf performances are inconclusive, ib.; and the evidence of the eye equally so, 249; Mr Palgrave's description of, considered, 250, 251; group of six typical Arabians depicted, and remarked on, 252, 253 et f.n. 3; "Greyleg's" history and points, 254-256; "Hermit" described, 256; size as a feature of, 256-258; "Rex," 256 et seq.; colour, 260 et seq.; mental characteristics, 267, 268.

Horse-boxes, travelling, proper fittings of, 316 et f.n. 1, 317 et f.n. 1.
Horse-breeding, list of peoples of the Tigris who pursue, 84 f.n. 1; practice of, among the Bedouin, 121-145; among the settled Arabs, 146-154.
Horse-dealer, the, of Arabia, 123 f.n. 1; his use of high-sounding names, 236; his representations as to "blood," 248 et f.n. 1; his search in our day for small Arabians, 259, 260; illustrative anecdote, ib.; his keenness for trade, 296, 297; his speculative character, 299, 300; in Bombay, 300; his risks and his caution in buying, 301; instances of his judgment in choosing racing Arabs, 306, 307; his liability to error, 307; his persuasive eloquence, 308; his tendency to represent every horse as desert born and bred, 312; how he manufactures the "Fort Adjutant's mark," 313.
Horsemanship, Bedouin, the, 138-140; a poet's description of, 143.
Horse-mart, Der as a, 68 et seq.; Egypt as a, 299; Bombay as a, ib. et seq.
Horse-pastures, the, of Australasia, 9 et f.n. 1.
Horse-provender among the Arabs, 80 f.n. 3.
Horse-racing, not practised by the Arabs, 131 et f.n. 3, 248 f.n. 1; in India, 304, 310, et passim.
Horse-shoe, the Asiatic (with illustration), 179, 180. See also Index i., art. NA'L.
Horse-shoe nails in El I'rāk, 203 f.n. 1.
Horses, European, is it possible to ward off decline in, by crossing with Arabs? 218; their good qualities would be developed, were they admitted to closer intimacy with their masters, 220, 221; the spread of their ears a point disliked by the Arabs, 312.
Horses, wild, can never have existed in peninsular Arabia, 7, 8, 74, 229; reported indications of, in Mongolia and Northern Thibet, 89 f.n. 1.
Hospitality of Amir Muhammad of Jabal Sham-mar, 43; Bedouin, ancient and modern instances of, 62 f.n. 2, 114.
Hump of the camel, the, a provision in time of leanness, 294 f.n. 1.
Hunter, the Arabian horse as a. See under Horse, the Arabian.
Hyder A'li, of Mysore, partly of Arab lineage, 93.
Hyderabad, the late Nizām of, his prohibition of the sale of intoxicants, 54 f.n. 4; Arab blood said to have been imported into India by Hyderabad Government, 187.

I

Illiterate condition of the Bedouin Arabs, the, 132, 247.
Immaculate Conception, doctrine of the, in how far preached by the Prophet Muhammad, 96 f.n. 1.
Inbreeding, practice of, by Arab horse-breeders, 243 et seq.
India, mad dogs in, 33 f.n. 2, 315 f.n. 1; the decadence of horse-breeding in, 91; the indigenous horses of, a century ago, ib., 187; importance of the Arabian horse to, 168; as a market for Arabian horses, 175; the Rajpūt's anxiety to keep his old breeds pure, 188, 189; pony-racing in, 239; the tat-tū (pony) of, ib. f.n. 1; the Government of, does not buy greys for the stud, 265 f.n. 1; horse-racing in, 304, 310,

et passim; facilities for the transport of horses from Dussorah to, 315; effects of its climate on Arabian horses, *ib.*, 316.
Intoxicants, use of, and the Arabs, 52 *et seq.*, 119.
Irrigation of the Arabian deserts, how it would affect the Bedouin, 50; in El Feāk, 79.
Ishmael, Abraham commanded to sacrifice, according to AL KUB-ĀN, 115, 116; his twelve sons the founders of twelve tribes of Arabs, 117, 118.
"Ishmaelitic," the, and the "Yemenite" Arabs, contrasts between, 118 *et seq.*
Islamism, its connections with Judaism, 101; in Arabia, a townsman's creed, 114; the Bedouin's position with regard to, 128, 129, 160; the question of the obligation of a Muslim people to yield obedience to a non-Muslim ruler, 163 f.n. 4; examples of its toleration of persons of other faiths, *ib.*
Israel, meaning of the name, 157; the close connection between, and Arabia, in ancient times, 100, 101; did the Semitic group which ultimately developed into "Israel" come originally from the Arabian desert? 103, *et* bk. ii. ch. ii. *passim.*
Israelites, the, deportations of, by Assyrian or Babylonian kings, 100; forbidden to breed or import horses, 157 *et* f.n. 1.
"Ivo," the N.S. Wales colt by "Chester," 195, 241, 242 *et* f.n. 1, 273.

J

Jewish names, changing of, when Islamism embraced, 106.
Jewish religion, connection between, and Islamism, 101.
Jewish settlements, ancient, on the Tigris and Euphrates, 100, 101.
Jews, conversion of, to Islamism, 101, 106 f.n. 3.

K

Kāthiāwār, colour and markings of the horses of, 226 f.n. 2.
Kerr, General Lord Mark, G.C.B., his views and practice of horsemanship, 141 f.n. 1.
Khar-ga hieroglyphics, or camel brands, the (with illustration), 67 *et* f.n. 3.
Kindness, the effect of, in forming the Arabian's character, 190, 191.
"Kingcraft," the Australian race-horse, 186.

L

"Laili" and the Maharājah Ranjit Singh, p. vi *et* f.n. 2 of prefixes of volume.
Lancer, the skill of a Sham-mar, 76.
Lane, Mr E. W., his suggestion as to origin of name "Arabia," 19 f.n. 2; his view of the Semitic languages, 103 f.n. 1; his Arabic lexicon, prefatory note *to* Index i., 324.
"Lanercost," the Arabian race-horse (with full-page illustration), 309.
Lawrence, author of *The Horse*, quoted regarding longevity in horses, 185 f.n. 2.

Layard, Sir H. A., a legend of Hātim's generosity related by, 62 f.n. 2; references to, 74, 149 f.n. 1; the subdivisions of the Sham-mar nation according to, 122 f.n. 5; a curious custom of desert warfare noted by, 124; his description of Shekh Sfūk's mare, *ib.* f.n. 1; costume as a traveller, 149 f.n. 1.
Locusts, 12; the reception of a flight of, in the settled parts of Arabia, 13; a source of food-supply to the nomads, *ib.*, 14.
Loin-ill, the disease of, in India, 314 *et* f.n. 1.
Longevity in exported Arabians, instances of, 185 f.n. 1; and in our own breeds, *ib.* f.n. 2.
Lyall, Mr C. J., his *Translations of Ancient Arabian Poetry* referred to, 49.

M

"MagdMa," show-name in England of the Bengal race-horse "Verdant Green," 192 *et* f.n. 1.
Mameluke bit, the, 130 *et* f.n. 1.
Management of domesticated animals by the Arabs, the, 196.
Maps of Arabia, 22 *et* f.ns. 1 and 2.
Marco Polo, description by, of a Tatar stud, 266; his account of the "Old Man of the Mountain," Index i., 330; his reference to the "kingdom of Mawsal," *ib.* 372; to Turkumānī horses, *ib.* 394.
Mare, the desert, *v.* the desert stallion, as a means of introducing the "Arab cross," 214, 215; pre-eminence ascribed to the, by the Arabs, 231 *et seq.*, 241.
Mare's milk. See under KUMIS in Index i.
"Marengo," Bonaparte's charger, 253 *et* f.n. 5.
"Markham Arabian," the, 138 *et* f.n. 1.
Markings and colours of horses, superstitions of the Bedouin Arabs regarding, 264.
Marriage, legislation of the Prophet Muhammad regarding, 17 f.n. 1; practice of the Bedouins as to consanguineous, 94 *et seq.*, 231.
Martin, W. C. L., *A History of the Horse* by, quoted, 204 f.n. 1.
Mary, the Virgin, the immaculate conception of, Gibbon's suggestion that this tenet was "borrowed from AL KUB-ĀN," 96 f.n. 1; the late Dean of Westminster's view, *ib.*; the Arab Prophet's teaching on this point, *ib.*
Mecca, the condition of modern, 19, 20, 160 *et* f.n. 3; no representative of a foreign power at, 47; dress worn by the pilgrim approaching, 143 f.n. 6; tombs destroyed by the Wahābīs at, 162 *et* f.n. 2.
Medina, the date-palms around, 12 f.n. 1; the city of, 28.
Mesopotamia, the application of this geographical term uncertain, 70 *et* f.n. 1, 71, 74, 111 f.n. 2.
"Minuet," the Arab race-horse, 306.
Mirage, the, 81 f.n. 5. See also SA-WĀB, in Index i.
"Monarch," the Arab race-horse, and the Goodwood Cup, 208.
Mongolia, wild horses of, 89 f.n. 1; horses of, 238 *et* f.n. 1.
Mosque, the term, 163 f.n. 2.
Mosul, 13, 125; no British consul at, 297.
Muhammad, the Prophet of Arabia, *v.* Index i.
Mule, the, not fully adapted for desert travel, 76; largely bred by the settled Arabs, 159; the Arab

tradition regarding the origin of its sterility, *ib.*;
the female follows the muleteer's riding-horse, 311.
Muslim, the followers of El Islâm properly known as, 101 f.n. 2.

N

"Najdî Arabs," remarks on this term as current among horsemen in India, 31.
Naming of horses, the, by the Arabs, 237.
Naturalisation of animals, some facts regarding the, 314. See also under Horse, the Arabian.
Navigators, the Arabs as, 21 *et* f.n. 1.
Nervousness, constitutional, in horses, as distinct from mere "inexperience," 195.
Niebuhr quoted on the delimitation of Arabia, 20.
"Nimrod," quoted on splint, 177.
Nolan, Capt., book on cavalry by, referred to, 198.
Nomadic races, the, of Arabia proper, 15, 59 f.n. 2.
Nose-bag, the horse's, 318 f.n. 1.

O

"Oranmore," the Arab race-horse, 207, 208.
Oriental Sporting Magazine, the, quoted regarding the Arab horse "Copenhagen" and the Goodwood Cup, 208; Esau bin Curtas quoted, as to *blood* in Arab horses, 248 f.n. 1; the Bombay *Oriental Sporting Magazine* and the "Fort Adjutant's mark," 313.
Origin of the Arabian horse. See under Horse, the Arabian.
Ottoman Government, the, now holds Al Ha-sâ, 30 *et* f.n. 2; and Wahabyism, 44, 45; influences the Najdian clans but slightly, 45; its position in Al Ja-zi-ra, 71, 72; has but a varying influence over the Bedouin nations of El I'râk, 119, 120; collection of the dues of, by the mounted police, 147; endeavours to stop the export of horses *vid* El I'râk, 161, 278, 296; its system of rule in El I'râk, 278; does not foster horse-breeding in El I'râk, *ib.*; its jealousy of Consuls, 297, 298.
Over-weighting, as a cause of defective action, 204 *et* f.n. 1.
Owen, Surgeon-Major, C.I.E., on wild horses, 89 f.n. 1.

P

Pad, or saddle, of the Bedouin, 141 (with illustration).
Paganism of ancient Arabia, features of the, 128 *et seq.*
Palgrave, Mr W. G., his assertion that the hordes of the Sha-râ-rât are of the genuine Bedouin controverted, 16; the delimitation of Arabia according to, 19; boundary given to Najd by, 32 f.n. 1; his journey across the Peninsula, 35, 36; his estimate of the population of Ja-bal Sham-mar, 39 f.n. 1; on the horse-yield of Najd, 57, 58; his estimate of the numbers of the Ae-ni-za and the Sham-mar nations, 63 f.n. 1; his statements in the *Ency. Brit.* on Arabian topics on many points misleading, 99 *et* f.n. 2; the Sha-râ-rât Arabs are not, as represented by him, sun-worshippers, 128; his contention that the true Arabian horse is inaccessible to foreigners shown to be erroneous, 210; his statements in the *Ency. Brit.* on the Najdi breed examined, 210-213; his view that the pure Arabian stock has never been subdivided, refuted, 236; his description of the A-mîr Fai-sal's horses criticised, 250, 251; his remarks on the colour of the genuine Arabian confuted, 260, 261.
Palmyra, or Tadmor, 66 *et* f.n. 1.
Pater, General, anecdote of, and his charger, 204 f.n. 1.
Pedigrees of Arabian horses written (with full-page illustration), 136; Arabs give the mare the pre-eminence in, 231; the true Bedouin will frankly tell all they know regarding, 247, 248.
Pedlars in the Arabian desert, 294 f.n. 2.
Pelly, General Sir Lewis, K.C.S.I., his journey to Ar Ri-âdh, 36 *et* f.n. 2; his description of the sandy desert, 37.
Peninsular Arabia, 25-61; nomadic nations of, 59 f.n. 2.
Percivall, Mr, on splint, 177; on coffin-joint lameness, 182.
Persia, the blood-horse in, 198 f.n. 1; the Persians as breeders and managers of horses, 239 f.n. 1.
Persian Gulf, the littoral of, at one time greater in extent than now, 78 f.n. 3.
Personification, love of the Arabs for, 34 f.n. 1.
Philology, remarks on, prefatory note to Index i., 324; science of, comparative, still in its infancy, Index i., 345, 346 f.n.
Physical aspect of the Arabs in connection with the question of their origin, 103.
Pococke, Dr R., quoted regarding site of "Ur of the Chaldees," 111 f.n. 2.
Poetical genius of the primitive Arabs, the, 135 *et* f.ns. 3, 4.
Pony, the, of India, 259 f.n. 1.
Pony-racing in India, effects of, 259, 260.
Pool, Mr Stanley Lane, and the "Table-talk" of the Prophet Muhammad, 93 f.n. 1.
Prehistoric horse, the, 225.
Presents, oriental diplomacy regarding the acceptance and rejection of, 42 f.n. 1; the giving of, among the Arabs, very often only another form of selling, 27, 296.
Proper names of the Arabs, 105; manufacture of Arabic proper names by Jewish converts, 106 *et seq.*
Purchasing the Arabian horse. See under Horse, the Arabian.
Purity of blood, claim to, by the Bedouin Arabs, 93 *et seq.*; their faith in, as horsemen, 137, 231, 267 *et passim,* 307.

R

"Raby," the Arab race-horse, 181 f.n. 1.
Rachel, of Scripture, her acts and traits typical of modern tent-life on the Euphrates, 110 f.n. 1; her tomb, *ib.*
Racing, buying Arabians with a view to, in Bombay, 304-308.
Raiding, across the Euphrates, 67; the Bedouin method

of, 112 f.n. 1, 127, 128; qualities required to make a horse excel in, 131, 248; the Bedouin horses expressly bred for, 242.
Rain, effect of, in Shá-mi-ya, described by Lady A. Blunt, 68.
Rainfall, the, of Najd, 50; of Shá-mi-ya, 67, 68; of El I'rák, 80.
Rajputâna, breeding of horses in, 189.
Rawlinson, General Sir H. C., quoted, 6 f.n. 1; his bay Arabian, 260; his estimate of the numbers of the Kurd nation, 282 f.n. 2.
"Red Hazard," the Arabian race-horse, 176, 306.
Religious beliefs, the, of the Bedouin Arabs, 128, 129, 160; Dr Wallin quoted regarding, 129 f.n. 1.
"Revenge," the Arabian race-horse, 270.
"Rex," the Arabian race-horse, his career (with full-page illustration), 236-258.
Riding-halter, the, of the Bedouin Arabs (with illustration), 140, 141.
Kingbone, 178.
Rivers, the, of Al Ja-zî-râ, difficult of access by reason of their steep banks, 73.
Roberts', General Lord, favourite Arab charger, 185 f.n. 1.
Ross, Dr, among the Sham-mar Bedouin, 75, 76.
Rous, Admiral, on the development of the English thoroughbred, 197; cited, 243 f.n. 3, 305.
Russell, Rev. John, his breed of terriers, 240 et f.n. 6.

S

Sabæans, the religion of the, 28 f.n. 2. See also Index i., f.n. to article Sá-bá, p. 382.
Saddlery, the, of the Bedouin (with illustration), 141, 240-244 *passim*; of the settled Arabs (with illustration), 147, 148.
Sadlier, Captain, his journey across the Arabian peninsula in 1819, 35; quoted, *ib.*
Sálár Jung, Sir, the late Nawáb, G.C.S.I., of Hyderabad, Arab lineage of, 95; an Argamak horse taken to, by a Hirâti dealer, 274.
Scott, Sir W., ballad by, quoted with reference to colour in horses, 267.
Seasons, the four, recognised by the Bedouin, 50 f.n. 2.
Self-command, the, of the Arabian horse, 267, 268.
Semite, explanation of the term, 92 f.n. 2.
Semitic languages, the, Lane's observations on, 105 f.n. 1; mystery of the triliteral root of, Index i., 345, 346 f.n.
Sheba, Queen of, visit of, to Solomon, 27.
Shetland cattle, dried fish as food of, 12.
Shoe, the Eastern horse- (with illustration), 179, 180; some novelties in (with illustrations), 201-203.
Shoe, the, of the Arabs (with illustration), 97 f.n. 4.
Shoeing horses, the necessity of, recognised by the Arabs, 179; their method of, and its effects, 179-181; in India and in Baghdad, 202, 203.
Sidney's *Book of the Horse* quoted, 165, 170, 257 f.n. 1.
Sinaitic peninsula, elimination of the, in considering the country of the Arabian horse, 25.
"Sir Benjamin," the Cape horse, 273.
Size, as a character in horses, 197.

Skene, Mr, the late, of Aleppo, on the horses of the desert, 212, 213; his purchases of Arabians, 213 et f.n. 2, 218.
Smith, Lieut.-Col. Ham, on the Arabian breed of horses, 261.
Smith, Prof. W. Robertson, *The Old Testament in the Jewish Church* by, referred to, 115 f.n. 4.
Solomon and the hoopoe, tradition regarding, 12 et f.n. 3; his genius for trading, 27; the myth of, and the seven colts, 226 et f.n. 3; his renown in Western Asia, 226; believed by the Arabs to have been one of them, 227; the legend regarding his sacrifice of certain mares, *ib.*; every genuine Arabian horse believed by many to derive his pedigree from strains preserved by, *ib. et seq.*
Spavine, 175, 176.
Speech of the Arabs, the, in connection with the question of their origin, 104 *et seq.*
Splint, 176, 177.
Sponge, use of the, in stable economy, 318 f.n. 2.
Spur, the Bedouin (with illustration), 142; use and abuse of the, 195 f.n. 1.
Stabling of Arabian horses, 317-319.
Stirrups, the advantage of being able to ride without, illustrated, 141 f.n. 1; an ornamental variety of (with illustration), 148.
"Stockings" in horses, Eastern ideas regarding, 264 et f.n. 2.
Strabo, his statement that Yemen contained neither horses nor mules considered, 27; on the ancient inhabitants of S. Arabia, 97.
Straight fore-legs, galloping with, 243.
Stud-book, the English, its beginning and history, 246, 247.
Stud-horses, the procuring of, from "Turkish Arabia," 284.
Sultán, H.I.M. the, of Turkey, 30 f.n. 2, 71, 147; the relations between, and the A-mir Muhammad of Jabal Sham-mar, 44, 45; his personality a formidable factor in Osmanli politics, 278.
Sun-worship, is it practised by any of the Arabs? 128, 129.
Superstitions of the Bedouin Arabs, the, regarding colours and markings of horses, 264.
Swiss merchant, a, robbed and stripped by the desert Arabs, 36 f.n. 5.
Syrian desert, the. See page references under Shá-mi-ya in Index i.

T

Tail of the Arab horse, set given to, by the Bedouin, 251.
Tattersall, the late Mr Richard, sentiments regarding Arabian horses, 169.
Tell el Amarna, in Upper Egypt, finding of Cuneiform Tablets at, 105 f.n. 1.
Tents, purchasing, in towns like Baghdad, 76 f.n. 1.
Thibet, Northern, accounts of wild horses in, 89 f.n. 1.
Thoroughbred, Admiral Rous on the progressive improvement of the English, 197; Mr Blunt's attempt to produce a new race of, 220, 246; sense in which the Arabian is, 94, 245-247; wherein consists the proof of "thorough-breeding"? 247 *et seq.*

Thunderstorm, an Arabian poet's description of a, translated, 49 with f.ns.
Tigris, the river, mixed population of valley of. 16, 84; scenery of the same tract, 81; list of horse-breeding nations of, 84 f.n. 1; the horses of its valley are of adulterated blood, 271.
Tigris-land. See under [El] 'Irâk, in Index i., for page references.
Time test, use of the, before buying Arabians for racing, 308 et seq.
Tobacco, the Bedouin's love of, 52, 164 et f.n. 2; not tolerated by Wahabyism, 164.
"Toeing," a defect of Arabian horses, 199, 200; attempts made to remedy this by means of novelties in horse-shoes, 202, 203; another remedy suggested, 204.
Toleration, examples of, shown by the Muslim, 163 f.n. 4.
Tombs, destruction of, by the Wahâbîs, 162 et f.n. 2.
"Touchstone," the race-horse, 199 f.n. 3, 243, 271.
Transcription of Arabic words in Roman letters, note on the, pp. ix, x of prefixes of volume.
Transport of Arab horses to England, the, 316 et f.n. 1, 317 et f.n. 1.
Travellers in Arabia, treatment of, 33 et f.n. 2; hints to, 149 et f.n. 1, 292-295.
Tripping. See Toeing.
Turkish Government. See Ottoman.
Turku-mân nation, article in *Blackwood's Magazine* quoted on history of the, 272.
Turku-mâ-ni horse, the, article in *Blackwood's Magazine* quoted on, 272; blood relationship between, and the Arabian, 273; the Argamak variety of, 274 et f.n. 1; mongrel Turku-mâ-nis often mistaken for large Arabians, 274-276.
Turnbull, Gen. and Mrs, Arab horse in the possession of, 185 f.n. 1.

U

Upton, Major, quoted, 7 f.n. 1, 213 f.n. 1; his purchase of mares from the Ae-ni-za, 218; his views on the origin and history of the Arabian breed, 228, 229, 246; chose his stud-horses from the Bedouin of the Euphrates, 270.
"Ur of the Chaldees," locality of, discussed, 111 f.n. 2.

V

Veiling of women, the, among the Arabs, 134 et f.n. 1.
"Venus," the Arabian race-horse, 270.
"Verdant Green," the Bengal-bred race-horse, 192 et f.n. 1.
Veterinary examination of Arabian horses, advisability of, as soon as possible after they have been brought to a civilised country, 320.

W

Wahabyism, has been twice repressed, 30 et f.n. 2;

its claim to the title of the true Is-lâm considered, 161 et f.n. 2; its primary aims, 162; failed to impress the Bedouin, *ib.*; found expression in the destruction of tombs, *ib.* et f.n. 2; the puritanical rigour of, 162-164; parallelisms between, and certain developments of Puritanism in Europe, 163, 164 et f.ns.; how, under its spread, the horse's importance was increased, 164; and his diffusion promoted, 165.
Wallin, Dr, of Finland, quoted regarding religious beliefs of nomadic Arabs, 129 f.n. 1.
Water, extreme importance attached to, in the East, 4, 5 et f.n. 1; the water of some localities favours animal growth more than that of others, 5; the value of running water in horse-breeding, 9 et f.n. 1; the Arab method of drawing, 47 f.n. 3; how the Bedouin contend against the want of, 48 et seq.; drought in Arabia, 50 et seq.; water not stored by the Bedouin, *ib.*; steep banks make the rivers of El I'râk difficult of access, 73.
Water-famine, description of a, in Arabia, 51.
Water-wheels on the Euphrates, 81 f.n. 2.
Weapons of Arabia, the, 104 f.n. 1; pre-Islamic ballad translated regarding ancient, *ib.*
Wellhausen, Prof., art. "Moses" in *Ency. Brit.* by, referred to regarding circumcision by Zipporah of her son, 113 f.n. 3; art. "Pentateuch" in *Ency. Brit.* by, quoted as to history of Ishmael, 115 f.n. 4; meaning of name Israel, according to, 157.
White asses, the, of Al Ha-sâ, 31.
White horses and mares, stud of, kept by a Tatar sovereign, 266.
White, the late Mr James, of Sydney, 214, 241 f.n. 1.
Wild horses. See Horses, wild.
William IV., King, dispersion of his stud of Arabian horses, 252 et f.n. 1.
Wine, the Bedouins' abstinence from, considered, 52 et seq., 119.
Wine-sellers' booths, flags used as signs for, in pagan Arabia, 106 f.n. 2.
Wood, Mr R., his work on the *Ruins of Palmyra* referred to, 66 f.n. 1.
Works consulted by the author, list of principal, pp. xi-xiii of prefixes of volume.
Würtemberg, the late King of, his stud of Arabians, 219.

Y

"Yemenite," the, and the "Ishmaelitic" Arabs, contrasts between, 118 et seq.
Yeok Tepe, as a centre for the purchase of Argamak horses, 274 f.n. 1.
Youatt, Mr W., quoted, 253.
"Young Revenge," the Arab race-horse, 270 f.n. 2, 307, 308.

Z

Zipporah, Moses' wife. See Index i.

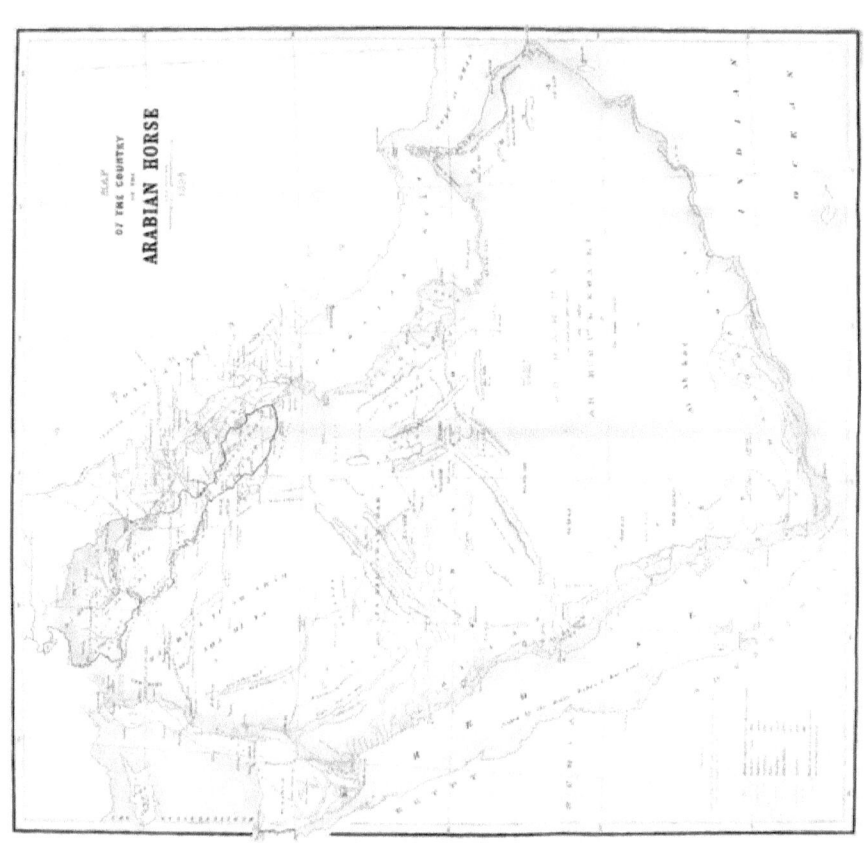

www.ingramcontent.com/pod-product-compliance
Lightning Source LLC
Chambersburg PA
CBHW032002300426
44117CB00008B/868